SEEING OURSELVES

Also by Raymond Tallis and published by Agenda

Logos: The Mystery of How We Make Sense of the World

Of Time and Lamentation: Reflections on Transience

Seeing Ourselves

RECLAIMING HUMANITY FROM GOD AND SCIENCE

Raymond Tallis

agenda
publishing

Dedicated to Jan Halák, philosopher and friend
and to Jerry Playfer, philosopher, physician and friend.

First edition published in 2020 by Agenda Publishing

Agenda Publishing Limited
The Core
Bath Lane
Newcastle Helix
Newcastle upon Tyne
NE4 5TF
www.agendapub.com

ISBN 978-1-78821-231-1

British Library Cataloguing-in-Publication Data
A catalogue record for this book is available from the British Library

Typeset by JS Typesetting Ltd, Porthcawl, Mid Glamorgan
Printed and bound in the UK by TJ International

Contents

Acknowledgements

Seeing Ourselves grew out of a series of seminars delivered in Autumn 2017 in the Department of Philosophy at Charles University Prague. I am grateful to Dr Jakub Jirsa, Head of Department, for responding so positively to what was essentially a self-invitation.

These seminars gave me an opportunity to revisit and to think again – and think harder – about some of my most longstanding preoccupations. More importantly, the series provided a framework in which topics that are often treated separately could be seen in relation to one another. It is one of the ironies of philosophy, which aspires to understanding "how things in the broadest possible sense of the term hang together in the broadest possible sense of the term",[1] that it shares the tendency of other academic disciplines to compartmentalization. I am therefore additionally indebted to you, my anticipated reader, for providing the occasion to attempt a synthesis of some of the strands of thought that have preoccupied me over the last half-century.

Chapter 3 on "I am and it is: persons and organisms" has benefitted greatly from reading Jan Halák's writings on Maurice Merleau-Ponty and conversations with him. Chapter 7 is deeply indebted to Mark O'Connor's thought-provoking, and indeed chapter-provoking, *To Be a Machine*. Some of the material in Chapter 8 was presented at one of Anthony Stadlen's Inner Circle seminars and in a paper on spiritual irredentism in part published in *Theology* thanks to Robin Gill. I met Robin through the kind offices of Brian Pearce who has tirelessly promoted dialogue between religious believers and infidels like me, and has both directly and indirectly been a stimulus to the thoughts in the final part of this book.

I am very grateful to Andrew Pinsent for carefully reading the text and making many very useful suggestions, most importantly that I should omit one section that would have alienated many potential readers while doing little to advance the arguments of the book.

It is a special pleasure to acknowledge the fantastic support of Steven Gerrard for over a decade. Without this support, much of my writing would not have seen the light of day.

Raymond Tallis

Preface

While it is not accurate to say that *Seeing Ourselves: Reclaiming Humanity from God and Science* begins with answers and ends with questions, this would be true to its fundamental intention. My aim is the relatively modest one of clearing away certain misunderstandings about our nature that stop us addressing philosophical questions to which we need answers. While I say "relatively modest", this aim may still seem to be wildly ambitious, in view of the domination of the collective conversation by views which I oppose and the numerous platforms they have. The task is analogous to cleaning the Augean stables while the horses are still evacuating their capacious bowels. Be that as it may, the most important question is: "What kinds of beings are we?"

Full disclosure: I am a secular humanist and a patron of Humanists UK (previously titled the British Humanist Association). It will be evident in what follows that I see this stance as a point of departure rather than of arrival. Humanism, for all its virtues, still lacks a philosophy that can compete in profundity with the religious beliefs it aims to displace.

Paramount among the many drivers to *Seeing Ourselves* are three beliefs. The first is that the work of humanism does not consist solely of – the admittedly important – tasks of distancing humanity from religious belief, highlighting the damage caused by religious institutions and the prejudices they validate, and challenging the ubiquitous hard power and soft influence they have in public life. Humanism has yet to develop a sufficiently clear idea of the "human" that the "-ism" is about. While anthropologists, psychologists, sociologists, historians, and many other thinkers, researchers, and scholars, in the sciences and the humanities, hold up secular mirrors to ourselves, they often fall short of inquiry at the most fundamental level.

Philosophy can – or should – make a decisive contribution to the endeavour to understand what kinds of beings we are, even if (as is too often the case), this takes the form of correcting the errors of other philosophers. It has perhaps contributed less than it should. In part this is down to an entirely honourable commitment to rigour, that has made philosophy often rather technical and encouraged philosophers to approach problems piecemeal. There is also a tendency to engage in a conversation with other philosophers equally inclined to arcane preoccupations. This is unsatisfactory: of all disciplines, philosophy, howsoever sophisticated, should remain in touch with the questions that first motivated its practitioners, questions shared with the most naïve inquirer. The inward gaze of academic philosophy is also rooted in an increasingly prevalent tendency, particularly among metaphysicians, to position their investigations in the shadow of natural science, and to concede much of the definition of human nature to biology, psychology and allied pursuits.

My second belief is central to the argument of this book. It is this: rejecting a supernatural account of humanity does not oblige us to embrace naturalism, as if this were the only alternative. It does not follow from the truth that we are not hand-made by God that we are simply organisms shaped by the forces of evolution; that, since we are not angels, we must be merely gifted chimps.

It might seem surprising that it is so difficult to persuade humans that they amount to more than organisms with a veneer of personhood. It is less surprising given the (often justified) prestige of science as the source of answers to the most general "What?", "Why?" and "How?" questions. Besides, simple untruths – "You are your brain", "Darwin has showed that we are just animals" – are easier to disseminate than complex truths. Hence the number of publications, and the impressive sales, of books that tell their readers that they are identical with their evolved brains – an idea, although wrong, is all too readily grasped.

Which brings me to the third, and perhaps most important, belief. It is rooted in a sense, sometimes overwhelming, of the mystery of ordinary human life. This sense can be liberated only when, first, we set aside the idea that such spiritual attitudes belong to, or are the exclusive preserve of, religion, and secondly, when we reject the naturalism that reduces us to pieces of nature. Part of the process of liberation will include an awareness of the rich cultural heritage we owe to religion. "How mighty are the works of Man!" is an appropriate response to entering an awe-inspiring cathedral dedicated to a non-existent God.

Much of what follows is structured around the questions that have preoccupied philosophers over the centuries and remain central today – for example, "What is personal identity?" and "Are we truly free?". My approach is essentially descriptive rather than explanatory. I offer "thick descriptions" (a term associated with the philosopher Gilbert Ryle and, through Clifford Geertz, with anthropology) to expose the inadequacy of reductive accounts of our nature, and clear the way to questions that humanist thought should address. While Wittgenstein's often cited injunction to philosophers is "don't think, but look!"[1] the looking must be guided by thinking as much as the thinking by the looking. There is much that is strange and unexplained, as well as glorious and monstrous, about us. That we cannot deny our selfhood and our agency, and the special mode of our being in time in which they are rooted, does not mean that we can explain them; but, equally, just because we cannot explain them (for example employing modes of explanation that have been developed in natural science) does not mean that they are unreal.

Seeing Ourselves, therefore, is often polemical, being directed against those who would diminish humanity, either through thinking of us in biological terms or simply through taking for granted or overlooking what is extraordinary in our nature. Even so, the book is ultimately a celebration. Behind the philosophical arguments there is a hunger for more wakefulness inspired by a feeling of love and gratitude (admittedly, all too intermittent) for the mystery of the most commonplace manifestations of our humanity. It is an endeavour to turn up the wattage of the light in which we see our everyday world.

Seeing Ourselves brings together the preoccupations of over half a century, addressed in 30 or more published works – mainly philosophy, but also poetry, fiction, and philosophical and non-philosophical essays – and an equal quantity of unpublished material. In many places I will be presenting arguments that have appeared in others of my publications, such as *The Explicit Animal: A Defence of Human Consciousness* (1990) and *Enemies of Hope: A Critique of Anti-Humanism* (1997, 1999) and most recently in *Aping Mankind: Neuromania, Darwinitis and the Misrepresentation of Humanity* (2011, 2016), *The Mystery of Human Being: God, Free Will, and the NHS* (2016) and *Of Time and Lamentation: Reflections on Transience* (2017). Rehearsing these ideas here reflects a wish, shared with most authors, to appeal to a wider readership. Beneath the calm prose of the pages that follow there is an exasperation, at times something more heated, that ideas which I believe to be wrong – and I also believe I have shown to be wrong – still dominate the discussion about human nature.

In places I will refer the reader to these other volumes where complex arguments are spelled out in greater detail. I am aware that self-citation can be irritating. It may seem like self-promotion.[2] Moreover, directing the reader to other publications may seem to relieve the author of backing up assertions and arguments as well as giving him or her more work to do. Although I have drawn on its predecessors, the present book stands on its own merits. *Hic Rhodus, hic salta. Seeing Ourselves*, therefore, is not merely a *Condensed Raymond Tallis*, even less an anthology, though the assiduous reader (note the insightful singular) of the works of RT will observe places where ideas, phrases, sentences, even occasionally paragraphs, and of course arguments, are repeated. This is not because they could not be improved upon but because this author could not improve on them.

The great American philosopher Willard Van Orman Quine (with whom I disagree extensively in the pages that follow) once warned "the more omnivorous of my readers (dear souls) that they are apt to experience a certain indefinable sense of *deja lu*"[3] on reading one of his papers. The omnivores in my own case are few and far between and they will discover that my thinking has not, however, ceased to evolve and re-expressing the thoughts expressed in previous books has prompted me to modify them. I have been surprised at the extent to which this has happened. As Lord Acton said, we should learn as much from writing books as from reading them. Each completed volume becomes another point of departure. Attempting this synthesis of my most longstanding thoughts scattered over many books has been no exception. They have been transformed by being brought together. I have been forced to think harder, to attempt to express things more clearly, and differently, to make new connections, and to see the limitations of earlier positions, not least to understand that they are part of a whole that I had not seen, and additionally to engage with more recent work in philosophy. The work of synthesis has brought to the centre of the cognitive field insights that have hovered tantalisingly on its edge, although that edge is just as alive with a sense of yet to be articulated possibilities.

What is missing, in a book that emphasizes our fundamental difference from all other creatures, as the foundation of thinking about ourselves in a new way, is a detailed account of *how we got to be so different*. It is not that I think such an account is not possible, though it is necessarily complex. It occupies most of a three-volume trilogy I published in the early noughties, whose arguments are not replicated in full here as the present volume is already large enough. In *The Hand: A Philosophical Inquiry into Human Being* and its two successors I offer a just-so story that gives a biological account of how we came to be so different from all other beasts, even our nearest primate kin.[4] Like them, we are born *inter faeces et urinam nascimur* but, unlike them, we humans comment wryly on this – and in Latin.

While humanism is an ethical and political stance, my focus is overwhelmingly on philosophical issues – mainly because (in common with many who write about the topic) I have little of interest to say about ethics or politics.

What little I have to contribute will be confined to Part III when I examine the question of whether or how humans can flourish without belief in God; whether they will be able to live with each other better, or worse, without a transcendental warrant for good behaviour and the threat of the judgement of an omniscient God to inhibit would-be malefactors.

Religion addresses hungers that are shared by believers and infidels alike. These hungers demand satisfaction. In the final chapter, I examine what I have called "spiritual irredentism" – reclaiming the human transcendence which we have projected into or donated to imaginary deities. While this may or may not be the most significant part of the book, it is certainly the most ambitious, and is perhaps the least successful. At any rate, it aims only to help start a conversation that might result in a humanism suitable for our still young twenty-first century.

Understanding, or at least seeing, our own nature is a worthwhile, if incompletable, goal. The struggle to do so is not a task we can individually outsource to others deemed to be experts. The issues covered in this book have generated hundreds, perhaps thousands, of academic papers, and many philosophers will have spent a productive life focused on just one of them. I am anxious above all that what I have to say should speak to anyone who aches for a better understanding, or at least a clearer view, of the world, notwithstanding the entirely justified suspicion that this is a task without a clear end or a definite direction and that even small gains may be taken back as we relapse into the preoccupations of daily life. The vast majority of such people are, like me, not professional philosophers. There will be places where the arguments are difficult for readers who have read little philosophy. Chapter 3 – on being an embodied subject – and Chapter 4 – on our mode of being in time – may require more work for those unfamiliar with the territory. The more difficult arguments are, however, necessary if we are to approach our human nature at the right depth. I would like to think that the non-philosophical reader will sense that the technical arguments represent a serious endeavour to see ourselves in a different light.

I have as far as possible avoided jargon and terms created to dazzle and convey the impression of quasi-scientific depth rather than to illuminate. I have not, however, been able entirely to do without technical terms, as they may capture aspects of things that do not usually concern us in daily life. Philosophizing is often, as the French philosopher Gilles Deleuze characterized it, "concept creation"[5] as a consequence of, or as a means to, putting pressure on our everyday intuitions. I have employed only two neologisms: "thatter" and the "thatosphere". They are not very beautiful (the second term is an ugly macaronic) but I hope I shall be forgiven inventing them, as they do a lot of work. At any rate, I have found them useful to highlight something unique and central to human life and to characterize the fabric of the human world.

A commitment to rigour and to engaging with the thoughts of some of the sharpest minds in contemporary philosophy – if only to dissent from them – has meant that *Seeing Ourselves* is longer than I had hoped and many readers would want. But I could not send it out in the world as a succession of inadequately supported assertions. In a couple of places, I have assigned some of the more technical or detailed arguments to appendices, an intermediate zone between the main text and footnotes. By this means, I would hope to reach out beyond that rare species the General Reader to the General Person.

I remain conscious of the presumption in taking up so much of the reader's time: the opportunity cost, in a life of finite duration, is an opportunity lost to read other books or to do other things. The reader in a hurry – who wants to read and run – might therefore appreciate a hint as to the central thought in this book before taking the plunge.

Human beings are like nothing else in the universe and what is exceptional about our nature has an ontological depth, best captured in the contrast between "is" of nature and "am" of human nature. This multi-faceted mystery is most intimately present in the contrast between the "I am" of the person and the "it is" of the human organism. That we are able to engage with this mystery is itself a second-order mystery. In trying to see humanity and our place in the universe we are rather like soluble fish endeavouring to become oceanographers. We are generated by the ocean, our lives are lived and made possible by the ocean, and yet we have some inkling of ourselves as other than the medium in which we live.

I hope this whets your appetite. Much of this book, like most of its predecessors, has been written in pubs and cafés where I am surrounded by people, beyond the horizon of the computer screen, who do not share my preoccupations. Little, if anything, of what I or anyone else have to say on them will matter to them much, if at all. The marginalization of philosophical thought in everyday life may be a consequence of secularization, even though religious thought is often reduced to verbal reflexes, to the commonplaces of common prayer recited rather than imagined or even understood. It is disheartening to think how so much careful argument conducted by some of the most scrupulous thinkers of the present day goes unheard and contributes little to the conversation we have about ourselves. Gregory of Nyssa, one of the Fathers of the Church, once complained that it was impossible to go for a haircut without someone wanting to engage him in a discussion about some finer point of doctrine. Those were the days! And just how distant they are, may be measured by the loud sound of barrel-scraping emitted by academic philosophers obliged by the government research assessment exercise (now called the Research Excellence Framework) to earn the marks set aside for public "impact" of their work.

There is the dream, more common than many philosophers would admit to, that philosophy might be influential "upstream" of the collective conversation which seems to be largely ignorant of their cognitive labours. It is captured beautifully in John Stuart Mill's essay on Bentham:

> But they [Bentham and Coleridge] were destined to renew a lesson given to mankind by every age, and always disregarded – to show that speculative philosophy, which to the superficial appears a thing so remote from the business of life and the outward interests of men, is in reality the thing on earth which most influences them, and in the long run overbears every other influence save those which it must itself obey.[6]

Philosophy seems to have been displaced far from the centre of the conversation we have with ourselves, appearing at times to be amateur and armchair, and at other times forbiddingly technical, losing its soul down the echoing corridors of academe, where footfalls are footnotes. Its very scrupulousness demands a patience that is hard to come by. In an age dominated by social media and in which the leader of what is called The Free World is a destructive, lying toddler elevated to office by reality television, the idea of the philosopher as a Shelleyan "unacknowledged legislator of the world" seems to take wishful thinking to new heights. But if we give up on the most serious, and sustained, attempts to see ourselves aright, then we truly are lost. There may be more direct ways of contributing to the well-being of our fellows than writing philosophy but the latter has a place not only in the Kingdom of Means but also in the Kingdom of Ends: like being in love or wakefulness, it is also an end in itself.

Perhaps the least visible aspect of *Seeing Ourselves* is that, notwithstanding the polemics, it is a work of gratitude for the mysterious gift – a term that remains legitimate even in the absence of any belief in a Divine Giver – of life and of the world in which its author has passed his days. It is a thank you, as I enter old age, to all those – known and unknown to me – who made my life possible, safe, largely healthy and, by historical standards, long; to the "choir invisible" (to use George Eliot's lovely phrase) of the dead, not to speak of the visible choir of the living who have mobilized their humanity to make life better for their fellows. I would like that gratitude, and the sense of wonder that may accompany it, to be shared.

This is not to promote the naïve Panglossian view that we are the best of all species in the best of all possible worlds. Hamlet's cry – "What a piece of work is man!" is uttered in the full knowledge that we are not infrequently a very nasty piece of work. Even so, I confess to the hope that, if we see ourselves, and extraordinary achievements, more clearly, we might be more inclined to make things better. At the very least, commemorating our common difference from the rest of nature is to profess a universalism that should encourage solidarity.

I would like you to enjoy this book and to share in the intellectual, even spiritual, joy I have had in writing it and experience the wonder, and thinking the thoughts, that prompted it. Writers solicit from unknown strangers what Simone Weil called "the purest of all gifts – attention". It should be earned by expressing a purified attention to the world. Perhaps as a result of reading *Seeing Ourselves* you will see the back of your hand, or the act of saying "see you next week", or of taking a train to another town, in an entirely different, brighter light.

PART I
Overture

CHAPTER 1

Humanism and anti-humanism

WHAT IS HUMANISM?

The reader will reasonably expect a definition of the -ism in question so we shall know what is being talked about. And I will offer one presently. But I am conscious that to start with a definition – while in accordance with tradition – may not be entirely appropriate. I say this because a key task of this book will be to characterize the object, or rather the subject, of humanism – our human being. I shall be working towards, rather than jumping off from, a (relatively) sharp-edged idea of "human being". Given, also, that humanism, like humanity, is a work in progress, definitions run the risk of premature foreclosure.

Nevertheless, we must begin somewhere. Here is an attempt, by British philosopher and humanist Stephen Law in his excellent introduction to humanism[1], to characterize an outlook whose boundaries, he concedes, are very elastic. Humanism, he says:

- Embraces agnosticism or atheism;
- Advocates the application of science and reason more generally to all areas of life;
- Assumes that this life is the only life we have;
- Argues that we should embrace an ethics informed by study of what human beings are actually like and what will help them flourish in this world;
- Asserts that we have individual moral autonomy: we should make our own judgements rather than handing over responsibility to an external authority;

- Affirms that life can have meaning without being bestowed from above by God;
- Argues that we should favour an open, democratic society in which the state takes a *neutral* position with respect to religion.

That is quite a headful – encompassing metaphysical, epistemological, cultural, ethical, and political positions – so let us simplify things by quoting a standard definition. Where better to look than the website of Humanists UK? There we learn that humanism is: "A non-religious ethical life-stance the essential elements of which are a commitment to human well-being and a reliance on reason, experience, and a naturalistic view of the world".[2]

This may seem straightforward, yet it invites critical examination. Those who are not humanists will resent the suggestion that "the commitment to human well-being and a reliance on reason" is a distinguishing mark of humanists. Others will point out that reason always operates within a framework of assumptions that have not themselves been reasoned into place and, indeed, may be unconscious or irrational. But it is the opening and closing phrases that warrant our most careful attention: "a non-religious ethical life-stance" and "a naturalistic view of the world".

For many humanists, "non-religious" implies *anti*-religious and that rejecting religion – and its privileged place in public life – is the central intellectual business of humanism. This means opposing, or even attacking, the conviction that, as the philosopher A. C. Grayling put it: "there is a powerful supernatural agency or agencies active in or upon the universe, with … responsibility for its existence, an interest in human beings and their behaviour, a set of desires respecting this latter ....[3] And the connected belief in "an all-powerful, all-wise, all-knowing, all-good Creator who intervenes in human affairs, to whom we owe worship in gratitude for the gift of life and his mercy towards us".[4] It is this which humanism opposes as part of a larger project of rejecting the appeal to agents – sprites, nature spirits, and other objects of superstition – deemed to be primitive.[5]

According to this view, it is only after we have disinfected our world picture of supernatural agencies that we are free to acknowledge that we are individually and collectively responsible for our individual and collective lives, though we must still recognize the extent to which personal freedom is constrained or enabled by historical, social, more broadly cultural, and natural circumstances. We are then liberated to embrace Enlightenment in the Kantian sense[6]: emancipation from a self-imposed minority or immaturity, which is due not to lack of understanding, but lack of courage to use one's reason, intellect and wisdom without the guidance of another. We would, to employ Kant's aphoristic summary of the spirit of the Enlightenment, *Sapere aude* – "Dare to be wise".

SOME THOUGHTS ON RELIGION

Humanism would be an impoverished outlook if it were defined only in terms of what it is against. Charles Taylor has pointed out in his monumental *A Secular Age*[7] that secularism is not merely what is left over when religion has been pushed to the margins – the so-called "subtractionist" view. It has itself been actively constructed; an alternative worldview with its own set of beliefs rather than merely an absence of belief.

For this reason, I will not fill too many pages adding to the long list of assaults on religion (sometimes entertaining but sometimes imbued by a smug superiority and a stubborn literal-mindedness) by scorched earth New Atheists, headed in the English language by Richard Dawkins, Sam Harris, Christopher Hitchens and Daniel Dennett – the Four Horsemen of the Non-Apocalypse. Some readers will be tired of what they would see as rather too well-worn paths of adversarial atheism – a journey through history and the Holy Books, crying "Gotcha" at every bout of spilled blood and every bloodthirsty sentiment. Rather, I will focus, in the chapters to come, on those larger truths about humanity that might form the basis of a positive secular worldview, rooted in an acknowledgement of the transcendence inherent in the human world. In the final chapters, I will advocate a "spiritual irredentism" that reclaims for humanity the transcendence we have donated to non-existent gods.

Nevertheless, the moral case against organized religion cannot be ignored. We need to be aware of the dangers that attend the passage from individual understanding to a collective form of behaviour, from vision to institution, that accompany any endeavour to transform our most profound existential hungers into something that has a prominent place in the way we live together and govern ourselves. There are perils attending the attempt to achieve what Hans Kung characterized as "a particular *social* realisation of a relationship to an absolute ground of meaning".[8] I shall therefore confine myself to a few observations on that issue.

How beliefs in the Almighty and their interpretation of His wishes have played into individual and human collective behaviour is a separate question from that of whether the universe (including ourselves) has been created by a Divine Agent, is driven by a Divine Will, and regulated by a Divine Intelligence. And even if worshipping God (or rival gods) has made humans behave more nastily to each other, this may say something about the nature of our belief, but nothing about whether the object of such beliefs exists.

Or does it? Daniel Kodaj[9] has argued that we cannot so clearly separate the cosmological and behavioural aspects of religious belief as follows:

1. Belief in God causes evil;
2. If God exists, then God wants us to believe in God;
3. If God exists, then God does not want us to do anything that causes evil;
4. Therefore – by (1) and (3) – if God exists, God does not want us to believe in God;
5. Therefore – by (2) and (4) – God does not exist.

On this basis, belief in God is "normatively self-refuting". Rationalist theists should therefore give up their faith. In short, the religiously inspired persecution, intolerance, brutal suppression of actual or suspected dissent, the subservience of women, and Holy wars, that have characterized religion throughout the ages add up to a case not only against the institution of religion but against the very existence of God.

If this argument is to prevail, then it must be belief in God *per se*, rather than religious doctrines and sacred texts, religious teachers, and religious institutions, that is a primary, and independent, cause of our behaving badly to each other. It does make a kind of sense. Gods are necessarily jealous because their rivals must be non-existent or flawed versions of themselves and the devout must be militantly jealous on their behalf. The notion of the sacred interacts with that of the blood sacrifice – of oneself and others. However, many deeply religious people – Christians, Jews, Muslims, and so on – do not feel the slightest desire to kill their fellow men – or not at least directly. There are other forces – historical, social, political – behind religious conflict. It is arguable that in the case of the Thirty Years' War, the most catastrophic of the European confessional wars, that brought more death and destruction than the Black Death, it was dynastic ambitions and territorial disputes that drove much of the conflict. (And the very fact that we speak of "confessional" wars, is an indirect reminder that most wars are non-confessional.) There is extensive historical scholarship "that identifies religious evil – whether in the modern or pre-modern world – as the result of complex political, economic, social, ethnic, nationalist" as well as specifically religious factors.[10] It might also be argued that religious believers behaved no worse than was dictated by the mores of the time when the religions were established or in the ascendant. While Pope Urban II launched the first Crusade in the belief that God wanted the Holy Land to be rid of Muslims, Pope John Paul II in 2000 declared the crusade to be a betrayal of the gospel and condemned it.[11]

Even religious terrorism may be regarded as a form of political terrorism, as is evident when it is perpetrated in pursuit of the long-term goal of establishing a caliphate. Robert Pape has argued that: "The data show that there is little connection between suicidal terrorism and Islamic fundamentalism, or any of the world's religions. [W]hat nearly all suicide terror attacks have in common is a specific secular and strategic goal: to compel modern democracies to withdraw military forces from territory that the terrorists consider to be their homeland."[12] In short, religion is more likely to be a pretext than a primary motivation, sacralising what is in fact a profane cause such as a sense of marginalization, alienation and social frustration.

We may grant this without in any way diminishing the role religion has played in magnifying and protracting conflict in virtue of being a marker of identity, fostering the collectivization and hence amplification of hatred, hostility and aggression. The Troubles in Northern Ireland, the slaughter in Bosnia, and the endless conflict between Israel and Palestine, have been at least in part fuelled by the fact that it is always easier to hate, harm, or even kill someone who is harming God or one's version of it. It is this that seems to make violence intrinsic to religion.

What is beyond dispute is that widespread religious belief is compatible with very high levels of nastiness. It is important to remember this when (as we shall discuss in Chapter 8), we are presented with the claim Dostoyevsky puts into the mouth of Ivan Karamazov that "if God does not exist everything is permitted"[13] and the suggestion that the rise of secular humanism would quickly lead to the establishment of Hell on earth. The unspeakable evil humans have done to each other with the tacit consent or active encouragement of believers and God's representatives on earth suggests that Karamazov's "everything" is *already* permitted in a world in which the existence of God is widely accepted. The default assumption that religious belief has been a constraint on bad behaviour, a brake on evil, would not cut much ice with those on the receiving end of Crusader violence, Sunnis being blown apart by Shias, or Rohingya Muslim victims of the genocidal intentions of an explicitly Buddhist nation.

In the end it should be admitted that we do not have the data to enable us to run the history of the world twice, with and then without religion, and to know whether religion has been overall an independent force for good or evil. After all, humans do not need a transcendental pretext, even less an established church, to treat each other abominably. For some commentators, the arguments for religion promoting beneficence and making people behave better are at least as strong as those for religion fomenting, justifying, and organizing conflict and cruelty and making people behave collectively and individually worse to each other.

The difficulty of judging the overall impact of at least one religion – Christianity – is captured in this passage from the British Humanist Association pamphlet *The Case for Secularism*:

> Christianity has been the dominant culture, so it is unsurprising that it has provided the vocabulary of both sides in most significant moral and social divisions. Those who argued for the abolition of the slave trade argued their case in terms of Christian values and so did the slave-traders. Many of those who sought to improve the atrocious working conditions in factories and mines invoked Christian values – and so did the factory owners and mine owners [who opposed reforms].[14]

And the historian J. C. D. Clark (from whom we shall hear more) has argued that "Egalitarianism was a religious principle for many centuries before it became a secular one: the idea that 'all men are created equal' has real leverage only when the emphasis is placed on the word 'created' and that term is construed literally".[15] It is possible, as Michael McGhee has put it, "to *define* out the bad, so that genuine religion can only be good".[16] Or, conversely, to define religion by its malign effects.

The same difficulties are encountered when we judge non-religiously inspired violence. When the horrors of the secular totalitarian states of the twentieth century are highlighted, secularists often argue that communism and fascism are religions only lightly disguised: creeds that permit no heresy; the worship of a God-like, infallible leader; unquestioning obedience enforced by apparatchiks spying on the inner and outer lives of the flock; and the promise of a future paradise, promulgated despite the present reality of earthly Hell. The millenarian dreams of communism, so the argument goes, have inherited the promises of religion. Even Hitler claimed to be inspired by the example of Jesus Christ Who, he claimed, led the fight against the Jews. This passage in *Mein Kampf* is noteworthy: "Hence ... I believe I am acting in accordance with the will of the Almighty Creator: *by defending myself against the Jew, I am fighting for the work of the lord*" (italics in original).[17]

The historical record – and any resolution of the question of whether the contribution of religion has been net positive or net negative – cannot guide us as to whether revival of religious belief would be desirable. Even if, to take an example, the Christian doctrine that values individuals equally, because they are equal in the sight of God, has had a role in the emergence of democracies based on a universal franchise, it would not follow from this that returning established religion to a central place in society would be supportive of the

democracies we now have or would, on the contrary, have regressive consequences. The past role of religion – for good or ill – gives us unreliable pointers
to its future influence in a different kind of society. The return to religion may
be associated with undesirable changes. The argument remains unresolved –
and unresolvable – and for this reason alone is ultimately unrewarding.

Dismissing religion simply as a collective act of self-harm that humanity
must get beyond also fails to acknowledge the extent to which even secular
societies are still in thrall to certain of its assumptions. We can point to a
vast, rich cultural legacy owing to, or inspired by, religious belief, that we
cannot forget without losing something irreplaceably precious in ourselves.
The legacy is not simply "out there" in the public realm, a collective heritage of
art, literature, architecture, and music. It is in the very fibre of our individual
and social being.

The atheist, existentialist, Marxist, Maoist, Jean-Paul Sartre highlighted
this:

> [W]e are all Christians, even today; the most radical disbelief is still
> Christian atheism. In other words, it retains, in spite of its destructive
> power, schemata which are controlling – very slightly for our think-
> ing, more for our imagination, above all for our sensibility. And the
> origins of these schemata are to be sought in centuries of Christianity
> of which we are the heirs whether we like it or not.[18]

One lesson is that we must judge humanism's "commitment to human
well-being" entirely on its fruits. Religious persecution, after all, was often
justified by the beneficent intention to save the souls of the persecuted from
eternal damnation. And, as we know from bitter experience, something that
starts out as a mission to improve human well-being can, when married to
untrammelled power, result in collective catastrophe. That great humanist
Albert Camus reminded us in L'homme Revolté, with reference to the Gulag, of
"slave camps [being established] under the flag of freedom, massacres justified
by philanthropy"[19]; "[A]s soon as a man … takes refuge in a doctrine, as soon
as he makes his crime reasonable, it multiplies like Reason herself and assumes
all the figures of a syllogism. It was unique like a cry; now it is universal like
science. Yesterday, it was put on trial; today it is the law."[20]

It is salutary to recall that, for speaking these truths, and for threatening the
morale of the French working class by exposing the truth about the Gulags,
Camus was excommunicated from the circle of the last century's most famous
and influential existential humanist and his one-time friend, Jean-Paul Sartre.
It is a reminder that not all persecution is by religious believers, murdering

others in the name of a God of Love, or Justice, or Peace, for the mortal sin of mis-worship.

Secular persecution is not an inevitable consequence of humanist ideals, only a reminder that we should evaluate them, as we evaluate religions, not by how good they sound but by how well they are applied. The path from the humanism of the early Marx to the horrors of the totalitarian states created in his name are no more inevitable than that which connects the Christian doctrine of love and peace with pogroms, murderous Crusades, the Albigensian genocide, the Thirty Years' War and the sponsorship of antisemitism that led to the Holocaust. That path has also been taken by the secular successors of the theocratic leaders – by Stalin, Mao, and Pol Pot and their followers – as hundreds of millions have learnt to their cost. It is a bitter irony that, under aggressively atheist tyranny, covert religious observance became an expression of a lost freedom.

Humanists therefore have a duty to remember that religion does not have a monopoly of organized, and institutionally justified violence. Yes, as Alister and Joanna McGrath point out,

> [religion] possesses a capacity to transcendentalize normal human conflicts and disagreements, transforming them into cosmic battles of good and evil in which the authority and will of a transcendent reality is implicated. Divine warfare is terrestrialized, its mandate transferred to affairs on earth. When this situation arises, the normal constraints and compromises that allow humans to solve potentially explosive problems are trumped.[21]

However: "[W]hen a society rejects the idea of God, it tends to transcendentalize alternatives – such as the ideals of liberty or equality. These now become quasi-divine authorities, which none are permitted to challenge".[22]

One current example will have to stand for many. At present, China's most sweeping internment programme since Mao has imprisoned a million or more Uighur Muslims for "transformation through education". The goal is to rid them of devotion to Islam.[23]

Lucretius' famous aphorism "*Tantum religio potuit suadere malorum*" – "to such heights of evil has religion been able to drive men" – may make the idea of an omnipotent, beneficent God, difficult to uphold. A more powerful argument for atheism, however – and one that I would like to think was decisive in my own case – is that any God that can be distilled from the 200 or so religions on offer seems to be a mass of contradictions. A deity who is self-caused, or who is both infinite and yet distinct from His creation, or who is eternal and unchanging and without location in space and time but nevertheless intervenes for good or ill in human affairs, or who is omnipotent and good and yet allows evil to thrive and suffering to continue unchecked, seems as attractive logically as a square circle. And while it is true that (notwithstanding the claims of certain physicists) we have no explanation of why there is a) something rather than nothing, b) there is life as well as dead matter, c) there is conscious life as well as life, and d) there are forms of conscious life that make at least partial sense of the world, these gaps in our understanding cannot be filled by means of a word – "God" – laden with historical baggage, used as a threat, a promise, or a curse. Whatever God may have or have not achieved "God" – or any meaning attached to Him – cannot emancipate the various modes of existence from their contingency[24] and stand for the possibility of explanation of the unexplained. Adding God to the ontological menagerie does not reduce the inexplicability of the universe; rather it redirects it upwards.

On the other hand, rational arguments against the existence of God may prompt the response from believers that experiencing God's presence is not the same as arriving at the conclusion of an argument; rather His reality is embraced through a leap of faith or felt as "a fire in the head" (as Nijinsky said in his Diary)[25] or in the heart.

At any rate, I remain agnostic about my own reasons for being a secular humanist and I will focus in what follows on the other, to me more interesting, aspect of humanism – which is to seek a positive vision, even an affirmation, of what humanity is. I will for this reason – and a disinclination to preach to the converted or the unconvertible – spend no more time on the arguments for (and against) the existence of God.

HUMANISM AND HISTORY: AN EXCULPATORY NOTE

> The present aeon, since 600 BC, stands in the sign of personal salvation. Only since this time has there been a notion of humanity because there is only one single category of personality and this is humanity.
>
> Béla Hamvas[26]

You may feel that the definition of humanism I have offered so far is a hopelessly inadequate starting place for engaging with a cluster of ideas, an aspiration, even a battle cry, that has had a complex history going back several millennia, albeit most of it before it was named. Let me develop it a little.

The modern term "humanist" was established in German educational theory and intellectual history in the early part of the nineteenth century.[27] It has then been applied, often retrospectively, to aspects of Enlightenment, Renaissance, and even Presocratic thought. The names with which it could be plausibly associated in western thought range from Xenophanes and Protagoras, to Epicurus and Seneca, Giovanni Pico della Mirandola, Montaigne, the eighteenth-century *Philosophes*, David Hume, Kant, Goethe, Auguste Comte, Miguel Unamuno, and Bertrand Russell. For some, humanism is a catch-all term for "the best that has been thought and said" in the great conversation that humanity – at least in its western manifestation – has had with itself.

Secular thought is not unique to the western tradition. As Amartya Sen has pointed out: "Indian traditions are often taken to be intimately associated with religion ... and yet Sanskrit and Pali have larger literatures on systematic atheism and agnosticism than perhaps in any other classical language".[28] It has been present most enduringly in China among the followers of Confucius.

Surely there is more to be said. A concept, a conception, a world picture, an ethos, a mode of collective self-awareness and self-assertion, an aspiration for humanity, that has such a long, if largely *avant la lettre* history, you might think, deserves more than a few paragraphs. This especially since "humanism" is a term steeped in politics and not all of it reducible to headline anti-clericalism, to the power play between Church and State, and modes of insurgency against secular hierarchies and priestly despotism, and those authorities that do not seem to exhibit "a commitment to human well-being and a reliance on reason". Humanism is a socio-political movement, a cry of freedom, a call to arms, a psychological and ethical stance, a defence of the right to think for one's self and to assert, as Giovanni Pico della Mirandola did, the dignity of man, who had been created "neither celestial nor earthly ... thy own free moulder and overcomer ... You alone have the power to develop and to grow according to free will".[29]

All this may be granted but, I am relieved to say, it is not relevant to the central purpose of this book. *Seeing Ourselves* will be a philosophical rather than an historical, political, or cultural inquiry into humanism. This is decreed in part by my own limited knowledge of the history of ideas, and absence of qualifications to say anything original about that history. The territory and its associated bibliography are huge: no life of finite duration could engage with the relevant literature and no book of finite duration could do it justice. Whether an ahistorical approach to humanism is serious flawed will be something you may judge when you have reached the end of the final chapter. Philosophy typically examines ideas with a minimal chaperoning by their history, only the slightest reference to the context in which they first arose, judging them on what seem to be their merits, on what they have to say to us now. If I narrow the scope of my inquiry it is for the sake of deepening it and connecting it with distinctively philosophical questions that are currently the subject of some of the most interesting and fruitful arguments in this discipline.

While I am in the business of managing your expectations, I ought to add that I will have nothing original and even less of interest to say about the *politics* of humanism or even the project of developing a distinctive humanist ethics. What little I have to say on the latter will be postponed until the final chapter when I touch on the question of whether, in the absence of divine commandments and the threat of what might result if one disobeys them, it is likely that people would behave well towards their fellows; whether, as is taught by many religions, the only path to goodness is through submission to the will of God.

SECULARISM IN RETREAT?

Secularism is far from achieving the global dominance anticipated by ill-informed infidels like me a few decades ago: it is not a done deal. It is easy, for someone coming from a relatively godless nation like the UK, to imagine that *Homo religiosus* is being consigned to history and to extrapolate from the emptiness of Anglican pews to worldwide secularization. The annual British Social Attitudes Survey showed a steady rise in the proportion of people declaring they have no religion, from 30 per cent in 1983 to 52 per cent in 2018.[30] According to a YouGov poll in 2013, 51 per cent of respondents "would not describe [themselves] as having values that are religious or spiritual".[31] Similar patterns are seen in other European countries.

These secularizing trends are not replicated throughout the globe. We do not need to look to theocratic states to see religion as not merely flourishing but resurgent. In communist China, for example, where Christianity is hardly the prescribed faith of the state, church membership is rising at an accelerating rate.[32] And according to a recent survey, the number of Christians in Africa has increased from 9 million in 1900 to an estimated 380 million in 2000.[33] Harriet Sherwood reminds us that 84 per cent of the world's population identifies with a religious group.[34] What is more, members of religious groups are generally younger and produce more children than those who have no religious affiliation. As a consequence, between 2015 and 2060, while the world's inhabitants are expected to increase by 32 per cent, the Muslim population is expected to rise by 70 per cent and Christians by 34 per cent. Meanwhile, the religiously unaffiliated will increase by 3 per cent. By contrast, in Europe, Christian deaths between 2010 and 2015 outnumbered births by nearly 6 million.

It has been suggested that secularization is going into reverse, not only for demographic reasons.[35] This passage from Peter Berger, one of the leading sociologists of religion over the last 50 years, is striking: "[A] whole body of literature by historians and social scientists loosely labelled 'secularization theory' is essentially mistaken ... The world today is massively religious, is *anything but* the secularized world that had been predicted (whether joyfully or despondently) by so many analysts of modernity".[36]

For this reason alone, a triumphalist reading of humanity's spiritual history is not justified. We may even be in a post-secularist age. As John Micklethwait and Adrian Wooldridge have pointed out, "God is Back".[37] The forms of worship are often evangelical, with a literal interpretation of the sacred texts, and religious beliefs are increasingly visible and influential in public life. One interpretation is that this is a triumph not so much of religion as of competing wares in a spiritual marketplace. God, texts, rituals, and memberships are products that are to be sold.

There are, at any rate, no grounds for an intellectual and cultural history that, to quote Jonathan Rée's ironical characterization of the secularization thesis, "draws an *a priori* straight line from a primitive 'natural' state and leading up to the ultimate summit of civilization", a cognitive advance from natural idiocy to rational efficiency and ultimately to a grown-up, disenchanted notion of humanity as "no more than an accidental efflorescence on the surface of a cooling planet, awaiting cosmic death and signifying nothing".[38] Equally unwarranted are "versions of secularism's history, whereby human nature steadily casts off its shackles of ignorance and superstition, finally emerging from a Bastille of the mind into the bright morning of truth".[39] This would anyway be open to question even if the expected secularization of increasingly rationalistic, contractual, bureaucratic, globalized societies had occurred as rapidly as once anticipated. After all, as Peter Harrison has argued, there is a case for seeing "secularisation as a natural outgrowth of this-worldly Protestantism" and even for "the origins of unbelief in the modern West" lying in "conceptions of moral responsibility and freedom generated from within Christianity itself".[40]

For these reasons if no other, humanism needs to look critically at some of its basic sociological and cultural assumptions. Its bill of fare may not be found sufficiently spiritually nourishing to a humanity assumed to be enlightened. While the "reliance on reason" flagged up in the Humanists UK mission statement quoted earlier is hardly contentious in societies in which science is the dominant cultural fact and public policy aspires to be evidence-based, or to appear so, the commitment to opposing unreason, evidence-free claims, and irrational hierarchies, must always be checked case-by-case. The findings are not always encouraging to the rational mind. One could be forgiven for sometimes suspecting that "superstition" – like ideology, or prejudice – is usually something to which others rather than ourselves are prone. What counts as evidence depends on how our inquiries are framed; and we are less likely to notice those injustices in the social order from which we ourselves, or those with whom we identify, benefit. The wearyingly familiar cry "check your privileges!" – in other words, be aware of the assumptions, the interests, the unexamined historical and cultural truths that shape your thought – does, after all, carry some weight. And the history of humanity furnishes us with countless instances where the application of reason in the absence of reasonableness, without an empathetic understanding of the situation to which it is applied, may be irrational. The disastrous dreams of quasi-scientific approaches to social organization in for example the Soviet Union and Maoist China – not to speak of the fantasies of the transhumanists that we shall discuss in the penultimate chapter – are salutary reminders of where unchecked reason may take us. As G. K. Chesterton pointed out, "a madman is not someone who has lost his reason but has lost everything but his reason".[41]

I will return to some of these questions in the final chapter. For the present, I will advance no further into what is an impenetrable thicket of tangled questions about the relationship between human history and the ideas its actors have about human nature.

CONTROVERSY AROUND THE VERY IDEA OF A DISTINCT HUMAN NATURE

Seeing Ourselves aims to look upstream of the kinds of claims that appear in the mission statements of humanist organizations, at least in part by attempting to delineate the nature of humanity more clearly, to highlight the essential and universal and distinctive features of humankind. I am inclined to characterize what I shall offer in the chapters to come as notes towards a definition of our "species being" – fully aware that the phrase raises much suspicion.

Granted, there are grounds for such suspicion. The notion of our "species being" is particularly associated with Marx and his quarrel with his older contemporary, the secular humanist Ludwig Feuerbach.[42] In the sixth of his theses on Feuerbach, written in 1845, Marx criticized Feuerbach's famous claim that the essence of religion reflected the essence of man. Against this, Marx argued, that man had no permanent and universal essence but was an ensemble of social relations that altered throughout history.

Marx's later views were more complex and allowed for a human nature in general which was modified in each historical epoch. Even so, the notion of a universal human nature, of an enduring human essence, is still treated with suspicion because it is seen as a key to concealing the accidents of history that shape what we are, thereby justifying as "natural" the often-oppressive situations in which many human beings live out wretched lives. In short, so the argument goes, the idea of an enduring human essence can be invoked to defend a status quo which, if it were seen clearly, would be seen to be indefensible.

Essentialist definitions of humankind can also, it is argued, lead to essentialist definitions of womankind and of anyone else that those who are doing the defining wish to freeze out from their own position of personal, political and monetary power and existential authority. They are implicated in the way European colonizers judged indigenous peoples as failing to meet the criteria for fully formed human beings, and as being closer to nature, and therefore appropriate for exploitation as beasts of burden. This was a concern that had a major influence on many thinkers, particularly certain Parisians prominent in the latter half of the twentieth century.[43]

It might further be argued that to aspire to characterize a human essence as something universal and stable is to go against one of the fundamental beliefs of humanism: that humans have a unique capacity to re-define, transform, and exceed themselves. It was Blaise Pascal, scarcely a humanist, who asserted that "L'homme passe infiniment l'homme"[44] – although history has taught us not to be too starry-eyed about the extent to which this is possible, or the direction which it might take, or the permanence of anything that might be deemed to be an advance. The idea of universal human characteristics might also seem to be at odds with existentialist humanism whose central thought was summarized in the motto: "existence precedes essence". Our lives, we are told, are not the unfolding of a predetermined essence. Any essence we have is post hoc, the product of our enactment of our freedom. We make ourselves through a life of freely chosen actions.

The most persuasive objection to specifying the universal characteristics of our species being is that any definition of what it is to be human, may be prescriptive rather than purely descriptive and shaped by the implicit ideology of those who are doing the characterizing. It will be a continuation of the very tendency, noted by Feuerbach, to develop our notion of God in our image. Our conception of humankind is fashioned after an image a sub-group of humanity may have of themselves. There are particular dangers where that image is an idealization. Many humans will then be deemed to have failed the test for being granted full humanity. Conveniently, this will justify reducing them to means to our ends, even enslavement. Even the generosity of spirit that motivated enlightenment thinkers such as Voltaire and Diderot, might turn into a universal aspiration for humanity that everyone should become more like themselves. The universalist, so the story goes, extends the hand of recognition on condition that the Other is not terribly Other or at least has the capacity to recover from his or her Otherness. To be fully human is to be male, white, European, middle class, able-bodied, and above all Parisian.

The mixed blessing of Enlightenment universalism is captured in this passage from Annette Gordon-Reed:

> While the Enlightenment (in all its different incarnations) nurtured anti-slavery sentiment, promoted personal liberty, made room for religious tolerance and provided a critique of cruel forms of punishment, like any extremely powerful idea or concept, it had negative effects that went along with the positive. Indeed, it can be difficult to grasp that features endemic to the system of thought – the impulse to categorize and put things into hierarchies, and the faith in the capacity to measure scientifically, as well as the very notion of progress – contributed to the need to classify not only ideas and things but also, alas, groups of people. Scholars have noted that it provided a basis, for those so inclined, to create a "science" of race and racial hierarchies that often justified the domination and ill-treatment of people classed as "inferior".[45]

The generous-spirited conviction expressed by the Roman playwright Terence in his play *Heauton Timorumenos* – "I am human; and nothing human is alien to me" – might be greeted with scepticism, given that the Roman Empire ran on slavery, were it not for the fact that Terence was the son of a slave and was himself a slave for the greater part of his short life. The sentiment is that we are, above all, members of the human race, citizens of the world with common needs, hopes, aspirations; that, if we understood ourselves properly, we would have similar fundamental values, notwithstanding that we are members of different tribes, of cultures divided by a profound difference of languages that give the world entirely different tastes, of modes of being-in-the-world.

Even the seemingly most generous and welcoming universalism, captured in the notion that we all belong to the Great Family of Man, has been criticized as passing over in silence the structures of oppression and of power that crush most people who have lived. It gives a definition of man (so we are told) that mirrors the class interests of our culture. According to a witty and mean-spirited essay by Roland Barthes, on a photographic exhibition in Paris on The Family of Man, he found examples of humanity "moralized and sentimentalized" and

"Nature and History confused at every turn".[46] He dismisses the focus in the exhibition on universal experiences, such as birth, childhood, work, laughter and death, as expressive of a sentimental humanism that overlooks the reality of irreducible differences, and of conflict and injustice.[47]

Defining the "species being" of humankind, therefore, is an exercise fraught with danger. The greatest danger is that of finding that some, perhaps most, people do not meet the entrance qualifications. They are deemed to be not human, or not yet, or no longer: thus, the "dehumanization challenge", discussed by Maria Kronfeldner.[48] We are only too aware where this may lead: the gas chambers for Jews, Roma people, or people with disability, or the Rohingya drowning in mud. Thus, the case for the prosecution.

While this is true to how things have sometimes turned out, it is unfair to the Terentian generosity of spirit that motivates the idea of universalism, the sense that the most important things about us are what we have in common. It underpins the Universal Declaration of Human Rights whose first article reads: "All human beings are born free and equal in dignity and rights. They are endowed with reason and conscience and should act towards one another in a spirit of brotherhood."[49] Of course, "brotherhood" should include "sisterhood". And, yes, this declaration is more conspicuous in the breach than in the observance. Nevertheless, it provides a benchmark against which we can measure our failings. To reject it would be to close off hope for a future in which all may flourish.

Even so, I owe you a more careful characterization of the nature of the inquiry into our "species being" that I shall be undertaking in the pages to come – if only to dispel the suspicion that my philosophical anthropology is not the captive of special interests or ideology, and to reassure you that this inquiry is sufficiently distant from essentialist anthropology as to be incapable of justifying the crimes of which the latter is sometimes justly, and sometimes unjustly, accused. The project of *Seeing Ourselves* is carried out, I believe, in such a way that the unaddressed question of who is seen and who is doing the seeing will not deliver an answer that will determine that some human beings are not part of the human family. The level at which the human universals, the clusters of typical capacities, are identified in the chapters that follow does not license the exclusion of any human beings from ranks of humanity and permits them to be treated as inferiors, as deficient, less than human, entities, who are at best mere means to an end. Nor does it overlook the huge variety of entirely valid ways of living a human life or the uniqueness of individual human beings. Rather it simply identifies a cluster of fundamental traits that are the most fundamental enablers of human life and human cultures. (Nor, incidentally, does it justify the cruel treatment of other species.)

Exploration of our nature as embodied subjects (Chapter 3), of our mode of being in – and out of – time (Chapter 4), of our selfhood (Chapter 5), and of our agency (Chapter 6), is not morally compromised in the way that the pursuit of human universals sometimes is, and which has made the very idea of "universalism" deeply suspect. To take one example. In Chapter 4, I identify the notions of "that" and "at" as designating key aspects of our distinctive human consciousness. These are scarcely terms that are open to ideological abuse. The "thatosphere", and the meta-fact that this sphere is constituted out of facts, hardly privileges one sub-group of humanity at the expense of others. To the contrary, it underlines our common human heritage, that has been forged in the vast verbal and non-verbal conversation that we have had with ourselves for hundreds of thousands of years.

My pre-emptive defence may prompt an opposite charge: given that it is conducted at a fundamental level, beneath politics, this inquiry is not only politically impotent, but distracts from that which is politically urgent, from the remediable sorrows and the iniquities suffered by humankind. It is consequently highly political in virtue of having no traction on the way things are ordered in the real world. If, as Berthold Brecht said, "to speak of trees is to pass over so many crimes in silence",[50] how can we defend labouring over definitions of humanity that speak of "intentionality", the "thatosphere" and other technicalities? On this issue, I am not entirely agnostic; for I have a stubborn faith that identifying, exploring, and – yes – celebrating the mystery of our humanity may in some indirect way have a beneficial effect on how we view, and hence treat, each other. This faith has somehow survived the fact that, as a doctor for many decades, the conversation – with my patients and colleagues – was rarely, if ever, of philosophy.

It is important, also, to distinguish what I regard as fundamental features of human beings from anything that might count as "entrance criteria", that determine whether an individual counts as a fully paid-up member of the human race. There is only one entrance criterion: a human being is someone whose parents are members of the biological species *H. sapiens.* That's it: having human parents is a necessary and sufficient condition of counting as a human being. The features that I examine as defining us are not additional "entrance qualifications" necessary for admission to the human race but simply fundamental characteristics that humans typically have. Although they are close to being universal, it is not necessary to have them to warrant being treated as a human being. There is a huge variation in capacities, talents, propensities, and personality traits. People with severe disabilities who are unable to engage with time in the way that is unique to humans, or lack a sustained sense of self, or have limited agency, are still humans with the rights of humans and we have obligations to them. In short, the features that I identity as unique to humanity are typical and universal, but not mandatory. We do not need to pass an examination to qualify as a human being.[51]

THE HUMANITIES AGAINST HUMANISM

It is a particularly bitter irony that some of the most sustained and elaborate attacks on humanism have come from within the academic humanities. In the latter half of the previous century, one would have in certain quarters to be possessed of a death wish to admit that one was a humanist. Much of the academic attack on humanism will have escaped the attention of most readers. What was fiercely debated in lecture halls, in specialist journals, and in international conferences, scarcely registered in the outside world. Terms such as "deconstruction", "postmodernism" and "poststructuralism" may have seeped out of the seminar room and the Groves of Hackademe but they made no impact on human affairs – a state of affairs that was guaranteed by the opacity and absurdity of the pronouncements of *maîtres à penser* echoed by their thousands of disciples teaching students who learned to replicate them in order to please their teachers and pass their exams. The legacy of this form of anti-humanism has been a lingering suspicion directed at anyone who advocates the kind of humanism to which this book is dedicated: at best they are politically naïve; at worst, they are malign upholders of race-class-gender prejudices.

The domination of humanities departments (in particular of literature) by anti-humanism was upheld by bad philosophy and worse linguistics. Those who want the full story of the dishonesty and cowardice of those whose academic self-advancement depended on spouting ideas that in many cases they could not understand, are welcome to read *Not Saussure: A Critique of Post-Saussurean Literary Theory*.[52] It is, however, fortunate that structuralist and poststructuralists ideas, so thrillingly subversive a few decades ago, are now regarded as old hat and those that propounded them, their priests, acolytes, and humble curates in hundreds of humanities departments both sides of the Atlantic and indeed worldwide, have long since retired from academe or indeed from life, being deconstructed in more literal ways than those that kept the professors busy for so many years spouting opacities or summarizing the total consciousness of great swathes of humanity in a handful of scornful sentences.

This should have cleared the decks for an approach to ourselves, to accepting that mankind, as a notion that, far from having had its day, is at a kind of beginning. But alas this version of the anti-humanities has been succeeded by something that is almost as bad. I am referring to *biologism*, which lies at the heart of our present concerns. After the uncritical rejection of science and the postmodernist (and ill-informed) dismissal of its claims to objective knowledge, there has in recent decades been an equally uncritical embrace of the dubious idea that the natural sciences, particularly the neurosciences, have something important to say about, even have the last word on, art, ethics, politics, the law, economics; that they may transform the study of those topics into a properly grounded discipline; or, more ambitiously, that brain science is, or will be, the key to understanding humanity. *Humanities* will (at last) come of age as *animalities*. New interdisciplinary pursuits have emerged prefixed by "neuro", "evolutionary", or even "neuro-evolutionary", embodying the hopes of advancing our understanding of the law, of ethics, of aesthetic experiences. The fact that collaboration with scientists with their expensive equipment can increase the grant income of academics in the humanities may not be irrelevant.

At any rate, there has been a trend towards explaining humanity by appeal to the science of the brain, understood as an organ designed to secure biological survival. "My brain made me do it", "we are evolved to behave in such-and-such a way individually and collectively" are the commonplaces of what passes for thought in many quarters.

Even philosophers are not immune to the "strong contagion" (to borrow Dr Johnson's phrase) of the white coat. Indeed, some philosophers embraced scientism in advance of practitioners of other humanities. Naturalism has been the default position of many in the analytical tradition. For Willard Van Orman Quine, who endeavoured to demonstrate a continuity in human cognitive development from "the irritation of nerve endings" to scientific theories[53], the "philosophy of science is philosophy enough".[54] It is up to science, not only to inform us about what exists but also to show us how we come to know what exists – indeed what science is and how it is possible. The logical positivists argued that the only knowledge worth having was scientific knowledge and that the traditional inquiries of the philosopher generated assertions that lacked truth value or empirical testability and were thus meaningless.

What we might call "science cringe" – the sense that philosophy is just playing round the edges of science to which it has little to contribute – is still alive and well in the writings of many philosophers. The philosophers' reliance on intuitions and arguments rather than the latest news from science in addressing metaphysical questions has been dismissed by science groupies in the discipline as primitive, a cognitive ox cart in the era of the jet engine.

More to the point, or so we are reminded, science has taught us how mis-leading intuitions are and how the truths about the real nature of things are often counter-intuitive. Quantum mechanics is crazy but powerful and true. Pre-Copernican metaphysics would maintain that the sun circles the earth and not vice versa. Philosophy is consequently best practised as the hand-maiden of science, perhaps contributing to its unification, not as something that is parallel to, or transcends, science.

BILL OF FARE

The intention to counter the capitulation of the humanities to the greater authority of science in advancing a fundamental understanding of our nature and, more specifically challenging a naturalism that is beholden to science, has played a key role in setting the agenda of the chapters that follow. My aim is to sketch the outlines of an image of our human being that may inform sub-sequent reflections on our collective future in the absence of religious beliefs propped up by institutions and tribal loyalties. An essential preliminary is to challenge the assumption that the only alternative to a supernatural under-standing of what we are must be one that sees us as pieces of nature.

A central target will be the seemingly self-evident presupposition – illus-trated in the mission statement of Humanists UK – that a justified respect for reason (assuming, that is, we can agree as what counts as the reasonable use of reason) and experience-based evidence (assuming we can agree on what counts as "experience" and what as interpretation) must lead to "a naturalistic view of the world" and warrants the belief that Della Mirandola's being that is "neither celestial nor earthly" is assumed to be entirely "earthly" because not "celestial".

The kind of naturalism I want to demolish has two aspects. The first is the assumption that "a naturalistic view of the world" must be one in which nature is to be understood ultimately in terms defined by the theories and discoveries of the natural sciences, whose queen is mathematical physics. And the second is the assumption that the human world, the human mode of being, can be included within the scope of the natural world. By this means, we arrive at the view that humanity is a piece of nature subject to the laws uncovered by science.

It has often been pointed out that naturalism is influenced by the dominant sciences of the day. Enlightenment naturalism was inspired by Newtonian mechanics and in some cases the idea of man as a little machine in the great machine of the cosmos. Late nineteenth-century naturalism was influenced by Darwinism and the idea of a Great (but continuous) Chain of Being, leading from gunk or primal slime at the bottom to you, the reader of this book, at the very top. Contemporary naturalistic accounts of humanity-as-animality have been shaped by neuroscience and the modern synthesis of evolutionary theory.

Scientism is an unsurprising consequence of science being the overwhelming cultural presence of our age. When we are faced with practical problems, even insoluble ones, we look to science, rather than (as the Psalmist would put it) to the hills, whence cometh our help. As Ernest Gellner expressed it: "while once upon a time there was science within the world, now it is as if the world were within science; science became the container, the world the content".[55] And we are gathered up within this container. It is necessary, I believe to reject this – without in anyway denying the benefits brought by science and the fact that it is the crowning cognitive achievement of humanity.

My first port of call (Chapter 2), therefore, will be to examine critically the kind of scientistic naturalism currently in the ascendant, manifested in two cognitive pathologies which I have christened "neuromania" and "Darwinitis". I hope I will persuade you that there is more to humanity than being a piece of nature; more to persons than being organisms. Contrasting us with other living beings, saying what we are not, is a way of highlighting what we are: *Omnis determinatio est negatio.* I shall next turn my attention to the distinctive features of humanity that elude interpretation in naturalistic terms. They are: our nature as embodied subjects rather than mere organisms (Chapter 3); our mode of being in and out of time (Chapter 4); personal identity or selfhood (Chapter 5); and agency (Chapter 6). These topics are interdependent: the extension through time that underpins our sense of selfhood is a necessary condition of our taking responsibility for our actions and being fully-fledged agents and it is implicit in our complex relationships to our bodies.

Much of what I will have to say will correspond to what Wittgenstein characterized as "assembling reminders for a purpose",[56] reminders that would be unnecessary were they not required to counteract the willed amnesia of many thinkers who are determined to erase the more complex features of humanity for the sake of a simplicity that promises to ease the process of gathering up human nature into nature period.

Notwithstanding our transcendence of our biological condition we are still beholden to the life of our bodies. The biological processes that permit us to live also decree that we shall die. The species *H. sapiens* is unique, however, in the degree to which its members are aware of the inevitability of death. Therein lies the truth of W. B. Yeats' seemingly paradoxical assertion that "man has created death":

Nor dread nor hope attend
A dying animal;
A man awaits his end
Dreading and hoping all; ...
He knows death to the bone –
Man has created death.[57]

Awareness of our necessary mortality haunts the last four chapters. The sometimes touching, often chilling, absurdities of the "transhumanist movement" and its technological battle against finitude are an instructive false path for humanism. In Chapter 7, I will focus especially on the idea, cherished by the evangelical wing of transhumanism, that we can secure immortality by arranging for our identities to be uploaded on to some other medium which is not subject to the ills to which the flesh is heir. This is not only the most absurd and extreme response to the threat of extinction but philosophically the most interesting because it draws on the idea – mainstream in much contemporary thought – that our identity is essentially "information" and that that information is reducible to the replicable states of material bodies.

In the third and final part – "Flourishing Without God" – I will examine the challenges that humanism must face when mankind tries to do without the consoling beliefs and rituals that come with religion. My starting point will be the profound mystery of humanity and of human life that becomes visible when the distorting lenses of naturalism are removed. If religion continues to play a part in secular life, its contribution may not be as a body of belief to be embraced but as an exemplar of the way to address the human predicament at a depth that does it justice. In Chapter 8, I will look at the hole left by the withdrawal of religion from secular societies: the "disenchantment of the world"; the lack of meaning in the universe, and of our lives within it; and the self-destruction of meaning in our lives as we move from one thing to the next, in a permanent state of "and then", of meanings that have no point of convergence or any accumulation.

The focus in Chapter 9 will be on the search for significance – in work and in making the world a better place. I will also argue that religious belief is not necessary for a society based on ethics and the rule of law. Nevertheless, religion offers something – beyond a putative basis for ethics – that is missing in secular belief. This sets the scene for the final chapter in which I examine ways in which we may reclaim ourselves from what we have hitherto donated to the gods via religious belief. I argue that "disenchantment" overlooks what is transcendent in us; that it bypasses the fundamental mystery of the emergence of the human subject in a subjectless universe, of "am" in Being. This provides the justification for reclaiming for humanity the transcendence that has been assigned to the gods. The means of doing so, however, remain problematic. Hence the final section of the final chapter, which looks to develop a framework for a dialogue between secular philosophy and religious thought.

We may distance ourselves from the answers provided by religion but the questions still remain.

PART II
Our Human Being

CHAPTER 2

Against naturalism: neither ape nor angel

SUPERNATURALISM, NATURALISM AND EXTRA-NATURALISM

There is an assumption – prevalent among humanists and indeed many secular philosophers[1] – that if we are not hand-crafted by God in His own image, we must be understood as the product of processes observed throughout nature. The claim is seductive given that naturalism, like humanism, is opposed to supernaturalism: since they have a common enemy, so the unspoken argument goes, humanism and naturalism must be allies.

As it turns out, naturalism proves to be a false friend. While it may have once liberated us from dogmatic religion and all the political and social powers that came with it, it is itself an alternative intellectual prison. Consistent naturalism leads to a denial of our agency: we are organisms acting out a biological script. In short, it is as anti-humanistic as religious belief. If the latter sees us as fallen, the former sees us as unrisen – which scarcely seems much of an improvement.

Clearly, we cannot proceed without specifying what is meant by "naturalism". It is, as Barry Stroud has pointed out in his beautiful paper "The Charm of Naturalism",[2] a term with a range of meanings. A commitment to naturalism, like a commitment to world peace, is unlikely to meet much opposition until one gets down to terms and conditions.[3]

At one extreme, there is the reductive, scientistic naturalism exemplified in D. M. Armstrong's assertion that "the natural world contains nothing but the entities recognized by physics".[4] This is hard-headed indeed: the world is the natural world; the natural world boils down to the physical world; and the physical world is the world according to physicists – an exsanguinated realm of quantities and patterns described by laws and equations. Less austere, is the claim that the natural world is the world as revealed by the natural sciences. In the case of human beings, the most relevant sciences are the biological sciences: scientism takes the form of biologism, whose classic statement is by the nineteenth-century philosopher and physiologist Ludwig Buchner: "The researches and discoveries of modern times can no longer allow us to doubt that man, with all he has and possesses, be it mental or corporeal, is a natural product like all other organic beings".[5]

A naturalized epistemology, grounding all our knowledge in the effects of the material world on our nervous system, rounds off this extreme scientism. As Quine wittily admits, this presents the challenge of explaining: "how we, physical denizens of the physical world, can have projected our scientific theory of that whole world from our meagre contacts with it: from the mere impacts of rays and particles on our surfaces and a few odds and ends such as the strain of walking uphill".[6]

Full-blown reductionist naturalism looks to the empirical laws discovered by natural science for answers to traditional questions of ontology, metaphysics and epistemology. Naturalism, Quine averred, is "the recognition that it is within science itself, and not in some prior philosophy, that reality is to be identified and described".[7] Philosophy, it appears, has very little of its own substance to bring to understanding the fundamental nature of things or even of our knowledge of them.

At the other extreme is an "expansive", liberal naturalism that allows the reality of states of affairs and of psychological phenomena disallowed or reduced by materialist naturalists. Expansive naturalism, as Stroud says, "does not amount to anything very substantive or controversial": it is "little more than a slogan or a banner raised to attract the admiration of those who agree that no supernatural agents are at work in the world".[8] Such a naturalism may be very hospitable indeed. Galen Strawson's "real naturalism", for example, encompasses panpsychism – the presence of mind throughout the universe – which he sees as an inescapable consequence of taking experience seriously.[9]

My main focus will be on biologism. It is, I will maintain, an obstacle to advancing our understanding of, or even seeing, our own nature; and it is a direct threat to humanism. It is at best boringly wrong and at worst dangerous. According to this form of naturalism, human beings, since they are not hand-made by God, and endowed with immortal souls, must simply be organisms; not being angels, we are simply apes. Most importantly, it is a direct challenge to the claim that human beings are fundamentally exceptional.

I am going to focus on two of the most prominent manifestations of biological naturalism: the intellectual diseases of "neuromania" and "Darwinitis".

The case that I shall present is set out in considerable – some might say pitiless – detail in *Aping Mankind*.[10] The purpose of doing so is to assert what should be sufficiently obvious: that there is a profound difference between humanity and animality, between ourselves and our nearest primate kin. My position has been expressed by the neuroscientist V. S. Ramachandran: "Humanity transcends apehood to the same degree by which life transcends mundane chemistry and physics".[11]

The arguments in this chapter will prepare the way for an examination of more fundamental aspects of our distinctive nature: the ways we are related to our bodies and how this has a radical influence on our experience and understanding of the world (Chapter 3); our mode of being in – and out of – time (Chapter 4); our identity as selves or persons (Chapter 5); and the agency that has enabled us to transform the world we live in (Chapter 6). I hope this will sufficiently clarify what I mean when I assert that, while we are not supernatural beings, neither are we natural parts of the natural world. We are *extra*-natural. This will clear the path to developing an agenda for a future humanist philosophical anthropology.

As someone who spent many decades researching in clinical neuroscience, I will not, in arguing for human uniqueness, ignore what the biological sciences tell us. My case will only be that such sciences do not provide sufficient evidence to overturn what we know from first-hand knowledge and experience about our unique nature.

What I will not address is *how* we became so different. I count myself a good Darwinian; consequently, I should, and do, feel obliged to accept that there must be a biological account of how we have escaped from biology, more specifically from apehood, to the degree that we have. Anyone who denies a supernatural account of humanity has an obligation to offer at least the outline of a plausible story as to what biological means enabled humanity to distance itself from nature. It is a long, and complex, story and I have offered a version of it in the first part of a trilogy published a decade or so ago.[12]

The story that I offer begins in the traditional place with the assumption of the upright position by our primate ancestors several million years ago, the liberation of our uniquely versatile hand from being a locomotor prop, and the domination of the visual sense. Assigning a central role to the distinctive properties of the human hand is strikingly unoriginal. It was first suggested by the Presocratic philosopher Anaxagoras, developed by Aristotle, and taken up by philosophers as disparate as Kant and Erasmus Darwin as well as by palaeontologists such as F. Wood Jones.

Irrespective of whether we yet have an explanation for how we humans got to be so different from all other beasts, including our nearest primate kin, the difference is real and irreducible. Although I will not provide a comprehensive "thick description" of the human condition, my offer will be more nutritious than the cognitive gruel that philosophy, even philosophical anthropology, often serves up. Only by such descriptions will we actually see what kinds of being we are and how we are fundamentally different from the rest of the animal kingdom.

One final preliminary point. I have sometimes been charged with claiming that animals are not conscious. Of course, they are: humans do not have the monopoly of consciousness. Animals are not Cartesian machines incapable of suffering. Their difference from us does not excuse us of the duty of concern for their welfare, insofar as it is compatible with our own. It is acceptable to swat flies but not to pull off their wings; and to eat meat to survive but not to farm without compassion.

RESISTANCE TO THE IDEA THAT WE ARE SPECIAL

The view that we are essentially or merely animal organisms seems to have a lot going for it. Many of the processes that produce us, sustain us, and destroy us are clearly biological. Given that I was a doctor for nearly 40 years, and working at various times as an obstetrician, a general physician, and a geriatrician, this is hardly likely to have escaped my attention. Psychologist Thomas Suddendorf has expressed very clearly what we have in common with birds, beasts and flowers:

> Like all living *organisms*, humans metabolize and reproduce. Your genome uses the same dictionary as a tulip and overlaps considerably with the genetic makeup of a banana. You are an *animal.* Like all animals, you have to eat other organisms – whether plant, fungus, or animal – for sustenance. You tend to approach things you want to eat while avoiding things that want to eat you, just as spiders do. You are a *vertebrate.* Like all vertebrates, your body has a spinal cord that leads up to the brain. Your skeleton is based on the same blueprint – four limbs and five digits – as that of a crocodile. You are a *mammal.* Like all placental mammals, you grew inside your mother and after birth received her milk (or someone else's). You are a *primate.* Like other primates, you have an immensely useful opposable thumb … You are a *hominid.* Like all hominids you have shoulders that allow your arms to fully rotate. Your closest living animal relative is a chimpanzee.[13]

Our flesh is heir to ills that many other animals inherit which is why animal research has guided us to better understanding and improved treatment of the diseases that plague us.

The point I will make is that our organic body is the beginning, not the end, of our story. It should not seem to be necessary to have to say this. Any arguments on this score could be settled by inviting the "animalizers" of humankind to compare the daily lives of animals lived in the natural world with human lives lived in the human world. Things are not, however, as straightforward as this for reasons it is worth touching on.

There are two main reasons why we might be inclined to deny that we are special. The first I have already mentioned: the (false) belief that, if we set aside supernatural accounts of what we are, then we are obliged to embrace naturalistic accounts, which reduce us, ultimately, to pieces of nature. The script, so the story goes, according to which we live our lives, or our lives are lived for us, is biological. To deny this, it is argued, is implicitly to regress to a pre-scientific, religious account of our nature and no self-respecting humanist would admit to this.

Which brings us to the second reason. We have known since Darwin that the processes that produced the organism *H. sapiens* are identical to those that produce grass and centipedes, blackbirds and chimpanzees. The differential survival and reproduction rates of spontaneous variants permits a process of natural selection that results in ever more complex and sophisticated organisms, culminating in creatures like you and me. To assert our fundamental differences from all other beasts, including those genetically closest to us seems, so it is claimed, to deny the truth of the most powerful theory in biology.

And the explanatory power of Darwin's theory is not in doubt; after all it has been supported by discoveries that had not been made, and by technologies he could not have imagined, when he published *On the Origin of Species* in 1859. Carbon dating, discovery of continental drift, more precise understanding of the genetics of natural selection, and demonstration of natural selection at work in experimental models using rapidly reproducing organisms such as bacteria, as well as the ever more detailed "joining of the dots" between species from the fossil record, have all contributed to justified belief in the theory of evolution as one of the most tested, and confirmed, as well as the most wide-ranging and visionary, theories human beings have ever had.

The naturalizers argue that anything that smacks of human exceptionalism seems a) to deny the fundamental characteristics that we have in common with other living creatures; and b) to propose an abrupt break between us and our fellow primates that is at odds with the overwhelming evidence of a continuous evolution from unicellular to complex creatures like ourselves. It is, perish the thought, to regress to pre-Darwinian biology.

There is also the suspicion that our belief that we are "special" is not unconnected with the fact that it is we who we are making the judgement. Humans give themselves top marks because they are both setting and marking the exam papers. It is hardly surprising, so the argument goes, that we have placed ourselves at the summit of the Great Chain of Being from gunk to readers of this book.

Besides, we are less likely to appreciate the extraordinary capacities of other species because we are not privy to them and because animals, being tested on things that matter to us, are playing an away match. As the leading primatologist Frans de Waal has argued, we may not be smart enough to see how smart *they* are.[14] We will fail to recognize that certain capacities, thought to be unique to humans, are evident in animals unless we learn how to look with unprejudiced gaze and the appropriate experimental techniques. Then the scales will fall from our eyes and we shall see that octopuses use coconut shells as tools, elephants classify humans by their age and their gender, chimpanzees have memories that in some respects outshine ours, and so on.

What is more, as Mary Midgley has argued, "Human beings are judged by their ideal performance, animals by their actual ones".[15] We have an inflated idea of our own cognitive capacities and the extent to which they are deployed in moment-to-moment living. Aristotle's definition of ourselves as "the rational animal" is a case in point. We are, so the argument goes, not unique in our capacity to deploy reason and reason plays a smaller part in our lives than we flatter ourselves to think. We do not proceed syllogistically from womb to tomb.

And there is a connected point. Even those who do acknowledge our exceptional nature often weaken their case by narrowly focusing on special skills, preoccupations, and faculties that are rarely deployed in everyday life and are somewhat unevenly distributed among human beings. The impulse to create art, the capacity for principled altruism, or a passion for science may be unique to humans; but human uniqueness extends far beyond this. It is wall-to-wall – being evident in our bad and ordinarily decent behaviour as well as in altruism – and, as I will discuss, uniqueness is as evident in the way we meet needs that we seem to share with animals, such as eating dinner, learning from experience, and grooming ourselves, as it is in sophisticated activities such as the one we are engaged in now.

Our estimates of the size of the gap between ourselves and other animals – notably our nearest primate kin – are also affected by how we view the beings each side of the gap. We can narrow the gap by adopting a grossly simplified

account of what is going on in human beings as they go about their daily business. The most extreme endeavour in that direction was the behaviourism that
dominated psychology in the first half of the twentieth century. The things
humans got up to were, it was claimed, solely the product of classical and
operant conditioning acting on an organism equipped with innate patterns of
reflex or instinctual responses to stimuli. The role of reflective or deliberative
consciousness was marginal or zilch. Thus the gap was closed between human
behaviour and that of other organisms.

The opposite approach to closing the gap between beasts and humans
is to ascribe complex modes of consciousness to the behaviour of animals.
Humanizing animals in this way makes it easy to animalize humans. Darwin
speculated that "the senses and the intuitions, the various emotions and
faculties, such as love, memory, attention, curiosity, imitation, reason, etc.
of which man boasts, may be found in an incipient or even sometimes in a
well-developed condition in the lower animals".[16] Suddendorf addresses this
gap-closing strategy by contrasting the approach of the "killjoys" – who have
a "lean" interpretation of animal behaviour – with the "romantics" – who tend
to "rich" interpretations. The killjoys adhere strictly to the "canon" proposed
by the nineteenth-century biologist Conwy Lloyd Morgan, according to which
we should not ascribe behaviour to a higher psychological faculty when it
can be ascribed to a lower one. The romantics are more inclined to attribute
behaviour to higher faculties, comparable to those seen in humans.

The case for the killjoys – with whom I align myself as will become obvious – is greatly strengthened by examining the overall activity of creatures in
whom putative signs of higher faculties have been identified. It is necessary to
look beyond individual actions and reflect on connected patterns of behaviour
and capacities or lack of them that they express. We should examine the lives
of animals and humans not a twitch at a time but a day at a time. If an animal
is thought to have a sophisticated mode of consciousness in one instance,
the question then arises as to why that sophistication does not manifest itself
elsewhere in its life.

Something as utterly basic and seemingly automated as wishing someone
"Good morning" is fundamentally different from a friendly exchange of barks
between dogs. It draws on complex customs and practices regulating human
greetings in general in different circumstances and the individual histories
and standing of the greeter and the greeted. The rules under which I may say
Good morning to an individual I bump into would fill many pages and draw
on many aspects of a uniquely human culture. There are also the abstract
notions entrained in greetings, such as that of a "morning". And this is before
we consider the grading of warmth and any meta-linguistic gaming that may

influence the tone of the salutation. Think about this the next time you are out walking in the park and are deciding whether and how to acknowledge a person walking towards you. You will find that your greeting is far from an automated response to a stimulus: it draws on many considerations relating to your own history, your sense of how you appear in the eyes of the other person, and of who that other is and where they fit into your world or your day, and your awareness of the general conventions governing greetings in public spaces.

Consider also a recent favourite of the romantics who want to ascribe complex psychological processes to non-human animals: the so-called "caching" behaviour of jays and other corvids. These birds hide food, intended for later consumption, from competitors. This behaviour has been intensely studied by Nicola Clayton, using many different, cunningly designed experiments.[17] How and where birds hide food, and for how long, is influenced by the kind of food that is being stored – perishable worms or stable nuts. This observation has been adduced as evidence of "mental time travel" and a sense of the future comparable to our own. If this were true, however, one would expect other manifestations of an idea of the future. But there are no such manifestations; and there is nothing, anyway, that comes near to the extraordinarily complex sense of the "not-yet" that is expressed in calendrical time.

If it is a matter of a difference of degree, it is one that is so great that it amounts to a difference in kind. But the degree/kind argument applies to many other characteristics that we (in my opinion correctly) regard as distinctive, through being uniquely developed and interconnected, in humans. Here are some examples: the use of sign systems; the conceptual and non-conceptual awareness of one's self and of the selves of others; the devising, making, storing, and employment of tools; and the capacity to travel mentally in time. We shall revisit the question of mental time travel in animals and humans in Chapter 4 when we shall consider the unique temporal depth of human consciousness and self-consciousness.

I cannot resist a further example of romantic interpretation. It concerns a creature that shows a remarkable capacity to predict the fluctuations in its natural habitat, to forecast the weather. As a result of pre-exposure to a changing environment, the creature's ability to cope with a later, different, state of affairs is enhanced: it knew what was coming and so was ready for it. And what is this talented organism, which shows such an impressive capacity to learn from experience how to anticipate and prepare for the future? It is a single-celled bacterium.[18]

In summary, there is a pincer movement on the gap between us and beasts: humans are described in beastly terms; and beasts are described in human terms. We have got so used to re-describing what goes on in ordinary animal life in such a way as to make it sound like what goes on in ordinary human life, that we no longer notice ourselves doing it. It exemplifies a wider error that I have christened the Fallacy of Misplaced Explicitness that enables thinkers to speak of squids "classifying the contents of the world", scrub-jays "planning", and even artefacts such as thermostats "making judgements".

It does not follow from the fact that our human lives and human world are profoundly different from the lives of other living creatures, that we can learn nothing about ourselves from the close study of other species. Jane Goodall, one of the great primatologists of recent years made this point:

> It is only through real understanding of the ways in which chimpan-zees and men show similarities of behaviour that we can reflect, with meaning, on the ways in which men and chimpanzees *differ*. And only then can we really begin to appreciate, in a biological and spiritual manner, the full extent of man's uniqueness.[19]

Suddendorf has expressed a similar sentiment: "The repeated comparison of human abilities with those of other animals will bring into sharper focus what it is about the human mind that sets us apart".[20] Ethological travels broaden the sense of one's own mind. We discover ourselves through our difference from other creatures.

In what follows, I shall begin by examining Darwinitis – the idea that evo-lutionary theory captures not only the nature of the human *organism* (*H. sapiens*) but also that of the human *person*. Looking at some seemingly basic activities such as feeding, learning, and grooming, will give an *entrée* into a distinctively human world. It will also provide a relevant background to our critique of neuromania: the conviction that we are our brains, themselves understood primarily as organs shaped by evolution directly or indirectly to serve the organism and maximize the chance of its survival and the replication of its genetic material.

The idea, incidentally, that we are our brains is associated with a sec-ondary delusion: that this is a brand new, cutting-edge discovery based on cutting-edge neuroscience. It is, of course, nothing of the kind. Its first clear statement was by Hippocrates:

> Men ought to know that it is from the brain and the brain only come joys, delights, laughter and sports, sorrows, grief and despondency, and lamentations. And by this, in a special manner, we acquire wisdom and knowledge, and know what are foul and what are fair, what are

bad and what are good, what are sweet, and what are unsavoury …
In these ways I am of the opinion that the brain exercises the greatest
power in man.[21]

And neuromania had many powerful advocates in the seventeenth and
eighteenth centuries, Hobbes and several of the Enlightenment *philosophes*
among them. The English chemist and philosopher Joseph Priestley asserted
that "the faculty of thinking is the result of a certain arrangement of parts of
matter", specifically that "sensation and thought do necessarily result from
the organisation of the brain".[22] In short, neuromania long antedates recent
advances in neurosciences and the development of exciting techniques such
as functional magnetic resonance imaging that have not only captured the
imagination of many thinkers but taken them hostage.

DARWINITIS

Darwinitis – the idea that *persons* are simply evolved *organisms* – derives
surface plausibility from the overlap between human and animal needs and
the behaviour arising out of them. To undermine that plausibility, let me take
three uncontroversial, and distinctly commonplace, examples: feeding, learning, and grooming. I want to use them to demonstrate something that should
be sufficiently obvious: that the evolution of a distinctively human culture
and of a human world as the unique theatre of our action has left nothing
unchanged, not even behaviour that seems to correspond to what we see in
animals.

Let us begin with something basic that is seen throughout the animal kingdom: feeding. Supposing you invite me out for a meal. Having learnt that you
have just taken on a big loan for a house, I choose the cheapest items on the
menu and falsely declare that I am full after the main course, to spare you the
expense of a pudding. A chimpanzee gives a banana to another chimpanzee
who eats it. Those afflicted by Darwinitis would like to say that the chimp and
I are doing similar things because we are both exhibiting "feeding behaviour"
or "shared feeding behaviour". This identity of description, however, obscures
huge differences between the chimp's behaviour and mine.

This may seem a rather exotic example loaded in favour of human distinct-
ness. So let's look more widely and examine the basic differences between
human dining and animal feeding.[23] Anyone who reflects on what takes place
at the most routine dinner table – the products of a vast number of deliberate
actions on the part of those sitting round it – will be on their guard when they

hear the phrase "feeding behaviour" applied to both humans and beasts. An ordinary human meal is the endpoint of a long journey away from biology. The ways in which dining is remote from feeding are protean.

Cooking is the most striking and has attracted much attention as a key moment in human evolution. Richard Wrangham has argued that this enabled hominins to take in more calories.[24] The extra calories could permit the growth of larger brains observed when *Homo habilis* was transformed into *Homo erectus*. Cooking requires the capacity to a) bring together the fuel necessary for fire; b) tend the flames; c) place the food in a primitive oven made of earth; and d) wait for the nutriments to reach a point between raw and oxidized, between under- and over-cooked. Central to the notion of cooking is the idea of the *ingredient* – naturally occurring (e.g. fruit) or processed material (such as flour) – that is kept in store for when it is needed to be united with other elements of a *recipe*.[25]

So many steps, so much expertise, imply a radically different relationship to nutriment than the grab-it-and-stuff-it-in of, say, chimps or the direct stuff-it-in of most animals or even the cache-it and eat it later of jays. Cooking is just one out of many steps away from animal feeding. In addition there is: eating regulated by the clock and even the calendar (the idea of dinner-time and its expression in meeting to eat by appointment); the complex structure of meals and the grammar of what goes with what; the symbolic, ritualistic, and celebratory aspects of meals; the multitude of items of tableware that have come from near and far; the journeys taken by the food to the table; the journeys undertaken by those who gather round the table; and the use of money as the all-purpose commodity to purchase food. Dining is a manifestation of a creature who has a normative sense that is not merely rule-following but rule-articulating, rule-checking and sometimes rule-challenging.

The customs and regulated practices around the sharing of food and the rituals of hospitality are but a few of the ways in which human dining is distanced from animal eating. Many of them are recent – perhaps a few thousand or tens of thousands of years; even so, they reveal indirectly the hinterland of mental faculties and capacities that made them possible. They require the sophisticated consciousness of an animal who does things explicitly and whose natural medium is a community of minds (of which more presently) that ultimately extends geographically across the globe and historically into the accumulated recollection of the race. The laid and laden table of the present day draws on four quarters of the earth and great tracts of past and present human consciousness.

Consider next, "learning behaviour". Let me first illustrate the difference by an example. I decide to improve my career prospects by signing up for a degree course which begins next year. I need to free up some time so I agree with my boss that I shall work harder this year in order to have a shorter working day next year. Now contrast this with the learning behaviour of a cow that, say, bumps into an electric wire and henceforth avoids that place. It could be said that both Daisy and I have been exhibiting learning behaviour. As with feeding, the difference between the two forms of behaviour is greater than the similarities.

The human example I have just given may again seem a little exotic but it illustrates a unique and prominent feature of human learning: that it is not something that merely happens; it is *done* deliberately and it is often *organized* and sometimes a long time in advance. Animal learning, by contrast, is typically an incidental outcome of the accidents of experience. This difference is connected with one that is even more fundamental: that humans actively learn and practise skills and deliberately memorize, while animals do not.[26] We do not see evidence of animals repeatedly doing things now for the sake of doing them better in future; or monitoring progress on the basis of episodic memory of performance and its successes and failures. Mental as well as physical rehearsal depend on a developed sense of one's self extended in time (something to which we shall return).

There is apparent imitation – as when a chimpanzee is prompted by observing what humans do to sweep a cage without understanding why – but there is no structured teaching, with time set aside, using dummy examples of behaviour, dry runs, rehearsals, and certainly nothing corresponding to a curriculum. Animals do not instruct their young, or not outside of Disneyland anyway.[27] The absence of teaching is often striking, as in this example from Suddendorf: "Where chimpanzees crack nuts with hammers and anvils [stones], it takes the young several years to learn the process. The mothers do not typically guide the young or help them along ... Active instruction could transmit this information far more quickly and effectively".[28]

To teach another involves a sophisticated sense of where the other is "at", and of the contents and states of their mind – what they need to know or understand and how to get them to know or understand it – which goes beyond any theory of mind that mainstream ethologists are inclined to ascribe even to the most tuned-in chimps. The teaching of the young also presupposes a sense of their future, the complex future of a life to come with its challenges, and a sense, implicit in education, that the nature of those challenges will be uncertain. We are prepared for eventualities that may never be realized. Teaching and learning is often a collective exercise – ranging from casual sharing of information to the inculcation of a standardized curriculum by methods that are reflected upon and argued over. Since time immemorial, teaching of the young by their elders has taken place in bespoke situations devoted to it, even though it is only over the last several thousand years that it has been mediated by purpose-created institutions. The pupil is not merely behaviourally or dispositionally shaped by experience but also acquires *factual* knowledge, information that is remote from sensory experience. For us, the acquisition of knowledge and skills, of becoming qualified and expert, is part of a narrative of a life that is led rather than merely lived.[29]

We are a long way from the accidents of experience that are the primary drivers of animal learning. Schooling occurs in an extra-biological space where individual experience, social learning, acquired knowledge, and our individual and collective life histories are connected. It is driven by the *shared intentionality*. Shared intentionality is, as Michael Tomasello has argued for many years, at the heart of human thinking, indeed human cognition.[30] It is: "the power of [human] minds to be jointly directed at objects, matters of fact, states of affairs, goals, or values. Collective intentionality comes in a variety of modes, including shared intention, joint attention, shared belief, collective acceptance, and collective emotion".[31]

One aspect of learning is acquiring the capacity to solve problems with increasing ease. Romantics are prone to attribute some problem-solving in animals to reason and insight, suggesting that they pick up on general principles and even have an elementary grasp of causation. Granted, there are the famous examples of Wolfgang Köhler's chimpanzees who accessed bananas that were attached to the ceiling of their enclosure by standing on boxes that they themselves had stacked. In most cases, however, problems are solved by trial and error and, as has often been shown, there are "astounding and persistent failures to solve simple problems".[32] The beasts don't *get* it. Any success ethologists may be tempted to ascribe to awareness of general principles can be more plausibly explained by associative learning with successful strategies randomly adopted being reinforced by rewards. There is imitation without understanding – rather as in cargo cult science; or (to take a homelier example) as when I imagined at the age of four that I could read because I could hold a newspaper in front of me and move my lips as I had seen my father do. The solutions animals find to problems do not require a sense of invisible forces, unobservable general causes, such as gravity. Indeed, the nearest non-human animals get to a sense of causation is a Humean association that does not, however, distinguish causation from accidental correlation. And the results – more precisely, the lack of them – are there for all to see.[33]

Problem-solving in non-human animals is confined to clear-cut, present situations and that are immediately related to biological needs, though unconscious instincts may have a greater reach. Animal inquiry, likewise, is related to the here-and-now, in contrast to the kind of inquiry seen in humans which, while not entirely disinterested, seeks general solutions to problems that may not be currently pressing. Such inquiries are often not of immediate practical relevance; even less do they address biological appetites. Mankind pays attention for its own sake. Indeed, a separation of inquiry from pay-off is what has made humans' science so powerful. The 600-year, collaborative journey from Copernican astronomy via mechanics to the Global Positioning System that will stop the human creature from getting lost in the wilderness is a particularly spectacular illustration of the patience built into human cognitive advance.[34]

So much for feeding and learning. Now, finally, the humble activity of grooming. I rise in the morning and brush my teeth. This involves an instrument (a toothbrush), amenities (running water) and materials (toothpaste). The action is linked to clock time and is part of a cluster of activities of "getting ready in the morning". There are complex intermediaries. The brush is manufactured from synthetic materials and bought and stored in the relevant place. The water is delivered to the toothbrusher by means of a distribution system that requires a multitude of engineering, bacteriological, and other technologies, that engages civil society in cooperative activities to ensure supply and safety and is underpinned by a system of billing secured by electronic systems that translate monitored consumption to invoices. And the toothpaste has been compounded according to formulae based (at least in theory) on dental knowledge.

I could go on but I imagine I have said sufficient to make visible the boundless hinterland behind the morning toothbrushing and establish the case for a fundamental difference between my grooming and the simple bodily attention involved in a cat licking itself clean or a chimpanzee removing its fleas or even having them removed by a fellow chimp.

The examples of feeding, learning, and grooming give us glimpses of something much, much bigger: a communal human world. This is built up out of shared cognition and it is a vast sphere of signs as pervasive as the biosphere of organic reality. One manifestation of this is the artefactscape of tools, instruments, devices, infrastructure, amenities, built environments, and cultivated spaces, maintained and regulated for the common good, in which we pass our lives. Another is the multidimensional lattice of facts, factoids, and possibilities we take account of as we act out our lives. All of these are the children of gestured, spoken and written language through which we share our consciousness and are enabled to work together with, or work against, each other in achieving shared and conflicting goals. Our individual experiences contribute to, and make sense of themselves in the light of, a body of shared knowledge – and expertise, rules, norms and sentiments – that belongs to everyone and no-one. Communities of minds, built up over decades, centuries and millennia, support and are supported by the intersecting, overlapping, interacting realms that enrich, extend, and deepen the theatre of our lives. I shall discuss the epistemological aspect of this – what I have called the "that-osphere" – in Chapter 4 because it is a key to the wide and ever-widening gap between ourselves and the other primates.

How different this shared world is from the environment which sustains the near-monadic lives even of the great apes! The difference is captured poignantly by Jane Goodall: "Sometimes when watching the chimpanzees, I have felt that because they have no human-like language, they are trapped within themselves ... How much more they might accomplish if they could *talk* to each other".[35]

As will be evident from what I have just said, it is not merely language in the narrow sense that marks the difference between the closed consciousness of animals and our awareness of a shared openness, of that which is "public". Nevertheless, the act of naming brings what-is into a public realm, a space that belongs to everyone in general and no-one in particular. It is a key step in the weaving of shared intentionality into a shared world, or shared worlds. We are talking to each other incessantly, even when we are silent, through the standing communications of the built environment, of the artefacts that embody centuries of shared ideas, and the millions of patented and unpatented ingenuities that underpin them; in the frozen speech of fabricated things – as well as of books, magazines, journals, hand-bills, bill-boards, newspapers, leaflets, notices, sign-posts – forbidding, permitting, exhorting, guiding, explaining; of the trademarks, identifiers, brand marks, covering every surface; and of the pavement delineated from the road, the cut lawn and the trimmed hedge, the ploughed field, uttering aspects of multiple interlocking shared and explicitly unshared worlds with their own spaces.

There is wall-to-wall, horizon-to-horizon, eloquence, speaking of "we" and "they", addressing "me", "us" and "them", expressing the commonality of our primary, secondary, tertiary and higher-order needs. The human world is a vast notice board, a pandiculation of past and present thoughts, ideas, inspirations, habits sanctified or staled by custom. Its visible, audible, tangible presence is a fabric of joined attention, expressed in the material structures we have inherited, a repository of our shared consciousness past and present, and the endeavour that made it possible.

So much distances our mind from the almost windowless consciousness of animals, who rarely exchange glances simply for the sake of togetherness and never even point out things to each other solely for the purpose of teaching or companionability – for cognitive togetherness.[36] Our world is in the keeping of a community of minds that we continue to maintain through endless join-ing of experiences, activities, and memories, and the standing state of shar-ing embodied in skills, possessions, and infrastructure had in common. This community goes beyond cognition narrowly construed to beliefs and hopes, prejudices and acceptances, and goals and ambitions, and sense-making that has developed under the influence of tradition, custom and practice. There is a virtuous circle by which the expanding population of others and the variety of interactions with them (including, ultimately, historical others) increases the kinds of interactions that are possible. My community of minds is worldwide and centuries deep, like those of all the readers of this book.

Some advocates of Darwinitis accept the reality of this huge gap but try to downplay its significance. They claim that it is opened, and kept open, by (unconscious) processes identical to those which drove the differentiation of species. Yes, they concede, there *are* fundamental differences between the bio-logical organism and the person shaped by culture. But, so it is argued, cultural transformation can be assimilated to Darwinism by a certain reading of cul-tural change as cultural "evolution" which operates by processes analogous to natural selection. There is differential survival of bits of human culture deter-mined by the extent to which they do or do not serve the basic needs of the organism, facilitating *its own* survival and, more importantly, its replication. These bits were christened "memes" by Richard Dawkins. A meme is a unit of cultural transmission analogous to the gene, the unit of biological transmis-sion.[37] Memes replicate themselves in the human brains that they infect like a virus: they leap from brain to brain via their phenotypical expression. They increase their own chance of replication if they increase the probability of survival of their unwitting carriers – you and me.

This is not the place for a detailed critique of meme theory – much beloved of the neurophilosopher Daniel Dennett – but a comment or two is appropriate because its fallacies are rooted in something fundamental to the anti-humanism of naturalist thought: the marginalization of deliberate action and conscious-ness, of insight and intelligence. Consider some of the examples of memes given by Dawkins: "words, music, visual images, styles of clothes, facial or hand gestures".[38] Each time a catch phrase is taken up by a new person, it is replicated; and if it looks to benefit the carrier – even of only by, for example, making her one of the "in-crowd" – it will survive to be replicated further. Memetic transmission is of items that have nothing to do with agency or consciousness. Cultural transformation is thereby presented as the result of the passive trans-mission from brain to brain of variations in ideas, techniques, and attitudes, that occur spontaneously, independent of deliberation or conscious adoption.

The most obvious objection to the theory is that memes such as fashions are, unlike genes, or viruses, clearly not particulate or self-defining. But there is a more profound objection. While it is evident that our collective cultural transformation is not directed or guided by any conscious individual or groups of individuals – at the very least because the outcomes of our collective actions are unforeseen – the ultimate drive for change must come from the insights, endeavours, efforts, and choices of individuals. This is true irrespective of whether the individuals are initiators or followers, inventors, marketers or consumers, originators, disseminators, or mere dittoheads, early or late adopters of technologies or of styles of living. When, for example, at university I persuaded a fellow student to stitch a large flower on the knee of my jeans, this was an instance of the unoriginal following of 1960s fashion, of a convention of unconventionality. But it was entirely conscious and involved quite a lot of cognitive effort. While the law of unintended consequences will be evident – especially where large numbers of people and large timescales are involved – cultural transformation will have as its necessary substrate the deliberate, conscious, goal-orientated actions of individuals or groups of people.

Whether it is the genius of Heisenberg discovering key elements of quantum mechanics, of the engineers seeing how to transform the notion of positrons into electronic circuits, of others using those principles to create for example mobile phones, of others marketing them, yet others buying them and learning how to use them (fiddling with the knobs, keeping the item charged, maintaining a directory of numbers), there is nothing in the resultant cultural transformation that is comparable to the processes by which a long-necked giraffe emerges or spiders acquire the capacity to weave webs. Darwinian evolution takes place mindlessly: the exquisite organisms with their extraordinary means of securing their survival are generated by natural selection and no-one is doing the selecting. By contrast, the cultural transformations that have brought humanity to its present condition remote from that of all other animals have been driven to a significant degree by intentions.

Nature may be a "blind watchmaker" (to use Richard Dawkins' arresting phrase) but humanity is a sighted watchmaker.[39] Without a multitude of deliberate intentions – never mind waking out of physical time sufficiently to wake to it (as we shall discuss in Chapter 4) – we could not have made a watch. The meanest "meme" involves numerous elements; we must choose them and put them together to allow them to replicate in our own practice. The style of cathedral building may evolve and be disseminated without anyone providing overall direction; but no cathedral – or even a single buttress – was built unconsciously. And copying a style is not a matter of blind replication: it involves many years of training, to acquire the necessary skills, and understanding fundamental principles of, say, the perpendicular style.

So much for Darwinitis. It is time to turn to the other intellectual malady associated with biological naturalism: neuromania

BRAINS AND CONSCIOUS PERSONS

Neuromania 1: brainifying the person and personifying the brain[40]

The most profound marker of the gap between humanity and animality is our extraordinarily complex, folded, reflective consciousness which is central to the way we exercise what seems like genuine freedom of choice as we pick our way through our lives. As we shall see, much of this is built on our capacity to transform individual sentience into shared experience and shared experience into objective knowledge. These should be recognized as presenting insuperable barriers to a biological interpretation of human nature.

This is where neuromania comes to the rescue by claiming that we *are* our brains; and our consciousness, our knowledge, our selves, and our agency, like the consciousness and activity of beasts, amount to brain function. Neuroscience we are told is, or soon will be, the key to unlocking human nature. The best way to advancing our understanding of persons will be to peer into the darkness of the skull using techniques that record neural activity. Given that brains are biological organs that have been generated by natural selection, Darwinitis is consequently upheld. Unfortunately (or, rather, fortunately) the endeavour to identify ourselves with our brains encounters serious, and seemingly insoluble, problems.

My critique of neuromania will have several strands:

1. The impossibility of accommodating the emergence and elaboration of consciousness within evolutionary theory;
2. The failure of neuroscience – ultimately a branch of physical science – to account for the intentionality (a term I shall explain presently) of mental contents;
3. The neurologically inexplicable transformation of sense perception into propositional or factual awareness and understanding that is amenable to unlimited elaboration into a vast body of knowledge; and
4. The development of a human world, in which we actively live our lives, offset from nature.

This will leave much unfinished business that will be picked up in subsequent chapters.

It would appear *a priori* highly unlikely that we could identify something *within* the experienced world – neural activity in a particular organ – as the basis of the totality of our experience. Surely, there must be a fundamental difference between what happens in things and our experience of what happens in things.[41] Nevertheless, there seems a strong prima facie case for identifying us with our brains. First, there is an intimate relationship between the brain and conscious and self-conscious activity. At a very elementary level, the world of which I am immediately aware appears to be that part of reality with which my brain is in causal contact. My immediate "where" is determined by the location of my brain. I am aware of this room because my brain is in this room and is in receipt of energy arising from it. If I move my brain by moving my body into the next room, I will be directly aware of the next room. Less radically, the redirection of my eyes, which are attached to my brain, so that I harvest light from different sources, will alter the visual reality available to me.

Of course, I can be projected outside of the immediate, physical surroundings of my brain by information mediated through language, by still and moving images, and by a multitude of other signs. But I can access these mediators only through their being in the vicinity of my brain so that they can impinge on it by activating my senses. A book may transport me to the Battle of Hastings, but it can do so only if it falls within my sensory field so that it can impinge on my brain. If my brain were removed, I would have no "here" at all.

Secondly, damage to my brain can alter the level of my consciousness; a bash on the head can extinguish my consciousness entirely. There is a consistent correlation between levels of consciousness – alert wakefulness, drowsiness, and deep coma – and patterns of neural activity. There is ample evidence of places in the brain where specific cognitive functions are most easily disrupted. Careful studies of the effect of injury to the brain suggests that conscious experience from the slightest tingle of sensation to the subtlest sense of self requires a functioning brain. Dramatic, indeed tragic, alterations in personality may result from, say, damage to the frontal lobes of the cerebral cortex. The dementia that afflicted Kant, arguably the greatest European philosopher of the last 500 years, is a particularly poignant reminder of this.[42] So far as we can tell, our minds die with our brains.

Thirdly, there is a correlation between contents of consciousness and observed neural activity. This, however, is not as close as is often thought – even in the case of something as basic as pain. Research has shown the supposed "pain neuromatrix" in the brain may be activated in patients who have a congenital insensitivity to pain.[43] Conversely, it has been shown that there is preserved awareness of pain in patients whose pain neuromatrix is absent due to damage.[44] In short, far from close correlation, there is double dissociation: capacity to experience pain without the relevant neural structures; and the relevant neural structures without the capacity to experience pain. If this is true of something as basic as pain, the hope of identification of higher mental functions, such as thought, belief, of ambition, with localized neural activity is indeed forlorn.

The observations cited so far licence only the conclusion that brain activity of the right kind is a *necessary* condition for consciousness but not that it is a *sufficient* condition. It is a necessary condition for you to buy this book that I should have written it. Alas, it is not a sufficient condition, otherwise I would be a very rich man. To take a less exotic example: for me to be knocked down by a tram in Prague, it is necessary that I should be in Prague; but, fortunately, given that I have a flat there, my being in Prague is not a sufficient condition. The correlation between brain activity and conscious experience does not prove that brain activity *causes* consciousness and even less that brain activity is identical to consciousness.

Fourthly, direct stimulation of the brain can give arise to episodes of awareness, which can sometimes be quite complex, suggesting to some that neural activity is not only correlated with consciousness but may cause it – or, indeed, *be* it. The findings in the classic studies of the neurosurgeon Wilder Penfield on waking patients are striking. He operated on patients with intractable epilepsy, with the aim of removing the areas of the brain that were responsible for triggering seizures while avoiding damage to parts of the brain that were associated with speech or other vital cognitive functions. He stimulated the brain in various places to identify those vital areas. He found that stimulation of certain parts of the brain could trigger rich, if fragmented, memories.[45] This seems to be direct evidence for the standalone brain to be able to sustain consciousness; but it is not as decisive as it may seem. The effects of brain stimulation are experienced only by already conscious, waking, subjects. What is more, in those few cases where complex experiences are had, they are revivification of memories that had been had in the past by the normal route of the subject being present at the events experienced. Their seeming reference is parasitic on the real reference of the memories had first time round. In many cases there is no conscious experience associated with any kind of stimulation.[46]

The slightly wobbly correlation between brain activity and consciousness may seem sufficient for sufferers from neuromania to draw the less radical conclusion that important similarities in the function and structure of human and other primate brains mean that we are essentially the same as other primates in all respects that matter. Similar brains, so the argument goes, will have been forged under comparable circumstances in order to discharge similar duties. This view drifts to the more radical claim that since we are, after all, our brains, and our brains are similar to other primate brains, we must be – despite surface differences – fundamentally similar to the "other" great apes. The flaw in the argument is in the starting assumption that *persons* are their brains. While it is clear that our conscious lives depend on having a brain in some kind of working order, it does not follow from this that our conscious lives consist of *being* a brain in some kind of working order. Even less does it follow that persons are identical with (their) brains.

The claim that "You are your brain" is easier to uphold when (as is so often the case), brains are described in personifying terms and persons, or at least psychological processes, are described in terms that would seem to apply to brains. Personification of the brain is pandemic in neuroscience and in "neurophilosophy". It is almost standard to talk of brains as "predicting", "calculating", "deciding", "knowing", etc. Even to describe the brain as "computing" is to ascribe to it functions that computers have only courtesy of persons. In the absence of conscious persons the transformation of inputs into outputs does not count as computation. Personifying brains is complemented by brainifying persons. It is standard to speak of people as "processing information", as if conscious persons were biological machines. If personification of brains and brainification of persons is resisted, the huge explanatory gap between brains and persons will become evident and evidently unbridgeable. We are permitted once more to see what is in front of our eyes and to acknowledge the vast difference between human persons and animal organisms.

Intentionality: about aboutness

This brings us to the most important concept – topic, truth, issue – in this book: intentionality. Intentionality – "the mark of the mental"[47] – lies at the root of the arguments presented and the claims made in this book. "Intentionality" not only marks a distance between conscious beings (human and non-human) and the material world but also, through its unique development in humans, opens up the huge gap between humans and other animals. Much of what I have to say in the next few pages is well-worn territory in philosophy but I will develop the central ideas in new ways. I shall subsequently argue that intentionality lies at the heart of our special relationship to our bodies, our mode of being in time, our selfhood, and our agency. En route to that argument will be a step-wise development of the notion that begins with its (seemingly) most straightforward manifestation – in the perceptions of objects like drinking glasses and trees – to the joined or shared intentionality that underpins our human world and the selves that populate it and is baked into an entire landscape of artefacts.

Intentionality was a term current in medieval philosophy. It was revived by Franz Brentano, the father of phenomenology, towards the end of the nineteenth century. There are many definitions. Here is one of the clearest: "the power of minds to be about, to represent, or to stand for, things, properties and states of affairs".[48] Mental elements such as perceptions, memories, beliefs, have "aboutness": they are directed to, or about, something sensed as being other than the perceiving, remembering, believing subject. This fundamental characteristic is not seen in material objects: stones, or their states, are not about anything – not about the earth on which they stand, other stones, or themselves. Nor are trees; nor, we presume, most lower animals. The term also captures something that is particularly evident in the gaze: directedness (towards) something. As Brentano put it, "we can define mental phenomena by saying that they are phenomena which contain an object intentionally within themselves".[49] They as it were "contain" the object by being about, reaching out to, and embracing, it.[50] The gaze contains, for example, the glass on the table.

Intentionality is not to be confused with "intention" in the everyday sense.[51] There is an overlap of sense, inasmuch as both perceptual consciousness and intentions are directed towards an object – a literal object in the case of perception and an aimed-at end in the case of the intention built into deliberate actions. Conscious (intentional) experiences add up to a sense of a shared world, independent of me, a shared outside populated by objects and events, something which we face individually and collectively in which I/you/we consciously pursue(s) ends and of which ultimately we form some kind of picture.

Intentionality is an awkward customer for philosophers of a materialist persuasion. The explanatory gap, evident even at the most fundamental level, between neural activity which is simply itself and conscious experiences which are about a world that is other than them has provoked a vast literature. What has attracted less attention, and causes problems even for more expansive naturalists is the transformation of intentionality in humans and its consequent role in underpinning the distinctive features of humanity that will be explored in the chapters to come.

Let us begin at the most basic level – perception. It is here that we most clearly encounter the (importantly erroneous) idea that consciousness is the result of a causal interaction between the brain and external objects or events, mediated by the energy arising from objects impinging on the brain via nerve endings. This is how the story goes. The brain, like the other organs of the body, and the things we perceive, is a material object. The activity triggered by the items we perceive is composed of material events; namely nerve impulses, which are waves of electrochemical discharges propagated along and between neurones. Unfortunately, there seems to be no "aboutness" built into the brain or its activity. This is underlined by the fact that most of the brain and the overwhelming majority of neural activity, even discharges in the cerebral cortex, are not associated with conscious experience.

This does not seem to trouble many neurophilosophers. Daniel Dennett characterizes "the prevailing wisdom" to which he subscribes, as being that:

> there is only one sort of stuff, namely *matter* – the physical stuff of physics, chemistry and physiology – and the mind is somehow nothing but a physical phenomenon. In short, the mind is the brain ... We can (in principle!) account for every mental phenomenon using *the same physical principles, laws and raw materials* that suffice to explain radioactivity, continental drift, photosynthesis, reproduction, nutrition and growth (emphasis added).[52]

This is endorsed by American philosopher John Searle, who also echoes (consciously or not) eighteenth-century philosopher and physiologist Pierre Cabanis: "Consciousness is an ordinary biological phenomenon comparable with growth, digestion or the secretion of bile".[53]

To undermine these confident assertions, and the idea that all conscious activity, even beliefs and thoughts can be reduced to what is observed in the material world – mass, charge, force or whatever – it is not necessary to look to complex conscious experiences such as being in love or solving quadratic equations. It is sufficient to consider something much more basic: seeing an object such as a glass in front of me.

Seeing the glass has two aspects. The first is the causal input into my brain arising from the glass: light energy entering my eyes and eventually stimulating my visual cortex. There is a set of events in the glass (cause C at time T_1) at the start of a causal sequence terminating in neural activity in the visual cortex (effect E at time T_2). The *inward* causal chain from C to E is a necessary condition of my true experience that there is a glass in front of me. It is not, however, a sufficient condition, or at least a sufficient explanation, of my experience; for there is a second aspect of that experience: the "aboutness". The events in the brain E at T_2 have somehow to "reach back" to the glass, via the intermediate events, to the events C in the glass at T_1 in order to be "about" the glass. The light getting into the eye (passing from the object to the eye – which we might call "telereception") and the gaze looking out (at the object "out there" – which we might call "teleprojection") are not the same. Indeed, they do not seem to belong to the same order of events, or indeed to the same kind of space. This is not to say that the gaze is a kind of quasi-physical or spiritual emanation that radiates in a direction opposite to the inward passage of light.[54]

The gaze looking out does not penetrate the same dimension as the light getting into the eyes: the "out there" of the perceived object is "out there" with respect not to the body of the perceiving subject but to the image we have of our body.[55] Looking is therefore not a literal kind of backward reaching, along the path of the light that has impinged on the visual system even less an emission in that direction. But neither is it something that fits into the causal nexus of the world as seen through the eyes of natural science – or even everyday common sense. There is nothing in the trains of spikes at the back of my brain that enables them to reconstruct a key part of their causal ancestry; namely the interaction between the glass and the light incident upon it.

This is already enough to undermine Dennett's claim that we can explain conscious perception using "*the same physical principles, laws and raw materials*" as explain radioactivity, photosynthesis or growth. If the electrical discharges in my visual cortex were sufficient to explain my awareness of the glass, they would have to grant to those discharges the capacity to be "of" or "about" the events upstream that caused them. The neural discharges in my skull would not only have mysteriously to be "about" the light coming from the glass; they would have to relocate the light on to the glass in order that it should reveal the latter and indeed conclude from this that the glass interfered with the light. Now, *contra* Dennett, there are *no* "physical principles, laws and raw materials" according to which (physical) events are a revelation of themselves (as in the case of, say, itches) or of their causes or (as in the case of seeing the glass) of an object implicated in the causes. Or not, at least, in the absence of a conscious subject retrospectively connecting the effect with its cause. But it is precisely the conscious subject that we are trying to explain. There is no "aboutness" in the principles, laws, and raw materials of physical nature. Even less are there discrete bounded worlds such as are keyed to individual subjects, in the material world.

It is worth dwelling on this a bit more because its vast implications are rarely fully appreciated. Imagine a billiard ball A colliding with another billiard ball B ("the" cause, Event 1), as a result of which B is set in motion ("the" effect, Event 2). I correctly attribute the movement of B (Event 2) to the impact of A (Event 1); Event 2, however, is not of itself a *revelation* of Event 1, even less of an enduring object, the billiard ball A. The reference back from Event 2 to Event 1 *requires* an observer, so it can hardly generate one. Causation operating in accordance with the physical principles observed throughout nature does not result in the revelation of one part of the universe (Event 1 or billiard ball A) by another (Event 2 or billiard ball B). The transfer of energy from one object to another does not make the one appear to the other. The interaction between two material objects does not make one present to the other. Presence is not an intrinsic property of a material object.

What we are challenging is the standard "causal theory of perception", according to which (to cite a classical formulation): "the perception is the terminus of a causal sequence involving at an earlier stage some event or process in the history of the perceived object".[56] Another, even more vulnerable formulation is that "perceptual consciousness is fundamentally an inference from an effect to a cause".[57] Given that "inferences" are the kinds of things that require a subject to perform, we have the strange situation whereby the subject who is constructed out of conscious experiences has the job of underpinning those conscious experiences.[58]

There are other problems. Firstly, there is the assumption (as in the description above) that the perception is the *terminus* of a causal sequence. That is very odd. Causal sequences in the material world do not have a terminus, except from the viewpoint of an interested subject – where it takes the form of an end or goal. But the subject and her interests rely on perceptions already being in place. Otherwise causal sequences are unending,[59] although individual causes may be lost in the noise of their consequences. And there is the related puzzle why this so-called "terminus" – the set of events constituting the neural basis of perception – should not only reach back up the causal chain to its ancestors but pause at an object such as a glass and not continue upstream until the Original Cause, perhaps the Big Bang, is reached.[60] That without consciousness there is no beginning or end of a causal chain can be highlighted in another way: in reality, causal relationships between discrete events are identified only *after* those events have been picked out by a (quite sophisticated) consciousness. They cannot therefore underpin consciousness. More specifically, it is impossible to see how the sum total of the neural activity of an individual brain could add up to a terminus where "the world" is received.

Secondly, the causal theory divides the honours for conscious experiences equally between two objects: the glass and the brain. However, the interaction between glass and brain that is supposed to generate consciousness exhibits an asymmetry not seen in the material world. The brain makes the glass visible but the glass does not make the brain visible. If the causal account were true, then we would expect either to see the glass make the brain appear to itself or causal events *downstream* of activity in the visual cortex make the brain appear to the objects that are involved in that activity. (This, of course, connects with the first point.) To put it another way, if appearance were the result of energy exchange between two objects rubbing against each other, then one might expect both objects to appear to one another. To take an example from another sense, if energy exchange entirely accounted for touch then it would be reasonable for the chair on which I am sitting to feel my bottom as for my bottom to feel the chair: the ontological equality of myself as an object among objects does not translate into a dialogue of equal partners. That ontological equality, however, is central to materialist naturalism.

The causal theory of perception, in which all parties are subject to the Dennettian edict of being subject to *the same physical principles, laws and raw materials* that operate elsewhere in nature offers nothing to explain the differentiation between the perceiving subject and object of perception; between the perceiver and the perceived. It does not account for the way perceptions get their content from the events in the environment that cause them. After all, the visibility of the glass is not a property or disposition of it: it does not have an intrinsic "look". This point is highlighted when we think of how that appearance may be altered by the *active* adjustments of looking, scanning, gazing, and scrutinizing, by setting the register of our perception (macroscopic or microscopic scale) and by manipulating the standing conditions (background light) that make the experiences possible. (We shall return to this point in Chapter 10, when we think of what the universe would be like before there are any conscious subjects.)

Thirdly, there is the problem that perceptions are typically about *objects*, or events located in objects. I experience or intuit not merely the light from the glass but the glass that the light illuminates. Objects are more than what is revealed through perceptions. The experience of the glass knows itself to be incomplete: it is of a mere part, aspect, or moment of its object which latter is other than, and more than, the perception. To arrive at that intuition becomes even more impressive – and mysterious – when it is suggested, as the hard-line naturalist Quine suggests, that objects like glasses and rocks and trees may be "theoretical posits" constructed on the basis of the impingement of energy on nerve endings – something we shall discuss in the next chapter; if, that is, the "object" that is implicated in the causation of the perception is itself built up out of perceptions. At any rate, Anthony Quinton identified as "the problem of perception" the need to give a satisfactory account of the relationship between sense-experience and material objects.[61] It is, as will already be evident, only part of the problem – the other is how there are sense-experiences at all – but it is clearly a major stumbling block to any materialist account of perception.

Finally, the gaze does not stop at the mere appearance of the object. The eye is rarely innocent. When I look at a glass, my gaze is a knowing one: the glass is an object of *knowledge* rather than of mere perception; something that is charged with practical possibilities; a possession – owned, say, by you rather than me; something satisfactory or unsatisfactory; important or irrelevant. I add this for the sake of completeness, though it is not as radical a point as those already made.[62]

The fundamental implausibility of the causal theory of perception is this: it proposes that differentiation into the (perceiving) subject and the (perceived) object, and the difference between the viewpoint and the items in the view, are generated by an exchange of energy between one part of the material world and another, or an interaction between two objects – one in the extracranial world (e.g. a glass) and one inside the cranium (the brain), such that the former is located inside its world by the latter.

Most of which I have said about basic intentionality is pretty obvious. The notion that *causes generate aboutness* – about themselves or about the items in which they take place – in virtue of their effects is manifestly untenable. Why on earth would philosophers as sharp as Dennett think otherwise? Why would he and others go further and make statements such as the following: "Colour vision is accomplished by a sophisticated system of information processing conducted entirely in spike trains, where colours are 'represented' by physical patterns of differences in spike trains that are not themselves colours"?[63]

One possible diagnosis is that aboutness can seem to be present in the absence of consciousness, as when material events seem to signify their causes. In fact, they do not signify anything in the absence of a conscious subject. Think of natural signs such as smoke "meaning" fire, puddles "meaning" rain, spots "meaning" measles. The smoke, the puddles, the spots are signs only to a conscious observer interpreting them. They are not in themselves *about* their causes or the things they might signify to a conscious interpreter. While *to a conscious observer* effects may be signs of their causes, they are not in themselves *about* their causes. This applies even in the case of images, such as reflections. The reflection of a pebble in a mirror – the interaction between the light from a pebble and the silver of the mirror – is not in itself "of" the pebble: it is not a representation of the pebble, or the presence of the pebble, or more precisely of the aspect of a pebble. The puddle does not detect or discern a cloud, even less *face* it as I face the world I am looking at. The isomorphism between the appearance of the pebble and the appearance of its image in a mirror does not alter this. The image is not a representation imbued with intentionality because there is no *re*presentation without a prior presentation. The relation between the object and its mirror image is not analogous to the relation between an object and the experience of that object. It becomes even more obviously true when we recall what we experience is an object but what is reflected in the mirror is not the object but part of the visual appearance of the object in a certain light at a certain distance from a certain angle.

The putative correlation between brain states and events in the outside world does not provide an explanation of how the former could be an image, or awareness, *of* the latter. In the absence of a conscious subject making observations and drawing inferences, no physical event reveals any other prior physical event. We could put this another way: givenness is not generated by causation. The sloppy thinking that permits the ascription of "aboutness" to events in the absence of a conscious subject leads to the kind of lunacy according to which everything in the universe is *information*, something we shall examine in Chapter 7.

Any lingering doubts on this score may be dispelled by imagining the consequences that would follow if an event's simply being an effect – which may be immediate or delayed – were sufficient to reveal its cause or counted as a revelation of its cause. The entire universe, which standard materialism thinks of as effects of preceding causes, would be a revelation of the entire universe; or, at the very least, each successive state of the universe would be a revelation of the immediately prior state. It follows that something more than causal connectedness in accordance with the laws of nature is clearly required to make event B a revelation of its cause, event A. Even more is needed for it to make event B a revelation of, or grounds for proposing, an *object* in which A takes place – the glass which interacts with the light in virtue of which the eye can see it.

We may safely conclude that the principles, etc. that Dennett refers to may apply to the transformation of light (electromagnetic activity) originating from the glass into nerve impulses (electrochemical activity) in the brain. But they offer nothing to account for the transformation of electromagnetic energy into visual experience – the *experience* of light, or *light as an experience*, or light as that *in virtue of which illuminated objects are revealed in a visual field*. It offers even less to explain how the reception of energy transmitted from the object to the eye resulting in excitation of the visual cortex is transformed into projection of the object as "out there", distinct from the brain and body of the owner of the cortex. Nor does it explain how a glass is experienced as the presence of something that transcends what is experienced of it such that I intuit that "there is more to this thing than meets my – or anyone else's – eye or other senses".

With the perception of *objects* such as glasses, we have reached something that lies at the heart of this book: *full-blown* intentionality – the directedness of consciousness on to something of which the subject is aware that exceeds, is other and more than, the experiences through which it is perceived. This is what is bundled up in the sense that the object is "over there", "other than me", and most importantly something "in itself"; that it has intrinsic characteristics which I may suspect (from previous experience or acquired knowledge) I am not, or not yet, experiencing. The three-dimensional nature of such an intentional object can be thrown into relief by the contrast with conscious contents that have only inchoate aboutness, for example itches and tingles, and ringing in ears, and floaters in the eyes. Tingles and the like do not efface themselves in something they are about, in something independent of experience and other than the body. We shall, however, discover in the next chapter, that the contrast is not as sharp, and the situation is more complex than appears at first sight. For the present we might note that bodily sensations such as pains that do not have obvious objects they are "about", nevertheless can be interpreted as being "about" something that is happening in our body. Indeed, the pain is about the state of a particular part of the body.

We could summarize the central argument of this section – which lies at the heart of pretty well everything that follows – in this way: while the laws and causal connections that we observe operating in the material world may explain *how the light gets into our heads* they do not explain *how our gaze looks out* – never mind the gaze that actively sees, that scrutinizes, the material world, or one that stares, or makes another person uncomfortable. Even less do those laws explain how we intuit an *outside* in which we locate objects such as glasses that are not only other than the gaze but also more than what is directly revealed to the gaze. There is no basis in the material events of the brain to create the basis of "outside" and "inside" or the subjective viewpoint that assigns items to the one realm or the other. If my perception of the room were inside my head, it is not possible to see how it is that I in fact perceive the room as surrounding my head. In short, the causal impact of material object on the material brain would not generate a world, with its nested outsides – this room, this house, this street, this town, this country, this planet – in which we locate ourselves as something within it. To put this another way, intentionality enables us to experience items as being not only "there" but "over there". The togetherness-and-apartness of the subject and her object of experience does not correspond to anything in the material world causally stitched together. The conscious mind is the opening up of Being to create the presence of beings to subjects.

Out of the intuition of the object as not only being out there, as being other than me, *but also available to everyone else*, as part of a *public* world, there arises the higher-order intentionality evident in consciously utilized signs, in assertions, in beliefs, and ultimately in theories. Such derived intentionality of sign systems is built on the first-order intentionality of perception – which is why (to quote Jerry Fodor, though I am not certain that this is what he meant to highlight by it) "the semantic proves permanently recalcitrant to integration in the natural order".[64] It is reflected in the many desperate – but necessarily futile – attempts to incorporate intentionality into the natural order.

A more radical attempt to deal with the embarrassment of intentionality is to get rid of it altogether. This is so widespread that it deserves a place in this discussion: its discrediting should be as public as possible. The position in question is called "eliminative materialism". Its advocates claim that items to which we ascribe aboutness or intentionality – such as perceptions and thoughts, not to speak of beliefs and desires – are unreal. They belong, so we are told, to a "folk psychology" which will be superseded when neuroscience completes its mission to describe the true nature of mind.

Let us start with naïve eliminativists such as Alex Rosenberg who wish to replace talk of mental contents, with their awkward "aboutness", by talk of neural discharges. As Rosenberg expresses it: "Consciousness is just another physical process. If physical processes cannot by themselves have or convey propositional content [i.e. have aboutness], then consciousness can't either".[65] In short, since causation or material events cannot generate intentionality, then there is no such thing as intentionality. Because they seem easier to deny, Rosenberg focuses on higher-order mental phenomena such as beliefs. It will be apparent that his arguments are pragmatically self-refuting. It should be obvious to Rosenberg that, in stating his position, he is describing his own beliefs. Those beliefs have aboutness: they are about "physical processes", "consciousness", "propositional content", etc.

The best-known eliminativist is the already name-checked Daniel Dennett, who also focuses on higher-level mental states such as beliefs. Given his claim that "the mind is somehow nothing but a physical phenomenon", it is easy to see why he has spent much of the half-century of his philosophical career trying to get rid of intentionality which is clearly an embarrassment for his materialism. As he himself says, "the Intentionalist thesis ... proclaims an unbridgeable gulf between the mental and the physical".[66] To which one can only respond: "You bet!".

Unlike Rosenberg, he is aware that intentionality cannot be eliminated by deploying arguments that are, after all, "about" something put forward by a conscious arguer. Dennett tries a subtler approach that doesn't at first seem as so obviously self-refuting as Rosenberg's.[67] He argues that the reason we believe in beliefs is that they help us to understand human behaviour. It makes sense, therefore, to adopt "an intentional stance" towards people, a stance which *ascribes* beliefs and desires to them: "all there is to being a true believer is being a system whose behaviour is reliably predictable by the intentional stance".[68] But, he argues, this doesn't mean that such items are real mental contents: they are abstractions. Ascribing beliefs is simply a useful strategy employed in daily life to help us make sense of what people are up to. By treating our fellows as rational agents who have desires, and beliefs as to how they might be fulfilled, we shall be better able to predict what they are going to do. Nevertheless, beliefs are *artefacts*: they are relics of "folk psychology", something to which a true science of the mind would not grant houseroom. In short, what residual validity the intentional stance will retain when folk psychology has been replaced by science, will be as a useful predictive instrument, not as a means of accessing an inner reality.

That this desperate endeavour to eliminate intentionality has been given so much air-time and indeed respectful attention is a measure of the commitment in certain quarters to materialist naturalism. Dennett, like Rosenberg, cannot deny that he himself has beliefs – most obviously about the nature of beliefs: he believes that they are artefacts. His philosophical beliefs are not merely items others ascribe to him in order to predict his behaviour – namely a propensity to make certain predictions about his behaviour. Secondly, Dennett's views challenge the reality of the distance between humans that behave in a certain way and mindless zombies that behave in a similar way. This may be what he wants to do; in which case he is in the position of denying consciousness. It is difficult to imagine how the idea of consciousness he discusses could arise in order to be argued over if the human race were a swarm of zombies. Or indeed, how zombies could form the idea of zombies. Thirdly, it is reasonable to assume that assigning beliefs, etc., to "systems" like you and me is helpful to the prediction of behaviour *because* systems like you and me actually have beliefs, etc. Why otherwise would they assist us to understand each other? It is difficult to imagine the (methodological) intentional stance without there being real intentional states. Why on earth would I ascribe beliefs to Dennett or he to me if neither of us, nor any of the human race, had beliefs and other items with aboutness? Fourthly, if beliefs and desires were mere abstractions, it is difficult to see how they would have any powers to influence the behaviour of the person who has them. And if they lacked such causal powers, what function would they have, why would we have them? And how, anyway, could anything without causal powers be part of the natural world that, according to Dennett, is the world period? Causes without descendent effects have no place in a materialist world picture, any more than effects without ancestor causes.

Dennett's account of beliefs does not eliminate the intentionality he wants to banish from his account of the world. The process of ascribing beliefs to other humans is an even more complex, higher-order intentional act than actually having beliefs. My belief that you have beliefs shaping your behaviour seems irreducibly a belief. More specifically, our belief that Dennett has beliefs about the nature of beliefs does not seem reducible to a mere intentional stance helping us to understand his behaviour. And we might even slyly point out that Dennett must believe that he himself has beliefs about beliefs – namely that they are illusions. At any rate there is something very odd about a strategy for deflating intentionality by appealing to the idea of a higher-order intentionality about beliefs that somehow function in absence of basic or first-order intentionality.

Dennett at times seems to retreat from his deconstruction of beliefs by suggesting that his position is more than merely instrumentalist about beliefs, desires, etc. Beliefs are objective phenomena, he concedes, but not entirely respectable, not being states of the brain. Unfortunately, he then confuses things even further by repeating his claim that beliefs are only things we ascribe to agents to predict their behaviour.[69] But then he fatally clarifies his position by asserting that systems such as thermostats and chess-playing computers also have beliefs that are causes of their behaviour because we can predict what they do by applying the intentional stance.[70] His discomfort with this view is evident in his claim that we can "attribute hemi-semi-demi-proto-quasi-pseudo-intentionality" to parts of persons (such as brains) as "it is precisely the enabling move that lets us see how on earth to get the whole wonderful person out of moving animal parts".[71] Really?

Intentionality and a human world

Our concern is to identify the nature of the gap between ourselves and other species, including even our nearest primate kin, and to examine the central role of intentionality. While the arguments I have presented so far demonstrate that conscious experiences do not fit into the materialist orthodoxy, you may think they are not relevant to our arguments about the fundamental difference between humans and beasts. After all, beasts, too, are conscious and seem to be conscious of an external world populated by objects outside of themselves. Our pressing task is to see how the distinctive intentionality of human consciousness underpins the huge and widening gap between humanity and animality.

A good place to start is at our consciousness of ordinary objects such as a glass. This is the ground floor of "full-blown" intentionality. I earlier pointed out that, when I see a glass in front of me, I see something that goes beyond my perception: I am aware that there is more to what I see than what I am seeing. The object "within" my perception is (justifiably) intuited as beyond my perception. The intentional object of perception is more than the content of the perception.

The correlative of full-blown intentionality is an object (or a state of affairs or a *mise-en-scène*) in what philosophers such as P. F. Strawson and Qassim Cassam have called "the weighty sense".[72] Such objects are explicitly experienced as things in themselves that may be accessed by, but not exhausted by, experience. The idea of objects "out there", "beyond me", "separate from the subject" is profound: it is the ground-floor of a subject/object division or a self/world division. Such objects are obdurate, not subordinate, not pliant to our cognitive bidding. They are also the substratum of an acknowledged public, shared, reality. This experience of an object is to be contrasted with sensory experiences – such as pains and tingles – that philosophers have described as merely "phenomenal" or "intransitive".[73]

So much for *full-blown* intentionality.[74] Belief in the continuing existence of an object that is not being perceived – so-called object permanence – and in the notions of causal relationships between objects, of force fields that operate on objects, are different aspects of the fundamental sense that objects are "in-themselves" and that they have intrinsic properties. This seems to be less well developed in non-human primates than in humans.[75] It is important to understand this because it is the key to something we shall come to: the limited extent to which animals share intelligence about an outside world and their joining of intentionality. It provides the connection between the fully-developed individual sense of Mummy still being real even when she is invisible because she is in the next room and the sophisticated collective sense that the sun still exists in the hours of darkness.

We are close to the place at which the fundamental differences between ourselves and other living creatures have their origin. The idea of an object-in-itself, that goes beyond my experiences, is the lynch-pin of a shared public space, of a space and time in which "we" are all situated, and subsequently of the idea of the world, and of Nature, apt for mythical interpretation and ultimately of scientific investigation.[76] The object that human perception is "of" or "about" is the ground floor of a shared outside. As we shall discuss in the next chapter, our sense of "objects in the weighty sense" is connected to our relationship to our own bodies, and our status as embodied, or "ambodied", subjects. The public realm where objects are located, however, is not built by each of us single-handedly or single-mindedly. Our awareness of things existing "out there" is of things existing in a common "there"; most importantly, existing for others. The sense of the public realm is interwoven with a sense of others' awareness, of the consciousness of our conspecifics. The public standing of objects, and hence of their nature as things-in-themselves is affirmed when they are the shared referents of pointing or discourse.

Although language has been the driver of the most spectacular advances of humanity from the state of nature, there is something deeper than language dividing ourselves from chimpanzees, something that language is built on. I want to suggest that chimpanzees cannot talk to each other because there is a relative underdevelopment of the full-blown intentionality that underpins a fully developed, shared outside, a common point of reference, a public world which is founded upon and underpins shared intentionality. The latter is that in virtue of which we *face* a human world that occupies a vast space we have together constructed and which distances us from nature – nature in the wider sense of the material universe and in the narrower sense of the biosphere. That space is ultimately populated with objects of cognition – facts, universals, abstract objects – that are non-natural, in addition to the materials of nature itself.

Intentionality is the crack through which the light of the distinctively human world pours in. The intentionality of mental contents is the ultimate origin of our unique human distance from the material world. The full-blown intentionality of object perception, is the platform, from which our human being that deviates ever more widely from nature, can take off. We do not have to think of mind as a Cartesian or other magic substance to see that it cannot be assimilated into nature. We have merely to recognize that human consciousness is not identical to neural impulses: without intentionality and its capacity to be joined or shared it would not be possible to see how the human and the natural world could be opened up. The sharing is "out there" – in a space where you and I are – not in the intra-cranial darkness.

The unique range, variety, and density of shared intentionality[77] permitting complex, sustained, cooperative behaviour – along the lines we have already discussed – has woven the cognitive fabric of the human world and built the boundless artefactscape with which we surround ourselves and which mediates our interactions with nature. Our being outside of ourselves in our consciousness of a world of material (and later abstract) objects that transcends our experiences is expanded through endless sharing of experience: from "seeing this" to "look at this!".

The sharing of attention, the convergence of consciousness, is evident in the earliest stage in child development.[78] Even very young children – 1 to 2 years – can understand "we-intentions" directed at joint actions.[79] Towards the end of the first year of life, infants incessantly point out things to others, for the sake of sharing experience. This mode of pointing – declarative as opposed to imperative ("gimme!") pointing – is universal in humans and absent in other primates in the wild. It presupposes and elaborates a mode of awareness, often called a second-order intentionality: the ascription to others of a viewpoint different from one's own that, nevertheless, looks on to a world "we" have in common. Pointing is a marker of capacities that permit elective, bespoke collaboration and social cooperation. The index finger by which we direct others' attention is a primordial seamstress of the fabric of the community of minds.

There are many other more powerful, complex, and layered modes of joining attention, also not seen in non-human animals. They are the very warp and weft of daily human life. Most notable are those that are mediated through speech and writing. Writing is obviously a recent development; but speech, too, is a relative *parvenu* in the history of hominids – between 40,000 and 100,000 years old – much more recent than earliest distinctive tool use which began with the pebble chopper some 2.8 million years ago. Among the many features of human language, the fact that its elements – words – are signs that are fabricated solely for the purpose of signifying rather than (as in the case of natural signs) occurring spontaneously and only incidentally signifying may be the most salient. They are not mere effects of causes but have been generated to serve communicative intent and hence are ultimately able to *propose* realities as well as respond to them, to entertain shared possibilities as well as register actualities – in short to point to absences that may or may not become presences.

Collectively, through the direct and indirect interaction of individual and groups of human beings over thousands of years, countless cognitive hook-ups, there is built up a tissue of knowledge and practice and understanding and togetherness that amounts to a community of minds. We find ever more elaborate ways to share intelligence and expertise and to collaborate in meeting our needs, even when they are seemingly primitive, as in acts of aggression. Chimpanzees get no closer to grand strategies than do participants in a spontaneous pub brawl. Their capacity to transmit any cultural development is to put it mildly patchy. A handful of tricks – termite fishing, cracking open a nut with a hammer, washing food – acquired in the absence of any sense of underlying principles or unaccompanied by a desire to share – is not significantly added to, even less purposively transmitted.[80]

We are now in a position to defend human exceptionalism against the claim that, since a) we are our brains and b) our brains are not very different from those of other primates, we cannot be fundamentally different from them. Full-blown intentionality is that in virtue of which we individually transcend our brains understood as material objects, or organs; and the joining or sharing of intentionality, adding up to collective consciousness, is that in virtue of which we collectively transcend nature, and individually live our lives in a world that is to a great degree outside of nature. It follows from this that it will not be possible to discover the human world or the human person in the individual brain. Trying to find the person by peering into the darkness inside the skull using brain imaging and other techniques is analogous to trying to hear the whispering of the woods by applying a stethoscope to individual acorns.

The distance between ourselves as persons and ourselves as organisms, and the difference between us and chimps, is not therefore to be found in our brains but in the fact that, courtesy of our brains, we have access to an extra-cerebral culture that we share with others and which has been transformed – and is being transformed at an accelerating pace – in the millions of years since humans forked off from the other primates. This distance originates in the very nature of human consciousness, in its "aboutness" that does not fit into the materialist world picture.

Those philosophers and neuroscientists who argue that, since neuroscience cannot find anything in the brain corresponding to propositional attitudes such as beliefs and thoughts, even less the self, such things are not really real, have things back to front. The correct conclusion is that brain science is not the right net for catching these indubitable realities. While they are indeed real, beliefs and desires are not to be found inside our heads. More generally, personhood is distant from, and not defined or constrained by, the characteristics of our biological brains shaped by evolutionary forces. Of course, personhood cannot continue without a brain. Chop my head off and my IQ falls; damage my brain sufficiently and my personality vanishes. Suddendorf's observation that it isn't clear "what is it about our brains that causes our minds to be so special"[81] is not in the slightest bit surprising. To seek the basis of human difference in the general characteristics of the human brain compared with other primate brains is to search in the wrong place. Likewise, those who seek the nature of human emotions such as love, or aesthetic experience, or a sense of justice, in brain activity, are also barking up the wrong tree. This tree, alas, has been so well tended that it has achieved the altitude of a Californian Redwood.

The development of the human mind is *extracorporeal* and consequently *extrabiological*, taking place in a cultural – technological, institutional, cognitive – sphere, a human realm experienced through individual participation in a community of minds. The rate of this development accelerates with time, as is illustrated by the pace of change of technologies. Over a million years separated the pebble chopper from the hand-axe while the discovery of electromagnetic fields was separated from the invention of mobile phones communicating through satellites by the mere blink of a couple of centuries.

Consciousness as a biological embarrassment

Behind biologism there looms a more profound reductionism – physicalism according to which, as pieces of living matter, we are *essentially* matter and, as such, subject to the laws of physics. The path to physicalism via biologism is described by Nobel-prize winning physicist Steven Weinberg: "The explanatory arrow points downwards from societies to people, to organs, to cells, to biochemistry, to chemistry, and ultimately to physics".[82] This is entirely consistent with Dennett's claim quoted earlier that mind is not only made out of the same stuff as the stuff described in physics but that it is a manifestation of *the same laws and principles*, etc. that govern the stuff that physics deals with. "Aboutness" – absent throughout all but a minute amount of the universe – becomes inexplicable, even when it is claimed that it is the product of a particular configuration of matter, such as is seen in the brains of higher organisms. Matter does not seem to have the wherewithal to climb out of itself and look on itself from without, never mind be capable of naming itself and identifying those laws and principles.

An increasing number of philosophers who appreciate this have embraced the more "expansive" philosophical naturalism to which I have already alluded. This fully accepts the reality of intentionality, and of experience, arguing that (as Galen Strawson put it) if you are not "a real realist about experience" you are not a real but a false naturalist.[83] You cannot be mistaken that you are having experiences because that mistake is an experience; or you would have to have experiences to make that mistake. Experience cannot be an illusion because the illusion of experience is itself an experience – of an illusion.

The claim that intentional experience is nowhere has been replaced, for some, by the opposite claim: that it is everywhere – a view called panpsychism. Panpsychists, aware that this is not how things look like through the lens of our most advanced theories, argue that science does not give us access to the intrinsic nature of matter, or the physical world, only its (mathematical) structural properties. All that science reveals to us, so the story goes, are the causal, or structural, or dispositional properties of the world and not its intrinsic properties. We do not therefore have sufficient grounds for believing that concrete reality is fundamentally or irreducibly non-experiential in character.

This seems undeniable. The panpsychist's next step, however, is less easy to accept. Given that experience is an undeniable aspect of reality and given also that this fits very awkwardly into an account of the material world (including organisms and their brains), there is a case – so the argument goes – for believing at the very least that *all* concrete phenomena have experiential as well as non-experiential properties. It is possible that consciousness is not confined to sentient beings or dependent on certain privileged configurations of matter such as brains. Some philosophers go even further and espouse a more radical panpsychism. They argue that we have no satisfactory grounds for maintaining that the physical world has anything more than experiential properties: there can be no experiential evidence for the existence of a reality beyond experience.

This is not the place to subject panpsychism to a detailed critique.[84] It is sufficient to note that, if we believe that experiential properties are everywhere, and Stuff and Sense were co-created at the Big Bang, it becomes even more difficult to understand the difference between pebbles and pains; or comprehend why individual people are conscious subjects, seeing the world from particular viewpoints – defined by their sensorium, their selfhood, their daily life – while individual rocks and trees are not; or account for the privileged relationship between brains and minds. In short, panpsychism seems a rather expensive way of not solving the mind–brain problem. We should be grateful, however, that it acknowledges that the puzzling relationship between the mental and the material is not just "a little local difficulty" that will eventually be sorted by advances in neuroscience.

More directly relevant to our present concerns, is this: Darwinism highlights (if inadvertently) a serious objection to Darwinitis, namely, that Darwinism gives no account of the *emergence* of consciousness from the material world of which lower organisms are a part. That failure is particularly conspicuous in the case of mental contents such as perceptions – with direct, full-blown intentionality – and beliefs and knowledge with derived intentionality, mediated most prominently by language the powerful, protean, all-purpose mediator of a boundless, and boundlessly shared, attention. There are at least two major obstacles to a materialist evolutionary account of human consciousness: the first is the question of the nature of the supposed competitive advantage conferred by being conscious; and the second is the question how, even if consciousness *did* confer survival benefit, it could have been generated between unconscious species; that, as a result of the blood bath of natural selection, the universe could get to know itself.

It is important not to approach the first question – What is the point of being aware of what is impacting on you or of having a sense of what you are? – from the wrong starting place. It is obvious that if you are a conscious being whose survival normally depends on being conscious it is better to stay that way. You are safer awake than in coma. But the relevant question is this: how did certain forms of living matter come to be dependent, as we are, on being conscious agents rather than unconscious mechanisms? The question that gains particular traction when we recall how metabolically expensive it is keeping alive the kind of brain to which materialists ascribe the capacity of consciousness – never mind the kind of brain said to be required for sharp perception, accurate belief, and a body of quality-controlled knowledge. And given, also, that pre-conscious processes do so much work, there is not much useful work left for consciousness to do.

To address this question properly, we need to go back to a putative moment when the first spark of consciousness was lit and ask what possible additional advantage would an organism with (say) an array of photosensitive cells gain from being *aware* of the light it is responding to? The "obvious" benefits vanish when we acknowledge:

a) That the best route to replication of the genome must be via utterly reliable mechanisms based on the (by definition) unbreakable laws of nature rather than the vagaries of (conscious) decision making;

b) Evolution should favour appropriate action, but it is not evident that this should have to be mediated by true belief or indeed any belief; and

c) That unconscious mechanisms have been perfectly adequate to bring about things that consciousness could not even dream of, such as the basis of the organism's self-maintenance (including its voluntary actions), the spectacular achievement of the development of the human brain *in utero*, and the entire evolutionary process.[85]

Conscious inessentialism – the thesis that seemingly intelligent actions could be carried out without conscious accompaniments – is discussed by Owen Flanagan.[86] He concludes, as I do, that explaining the evolution of consciousness (or, to use a less prejudicial term, the emergence of consciousness) is as hard as explaining consciousness itself. Explanations of the form "consciousness is necessary for such and such a function" simply moves the problem on. If, say, consciousness is necessary for learning and plasticity, then we have to ask why is it not always necessary for learning and plasticity. In most cases, learning and plasticity do not require the conscious participation of the organism. Readers may recall the perceptive bacterium mentioned earlier in the chapter. Discriminative behaviour necessary for survival can be entirely based in evolved unconscious mechanisms. After all, mechanical causation seems to have delivered everything that is needed for life without the help of sentience, never mind sophisticated intentional consciousness. Indeed, some psychologists have argued, along with Ran Hassin, that "unconscious processes can carry out *every* fundamental-level function that conscious processes can perform".[87] The redundancy of consciousness is close to the notion of mental phenomena as "causally inert epiphenomena" (Stanley Klein's phrase) and the conscious person as a rather expensive luxury that cannot be explained by natural selection.

One of the ironies is that the more clearly we understand the neural basis of seemingly very sophisticated behaviour such as jamming avoidance in weakly electrical fish or sound localization in barn owls, the less we need to invoke subjective consciousness. This is the most obvious reason why it is difficult to see how being consciously concerned about itself could make a creature less vulnerable. Yoram Gutfreund asked, "Why does an antelope being chased by a lioness need to suffer terrible fear while its body is responding so efficiently to threat?"[88] The more we understand about the neural basis of behaviour the less we need to invoke subjectivity; conscious subjectivity thus becomes *more* mysterious with increased neural explanation of behaviour. The theologian Richard Oxenberg points out that the supposed efficacy of subjective experience in giving a beast an edge over the competition, suggesting that a subjective state (e.g. pain) has physical efficacy above that of any state corresponding to it (e.g. firing in certain nerve fibres), is at odds with materialism, since consciousness would be at best epiphenomenal: that is to say, it would be a spin-off from the brain but not do any work.[89] Epiphenomenal consciousness puts materialists in the awkward position of accepting the existence of events having causal ancestors and no causal descendants. Besides, nothing causally inert can make a difference, least of all conferring an edge in the battle for survival.

The achievements of organisms that we may safely assume are not conscious of what they are doing, even less self-conscious about doing it, are staggering. Tropical ants build a trap to catch insect prey nearly 50 times weightier than themselves. The prey – a grasshopper or some such – steps into a swiss cheese of holes occupied by ants ready to tear off the limbs of the giant. As it moves from hole to hole in its endeavour to escape, it loses limb after limb and is immobilized and thus available to be eaten. This complex, cooperative but standardized task is accomplished without any one of the ants entertaining the idea of the overall plan.[90]

Given that so much can be achieved without any consciousness, never mind mental states with full-blown intentionality, the question of the marginal advantage it confers remains unanswered. It has been suggested that mobile animals must differentiate events arising in their bodies from those arising out of the environment. However, that differentiation could be achieved without consciousness, as it is in the case of mobile single-cell organisms. What is more, the differentiation has nothing to do with the distinction between "self" and "other", which seems to bring no benefit to what have been described as "coherent macroscopic actors". Experience seems to bring little to the party; whence we may assume that subjectivity, selfhood, and personhood, bring even less. The distinct value of subjective experience – of feeling what impacts on me and feeling what it is like to be a certain organism – so that the "it is" of the organism becomes the "I am" of the person is elusive.

The force of the second question about the emergence of consciousness as the result of the evolutionary process is felt more strongly if we ration our use of anthropomorphic terms such as "competition". Natural selection can act only on what is already available. It seems inconceivable that it could *generate*, even less requisition, entirely novel properties such as consciousness. The clash between forms of organic matter over limited means to life seems hardly likely to give rise to something that goes beyond the material world, namely intentionality.

If natural selection does not seem a plausible source of sentience – such that photosensitive cells become aware of the light that impinges on them – it is even less plausible as a cause of: pieces of the material world becoming conscious of being located in a world outside of themselves; or becoming viewpoints that care for themselves; beings for whom matter is (for example) resistance to goal-directed effort; and, ultimately, pieces of matter mattering to a piece of matter that matters to itself, and consequently acquiring a mouth to name itself.

Thomas Nagel expressed this with characteristic clarity:

> [Evolution] may explain why creatures with vision or reason will survive, but it does not explain how vision or reasoning are possible. [...]. The possibility of minds forming progressively more objective conceptions of reality is not something the theory of natural selection can attempt to explain ... since it does not explain possibilities at all, but only selection among them.[91]

This is echoed by Galen Strawson: "Experience must exist before it has adaptive value in order to be available to be moulded to some adaptive purpose by evolution. Evolution by natural selection can only work with materials that already exist."[92]

In summary, evolutionary theory, which describes a mindless process of the origin of species, starting in a mindless cosmos, fails at a fundamental level to account for our distinctive nature: it cannot explain the emergence of the consciousness out of insentience or the conscious subject out of sentience. What is more, the spectacular "achievements" of the overwhelmingly mindless evolutionary process throw the usefulness of mind into question.

The panpsychist idea that mind is there at the beginning, in the raw material on which evolutionary forces operate, simply creates new problems. The most obvious is trying to make sense of the very idea of mind being present in the microscopic constituents of the material world. A prominent contemporary advocate of panpsychism Philip Goff asserts with admirable consistency that "electrons have an inner life".[93] What gathers up the angel dust of experience diffused through the elements of the natural world into the kind of mind you and I have? No answer is forthcoming. The attempt to close the gap between humanity and the non-human world by claiming that mind is everywhere appears to be at least as ill-conceived as the endeavour to close that gap by reducing the mind to brain activity.

CONCLUDING THOUGHTS

Our present concern is the difference between ourselves and other living beings. The lack of a materialist explanation of consciousness is a serious objection to the kind of naturalism that sees us solely as organisms generated by (material) evolutionary forces. The difference between persons and sentient organisms is another issue. This difference has arisen out of the intentionality of our conscious minds. Shared intentionality is the driver of the widening gap between ourselves and nature, evident most clearly in the distance between ourselves and our nearest animal kin, and lies at the heart of the human world. The gap between the activity of evolved brains and what happens in the community of minds to which they give us access justifies the claim that we are *not* (just) organisms, or mere parts of organisms (such as brains). Our personhood is neither entirely part of nature nor supernatural. It is extra-natural.

There are clearly vast differences – in structure and function, behaviour, and sensory range – between (say) oysters and giraffes. The difference between humanity and animality, however, is a different kind of difference: a difference that permits us to live in a world rather than being cocooned in an environment in which there is a necessarily tight fit between needs, the resources to meet them, and the means by which the resources are detected and accessed. The difference may be highlighted by contrasting the animal *umwelt* which all sentient creatures possess, and having a world-picture which is a capacity unique to human beings.

Unlike non-human animals, *we* spend relatively little of our time directly moving towards what is of biological benefit and away from what is biologically detrimental – or not by literally altering the spatio-temporal gap between the body and the promise or the threat. Our approaches and retreats are in a different kind of space. Much of our behaviour is driven not by stimuli from our surroundings but by facts, duties, and roles, set out in schematized (clock and calendar) time. As we cooperate in creating or at least cultivating the means of our own subsistence, in attending to secondary, tertiary and higher-order needs, and in maintaining the artefacts that support us in work and play, health and sickness, discharging defined roles according to tabled time, we lead lives that are remote from those of other denizens of the natural world.

For us (as I will discuss in Chapter 4) "thatter" is as important as matter. We live in a "thatosphere" where we take account of facts as much as of forces that impinge on us and stuffs that we negotiate. As for facts, they are not themselves part of the physical world. Matters of fact are not made of matter. Facts are not part of an order of things that is composed of masses, charges, forces, energies, and the like. That is why, to reiterate Fodor, "the semantic proves permanently recalcitrant to integration in the natural order".[94]

The elaboration of "aboutness" in a growing body of knowledge – know-how interacting with know-that – that guides our behaviour is one aspect of our being *explicit* animals who do things for reasons, responding to rules which we consult, lay down, or challenge. We mediate our way of being through principles, norms, and institutions, and differentiate ourselves into office holders in a society in which we embrace or are allocated roles, that build on our skills that we have actively acquired and endeavour to enhance. The means to survival – the hunting and gathering once shared with other animals – are transformed into the tasks of creating the means of our subsistence or engaging in activities indirectly related to this, mediated via labour, exchange, and that all-purpose means of exchange – money. Consumption becomes the indirect reward of production or supporting production. We outsource tasks to others. The division of labour – with hierarchies and graded responsibilities and stipulated powers – extends the principle whereby two hands can do things that one hand could not conceive and two-legged walking far exceeds what can be achieved by hopping.

I guess that there would be few philosophers inclined to challenge these observations about our everyday life. They are, however, incontrovertible evidence that, contrary to the claims of writers such as Dennett, our competencies, unlike those evident throughout the natural world, are shot through with comprehension.[95] There are many things we could not do, or would not do, without knowing why we are doing them. Indeed, the vast majority of activities that fill our days would not be undertaken if we did not have an idea of why we are doing them.

Other species have minds and, in the case of higher mammals, complex minds. And this may prompt the objection that in comparing ourselves with non-human animals I have homogenized "animals" and homogenized the human mind. But by focusing on intentionality, I have highlighted the unique way in which we offset the world so that we *face* it. Intentionality is the seed of our evolving human wakefulness in virtue of which ultimately we come to locate ourselves in a universe defined by objective facts. This is something that a naturalism which sees us simply as organisms – as material objects wired into the material world – cannot accommodate. Full-blown intentionality opens the long path, taken uniquely by humans, that leads from sentience to sentences. Our minds are as remote from the sentience of animals as a three-piece suit saved up for and bought in a shop is from a pelt that is secreted. Unwired from nature we face it across, or through the mediation of, the human world.

A naturalism that cannot, or will not, accommodate intentionality, because it wants to identify consciousness with neural activity, implicitly opposes the humanist view of humanity and of the human world. Hence our rejection of this almost standard view (though it is rarely expressed so baldly) as to what Darwin is supposed to have shown us about ourselves:

> Since Darwin's *Origin of Species* and *Descent of Man* ... we have known that man is a part of nature ... If man is a natural, a wild, an evolving species, not essentially different in this respect from all others ... then the works of man, however precious, are as natural as those of beaver, termite, or of any other species that dramatically modifies the habitat.[96]

The present chapter has been devoted to dismantling the claim that "man is part of nature" and that his works, too, are natural. Full-blown intentionality ultimately lies at the root of other aspects of our selves that have been identified as the unique characteristics of our "species being" – language, irony, art, currency, medication, trade, long-term strategies:

> from having a soul, being aware of ourselves, time or death, through being rational, linguistic, or conceptual beings, to being jokers, tool-users, self-recognizers, other-recognizers, inhabitants of an objective world, truth-trackers, capable of meta-cognition, pursuers of moral, aesthetic, or epistemic goals for their own sake.[97]

Let me, finally, reiterate an earlier point. My purpose in highlighting the profound difference between humans and other creatures is not to justify treating animals without compassion, even less denying their capacity for suffering. I have no doubt whatsoever that a dog that appears to be howling with pain is really in pain. Indirect evidence from wound tending which is seen in crustaceans but not in insects has suggested to some that even beasts as lowly as decapod crustaceans are capable of experiencing pain.[98]

Nor am I even claiming that we are "superior" to animals. The thesis that we are different from them, in a manner that is different from the differences seen between other animals, should lead us to consider ourselves as *incommensurate* with them. This is true especially because we hold the measuring tools. If we have judged ourselves as superior, as opposed to different in a fundamentally different way, this may be because we have often ventriloquized thoughts about ourselves through a god we have invented – something else a humanist should resist.

Addendum
Some observations on animal cognition: making it tougher for killjoys

We killjoys sometimes make life easier for ourselves by considering animal consciousness from a distance sufficient to enable us to overlook the often-remarkable capacities of individual species. We talk about "reactions", "associative learning", "mechanisms", "programmes" and "instinct" – terms that apply equally to the behaviour of ants and apes. The purpose of what follows is to look closely at some individual species and their remarkable capabilities, to put the notion of humans versus (all) animals, man versus beast, to the test.

A good place to begin is with bees. They have only a million neurons, compared with the 9 billion neurons in the reader's brain – though they are widely branched and richly connected. Lars Chittka's "Bee Cognition" should be mandatory reading for anyone persuaded by the views advanced in this chapter and, indeed, this book. It is a reminder that the central thesis of human exceptionalism has to be specified carefully. Chittka reminds us of the rich behavioural repertoire of social insects: "that orchestrate life in the colony, facilitate the construction of a communal home, secure a steady stream of appropriate food for their young, defending the colony and regulating its climate".[99]

This is usually dismissed as "just instinct". Instinct it is, but the "just" is not justified. In the case of bees, the provisioning of their young in a specially constructed nest, required a precise spatial memory in addition to extraordinary home construction skills because "evolution does not take kindly to a mother who forgets the location of her offspring". There is also the vital capacity to learn to identify and remember – and to communicate through their dances – the spatial location of those flowers that are the richest source of energy. Bees can remember multiple foraging locations and even the time of day when each one is profitable. And they have to learn this quickly, given that life expectancy is only a few weeks, and they often employ the short cut of copying the flower choices of more experienced individuals. Some individuals spontaneously dance in the night, when no foraging takes place, apparently consolidating the memory of a location they had visited the previous day. Bees also learn the shortest route between all the best locations, to gather the maximum of pollen in the shortest mileage – a feat that requires integrating a "rich library of landmark memories with celestial cues", to permit orientation, and the capacity to consider the time of the day when using the sun as a compass.

And we have not even considered what the bee has to learn if it is to harvest the riches it finds when it alights on a promising flower. The manipulation techniques required to extract nectar or pollen are often complex and may require numerous trials to master, particularly as the bees may have to avoid or deal with waiting predators, often cunningly concealed. Bees can also cope with situations that do not occur in nature. They can, for example, learn how to pull an artificial flower doped with sucrose from under a transparent table by means of a string. Some bees are quicker off the mark than others and the dimmer bees can solve the task by observing and then imitating the brighter ones.

I have not, of course, touched on their most conspicuous collective achievement: the creation of the aesthetically beautiful and mathematically precise honeycomb. Most astounding is the architectural flexibility that may be necessitated by, for example, the foundations being turned upside down. But I have said enough to discredit any easy dismissal of the cognitive capacities even of creatures as small as and evolutionarily distant as bees in which we have seen consciousness-like, even quasi-intelligent, behaviour. A fundamental difference, however, remains between bee and human construction. The bees do not have an explicit plan for the honeycomb: design and build are not separated. And there is no discretion as to whether the efforts of individual bees should be put into honeycomb construction or some other beneficial activity. Bees are automata: their activities fulfil competencies without comprehension or intention. It seems more plausible to conclude from their complex behaviour not that they have extraordinary conscious cognitive activity but that much can be achieved without conscious cognitive activity; that they are programmed to do what they do without having to know what they are doing or why they are doing it.

Let us say a little more about something we have made much of in our endeavour to pinpoint what distinguishes man from beast: cooperative behaviour. It has been extensively examined in animals through a cooperative pulling task. In this task, "two or more animals pull rewards to themselves via an apparatus they cannot successfully operate alone".[100] In a typical set up, two animals have to pull at either end of a string looped through a moveable platform to bring a reward closer. If only one end is pulled, the string slips out and the platform can no longer be pulled. There is evidence of understanding the principle of cooperation if one animal waits to be joined by a partner or actively solicits help. The team members take account of each other's behaviour to pursue their common goal.

Although many animals seem to work together in cooperative pulling tasks, the conclusions from experiments seem to be mixed. The most consistent evidence of understanding cooperation comes from primates – as expected – but also from some birds such as ravens, which will wait for their partners after many trials. Tellingly, the chimpanzees performed rather badly, making it difficult to correlate with intelligence or insight. And, of course, even the most accomplished cooperative pulling comes nowhere near the long-term cooperative projects that are ubiquitous in human life, where we all pull together in maintaining the material and social fabric of our lives. And it falls hugely short of the kind of cooperation that results in the formation of a honeycomb, though the latter is not the result of a shared plan envisaged by the thousands of individuals contributing to the finished product. A comparison of either cooperative pulling or honeycomb creation with the building of a cathedral according to a preconceived plan is sufficient to throw the difference into relief.

Some recent research appears to question one of the most widely accepted differences between ourselves and our nearest primate kin: the limited development in apes of the sense of other individuals having a mind and, in particular, entertaining beliefs that may be mistaken, so that their actions are not driven by reality but beliefs about reality, which may be false. Krupenye and colleagues[101] found that in three species of great apes, some individuals seemed to anticipate another individual acting on a location not where an object was but where the latter falsely believed it to be, even though the observers themselves knew that the object was no longer there. In humans, it is only after age four that children pass traditional false belief tests in which they explicitly predict a mistaken agent's future actions.

This is impressive but there is still a gulf between the episodic sense of the other as possibly being mistaken and a sustained sense of the other having a viewpoint different from one's own. The latter is expressed throughout social life, beginning with declarative pointing (not seen in any non-human animal), proceeding to informing others of things they are thought to be unaware of, through to teaching and instruction. In short, the ape's theory of other apes' minds is confined to twinkles of insight rather than a full-blown awareness of the other as having an entire and different world.

We may infer this because very little social coordination in non-human animals is mediated through, or underpinned by, collective intentionality. Rakocky and Tomasello (the latter one of the authors of the paper just discussed) have pointed out that, in the case of chimpanzees, "There is nothing that would be called collaboration in the narrow sense of joint intentions based on coordinated plans".[102] Joint intention is a necessary condition for engagement in elective, bespoke collaborations that mark the individual and shared narratives of our lives. Such collaboration is not to be confused with herd behaviour, where the individual members of the herd may simply have the same goals but do not consciously plan joint working to achieve those goals. The difference is between, say, queueing and teamwork.

CHAPTER 3

I am and it is: persons and organisms

We are neither apes nor angels; neither mere organisms nor disembodied spirits passing through nature from a pre-natal to a post-mortem eternity. Nor are we flesh and spirit combined in percentages to be determined by our propensity to romanticism or realism about humanity. No; we are *embodied subjects*. It is this that I want to explore in the present chapter. Like the last chapter, it is haunted by the mystery of intentionality.

Intentionality accounts for the distance between the organism *H. sapiens* and the human person. More specifically, full-blown, shared intentionality, creating a community of minds, a public space, an explicitly shared world, is the key to our distance from nature and our status as individuals *facing* a common world populated by objects and subjects that are intuited as being other than ourselves and as having hidden as well as manifest properties. Our exploration of embodiment will eventually lead to a suggestion as to how we arrive at the notion of "physical" objects that have an existence, a reality, properties, that lie beyond our experiences – at the idea of an object as a thing-in-itself. I hope this part of the inquiry will address lingering doubts about the reality of the profound gulf between ourselves and beasts; between humans who have world pictures and beasts that are wired into, or attuned to, an *umwelt*, an environment.

The distinctive intentionality of human consciousness involves two fully developed partners. The first is a subject or self which has – even "owns" – its experiences; and the second is the object of those experiences, encountered as something in-itself, distinct from the experience and, indeed, from the subject of the experience. This form of intentionality is able to develop from a first-order level of the experience enjoyed by most higher animals to second-ary and higher-level intentionality unique to humans.

Higher-level intentionality has many manifestations. The most obvious are signs that have been deliberately generated in order to be "about" something that a subject wants to share with other subjects: individual gestures and a thousand verbal and non-verbal sign systems. These create, expand, and main-tain the human world. They distance us from nature, even when they serve biological needs, such as for food, shelter, and protection from predators and natural disasters. Using arbitrary and conventional sign systems that have to be learned and taught, the intentional consciousness of the subject expands further into a "beyond" woven out of (for example) quoted testimony, fac-tual knowledge, and shared history that all may draw upon. This forms the fabric of the multiple communities to which we belong and which have their distinctive, personalized echo in each of us, as we engage with, and reflect upon, them. It is the theatre of our individual, joined, and collective human agency, the platform from which we are able to change both ourselves and our worlds. Another world-making aspect of second-order intentionality is explicit memory. Memory explicitly connects itself with our own past and the world to which it belongs plays a central role in the establishment of the subject as a self and the latter as an agent. It is the basis of institutions – stand-ing promises – and of the shared histories that underpin our many modes of cooperation and co-habitation.

The relevance of this to our concern with the embodied subject is that at the heart of the human world, by which we are offset from the natural order, is the co-emergence of the "I" of the subject and the "it" of the object, in an iterative or circular process replicated in all of us in the earlier years of cog-nitive development. Full-blown intentionality corresponding to awareness of external objects that have only partially disclosed properties requires not only sentience but also an embodied subject to which experiences can be ascribed. The relationship between the "I" of the subject and the "it" of material objects (including the primordial object of the human body) is the theme of the pres-ent chapter.

The conception of ourselves as embodied subjects is particularly associated with the great philosopher Maurice Merleau-Ponty whom I read (with profit) at an impressionable age. I will not, however, be closely following the outlines of his thought. To some extent this is because my aim in this chapter is less an endeavour to correct the Cartesian error of seeing us as ghosts in machines, or the opposite error of seeing us as physiological machines, than an investi-gation, even a celebration, of the complexity of the relationships we have to our bodies which, I will argue, underpins the ontology of everyday human life – our sense of what kinds of things there are "out there". While, as we have seen in the previous chapter, some primatologists believe that other species share in that ontology to a degree, there is an undeniable difference between inklings and explicit awareness; between objects as registered in non-human consciousness and things existing in themselves being located in a public realm inhabited by human beings. Our full-blown intentionality is the path to humanity's unique metaphysical take on what-is that ascribes intrinsic properties and relations, including causal relations, to objects. Humans have travelled so far along that path that the argument as to whether our differences from (for example) chimpanzees are of kind or just a matter of degree are vacuous.

ONTOLOGICAL SNOBBERY: HATRED OF THE BODY

We are, of course, as inseparable from our bodies as any other living creature: that is the force of the description of us as *em*bodied subjects. You are unimaginable without the body that is holding this book in order to present to your gaze the sentences you are currently reading. Body and person are like the recto and verso of a sheet of paper – at least in the sense that you cannot have the one without the other, although there are other ways in which this analogy fails. Body and person, for example, do not occupy the same space in the sense of having shared boundaries.

Our embodiment has been a source of grief for many body-hating philosophers. For Plato it constitutes a kind of ontological slumming: an ultimate, total embrace, stifling ideas that are only badly imprinted on or realized in the flesh. The body and its experiences are an obstacle to our accessing truth; and its appetites distract us from the pursuit of wisdom.[1] Fully to entertain ideas, we have to rise above our carnal station. The embodied subject is the imprisoned subject. For many theologians, Pascal's thinking reed is a stinking reed, though surprisingly it was good enough for the Son of God who, we are told, wept, bled, and breathed and spoke with his mouth, and died through injuries inflicted on him. Christianity is an incarnational religion, however ill-at-ease its practitioners have been with the flesh and its appetites.

Hatred of the body is perhaps a response to something adumbrated in Roger Scruton's reference to "the metaphysical predicament of the human being in the deep clash contained in the words 'I am', the one affirming transcendence and the other denying it".[2] I would rather characterize the clash as being between "I" of the subject and the "it" of the body; or, more precisely, between the "I am" of Raymond Tallis (RT) and the "it is" of Raymond Tallis' body; more precisely still (as we shall discuss) between "am" and "is", which is not merely an opposition created by an accident of grammar. We are transcendental subjects fastened to inescapable empirical predicates dependent on our organic being for individual realization. We are not (for example) minds temporarily or accidentally caught up in bodies, if only because there could not be a point of intersection, even less causal interaction, between minds that are not located or extended in space and a body that is both located and spatially extended.

The Czech philosopher Jan Patočka put it this way: "The way from the transcendental subject to humans leads through corporeity".[3] This is not a Fall from Platonic grace since there is no transcendental subject without a living body. The body is the necessary condition of what Patocka called the "situatedness" of our existence: our being in the world, enmeshed in a multiplicity of relations. Without such situatedness, our lives would lack an agenda, would have no definite narrative. As Patocka said, paraphrasing Husserl: "Humans are integrated into the world ... by virtue of their *corporeity*".[4] A disembodied Plato would not have met and argued with Socrates, even less fretted over the obstacles that the body seemed to him to place in the way of philosophical understanding. My body is that in virtue of which that I do not merely *have* a point of view but I *am* a point of view, or more broadly, a point – or blob – of concern, according to which I am not only at the centre but also at the edge of things, aware from time to time of being an insignificant creature in a large world that is revealed to me. One manifestation of the necessity of embodiment is that perception has to have a locus of origin: I have to look *from* somewhere in order to look *at* anywhere. This ground-floor truth is underlined by the close connection between perception and bodily skills expressed in the actions necessary to direct perception and the continuous interaction between perception and ongoing action. For being in the world is not a spectator sport: we are in it in virtue of engaging with it.

Let us therefore examine the *em* of embodiment through some of the ways we both *are* our bodies and distanced from them.

ASPECTS OF EMBODIMENT: EM AND AM

Being my body: aspects of carnal presupposition

There is an obvious sense in which I *am* my body. "I am RT'" is not the lifelong iteration of a discarnate ghost. The impersonal, inhuman being of my animal flesh somehow permits my first-person, human being and consequently also the second- and third-person being – myself as a "you" or a "he" – sustained by first-person being.

At the most elementary level, I *am* most immediately *where* my body *is:* if I am in the kitchen, my body is in the kitchen. I am at a specific address because this item in trousers is at that address. When I stand up, it becomes upright. When I dress myself, I put clothes on my body. (The question of who is wearing my trousers is readily settled. But the relationship between the "who" and the "what" is not so readily settled as we shall see.) If you want to point to RT, you point to RT's body. If the latter moves, I move, though when I move, there is no clear-cut hierarchy of the mover and the moved. (By contrast, when I move an extra-corporeal object such as a chair, it is clear which is the agent and which the patient.)

There are, of course, many other modes of being here or there, but localized space occupancy courtesy of our flesh is fundamental. Being literal minded for a moment, we may think of the body as delivering the (non-mathematical) 0, 0, 0 of the co-ordinates of the framework of movement: the point from which I am always setting out. Head-to-toe supplies the vertical axis, left-to-right the horizontal axis, and from back-to-front the axis of depth.[5] My body is the reference point or (more accurately) the reference blob from which I interact with what-is, and in virtue of which a part of what-is is established as the "surroundings" I have to deal with. My body, in sum, is the presupposed platform for actions and for the reception of a perceived world; for the need for action and the possibility of perception.[6] A disembodied view would be a view from nowhere and this would not be a view of everything but of nothing. My body is not only the primary viewpoint or view-blob on, and the fundamental *point d'appui* to, the world, however much absence of mind permits me virtually to occupy any number and kinds of elsewhere, to be "miles away". It is also the condition of there being a world that is my world, of my having surroundings that are themselves further surrounded, of contexts that have wider contexts, that are often shared or even ownerless.

We can characterize the "am" relationship in "I am my body" in another way: my body is the possibility, the necessary condition, of "I". It is the place where happening meets doing or happening creates the possibility of, and necessity for, doing. The state of my body – its development, its health, its decay – of course hugely influences what I experience and what I can do or whether indeed I can experience or do anything at all. "Our flesh surrounds us with its own decisions" the great English metaphysical poet Philip Larkin wrote.[7] More than surrounded: we are invaded, forced to live out, those decisions. A rising tide of ill-being may signal the final engulfment as the body closes over the subjective spaces it has made possible and the "I" drowns in an "it" whose posthumous fate thankfully has nothing to do with us. Our body comes to seem like our mortal enemy – its final embrace total and lethal – in virtue of being the condition of our mortality. It precedes our "I" and will outlast it. Sudden death seems like the murder of "I" by "it".

Nothing in what I have said so far would justify a report to the Royal Society. But now things get a little more difficult as we try to determine the extent to which "I am my body" does or does not boil down to a banal statement of the identity of something with itself; of "x is x". "I am my body" does not reduce to:

"RT *is* RT's body"
"RT's body is RT's body"
"This body is this body".

One way of capturing the divergence between "am" and "is" would be to remind ourselves that our biography is not the summed material or biological history of our flesh. Richard Jefferies' beautiful autobiography *The Story of My Heart* was not, for example, a long ECG trace or a succession of coronary angiograms. Indeed, my body, unlike my life, has no intrinsic narrative. Of course, I can tease out threads of a story – successive images of my face, a timeline of my serum potassium, or a cardiac tracing. But these banal sequences are not self-teasing or self-telling and are intrinsically meaningless. And this is just as true of the story of my brain – a physical object subject to the laws of nature – with its showers and waves of spikes in different parts of the neural stuff. *I* have a C(urriculum) V(itae), while my body's V is without C: the organism is a multitude of unfolding sequences of coordinated events rather than a life that is led. That is why we cannot conclude from the fact that I do not know much about how my body "works" that I am (entirely) my body's puppet. To return to Philip Larkin, "Our flesh surrounds us with its own decisions", for sure; but we are distanced from those (quasi-)decisions – hence "*our* flesh" and "*surrounds*" us.

In sum, I and my body develop over time in ways that are inseparable and yet divergent. When I travel to London, my body of course transits to London but I, not it, am the traveller. I travel, while it moves or is moved.

Being my body: the body schema

We shall shortly unpack some of the ways in which we are distanced from our bodies but before I do so, I want to look at the fringes of the "am" relationship, the penumbra of strict "is", strict A = A, identity. It is what we might call the carnal assumption that "this" – my body – is "me". It constitutes the epicentre of my feeling that "I am here" and "I am doing this".

There are various ways in which we could capture this sense of identification with my body: my body as platform; as the nearest part of the world; as the origin or source of what I do; as a point of initial departure; as something that is prior to any discovery about myself or the world. More broadly we can think of it as the material guarantor and the most intimate – even beyond "intimate" – content of what we take for granted when, as we overwhelmingly do, we take ourselves for granted. The most obvious and continuous aspect of this is the merging between bodily sensations and the moments of my life. A headache is a pain in my head, yes; but also a pain in my present moment; indeed, it is I, not my head, that is in pain. I have compulsory ownership of the headache and am forced to live it out.

The philosophical and biological literature has recently dwelt on another aspect of my being my body, generating a fascinating set of reminders of our moment to moment existence. It is captured in the notion of the "body schema".[8] Narrowly construed, a body schema is "a preconscious standard against which ... motor changes are measured".[9] More broadly and fundamentally, it is "a practical intuitive diagram of my relationships with the world, a 'register' where all of my attitudes and actions are 'noted', and which therefore provides the reference norm in contrast to which I perceive something as specifically spatially and temporally related to my body".[10] The body schema is "a point from which there is something to do in the world".[11] It lies at the root of the distinction between "here" and "there" or "in here" and "over there", "inside and outside", and marks in a broad brush fashion the border of "I" and "it". There is nothing merely schematic or diagrammatic about it, however: it is infused with the blush of livingness. The body schema is the first storey of the ascent from sentient organism to a person, a divided being aware of the contrast between the "am" of me and the "it" of the body.

The body schema, then, is a carnal presupposition in which much is taken for granted. It may become explicit in action, as when the presupposed unity of my body is enacted as an explicit unity of its engagement in action. Consider my sense of the "where" of my head. It is located in a sensory field woven out of what it sees, hears, and touches. But my head is also experienced as part of my body. As such, it is elevated some 60 centimetres above my buttocks. The intervening fleshly structures that make this sensed state of elevation possible, however, are not directly vouched for. There isn't a spatially and temporally continuous shirt of sensation, even less a solid mass of awareness, broadcasting my torso and its contents, as it were "colouring in" the gap between my head that is currently looking at this sentence and my buttocks reporting the hardness of the item of the chair I am sitting on. Nevertheless, patchy, intermittent reports are sufficient to validate the assumption, based on a kind of material logic, that there must be a continuity of fleshly support between my pelvic girdle and my neck. The body schema is a presupposition filling in the gaps between those parts that are actually being experienced. If I use my head in order to head a ball, as I jump up to ensure that the trajectory of my head intersects with that of the ball, the unity of my feet, my legs, my pelvis, my trunk, my neck, and my head, are made explicit. My body schema is thus the link between the fact that I experience my body patchily and the equally solid fact that I live it as a whole.

It is evident that my carnal being is experienced both as unitary and as multiple, with different parts being mobilized, attended to and cared for at any given time. The form of the emergence of "a whole" is quite different from that which we see when, say, molecules of H_2O add up to a shiny drop or a face emerges from printed dots. While my experience of my body is always of a subset of parts of or locations in my body, there is still the permanent possibility of sensation inherent in all of my body. At any moment, for example, my arm can be the subject of pleasure or of pain, even though at present the focus is on, and the experience is in, other parts of my body. In this sense, the schema is an envelope of exposure or susceptibility as well as the unfolding platform of my agency. And the very idea of a schema is only the surface of the presuppositions upon which my moment-to-moment coherent bodily existence is supported. This awareness, often at a subconscious level, of the position and disposition and ongoing movement of the body, independent of vision, is necessary for the most basic of actions – such as reaching for something, looking around, or even sitting still – upon which more complex actions are built. The body schema, as the ground floor of our relationship to our body, where "it" becomes "I" and "I" become "it", curates our double nature as object and subject.[12] It marks how we are located in space because we locate ourselves in, inhabit, space through the assumption – in both senses of "taking up" and "presupposing" – of our body.

Given that the body is a point of reference, of *initiation*, of origin – the place at which the power to act on things and the vulnerability to be changed by things intersect, we might reasonably assume that the body schema is present in some form in other species. How otherwise could they get about, and do all that has to be done when leaping from branch to branch or stalking a prey? That is of course true. What is less well-developed in non-human animals, however, is the intuition of the/my body-as-object, an object whose existence transcends our experience of it. The "objectification" of the embodied subject is a key step in developing the pre-scientific, even pre-reflective, "folk" ontology that characterizes the human world of material objects.

We shall return to this issue presently when we have examined other relationships we have to our bodies that widen, or mark the widening of, the interval between "I" and "it" and have prepared the way for the full-blown sense of "it" which enhances "I" by contrast.

Owning my body

"Every man has a property in his own person".   John Locke[13]

One marker of the gap between the "it" of my body and the "I" that is me is the possessive pronoun in the phrase *"my* body". There is a complex relationship of ownership between me and it. My body as my most intimate and enduring "property" has endless personal, sexual, social, political, and cultural ramifications. When we are dead, ownership belongs to the state – to no-one in particular, to an institution. Prior to that, we are (to steal and misuse Shakespeare's phrase) to some extent "the Lords and owners of our faces"[14] – and of our arms and legs and the rest.

Ownership is expressed in many ways; for example, the right not to be touched without consent and the criminal law on assault and battery. As its owner, I can donate parts of my body to others – my blood to a blood bank, my organs for transplantation. I can envisage my future (dead) body as a donor kebab – a potential smorgasbord of benefactions. Ownership can be compromised by the violations of others in the misuse of power, most intimately in sexual enslavement, most commonly in working as a wage slave whose every hour is appropriated by another. The control of the body exemplified in regulating the posture of a soldier standing to attention is an outward manifestation of control of the person.

Ownership can be asserted from within, as when I measure, and then seek to adjust, the properties of my body. Think of the common preoccupation with "my weight" or my complexion and other parameters that concern me. Or in my concern with "my well-being"; or (to phrase this in the argot of current obsessions) "my wellness" as if one could own the token of an abstract state instantiated in my flesh.

Of course, my "possession" of my body is fundamentally different from that of other objects. My flesh is not something I acquire during my life or could dispose of at will (not at least so long as I am alive). It is a necessarily pre-natal possession – just as my nakedness is "my birthday suit" – and is the necessary precondition of all other ownership as well as that which necessitates my having possessions. And there is something not quite legitimate about extrapolating ownership from "my arm" or "my leg" or "my eyes" or even "my weight" or "my appearance" to "my body" – that is to say, my body as a whole. I cannot, after all, *discover* that my body is mine. We do not bump into our bodies, even less bump into them and wonder whose they are. I do not encounter my body from without, from some place that transcends both the corporeal and extra-corporeal realms of material objects. And it would be very odd to think of experiences of our bodies from within (that I will discuss presently) as that in virtue of which I am apprised that my body is mine.

Ownership can, importantly, slip into objectification, where my body or more often part of it is experienced as an object – in my own gaze, in the gaze of others, or in my own gaze tinted by the imagined gaze of others. In pathological states, the body-as-object may lose its subjective dimension: a patient may fail to recognize parts of her body as her own, and even hate it as in the condition of misoplegia which sometimes occurs in patients with hemiplegic stroke. I had one such patient who sometimes tried to throw one of her limbs out of bed. She christened it "Thatcher" to express her loathing of it. In the so-called "alien hand syndrome", the subject may fail to feel a sense of ownership of her actions: the hand may seem to reach for objects and manipulate them without the owner wanting this to happen. Indeed, she may use the unaffected hand to restrain its delinquent partner. Such an attitude cannot be extended to one's body as a whole: my body could not cast itself aside, not the least because it is the precondition of any action.

The sense of the body as visible object underwrites that strangest of all (quasi-) possessions which I call "my appearance" – something that is susceptible to being judged as beautiful, ugly, slim, fat, old, young, or more elusively as impressive or unimpressive, reassuring or unnerving. We have entered the zone where the body-as-object melts into the person-as-subject or and thence as objectified subject. My physical appearance becomes the figure one cuts, and the beginning of a narrative as to how I appear in the eyes of others. There is a complex relationship between my sense of myself on the one hand and, on the other, my awareness of my material presence and what is visible to my own and others' senses. Being aware, for example, of the stupid grin on my face incorporates both subjectivity and objectivity. The example illustrates how I may emphatically reject something that is mine precisely *because* I am inseparable from it.

Cosmetics, tribal markings, tattoos, hairstyles, jewellery, costumes, uniforms – these are some of the ways we may appropriate our own appearance to make it work for, rather than against, us and express an acceptable part of ourselves. As such, if it is to be intelligible, our "look" must be at least in part a product of the collective, the "them", signifying an allegiance, status, a role or office, a provenance, in the endeavour to attract, dominate, or simply rise above, the helplessness of visibility. This is doomed, if only because we cannot know (even less *be*) what we look like: there are too many eyes attached to too many conjectured – but in fact unknowable – judgements. Cultivating a particular type of "look" – which may depend on observing, research-ing, or buying the wherewithal for, a particular kind of appearance – is an extraordinarily complex way of encountering one's self through the eyes of the Other.

My ownership of my body is rooted in a, sometimes helpless, awareness of others' awareness of me. The internalized public gaze we train on our own body, even if transformed into something as intimate as embarrassment, is another driver to the sense of our bodies as objects belonging to a common world. An involuntary blush may transform my body from something like a carnal presupposition to the source of an explicit sense of being carnally nailed to a particular object. Ownership under such circumstances – among many others – has to be protected, affirmed, and not infrequently rescued. This marks a widening distance from the "am-is" penumbra around the body schema.

My body as agent

Getting our appearance to work for us is an intimate manifestation of another way in which our relationship to, and hence distance from, our body is elab-orated: our making it the primary agent of our agency.[15] Our bodies – most prodigiously our grasping, grubbing, groping, cupping, catching, pulling, pushing, squeezing, fingering, dabbing, caressing, scratching, waving, thread-ing, twisting hands – are the most versatile and ubiquitous of our immediate agents.

In many, perhaps most, of our actions, of course, there is no explicit dis-tance between our doing and the flesh with which we do it: we simply stand up or walk, say, rather than "do standing up" or "walk with our legs". Even so, a gap can appear, especially when my body fails. A paralysed arm can become a dead weight which I lift with my other arm. Walking with stiff or wobbly legs can become "doing walking". Even breathing can become an action for a person with respiratory problems: fighting for one's breath may take up a large proportion of one's agency. And any action performed with difficulty, even something as simple as threading a needle, may seem like a battle with something reluctantly obeying our command, like a truculent, idle child.

I can, when appropriate, take control of those things that usually occur spontaneously, elevating bodily happenings into my doings. Breathing continues for the most part without my doing it, notably when I am asleep, but I may still "do breathing" as when I "take a deep breath" for a variety of reasons – such as prior to singing a song, diving into water, or as an effort to control my temper. There is an interesting modulation of the gap between the "I" and the "it" when I "take the weight off my legs" by sitting down, or force my finger into a glove, or my body into a wetsuit. Over a long term, I may exercise my body in a gymnasium to transform it. Supplementing my daily work (which, being largely sedentary, is insufficiently physically challenging) with a "work-out", I employ my embodied agency to reduce my or its weight, increase my or its fitness, or hone a skill. Thus, the embodied agent acts on itself to enhance its agency, something we shall revisit in Chapter 6.

Agency often involves making a portion of my body a thing on a level of, interacting with, other things. In such instances, our bodies or parts of them are explicit tools: the user and the used are distinct. I may, for example, employ my fist as a crude hammer or use my body to pull off a gymnastic trick, such as doing a handstand. The calculated use of gestures is an obvious instance of this – and we shall return presently, to one such gesture, pointing. More crudely, we may directly exploit the physical properties of our bodies, such as their opacity – as when I stand up deliberately to block your view – or deploy my weight to squash the contents of an over-filled suitcase I am trying to close. Such carnal tools may operate on the body, as when I put my fingers in my ears to block out sound or use my hand to shade my eyes. That is why we need to be cautious when we refer to the body as agent: we may mean part of the body rather than the body as a whole. At any rate, we can see that, notwithstanding the body schema discussed earlier, it is not utilized as a whole.

The central (and perhaps too obvious) point is that the body is the primary agent of my agency, being the first and last link in the behavioural chain. Additionally, while I may aim at my goals through a large number of intermediate causes, often delegating agency to others or to machinery, direct fleshly agency is the first intuition of causation. Grasping, tearing, banging, throwing material objects give us primordial demonstrations of the causal connectedness of that which is outside of us. Beyond this, I may employ a variety of artefacts, tools, devices, and commodities, in fulfilling my intentions and meeting my needs, desires, and responsibilities, but the body is the final common pathway. A plane may take me to my destination but I have to board it. A book may inform or entertain me but I have to get hold of it and read it, using my hands and eyes respectively.

Even in actions where the body is a minor presence, such as acquiring the information from a book, it is still present at many stages: as when I see the book advertised, in obtaining it (by something as grossly physical as going to a shop or more refined as pressing a keyboard to order it online), in picking it up, moving to a lighted place, holding it, and turning over the pages. The reader-as-bodily-agent operates at many levels – from the macroscopic action of walking to the bookshop, to smaller-scale actions such as turning down pages. There are over-arching and subordinate elements in the action illustrated by fetching the book from the adjacent room to using a pen to underline a passage. The hierarchy of actions is something else we shall return to in Chapter 6.

The interaction between my use of my body as the ubiquitous primary agent of my agency reaches extraordinary levels of complexity when I exploit my visibility in order to communicate. Even in the case of the most primitive gestures, such as pointing or waving, I transform what is visible to others of my body into a source of meant meaning. Transmitting such meanings depends, of course, on my sense of your appreciation of what I am trying to convey through my movements. Gesticulation has been described as the product of the integration of body and mind, particularly in the case of the use of bodily postures, such as nodding in agreement.[16] My awareness of how I appear in others' eyes may energize other aspects of my agency. We experience social causation through our desire to please or vex others: we are equally agents in obedience and disobedience; and even more so when we manipulate others to get them to act on our behalf.

We are now on the threshold of a topic of oceanic breadth and depth: emitting sounds to convey meant meanings. I am of course referring to speech. It is wise to withdraw at this point to avoid drowning.

There is another kind of use of the appearance of one's body: as a primitive measuring device. This is signified in the names we give to primordial units of measurement: such as "feet" (and their twelve parts – *uncia* or inches), hands (measuring the height of horses), and "cubits" (forearm length). To see parts of one's own body as an instance of, say, length involves objectification and a double abstraction as the part in question is reduced to a quantitative parameter applied to an external object also reduced to a quantitative parameter. It is an extraordinary thing to do with one's own body and an egregious example of the joining of intentionality with others: relating one's body as an object in public space to other objects in public space. This distancing from one's body lies at the root of science that liberates our perspectives from the constraints of experience; it is an essential step towards a world picture in which the world is presented as a system of magnitudes.

My body as object of (factual) knowledge

We have highlighted a gap between on the one hand *being* (or more accurately "amming") our body and on the other *encountering it* as something other than ourselves. While our body is not primarily a thing among things we can encounter it as such and indeed can distance ourselves further from our bodies. This is most pronounced when our bodies are objects of factual knowledge – the most striking expression of our capacity to see them, or parts of them, as objects, or (even more striking) as instances of a certain type of object. There are many things *I* – and indeed others – know about *it*, my body.

Before we reach this stage, much has to happen. The most interesting and significant event in creating the wide gap between "amming" and "knowing" is the "discovery" that my body – in particular its visible outlying parts such as my feet, and more importantly my hands – is indeed mine or me. When babies see their hands, they do not at first know that they belong to them. They will play with one hand exploring the other, as if it was an external object, prior to using them to pull at blankets and clothes. This is beautifully and wittily captured by the novelist Anthony Burgess. The speaker in the passage has a baby on his knee: "He told off point after point on the child's downy head, ear to ear, occiput to brow, while the child gazed like a drunk at the wonder of its own fingers".[17]

The existential contradiction between my being my body and experiencing it as an object of knowledge, is explored in a famous passage in Sartre's *Nausea*. The novel's anti-hero Antoine Roquentin catches sight of his own hand:

> I see my hand spread out on the table. It is alive – it is me. It is lying on its back. It shows me its fat underbelly. It looks like an animal upside down. The fingers are the paws. I amuse myself by making them move about very quickly, like the claws of a crab that has fallen upside down … I feel my hand. It is me, these two animals moving about at the end of my arms …[18]

The knowledge relation to the body – that goes beyond ownership – first becomes fully evident when experience of it is mediated. Archetypically this occurs when I catch sight of myself in a mirror – such that I might, for example, see that I have a spot on my forehead that had not otherwise declared itself to me or that I am tanned or looking smart or shabby or have a silly grin. I have a sense of my body as being an involuntary spectacle; as an object of knowledge for (and judgement by) others. This mode of bodily-being-for-others is important and can become extraordinarily entangled but I want to focus on the sense in which I am for myself and am not my body. The distance from our bodies opened up by the mirror image – in virtue of which our "heremost" here is over there – may sometimes be alienating in a way that is more ordinary but no less startling than that reported by Sartre's hero. The other day I saw an elderly man walking towards me. It turned out to be a reflection in a plate glass window: my own. I wonder, sometimes, given the gradual divergence between my idea of my appearance and its reality, whether I would be able to pick myself out of an identity parade. The point is that there is a level of knowledge at which I can be unsure which body is mine – something that is not possible at the level of experience.

The displacement from my body that begins with my own gaze at my body, a gaze coloured by the real or imagined judgement of particular others or a general normative Other, ends with the virtual encounters with the rumour of our body in the form of general facts about them. As humanity advances cognitively, we individually share in that advance. The increasing body of knowledge about the stuff of the human organism opens up ever greater distances between me and the flesh in which I am embodied. Knowledge is intrinsically public. Indeed, some information may belong to others while I am denied it. The public/private divide does not map on to that between exterior and interior of the body: a surgeon may know the look and disposition of my abdominal contents better than I do. Indeed, my spleen is more "outside of me" than my skin or even another's familiar face. As knowledge of the basic anatomy of the body – that there is an item such as a bladder next to the rectum or even an exotic organ such as the spleen – becomes more widely disseminated, I may know less about my body than many others do. Factual knowledge is not accessible to direct experience. This applies even to basic parameters – such as my height in feet and inches, or weight in pounds and ounces. I cannot arrive at my weight in kilograms by introspection, although I may episodically experience my heaviness.

Facts about my body, like all facts, while ultimately checkable against experience, lie beyond experience, being tethered to no particular sense. *Facts* neither glow, hum, nor smell: they are as scentless as a metal rose. Robert Graves' "cool web of language" points to the inaudible and invisible realm of objective knowledge which ultimately leads to the view from nowhere, or at least no-one. That is why we cannot experience the experiences of others – know what it is like for them to have an experience – through the facts of their body, even facts about their sense organs. Knowledge does not taste of experience. After all, knowing that one is eating a pineapple does not oblige a pineapple to deliver its taste if one lacks the taste buds. Nor, conversely, does tasting a pineapple carry within it the knowledge that it is a pineapple one is tasting.

Experiences will never be fact-shaped, even less equation-shaped. When I take my temperature, the resulting figure does not accommodate what it is like to be feverish; and the thermodynamic realities behind raised temperature – increased average molecular velocity, etc. – are not experienced by me. As many philosophers have pointed out, we could have complete knowledge (whatever that is!) of the science of colour vision and still not know what it is like to see the colour red. We are particularly aware that "our flesh surrounds us with its own decisions" when we are apprised of the result of a medical test, which may translate ultimately into a unique experience, but which is not the slightest bit personal. Biomedical knowledge of our body is a post-personal or supra-personal awareness of the pre-personal or sub-personal organism that makes our personal existence possible.

Knowledge, being generated collaboratively and communicated within and between epistemic communities, enables us to take a less egocentric, indeed less anthropocentric, cognitive stance to our flesh. We see our body as a site of biological, chemical, physical processes that are shared with other humans, many other species, and even with other material objects, as in the case of the tensile strength of my tendons or the viscosity of my blood. The impersonal, general nature of knowledge applies as much to what is going on in my brain as to what is happening in my kidneys.

We sometimes see those biological processes at work but are generally unaware of them. Even in the case of those that are visible – as when we extrude pus, or form scars – much of what is happening is largely hidden from us. The gathering of fibroblasts that lies at the heart of wound healing is a secret process. There is no imaginable experience corresponding to much that is known about our bodies. The Krebs cycle that lies at the heart of the energetic transactions in the cells is not something that can be experienced. This is true of the thousands of other metabolic pathways and processes that bioscience has revealed to be essential for my continuing existence. What is more, most of what happens in my body as picked out by the biological sciences occurs at a scale below that to which we are attuned. Besides, biomedical science operates at different scales of observation competing for our potential attention. Unmediated bodily awareness could not simultaneously be aware of events at bodily, organ, cellular, and molecular level.

Being my body, therefore, does not consist of tracking or experiencing its objective properties. Facts are not merely impersonal: they are apersonal. That is why I cannot experience the truths that I spent five years as a student acquiring at medical school. And the more we learn about flesh in general, and are conscious that our own flesh is a particular helping of the stuff, the more we are aware of how little we know of the particularities of our own flesh. I know that I must have a spleen of a certain size, a blood pressure, a serum potassium, and a certain number of lymphocytes but I cannot access the numerical values of these parameters by attending to my bodily sensations. More seriously, introspection tells me nothing about the cancer that may or may not be growing in the depths.

Biological knowledge concerns my flesh as *anyone's* flesh. Our body as a body of knowledge is effectively ownerless, a site of processes that get on with themselves as unshaped by me as the events happening in trees or in the moon. Our cells are little zombies, our bodies largely mindless and beneath the radar of consciousness. Incorporated in the seemingly simple thought that "My blood pressure is too high" is a huge slice of our shared body of knowledge that draws on intelligence – about how the body "works"; about certain measurements that can be extracted from its ongoing business; about the significance of abnormal values; and about the steps to be taken to pre-empt any adverse consequences of abnormality – interposed between me and the flesh that folds up when I sit down.

Through knowledge, therefore, we come upon our bodies from far off, from random places in the nexus of facts curated by the community of minds. The gap between our flesh and the body of knowledge we may have about it and may deploy in our care for it – as when we go to the chemist to cash a prescription that is the product of a huge enterprise of inquiry into the chemistry, biochemistry, physiology, pharmacodynamics, etc., of the human organism – is an everyday, and yet startling, example of the distances that are opened up in our lives by the seed that is full-blown intentionality flowering into the objective knowledge made possible through the secondary intentionality of factual propositions. We shall revisit facts in the next chapter – and discover that there is nothing matter of fact about them.

Other modes of being related to our bodies

Reference to medical knowledge brings us naturally to another dimension of the distance opened between us and our bodies; namely, our caring for them – feeding, warming, laundering, and generally looking after them.

Of course, animals care for their bodies. Indeed, the greater part of their lives may be described as body-care; but in humans that care is utterly transformed, as we noted in the previous chapter when we examined the humble activity of brushing one's teeth. There are less direct ways than feeding, watering, grooming, etc., of caring for ourselves. Taking tablets that dissolve into the darkness of the body to lower one's blood pressure to prevent strokes and heart attacks is one of many ways in which the embodied subject cares for his/her body, and the person looks after the organism that is his/her body – under the cognitive direction of the collective wisdom.

Exercising one's body with the aim of postponing its decline may seem less exotic than popping pills but it involves no less complex a relationship to one's flesh, including envisaging in very general terms its possible condition at an unspecified future date. This caring is mediated by knowledge – for example regarding an appropriate regime – and by complex observations on one's body that may also be guided by know-how and know-that as how to make the observations and how to interpret them. The use of one's hand, applied to one's own wrist to take one's pulse may seem simple but it is a highly esoteric mode of bodily self-encounter, in which the one part of the body, the fingers, recruits a watch to obtain information about another part – the heart. Knowledge transforms our mode of ownership of our bodies, our agency, and our self-care.

There are many other ways of being related to our bodies, most notably suffering or enjoying them or, more precisely, parts of them. The experience of pain or disability, or fatigue, lassitude, nausea, the joy of sunbathing, stretching cramped limbs, giving way to tiredness, or experiencing sexual pleasure, are a few. They do not fit comfortably into the categories of ownership or knowledge. The non-elective nature of many experiences arising from our bodies – for example pains and itches that have imperative content – makes them alien. When I am tired, or sinking into a delicious sleep, or struggling with the effort of walking uphill, or feeling nauseated or bloated after over-eating, or relishing the pleasure of a hot bath, bodily experience comes closer to defining what I am at that time. Indeed, there seems to be a greater equality between the "am" and the "it". "My" tiredness at least as much possesses me as I possess it and, in the case of a drowsiness that may be heading towards a deep coma, "I" is progressively engulfed in "it". But "getting closer", short of unconsciousness, is not merging. On that final struggle up the slope to the top of the mountain, we still have space to talk to our companions, even to get annoyed with them for setting too fast or slow a pace, or for requiring us to talk and walk at the same time.

Even so, there are relations that are sometimes so intimate or engulfing as temporally to narrow the distance between the *relata* – between the "I" and the "it" – and to suggest another way of thinking about our condition of being embodied subjects. It is the "What it is like to be" dimension of our being our body, such that the matter of our flesh is that in virtue of which matter, or a portion of it, matters.

EMBODIMENT AND WHAT IT IS LIKE TO BE SOMEONE

Is there something it is like to be a body?

Non-philosophers will be astonished by the extent to which the notion of "What it is like to be" has dominated the philosophy of mind since it was first introduced into the conversation in the 1970s by Timothy Sprigge and subsequently popularized by Thomas Nagel in his famous paper "What it is like to be a bat?": "[No] matter how the form [of phenomenal consciousness] may vary, the fact that an organism has conscious experience *at all* means, basically, that there is something that it is like to *be* that organism".[19] There is something like it is to be a conscious being, whereas there isn't something like it is to be a material object such as a pebble. Pebbles do not experience their states. Even less do they register what or that they are over time. They do not enjoy the partial self-transparency, the privileged awareness, of the embodied subject, whose limits we have just highlighted. They are selfless and worldless.

Philosophers have used this rather obvious fact to challenge the claim that consciousness can be reduced to functional connections between inputs of experience and outputs of behaviour. Functionalism overlooks the something "in the middle", which cannot be captured by objective observations of what organisms get up to, how they react (outputs) in response to stimuli (inputs). The missing element is the "what it is like to be" that organism: behaviour or dispositions to behave are not constitutive of mental states.

The appeal to "what it is like" has been criticized by some philosophers, for example P. M. S. Hacker.[20] Hacker distinguishes between intransitive consciousness "which is a matter of being awake rather than asleep or otherwise unconscious" and transitive consciousness "which is a matter of being conscious *of* something or other".[21] These quite different modes of consciousness – and intermediate ones, like being tired – tend, he argues, to be conflated in "what it is like to be"-talk. Hacker rejects the claim "that for every differentiable experience, there is a specific way it feels to have it"; "The notion of a quale – the singular of qualia – equivocates between signifying whatever it is like for a person to have experience E and experience E itself".[22]

While this is importantly true, it may miss the point of "what it is like to be"-talk: that there is something that it is like to be RT while there is not anything like it is to be a pebble, a storm, or a tree. A pebble may be heavy, opaque, or hard, but it is none of these things for itself; it doesn't feel itself being hard or heavy. That is why objective observations of a pebble may get us ever closer to what a pebble is but not to what it is like to be RT. "What it is like"-talk is a salutary reminder, to those who subscribe to the idea that neuroscience will eventually reveal the true nature of consciousness, of something that should have been pretty obvious: that if you are going to understand consciousness, you have to take into account the fact that conscious beings cannot be defined by, captured by, objective facts about them, not even when these include objective facts about their bodies and brains.

I could have complete information about (for example) what happens in a brain when an individual sees the colour green and still (if I am colour blind) not know what it is like to experience that colour. The gap between (objectively) observable neural activity and unobservable experience could not be closed by ever more careful observation of neural activity. A full transcript of the neural discharges associated with looking at grass, leaves, and a patch of green paint, would not bring a colour blind individual closer to knowing what it is like to see green. To say this is only to argue that you cannot get back to immediate experience from objective knowledge by acquiring ever more sophisticated and complete knowledge. The reason for this is important: knowledge is reached at the end of a journey that begins with moving beyond sense experience by means of impersonal means of investigation. The accumulation of objective knowledge cannot bring us closer to experience; indeed, it only takes us further away from experience. Tastes or smells or colour experiences cannot be unpacked as facts because, as we noted earlier, facts have no taste or smell or colour. Scentless, colourless everyday facts – such as "That the cat is in the garden" – mark a half-way point in the journey from an experienced world of experienced qualities to the scientific realm of primary qualities and pure quantities. (We will have more about the nature of facts in the next chapter.)

The appreciation that conscious, but more importantly self-conscious, organisms, such as you and me experience ourselves in a way that is unobservable from without, or inferable from behavioural, functional, or causal connections, has been rated as a *discovery* – or rediscovery among philosophers. What has been discovered is the so-called "hard problem of consciousness" (as if there were any other).[23] Fortunately, this somewhat depressing tale of an excessively long journey to the recovery of the blindingly obvious is not our concern. However, the phrase "what it is like to be" helps to give another hand-hold on the mystery of embodied subjectivity – the mystery of the person who, courtesy of his body, and in his body, suffers and enjoys experiences, knows a world, and lives a life unfolding in a multiplicity of biographical stories. "What it's like to be"-talk can usefully highlight the not-at-all-straightforward nature of our relationship to our body.

We already noted that the story of the body – cyclical recurrent events (circulation of the blood, beating of the heart, etc.) on a background of initial growth development and ultimate deterioration – is not the story of a human life. What it is like to be RT (or indeed what RT is like for others) is not the same as what a certain body gets up to: being RT is not the (continuous, total) self-intimation of RT's body. Indeed, there cannot be a "what it is like to be a *thing*", even where the thing in question is a living organism. "What it is like to be RT" is not a stable, distinctive state, even less that of a thing. Even for an embodied subject such as RT, there are great tracts within his body *qua* organism that are simply unknown to him. The greater part of RT's carnal being is silent for most of the time and some for all the time: the blush of awareness is patchy and intermittently distributed. There is a limit to the epistemically privileged introspective access to my body: my body is not transparent to the "I".

We shouldn't complain about this. If my body were *not* largely experientially silent, then its global, continuous, self-broadcasting would get in the way of the extra-corporeal awareness necessary for my perceiving, making sense of, engaging with, and navigating through the world. If I am to be open to the world, then my body has largely to get itself out of the way, to be transparent.[24] "That this is going on in my body" does not automatically translate into "that this is going on in me". In fact, it does so only rarely. The Krebs cycle generating energy necessary for cellular life is also necessary for the continuation of the conscious subject but could not, as we noted just now, itself be experienced.

We could press this conclusion further by asking further questions. What would it be like being even a part of my body? What experience would be faithful to it? I may feel a pain in my otherwise silent kidney when I have a renal stone but this is not the organ in question disclosing itself. It is I who feel the pain, not the kidney: the pain that I feel in my kidney is not a pain the kidney feels in itself. More to the point, there is no sensation corresponding to a normally functioning kidney and any sensation would anyway not be "what it is like" for that kidney to be itself. And to develop an earlier point, concerning the issue of the *scale* at which we seek what it is like to be: there are no intrinsic scales – they are applied from without. So, any "what it is like to be" could be sought with equal justification (or lack of it) at the level of single cells as at that of whole organs. This absurd conclusion applies equally to those parts of the body that are typically not silent in our lives – for example, our rib cage moving up and down as we breathe, our heart beating, our guts speaking fluent borborygmi as they go about their serious business of ushering excrement towards the body's south-facing plughole.

What is more, it is difficult to know what sense we would make of constant self-broadcasting. Wittgenstein's famous observation that "if a lion could speak, we could not understand him"[25] must be even more applicable to the body: "if my body could speak, I could not understand it". It would not speak English, or even a biological Esperanto such as Humanish, that is for sure.

It is clear, then, that being RT is not to be conflated with "what it is like to be RT's body" because there is no such thing. This gives an opportunity to take another dig at neuromania and the fantasy that to understand the "it" of brain activity is to understand the "I" of the person.

Is there something it is like to be a brain?

For the prophets of neuromania whom we discussed in the last chapter, persons *are* their brains: I am the neural material, or the activity of the neural material, inside my skull or some of it at least. Consequently, what it is like to be RT becomes what it is like to be a certain brain or the electrochemical activity within that brain. Several questions immediately arise.

First, even neuromaniacs would agree that not *all* neural activity contributes to, or is, the "what it is like" to be the brain that hosts it. For example, the so-called neural correlates of consciousness – defined as "the minimal neural mechanisms that are jointly sufficient for any one specific conscious percept" – are confined to activity in a very small proportion of cerebral tissue, mainly according to one view in the so-called "hot zone" of the posterior cerebral cortex.[26] Many areas, with large numbers of neurones, and rich inputs and outputs, do not contribute directly to the content of experience. Individuals who lack a cerebellum, which has four times as many neurones as the cerebral cortex and is densely connected with the rest of the brain, appear to have no impairment of consciousness. What is more, nerve impulses are connected with each other and travel from place to place. It seems improbable that waves of neural activity acquires their status of being conscious or associated with consciousness by travelling from one part of the brain to another. Metaphysical promotion is (surely) not so easily earned. Travel broadens the mind; but hardly permits something essentially mindless to broaden into a mind; or allows "it" to be transformed into "am".

If activity in that small part of the brain which is implicated in consciousness amounted to a "what it is like", it would be unclear what it is that is experiencing what is it like to be itself. The "hot zone"? The hot zone plus critical pathways that feed into the hot zone from midline structures? Or something more widely spread? Such islands of activity, even if *per impossibile* they were granted – as an intrinsic property – a level of pooled being that permits the activity in individual neurones to add up to a unity, would hardly be the entire organ disclosing itself to itself. Nor would it, however, amount even to the self-disclosure of the subset of neurones whose activity is implicated in consciousness.

One conclusion, therefore, at least seems justified: conscious experiences are *not* the self-disclosure of the intrinsic properties of neurones. Indeed, to subscribe to the notion that there is a "what it is like" at the level of neuro-chemical discharges would be to move in the direction of a panpsychism that neurophilosophers would reject straight off. And even panpsychism would run into great difficulty, not the least in explaining what is distinctive about a nervous system that would enable it to gather up the mentality scattered through the material world into a conscious person with a macroscopic, coherent, sustained viewpoint on a world. Besides, "what it is like to be RT" is to be someone aware of a world, living in a world, engaging with that world, being judged by and being aware of being judged by, of being threatened and promised, obstructed and permitted, by that world and its population of con-scious subjects. As for that world, it includes RT's own body both as an item within it and as the foundation of the many different relationships RT has to it. In short, the "it" in "what it is like" is not the brain or my brain as a whole but to be in a world out there, which includes being a body in that world, being itself in part experienced. As I mentioned earlier with reference to my body as a whole, my brain would deliver on its supposed job description only by *getting itself out of the way* – by being transitively "about" something other than itself. More generally, the brain, or the body's self-intimation (if that were conceivable) would not amount to intimation of a world.

To pick up on Peter Hacker's point, the focus on "what-it-is-like" conflates experience with what it is experience *of*, the phenomenal character of expe-rience with the character of what is experienced. In the case of an itch, that may be acceptable: an itch if it is about itself is about an instance of itching (although in fact most itches are about more than themselves). But this is not applicable in the case of vision. When it comes to describing what it is like to see a scene, the description will largely be taken up with the contents of the scene. Indeed, if one is truly seeing a scene, the fact, act, or process of seeing it is not visible or not obtrusively so.[27] And this character of transitivity applies with greater force to propositional attitudes such as expectation, hope, and fear. If, say, my fears were connected with bodily states such as a rapid heart rate, those states would have to get themselves out of the way to deliver the relevant intentional content. My worry about your health may be signalled by bodily events, such as a fast heart rate, but that is not what my worry *is*. An ECG – or even an EEG recording of my brain waves – would not reveal anything about the object of my concern.

The gap between neural activity and conscious experience – underlined by the contrast between our mediated knowledge of what the neurones are up to and our immediate awareness of our (own) experiences – cannot be eliminated. Consider the well-known thought experiment in which I look at the activity of my own brain using an "autocerebroscope". What I see on the screen of the cerebroscope – trains of neural activity, or markers thereof – is something quite other than my experience of *seeing* the trains of neural activity associated with my seeing. The neural activity is apparently mindless but visible; by contrast, seeing is clearly mindful but necessarily invisible – I see sights not my sight. I may of course infer indirectly *that* I am seeing the neural activity through the same means that I may infer that you are seeing something – by looking at the position of your eyes and the direction of your gaze – but that is not the same as seeing your sight, seeing your seeing as opposed to seeing (or making an accurate guess about) what you are seeing.[28]

The cerebral cortex examined objectively looks as innocent of awareness as does the cerebellum; and the latter, not being engaged in consciousness, is as innocent as the kidney. My brain is as ignorant of the fact that it is inside my skull as my left kidney is of its status as being one of a pair. And the claim that "I am my brain" raises the question of the origin of the "who" whose brain it is. And where did that possessive creep in? How did my brain come to be owned? My brain, looked at through the authoritative gaze of neuroscience, is I-less.

For these reasons, the "What it is like to be" argument still delivers a key insight: that, for a conscious being, there is something that it is like to be it and this is not true of any imaginable material objects, which do not seem to have the wherewithal to register what it is like to be themselves or states of themselves.

To pick up on an earlier point: inside my skin it is *terra* largely *incognita*.[29] Subcutaneous, and for most of the time cutaneous, realities, come to my attention usually when they are under stress, malfunctioning or diseased. My appendix, for example, will speak to me only when it is inflamed and it would hardly be speaking in its own language. (So far, so good: not a peep in 70 years; and long may things remain thus!) A muscle will precipitate out of the implicit schema of my body when it is pulled. Of course, as my health worsens, so more of my body will obtrude into my daily life: "it is" will encroach on "I am". Illness reveals the foreignness of the body from which we are inseparable. Acute illness is a temporary convergence of my life with organic processes; chronic, progressive, severe illness is the gradual shaping of my CV by the unfolding of experienced pathophysiological processes. Nothing, however, of what lies within that shape – medical attention, interference with other plans, disappointments, limitations – is my body speaking.

Even as the end approaches, there remains a residual distance between the fortunes of the body and the person, if only measured in hope and hope-lessness, the expectation of a better tomorrow or a worse next week, even as we drown in a sea of reminders that we transcend our bodies only with their permission, the health of the organism being the necessary condition of our being distanced from it. Eventually, however, body and person share a common end, though the body has a posthumous existence that seems to be denied to a person. Which is no bad thing: no-one wants to be around when the worms set to work. As the body closes over us, there ceases to be a "what it is like" to be ourselves.

We are closing in on a profound mystery. How does the "I am" take root, flourish, or suffer, in, or courtesy of, the "It is" of the body? The machinery of the flesh, however exquisite, seems stony ground for the human subject. This puzzle is a microscopic expression of the macroscopic mystery of the emergence of the conscious subject in an insentient material world, a theme we shall revisit in Chapter 10.

CONCLUDING THOUGHTS

We have touched only superficially on what Patocka called the "lived corpo-reity"[30] of being a situated bodily agent. I shall be content if I have persuaded you that to see persons as mere organisms, as opposed to embodied subjects, is to bypass most of what is interesting and distinctive about us; if I have italicized the complexity of our relations to our own human bodies; and if I have reminded you of what a strange business it is being-and-not-being an oddly-shaped, fluid-irrigated, object, with hollows expanding and contracting as it breathes – such as the one that is reading this paragraph – that for the most part gets on with its own business without requiring or even consulting us.

Embodiment spans the huge, and yet elusive, gap within human being between the person and the organism. This – the relationship between the "it" and the "I" is a profound puzzle we shall revisit in future chapters when (in Chapter 5) we consider the relationship between the body and the self and, near the end of this book, when (in Chapter 10) we try to envisage the irrup-tion of the conscious subject in a mindless universe and, as a result, discover that the business we have left unfinished here is, alas, unfinishable, for we shall have moved, beyond the limits of polemic, to the realm of mystery.

It is courtesy of being this object in our own way that we live lives whose stories are subtended at many angles to the organic processes that make them possible. The distance between the subject and the body – between "I am" and "it is" – is widened by the elaboration of intentionality into a semiosphere – a realm of signs at least as complex as that of the biosphere – and a realm of "that" as in "that x is the case". What I have called the "thatosphere" will lie at the heart of the exploration in the next chapter. This chapter shall, among other things, examine the unique relationship to time that lies at the root of selfhood and makes agency possible – the themes respectively of Chapters 5 and 6. In the coming pages, there will be several iterations of a circle: the lived sense of our body as object will be reinforced by, and itself reinforce, our agency and our sense of being agents, our selfhood, and our mode of being in (and out of) time.

Addendum
Ambodiment: the I and the it

There is a deep mystery around the relationship between the first-person who *am* and the third-person or no-person of the body that *is*. While ambodiment is the ultimate embrace, and RT is the body that is pointed out when he is pointed out, and they are inseparable – as inseparable, as I have suggested, as the recto and verso of a sheet of paper – there nevertheless remains a distance between RT and his body. It is time to return to where we began: the fundamental tension at the heart of embodiment and what we may call the difficulty of getting an "I am" out of an "it is".

Some readers may detect the echo of a philosophical problem, first put into circulation by David Hume in his *Treatise of Human Nature*, of deriving an "ought" from an "is": "The distinction of vice and virtue is not founded merely on the relations between objects; nor is perceived by reason".[31] There is nothing in the material world, in nature, that seems capable of generating norms. Matter ain't a normative stuff: pebbles, for example, do not deplore or applaud.[32] I would like to suggest that the difficulty of getting "ought" out of "is" is an aspect of a wider challenge of finding a basis for mattering in matter. And this is in turn a surface manifestation of the difficulty of *finding an "am" in an "is"*; or getting an "I" out of an "it"; or "I am" out of "it is".

The difficulty is highlighted by the various complex quasi-external relationships between the "I" and the body that we discussed in this chapter: ownership, caring, using, suffering, and above all knowing. Of course, RT is represented to some extent in both places of the two-place relationship: the body I possess, care for, use (as the immediate agent of my agency), suffer, and so on is *my* body. Nevertheless, the distance underlines the non- or incomplete identity between me and my body. Those muscles that are so identified with my agency, may prove to have properties independent of me – as when they twitch or they grip me with cramp. Or when I am the helpless spectator of their decline. Then my body seems less like a possession, an asset, capital, than a curse.

The problem of getting an "I am" out of an "it is" is, I will argue, the result of starting in the wrong place, approaching RT's body as primarily a material object with general properties that, as items of knowledge, belong to no-one. If we treat the human body as an object like any other, then we shall indeed find it metaphysically infertile ground for an "I" to take root. We might be tempted to go further and join many contemporary philosophers in denying the reality of the "I" that "am" and give ontological priority to the "it" that is. Because it is not visible to the objective gaze, so the argument goes, the "I", the first-person, has at best marginal existence – "a narrative centre of gravity", a mere vanishing point of consciousness, a secular soul lacking theological underpinning, or a Cartesian hangover – as we shall discuss in Chapter 5.

I want to argue that questioning the reality of the "I" in view of the indubitable "itness" of the body (and in particular the brain) is to draw precisely the wrong conclusion about the relationship between "I" and "it". More precisely, I will suggest that the third-person or impersonal reality of objects is inseparably connected with the first-person reality of subjects – something that sounds suspiciously Kantian, though it need not be.

To understand this, we need to dig deeper into the unique nature of the human body. Yes, it is an object, and often, as when I sit on a chair, and my flesh is in dialogue with its wood, it seems like a thing among things, with the two objects in contact, communicating through the laws of mechanical nature. But the body has a special place in our world, though just how, or in what way, it is special is both obvious and difficult to grasp. My being in this room requires that my body is in this room and yet it is not the same as my body being in this room.

There is a crucial respect in which the body-as-object is special; namely that it is the primordial, paradigm object. More precisely, I will argue, it is *that in virtue of which we have the concept of an object with properties other than, even alien to, ourselves.* It is through our relationship to our own bodies that we are able to intuit beyond our experiences of extra-corporeal objects that they are in-themselves and have intrinsic properties. Appreciating the ontologically privileged status of the body throws open the possibility of transforming the problem of the relationship between "I" and the "it". Far from "am" having to grow into "it", a fully-fledged notion of "it" is built into the sense of "am", of the embodied subject. At the very least, "I" and "it" are co-dependent.

Let me develop this further. It is our own status as embodied subjects that gives us the sense of "objects in the weighty sense" – to use a crucial term from the philosopher P. F. Strawson. It refers to items that are "independently existing objects forming a unified spatio-temporal system".[33] Such objects continue to exist when they are not perceived. They have an existence that transcends the subject's necessarily perspectival perceptions of them.[34] The intuition of the reality of such objects is expressed in the notion that they are made of "matter". Matter is the basic designation of the in-itself of objects that are not merely hallucinations: it is the stuff underpinning and hence going beyond sense experiences. They are opaque in the sense of being incompletely revealed by our experience.

The ontological opacity of objects is not diminished even in those cases – such as a glass – where they are transparent in the usual sense. Glass still has hidden properties in virtue of which it is visible. If it were 100 per cent trans-parent to all senses, it would be imperceptible. Some hidden properties may be revealed by further ordinary inspection or scientific inquiry. The inquiry, however, is without end, as we know from the present condition of fundamen-tal physics where the two most powerful theories in the science of matter are yet to be reconciled, never mind to be united.[35]

There is no definitive account of the stuff of objects. It is our own status as embodied subjects that gives us the sense of "objects in the weighty sense". It is in virtue of our being and yet not-being our organic body, of being iden-tified with an object that we only incompletely – or patchily – colonize with our awareness and agency, that we develop the sense of an object – our own body – in its full otherness, and hence, by extrapolation, of the opaque "it" that forms the substance of the world. If that seems too extreme – and to be at odds with the apparent fact that "it" (the universe) precedes humans that are bearers of first-person consciousness – we could argue that "am" and "is" develop in parallel, through something like a dialectical process. The sense that I-the-person *am* and it-the-body *is* grow in parallel. The important point is that we *live* something that we can only incompletely *experience*. Our lived body is our primordial experience of something that transcends experience.

These are large and perhaps rather puzzling claims, so let us begin with something relatively straightforward: my experience of my hand.[36] When I look at the back of my hand I see an object that I know, from immediate experience, has parts that lie beyond what I see. Such parts belong to its under-surface and interior. I can, for example, feel my (currently invisible) palm through the pressure on its flesh of the table on which it is resting. I can directly intuit its interior, courtesy of a variety of sensations such as its weight and warmth, and sometimes through localized experiences such as pains. These testify to an "in here" hidden from the vision that discloses the hand as "out there". That "in here" is hidden from everyone else: you cannot sense my pain just as I cannot sense yours. I thus experience my hand from within *and* from without – as I do other parts of my body.

It is worth reflecting on this a bit further before proceeding to the larger claims. When I directly feel the hand that I am also looking at, I am in receipt of parallel streams of experience of the same object. Each stream is exposed by the other as being incomplete. The warmth of, or the pressure on, or a pain in, my hand betrays that there is more to my hand than I can see; and the visual appearance of my hand – for example the shadows cast on my skin by the veins on the dorsum – discloses that there is more to it than I can directly feel. We thus have the cross-sensory equivalent of the depth perception that is afforded by binocular vision – in this case, two sensory modalities as opposed to two eyes. The object perceived in two different ways *simultaneously* has a depth that reveals it as being more than is provided by a single sense.

But I am moving too fast. When I pick up and examine a cup, I can feel tactile properties I can't see (such as the coolness of the porcelain). I can see visual appearances (for example the shadows cast by my fingers) to which there correspond no tactile sensation. We need therefore to clarify in what way the experience of our own body, as opposed to extra-corporeal items such as cups, is unique.

Firstly, the different aspects of my hand – what I can see and what I can feel – are unified in agency, as when I grasp an object. The hand has a lived unity corresponding to the experiential stereopsis. Secondly, (and this is the more important point), whereas lifting up and looking at a cup afford differ-ent experiences of it – thereby indicating that each sensory modality yields an experience of something that is more than that experience – the different senses do not have such a fundamentally different angle of approach to the cup as they do when the item I am experiencing is a part of my own body. There is nothing in my experiencing the cup comparable to the double aspect of my hand: an external aspect revealed from without *plus* the "from within" of my hand apprehended immediately through its warmth or weight or feeling of discomfort.

The dissociation between perception courtesy of a distance sense such as vision (external or mediated access) and the seemingly unmediated awareness arising out of the hand's sensation of itself (internal, or immediate access) is most clearly evident when my hand is in action: I can feel but cannot see the *effort* in the grip. What is more, *you* cannot feel the effort in my grip, although you may infer it from what you see. Vision, which locates the object as "out there" is complemented by proprioceptive awareness that illuminates the "in here" of the object that is not accessible to anyone else. I suffer and enjoy my body in the way that you cannot. The "in-hereness" of proprioception and other immediate senses such as the feeling of warmth or pain is underlined by its inescapability. While seeing my body can be interrupted by closing my eyes, feeling it (particularly when it is in pain) cannot be extinguished in this way.

This is why tactile and proprioceptive experience locates my body firmly in my subjectivity, though on the edge of objectivity, while seeing it – parts of it directly or perhaps a whole indirectly courtesy of a mirror – locates it at a distance from subjectivity. This double status is at the root of the various two-place relationships we discussed in the text, as when we referred to our bodies or parts of them as if they were possessions: "my hand", "my face", "my body". I am at both ends of the relationship.

The two fundamentally different modes of access to my body reveal the ontological depth of my-body-as-object. Another aspect of this stereopsis is to be found in the body schema which we discussed in the main text. It underpins the sense of being my body as a unity, reinforced as I move head, arms, legs, and belly as a whole, though my body is only patchily illuminated, from within and without, by awareness. I therefore directly experience my body as an object transcending what at a particular moment (or, indeed, any moment) I experience of it. This wholeness-despite-incomplete-perception applies equally to parts of my body. When I look in the mirror, I can feel the back of the head that I cannot see. I can see my face but not the moistness I can feel in my closed mouth, or the slight ache in my temples or the ringing in my ears. I have the doubtful privilege that others do not share of being able to *see* that my headache is invisible.

The interiority of sensations is not, of course, identical with the interiority of the organs of my body. After all, you will not be able to see your guts but a surgeon might, although with his assistance or that of some device you might be able to see them. What remains interior in the sense relevant to the ontological depth of the body is something that cannot be made public. There is an *essential* privacy about what is revealed to proprioception, in contrast to what is revealed to distance senses such as sight and sound. That privacy underlined by the lack of spatial relations between items that are regarded as "inner" and those that are "outer". When I am having a thought and scratching my head at the same time, the itch and the thought are not related in the way that my brain and my forehead are.[37] Likewise, my headache is not in the darkened room in which I am lying down in the way that my head is.

I have, I hope, set the scene for my claim about the connection between our experience of our own body and our intuition of objects that have the status of belonging to the opaque realm of "it"; objects that we know through perception and yet, we believe, transcend perception. By offering the (human) body as a starting point, we shall avoid travelling in a sceptical path that has led many otherwise sensible thinkers to find our knowledge of material objects, and even the status of objects themselves, problematic.

I am thinking of Hume's opinion in his *Treatise of Human Nature* that "bodies" are mere fictions constructed out of sense impressions;[38] and Quine's assertion in "Two Dogmas of Empiricism" that objects are "cultural posits" fashioned out of "irritations on our sensory surfaces" and on a comparable "epistemological footing" as Homer's Gods.[39] As Kant (who reported that he had been woken by Hume out of his "dogmatic slumber") argued, we cannot know any "thing-in-itself" by unaided perception. Unfortunately, he went on to argue that stable objects in a spatio-temporally coherent world were the product of the synthetic activity of the mind that gathered up our experiences into the impression of things that transcend experiences. Even more unfortunately, he postulated a realm of things-in-themselves that lay beyond the reach of our experiences. However, his puzzle is well founded: how could we *experience* objects as being more than constructs out of experiences? What on earth could justify the belief that the world is populated by items made up of stuff that is more than, and hence lies beyond, our experience?

For Kant, the existence of a realm of things-in-themselves was a necessary conclusion we arrive at by reason. The trouble is that the referent of reason cannot be ascribed any particular content or location in space and time. The suggestion that the source of our sense of objects that transcend our experiences, that are coherent and enduring, is our experience of our own body which is experienced from both within and without seems more promising. Epistemic stereopsis – combining proprioception and distance perception – gives it the ontological depth we require of, or ascribe to, a real experience-independent object. The one object that could not be a Humean "fiction" or a Quinean "posit" is our own body. That body, in virtue of being both an object of external perception *and* experienced, indeed *lived*, from within, has the ontological depth of a being that is more than just the sum total of my and others' experiences of it. This relationship to our body is the existential root of our awareness of extra-corporeal material things as "objects in the weighty sense" that are both capable of being perceived and of existing unperceived. The lived weight and the existential unity of a body that is *experienced – suffered, enjoyed, lived – as going beyond my experience of it* is a key to the passage from epistemic stereopsis to ontological depth.

I can envisage several objections to the argument I have just presented, not the least that I may seem to have jumped across from bodily experiences that give the sense of a real, external material world to a claim about the reality of that world. Let me deal with the most pressing.

Firstly, the knowledge-from-within-and-from-without argument might not withstand Cartesian doubt. How can I know with certainty that I really do have a body, located in an extra-mental world? Could my body be an hallucination? Descartes' *cogito* argument – "I think therefore I am" – finds a bedrock of certainty in the fact that I am thinking. I cannot without self-contradiction seriously entertain the thought that I am not thinking. But the scope of what is placed beyond doubt by the argument, is severely limited.[40] I can be certain, Descartes might argue, only that I am a thinking being – or that there are thoughts happening – not that I am an *embodied* thinking being.

This was countered by P. F. Strawson, who pointed out, in *Individuals*, that the (singular) identity implicit in "I" depends on the occupancy of a unique location in space. It is incoherent to limit the "I" that I "am" to current thoughts (or indeed perceptions) as they do not occupy space. If I am to have an identity – in short if "I" is to have a reference and "I am" is to be realized in having token experiences and token thoughts – then the I in question must be inseparable from a means of occupying space: it must be embodied. The subject that "I am" requires the body, the "it is". No entity could be a free-floating bundle of perceptions; even less of untokenized thoughts, least of all, the thought that "I think therefore I am". If thoughts were entirely general, and not instantiated in virtue of occurring to an individual located in space and time, they would lack a specific reference. This is equally true of the very sense organs by which I perceive the world: they, too, must be located in a body itself localized in space and time if perception is to have (justified) particular content – so that I see "this" (over here) rather than "that" (elsewhere).

It follows, that, given my indubitable condition as an individual who experiences the world from a viewpoint, and entertains thoughts that have definite referents, I cannot be mistaken that my body exists. That I am embodied is what philosophers have called a "hinge commitment". Being possessed of a coherent viewpoint, unified across seemingly spatially localized and spatially separate sources of sense experience, themselves situated among that which they perceive, as individual in his or her environment, is inconceivable without a spatially localized, and space-occupying body. That body must in turn be conceived as a kind of whole, notwithstanding the patchiness of its owner's experience of it or indeed any given part of it.

So my body, the paradigm of the material object, the "it", that continues in the absence of being perceived, could not be an hallucination. Its continuity and wholeness and solidity is, furthermore, lived, affirmed in the felt needs and related actions, that presuppose my body in different ways. We are not spectators of a mere veil of appearance, least of all the appearance of our body. The unity presupposed in an action as straightforward as walking towards a visible goal implicitly fills in the dark places between the patches of flesh illuminated by sensory awareness and agency. A body of this nature – as the agent of one's agency – is resistant to being dissolved into mere sensation or to being assimilated to a Cartesian dream state.[41] Certainty, therefore, extends beyond the Cartesian limits to encompass at least one type of material object that transcends sense experience: the bodies of conscious human beings.

So, I could not be mistaken in believing that I am embodied. But what about extra-corporeal objects such as sticks and stones and mountains? Are we entitled, on the basis of the story so far, to conclude that they, too, are real, that they are more than our experiences of them? Could we not be mistaken in ascribing to them a reality independent of our experiences? No; and here's why. If my body, with its interacting parts, were real but the things it acted upon were merely fictions or Quinean "posits", there would be an impossibly lopsided, indeed one-sided, coupling between a real, physical body, and a world of fictional items. What sense could be made of this? We could not rationally consider that they are hallucinations cooked up in our brains. After all, the nervous system – central to this understanding of the origin of knowledge – would also be a posit, which makes its role in positing objects on the basis of events or forces that impinge on the brain somewhat difficult to understand. And the impingements from objects in the vicinity would have no basis. And the nervous system would have to cook up not only itself but also the items that interact with it to generate the experiences out of which objects are constructed.

In short, the reality of extra-corporeal objects is intimately connected with the reality of the living body. We have already mentioned the reciprocity between the hand that touches and the object it touches. And the sense of extra-corporeal things is underpinned by more than passively received evidence. Our interactions with them are imbued with effort, pain, carnal heaviness, resistance, struggle. These reach into the heart of our sense of our self and what we are and of the reality of the world. Quine's "strain of walking uphill" points to an ontological democracy in which the body of the walker and the hill she is climbing are interacting in the same realm. This democracy is underlined by, for example, my feeling the resistance of a stone to be lifted and the resistance of my arm to being lifted – or the weight of an external object and my arm that is lifting it.

What is most importantly granted to me through my embodiment – more precisely ambodiment – is what we might call "existential reassurance". In virtue of the "I am" that grows in and haunts – and appropriates and distances itself from – this body, I have a sense of an "it is" that is in the first instance applicable to my body and thence to material objects beyond my body. The combination of first-person being or "am-ing" my body and experiencing it as an object, most strikingly when I look at myself in a mirror, awakens the sense of the "it-is-in-itself" of the objects in the world that surrounds me.[42] We may think of our bodies as the point of convergence between knowing and being, between epistemology and ontology, with our lived being providing the ultimate warrant for our knowledge; or ambodiment closing the gap between the experience of the object on the one hand and, on the other, the object that is experienced as being more than what is experienced of it.

At any rate, it seems that the existential stereoscopy of perceived (and possibly the *con*ceived) image of the body on the one hand and lived carnality on the other makes our own body the paradigm of the ontological depth we ascribe to the things we encounter in the world as objects of perception. This existential stereoscopy is highlighted in effortful activity, when we simultaneously see and feel our agency as a bodily cost. It is under such circumstances, also, that we encounter reality as matter – as stuff that is impenetrable, heavy, resistant, even hostile; as the substrate of *work*. It is the strongest justification of the projection of what we have learned about what-is from our own bodies to the extra-corporeal world. At a more immediate level, the production of sweat as we struggle with the physical world (including our own bodies when we exercise) delivers an objective sight (the glistening) and touch (the tickle of the trickle), immediate signs, of a hidden process going on in our body, and direct awareness of our own will and effort – all of which adds up to a three-dimensional ontological revelation.

This seems to dispose of one objection to the idea that our experience of our bodies that straddles the "I" of the subjective and the "it" of the objects delivers knowledge of external objects that is proof against scepticism: namely, that it muddles an ontological question about what kinds of things there are out there with an epistemological question about what we know, or think we know, is out there and the grounds for our knowledge of what kinds of things there are. The embodied subject as a point of convergence of the ontological and the epistemological is realized in the body-as-object-and-subject. The grounds for our believing in the existence of objects out there that transcend our experience – though they are the source of our experience – are to be found in our being (suffering, enjoying, striving) lived bodies which we know from within transcend our experience. The ontological reality of the body is a necessary condition of there being a knowing subject and hence justifies the sense that there are objects that transcend experience. Our sense of objects in the weighty sense being "out there" originates from our incontrovertible sense that our own bodies are objects in the weighty sense. If (as we must) we concede the latter, then – given the kinds of interactions between our bodies and the extra-corporeal world – we must also accept the reality of objects in the weighty sense beyond our bodies.

"Am-ing" is the mode of being that closes the gap between the epistemic and the ontological in lived, suffered, enjoyed, reality. Living goes deeper than knowing, not the least because it is the necessary condition of knowing, though knowledge seems to transcend organic living and, of course, in humans vastly extends its scope. We may express this another way by seeing the object in the weighty sense as both the starting point from which knowledge arises and the end-point towards which knowledge aspires. The object as a Quinean "posit" is posited by an embodied subject whose reality cannot be in doubt as it is a necessary condition of positing. Disembodied spirits could not "posit" objects – particulars located in space and time, spatially and temporally related to themselves.

While the lived experience of our bodies is the ultimate source of our (justified) sense of the independent reality of objects in a world out there, transcending our experiences, it is only a starting point. Because I am an embodied perceiver, enjoying successive perceptions, I can perceive *that* I perceive from a certain, restricted viewpoint. Looking at this table in front of me, I see it from a certain angle; but more importantly I see *that* I see it from a certain angle. This awareness of my own perspective is courtesy of the fact that my viewpoint is incarnate in an object – my body or at least my head – that is also visible to me. The explicit awareness of perspective awakens the sense of other perspectives, future ways of seeing, that are also available, underlining that the visible object is not exhausted by what is presently seen. The object has a back, an inside, an underside (consider a carpet in my lounge I have walked on for years). These are presently not visible but are implicit in a viewpoint whose restrictions are made explicit in the viewing body that can see itself. The intuition that, if the seen object is real, "there is more to come" is validated by the experience of touching the object, feeling its temperature, resistance, weight and so on: touching justifies seeing's believing. This is the opening to shared, validated, quantitative experience that is a realm of knowledge far beyond that which can be lived.

The successive experiences of the object are separated in time. As Kant pointed out, they need to be *bound* together; or rather their succession needs to be such that the elements are in some way co-present as evidence that the object transcends any given experience. The basis for this – that Kant located in the synthetic activity of a strangely bodiless mind – is to be found in our experience of ourselves as embodied subjects. We could not, in short, generate objects from successive experiences if we were not ourselves identified with an object that transcends our experiences whose successive moments are bound together.

Unlike Kant's transcendental subject (which we shall touch on shortly) the body, or the embodied subject, *is* located in space and time and is, under one aspect, an object among objects. In this more democratic ontology, the lived body bumps up against other objects, and experiences modes of reciprocity such that it is pushed by the things it pushes against. As I press a solid object, it presses me, sometimes leaving the marks of its pressure. The embodied subject falls, as other objects do, under the influence of gravity. Finally, it is visible, tangible, audible, to other embodied subjects or indeed to other sentient creatures. This democracy is reflected in the microcosm of my body. If my legs are crossed, there is an equivalence between the two legs: the leg on top presses downwards on the leg underneath and the leg underneath presses upwards on the leg on top. More importantly, both legs have an external surface revealed through contact but, at the same time, an inner experience not shared with the other leg. The pain in the lower leg squashed underneath is not experienced in the leg on top.

The democracy extends of course to the chair on which I am sitting, which reciprocates the pressure from my legs by pressing on them: action and reaction are equal and opposite and equally applicable to the sitter and the sat-upon. Another expression of this democracy is in the act of weighing myself, using the same scales as I use to weigh the suitcase I am taking on a plane. There is, however, a limit to this reciprocity. When I sit on a chair, while it presses upwards on the backside that is pressing down on it, it does not acknowledge me or my backside in the way that I acknowledge it.

There has been an important omission in my unpacking of the "it is" from the "I am". It is the shared nature of human experience. Yes, we may imagine that, as the developing infant discovers his own body as something he is and is not, so he deepens his sense of an objective world that has a reality that is both public, being exposed to any number of others, and is intrinsic to it and hence to be uncovered by further experience. Our body is first lived and only gradually encountered as an object. It takes an infant some time to find its hands, to discover its mouth with its hands, and to connect his toes with the complex of hand-and-mouth that lies at its centre. Subsequently, living our discovered body still retains its priority over encountering it: we encounter parts of our body *from* a body that is lived. But the co-discovery of "I" and "it" is not a single-handed achievement. It is inseparable from the infant's awareness of a world that is in the keeping of others, just as the "I" grows in a multi-layered matrix of "we" upheld by the "you" of special, and then more numerous and less special, others. "We are born in someone's arms"[43] as Patočka so poignantly expressed it; and we develop in the marsupialized space of the breasts, arms, and warmth of our mothers – and this is in part true of our world. In this connection, it is highly pertinent that reasoning about hidden objects (and whether things still exist independently of whether we can still perceive them) and recognizing one's image in the mirror (a marker of emerging self-awareness) seem to be connected.[44] Our sense of others as equals is entangled with our sense of the objects we perceive as being accessible to others: that you and I belong to a common, public space, available to us all.

Thus the case for arguing that there is no "it" without an "I", just as there is no opacity without vision (or vision without opacity). The "it" of the objective view may seem, falsely, to be the product of a cognitively superior, ultimately scientific, understanding, so that the "it" facts about our human being, understood as *the* truths of the human organism, marginalize or trump our first-person I-truths. In part, this is because the realm of "it", as opposed to "I" is a public cognitive space to which norms ("true" or "false", "accurate" or "inaccurate") apply. As Kant put it, "Error is a burden only to the understanding".[45] "Pure" sensation, not subject to the tribunal of judgement, cannot be false – or even true. The expanded cognitive space of objective or at least agreed knowledge extends boundlessly beyond what is currently visible or audible, or in any other way sensible. It seems to partake of the "really real", as opposed to the merely "real to me" or "real to him". Truly objective truth ultimately is seen as that which is uncovered by measurement which has standards that seem to liberate it from the vagaries of the subject with her individual perspective.

The personal "I am" cannot seem to find a foothold in the no-personal places of the body and the brain understood as primarily objects of factual knowledge. The body seen through the eyes of objective science, seems to offer nothing to allow a subject to take root and flourish. What I have argued is that we can (indeed should) turn this on its head: "it is" is rooted in the experience of being, more precisely *living*, a body that we are aware of as only incompletely experiencing. There is no third- or no-person world without a first-person one: the latter is necessary to turn is into "is" or "is-in-itself". Neither, however, is more fundamental than the other.[46]

This view, which leans neither to Kantian idealism nor Quinean materialism, overlaps with a view expressed by Merleau-Ponty that "the very idea of the ontological dimension of objects must be traced back to the context of the constitution of the object in our (bodily) experience".[47] It undermines the standard physicalist assumption that the conscious subject, the "I", is the product of the causal interaction between extra-corporeal objects (and events and energies) and other objects (notably brains). While it is obvious that "I am because it [my body] is", there is an important sense in which "It [my body as object in the weighty sense] is because I am". An ontology of physical objects arises out of the existentially justified epistemic stereopsis of the embodied subject. Epistemic stereopsis of our body – that is the object and the subject of consciousness – delivers ontological depth. Two eyes give spatial depth; two senses give the object further depth; two perspectives on our own body – from within and without, seemingly unmediated and mediated respectively – gives ontological depth.[48]

CHAPTER 4

Human being: in and out of time

In the last chapter we reflected on the mind-boggling complexity of our relationship to our bodies. While there is a fundamental sense in which those bodies are objects among the other objects of the world, on all fours with tables, chairs, pebbles, and clouds, they are also the basis of our being viewpoints on what-is and hence upholders of a world in which objects are located. The lived stereoscopy of our bodily awareness underpins our intuition that objects have an existence in themselves independent, or truly outside of, ourselves as perceiving subjects inhabiting a world populated with such objects.

We have left much business unfinished, some of which can be gathered under the headings of "selfhood" or "personal identity" and "agency". I will delay discussion of these concepts until we have further explored their hinterland in order that our investigation might be conducted at the right depth. The present chapter is devoted to our mode of being in – and out of – time. This might seem a long way from our topic of humanism but in fact it lies at its very core. Our unique relationship to time is the basis of the extended subject that is the self and the conscious human agent. As such it is central to our distinctively human being.

I am conscious that the previous chapter and what I will have to say in the present may be hard going for non-philosophers. Stick with me, however – and take heart because the remaining chapters will be easier to understand. The burden of the present chapter is that persons are extended in time in a manner that is fundamentally different from the way that material objects (including organisms) are located in time. Indeed, our entire mode of being in time is unique to human beings.[1]

The phenomenology of human time is a vast topic. Mentioning just two names from what in the UK is called "continental" philosophy – Husserl and Heidegger – will be sufficient to those who are familiar with these names to indicate the importance of the topic as it has flowered in philosophical discourse. My concern with our extendedness through time is deeply unoriginal; but my take on this matter is, I believe, original. In order that we shall not drown, I want to tether our reflections to two small words: "at" – as in "at such-and-such a time" – which makes time explicit; and "that" as in "that such-and-such is the case" which points out of time to a timeless zone.

"At" and "that" mark the distance between human time on the one hand and, on the other, the time of the natural world especially as it is seen through the lens of the physical sciences. It is in virtue of the relationship signified by "at" that, unlike non-human animals, we are both in time and out of it; and it is as a result of "that" that we can project ourselves out of time altogether. Central to my argument is the claim that the time of physics – typically signified by the symbol (little) "t" – far from being the fundamental temporal reality is a late derivative of these modes of being inside and outside of time that characterize human time.

More specifically, "at" – as in "at such-and-such a time" – is a marker of the distance between on the one hand the time of the organism (of our bodies and the biological events that take place inside them) and, on the other, the time of the embodied subject, the self or the person (and of the community of selves and persons who have built and maintained the human world). "That", as in "that such-and-such is the case", is the marker of a sphere I have called the "thatosphere". This is a sphere, ultimately founded in our capacity for shared intentionality, to which knowledge belongs and which forms the fabric of the community of human minds. The thatosphere is, in an important sense timeless. This truth has been the source of a major (perhaps *the* major) strand of philosophical thought in the West. We shall return to this presently.

A GLANCE AT SPACE

I shall discuss "at", and "that" in relation to time and timelessness; however, both terms also apply to our mode of being connected with space. Our bodies are located in space but we inhabit space from a virtual outside. The space of personhood is not the space of physics or even of the biological body and the processes that keep it ticking over. I will, however, focus on time rather than space because it also underpins most directly the mode in which the enduring self is internally connected and is the condition of the possibility of agency

– the themes of the next two chapters. A few words on space are, however, in order.

As I stand here now, my body is physically located in a space that could be described by coordinates belonging to a frame of reference that also define the location of the material objects around me: the table, the door, and the sun. Yes, my body is physically surrounded: that is why, or how, I can sit on a chair, reach for a glass, cross a road, or look at the sun. This does not however define my *situation*: *I* am not "in" space in the way that my body is. An obvious manifestation of this is that I am not *confined* to my spatial location in the way that the tables, doors and the sun are. I am conscious of where I am at, am conscious of being surrounded, in the way that they are not. They do not have an outside-of-themselves – except to the extent that I or some other conscious being ascribe an outside to them. The pebble is not "on the beach" any more than it is "in Cornwall" or "on Earth" in the sense of situating itself there. My spatial "at" is many-layered, being defined not solely or even primarily by the envelope of my body or the items encircling me, but by places defined by my interests, agency, thoughts and knowledge. The space of my occupation is not the space of my preoccupation. Hence, depending on my preoccupations, I am "in a café" or "in Bramhall", or "near Manchester", or "200 miles from London" or "a long way from home". Explicit distances, highlighted by salience, are profoundly different from the spatial intervals identified in physics. This would be true even if special relativity had not demonstrated, at least to the satisfaction of most physicists, that space and time do not have separate reality, such that there is only space-time and the apportioning of the spatiotemporal separation between events into spatial distances and temporal intervals depends on the relationship between the frame of reference of the observer and that which is observed – of which more presently.

Of even greater importance, my location is defined to some extent factually. To be "at such-and-such a place" is to be connected to a nexus of expectations, or presuppositions, that are ripe to be expressed as factual possibilities some of which may prompt or justify actions. And – to anticipate an argument we shall make with respect to time – facts are spaceless. Even a seemingly spatial fact such as *that* "X is ten miles from Y" is not itself located in space. The spacelessness of other facts such as "This is my tenth visit to this café" or "The owner of this café does not pay taxes" hardly requires labouring. When I tear up a piece of paper I do not tear up the facts that are reported on it, dividing them into spatially separate parts; and though people talk about "the facts on the ground", they are not situated on the surface of the earth beneath the trees and above the worms. The Battle of Hastings took place in Hastings but *the fact that* there was such a battle is not located in the South of England or anywhere else – except metaphorically "inside" the minds of those who are thinking about it. Likewise, the fact that I am in Stockport station is not located inside, or outside, railway property.

Whatever I have to say about human mode of being in and out of time, therefore, applies equally to our being in and out of space. They both contribute to our extra-natural mode of being that, as I will discuss in Chapter 6, permits us to act as agents from a virtual outside – that of the human world. Human space, like human time, is folded, layered, bordered and opened, having a multiplicity of kinds of insides and outsides, invaginated and extravasated, separated and overlapped and nested. Between trouser pockets, where we keep our hands warm, to intergalactic light years revealed by radio telescopes there are a thousand modes of extendedness defined by innumerable kinds of limits, bounds and borders. None of these is captured by space of the physicist. The *places* to which we are guided by GPS are not known to physics. The space of the physicist is featureless – an entirely expected consequence of its being deprived of all qualities except those that are reduced to numerical measures of quantity. While it is possible to distinguish point 2,4,17 from 3,6,12, these points borrow their distinctiveness from outside – from a gaze that supplies them a frame of reference.

That is all I am going to say about space. Time to return to time.

TIME

Introducing "at"

Let us begin with "at" as in "at noon".[2] I want to argue that there is no "at" in the physical world.[3] "At" is important because without "at" there could be no communal human life, of which the discipline of physics is a small but very distinguished part. The true nature of "at" is concealed because it is often hidden away in designations such as "t", or "t_1" or "t_2" where "at" is rolled up into the letter that designates a moment in a universe of physical events or, more precisely, of events assimilated into physical theory.

To unmask the true nature of "at" it is necessary to engage with the most authoritative account of the natural world: physics.[4] Let us begin with a famous – and seemingly entirely straightforward – passage from Einstein's first paper on relativity. It marked his joyful embarkation on the intellectual adventure that ended with perhaps the greatest of all scientific theories. Here is the passage in question: "All our judgements in which time takes a part are always judgements of simultaneous events. When I say, for example, 'The train arrives here *at* 7, that means that 'the passage of the little hand of my watch at the place marked 7 and the arrival of the train are simultaneous events'".[5]

It all sounds very innocent, even banal. But it is revolutionary. For the "simultaneity" of spatially separated events, as Einstein makes clear, is a *judgement* made by an observer and it does not correspond to anything in the physical world in the absence of observers. This is the basis of the famous, indeed, notorious paradoxes of relativity theory. Before we focus on this, there is something we should not overlook: the two events – the arrival of the little hand at the place marked 7 and the arrival of the train – are not entirely comparable. We can see this more easily if we choose a different example, one that lacks the human significance of the arrival of a train – say a flash of lightning occurring at 7 o'clock. The lightning flash is entirely physical. The little hand of the clock reaching 7 has two aspects. It is a physical event, yes; but in addition, it is also a sign, revealing what time it is; it would be therefore something fundamentally different for a non-human animal incapapble of telling the time or conceiving doing so. As such it does not belong to the same realm as other physical events.

Einstein wants to highlight how the time of occurrence of an event is not something definite or absolute located in a universal clock. *When* something happens depends on the relationship between the frame of reference from which it is viewed and the frame of reference in which that something takes place. From this we may conclude that "at time t" – in this case 7 o'clock – is not an intrinsic characteristic of physical events but of an *observed* relationship between them. The connection of events with explicit times, their taking place *at* a time, is observer-dependent. The train entering the station "at 7 p.m." is true only for an observer using a clock that is close to the train. If the clock was a light-year away from the train, the train would enter the station "at 7 p.m." a year later than it would enter as noted by the nearby clock. And the first clock would not be more accurate according to some absolute standard than the second clock.

Several consequences follow from this: there is no intrinsic time at which events take place; the order and the duration of, and the interval between, events is observer-relative. Two distant events A and B may be judged, with equal validity, as simultaneous or successive depending on the inertial frame of reference from which they are viewed; and if, non-simultaneous, whether A follows B or, on the contrary, B follows A is again frame-dependent. In short, whether the train came into the station at 7 o'clock is not intrinsic to the physical event in question. In the absence of viewpoint, we cannot say that a physical event E took place at any particular time. It did not, for example, take place at the equivalent of 7 o'clock in some global time scheme. There is nothing, in short, to underpin "at" in the physical world.

Behind this conclusion is the central dogma of physical science: that there is no reality beyond observed, or at least observable-in-principle, reality.[6] Ernst Mach, the philosopher and physicist who hugely influenced the early Einstein, asserted that space and time are real only insofar as they are observed, indeed measured. (He argued this against the Newtonian idea of an absolute space and time that was independent of measurement or indeed experience.) There is a profound consequence of this extreme empiricism: the observer must be part of the physical world, interacting with it. But consciousness, and conscious subjects, as we saw in Chapter 2, sit awkwardly alongside "mass", "energy", "charge" and the other elements that physical science grants to nature. Likewise, the *viewpoint* necessary to establish and uphold the inertial frame of reference from which actual values can be assigned to locations and intervals in space and time also fit in rather awkwardly. Once frames of reference have been established or defined, then it's business as usual.

This may seem rather shocking for tough-minded physics, almost as shocking as the explicit observer-dependence of quantum reality that Einstein resisted and which contributed to his ultimately distancing himself from Machian philosophy of science. At the very least, it made the idea of a temporal order of events in the absence of a conscious observer problematic – as Herman Weyl (*vide infra*) pointed out.

All of this seems less upsetting than it should because "at time t" is incorporated into a mathematical schema and its human origin is concealed. Physicists sterilize the notion of viewpoint, disinfecting it of conscious subjects, by representing a frame of reference as a purely mathematical coordinate system that confers numerical values upon spatio-temporal points and consequently upon the events that take place within them. Despite their respectable mathematical appearance, however, coordinate systems are *not* part of the physical world. Material nature does not populate herself with coordinate systems, anchored to the origin of its axes located at point 0,0,0,0. In short, in the absence of a spontaneous blizzard of quartets of zeroes, there is no "at" defining the location of events. Consequently, the "at" of an event is not inherent in the event or the location, itself composed of other events, assigned to it. In the absence of an observer, there is no frame of reference and consequently no temporal order, or time of occurrence, of events. This goes beyond the truism that we need an observer for anything to be *registered* as happening.

The "observer" who fits so badly into the physicists' view of the natural world has somehow to be accommodated, if only because she privileges one frame of reference over another – a viewpoint without which actual times cannot be assigned to events. How is this to be achieved? By this means: conflating the observer who uses measuring devices such as a clock with a clock itself or the material of which it is made – so that the fingers on the clock reaching a particular point becomes an event like any other physical event: fingers arriving at 7 o'clock and train arriving at the station are of the same kind. It is as if clocks could do what they have to do without a conscious observer to assign location, size, and order to events – as if clocks left to themselves could "tell the time". Here is the conflation at work: "It is true that for the sake of convenience authors of works on [relativity] have often introduced 'observers' who are assumed to perceive the phenomena. *But these observers can just as well be replaced by recording instruments, and whether or not they are living and conscious is irrelevant*" (emphasis added).[7] Bertrand Russell, in his *ABC of Relativity*, dismissed the idea that the observer must be "a human being, or at least a mind" and asserted that it was "just as likely to be a photographic plate or a clock".[8]

It should hardly be necessary to point out that no physical entity in and of itself is a clock. A source of regular ("isochronous") periodic activity does not tell the time on its own because it needs someone to ask it, to want to know it, and to provide a frame of reference which will give time a definitive value. What it needs are those beings who make measurements and use devices called clocks: conscious observers who cannot be substituted for by (say) photographic plates. There are no readings without readers, even though the event that is read may be separated from the event of the reading.

The idea of the time on a clock as a purely physical phenomenon, disinfected of any conscious observer, is unacceptable. It is hardly surprising, therefore, that along with other measuring devices such as measuring rods, clocks fit very awkwardly into physical theory. Einstein himself was uneasy about their status. Speaking nearly 50 years after the glad, confident morning of his first relativity paper he admitted that he did not know how to deal with them:

> One is struck by the fact that the theory [relativity] ... introduces two kinds of physical things, i.e. (1) measuring rods and clocks, and (2) all other things, e.g., the electromagnetic field, the material point, etc. This, in a certain sense, is inconsistent ...; strictly speaking, measuring rods and clocks would have to be represented as solutions of the basic equations (objects consisting of moving atomic configurations) not, as it were, theoretically self-sufficient entities.[9]

As philosopher of physics Tim Maudlin has put it: "A term like 'clock' unlike 'light ray' or massive particle cannot appear in the statement of any fundamental law".[10]

This is no trivial point. Clocks do not fit into the world as described by relativity theory in which they figure so centrally. They are an embarrassment and yet indispensable. This, to reiterate, is an expression of the fact that they are ultimately inseparable from observers – who are necessary not only to settle the frame of reference required to allocate events to times of occurrence, but also to turn periodic events into timing devices.

If physics cannot accommodate conscious observers and hence clocks (which require conscious observers), there is no "at time t". To measure time (and space) is to approach time (and space) from without; to stand outside of time and space understood as physical realities. As for mobilizing laws derived from using clocks and measuring rods to make predictions about future states of the world or retrodictions regarding its past states – the very stuff of science – this is even less possible to fit into a world reduced to physical laws, states, elements and stuffs. To anticipate, there are no *facts* in nature – not even, or especially, the facts of nature.[11]

The narrow conclusion from what has been said so far is that, if the story told by physics were a complete account of the universe, then there would be no physics, given that there would be no place for the observers with their frames of reference who are central to relativity theory, and who generate the observations upon which the theory depends. The reduction of clocks to physical processes would seem to saw off the very branch on which fundamental physics is seated. There are, however, implications that go beyond this; indeed, we have opened up a path to understanding our special place in the scheme of things. The sense that something takes place "at" such and such a time – which ultimately leads, via organized collective daily life, to the collective cognitive monument that is science – has many more consequences that separate human life from the processes of the material world.

When I situate an event in (clock-)time "t", I a) connect it with other events and b) with other times. Consider first other events. By linking event E explicitly with a particular time t – the time *at* which it happens – I potentially relate it to the set of events also taking place at time t, even if time "t" understood as a single universe-wide moment is absent from physics. For the *experience* of simultaneity (of the things happening at a particular time) cannot be denied. It is extended to a set of events falling within the consciousness of an individual subject, or a group of subjects having shared experiences. There is the idea of a *moment*. It is not a mathematical instant but a nice fat Now that encompasses all the events that I or a co-present we are currently experiencing. The intuited scope of 7 o'clock extends beyond the horizon of perceptions to a world that I am aware is largely unperceived. While it may be an illusion from the standpoint of physics, the Common Now is a shared, lived reality. A vast number of events are encircled by its embrace.

It should not come as a surprise that a scientist as philosophically astute as Einstein should admit that the absence of the present, of the common "Now", from physical science worried him. As the philosopher Rudolf Carnap reported:

> Once Einstein said that the problem of Now worried him. He explained that the experience of the Now means something special for man, something essentially different from the past and the future but that this difference does not and cannot occur within physics. That this experience cannot be grasped by science seemed to him a matter for painful but inevitable resignation.[12]

The reasons for the absence of Now are explained by philosopher of physics Steven Savitt:

> If each inertial frame has its own set of simultaneous events, and the principle of relativity states that no physical experiment or system (and *we human beings are physical systems* as well) can distinguish one such frame or another as (say) genuinely at rest, then we are able to discern no particular set of simultaneous events as constituting the now or the present.[13] (emphasis added, added for reasons that will shortly become apparent.)

As might be expected, moments designated as "past" and or as "future" also go the way of the Now, because there is no reference point that would determine them as past or future. "Not yet" and "no longer" lose their distinctive nature as physics ascends from the viewpoint of a conscious observer. Without the conscious observer, there is no basis for assigning a privileged status to a certain moment, to a temporal slice (or foliation, to use the technical term) through the four-dimensional manifold of space-time. The conscious observer, the now, the future, and the past, have no place in physical science.

Which brings us to the second point. Time made explicit as "at t_1" is opened up to other times: 7 o'clock takes its place in a series, such as 5 past 7, half past 8, and so on. Connecting an event with its (own) time, therefore links it up both with other times, and with other events occurring at other times, manifest in the structured time of the clock and, beyond this, of the calendar. While making a time explicit as (say) "at t_1" is essential for the physicist's vision of the world, it also marks a distance from the physical world. Since no material event – not even those taking place in our bodies – has a relationship to a time scheme as an intrinsic property, relating to those time schemes separates us from the physical time of the material world. Einstein's discomfort about the status of clocks was clearly well-founded.

Connecting events with times, and consequently locating them in time schemes, generates a second-order temporal "at". The relationship between an event and a time is supplemented by a different kind of relationship between one time and another time, or between a time and an entire time scheme. Let us suppose it is determined that event E occurs at time t_2. This also means that it occurs between t_1 and t_3. The train comes in at 7 o'clock and this event is also located between 6:55 and 7:05. Moreover, we are talking about 7 o'clock on Wednesday which is between Tuesday and Thursday.

The story has only just begun. The time of the timetable – as is most explicit in transport systems, but is ubiquitous in our human life of appointments and promises, contracts and cooperation – extends into a distant future and the records of punctuality reach into the distant past. "At" is thus the opening through which time becomes explicitly set out and can then be extended indefinitely from the present, courtesy of clocks, calendars, and historical records. Told time is located in an abstract framework that brings together moments, eras, events, and histories in a way that is unknown to the physical world. There is no 5 o'clock on the sun as Wittgenstein pointed out; but there is no 5 o'clock anywhere in the physical world.

The sense of events occurring "at" such and such a time and of ourselves (our experience of our bodies and the surrounding world and our thoughts) being "at" the time at which they occur, thus distances ourselves from the physical world. That distance is extended by the explicit sense of the "at" being shared with other people, highlighted by joint attention and presupposed and realized in joint enterprises, delivered in a Common Now, connected with a common Yesterday and Tomorrow, a common Last Week and Next Week, Last Year and Next Year that is available to a multiplicity of agents. While the sharing of Now is most clearly evident when we work or plan together, it is presupposed in any coordinated action, for example when we engage in conversation. Out of these interactions arises the ordered sequence of events and times that is history; and the more parochial but no less exotic, awareness of the story of our individual lives and the sense that we are at a particular time of ourself or in our lives.

The distance between the way the organism that is my body is in time and the way I relate to time is evident even in the earliest manifestations of "clocking" time. Consider the most primitive of all clocks – the "peasant's clock"[14] – that exploits the shadow cast by one's own body. You and I agree to meet when (for example) our shadows are as long as our bodies. Given that the relationship between the length of a shadow and that of the object casting it depends on the angle of the sun that is the same for everyone, the appointment can be honoured.

It is worth unpacking the complex cognitive background to this seemingly simple arrangement. There is the knowledge of the shadow-casting property of one's own body-as-object. There is the joint exploitation of that knowledge. There is a shared understanding that the shadow can be reduced to a parameter (length) which it has in common with its body. There is the appreciation (also shared) that the length of the shadow has a definite ratio to that of the body, that this varies according to the position of the sun, and that this is true of all our bodies: there is nothing special about my body. On top of this, there is the sense that others can appreciate and use these implicit principles of the peasant's clock. That is not the end of the story. The transformation of the position of the sun judged by the ratio of the length of shadows to the bodies that cast them into "times of the day" *at* which appointments can be fixed is yet another complex notion upon which the seemingly primitive peasant's clock depends.[15]

The relationship between "at t" and the time scheme to which it belongs confers form, structure, and stability upon, as well as underlining, our common occupancy of, "hitherto" and "about to", "no longer" and "not yet", "yesterday" and "tomorrow", "last week" and "next year".[16] The "at" of time translated into an "o'clock" underpins innumerable agreements based on joined intentions that enable our separate agencies to be orchestrated into cooperative effort, whereby individual powers are directly and indirectly aggregated to collective strength. A society is above all a huge meshwork of timed commitments, of promises informal and contractual, voluntary and imposed.

We are unique beings in virtue of our locating physical events *at* a particular time, in connecting those times with other times to gather them up into a schema at which other events happen, and, in virtue of timing them, ascribing a duration and rate to them. Man is the clock-watching, clock-governed animal. Humans, we might say, are the only beings whose temporality includes telling the time, and in locating themselves in the time that is told. While the material world – clouds, pebbles, trees, insects – unfolds in time, it does not do so by moving from "at" one time to "at" another time. (I will return presently to the question of whether or in what sense "higher" non-human animals such as apes exist in time).

By thus locating ourselves, we are in an important sense outside of the time that we are, in another sense, within. My kidneys at t_2 are not, of themselves, located between t_1 and t_3. It is only because I, Raymond Tallis, am (explicitly) at t_2 that I am between t_1 and t_3; that I am a being who transforms his unfolding through successive states into a temporally connected lattice of events, some of which add up to my biography. The brain (at least as the level of neural events) cannot, any more than the kidney, curate its (absent) past states or entertain (absent) future ones. The absent cannot be present in biological material in order to make the present state explicitly "present" in contrast with a remembered past and an anticipated future.

The sense in which we are outside of time when we tell the time or time events is worth exploring a bit more. Someone asks, "What time is it?". I look at the clock and on the basis of the position of the fingers report that it is 12 noon. There is a sense that my action of looking at the clock and my experience of seeing the clock face take place at 12 noon. I may seem, therefore, still to remain within physical time when I am telling the time. This is not so. To see – and to report – *that* it is 12 noon, it is to come upon the time I am "in" from without. Nothing else around me, not even the clock, is telling the time, and hence is outside of time in this sense. Something else is connected with this. The experience of an event such as the clock fingers reaching 12 noon does not occur at the same time as my experience of seeing the clock face showing that it is 12 noon. Or not in the same sense that the fingers reaching 12 noon (E_1) is at the same time as the clock chiming 12 noon (E_2). Event E_1 and my experience of E_1 are not temporally related in the way that Event E_1 and Event E_2 are temporally related. Consciousness is not part of the temporal schema of physics, if only because it delivers the frame of reference that underpins temporal relations observed and measured in physics.

That material events do not assign times – temporal locations, relations or durations – to themselves is obvious. It is precisely because it is so obvious that its profound significance is overlooked. Einstein's unease with the presence of clocks (and measuring rods) in a fundamental theory of the natural world is not as widely shared as it should be. No material event is "at 7 o'clock" without the assistance of a clock; and no clock is "at 7 o'clock" without the assistance of an observer. The spatio-temporal scheme of the physicist is not a natural phenomenon, finally uncovered by the natural sciences, but something that is in a sense imposed. It lies at the *end* of a journey of human consciousness, not at the beginning of a putative journey from the Big Bang that led finally to human consciousness. Importantly, from the point of view of the present discussion, "at" gives a *width* to the present that far exceeds any notional mathematical instant or even the so-called "specious present".[17]

Which is a rather roundabout way of explaining why I highlighted the phrase *"human beings are physical systems"* in the passage from Steven Savitt cited above. This combines a banal truth with an important untruth. Of course, we are physical objects at one level – that is what the peasant's clock exploits: we cast shadows just as do rocks and trees. But at the level at which we record time, and assign event E to time t_1 and, even more, at which we experience a given moment as the present, as belonging to a Common Now, we are more than physical systems. Savitt asserts that "we are able to discern no particular set of simultaneous events as constituting the now or the present".[18] It is *physics* that is unable to discern such sets of simultaneous events. There is no "present" in physical systems. Since we *do* distinguish "now" from all the other moments in time, the assumption that we are (just) "physical systems" must be rejected.[19]

Einstein's initial embrace of Mach's principle that there is no reality beyond that which can be observed, and time is only (frame-dependent) measured time, led entirely predictably to the conclusion that, in the absence of actual or potential experience, nothing happens at a particular time. But if event E does not happen at any particular time, there is an important sense in which it doesn't happen at all. Universal non-happening is the unsurprising consequence of seeing the universe as a 4-dimensional spatio-temporal block, viewed from no-one's viewpoint. Hence the famous claim by the mathematical physicist Herman Weyl: "The objective world simply *is*, it does not *happen*. Only to the gaze of my consciousness, crawling upward along the lifeline of my body, does a section of this world come to life as a fleeting image in space which continually changes in time".[20]

It will not have escaped your attention that the "crawling" of (someone's) consciousness along the lifeline of (someone's) body sounds like a happening – a process if not an event, which miraculously escapes the general veto on processes or events occurring at definite times.[21] Be that as it may, Weyl's frozen world is deeply reminiscent of the unchanging block universe of Parmenides. Indeed, Einstein accepted the title of "The Parmenidean" from Karl Popper.[22] Such are the ultimate unhappy consequences of denying that, in the absence of a frame of reference erected and inhabited by an observer or observers, there is no definite time at which events occur nor any definite temporal relationship between them. A universe without such relationships is essentially a tenseless, indeed timeless, mathematical structure in which successive events are simultaneous with and before and after one another. It can be unfrozen, it appears, only by the insertion of a conscious subject who clearly does not and cannot belong to the physical world, and certainly not the physical world as seen through the eyes of physics.

In conclusion, if the world according to physics were the true story of the sum total of everything, there would be no physics. The notion of observers as "complex physical systems" overlooks their essential nature, that distances them from the rest of the universe. They would not have the capacity to turn sources of periodic events occurring at equal time intervals into clocks or marked pieces of wood into measuring rods. There could be no more powerful testimony to the reality of that distance between human observers and the physical world than the existence and activity of a certain Herr Einstein developing his special theory of relativity in 1905. Mathematical space-time is not real space and time, the space where things happen, where action takes place, where our individual and collective destiny is forged.

The absence of clocks and other measuring devices in the fundamental laws of the physical world, and of "at" in the material world of space–time, is a surface manifestation of something we shall examine in more detail in the final chapter: the impossibility of understanding the place of the subject in the world described by natural science.

The flowering of "at"

You may think that we have drifted a long way from our topic: the distinctive nature of human being. The exploration of "at t", however, is a way of highlighting the profound distance between ourselves and our organic, indeed our physical, basis. To take this exploration a little closer to the task of developing a philosophical basis for humanism, let us observe the flowering of the seed that is "at", through the joining of attention, into the clock and calendrical time that transcends the experiential order of autobiographical time and thereby orchestrates our everyday lives and allows them to be entirely different from those of all other animals.

We touched on the "sideways" expansion of "at" when we envisaged how, for example, "at noon" would be located in, and connected with, forenoon and afternoon. Any given moment is located in an expanded framework within which its "at" finds its place; it is both located and dis-located. To be consciously "at" a time is to be beyond that time, just as to be looking out of a window is to be outside the room one is in. "At" allows the indefinite expansion of "now" to "today", or even larger stretches of time centred on "now" such as "nowadays" or "this week" or "this year". These informal extensions, tethered in the first instance to natural phenomena, such as sunset, prefiguring the invisible sunrise on the far side of darkness, lay down the foundation for more formal structuring of past and future: clock and calendrical time. The latter has no intrinsic limits, particular when humans join attention in the boundless community of minds, and generations share their consciousness in a collective history, a shared chronicle, ultimately relayed through speech and writing.[23] The "at" of "at t" is distant from the durationless instant of the physicist, the temporal *punctum* fused with an equally punctate item of space in a space-time point.

It is almost equally distant from the so-called "specious present" talked of by psychologists, who imagine that the present is defined by or confined to a narrow band of experience, centred at a point in time. This image of a narrowly constricted consciousness does no justice to the reality of the human present. My present moment, as I sit here typing, is charged with the past, indeed many pasts, and reaches towards the future, indeed many futures. The presence of the past is implicit in the continuous unfolding sense I make of what is happening "now", being necessary even for me to recognize what is around me and what I am doing. Yes, there is a sense in which I am in this moment; but I am also in the morning, in 2019, in my seventies. In addition, the presence of the past is an explicit resource I draw upon to guide my agency. The presence of the future is also implicit in the sense of the continuation and ongoingness of what is presently happening and I am doing and explicit in the things I anticipate and what I wish to achieve. It is publicly visible in our cooperative activity directed towards specific goals. While the (rich, complex) past and future are accessed through episodic memories and the idea of particular goals, the crucial development is that remembered experiences, anticipated events, commitments, plans, and so on, are often located in public clock, calendar, and historical time. This form of time is an essential vessel for the collective consciousness and the shared identity of communities.

To conclude, material events – including those that constitute the life of our organism – do not occur *at* the time of their occurrence in the absence of a conscious subject to fasten them to their times. The "at" distinguishes the event from its time of occurrence in order to connect the two explicitly and it is the key to the expansion of time consciousness from a putative specious present to a tensed awareness of an indefinite past and future and a more formal clock and calendrical time. The latter in turn feeds back into our tensed awareness, extending them into something collectively curated as "our past" or "history" and "our future" or "destiny". As a consequence, when we are born, we enter "A web of human relationships which is ... woven by the deeds and words of innumerable persons, by the living as well as the dead".[24]

A shared history and collective future is a long way down the track but that track is opened up by "at". Without "at", there is no temporal tagging of events, no explicit order, no gathering up of aspects of becoming into measured duration. "At" locates events outside of themselves allowing them to be connected together as sequences, and at the same time to be separated as elements of sequences. It opens up time from notional mathematical instants in which every state or phase of the universe is identified with itself. It allows time itself to be taken a moment, an hour, a day, a week, or a year at a time. Statements of timeless fact can represent, or re-present, the contents of one time at another time. This also provides, as we shall discuss in Chapter 6, an important part of those conditions that make possible the many-layered, many-stranded, multi-thematic ongoingness of agency.[25]

Human futures, animal futures

I have done scant justice to the richness of the "now" and to the human futures and pasts that nourish and inflate it beyond putative "present moments", borrowing temporal depth from either side of a notional, extensionless mathematical instant, for which there is no "at". I hope, however, I have said enough to highlight what is distinctive about human time when compared with time as it figures in the physical sciences. The top and bottom of it is that the time of the embodied subject is not the time of the material of the human body.

We need, however, to do a bit more work if we are fully to characterize the extent to which our relationship to time is a source of our fundamental difference from other living creatures, and the basis of our genuine, and otherwise inexplicable, individual agency and the shared agency of communal life. An essential step will be to return to something we have already flagged up as central to our distinctively human nature: the "full-blown" intentionality identified and discussed in the previous two chapters as being unique to, or at least uniquely developed, in humans. Such intentionality is manifest in the "at" of "at time t".

To locate an event in time, as opposed merely to experiencing it unfolding in an implicit present moment, requires that the event should be identified as lying beyond, as being more than, the experiences that give access to it. Appreciating the independent reality of what is "there" as "out there", and "what is happening" as "what is happening out there", as "other", complements the subject's developed sense of his or her subjectivity. The intentionality we share with innumerable others in the great conversation of society extends "at" – our temporal location – indefinitely until what is happening at any given moment potentially takes its place in a history belonging to groups, cultures, and nations. The temporal forest growing out of the seed of "at" makes it possible for us to talk of, and plan for, personal futures often connected with the collective futures of our fellows, and to draw on the private pasts of individual experience, itself potentially located in a collective past. Our individual and joint foresight is rooted in mind-sharing, world-sharing, and life-sharing.

Some biologists have argued that non-human animals also have a developed sense of the future – to which they can travel mentally. In addition, it is claimed, they have a sense of a past, based on episodic, personal memories, a past that is more than its implicit presence in altered responsiveness such as is seen in conditioning. Let us examine the claims for mental[26] time travel to the future seen in relatively humble creatures such as corvids.

It will be recalled from Chapter 2 that corvids (members of the crow family that include ravens, jays and magpies) hide food for later consumption – so-called "caching". Research by Cambridge University ethologist Nicola Clayton[27] has investigated the tactics used by these birds to protect their caches of hidden food from theft. She and her team observed that the birds would hide food differently if they were aware of having been observed by others. From this they drew the conclusion that corvids had a sense of a future – the future possibility of pilfering by other birds. Other experiments investigated another aspect of apparent future-orientation: the seeming capacity of jays to anticipate their own needs. In one experiment, satiated crows, confined to certain rooms, would preferentially store food in the rooms where they had not previously been given food. This would seem to suggest that, notwithstanding their present satiation, they could envisage their own future hunger – a future state of themselves – and, in addition, the potential lack of wherewithal to meet it in those rooms where, from their previous experience, food would not be available. Great care was taken to ensure that this behaviour could not be explained merely by associative learning.

The sense of a specific, individual future is the mirror image of the sense of a specific, individual past. Clayton has carried out ingenious experiments which, she claims, demonstrate that jays remember what they cached, where they cached it, when they cached it – in short that they have episodic memories of past actions. Suddendorf, who is critical of Clayton's conclusions on episodic memory, summarizes her findings as follows:

> [Birds] adjust their search differently for cached worms, which rot quickly, and peanuts, which keep fresh longer, depending on how long ago they stored them. They do not bother searching for worms if they had been stored a long time ago because they would be rotten. Jays show this search pattern even when there are no cues, such as smell, to guide them. The researchers conclude that the birds have memory for the past occasion on which they stored these foods.[28]

This is striking: if the jays are prevented from recovering their caches long enough, they will recover only non-perishable items such as peanuts and not the usually more favoured but perishable items such as mealworms.

Suddendorf's killjoy explanation of Clayton's findings (with which this killjoy concurs) is that the jays can know what food is where and whether it is past its sell-by date without having to remember the episode of caching it. The birds may learn from experience that worms are not worth searching for once the memory of their location (not the experience of caching them) has weakened beyond a certain point, while with nuts this does not apply. This could all be driven without conscious recall of an act performed by themselves. Their what-when-where memory of the action is not suffused by a sense of "who".

There are other reasons for preferring a killjoy to a romantic interpretation of what is going on in corvids' minds and for thinking that they are "stuck in time" rather than (to use Clayton's lovely term) "chronesthetic creatures".[29] For example, young children do not pass tests, similar to those passed by the corvids, until they are over four years of age in the case of social cognition and over eight years in the case of physical cognition. This should raise doubts about what the tests actually test and ring alarm bells over the generous interpretation of the mental faculties behind the corvids' behaviour.[30] Surely, we cannot believe that corvids are more advanced mental time travellers than young children. After all, eight-year olds, and indeed four-year olds, are able to look forward to their birthday and Christmas many days hence and can dread events that might happen the following day or next week. And eight-year olds are capable of sharing episodic memories. They are better, not worse, than bird-brained. As a fellow killjoy has said of an evolutionarily more recent species: "The squirrel that stashes a nut in my yard 'knows' about the future in approximately the same way that a falling rock 'knows' about the laws of gravity".[31] This may seem a little harsh but Wittgenstein surely hit the nail on the head when he noted that "a dog is afraid his master will beat him; but not, he is afraid his master will beat him tomorrow".[32]

It may be appropriate to be agnostic about the reality of episodic memories nourishing future-orientation in jays. The most telling fact is that there is no other evidence that it is a general faculty. Its manifestations do not seem to extend much beyond cache-protection tactics ("By their fruit shall ye know them"). As Suddendorf points out "the future directed comprehension [of scrub jays] seems limited to a particular type of problem and shows none of the open-ended flexibility evident in humans".[33]

Before granting corvids human-like temporal depth, we should therefore require evidence that such behaviour is part of a nexus of behaviours anchored in a many-layered future. While corvids may have "where-what-when" memories of the circumstances of caching that influence plans for feeding to come, there is no evidence of "at" a time (future, past, or present) in the corvid's time sense. In sharp contrast to the restricted future of corvids tied to a particular function, the human future is boundless and open. What is more, it is explicitly shared ("our" and "their" future as well as "my" future). That our mental time travel is frequently joint is evident in the making and keeping of appointments, not to speak of planning, and reminiscing. Moreover, as we shall see, at-time is extended and structured through "that" – the second of our two key words – into a realm woven out of, and densely populated with, facts, and ordered by clocks and calendars. It is essential to the very architecture of human world. Human life is dominated by a personal or shared (we-personal) future which we work, singly or collectively to bring about, to secure, or to protect. The seemingly banal agreement to "see you with Bill and Jean at 6 next Wednesday" draws on a mode of consciousness that is not only remote from nature but also from that of all other living creatures.

It is worth developing this point. We are creatures who live by appointments. The appointment is the key to cooperative activity in complex, ordered communities; it is a primordial underpinning of a contractual society. Appointment-regulated activity is remote from the instinct-driven or reactive behaviour typical of animals. Appointments are often voluntary. More importantly, they are "bespoke" in several respects: they involve a singular "I" and a singular "you" or an "I" and a "they" and unique intersections in the stories of two or more lives; they have a singular, explicit purpose (even though that purpose can be described in general terms); they involve commitment; finally, unlike, say, instinctive or reactive behaviour with proximate triggers, they have to be remembered. They may be extremely complex as when we "turn up" to a day's work, attend a conference, or go to a sporting event. Our lives are coordinated, so that we can work collaboratively to meet our primary and secondary needs and wants, directly and indirectly, by converging on a pre-determined "at" in a clocked or calendrical landscape of "that" (*vide infra*). We can even make an appointment with our own consciousness as when we set an alarm clock to wake us in the morning. Our being in and out of time is also revealed through our many modes of waiting. And, finally, appointments – and associated disappointments – are manifestations of something fundamental to the moral fibre of society. The blame and guilt that follows from breaches of agreements are a marker of, and highlight, our temporal depth, and this is one of the many ways that our mode of being in and out of time provides a backbone to our sense of self.[34]

THE THATOSPHERE

The realm of facts

Our mode of being out of physical time is also reflected in the "that" relationship which we humans have to what is happening around and within us.

"That" creates the building bricks of the human world and is woven out of trillions of episodes of shared intentionality and joined attention.[35] Such sharing and joining of consciousness is not merely episodic but is a standing condition, baked into the boundless artefactscape – infrastructure, built environment, amenities – populated with countless tools, gadgets, consumables, institutions, in which we pass so much of our lives.

For the present, I want to keep it simple so that the overall point about the thatosphere is not lost. To this end, I will focus on what we might call "propositional awareness". It is seen most straightforwardly in what is asserted in declarative sentences of the general form "[That] X is the case", or "[That] X is not the case" or "[That] X might be/or might not be the case". Centre stage will be facts; and I hope to persuade you that there is nothing matter of fact about facts, about factual truths that are supervenient on what-is. They are a dazzling reminder of the strange super-fact that Being or the Universe, or the Whatever, is *given* to us, that this givenness depends on us to take it, and that we shape that givenness into networks of information.

At this point philosophers among my readers might expect me to do a little work in teasing out the relationships between propositions, sentences, thoughts, knowns, facts, statements, speech acts, truths, and other items that have figured so largely in analytical philosophy. I have tried to do this on previous occasions and, like many before me, have failed to produce a coherent account of those relationships. I am not inclined to try again because (with apologies to Kant for misusing his aphorism) I have concluded that "out of the crooked timber of human discourse no straight thing was ever made".[36] This may make many philosophers cry out in exasperation. Surely, they may say, if philosophy is anything it is about getting straight the geography of the concepts in which we talk about items such as "propositions" and so on. The experience of 100 years in which this was a central preoccupation of analytical philosophy has only confirmed that straightening the crooked timber of human discourse is a forlorn hope. At any rate, the important thing is not how these terms divide the territory between them but that they are *all* fully accredited denizens of the thatosphere. In their different ways they give us an entrée into the area of our present interest. What is common to them all – and what is central to our present concern – is a non-physical *distance* marked by the intentionality of "that", a mode of full-blown intentionality most easily illustrated by factual statements.

Consider the simple assertion "[that] X is the case". How does this relate to the claim about our being "outside" of time? Very simple: facts, unlike experiences or material happenings, are not occurrent events located in time. The Battle of Hastings lasted for a few hours in 1066; but *the fact that* it lasted for a few hours and that it took place in 1066 is true for all time. There is a distance between what is said about events taking place in the physical world and the physical world in which those events took place. Once true, facts are always true. Factual assertions, for all that they take place at a particular time, and pass away in the sense of being completed, therefore have a splinter of eternity at their heart. It was this, perhaps, that motivated Plato's rather elevated conception of the nature of the universals used in discourse as unchanging Forms or Ideas located in a (Platonic) heaven. Facts are cryogenically preserved reality. The transition from seeing an event to asserting that an event has taken place removes the dynamism, the transience, out of change.

This characteristic of facts tends to be overlooked. It is easy to see why: the tokens in which they are expressed, spoken or written sentences, are transient puffs of air or fading ink. When I assert that the Battle of Hastings took place in 1066, the assertion itself takes place at (say) 12 noon on a particular day in 2018 and is over and done with. The fact, however, remains. But even if we do not confuse assertions with the facts they assert, there may be another reason for missing the splinter of eternity: we may conflate the eternal nature of facts with the transience of the states of affairs they refer to.[37] The important point is that we can say of any event E that it happened at time t but we cannot say of the *fact that* E happened that it happened at t or indeed any time. The Battle of Hastings took place in 1066 but *the fact that it took place* did not take place in 1066 or any other time. That is why the assertions to the effect that the battle happened can be asserted at any time, with no detriment to the truth of the assertion. My saying in 1067 that the Battle of Hastings took place in 1066 is no more or less true than my making this statement in 2019. The "that" lifts the utterance out of time, even though, as a physical occurrence, the token assertion to the effect *that* it happened must itself happen at a particular time and have a certain duration. The utterance is outside that of which it speaks and picks out an event or state of affairs thereby making it into its own truth-maker – that which makes it true. This is the deep truth behind Jerry Fodor's observation, quoted in Chapter 2, that "the semantic proves permanently recalcitrant to integration in the natural order".[38] The thatosphere, to which facts belong, lies outside of the natural world and the biosphere, beyond the flesh, and out of the reach of incessant becoming. The facts are not "on the ground" – or in the trees, in the heads of chimps, or in the neural discharges of human brains. Factual knowledge is unique to humans: there is only one animal in The Knower's Ark.

It is easy to see why facts are an embarrassment to those who would wish to naturalize human knowledge. There have been many attempts to deal with this. One of the best-known is that of Quine who acknowledges the central role played by discourse in the passage "from stimulus to science" (to echo the title of his final book).[39] He wants, however, to naturalize discourse. He claims that there is a continuity between being in the receipt of stimuli that trigger what he calls "neural intake" and the eventual development, via facts generated by observations, of natural science at the highest level. This is important to his overall project of reinserting human discourse, and hence humanity, into the natural world. He does not shrink from bold assertions: "This human subject is accorded a certain … input – certain patterns of irradiation in certain frequencies, for instance – and in the fulness of time the subject delivers as output a description of the three-dimensional external world and its history".[40]

Quine's case that we are, as it were stung or tickled into science, depends on collapsing the gap – marked by "that" – between human discourse and the realm of natural stuffs and forces. He argues that the ground floor, and the platform of discourse, and the starting point of our acquisition of knowledge, is "the observation sentence" which (so he believes) is directly tied to the stimulation of sensory nerves. There is therefore an uninterrupted causal pathway going from an event or state of affairs occurring in the natural world, to a human experience, thence to an utterance of a sentence that reports the experience, and sends it onwards to a recipient of the information about the experience, who has a further sensory experience that in some sense represents the state of affairs that triggered the utterance in the speaker. This pathway belongs entirely to the material world: "knowledge, mind and meaning are part of the same world that they have to do with, and that they are to be studied in the same empirical spirit that animates natural science".[41]

The most obvious problem with this claim is something we noted in the last chapter with respect to our bodies: the facts that make up knowledge, including knowledge of my own body, are remote from sense experience and from any material (e.g. neural) interaction between the body and its material environment. This remoteness is betrayed by the meta-fact that facts are not audible or visible; they have no smell or taste. Indeed, they do not even have primary qualities such as size and shape. In entering the realm of knowledge, we take leave of our senses. Any sensory features of sentences that convey knowledge are irrelevant; indeed, they may be a distraction. The more flavourless the sentence, the more its content shines through: statements are most likely to be heard as mere sounds when they are not understood, when they make no sense. This point is particularly clear in the case of thought, when the tone or loudness of the voice in which those of us who hear our thoughts hear them is quite irrelevant. The referent of thoughts is not determined by any experienced property of them – something that is a radical consequence of the so-called arbitrariness of linguistic signs: their sound is not shaped by that to which they refer. There is nothing apple-like about the word "apple". More generally, their phenomenal qualities are contaminants that have to be looked through or past.

The other side of the gap between experiences and facts is that (for example) no cognitive work is required for me to feel pain; but to know that what I am feeling is called pain, or that it may be due to some condition, and that it occurred in a structure called a cartilage, does require such work.

And that is just for a start. What is missing from Quine's system is the "that" which gives facts their timelessness. That is why there are no such things as *brute* facts, the kinds of facts that are, as it were, secreted by nature herself or are the direct effect of material causes. The correlative of this is that brutes do not have access to, or deal in, facts.[42] The "thatter" we access at time t is about the world beyond, or embedded in, time t. To this extent the fact is uncoupled from the world at time t. The thatosphere is woven out of facts curated by the sum of us and which, for each of us at any given time, is largely absent. While in part this world may be delivered to us by our own past or present experience, it reaches us much more commonly through the testimony of others.

Quine, as we have seen, regards speakers as being as it were stung into speech. The meaning of what they say is, he argues, mechanically triggered by material events that count as stimuli. This sustains the naturalistic idea of a continuous causal chain between the organism and thatter. It will be evident from our discussion in Chapter 2 that it collapses many layers of intentionality: the first-order intentionality of experience; the second-order intentionality of memory (of which more presently); and the higher-order intentionality of meant, and understood, meaning. It also overlooks the most obvious features of ordinary discourse. The thatosphere feeds the chattersphere, in which we exchange commonplaces, drawing on our vast hoard of things, relevant or irrelevant, we might want to say. What we actually say on a particular occasion may be influenced by conventions but is not dictated, even less physically caused, by them. The convention may require us to say something but not necessarily to say something in particular. Indeed, we may rack our brains for things to say. Or we may think twice before saying anything. While conversation may serve various practical purposes, these purposes do not closely prescribe its contents. In Chapter 2, I unpacked some of the complex modes of self-consciousness and decision-making behind whether and how we decide to deploy the ultimate commonplace: "Good morning". The deeper point is this. When we share intelligence with others, we *intend* the things we say. We intend to share the states of affairs our utterances are about, to deposit them in the minds of our interlocutors. Such intentions are prompted by an idea of a future rather than being, as it were, pushed from behind.

Discourse, in short, is not in the slightest bit like a response to a stimulus, a collection of links in a continuous causal chain connecting experience with verbal behaviour and verbal behaviour with the replication of that experience in another person. Even leaving aside the inevitable failure of any theory that relies on translating intentionality into causal relationships, there are many other deficiencies with Quine's story. Mere stimuli know nothing of the typical *context* of speech, the necessary framework of communication. The latter include, at the very least, appreciation of the fact that I know that my intended recipient knows, or at least assumes, that the sounds I am producing have meant meanings intended for her consumption. Additionally, I must know, or assume, that successful reception of my meaning will depend on the recipient's having a sense of the context of my utterance. This will give her clues as to what I mean: there is an intimate interweaving of what I am telling you and why I am telling it to you. Both draw deeply on the thatosphere. Quine's "observation sentences" are not mere ejaculations in response to external triggers provided by what is observed. There is a distance between my crying out when I step on a thorn and my explaining to you what it is that which has caused me to cry out; and there is the huge gap between an infant howling with hunger and a conversation between the anxious mother of the baby and the district nursing about the crying.

Any doubt on the question of whether utterances are causally wired into material occasions can be dispelled by noting how often we *seek out* our interlocuters. We "pop" round to tell someone something; and that something is typically not an ongoing stimulus or presence but an event or process or state of affairs pickled as a fact or possible fact. There is, in short, a great (nonnatural) space between external events and our reports of or comments on them, a space that is not crossed by causal chains subservient to the laws of nature. Meaning something we say is an action, not a reaction: it is an intended intentionality. Meant meaning lies at the heart of our cognitive expansion from a world defined by sense experience to one revealed through factual knowledge communicated by and to others – knowledge that in turn creates the basis for further interruptions to and relays for our senses.

Quine at least accepts that our knowledge of the world is not built up stimulus by stimulus, sentence by sentence. There is "a holism of meaning" and the relations between sentences and stimulation of nerve endings is mediated by many other sentences. This does nothing, however, to mitigate his Original Sin: that of collapsing the distance between discourse and that which is spoken of, between the knower and the known, and between nature and the science that discovers and describes its laws. He squashes "That" flat. The thatosphere, the community of knowers including scientists, is downgraded into a nexus of organisms wired into the world and into each other, rather like ants in a colony. By this means, we lose the space from which we view, we are able to *face*, the natural and human world.

Facts, to reiterate, are not like physical events, or processes, that take place at a particular time, which occupy and/or affect a certain quantity of space, and are causally wired into material events and processes. To see their true nature, we need to recognize that they are further developments of intentionality. The counter-causal direction of intentionality is transformed into the extra-causal direction of human awareness of facts. Facts, not being material items located in space or in time, do not carry a Quinean energy of impingement with them, though the tokens in which they are expressed might. While the present state of England may be at least in part due to the long-term effects of the Battle of Hastings, the fact that a battle took place at Hastings in 1066 does not have that kind of causal effect. The backward glance of memory is in the counter-causal direction and the fact on which it is directed does not belong to the causal nexus of which the battle was a part – except in the trivial sense that the occurrence of the battle may have prompted people to believe that there was such a battle and to assert that it took place. While factual knowledge is ultimately *warranted* by experience, it nevertheless belongs to a temporal order outside that which is directly revealed by sense experience. It is not part of the causal nexus that connects the natural world. Knowledge is a key element of that "human outside" from which we can act on the material world as more or less free agents.

The timelessness of facts enables us to time travel in a shared way that goes beyond the time travel of individual episodic memory. You and I can talk about the Battle of Hastings, about what happened yesterday, about what is planned for tomorrow, and about the future of our planet. The landscape of facts is a cognitive commons available to a limitless plurality of agents, being intrinsically remote from the appetites, and desires of individual embodied subjects, though they may indirectly serve them. Individual facts have a potentially boundless community.

Timeless facts have an important role in expanding the triptych of tensed time. We have already noted that the present, the future, and the past cannot be accommodated in physics. They are nonetheless real – as my guilt over what I did yesterday and our shared plans for tomorrow make clear. If physics were the whole story of everything, then the future and the past would not be possible even as illusions. Nor could we invent those temporal realms because, if we were physical objects, we would not have the wherewithal to do so. More to our present point is the transformation of the reality we share with others by populating the past and future with a nexus of facts.

Weaving the thatosphere

Quine's idea of a straight-line journey from tickled up sensory endings to the cognitive monument that is science goes off the rails even before we get to language, because it overlooks the space necessary for truth to be able to supervene on being – or in the case of fictional objects, non-being. This requires the distance of "aboutness". What is more, the role of intentionality in the generation of facts – or the transformation of happenings into "*that* such-and-such happened" – is supplemented by the testimony of others. Thus, we arrive back at something central to humanity: the joining of attention, which as we noted in Chapter 2, is not developed in non-human animals to anything like the extent it is in humans.

Let us revisit one of the earliest examples of shared intentionality (in child development, and possibly in the development of humanity): declarative pointing which enables us to share "noticings" with another, without necessarily articulating them.[43] Linguists, as we noted, distinguish declarative from imperative pointing. Imperative pointing – effectively "Gimme!" – is seen in some primates in captivity. Declarative pointing – the sharing of experience often just for its own sake – is a human universal and not seen in other species. Children from about a year onwards are incessantly pointing out things to anyone who will pay attention, most notably their parents. Their frantic need to share what they have seen is delighting and fatiguing in equal proportion. Declarative pointing wishes to *give* unlike imperative pointing that wishes to take or to be given.[44] A crucial bridge to speech, it stands on a platform of many prior faculties. Awareness that others occupy a different viewpoint from myself, so that they may be unaware of something of which I am aware, is central. The employment of one's finger, hand, or arm, as a pointer presupposes an external stance on one's body such that one is able to exploit its visibility to others as a device for picking out something one wants another to attend to.

The layers of intentionality in declarative pointing are worth teasing out. Supposing a small child points a cat out to you. There is the intentionality of her seeing the cat, more specifically seeing it as an object in the weighty sense: its having an existence in itself as the condition of its public availability and the child's presupposition that it is thus available to you. Next, it underlines the child's intentional relation to the cat by making visible her awareness of it. Her outstretched arm is a carnal echo of her outward gaze. In addition, she is intentionally aware that I have an intentional consciousness of her arm, and, more broadly, a consciousness that has a viewpoint and contents different from mine. Specifically, while the child surmises that I can see her arm, she also thinks that I have not seen, or at least not noticed, the cat. She has, in short, a second-order intentional awareness of my awareness and its limitations. Through her gesture she aims to redirect my awareness so that she can share the intentional object – the cat – with me. All of these faculties are developed, if inchoately, before the acquisition of fluent speech, though they are presupposed in speech. Speech makes many other demands; for example, understanding the relationship between sounds and objects so that the former can mean or refer to the latter.

The relevance of pointing to our concern with the thatosphere is not merely that it is proto-linguistic, a "See that!" which lies on the threshold of "thatter", of shared "That X is [the case]". It is intermediate between the direct intentionality of perception and the complexly mediated intentionality of speech and thoughts. In addition, it is another mode of reaching across the space of "that": the object of joined attention has been partially lifted from where it is located by perception to a shared space and time. This is the first step on the road to the expansion of the thatosphere. The latter is without obvious limits and is populated by any number and many kinds of objects of knowledge: things present and absent, particular and general, past or present, real or imaginary.[45]

Pointing, that explicitly singles out an extra-corporeal item for the sake of another, can be seen as an important step in the long journey of transcendence into a common human world. This corporeal gesture highlights the connection between on the one hand the genesis of the thatosphere and on the other the complex relationships we have to our bodies arising out of our status as embodied subjects who discover themselves as objects in a world sustained by a community of minds. Unpacking what is involved in the seemingly very basic gesture of pointing is sufficient to expose the fundamental error – one is tempted to say that it is assiduously point-missing – of Quine's naturalization of meaning and his endeavour to reinsert the thatosphere into the realm of mechanical causes, forces and materials that physics makes sense of.

It is interesting to reflect on Quine's commitment to the causal theory of perception and knowledge given that it gets him into so much trouble. It will be recalled that he regards all objects as "theoretical": "Even our most primordial objects, bodies, are already theoretical".[46] Objects, he says, are "posits" – things that we posit. While to say this is not to "patronize" them (to use Quine's own witty phrase), it is clear that they are not entirely authenticated or underwritten by direct or indirect causal influences they have on our nervous systems. The subject who is (actively) positing objects cannot at the same time be a passive recipient of causal influences arising from objects that exist independently of perception and the mind.[47] This push-back, according to which objects are constructs, would breach the causal continuum. It is a huge concession. It puts into question Quine's often-stated belief that the very process of building physical theories can be investigated in terms of the items and forces invoked by those theories, in short by *physical* items and forces. By the same token it undermines the claim that epistemology is part of natural science, and the philosophy of physics will explain physics by applying physics.[48]

The salient point for our present concerns is this: the thatosphere cannot be assimilated into the biosphere and ultimately the geosphere. The failure to rehouse the thatosphere in the material world – even at the rather basic level of objects that have a public existence available to a multiplicity of perceivers and agents – is clearly not for the want of Quinean effort. The *significance* of utterances cannot be gathered into the physical world of the sounds of sculptured, exhaled air, that are indeed subject to the laws of physical nature. As physical events, they are not even "noises", since sound is a secondary quality. The meaning of factual statements belongs to the thatosphere whose elements as we have seen have a splinter of eternity at their heart which resists capitulation to the "done and dusted" of events that give way to their effects.

This observation is fatal for the causal theory of knowledge; for the idea that knowledge is merely an effect of the known (understood as sources of energy) on the body (or brain) of the knower and our cognitive functions are merely a way of wiring us more efficiently into the biomaterial world. On the contrary, our factual knowledge distances us from it, liberates us from the bumped-into realm of physical things, of the interactions between the organic body and material world. No amount of ingenuity can explain how, or demonstrate that, light energy generates our understanding of the physics of light by processes analogous (to borrow an example from Dennett) to that by which light is turned by leaves into sugar.[49] Energy exchanges between the body and extracorporeal reality – events, objects, and material states of affairs – do not change themselves into truth-makers (even less falsity-makers) of the claim that they happened simply in virtue of happening or existing.[50] That which is does not spontaneously generate (the fact) *that* it is. There is nothing natural about the facts of nature or nature presented as facts.

Another sign that facts, the utterances that express them, and the knowledge or untruths that they convey, do not belong to the physical world of impingements on sense endings is captured in a phrase that Quine himself used to illustrate the holism according to which little of our knowledge is directly answerable to sense experience. It is exposed to "the tribunal of experience" "corporately" and indirectly.[51] The sideways and every-which-ways connectivity of true beliefs is nothing like the connectivity of causal chains linking events occurring in material objects. The material world is not, for example, characterized by "If-then", "General principle-individual instance", etc., relationships that govern our judgement of the compatibility of beliefs.

There is no consistency or inconsistency in the material world: items are not side-by-side in this way. The universe is not a bag of (frozen) p's and not-p's.[52]

Perception can be a source of facts only if our conceptual faculties are already mobilized. Knowledge, elevated above individual experience, belongs to no-one. Its ownerless facts have no source tag, no personal context. They are fragments of standing collective intentionality. As is particularly clear in the case of written down facts, they are the frozen possibility of shared aware-ness. Appreciating the extent to which the web of beliefs (and the practices that both underpin, and are underpinned by, them) extends beyond individual minds (with their associated sensoria) to communities, cultures, and disci-plines, to cultural epochs and beyond, reveals how the gap between the causal network and the thatosphere grows limitlessly. This is the sense in which we are insulated by the thatosphere from the material world and offset from the biosphere.[53]

SUMMARIZING THOUGHTS

Our human being is incessant becoming: this is true both of the person and the body. Much of what is unique about ourselves as persons is our mode of being in, and out of, time, which is quite different from that of our bodies or indeed any material object. Our distinctive modes of being in time are captured by two key terms: "at" and "that". At a fundamental level, they are connected: they are both developments of the intentionality initially made explicit in the distance senses, most notably in the gaze that is a gaze "at" and sees the near reaches of "that". My body, by contrast, is not "at" the times it exists in the way that I am at those times. My kidneys, for example, are not in Wednesday, even less in a clock time situated in Wednesday or a Wednesday that is situated in calendar time. Nor is it "that" in the sense of being a clus-ter of true facts about the states it, or its surrounding world, is in. The same applies to the brain.

"At" and "that" act as the source of temporal schemata that are containers, such as "Wednesday", as well as that which is contained in those schemata – such as the facts about what happened on Wednesday. "At" and "that" interact. The at-related temporal schema becomes increasingly densely characterized as factual that-contents are ascribed to it; and an increasingly elaborated schema is able to house more contents. Since events are eternized through being artic-ulated as the referents of meaningful assertions, things that happened in dif-ferent nows can be side-by-side in a kind of space which encompasses "that which is", "that which was", or even (though problematically) "that which will be". The past and future are sown with happenings: past happenings that enjoy a posthumous existence in the acknowledged fact that they happened in the past; future happenings that have a pre-natal existence as the acknowledged possibility (for the most part counterfactual) that they might happen in the future. The now is consequently situated in a richer soil. Additionally, now can itself expand from (say) the specious present of psychology to the "today" or "nowadays" that we share. "That" permits the co-presence of facts whose truth-makers can be any distance apart (the current pain in my toe, the state of the country, the Battle of Hastings), and thereby widens "at" to a *landscape* of days and years, which form the sense-making background to our lives. And it is here that we find the complex relationships between our autobiographical sense of being extended in time – upheld by visits to events in our past – and the objective temporal addresses we give them.[54]

The uniquely developed human capacity for mental time travel[55] – and our ability to, for example, exercise our imagination, and populate the future with possibilities – is itself possible because in the thatosphere linear time and the fixed temporal order observed in the material world are not mandatory. The symbols that refer to individual events through general meaning allows an intersection of time and timelessness.[56] For this, and other reasons, human becoming, the successive moments of our lives, are fundamentally different from the becoming of our bodies. The unfolding of meaning, narrowly expressed in the passage from premise to conclusion, more broadly in progress towards a goal, is fundamentally different from the passage from cause to effect.

One final point. Intentionality has made yet another starring appearance. Although it has a well-established place in the philosophy of consciousness, of mind, and of language, its significance still has not been fully grasped. What we have explored in this chapter is yet another of the ways it opens up a widening gap between ourselves and nature, between human lives and the natural world. No wonder philosophers inclined to materialist or physicalist versions of naturalism hate intentionality so much – or at any rate do their level best to deny its importance or even its existence.[57]

CHAPTER 5

The elusive, inescapable self

The scene is now set for a discussion of what may be variously called the subject, the "I", the ego, the person, or the self. As if that were not sufficient as a source of confusion, there is a range of terms available for describing what is at issue – first-person being, personal identity, the self, and so on. Given that the scope of these words is individually contested, with edges that are at best fuzzy, it is hardly surprising that the relationship between them is somewhat confusing. I shall again refrain from attempting to straighten out "the crooked timber of human discourse". The self will be my main focus, or at least my term of choice, and while the concept seems nebulous this does not mean that its object is mist. I shall also look sideways at the rest of the cast of characters, notably "personal identity" which, due to the massive presence of the recently deceased Oxford philosopher Derek Parfit, has occupied centre stage.

Selfhood is central to our distinctive human nature, to our sense of the kinds of beings we are, and it is inseparable from the agency on which our claim to dignity rests. Trying to get a clear idea of the self is therefore essential to any endeavour to develop a truly humanist philosophical anthropology. This is particularly urgent in view of the fact that many philosophers and others deny or diminish the reality of the self.

In the last two chapters, we have reminded ourselves of certain fundamental, pervasive characteristics of the embodied human subject. The ways we are related to our own bodies, and our mode of being in time and relating to the thatosphere, are extraordinarily complex. They most certainly go deeper than any particular ideology, bourgeois or otherwise. It is these characteristics that will provide the starting place for our understanding of what it is to be a self.

But we first have to address the views of those who deny that there is such a thing.

AUTOCIDAL TENDENCIES IN PHILOSOPHY

The self as a fiction

The self seems to everyday observation to be inescapable. This is reflected in the familiar saying that wherever you travel you take yourself with you. Raymond Tallis is awaiting Raymond Tallis whatever destination he arrives at, having accompanied him all the way. He cannot entirely shed, though he may modify, his habits – of behaviour, of reaction, of thought – or his limitations – never mind his duties or the world's expectations of him. Nor can he escape his past or the demands of a future towards which he is orientated. And yet, when he looks for himself through the eyes of certain philosophers, he seems to dissolve in their gaze. The self shares the paradox of "Now" of appearing to be at once elusive and inescapable.

The *locus classicus* in western philosophy for the dissolution of the self is David Hume's *Treatise of Human Nature*. Hume found his self dissolving in his philosophical gaze even as he looked for it:

> There are some philosophers who imagine we are every moment intimately conscious of what we call our *self* … For my part, when I enter most intimately into what I call *myself*, I always stumble on some particular perception or other, of heat, or cold, light or shade, love or hatred, pain or pleasure. I can never catch *myself* at any time without a perception and can never observe but the perception.[1]

It should hardly amount to a shock to find that the self is not empirically discoverable, a distinct item of knowledge in which the knower and the known are the same. What is perhaps more shocking is his conclusion that the train of his perceptions was not united by identity: "[I]identity is nothing really belonging to these different perceptions, and uniting them together, but is merely a quality which we attribute to them, because of the union of their ideas [i.e. the ideas of them] in the imagination when we reflect upon them".[2] At any rate, we do not have an identity based on the experience that "we are every moment intimately conscious of what we call our *self*".[3]

The very fact of Hume making an argument against his being, or having, a self seems to be at odds with its conclusion. There is, or was, self-evidently much more to the peerless philosopher than a succession of perceptions. As for those perceptions, they appeared to be connected by more than mere temporal succession of, or even causal linkage. They had a common ownership that allowed the owner – one David Hume – to claim them as his own and, because of this, to be able to access them in a way that no one else could. There was, that is to say, more to David Hume than what he characterized as "a bundle or collection of different perceptions, which succeed each other with an inconceivable rapidity, and are in perpetual flux and movement".[4] If this were denied, how otherwise could we explain the *fiction* of the unitary or coherent self.[5] Or indeed, explain Hume's own notion of himself as a *bundle* or *collection* of different perceptions?[6] In virtue of what principle of connection were his different perceptions his, or at least ascribed to the same bundle or the same collection? Who or what bundled the bundle? If it is merely a matter of the imagination that they belong together, who or what is doing the imagining that unites them as belonging to the same (non-existent) self? My experiences are connected with one another in the way that they are not connected with the experiences you are having. As has often been pointed out, a succession of perceptions does not deliver even the perception of succession – not even the perception of a succession of perceptions. If each of a thousand people heard one of the thousand successive notes of, say, Beethoven's Fifth, there would be no-one experiencing the opening movement of the symphony.[7]

So, there must be something other than the components of the bundle in order for the self to be bundled together; something connecting the flux of perceptions with one another and with the genial Scotsman who reported his findings in a large, coherent treatise that he worked on for several years. His experiences could not belong to the series called David Hume's experiences without belonging to *someone* – to David Hume their implicit owner or subject. They could belong to each other only if in some sense they are co-owned, by a self to whom they are ascribed, who experiences them. We need this because the experiences do not even have shared spatial proximity as in the case of (say) the drops of moisture that all qualify as belonging to a single cloud.[8]

Of course, they do not need to be *marked* as mine by some particular characteristic because mineness is built into the fact that I am experiencing them. There is a pre-reflective continuing me-ness that permeates all our experiences. The "I" that "owns" the experiences does not have to justify or prove its ownership by the brand-marking them or by some other proof of common identity, that Hume seemed to be looking for. A sustained sense of I, of personal identity, pervading experience is a prior condition of my experiencing a coherent world. It could hardly be a conclusion that I arrive at as a result of finding, through introspection, a similarity between my successive mental states or finding causal relations between them. I may discover all sorts of things about myself – including that I am Raymond Tallis – but not that I am a self. To put this another way, I could no more discover that I am an "I" than I could discover that I am. The "I" adds nothing to what is already bundled into "am": "am" is the mode of being of "I". Human consciousness is self-conscious: it has what some philosophers call immanent reflexivity.[9] That I *am* what I am is the fundamental presupposition of my existence, the contingency that I embrace as the taken-for-granted me. We could turn Hume's observation on its head: the fact that individual perceptions do *not* bear the stamp of the individual whose perceptions they are – rather they are transparently given over to that which they are experiences of – is proof that there is more to the "self" than a succession of perceptions.

This, then, is Hume's basic mistake. He incorrectly expects that the self will be a distinct object of perception and concludes, from the fact that it cannot be perceived in, or as brand-marking, the flux of perceptions, that it is a fiction. If, however, the self had to be an object of experience or if "selfness" should be a perceptible quality, we would run into two problems. First, there would have to be some feature – a self-tint – present in all of an individual's perceptions. This would clearly get in the way of the transitivity or transparency of perceptions we discussed in Chapter 3. Secondly, there would be the threat of an infinite regression: the self that is aware of its perceptions would have itself to be perceived and that self-perception would also have to be perceived and so on. Against Hume, therefore, we must think of the self as presupposed in, an inescapable feature of, our life, not something added on.

But I am getting ahead of myself. Suffice it to note for the present that anyone inclined to defend Hume's deconstruction of the self might reflect on this: in the passage I have just quoted in which he reports his failure to find himself, there are six references to a person – *le bon David* himself. These references seem to be to someone who, to all appearances, transcends the perceptions of heat and cold, etc., that he experiences, not the least in virtue of being able to support his claim that they do not correspond an experience of a self. Denying the reality of a self as Hume does requires, it seems, quite a lot of self. It is difficult, surely, to maintain that there is no fully paid-up referent of "I" and hence there is no "I", when there is someone who was called David Hume, immiscible with others, and internally coherent, referring to himself.

Hume may have been aware of his arguing backfiring in this way when he admitted, with the honesty so characteristic of his writing, that all his hopes of a theory that will explain the illusion of the self, if the self is an illusion: "vanish when I come to explain the principles, that unite our successive perceptions in our thought or consciousness. I cannot discover any theory, which gives me satisfaction on this head ... For my part, I must plea the privilege of a sceptic, and confess, that this difficulty is too hard for my understanding".[10] David Hume, in short, could not explain how, if it was false belief, he came to believe that there was an entity called David Hume that or who wrote *A Treatise of Human Nature*, was a going concern from 1711–76, and acquired enduring fame for denying that he was more than a succession of ownerless experiences.

Even if we downsize the self from a soul or a Cartesian substance to, for example, "the principle of unity" connecting the experiences, thoughts, memories, capabilities, appetites, beliefs, and moral propensities of a person, it remains an elusive idea. No wonder otherwise quite sensible philosophers question its existence. Hence the strong autocidal tendency in contemporary philosophy.

One of the most prominent contemporary autocides is Daniel Dennett. This will come as no surprise to those who recall from Chapter 3 his assault on the reality of intentionality and basic mental contents such as qualia. His autocidal tendencies are linked with his naturalistic stance. Since selves don't fit into the physical world as described by natural science, they should be excluded from the world picture of any self-respecting thinker. Any substantive notion of the self must be a Cartesian hangover, or (for a vocal atheist) something worse – a sibling of the eternal soul or free-standing immaterial spirit haunting the biological machinery.[11]

The self causes particular problems for those such as Dennett who identify the conscious human subject with brain activity. Given that there is nothing in the distributed activity of the brain corresponding to anything as organized and coherent as a self, neuromaniacs conclude that it must be a construct to which nothing in-itself corresponds. It is like the notion of a centre of gravity: "A centre of gravity is not an atom or a subatomic particle or any other physical item in the world. It has no mass; it has no colour; it has no physical properties at all, except for spatio-temporal location ... It is a purely abstract object. It is, if you like, a theorist's fiction. It is not one of the real things in the universe in addition to the atoms".[12] The abstract idea of the centre of gravity of a rock is simply something that is useful in anticipating its behaviour under a wide variety of conditions. The self is even more ontologically dubious than the physical centre of gravity as, unlike the latter, it lacks spatio-temporal location. It is a fictional entity invoked to confer coherence upon all the things we say about ourselves and all that we internalize of what the world says about us.[13]

The ingenuity deployed by autocidal selves such as Daniel D. in pursuit of their goal of demonstrating their own non-existence is impressive. We should not dwell too long on his claim that his own existence as a self is mere *abstractum*, or a user illusion, but it is worth making a couple of points, similar to those we made in response to Hume's denial of the self.

Firstly, if what Dennett says is true, there is no-one to recount, even less to put together, the stories Dennett tells about his self; no "user" to house what he calls the "user illusion". After all, a rock's centre of gravity is not something it ascribes to itself but something we (drawing on the collective "we" of scientific discourses) ascribe to it. But my sense of being a self is a self-ascription. In short, if the self is a fiction, it is one which I – presumably a non-fictional I – propose and embrace. As Ulrich Meixner has expressed it "The fictional subject of experience is incoherent, since it involves the incoherent idea that I, for example, am an illusion of myself".[14]

Secondly, the kind of work that Dennett acknowledges is required to manufacture a self looks like the kind of work that only a self could carry out. He addresses this objection by invoking the analogy of an unconscious novel-writing machine called Gilbert which has had information fed into it and programmes for story writing. It begins its story with "Call me Gilbert", echoing the opening of Herman Melville's *Moby Dick*. It writes its own fictional autobiography but while the subject of the fiction is a self, the writer of the fiction is not: it is a selfless machine. That, he claims, is how we can have a fictional self created by something that is not a self. The analogy doesn't work: it is impossible for a device to generate a narrative of something that has unity at a time and over time – a narrative that is explicitly about itself – without the kind of self-consciousness that we ascribe to selves that are not mere fictions. Something else has to gather up the successive states of the machine. Gilbert's fictional self parasitizes the consciousness of readers who are real selves.[15]

The idea that the self is a fiction has generated an extensive sociological and psychological as well as philosophical literature that lies beyond the scope of our present concerns. It is worth, however, noting that there are some quarter-truths in the idea that personal identity is in part a narrative construct that can be woven out of stories that may or may not have a beginning, a middle, and an end, but at the very least gather up the "and then ... and then ..." of our hours and days into something more coherent. After all, the way we talk (or think) about ourselves can influence our sense of the kind of person we are – what we expect of ourselves, the way we judge, value, esteem ourselves. And, likewise, we can internalize others' judgements on us. The very process of making ourselves intelligible to ourselves involves stories, fragments, judgements using the language we share with others. We often encounter ourselves as the protagonists of stories about our lives, when we look back in gladness, sadness, joy, or regret, or look forward in hope, determination, or aspiration to become the actors of our ideals.

All of this, however, operates at a higher-order level and would not be possible without a prior enduring sense of one's self already being in place. The narratives must have a narrator at their heart; the woven tapestry must have a weaver. The idea that a persisting subject exists only by a narrative appropriation of different experiences over time is clearly circular. If I can tell a story to persuade myself that I am what I am, then I don't need to tell a story to make this true.[16] The point is that we cannot talk, even nag, ourselves into connected, sustained first-person being because the latter is presupposed in making sense of what we are: it is a prior condition of the different narratives converging on, or being anchored to, a single hero or heroine. An unspoken "I" has to glue together all the stories, and the spoken I, the subject of the sentences, is an indissoluble core that does not dissolve into those things that are predicated of her. And while it may be argued, with some validity, that it is others that talk us into first-person being, that we are born not only into someone's arms but also into everyone's discourse, the intuition that "I am this" (this person, this self) is not something that can be outsourced to others.[17] We cannot third-person talk ourselves, or be talked by others, into believing, even less having, first-person being.

The essential point is this: if the self really were a construct, you would have to have something like a self to do the work of construction, something like a self to forge and sustain a self through narratives, generated by one's self or internalized through others, or to have this as a fundamental lifelong project. It would take a lifelong self to fake a lifelong self.

According to the virtual self theory,[18] selves are virtual entities, lifelong hallucinations, generated by the brain. Nothing corresponds to these self-representations, just as nothing corresponds to the pink elephants seen by a person in the grip of an alcoholic psychosis. As Tom McClelland, a critic of this deconstruction of the self, has pointed out, "denying the existence of the self is hard to reconcile with accepting the existence of self-representations, for self-representations must surely have a bearer that can be appropriately described as the self".[19] It takes a self to experience a self so that self cannot be an hallucination. We cannot discover that we were fooled by ourselves into thinking we are selves.

An alternative view is to accept that, yes, the self that I resume when I wake up each morning is undeniably real – it is not an hallucination – but that "it is systematically misrepresented by us",[20] inasmuch as it does not look like anything that science can discover. As McClelland points out, "We should regard the bearer of our self-representation as the self, even if that entity diverges dramatically from the way we represent that self to be".[21] Misrepresentations of the self require as much self as correct representations of it. So the self is real, after all, but is not as it appears to us to be.

This is a compromise designed to appease those who feel obliged to challenge the way we think about ourselves because science (notably the neurosciences) cannot find anything corresponding to the self as usually conceived. This argument should cut no ice. The fact that objective science cannot detect the principle of subjectivity as expressed in the self is no more surprising than that we cannot hear light or taste thoughts or be literally dazzled by reading the words "blinding light". It is the very principle of objective, quantitative science to get the self out of the way, shedding the subjective dimension of experience, the perspectival givenness of consciousness. That is why the human subjects who made science possible are not visible to science. Einstein is nowhere in the general theory of relativity.

And the brain seems the wrong kind of entity to create the "user illusion" or the "hallucination" of the self. How would the brain – a material object – manage this? How would the scattered processes stitch themselves together into the illusion of being stitched together? And there is the further question as to how the brain, confined to its successive moments as material objects are, would be able to undertake mental time travel to its own future in order so to act as to care for itself.[22]

The very idea that I have been fundamentally wrong about the fact that there I am a self therefore seems implausible. I can of course be mistaken over empirical facts about myself – such as that I weigh so many kilograms or even that I am Raymond Tallis – but not about myself at a metaphysical level. Talk about "representation" and "misrepresentation" of the self also overlooks the fact that the self is *not* merely a passively experienced gift: it is something that is affirmed, actively shaped, sought for – and, of course, affirmed, shaped, and sought for by other selves. These are just some of the dimensions of the self as the enduring bearer of conscious experience over time, and we shall return to them.

The basic argument is that, if the self were constructed, it would require a self to construct it and a lifelong self to sustain it lifelong. This should give pause to those who defer to objective science to tell us about the nature of the self. If a brain cannot make a self, it presumably cannot make the hallucination or even the illusion of the self. How would such an entity arise in the material world of causally closed physicalism?[23]

Brain-shrinking the self

Relying on the brain sciences to tell us what we are leads to some enjoyably absurd consequences. Nick Chater's recent book *The Mind is Flat* is devoted to the notion that "mental depth" is an illusion: the surface is all that there is.[24] Indeed, mental breadth is also an illusion. "To believe that we have constructed a 'picture' of the visual world in our minds is to fall for the illusion of mental depth, hook, line, and sinker".[25] His idea is of the mind as something entirely "in-the-moment": it is pin-point.[26] If we disagree with this, it is because we are brain-washed by our brains: "almost everything we know about our minds is a hoax, played on us by our brains".[27] A hoax that Chater, despite presumably relying on his brain, has mysteriously unmasked. The grounds for this extraordinary claim are worth examining because they give us further insights into the neuromania discussed in Chapter 2.

For Chater, the most compelling evidence comes from our sensory experience. It seems to deliver a picture that is loaded into our mind as a coherent and unified whole. Experiments, however, show that it is "glimpsed, piece by piece, through a narrow window"[28] because our visual acuity is sharply concentrated on a minute area of the retina. You may feel that you are looking at a page of print but what you are seeing is delivered one word at a time, with everything else being ignored. The visual *field* – corresponding, for example, to a view of a room or a landscape or a crowd – is therefore an illusion. The feeling that we are simultaneously grasping a "whole" is the result of being fooled by our brain into thinking "that we 'see' the stable, rich, colourful world before us in a single visual gulp, whereas the truth is that our visual connection with the world is no more than a series of localized 'nibbles'".[29] What applies to perception, applies *a fortiori* to thought, feelings, to the exercise of our will, and to our sense of being unified or coherent selves. To conceive of our mind as more than fleeting fragments and to think of ourselves as having inner depths is to fall victim to a Grand Illusion. The impression that "we see pages full of words, roomfuls of people, scenes full of objects rich in colour and detail … is entirely mistaken".[30]

This conclusion is, of course, absurd.[31] The world *is* rich; so, to see a rich world is not to be the victim of any illusion. The seething vista of events and objects that is the moment-to-moment appearance of the world around us is real. I see a room or a landscape, as opposed to pin-pricks of sense data, because there *is* a room, a landscape, or a crowd to see, not a heap or succession of pin-pricks. If there is an illusion, it is a modest one about the processes underlying visual consciousness, not a grand one about the objects of consciousness. Or rather – since most of us are not up to speed with the latest research in the psychology and physiology of perception – an unawareness of those processes. If, however, we *were* aware of those processes as we looked around us, we would be blinded by distractions. At any rate, since as Jonathan Cohen points out, ordinary subjects "do not hold beliefs about visual representations, they do not hold false beliefs about visual representations".[32] The illusion would be an illusion only for those who believe that our visual experiences are realist pictures in the head, mirror images of our surroundings. That they are not mirror images is merely another nail in the coffin of the bankrupt representational theory of mind[33] that requires a succession of spectators to look at those pictures. Visual awareness is not the generation of an endless album of photographs imprinted on the substance of the mind.

The idea that perception is fragmentary and the experience of a rich visual field must be an illusion is therefore ill-founded; and the notion that the mind, or the self, lacks depth is even more daft, as the very existence of Nick Chater's own book proves. If his mind were a succession of moments, and there were nothing corresponding to enduring mental phenomena such as sustained intentions and beliefs, it is difficult to see how he could have been sufficiently "together" to write a book (which was presumably planned, researched, and written over several years) in support of these beliefs. Our coherence has its limits, of course, as some experiments show, but the very research necessary to demonstrate these limits itself requires a coherence within and between individuals (scientists) that (to put it mildly) far exceeds the showers of perceptual sequins to which Chater would reduce the mind. *The Mind is Flat* could not have been produced by a mind that is flat in the way that Chater says his mind is; by a series of wafer-thin temporal slices of a brain, given that as we discussed in the previous chapter, those slices would not be open to one another. The thesis he has about the mind could not be entertained by any mind that is as he portrays it. Nor could he have the coherent, bespoke, chosen life, that makes complex, interlocking sense to itself and the lives of others, necessary to bring a book to publication.

In short, the existence of Chater's book is the most powerful imaginable refutation of the thesis contained between its covers.[34] Given this, the reader may wonder why she is being asked to spend time on what is obviously a daft claim. One reason is that it is a particularly clear example of the tendency to take empirical science as having the capacity to overturn our fundamental intuitions about our own nature: the assumption that if neuroscience can't accommodate it, if there is no neural self-module in the brain, then the self does not exist. Chater's book is a useful aid to the project of teaching us "to pass from a piece of disguised nonsense to something that is patent nonsense".[35]

Additionally, *The Mind is Flat* illustrates something we discussed in Chapter 2: how the project of reducing persons or selves to their brains – what we may call "brainifying" the person – invariably involves personifying the brain and treating it as if it were a kind of person. The brain in Chater's book perpetrates "hoaxes", "solves problems", "is continuously scrambling to link together scraps of sensory information", and in trying to organize and interpret them, "brings the full range of past experience and knowledge to find meaning in current experience", and so on. The illusory depths ascribed by Chater's "flat mind" to itself are, so he claims, the properties of the brain. Conscious experience, which includes the illusion of "a continuously flowing stream of consciousness" (and the sense that we are extended in time), is simply a report of "the brain's *interpretation*". In reality: "talk of being conscious of one's *self* is incoherent nonsense – 'selves', after all, aren't part of the sensory world. And all 'higher' forms of consciousness (being conscious of being self-conscious), though beloved of some philosophers, are nonsense on stilts".[36]

There is good reason for suspecting that Chater does not believe what he says about the self. "There is the bit where you say it and the bit where you take it back" J. L. Austin once said caustically about certain philosophers who claimed to adhere to counterintuitive views. And Chater "takes it back" in spades. For example, he tells us that "what makes each of us unique is our individual and particular history – our own specific trail of precedents in thought and action. We are each unique, in short, because of the endless variety of our layered history of thoughts and actions".[37] Layered? What happened to the flatness of the mind? His entire book from the subtitle onwards has been devoted to attacking the very idea of depth. And this is not just a momentary aberration: "These past patterns of thought, and their traces in memory, *under*pin our remarkable mental abilities, shape how we behave and make each of us unique. So, in a sense, we do, after all, possess some inner mental landscape".[38]

This would be very odd, if the mind really were the brain and the self a brain module or some such. The brain is a material object, whose enduring existence can be divided into a succession of time-slices. Unlike a self, the brain's state at any given time is what it is and what it is cannot reach either to what it has been or what it will be, even less to the timeless zone of general meanings. The self, however, is not a succession of time slices, as we discussed in the previous chapter. RT at 12 noon is not confined to 12 noon in the way that his body or brain is confined to 12 noon. It is impossible, therefore, to see how the brain could coin the ideas of the self and of higher modes of self-consciousness. How could a temporally flat brain acquire the capacity, to deceive the mind into thinking that it is not flat, to deceive us into thinking that we are or have selves? It seems as if the brain can borrow the properties of non-existent minds (persons, selves) so that it can then provide minds (persons, selves) with their most distinctive, non-flat, properties – or to deceive them into thinking they have such properties.

Spreading the self thin

Panpsychists have also tried to shrink the self or the conscious subject, because it fits awkwardly into their vision. Unable to explain how mind emerged out of the material world, they proposed that it was universally present from the beginning. Unfortunately, this simply moves the problem on. As Janko Nešić has expressed it, "if everything in nature is endowed with a modicum of consciousness some kind of emergence [will be necessary] in order to account for the production of high-level subjects".[39] People like you and me.

To minimize this challenge, some panpsychists have "deflated" the self, denying that it is unified or enduring. There are no persistent subjects. More radically still, others have denied "that experiences must have subjects at all, or at least denying that subjects are metaphysically or conceptually simple entities".[40] There are only episodes of experience belonging to no-one.

Deflating the subject in this way – delivering a seemingly selfless consciousness, lacking ownership, a viewpoint, or even aboutness – is intended to narrow the otherwise inexplicable gap (to be crossed by just-like-that "emergence") between the universal twinkling of consciousness in the material world and the high-level consciousness of subjects who have their own first-person viewpoints on the world and arrive at and develop such viewpoints through putting together the experiences they have and own and reflecting on them, over a life-time of awareness.

Predictably, this creates a problem that is at least as big as the one it purports to solve. If subjects boiled down to disconnected episodes of experience, then it would be difficult to see how they could have a unified conscious field, never mind relate a present to a past and future that is uniquely their own, or how they could inhabit, occupy, or build up a world shared with others. Even less would there be any basis for the interpersonal dimension of personal identity. Trickles of ownerless episodes of subjectivity, unconnected by co-ownership of a world, would have little by which to relate to one another. There wouldn't even be the wherewithal to survive the nightly interruptions of sleep or the capacity to "pull ourselves together" in order to attend to something or perform an action better.

We cannot therefore accept that human experiences are free floating, untethered to any subject, though it is necessary for experience to be transitive: to be about something other than myself, the experiencer. We need to maintain the distinction between *awareness of self* and *awareness of experience* that is implicitly "my" experience. The subject makes experience two-faced: looking outward to the world; and inward to the self.

OUTSOURCING THE SELF

Philosophers who dissolve, demolish, or deconstruct the self are left with the task of explaining the robust intuition that we have an enduring identity. The alternative to denying the reality of the self is to cut it down to size or by some other means make it less threatening to the naturalistic viewpoint. Hence the fashion in contemporary Anglophone philosophy for seeking a *reductive* account of the self; one, at least that undermines the special nature of the self. Many attempt to do this by *outsourcing* our identity to a material object which somehow magically translates into a sense of personal depth and adds up to a biography. They seek enduring I-hood in the enduring it-hood of a piece of living matter – the body or the brain or part of the brain. Those who do not appeal to the relative permanence of the body look to the connectedness and continuity of the stream of experience.[41] We shall deal with these in turn.

Bodies, brains, bits of brain, and personal identity

Contemporary Anglophone philosophy about personal identity has been dominated by arguments driven by reflections on, and quarrels over, the supposed implications of thought experiments involving brain transplants and the like. Philosophers invite each other to consider whether, for example, Mrs A would continue to exist if more than 50 per cent of her brain tissue were implanted into the body of Mrs B who has had her brain removed. Or to decide whether, if A's brain were taken from her body and kept alive in a vat, the resulting complex of brain-plus-vat would amount to a continuation of A's existence. Or to attempt to make coherent sense of the scenario in which two halves of A's brain, each (we are to suppose) sufficient to support an independent person, were transplanted into two bodies whose brain contents had been removed. Would there be two duplicate A's each with a legitimate claim to be A and quarrelling over her estate?

The primary purpose of these thought experiments – that are particularly associated with Derek Parfit and the many philosophers who argued with him for over 40 years – is to make visible our customary intuitions about selfhood and personal identity, what would count as a continuation of our existence, and what is at stake in our concern for our future. In Parfit's case the thought experiments were used to challenge those intuitions and also the notion that our continuing identity is what truly matters. His ultimate motive was to justify a form of truly disinterested utilitarian ethics, that would be resistant to the criticisms to which utilitarianism has been exposed.

The ethical implications are beyond our present agenda. I mention the thought experiments not just to dismiss them as a way of proceeding in the philosophy of personal identity even though I am very dubious about their value: they seem to conflate logical, metaphysical, and biological possibility in a manner that does not make for clear thought. The seemingly endless arguments about their implications still unresolved after over half a century is empirical evidence of their limited capacity to cast light. However, I am interested in the assumptions about the relationship between ourselves and our bodies that they highlight and which I believe to be mistaken but instructively so.

A good place to visit the state of the discussion is the debate between Parfit[42] and the so-called "animalists" one of whose most eloquent spokespersons is Eric Olson.[43] Confusingly, the argument is sometimes framed in terms of whether we are or are not "human beings". What is at issue between these two philosophers is the extent to which we are to be identified with our bodies; that is to say, whether we are human animals.

In places in his writing, Parfit highlighted psychological connectedness and continuity as the basis for enduring personal identity. He also invoked the brain because the succession of psychological states did not seem to have enough within it to hold itself together: it needed help. As Olson expresses it, for Parfit, "our persistence through time consists of two factors: our unique psychological continuity and persistence of enough of the same brain".[44] The "enough" is the amount required to constitute the conscious thinking and controlling parts of human beings. As Parfit himself says, "What makes different experiences the experiences of a single person is their being either changes in the states of, or at least causally related to, the same brain".[45] The unsatisfactory suggestion that there seem to be *two* sources of our persistence is dealt with by the even more unsatisfactory suggestion that they are essentially the same because the psychological elements are neural events in the "thinking part" of the brain or effects of those events. We have already seen that we have reasonable grounds for questioning this identity relation between brain activity and conscious phenomena such as thoughts. And there are even more problems with invoking a causal relation, as we have noted. But let this pass for the present.

Olson's own ("animalist") view, by contrast, is that our identity is inseparable from our status as (whole) organisms: our conditions of persistence are the same as those of animals. Olson's merging of personal with bodily identity seems to squeeze out all the complex relations we have to our bodies that we discussed in Chapter 3. For Olson, instead of (for example) *having* our bodies, we *are* them. The identity Olson proposes is, so it would seem, an "is identity" rather than an "am identity": "I am" boils down to the "it is" of the body.

Olson argues against Parfit's view that we are identical only with those parts of the body that he deems necessary and sufficient to maintain ourselves as psychological continua – our brains or, rather, just a part of them, our forebrains. Among Olson's many arguments is that if we really were identical with a part of our brain, we must be a few inches tall and weigh a few pounds. And we would somehow be grey, wrinkled, and soggy: very short and not terribly personable.[46] Olson's alternative view, however, that we are identical with our entire body and that our life is to be the life of a human organism, is clearly doomed. If we say that "Raymond Tallis is thinking" means "Raymond Tallis' body is thinking" we will be flattering our kidneys, liver, and toe-nails, which seem to have little to do with thought. I may think I can solve Fermat's Last Theorem but I am sure it is not my body that pulls off the mathematics if I can.[47] And animalism is unclear whether it means that I am my body, I am that part of my body which is experiencable, or my experiences of my body.

By limiting the material basis of personal identity to bits of the brain Parfit does not, however, address the problem associated with Olson's "animalism" for at least two reasons.

Firstly, there are problems with a standalone forebrain as the basis of our identity. Contrary to those who imagine we could sustain a part of the brain in a vat full of nutrients, its function cannot be separated from that of the remainder of the brain plus all the bodily structures that feed into and out of the brain. Even neuromaniacs would argue that the forebrain does not, for example, maintain wakefulness without input from the reticular formation in the brain stem; that the brain stem in turn draws on input from many sources including ascending sensory pathways; and that the latter have to be maintained by, and *get their meaningful contents* from, a complex, supportive, organic environment beginning with the rest of the body. A vat full of the most delicious nutriments could not underpin such meaning. There is no viewpoint, a *point d'appui* for agency, without embodiment to underpin needs, make actions possible as well as necessary, and to give both their meaning. "Embrainment" falls short of embodiment. While there is a division of labour in the human body, it is not possible to carve out, as a continuous slice of living matter, all that is necessary to sustain a person.

Secondly, it is not clear that a brain separated from a body would have the memories and thoughts of a living person; that as a handless, legless, chest-less, faceless, spineless, etc-less entity, I would make any sense of memories I formed when I had hands, legs, a chest, a face, and a spine. What is more, as we shall discuss at the end of this chapter, and in more detail in Chapter 7, it is not possible to imagine a self continuing in the absence of a world populated by other selves.

Parfit's brain-part position, therefore, is no less flawed than Olson's whole-body animalism. Their differences prove to be less interesting than what they have in common and what motivates both views. At the heart of both visions is an awareness of the Humean difficulty of finding a basis for the continuity and connectedness of the self over time in the flow of purely psychological items such as perceptions. Parfit and Olson therefore endeavour to *outsource* the task of providing that continuity to a material object, to the brute physical continuity or connectedness either of the putative thinking parts of our bodies such as our forebrains (Parfit) or of the entire animal organism (Olson). For Parfit, the brain holds the self together. For Olson the body holds the self together. They seek the persistence, or the unity, of the "who" in the persistence, or the unity of a fleshly "what". While such a view fails to take account of the complexity of the relationship between the "I am" of the person and the "it is" of the body, there is an important failure, connected with what we discussed in Chapter 4. It does not reflect the *temporal depth* of the human subject, of the "I": such depth cannot be found in a material object; not even a living one such as the human body or its brain. But I want to focus on other considerations.

There are two closely connected strands to our opposition to both Parfit and to Olson. First, as Hume pointed out, material objects do not deliver their own persistence, continuity, or unity rooted. Secondly, you cannot get a who out of a what, the story of the person out of the successive states of the organism.

Let us begin with Hume who argued,

> [T]hat we have no idea of external substance, distinct from the ideas of particular qualities. This must pave the way for a like principle with regard to the mind, that we have no notion of it, distinct from particular perceptions [...] The identity which we ascribe to the mind of man is only a fictitious one, *and of a like kind with that which we ascribe to vegetable and animal bodies.*[48]

Hume's grounds for arguing that all objects are fictitious is that the spatio-temporal limits of an object, the bounds of its identity, are dependent on the criteria we choose to determine whether or not an entity has remained the same entity, in the face of change. There are no intrinsic criteria for deciding when an object has changed sufficiently to justify saying that it is no longer the same object. Our decision will depend not on the quantity of change but the speed, continuity, smoothness and proportionality of change. That is why my two-year-old body is regarded as the same object as the body of the 70+ year old who is typing this sentence. The day-to-day changes are usually imperceptible. Imperceptibility, however, is in the eye of the beholder. That these are subjective criteria, and are not intrinsic to the object, is evidenced by the fact that the material of the object can be entirely replaced but, so long as this is gradual, we still grant that it has continued in existence: it is the same thing.[49] We are also more tolerant of change in the case of living creatures – for example a sapling turning into a great tree, or a toddler turning into a 70-year old – because there is, Hume says, "a *sympathy* of parts to their *common end*, and suppose that they bear to each other the reciprocal relation of cause and effect in all their actions and operations".[50] In the case of my body, the two-year-old and the septuagenarian belong to the life-course of a single organism.

What this highlights is that insentient objects don't deliver their own identity – their own "id-entity", their own status as being "same-entity". They are not self-stipulating. After all, they do not specify their own spatial or temporal boundaries. It is the acuity of our attention, perhaps directed by a description, that will define what counts as the entity that has identity – whether an item is a whole (a pebble) or a part (of a scree). Of course, once we use the same referring term, we have the basis for saying of something that it has a persistent identity: "Pebble 17 is Pebble 17", no ifs or buts, no vagueness, no fluffy edges. The pebble does not, however, pick itself out. A pebble may be eroded and yet deemed over a certain period of time to be the same pebble. If it is smashed in a single blow, then it will be regarded as having being transformed into something else – shale or powder.

Something analogous may seem to apply in the case of personal identity. My belief that the succession of my ever-changing perceptions is regarded as belonging to, or occurring in, to the same self depends on the fact that the rate of change is sluggish: the sum total of my experiences at time t_1 is only trivially different from the sum total at time t_2 if the interval between the two times is modest.

As an explanation of our intuitions that we, or someone else, count as the same person over time, this does not however seem to work. The obvious reason is that the life history of our body is not present to us at any time so that its present state can be compared with its sum at other times. Indeed, the very process of reviewing its states, with the aim of determining the degree of resemblance between successive moments of our lives, would seem to presuppose the existence of the self to lay claim to those states as a) its own, and b) available to be summed. Without the self as the single, enduring "owner" of the states, the sense of the enduring self – real or illusory – would not be possible.

Although it may not have been Hume's intention, this argument should be sufficient to discourage those who would seek the unity and endurance-over-time of the self, or the guarantor of it, in the unity and identity of the body.

What is more, given the dialectical relationship we observed between the "am" and "is" in the embodied subject, it would seem that self and material organism – two "fictions" – would have to stand surety for each other's identity, taking in each other's washing: they would have to acquire their oneness from each other. The persistence, unity, and identity of a *who* would have to be found in the persistence, unity, and identity of a piece of a *what*, namely the living meat of the body or part of it; and the persistence, unity, and identity of the meat would have to be underwritten by the synthetic activity of the *who* gathering its parts (neurones, arms, feet) and its duration over time into one. The Parfitian-Olsonian notion of personal identity would seem therefore to have to help itself to two items that Hume called "fictions" – that of the object (in Parfit's case the brain, in Olson's the body) and that of the self – to confer unity, persistence and hence the sought-for reality on each other. The very processes, according to Hume, that bundle me into a unity are also required to confer unity on my body or part of it.

In Chapter 3 we developed a different take on the interdependence between the "I" who am and the body that is. As Kim Atkins has put it: "objects of outer perception gain their status as enduring, independent objects on condition of a subject's capacity for self-ascription".[51] It is not necessary to embrace Kantian idealism to accept the co-production of a) the enduring, unified embodied self, and b) the sense of objects that have an existence and a unity that transcends our perception of them. Significantly, the evidence from childhood development suggests that the sense of self and of object permanency seem to be acquired at the same time. Understanding that things exist independently of their being perceived coincides with, for example, recognizing one's self in a mirror.[52]

At any rate, the outsourcing of the continuity of the self to a (material) body, or the connectedness of the self to the connectedness of successive states of the brain, is manifestly circular, which, though true, is not the result that either Parfit or Olson would have welcomed. Atkins again: "The unity of consciousness as a fact (i.e. from an external/third-person perspective) presupposes the first-person activity of self-ascription, at the same time that such activity presupposes the unity of consciousness as a fact".[53]

How could so many reasonably sharp philosophers miss this seemingly obvious objection to outsourcing the continuity and unity of the self to the persistence of a material object (the brain) that is the putative source of a connected or continuous stream of psychological events? Qassim Cassam, cited by Atkins, offers a plausible explanation:[54] the confusion, or conflation, between two questions that arise when we are considering the identity of persons. The conflation is between: a) an internal question looking from within consciousness of "what *within* a given mental life underpins experience"; and b) an external question, looking *at* consciousness namely "what the unity of consciousness in a given life consists in?". Parfit most blatantly collapses the two questions: he reduces my personal identity to the objective markers by which I may be identified.[55] This is consistent with Parfit's ambition to show that it is possible to describe our identity in terms of entirely impersonal facts, so that personal identity becomes "unimportant" – a necessary step to a pure utilitarianism from which we genuinely treat all persons the same and consider only the sum total of human happiness. The essence of personal identity, he seems to believe, is something revealed to an impersonal viewpoint.

At any rate, we cannot look to material objects – not even living objects such as the animal body, or parts of living bodies such as brains or forebrains – to secure the continuing identity of the self since both the endurance and unity of objects and the continuity and unity of enduring subjects have the same ultimate source. An object such as the human body that is itself a bundle could not tie together "the bundle ... of different perceptions, which succeed each other with inconceivable rapidity, and are in perpetual flux and movement".[56] Being associated with a thing (a living body), howsoever intimately, will not of itself rescue us from being an unbundled flux of impressions. Even if we were to break with Hume and many empiricist philosophers since him and claim that objects really do have a substantial reality "distinct from the ideas of particular qualities", we still could not rely on thinghood to rescue selfhood, in the hope that the stability and continuity of things (such as the body or the brain) would deliver the coherence, reality, unity, and persistence of the self and license a reductionist notion of personal identity. To see why we need to revisit the arguments made in the previous two chapters.

The time of my body and the time of myself

There are other reasons for *not* trying to find the self in the organic body or the brain.

In Chapter 3 we observed that my curriculum vitae cannot be extracted from, even less identified with, the life of the impersonal organism that is my body. Granted, the capacity of the body to change and yet remain essentially the same – evident in the homoeostatic mechanisms that secure the dynamic equilibrium conserving living flesh that is identifiably mine from year to year – seems to mirror the characteristic of a self that is likewise changing from moment to moment while in some important respects being conserved. Nevertheless, the stories of Raymond Tallis and of Raymond Tallis' body-qua-organism have only a distant relationship to one another. The most important reason for this is that self-hood *at* a time and over time is fundamentally different from the way the human body (and any other material object) is in time. We discussed this in Chapter 4 but the reader might find a rehearsal of the key arguments helpful.

My body, or any part of it such as the brain, at time t_1 is confined to t_1. It does not, of course, make this connection of its own accord, there is no "atness" in its temporality. Likewise, while my body is located in any space S that it physically occupies, it does not, *qua* material object, connect that space with space-in-general, even less with human spaces such as "home", "library", "base camp", etc. By contrast, *my* being at time t_1 is connected with other times and spaces, both as part of an objective schema (e.g. 12 noon as a location in clock and calendrical time) and as a semi-private landscape of times flagged up by past experiences and anticipated future ones, by past actions and future duties, by regrets and hopes, hurries and dawdles, and so on. My self could not be a succession of time slices of the physical entity that is my body, even if the time of that body could be sliced. Similarly, the position P of my body is not intrinsic to it: it is located *by me* – or some other subject or observer – in objective geometrical and geographical space, or in (more homely, subjective) domestic space, such that my here is connected with a nexus of heres and theres and elsewheres.

The fundamental difference between the life that I live and my living body, between a person with an identity and an organism, is not therefore erased by shrinking the living tissue in question from a body to a forebrain. In the quarrel between them, both Olson and Parfit miss the point. I am no more a succession of the states of my forebrain that I am of my body. My every moment, unlike that of my brain, has temporal depth. I am not a succession of instants: they would be meaningless, as is Chater's flat mind-brain discussed earlier. Additionally, there is a unity of my conscious self at a given time such that the multiplicity of conscious activities – associated with a multitude of sensations within and across sensory modalities in a conscious field, along with thoughts, memories and emotions, an implicit body schema and an explicit body image, amounting to a conscious moment – add up in a way that neural activity does not. Neural discharges do not know that they belong to each other. Their co-belonging is not self-forged: it is in the eye of a beholder. To make things worse, the elements of the moment of consciousness must not only be brought together, they must also be kept distinct – as is evident from the irreducible richness of the moment which I can appreciate in the simultaneity of the kinds of conscious contents I have mentioned. If (for example) the conscious field were unified by a mechanism by which all relevant neural pathways converged on a single "master-neurone for the conscious moment", it would be difficult to see how experience would retain its manifest multiplicity, with sights and sounds, memories and thoughts, being kept apart. It also assumes that the activity in a "higher-level" neurone, in which different sensory or cognitive pathways merge, would somehow be "about" the activity in those lower neurones, but brought together, to deliver a higher-order aboutness.[57] More generally, without separateness there is no issue of a unity requiring to be achieved; and with separateness, unity seems unachievable, or not at least given within the experience. Experiences would not even amount to a *succession* of moments in a Humean "flux". If we deny the reality of the "I", the continuing subject of my experiences, we lack any basis for the coherence within the conscious field.

The troubles of those who would outsource the self, the person and his or her identity, to the body or the brain, have hardly started. The million-threaded unity of the self *over time* presents even greater problems. The sense in which material objects such as bodies and brains hold together does not match the way the self holds together in full awareness of its own changes and its multiplicity. Irrespective of whether or not he is deluded in believing in himself as a self, it cannot be denied that the innumerable moments of "Raymond Tallis" belong to other moments in a life that is coherent over time and not a mere succession. My sense of who I am, of where I have come from (in the widest sense), of what I ought to do, and where I am going, of the narratives Dennett seems to take for granted, could not be merely the successive states of the material object that is his body or the smaller material object that is his forebrain.

Our attention has slipped from the synchronic unity or unities of consciousness – that is, unity at a particular time – to the diachronic unities of consciousness – that is, the unities over time. This is, as we shall see, not an accident, nor even a mistake. What I am at a particular moment is impregnated with a many-layered sense of what I have been and a many-layered sense of a future towards which I am directed. My over-arching sense of myself at any given time t_1 locates me in a meaningful *situation* that is not merely a consequence of what has happened in the past but itself has temporal depth: the past is *present* as a pointer to the future that is also present as live possibilities, goals, the target of expectations or intentions. Memory is important for unity *at* a time, as well as unity *over* time because my sense of me-now is of an ongoing someone continuing on the basis of implicit and explicit sense-making and *re*-cognition. My being "deep in time" is experienced *at* a time: as we noted in the previous chapter, the "now" – which gains part of its content through contrast with the "no longer" and the "not yet" – is situated in a present that may be a few seconds, an afternoon, today, "nowadays", this year, and so on. The length of my past, the distance between now and (say) my looked-forward-to summer holiday – all these all have to be experienced or thought of at a particular time. There is nothing that could correspond to this in the electrical activity of neural tissue: there are no afternoons in the brain – no "after", no "noon", and no evening-to-come. At every moment, the brain is what it is at that moment. By contrast, what I am at any moment is inseparable from what I have been and what I will be.[58]

That is why my identity *at* a time cannot be extricated from my identity *over* time. What makes a pebble the same pebble at t_1 as at t_2 is that it is unchanged between the two times or, if it is changed, the change is continuous and (by some scale) gradual, as Hume noted. And it is also true that I am the same person at t_1 and at t_2 if and only if either I am relatively unchanged between the two times or there are no discontinuities. This, however, is not enough. For RT at t_2 to be the same as RT at t_1, they have to be in *explicit* contact so that the former reaches out to, is aware of, and "owns" the latter. No such explicit internal connectedness is required of a pebble because any identity it has is conferred from without – by someone like you or me.

Highlighting the synchronic and diachronic unities of the self makes it easier to see the misconception behind Hume's conclusion that the self must be a fiction because he can't find it by inspecting the pell-mell of experiences. What is central to selfhood is connectedness over time. The need for something to hold everything together remains. To this extent, those such as Parfit and Olson who would outsource personal identity to something other than the flux of experiences have at least progressed beyond Hume. Unfortunately, as will by now be evident, the belief that a material object can underpin the self, and bundle together the bundle of experiences, is mistaken. Bodies and brains cannot experience ownership of the events taking place in them and they do not *experience* their stability over time. Certainly, they cannot sum their distinct and successive states into something that is the owner of these states; even less can they adopt the semi-external relationship that ownership of perceptions constitutes. The human organism does not own its properties or its temporal extension – even less its future or past.

THE PSYCHOLOGICAL BASIS FOR PERSONAL IDENTITY

Psychological continuity and connectedness

We cannot outsource the unity and endurance of the self to the stability and continuity, the (scale-relative, and hence observer-relative) sluggishness and the internal cohesion, of an objective body or body-part. We need therefore to look elsewhere for the enduring, unifying subject of experience. The search therefore switches to something *within* the flux of experiences, or more generally psychological events, that will correspond to the self.

It would be neither plausible nor explanatorily helpful to propose that there is a distinctive colouring common to all my experiences brand-marking them as mine. The common ownership of my experiences must be presupposed, rather than being discoverable through our experiences that have a common empirically observable trait. A common contemporary way of presenting Hume's concern is to see it less as a search for a specific perceptual marker of the self or of the sense of the self than as a search for criteria by which a person RT at time t_1 shall count as the same person RT at time t_2. The question arises with particular force because we are ordinarily subject to profound changes – of circumstance, of preoccupations, of the things we feel are important, even of character – as part of normal, healthy development. Hence the appeal to *psychological* continuity and connectedness (*vide infra*) as the basis for personal identity and the enduring self. This continuity and connectedness, what is more, is extrinsic to the elements in the flux of perceptions. The relations between perceptions P_1 and P_2 are not intrinsic properties of those perceptions: they do not have to assert their common allegiance through sharing the same brand-mark.

We have arrived at territory so well-trodden that the paths are shiny and at arguments that go back before Hume at least as far as John Locke, who focused on psychological sameness over time, as the criterion for establishing, and defining a person as "a thinking intelligent being that has reason and reflection and can consider itself as itself, the same thinking thing in different times and places".[59] This characterization of what counts as selfhood combines both synchronic unity – "consider itself as itself" – and diachronic unity – "the same thinking thing in different times and places". The former seems like the affirmation "That I am" and the latter the affirmation "That I still am" or "I am the same I as I was".

It is clear that the continuation – changing but essentially unchanged – of myself over time does not consist simply of an iteration of some core, contentless "I", of a logical or grammatical subject. The self has to be sustained, nourished, given content by the influx of events and their accompanying experiences, and also by the awareness that comes from voluntary activity in response to, and shaping, experiences. At the same time, there has to be intrinsic continuity of the elements; hence the emphasis by Parfit on psychological linkage and connectedness. We are entities "that can think about themselves, and whose continued existence essentially involves psychological continuity".[60] This being the case, "a human embryo or foetus" that cannot think about itself is not a person. A foetus is something that only subsequently develops into the body of a Lockean person.[61] However, Locke foregrounds the "psychological continuity and connectedness that, in ordinary cases, hold between different parts of a person's life".[62]

It is worth clarifying Parfit's distinction between continuity and connectedess.[63] *Psychological connectedness* is the holding of particular direct psychological connections. It is based on several elements: a) direct memory connections, as when I remember having some of the experiences I had 20 years ago; b) the sort of connection holding between my intention to do something and a later act in which the intention is carried out; and c) the successive moments of a continually held belief or experienced desire. Psychological continuity is formed of overlapping "chains of strong connections" where strong connections are a matter of there being enough direct connections between the self at successive times. "Enough" cannot be defined *a priori* but Parfit favours something like 50 per cent overlap – an admirably democratic way of deciding on whether one should count as the same self.[64]

But "insourcing" – or inward outsourcing – of enduring personal identity to psychological connectedness and continuity brings problems of its own. In the case of connectedess, it would seem that, far from delivering the sense of personal identity, it would be *presupposed* by it. My experience now (say in 2019) of an experience I had then (say in 1970) would count as a memory in 2019 of an experience I had in 1970 only if I already had a sense that what happened in 1970 happened to *me*. Memory would provide the connection necessary to highlight continuing identity if and only if identity had already been established. And there are greater problems with psychological continuity as a source of enduring identity. How would a succession of totalled experiences, not themselves bearing the mark of identity, happening to or in an individual person, amount to a continuity sufficient to sustain sameness of identity? How would what is handed over from day to day *add itself up* in order to underwrite the claim that RT on 12 June is close enough to RT on 13 June to count as the same person? After all, the actual perceptual contents are of necessity highly variable, being shaped to a very great significant degree by the highly variable circumstances in which I find myself. My experiences as a teenager at a party in 1964, as a doctor running a clinic in 1985, and as a retiree writing this paragraph in 2019, are profoundly different. Even so, I have no doubt that Raymond Tallis is the protagonist of each and that RT_{1964}, RT_{1985} and RT_{2019} are the same person in any sense that matters; that the cumulative total that is my formal CV and informal biography is correctly ascribed to the one person in successive decades.

The appeal to a gradually changing sum total of psychological elements as the basis of the continuity of the self is problematic in other ways. Two are worthy of particular attention.

The first is the multiplicity of the strands of connectivity between moments of consciousness. Let us just take a couple. There is the succession of experiences within and around our bodies. Their coherence lies not within us but outside of us. Consider for example, the successive visual fields in which I am immersed when the tram I am sitting on goes round a corner. The outside is in charge. They will become part of my self only in retrospect when they have been transformed from experiences to memories. At the same time, there will also be a succession of preoccupations that may have little to do with my sensory experiences, such that the latter will receive scant, intermittent attention. The upper surface of these preoccupations are trains of thought, with their own associative logic. I overhear a tune, remember the concert when I last heard it, recall the programme notes, think about the cultural references in those notes – Haydn, *sturm und drang* – be drawn to remember my autodidactic youth when I first encountered these terms, my solitary walks, attempts at poetry, and then wake up to the realization that I have reached my tram stop. These will feed into my accumulative self but will sit awkwardly with the (relatively) passive reception of the world around me and the (relatively) active trains of thought. The relationships in each series are different: successive experiences are prompted by successive encounters with the physical world which orchestrates them; whereas successive thoughts prompt their own successors. This highlights how connectedness and continuity are not in any sense simple or transparent.[65]

The other problem is particularly vexing. It is the seeming conflict between continuity – RT at time t_1 is only slightly different (as a psychological sum) from RT at adjacent time t_2 – and connectedness. My random recollections in my old age of my childhood, and an access of childhood memories, is an irruption, a discontinuity. Personal memories may vouch for RT in 1959 being the same as RT in 2019 but they represent a big jump, a flashback. I have to pull myself together to pay attention to the job, and the RT, at hand in 2019.

The appeal to "insourcing" our identity by finding it in psychological connectedness or continuity therefore seems problematic. More broadly, the ambition, common among many contemporary philosophers as well as Parfit, to produce a reductionist account of personal identity – to locate it in something that can be described in impersonal terms – irrespective of whether the material invoked is neural activity or free-floating streams of psychological material – misses the point of what personal identity and selfhood are. Reductionists deny that the self is some kind of thing in addition to bodies and the succession of connected experiences. But one can be an anti-reductionist without reifying the self or invoking "some special entity, such as a Cartesian Ego, whose existence must be all or nothing".[66] Nor does anti-reductionism commit one to what Parfit calls – in order to dismiss it – "a further fact" additional to psychological and bodily (or brain) continuity. It is not a fact that defenders of the self are after. Unless, that is, we classify as "a further fact" as our referring intelligibly to ourselves as "I", and that "I" has temporal depth and worldly width. "I" is not the realm where further (objective) facts are to be located. The "am" of "I am" is not an objective factual addition to the "is" of the body and its world and of certain psychological states seen from a quasi-outside; but it is nonetheless non-reductively real.[67]

Memory and personal identity

Memory as it is understood in psychological science encompasses a multitude of cognitive and even non-cognitive capacities. Indeed, its application in psychology is so broad that it threatens to become meaningless, as pointed out by American psychologist Stanley Klein in an article that should be required reading for all students of psychology: "When an initial act of registration produces a mental state, that state may be a memory. But it also may be knowledge, skill, belief, dream, plan, imagination, decision, judgement, feeling of familiarity, act of categorization, an idea, a hope, fear, and so on".[68]

The wider the scope of the term "memory", the further it drifts from self-consciousness and its home base in conscious recall of "an event that happened to myself" and the further it slides from the very character of memory central to the connectedness that we intuitively feel is what delivers the sense of personal identity. The kind of memory central to personal identity is fundamentally different from: semantic memory (of facts); from what Henri Bergson called "habit-memory" (implicit in learned behaviour or altered reactions to stimuli, manifest in the performance of habitual acts); from the "memory" ascribed to artefacts such as computers; and from the "memory" supposedly inscribed in the changed properties of material substances exposed to the impact of single or repeated events.

Real memory, Klein points out, is not just *from* the past but also explicitly *about* the past: the past is experienced *as* the past. This rules out implicit, unconscious, and dispositional memories as central to the idea of memory: "[t]he fact that events in one's past determine our success in engaging in current thought or behaviour is a necessary, but not a sufficient, condition to sanction the conclusion that a thought or behaviour is an act of memory".[69]

Klein argues powerfully for re-anchoring the notion of memory to "a direct, non-inferential feeling of reacquaintance with one's past ... linking content retrieved from storage with autonoetic awareness during retrieval. On this view, memory is not the content of experience but the manner in which the content is experienced."[70]

Autonoetic memories are memories in which one is aware of having personally experienced the relevant events. They are infused with the sense "that I was there", "that this happened to me", "that I was in that world", in short, "that *I was*". Autonoetic memories are memories, in short, of events that are not only personally experienced but of which we are aware of their having been personally experienced. These memories are of events and states of affairs that are recalled as being seen from a certain angle and consequently situated in a past world cognate to one's past self. They are constitutively unique (and irreplaceable). Semantic memories do not have the personal mode of presentation of autonoetic memories. (It would be difficult to imagine how "Africa has a growing population" could be translated into personal experiences, though there may be a personal experience corresponding to the event of the fact being learned from a teacher.)

Memories that will contribute to our sense of personal identity must have this character of being not only the product of our past experience (as, for example, acquired skills such as being able to ride a bicycle typically are), or being *about* the past (as is the case with factual memories of what has happened) or merely having been acquired in the past. They must, in addition, be directed to the past, a past that is seen as one's own past, as being part of "my" life: they have a "me-ness" or "mineness". Such memories, in short, are not merely present effects of past experiences; they are present experiences that have past-events-experienced-by-me as their explicit intentional object. They offer an experience of the past *as* past and a part of the past that is *my* past.[71]

Identifying autonoetic memories as the key to the threads, connecting present and past, germane to a sense of personal identity highlights something that is sufficiently obvious: that memories will deliver these connections only if they are (already) imbued with an autobiographical sense – with the sense that what is recalled was experienced by, happened to, me and was located in a past world that was *my* world at the time. The connectedness over time will be established only if "now" that recalls the memory is "me-now" (which we may take for granted) and "then" (the past) is "me-then" (or my-then) which cannot be taken for granted. In short, autonoetic memories will provide a sense of a continuing self only if they are already tagged with "me". This requirement shows that "I did X" cannot be reduced to "Such and such a living body/brain did X" or even "A person usually called Raymond Tallis did X".

Objectively observable causal connections between the experiences that are remembered and the memory of the experience – in some way putatively connected with a succession of events in the forebrain – would not deliver this sense. It is important to stress this, as the idea of such a causal connection is crucial to the reductionist account of personal identity. Because this view is so widespread, it's worth examining it a bit further. Let us call the event that supposedly caused the experience "*E*" and the experience of it a perception "*P*". And let us call the memory of *P* "*M*". Reductionists postulate the following causal sequence:

$$E \text{ (cause)} \rightarrow P \text{ (effect/cause)} \rightarrow M \text{ (effect)}$$

This putative sequence – event *E* causes perception *P* and perception *P* causes memory *M* – does not capture what happens when I remember an event that happened to me as something that happened to *me*.[72] We saw in Chapter 2 how *P* being about *E* is not explicable causally, with *E* being the cause of *P*. A causal account of the relationship between *P* and *M* equally does not offer anything that would account for the memory *M*, even less that it belongs to "me-now" and the experience *P* that it remembers belongs to "me-then". Furthermore, putative causal connections between my successive conscious states would not deliver a cumulative sense of self (illusory or not) unless each state was (already) connected with me.

The reductionist account that locates personal identity in the connectedness and continuity of psychological contents glued together either by direct causal relations with each other or by a common causal substrate in a body, a brain, or a part of a brain is therefore clearly flawed. If enduring personal identity relied on the connectedness and continuity of psychological contents, those contents would already have to be steeped in a sense of personal identity.[73] It is only in virtue of ignoring the phenomenal character of memory – the manner in which it is experienced as opposed to a causal chain that is supposed to generate it – that an impersonal account of personal identity looks plausible or even possible.

The critical, irreplaceable, role played by autonoetic memories in establishing personal identity is also highly pertinent to our quest to characterize the difference between human beings and non-human animals, between persons and organisms. Endel Tulving's magisterial summary of the evidence and arguments for believing that autonoetic memory is unique to humans is unanswerable. While there has been a small amount of somewhat dubious, and certainly patchy, evidence to the contrary,[74] the limited or absent development of autonoetic memory in non-human animals is precisely what we might expect, given that (as discussed in the previous chapter) they are not mental time travellers and they do not appear to have a sense of self-over-time to make it possible to assign memories to a past that is their own past.[75] As Tulving put it: "It is the self that engages in the mental activity that is referred to in mental time travel. There can be no travel without a traveller".[76]

Autonoetic memory is the most profound manifestation of our deeply personal psychological connectedness. This inner connectedness between distant moments of a personal world, and the ability to be truly both at time t_1 *and* at time t_2 – a double "at" – is to be outside of time. The most striking instances are the kinds of involuntary memory that lay at the heart of Proust's monumental autobiographical novel. Many readers will be familiar with the famous passage from his mighty act of self-excavation, where he reflects on the overwhelming effect of the involuntary memory prompted by eating the madeleine: "[M]y anxiety on the subject of my death had ceased at the moment when I had unconsciously recognized the taste of the little madeleine since the being which at that moment I had been was an extra-temporal being, and therefore unalarmed by the vicissitudes of the future".[77] We value the past for itself, as a mode of self-affirmation, and not (as scientism would have it) merely as a guide to a future that will promote our (biological) survival. It is additionally a way of valuing our personal identity and (where the memory is shared) that of our fellows. It is a reminder of what truly matters.

While Proustian involuntary memory is justly celebrated, ordinary autonoetic memory is equally mysterious and a cause for wonder. So, too, is its extension, through shared or joined intentionality, from "I" to "we". Reminiscing, shared time travel to specific events experienced by more than one party – "Do you remember when we ...?", "Do you remember what it was like when the children were young?" – is nothing short of miraculous. And the fact that we enjoy it so much is an affirmation of the "we" of the most extraordinary kind, as one person points to an absent place in the past and the other persons looks and sees it.

The mirror image of autonoetic memory is time travel into a specific future that concerns one's self. I can imagine myself going to the dentist at a time agreed by appointment, rehearsing the event on the basis of past experiences, and planning to take a couple of painkillers an hour or so in advance. Even more complex time travel is the darting back and forth expressed in, say, anticipating the (backwards-facing) regret I might feel after I have done something I plan to do tomorrow. The distinctive nature of the future is that it exists only insofar as it is actively posited. While the past is to a greater or lesser extent inherited by the present – it in part (but only in part) curates itself, the future has to be actively envisaged if it is to come into being. (This touches on something to which we shall return: that personal identity is not just an objective fact, a mere given that looks after itself.)

The key point is that no memory that was a mere effect of past events that had impinged on the brain would deliver a sense of personal identity unless that sense was already established in the individual recalling his/her past. The sense of self has to be implicitly present in the me-now – in the moment-to-moment "I" – if the me-then is going to be affirmed through a present memory of the past. Without the fundamental intuition *that I am*, which is not an impersonal matter of fact, there can be no *that I was* to give a personal home to the memories. "*That I am*" is no mere tautology. It is fundamentally different from "A is A" or "Raymond Tallis is Raymond Tallis" – as I hope the discussion in the previous two chapters has made apparent. At any rate, the intuitions *that I am* and *that I was* are the necessary condition of autonoetic memory having authentic autobiographical status delivering temporal depth and extensity to the self. No memories could deliver extended personal identity to an individual who did not already have a sense of self. The diachronic sense of persisting identity must depend upon (as well as feed into and enrich) the moment-to-moment, synchronic sense of my self. "That event happened to me" must stand on the sense, operating at the time of the event, that "This is happening to *me*" where the me in question has temporal depth. The self at any time is a self that is beyond that time.

We are in the vicinity of an argument that Bishop Butler presented against John Locke. Locke claimed that so long as an individual possesses memories, the individual remembering and the individual whose experiences are remembered are the same. Against this, Butler pointed out that for memories to reassure Raymond Tallis of his sameness at time t_1 and time t_2, he must already be sure that the memories are not only true but they are his own memories, of events that really happened to him, and that he is justified in believing in their truth. Hence RT's identity must be *presupposed* when he locates memories in his (own) past; in which case, the memories cannot form the basis of personal identity. It is "self-evident", Butler argues, "that consciousness of personal identity presupposes and cannot constitute personal identity".[78]

Parfit tries to get around this charge of circularity by introducing the concept of a "quasi-memory" of past experience:

> I have an accurate quasi-memory of a past experience if:
>
> (1) I seem to remember having an experience,
> (2) *someone* did have this experience,
>
> and

(3) my apparent memory is causally dependent, in the right kind of way, on that past experience.[79]

As an exercise in point-missing, this would be hard to beat. It breaks down into two steps the process of arriving at the awareness that my memories are mine in the fundamental sense that they are of experiences had by me. The first step is the assumption that *someone* (anyone) had the experience I recall. The second step is supposedly provided by the objective fact that the experience and the memory are causally related in "the right kind of way". Regarding the first step, it is difficult to imagine how we could entertain the idea of an experience had by a generic *someone* without specifying who that someone is – except via a verbal report which is clearly derivative, and higher order. Not only is this deeply untrue to the immediate awareness evident in autonoetic memories, it would be no less absurd than my claiming to be aware that there is someone in the room and then wondering whether that someone is me. Secondly, the long chain of causation connecting the past experience and the present memory (which may be separated by decades) will, in the overwhelming majority of instances, be entirely hidden from me. At any rate, it is difficult to imagine an internal auditor checking that there is a causal link and one "of the right kind", between an experience and the memory of it, who would then sign off the account of the memory as being truly a memory of his own past, and consequently being able to uphold his sense of a "me-then" being identical with a "me-now". If the auditor were someone else – a neuroscientist or a detective – then we would find ourselves in the odd situation of requiring someone else to assure us that our remembered past really belongs to us. This may be necessary in cases of total amnesia – so that we have to be taught our own past – but it clearly could not be the norm that everyone tutors everyone else. If we did not typically connect with our own autonoetic memories, then there would be no past, or not one available for sharing, which is one of the fundamental bases of the community of minds.[80]

It will be evident that Parfit's ambition to arrive at personal identity by impersonal means, by the route of factual, objective truths, is misconceived. Without sameness of person, there is no psychological continuity, only a succession of experiences such as we may suppose is the inner life of animals – or of Humean, as opposed to human, beings. Our sameness of person is rooted in an essential, underived, sense of self, of my being one who experiences what I experience. The fundamental point is that "I am" or personal identity cannot be translated into, or reduced to, "it is"; nor can the continuity of the "I" be outsourced to causal chains ultimately housed by a material object such as the brain.

OTHER SOURCES OF THE SELF

Other selves

We have focused on memory because it seems central to personal identity over time.[81] My human being, however, is not only something I am merely aware of as a given, a passively received inheritance from the past, but also something that is affirmed, sought, expects or longs to be recognized, lived, enacted. It is upstream of the opposition between the passive receipt of something merely given and something that is actively made. This is another fundamental difference between the "am" of I and the "is" of (for example) a persisting organism whose successive states are also effects of prior causes. We do not ordinarily think of objects (for example) affirming their own identity. Or, closer to home, when I say "I did that", my owning up to it, or claiming the credit for it, is not merely a present phase of the flow of psychological material asserting that "An earlier part of the present flow of psychological material did it".

As we have seen, the kinds of memories that will deliver personal identity over time are those that are identity-involving, that are *embraced* as "mine", or "me". To bypass this – as the impersonalizers of personal identity try to do – is to make the truths about our identity something that does not require our participation. It is at odds with the broader fact that living my life is not purely passive, mere endurance. At the very least, the moments of our lives reach out to each other: we curate ourselves with and without the assistance of other people by reaching back and forward in time. This is quite unlike the mere persistence of an object through inertia in virtue of which its later states are very close to its earlier states. A self is *asserted*. It is in part maintained through self-interest.[82] Our human being is a matter of concern for itself; our memories *matter*.

This is the beginning of a necessary addition to a story that has so far placed episodic, autonoetic, autobiographical memories at the centre of memory and accepts the key role of memory in establishing the sense of continuing personal identity. There are two *caveats* to be entered supporting the position that such memories are a necessary but not a sufficient condition of personal identity. First, as we have argued, such memories would not be *auto*noetic without the prior sense of a self to which they can be ascribed. They are a marker of my extension over time only because I have a sense of myself *at* a time, including the present moment when I experience the memories as belonging to *my* past. There is a second *caveat* that I want to develop in what follows.

It is highly improbable that the continuity of the self and something as important to us as personal identity can be entrusted to episodic memories (or anticipations), notwithstanding their Proustian specialness and the fact that they seem to be unique to humans. They are, after all, random, subject to caprice, and at risk of being marginalized when something important – engrossing or urgent – is going on in our lives. The hurry of the moment has little room for reminiscence. What we actually remember is only a small part of what is available to be remembered; and what is available to be remembered is only a minute part of what has been experienced. We small-sample ourselves. It would be absurd to think that we could maintain our identity only by keeping tabs on *all* our past, having ourselves constantly in mind – particularly as this would require that every moment should house a representative sample of all other moments. If I continuously remembered everything, I would not only be unable to "move on" in the pop psychological sense: I would not be able to move. The past would blot out the present and successive layers of the past would blot out every other layer. At any rate, each day could not house the sum total of all other days. Given this, how is it that my very patchy recollection of my student days or of my middle age does not undermine my claim to have a fully-fledged personal identity or to be a fully-formed self who has lasted more decades than I care to recall? While we privilege conscious contents – because to be a continuous self seems to require continuous self-awareness, to be a self is inseparable from being aware of being a self – they do not seem to provide a complete internal skeleton sufficient to hold the self together over time.

Manifestly, we need to look to other personal characteristics that have the twin virtues of being standing, or relatively enduring, psychological states rather than occurrent events and of seeming to be able to look after themselves without being consciously maintained. These include habits, skills, faculties, competencies, talents, convictions, preferences, tastes, preoccupations, interests – even trivial ones such as lifelong allegiance to a football team – and access to a body of knowledge, including parochial knowledge about one's own world and certain people in it. Additionally, and most importantly, there are markers of character such as convictions, moral traits, and values, that fasten together our personal past, present, and future. While such standing characteristics may seem to constrain us, they also confer a robustness upon our identity. Importantly, they survive intermissions of wakefulness, most obviously our nightly sleep. They support a sense of being "ourselves" and of being familiar to ourselves – and indeed (to anticipate something important) to *others*. Beyond these items there is the continuum of our body not as a material object – we have dealt with that – but as it is evident to us in familiar sensations, including its visible appearance to ourselves, and as the primary agent of our agency.

None of this, of course, renders memories which lie at the heart of our sense of sustained personal identity less important. Indeed, it may be pointed out, the very fact that standing psychological states can to some extent look after themselves, the less explicitly present they are to us, the less they constitute a sense of our being a – or our – self. Consider the possession of a body of knowledge. To take a particularly unpromising example, the fact that I have possessed the semantic memory of the date of the battle of Hastings for 60 or more years contributes nothing to binding the self of those years together. And while the ready access I have to the knowledge I acquired at medical school seems to offer more to maintaining my identity and my sense of it than my possession of single facts, that body of knowledge still does not deliver the core of a sense of self. It is, after all, accessed randomly and does not unify itself.

More damagingly, a piece of knowledge, even if personalized to the extent of being tokenized in my recalling it, is *essentially impersonal*. Facts are own-erless; they belong to no-one in particular. There is nothing personal about the fact that the Battle of Hastings took place in 1066. Yes, I may take personal pride in being able to recall that date – clever me for remembering it! – but it is not identity-involving in the way that my recollection of (say) walking in the hills yesterday is identity-involving. Moreover, facts not only being available to any- and everyone but also timeless (see Chapter 4), have no "pastness" associated with them. My take on world history – even if my grasp of it were more impressive than it is – would not amount to a coherent slice of *my* past; while it may buttress my sense of the kind of person I am, it could not do so in the absence of an established personal identity.

This does not alter the fact that, while the endoskeleton of autonoetic memory is an indispensable marker of my continuity over time, more is needed to support my sense of being an enduring self. Some of that "more" comes from the crucial fact that I am not merely the site or even the spectator of my life. I am an agent. In the next chapter we shall discuss how agency draws on the temporal depth of the self. For the present, it is important to appreciate that the reverse is also true: that the depth of the self is maintained by activities that are explicitly extended over time. My enduring self is both expressed in and reinforced by plans, projects, responsibilities, commitments, duties, offices, roles, citizenship, that may extend over hours, days, weeks, years, or even be lifelong. It is this that makes the person Raymond Tallis, far from being elusive or illusory, inescapable. Past promises make present demands and they bind us, sometimes nail us, to a future which is uniquely ours. That future connects with, and existentially honours, the past in which the appointments and promises were made, and larger-scale commitments, such as are expressed in our professional and family roles, were undertaken. Ambitions, dreams, struggles, literal and metaphorical debts that have to be discharged, projects – these all bind our days each to each, occasioning thousands of actions directed towards prescribed goals. They form the warp and weft of narratives – ranging from scraps to full-blown depositions – which transform the scalar flux of the Humean bundle to a vector person, weaving and being woven by meanings that extend over time. These aspects of personhood would warrant an entire series of chapters. They are, however, the indispensable surface manifestations of a unity that they presuppose – and reinforce.

These binding activities do not leave continuous memories. Even discrete and moderate-sized actions such as "taking the train from Stockport to Manchester" would be recalled, if at all, only as a few events marking the trajectory between start and finish. While I must have experienced all the intermediate places on the journey, assuming I did not fall asleep, what I recall is not of a two-hour continuum. Recollection stands in relation to moment-to-moment experience rather as the successive observations of two positions on a clock-face signal the gradual passage of the fingers from one position to another. In such a case we note *that* change has taken place – one o'clock has been replaced by five past one – even if one cannot see the changes. This difference between observing change and noting that change takes place is replicated at many scales over our long lives – *that* the day has got later, the season has come and gone, the years have flown, the junior posts are completed and seniority is achieved, seniority has led to retirement. At such a scale, autobiographical memory becomes scattered, pressed flowers of facts about one's self. Personal identity does not require us to keep tabs on, or even retain access to, all the experience we own as ours.

Our large-scale actions are connected with another important source of the adhesive that binds us to ourselves over time: the shared world to which we belong. Our identity does not have to be entirely self-curated because it is also maintained by the expectations of others of whom we in turn have expectations – in my case as a son, brother, husband, father, friend, colleague – expectations that are central to the sustained sense we make of ourselves. This is most obvious in the case of those formalized roles called jobs. I was a doctor for nearly 40 years and in the course of discharging my duties I travelled back and forth along threads in a network of obligations – to see patients, to attend clinics, to do ward rounds, to make certain decisions, to take responsibility for them, and so on. These obligations – reinforced by justified expectations agreed with others which we know we have to fulfil, and underpinned by reciprocity whose uppermost surface is contractual obligation – strengthen our inner coherence.

My obligations and entitlements are not infrequently attached to me via my name coming out of the mouths of others or placed on numerous documents written by or about me. That name, as the common reference of many facts and other discursive elements asserted of me, fattens up the identity of "Raymond Tallis" which still, of course, has to be underwritten from within. They feed into, and validate, those countless narratives and narrative fragments by means of which we make ourselves intelligible to ourselves and connect ourselves, via relatively stable, even timeless general senses to our own past and future. Such glue is linked with the standing recognition of the community of fellows to whom we explain ourselves and by whom we are explained. Our proper names attach us to and extend the acknowledgement we may expect from others. That is why, when I say "I am Raymond Tallis", this connects a bald statement of singular identity to many things, such as a complex of entitlements.

The sense we make of ourselves through the many lenses of the sense we suspect others make of us may be extraordinarily complicated as noted in Chapter 3 when we reflected on the ways we possess our bodies and our bodies are possessed through our appearance to others. The modes of embarrassment and shame and pride may be enormously complicated: reflections of the kind "he thinks that I think that he thinks this of me" have no intrinsic limits. In the public realm, where our sense of our self is co-produced with many others, we shall forge a multitude of nested identities. Nevertheless, the rock, or anchor, or centre-point of the existential tautology – "I am this" – that gives all our public identities their personal substance means that we do not dissipate with our fellow humans into mere hive-minds, a gauze of unattached awareness belonging to no-one. We are liberated from our bodies by our engagement with the human world; but we are also set apart from that world by our bodies with their unique trajectories through space and time from birth to death.

That our personal identities are individual, though they are sustained, as well as shaped and elaborated by things that are not unique to us – though we shall have a unique "take" on them – will not come as a revelation to non-philosophers. The public roles we assume as contributors to shared and collective enterprises are the cladding or scaffolding that maintains the self. They create an exoskeleton, a carapace. "I am a doctor" makes an element of my personal identity a standing condition, though it is necessarily expressed in occurrent events tagged to my individual self.

Our responsibilities to others constitute a dimension of the self that flips it over from elusiveness to inescapability: accountability. We can be skewered by guilt over mistakes and sins that were committed decades ago. The fact that the less we care about the consequences of our actions, the less – or the shorter time – we feel responsible for them illustrates how we cannot safely place personal identity solely in the keeping of our own memory, our capacity or inclination to remember. Our identity is reinforced by our being held to account for our actions and by wider expectations others have of our behaviour and attitudes. Others quite rightly expect consistency of us – a requirement extending to varying degrees to our outlook, moods, modes of attunement to the world, manner of speaking, propensity to kindness and sternness, humility or scorn, or selfishness or concern for others, being a miserable sod or a cheerful bugger. The vice of all vices is inconsistency, or unpredictability. It undermines the fundamental implicit contract by which we support each other through mutual recognition, which in turn relies on that which can be recognized. What we call integrity etymologically connects the notion of having strong moral principles with being whole or undivided.

It is here that the metaphysics of selfhood spreads out into a phenomenology of the (social) self as it is evident to others as well as one's self. The outer face of the enduring self is that which others can see, enjoy, or endure, as moods are expressed or indulged, talents exercised, and roles discharged.

We cannot of course hand over the curating of our identity to others. After all, we can be misunderstood, or feel that we are. So far as we get to know of others' judgements, we may consider them woefully incomplete, at times unfair. Our public persona may sometimes seem like the sum of others' misunderstandings, even though we may collude in, or actively foster, those that are more flattering. For this reason alone, the externally mediated sense of self-over-time cannot replace the immediate sense of self-over-time that comes most intimately from autonoetic memory. The latter is gold coinage underwriting the paper currency of the public persona or the CV. The existential intuition *That I am* and *That I still am* and *That I am the same person* are not superseded by the supplementary scaffolding applied by the community of minds. In the absence of those modes of awareness that directly deliver the sense of self at any given time and the sense of self over time, the external supports would have nothing to be attached to. The enduring *I am* cannot be referred to, derived from, social supports any more than it can be outsourced to the "it is" of our bodies, our brains, or bits of our brains.

Mutual affirmation

One reflection of the irreducibility of the self is to be found in our irreplaceability, in the value we place on each other. The meaning and significance of simply being together goes beyond any instrumental value to be found in cooperation to meet shared needs, in forming duos and trios and teams, and infinitely variable combinations (and ways of combining), of joint and several. Humans are creatures who get together for the sake of togethering, of companionable coexistence, to affirm each other's reality. One of the greatest – as well as the most mysterious – joys of human life is to share experiences and subsequently to be able to share memories. While "Do you remember ...?" may refer to something that may seem trivial to others, it seeks acknowledgement of the reality of a past that is *our* past and hence *my* past and hence far from trivial. We are the co-curators of each other's days of yore. Reminding one another of a shared experience as a marker of a shared past is a delightful, bespoke validation of our sense of personal identity. While "we-mode" memories seem half-way between on the one hand I-mode experiences and on the other public, impersonal facts, capturing objective realities, the aura of the personal is not diminished.

From others we get, and to others we grant, the form of cognition that we term "*recognition*". It is a crucial affirmation of our sense of ourselves at every level from the most private to the most overtly political. At the surface level, ordinary expectations that come from others – so that when I enter a clinic in a white coat, I know what to expect of others' expectations, or when I open my front door, my wife knows I am not an intruder, and tells me that the post has arrived instead of calling for the police – maintain our sense of self. They allow the stream of consciousness to be the basis of a standing identity rather than a mere endlessly extended "and then ... and then ... and then" of a Humean flux.

The "*re*" in the re-cognition I receive from others is an external warrant of that persistence we seek when we look for the basis of personal identity, although – to reiterate perhaps once too often – it cannot replace the immediate self-recognition of "*that I am*". Third-person recognition would not be alone sufficient to deliver the sense of self over time, if only because it depends on our recognizing those who recognize us, something established through remembered experience. I remain the primary curator of myself; others are only assistant curators. They, or the material and social worlds they have created, are there to help me resume myself, assisting the daily miracle of the resurrection of "me", when I wake from deep sleep, from the effects of psycho-active drugs, or from coma. They cannot, however, replace autonoetic memories, which close the distance between the internal connectivity of one's self and the merely causal relationships between past events one has experienced and their present consequences.[83]

This brings us close to the heart of the matter: beyond the notional core of an existential self-iteration, personal identity is inseparable from *inter*personal identity; the "I" cannot develop fully without participating in "we". We-self and I-self develop in parallel – the sense of enduring personal identity is bolstered by continuities outside of ourselves, even though the interpersonal can live only in individuals: it does not float freely. The stories we tell ourselves about ourselves are at least in part stories we are telling real or imaginary, individual or general, others and the stories about ourselves others have told us. Shared mental time travel – as we plan what we are going to do tomorrow, reminisce about our holiday last year – upholds, affirms, and fills in the sense of our selves. Because at the most fundamental level, my sense of myself is italicized by my sense of others' sense of myself, there is no fundamental problem of other minds. That your mind exists is no more in doubt than that my mind exists.

Selves are no less individual for their interpersonal dimension. We do not dissolve into an ensemble of relations or, worse, into a sea of generalized discourse. Our selves are internally stitched through the coherence of our (own) days. Our preoccupations are inescapably self-centred: that is a condition of our taking responsibility for our own lives. What is more, there is an impermeable barrier between ourselves and other selves evidenced by the fact that our knowledge of others' conscious experience and their lives is mediated, distant, intermittent and often, perhaps mainly, guesswork. Even the closest relationship, the most intimate co-habitation, is marked by long intermissions of knowledge of what he/she is experiencing, doing or feeling and ignorance of the internal connectedness that is represented in her involuntary memory, the internal soliloquy, or the moment-to-moment ebb and flow of her emotions. There is something continuously hidden about each of us. We have to tell each other what we are feeling, thinking about, hoping, worrying over. We may choose not to; and we could never reveal ourselves completely to others. Candour falls far short of transparency.

While our encounter with ourselves is often mediated by the intelligibility drawn from the thatosphere – "I" is "we-tinged" all the way down – there is an irreducible core of "me" that resists being dissolved in the common world. Though we incessantly mutter to and about ourselves and our private thoughts are necessarily cast in the language of the tribe, our token thoughts fit into a nexus of understanding and concern that is unique to us. Likewise, while inside our skin there are universal metabolic processes, we undergo our awareness of those processes in our personalized days. The intersections between our experienced body, the experiences the body permits us, our history of experience, knowledge, understanding, and concerns, and our articulation of our situation, are integrated into an individuality that is resistant to dissolution into the general unfolding of the natural world, or the sea of culture. Although the personal is *irreducibly* interpersonal, persons do not dissolve in the interpersonal. Just as persons are sustained by the interpersonal, the interpersonal has to be realized in persons.

We have set aside the expectation that the self, if it were real, must be the kind of super percept Hume sought in vain. We would not, after all, expect the visual field to be everywhere haunted by the ghost-image of the visual apparatus. And it is not an "I think" that Kant rather donnishly considered must accompany all his perceptions, that holds the self together.[84] Rather, the self is a *presupposition* most fully realized in autonoetic memories that connect a present that is mine with a past that is mine. Autonoetic memories would not deliver a sustained, substantial sense of personal identity were those memories not themselves infused with a sense of self, with the existential intuition *that I am*, that is at the heart of the experiences that are remembered and of the remembering. This must be a presupposition, not something that can be discovered in the properties of the flux of experience or derived from some other source. Nevertheless, we need the giant mnemonic of the shared social world – that makes relatively stable sense of us and of which we make relatively stable sense – to supplement the primary material of selfhood.

It is this relationship between self and world that gets us out of the circularity that Bishop Butler pointed out in response to Locke's reduction of personal identity to the connectedness of memory. There is a reciprocal inherence between ourselves and others, though in virtue of the fact that we draw on different populations of people, in different ways (including the ubiquitous implicit presence of others in the intelligible public world), we are not fused or dissolved into each other or (God forbid) a post-humanist "system of signs". "It takes a village to raise a child" – yes, and a world to sustain a self.

Notes on the body and the human world

Time for a corrective to our corrective. We cannot cut out entirely the middle term between individual consciousness and society: the organic material of my body or part of it such as my brain. Yes, we rejected Olson's identification of personal identity with the human organism. And we were not persuaded by Parfit's appeal to the forebrain to underpin what I am. Even so, the story we have addressed so far has been somewhat ethereal. We need "to bring up the bodies" for several fairly clear reasons.

While we cannot delegate the sense of our continuing identity to the permanence and stability of the body, the very idea of our identity without a body is empty. It is the "it" necessary to provide an objective, numerical identity to the "I" in "I am". More specifically, the body is the condition of our being situated, of having a particular life. It is the ultimate framework within which my experiences, which are owned are co-owned, are unified, even though its organic unity and continuity does not of itself deliver ownership or the sense that the experiences I have are mine. Let's think about this role of the body a little further.

First, the flux of experience has to have a locus that justifies a particular content. Vision, without eyes located in a body to provide a viewpoint, would be a view from nowhere giving a view of and on nothing in particular – and hence nothing. The world revealed from no perspective would be a world unrevealed. The same applies to the other doors of perception and also to the proprioceptive and interoceptive platform of our experiences – the body image and body schema we discussed in Chapter 3. In short, we are at the most basic level a lived perspective, or a "take" on, what there is, and embodiment is the key to that.

Secondly, there can be no community of minds, no interpersonal realm, without a co-presence of communicating bodies. The most basic form of recognition – by family, friends, neighbours, colleagues, once-met acquaintances – is identification through bodily presence. My body is the condition, and location, of my personal presence – notwithstanding that this physical presence is supplemented by a derivative presence mediated through my multi-modal, multi-layered footprint in the world. My body, in short, is the ground floor of my identity-for-others, the fundamental condition of the necessary third-person input into my first-person being. Available to be encountered and re-encountered indefinitely, my body is the trigger for, and point of convergence of, a set of expectations that are expectations of me.

We can link this with a response to Butler's critique of Locke's memory-based account of personal identity. If my persistent identity were underwritten solely by memories, to revisit Bishop Butler's question, how could I know that these memories were mine or of things that happened to me? Would I not already need to be in possession of a criterion of personal identity to confirm that the things I remember truly were of experiences *I* had had and of events that had happened to *me*? The question at one level (not the most fundamental) is about knowledge and its justification; more broadly it is about a coherent account of the world, or at least a salient part of it. This clearly cannot be provided from within the flux of experience, which might be contaminated with hallucinations.[85] Enter the body, the necessary foundation for interpersonal corroboration.

The publicly visible spatio-temporal audit trail provided by my body is the ultimate foundation of the audit trail separating true from false quasi-memories.

If I remember being in my house all yesterday afternoon and you remember me being in my office all afternoon, something has to give. Eye-witness testimony from a third party may settle the dispute. The body provides a constraint on the succession of possibilities – of what I was doing and what I experienced and where and when. Irrespective of how my mind may "wander", I cannot bodily, and observably be, in Manchester and New York in the same hour acting in the streets of both cities. My memory claims can be subject to interpersonal warrant and the interpersonal is ultimately founded on the inter-corporeal. An obvious example would be a memory I have of meeting you. If I was there "in person" I was there "in body". This is connected with the fact that, however discontinuous psychological contents are, there is an enduring, continuous point of view underwritten by the body, though not (it hardly needs reiterating) identical with that body's (also continuous) history.

These observations about the role of the body are, as already emphasized, a corrective to a corrective. Let us retrace our steps. Earlier, we rejected the idea that personal identity is to be found in the persistence of our body or our brain. The explorations in Chapters 3 and 4 highlighted the important distances between ourselves and our bodies, central to our nature as persons. And so (Corrective 1) we switched our attention to the psychological continuity and connectedness that hold between different parts of a person's life. This would provide the basis of the sense of persisting identity over time, however, if and only if we already had a sense of our identity at a particular time expressed in the existential intuition *that I am* (*this*). What is more, an interpersonal scaffold was also necessary to give stability and support to that sense of enduring identity. And this, too, constitutes a trellis to provide individual episodic memories with a location and the truth warrant that comes from a structured landscape of shared reality. It takes a community to maintain a self, though selves are the very material of a community. Cue for Corrective 2: re-enter the body as being necessary for our having actual, particular, experiences (perceiving *this* rather than *that*, perceiving anything in particular) and for our being identifiable to others, as a back-up to the connection of autonoetic memory with the identity of a person. Now that the role of the body has been acknowledged, it is time now for a third corrective, based on the observations made in Chapter 3.

While our body is a necessary condition of having a flux of particular experiences, and it is equally necessary as a condition of that flux being transformed into the underpinning of a standing self, it is – for all the reasons we have given earlier – not to be identified with myself. Its successive biological states do not amount to an "I". Indeed, my moment-to-moment identity does not reside in the successive states of any physical thing,[86] not even where that thing is my body, the necessary condition of my existence, from which I am inseparable, and which is pointed to when someone wants to draw attention to Raymond Tallis.

CONCLUDING THOUGHTS ON PERSONAL IDENTITY

To say that our self is not a thing, nor identical with a thing such as a body or a brain, is not to say that it is nothing. The autocides are wrong. Nor is it to propose that, if human beings are not simply Humean fluxes of impressions, they must be supernatural, immaterial beings, Cartesian egos, or the like. Nor is personal identity a mere "additional" fact. We cannot find any ontological category for it. A self is a self. Its elusive, even nebulous, nature does not disprove its reality;[87] more specifically, it does not justify denying the undeniable, the capacity of each one of us to gather ourselves up and act as a unity that incorporates many years of many kinds of experience. The backward reach of autonoetic memory is like nothing else in nature and yet it is indubitably real. Although it is deeply mysterious, it is not a fantasy that I can say to someone, "Do you remember our holiday last summer?" and she will confirm that she remembers it and even elaborate on the memory. The shared recall is not an hallucination *à deux*.

The undoubted dependency of the "I" of Raymond Tallis on the "it" of Raymond Tallis' body is all the more disturbing for being intimate and higher-level, affecting not only basic awareness and motility but his very character. We may be unaware of changes in ourselves arising from changes inside our body – because we are judge, jury, and defendant, as expressed by neurosurgeon, Henry Marsh: "The person with frontal lobe dementia rarely has any insight into it – how can the 'I' know that it has changed? It has nothing to compare itself with. How can I know if I am the same person today as I was yesterday? I can only assume that I am."[88] In dementia, which particularly attacks memory, we cannot see that we are changed, or by how much, at the most fundamental or truly first-person level, because, if we have changed, the viewpoint from which we are viewing ourselves has also changed. We cannot get outside of ourselves to compare how we were at time t_1 and how we are now at time t_2 and see their difference.

We rightly think of dementia as an appalling tragedy for the person who suffers it. From the standpoint of a philosophy that would reduce person-hood in the way that Parfit attempts, it would not seem to be so. This helps us to understand the motivation behind Parfit's wish to reduce the person in the way that he does. He argues that: "If some future person would be uniquely psychologically continuous with me as I am now, and this continuity would have its normal cause, enough of the same brain, this person would be me".[89] Given that "enough of the same brain" is ill-defined, it is possible, Parfit would argue, to see that the person with fronto-temporal dementia is the same person as the pre-morbid individual. Her condition would therefore not be tragic.

Parfit takes this further and argues that personal identity is not what matters in survival, given that personal identity is no more than the connectedness of the psychological stream and the cerebral underpinning necessary to secure this. But we have seen that Parfit's reductionist account of the person leaves it entirely obscure how these successive psychological effects of cerebral causes not only join hands with each other (in the way that for example autonoetic memories do with the experience they are of) but also recognize their common allegiance to a single identity. The important thing for Parfit is that the elements of personal identity can be characterized as impersonal *facts*. The *what* seems to be the last word on the *who*. For this reason, he argues, it is irrational to fear death because this is only the end of these impersonal facts and not of personal identity:

> Consider the fact that, in a few years, I shall be dead. This fact can seem depressing. But the reality is only this. After a certain time, none of the thoughts and experiences that occur will be directly causally related to this brain or be connected in certain ways to these present experiences. That is all this fact involves. And, in that redescription, my death seems to disappear.[90]

We should not therefore take death hard, or even personally, because the person who dies is not something additional to impersonal brain states and psychological elements floating free of any self.

It would be difficult to draw comfort from his stance, even if the underlying arguments were persuasive. The conclusion makes sense only to one who disregards the value we place on the past (as well as the future) for its own sake – as expressed in nostalgia, in the existentially profound recreation of reminiscing with others about a shared past, and thus affirming its reality, and its significance, quite independently of any practical use it may have. Such self-valuing is inseparable from personal identity.

While Hume distinguishes "personal identity, as it regards our thought or imagination and as it regards our passions or the concern we take in it",[91] the latter is not a narrowly egocentric attitude. It is expressed in the Heideggerian sense that human being or *Da-sein* is "that being whose being is an issue for itself".[92] Being an issue for one's self is the basis for the value we place on others, as well as ourselves, and on the world in which we live. It is bound up with the interpersonal underpinnings of personal identity, the centrality of *recognition* to our distinctly human being. Reducing personal identity to a discrete flux rooted in a discrete object (the embodied brain) overlooks how much our personal identity is co-produced with the identity of others; how much "I" is rooted in "we"; how the first-person singular is inseparable from the first-person plural, and the second and third person. Our identity in short, is inseparable from our being-with, and being valued by and valuing, others.

That is why personal identity, far from being "unimportant" (Parfit's judgement) is of supreme importance. Lucretius famously argued that we should not fear death because "he who is no more cannot be wretched".[93] But even if we accept (or try to accept) the Lucretian reassurance regarding our own death, we still fear the death of those we love. Our sense of ourselves, our identity, is inseparable from our being, in every sense of the word, shaped by and mutually invested in others. We consequently fear the loss of others and suffer sorely from bereavement, which is as much as anything a loss of ourselves. *I* may not suffer the loss of myself when I die but others (at least I hope) will.

It is the failure to acknowledge the centrality of others to personal identity that gives apparent plausibility and relevance to the endlessly debated thought experiments, centred on the idea of the "teletransportation" of *individual* brains or their "information content" to distant places, that have been so central to Parfit-inspired discussions of personal identity. We shall return to them in Chapter 7. Suffice it for the present to note that such thought experiments overlook the community of minds and indeed the outside world where personal identity has its public reality. In this interpersonal realm it is connected with *identification* (with a family, a group, a cause, a culture) – something that is embraced, even struggled for, and granted or imposed – and, behind this, the mutual acknowledgement and recognition that we discussed earlier.

The existential intuition *that I am* – and the sense that our identity is something we seek to embrace and is the point of convergence of all our valuation of things – is connected with what is missing in the reductionist idea of personal identity. It has no place for our valuing ourselves, in part through being valued by others, and the values of the community of minds in which our identity is forged and forges itself. It is hardly surprising that, as Roger Scruton said of Parfit's gigantic magnum opus *On What Matters*: "Nothing that really matters to human beings – their loves, attachments, their delights, aesthetic values, and spiritual needs occurs in Parfit's interminable narrative. All is swept into a corner by the great broom of utilitarian reasoning, to be left there in a heap of dust".[94]

Of course, from the purified objective, even autistic, viewpoint underpinning Parfit's ambition for perfecting utilitarian thought, the individual person does not matter as much as the sum total of all the experiences of all people that on earth do dwell. But that sum total can itself matter only to (individual) subjects. We cannot set aside the subject and still retain mattering. Our singularity, and irreplaceability, is gathered up in the idea of the over-arching individual self to whom experiences and life events can be attached and through whom they are related. Such a self cannot be translated into the successive states of a persistent, functioning brain and the psychological stream supposedly generated by them.

If personal identity does not matter, then very little that we value in our human lives does. We would be content with the lives of animals. But we are not thus content; and, anyway, our lives are not those of animals whose self is scarcely developed. And it could scarcely be an illusion that I have a continuous sense of being myself, if I can have privileged access through autonoetic and other memory to past experience, to knowledge about myself (even over esoteric things such as whether I have ever engaged in hand-to-paw conflict with a wolf) and, through this, to a past world I inhabited from a unique perspective, and can regulate my future on the basis of this capacity.

In this chapter we have been addressing the humanist challenge of finding an understanding of the self that locates it in the right place between (say) a Cartesian substance (and its ancestors such as the soul), a Humean flux rather haphazardly internally stitched with memory, a Kantian transcendental subject located outside the phenomenal world but the principle in or a vanishing point of a field of consciousness, or a Sartrean nothingness. What Wittgenstein said of a sensation (such as pain) – that "It is not a *something*, but not a *nothing* either"[95] – should apply to a self, to whatever it is that is identified when we think of personal identity as something that matters. It is not easy to assign the self a place between an entity, a container for entities, and a non-entity. But we cannot dodge the problem by denying its existence. This – and Descartes-phobia – may explain why the self has such a bad reputation among some philosophers. The postmodernist, Dennettian, Chaterian, and panpsychist and Parfitian deflations are some of the indignities to which it has been subjected in order to put it into its place as ontologically inferior.

It is only because we are, at any given time, real selves extended over time, that we can be true agents. And there is no doubt that we are such agents and can be responsible for our actions. Because we own some of our past, we can own up to it. I have reached the topic of the next chapter: agency.

CHAPTER 6

The mystery of human agency

We are now equipped to examine something that many philosophers – not to speak of myself as an anguished teenager – believe that reason obliges us to deny: human agency. I will argue that we have an important measure of freedom. At the heart of our freedom is the special relationship that we, as persons rather than organisms, have to time, a relationship manifested in our selfhood and our enduring identity. Selfhood and agency develop in parallel. We realize ourselves through our struggles as agents with the world and our selfhood underpins our agency.

A valid defence of the reality of our freedom must be a cornerstone of humanist philosophy. "Freedom" the English historian Edward Gibbon said "is the first wish of our heart, the first blessing of our nature"[1] – notwithstanding that there are times when the way we exercise it suggests that it may also be our primordial curse. Any version of Della Mirandola's "dignity of man" must presuppose that we are not the playthings of nature. If we have no agency, our lives are no more imbued with purpose than those of other primates; or, if that seems a little harsh on our nearest animal kin, than the lives of insects whose sole end (unknown to themselves) is to create more insects.

DETERMINISM

Opening shots

The case against our being free agents is sufficiently well-rehearsed as to require little telling. Briefly, it takes its rise from the undeniable fact that we are embodied in material organisms which, it is to be assumed, are subject to the laws of nature. Such laws are, by *definition*, unbreakable, admitting no exceptions. We are, it seems, frog-marched from birth to death along tramlines laid down by those laws which have their local and universal expression in the way effects inescapably follow causes. Every material event in my body has a material cause within or beyond my body operating in accordance with physical laws. Although those laws are expressed differently at different levels – at the level of atoms or whole, macroscopic organisms – they are equally unnegotiable. The causes have other causes and they have other causes in turn. Their causal ancestry therefore extends beyond anything that could possibly lie within the scope of any free will you and I might care to exercise. Our lives it seems are simply local expressions of the universal habits of a material world. The processes that brought you to read this page are fundamentally no more tractable than those that govern the interactions between the seat you may be sitting on and the floor that supports that seat.

The determinist case seems even tighter when we recall how we *rely* on the unbreakable laws of nature and the rigidly deterministic relationship between cause and effect when we act with the intention of bringing about certain outcomes. Any downstream loosening of the law-governed connectedness of the material world, and of our interactions with it, would be incompatible with our achieving our ends or indeed with our continuing survival. I could not walk towards something I need, or away from something I fear, if my body and the material world were not subject to mechanical principles. And this dependency on 100 per cent reliable nature applies at every level from the individual cells of which I am made to the overall beast that is writing this sentence.

If we are to have free will, it seems, we need to be to some degree *outside of* the very nature that has fashioned us, implanted the basic needs that directly or indirectly prompt most of our actions, and created the order that enables us to meet those needs. If this is not possible, then we cannot be points of origin shaping our local bit of the universe, any more than bubbles could guide the stream on which they float. We cannot, as it were, *get behind* the causes of which we are effects to direct those causes to fulfil freely chosen intentions.

Some think that the very idea of our being agents is a superstitious hangover from the idea that the universe is driven by the agency of God and that, by His permission, we are privileged beings who are granted a share in that agency. According to the narrative of the Qur'an, and its story of the creation, it was free will that distinguished humanity from the rest of nature. The Islamic story begins with a statement of intention by God to the assembly of angels: "I will create a vicegerent on earth".[2] Slim chance, then, that we might be free in any sense that matters to us, a sense succinctly summarized by Robert Kane: "the power of agents to be the ultimate creators (or originators) and sustainers of their own ends and purposes".[3]

Freedom of the will in Kane's sense would require that:

1. We can truly say, of at least some of our behaviour, that "the buck starts here";
2. Our actions have deflected the course of events rather than merely been part of a predetermined flow;
3. They express something within us that we can truly own and for which we take credit or blame; and
4. Any given action is one of several possibilities genuinely open to us such that we could have done or chosen otherwise.

Your brain made you do it

In recent decades as the traditional case against free will has been apparently reinforced by arguments arising from an interpretation of neuroscience – so called "neurodeterminism". Neurodeterminism seemed to have been placed on an empirical footing by a famous set of experiments, carried out by the neurophysiologist Benjamin Libet in the 1980s and repeated and refined many times since then.[4] It has been claimed that they demonstrate that our brain makes decisions to act before our conscious mind is aware of them, so those "decisions" are not really *ours* at all.

What did Libet do and what did he find? In a typical experiment, Libet's subjects are instructed to make a simple movement – such as to bend their wrist – in their own time. The action is self-initiated not in response to an instruction. It would appear therefore to be truly voluntary, not merely a reaction to a stimulus. The subjects are also asked to register the time at which they felt the urge or intention to move, by noting the position of a dot on an oscilloscope timer. In addition, using an electroencephalogram, the experimenter records an activity in the brain that indicates a readiness to move. This so-called "readiness potential" (RP) is observed in the part of the cerebral cortex that standard neuroscience deem is most closely associated with voluntary movement. The RP occurs about half a second before activity in the relevant muscles of the arm or hand, as recorded by an electromyogram, because it takes time for the neural activity in the cortex to translate into events in the relevant muscles.

All very straightforward. What, however, caused considerable excitement or concern (depending on your viewpoint) was that the RP occurred a consistent third of a second *before* the time at which the subjects reported being aware of a decision to move. Libet concluded from this that the *brain* had "decided" to initiate, or at least to prepare to initiate, the act before there was any reported subjective awareness of a decision having been made. Put more simply, the cerebral causes of our actions seem to occur *before* our conscious awareness of deciding to perform them.

Even more alarming to some, are more recent studies by John-Dylan Haynes and colleagues. They asked subjects to press a button with the index finger of the left or right hand in their own time, while a scanner recorded which parts of the brain were active. Again, subjects would time the decision they made to choose a hand – on this occasion by remembering a letter which was shown on the screen when the decision was made. The patterns of neural activity predictive of whether the subject would choose either left or right hand occurred 7 seconds *before* the subjects were aware of having made a choice.[5] The brain, it is claimed, is making the decision before the person.

The apparent significance of these findings was spelled out by neuroscientist and philosopher Patrick Haggard who argued that:

> although we may experience that our conscious decisions and our thoughts cause our actions, these experiences are in fact based on readouts of brain activity in a network of brain areas that control voluntary action ... The notion that free will is merely a feeling that occurs after consciously inaccessible circuits make a decision can be unsettling.[6]

Not only unsettling. For some, it has settled the matter. As psychologist Sue Blackmore put it: "Mind over matter? Many philosophers and scientists have argued that free will is an illusion. Unlike all of them, Benjamin Libet has found a way to test it".[7] Evolutionary biologist Jerry Coyne has argued that "So it is with all of ... our choices: not one of them results from a free and conscious decision on our part. There is no freedom of choice ... no free will".[8] Our belief that we are responsible for our actions is no longer valid. All activity is passivity.

Thus, the views of those whom Eddy Nahmias has called the "willusionists".[9] While many have questioned the significance of the neural activity – such as the RP – that has been used as a marker of the brain "making a decision to act" in advance of conscious awareness of the actor,[10] these technical questions are less important, and indeed philosophically less interesting, than the fundamental misunderstanding of the nature of human action and what it is to exercise free will betrayed in the very design of the experiments.

ACTIONS

Neurodeterminist misrepresentation of the nature of voluntary action[11]

The first thing that should strike anyone evaluating the philosophical significance of these neurological studies is the *triviality* of the actions and of the choices required of their subjects.[12] For example, the choice between a left and right hand is entirely without meaning: nothing of material importance is at stake. Flexing one's hand, solely in response to an urge to flex one's hand, is a piffling movement. It is little more than a twitch. It is scarcely something that would warrant a diary entry: "Today I bent my left wrist".

Of much greater significance for our understanding of the nature of free action is that the trivial events connected with the observed brain activity were really small parts of whole actions that belonged to something much, much bigger and which *would* warrant a diary entry: "Today I went to Dr Libet's laboratory and took part in an experiment". *This* action was hardly something that we could imagine being built out of little meaningless movements such as the hand flexion Libet requested of his subjects. Ninety-nine point nine per cent of the visit was beyond the scope of the experiment and, indeed, the laboratory. Voluntary participation in the experiment, to which the hand flexing owed any sense and purpose, began at least as far back as getting up in the morning to visit the laboratory. It involved consenting to take part in a procedure whose nature, purpose and safety was fully understood; and it required (among many other things) listening to and understanding and agreeing to the instructions that were received – and *then* deciding to carry out the instruction. In other words, the self-timed psychological event, the "urge" to move the finger, was preceded by many relevant events and intentions that were located minutes, hours, perhaps days, before the wrist flexion. These conferred the meaning upon the finger movement and accounted for its actually taking place at the time it did. Without this context, it is unlikely that the subject would have sat in a chair in the lab, flexing her hand at intervals.

The real story, therefore, was not just the flexing of the wrist. Nor, indeed, the flexing of a wrist *plus* timing of one's own urge to make a movement (an element of the experiment that is somewhat overlooked).[13] The real story was one of a sustained and complex resolve being maintained over a long time, way beyond that of brain events observed by the scientists. "Taking part in Dr Libet's experiment" included many large items of behaviour: making sure one was available at the appointed time (remembering to set the alarm clock in advance so as not to oversleep); wearing appropriate clothes as laid out in the letter of invitation (remembering to iron them the night before); finding one's way to the laboratory (road, building, room, and not forgetting to take the map); using transport to get to the laboratory (checking the bus times in advance), or driving one's self and parking one's car (keeping the receipt for the parking charges in order to claim back expenses); and so on. The total of these components of the visit to the laboratory amounted to many thousands, perhaps hundreds of thousands, of integrated motor events and involved many choices all orchestrated and subordinated to achieving a rather complex goal. The movement of the wrist, which would not have taken part except as part of *volunteering* to take part in the experiment, was quite likely part of an even greater intentional whole, such as "wanting to help those clever scientists understand the brain as it might one day help doctors to treat my child's brain injury more effectively". None of this could have been achieved unconsciously.

The point is this. The apparent importance of the fact that the self-timed intentions of the empty movement seemed to *follow*, rather than *succeed*, the RP – supposedly a marker of the brain "making a decision" – tells us nothing about the operation of ordinary free will. It seems to do so only if we accept a grossly distorted, indeed impoverished, idea of what constitutes an action in real life.[14] It even more radically traduces the very idea of volition, whose expression is not broken up into individual, isolated physical movements. Even less are those actions that comprise taking part in the experiment the outcome of binary choices – flexing or not flexing a wrist; moving one hand rather than another. Our path through life is not made up of a series of Left vs Right branches of a fork – such as moving the right hand or the left. If we have reached the point where we have to make a binary choice, much of the work of agency has already been completed. This is evident where there is genuine equipoise, when we might be inclined to hand over our choice to the toss of a coin. We resort to coin-tossing when each branch of the fork seems equally expressive, or inexpressive, of our agency.[15]

Freedom of the will operates in a *field*: it is not a linear succession or collection of atomic intentions/causes bringing about atomic material events that are their direct effects. Its expression arises out of, and is directed towards, a multi-dimensional self-world. The Libet model of agency

$$\text{Urge (Intention)} \rightarrow \text{Action}$$

misrepresents how volition is expressed in our lives. Even if Libet's discovery that a brain event (the RP) precedes the Urge (Intention) were accurate, therefore, it would tell us nothing about the reality or otherwise of free will. The experiment traduces the irreducibly complex ways of volition. The human agent operates out of a temporally deep world, rich in multi-layered explicit meanings that give her actions the bespoke purpose without which they would not take place.[16] What's more, to isolate the "urge" or "intention" as a discrete cause of action would be to require that it should have no causal antecedents – it should be formed independently of the material world though it is obliged to have causal descendants – the action. (This is the opposite error to the epiphenomenal idea of consciousness as something that has causal ancestors but no causal descendants.)

One of the most intimate conditions of volition is arousal and wakefulness. Setting an alarm clock is a reminder of how we can coerce ourselves to attend to the necessary conditions of our competence. "Shaping up", "snapping out of it", "getting a grip", battling drowsiness, arranging to ambush one's future self by means of notes left in a prominent place, are just a few examples of how we act upon ourselves to maximize the global mental state necessary for the operation of our free will. The complex temporality of leaving our future selves reminders of things we should not forget to do should also give determinists pause.

It is easy also to forget that Libet's experiment, like all research, is a cooperative exercise, not only between the subject and the experimenter but also between the experimenter and an extended community of fellow scientists whose technologies (consciously created and consciously used) and skills (consciously deployed) have been and continue to be necessary for designing the experiment and carrying it out. The rationale of the subject's participation in the experiment has multiple and complex roots in this interpersonal realm. It is scarcely surprising, therefore, that the rationale of the experiment into which the volunteer buys cannot be discovered in the fractions-of-a-second interval between one set of neural discharges (supposedly constituting "preparation to act") and another (supposedly constituting the intention to do so). The action has tentacular roots not only in the subject's intention to take part in the experiment, expressed in her determination to find her way to the laboratory, but also in the experimenter Dr Libet spending many months learning the relevant neuroscience techniques, dreaming up the study, and writing grant applications to fund it. It is ironical that nothing could be a more striking expression of human freedom than the performance of an experiment on another human being, with their informed consent, that is subsequently claimed to demonstrate that such freedom is unreal.

All of this shows the absurdity of philosopher and neuroscientist Sam Harris' claim that neuroscience has exposed free will as an illusion, on the grounds that "if we were to detect [people's] conscious choices on a brain scanner seconds before they were aware of them ... this would directly challenge their status as conscious agents in control of their inner lives".[17] Nevertheless, it has justified the claim that, as willusionist Coyne has expressed it, "true 'free will' ... would require us to step outside of our brain's structure and modify how it works".[18] We need, therefore, to address this seeming killer determinist argument that to be free agents we would have to act upon ourselves from the outside – like Baron Munchausen pulling himself up by his own hair. To understand free will, our ability to exercise leverage on ourselves and the world, we need to understand that *outside*.

Real actions in the real world

We don't have to look very far, or very hard, to find clues as to the nature of the outside. The possibility of ourselves as agents has its origins in our temporal depth. Our actions draw on many layers of our past that are not reducible to previous moments in physical time. The "time" we are talking about is of the kind we discussed in Chapter 4. It is central to what lay behind that wrist movement in Libet's laboratory – the subject's commitment to honouring the appointment, the skill to navigate, with the aid of written instructions, to the laboratory where the experiment is to be held, the cultivation of good relationships with a neighbour to mind the children while one attends for the experiment, the ability to understand a long explanation of its nature and purpose, and an attitude of trust to the experimenters wiring you up to machines. The clue, in short, lies in the complex reality of our everyday human actions and abilities which draw on near and remote layers of an actual (individual and shared) past and an imagined (shared and individual) future.

Each of these abilities mobilizes different timeframes and a different kind of relationship to them. Multiple modes of "at" and strata of "that" and the "thatosphere" are brought into play. Against this background, it becomes self-evidently absurd to think that the 300-millisecond time relationship between the RP and the subjective sense of the intention to move, would reveal anything about what it is to participate in the experiment. It would have even less to contribute to the argument as to whether or not we are free outside of the laboratory.

The causally closed realm of the material brain is not the place where actions are forged. It is in the thatosphere that we find the "outside" that is in play when we perform a truly voluntary action. The person who moves her wrist as the executor of the key part of the experiment is not, in so doing, confined to the time at which the wrist moves or the "urge" to do so is felt. Moreover, the clock time of the subjectively noted intention is not the time upon which the intention draws: the intention derives its rationale from a multiplicity of times. That is why this or any other subjective manifestation of intention is not to be identified with a physical event in the brain or indeed any isolated event. Intention does not belong to the timeframe in which the Readiness Potential is located.

The determinist conclusion from the experiments of Libet and others illustrates how the case against freedom is rooted in a very impoverished, indeed distorted, conception of what constitutes an action in real life. To think of an intention as an isolated event occurring at a particular time is to succumb to a misunderstanding even more profound than would be that of treating in isolation individual words or letters that comprise a novel. The intention to move the wrist belongs to a self addressed to, and addressed by, (a part of) the human world. If, however, you want to make voluntary actions seem involuntary the first thing you must do is strip away their context – the person from whom they originate, the soil from which they grow, the world to which they are addressed – and then effectively break them down into small, physical elements. This gets you well on the way to eliminating the difference between a twitch and a deliberate action; between a mere reaction and a carefully planned fulfilment of an aim; between someone *in*voluntarily taking part in the experiment, having been carried to the lab in a coma and woken up simply to move her wrist, and her participating in it "because I want to help those clever scientists".[19]

I could, for example, decompose the process of writing this page into physiological events such as the formation and rupture of cross-bridges in the fibres of my hand muscles when they contract. Now it is perfectly obvious that I could not *do* the physiology of my movements: I would not know how to make or unmake a muscle cross-bridge if I tried. Does it follow from this that I am not writing this page freely or that I am not really intending to write it or that it has no relation to the intentions I formed during the days when I first started planning it? No; all that this demonstrates is that atomic fragments of actions shorn of the frame of reference that give them meaning, cannot – and need not – be separately intended, and that it is misguided to look for the freedom of my free act at that level. Real actions are indissoluble wholes, orchestrated by higher-order intentions that issue not from bodies but from persons. This extra-cerebral realm – and not brains or bits of brains – is where we should look when we are trying to find the locus of our free will, even though, of course, the brain is a necessary condition of our being able to act.

Our intentions are interconnected with each other as are our decisions and our plans. Unlike local causes, they are not linear pushes; rather they are inseparably woven into a landscape, a fabric, of embraced significance – rooted ultimately in our sense of who and what we are and where we are in our lives. For this reason, typical actions do not have to be propelled into existence by specific intentions; for the most part, they unfold without explicit decisions – except broad-brush ones – at every node; and they are pulled towards an envisaged future, rather than pushed by an unchosen past. When I am walking to the pub to meet you, there isn't a separate decision corresponding to every one of the hundreds of steps I take to get there. The drivers of our actions are not quasi-causes located immediately prior to the actions. More generally, the power to make discrete choices is exercised within a *field* of freedom that creates the context within which any "A or B" – or "Yes vs No" – choices are made.

Ordinary actions incorporate vast numbers of physical events arranged *hierarchically* with subordinate elements serving superordinate or over-arching purposes. As we shall discuss presently, such events are *requisitioned* as the means to bring about certain intermediate ends, themselves means to further ends, often involving tools and machines that facilitate or deputize for other intermediate steps. They are composite, and the tools they requisition are themselves assembled out of many parts. Seen in this light, it is evident that an action is an event that would not have taken place unless it had fulfilled a purpose explicitly entertained by an agent bent on making it happen or preventing something else from happening. Its conditions are entirely different from those that make an event the result of a cause in the causally closed material world: mass, energy, charge, etc.

Let us think again about the elements that make up the subject's participation in Libet's experiment. As a succession of physical movements, they would seem to have negligible probability of co-occurring spontaneously: only a goal-orientated conscious agent could account for them. Consider the subject's journey to put the money into the car parking machine and the half hour of sitting still in Libet's waiting room and the movement of the hand a few minutes later. They would not have occurred in the same morning had they not all been requisitioned by a single over-riding intention: to take part in Dr Libet's experiment. The improbability of that succession of events taking place by chance or by the operation of the laws of nature would approximate to zero. We hardly need to multiply the length of these odds by the odds stacked against all other things the subject fits into that busy day to make our case.[20] And that is true of the actions that make up the foreground of an ordinary busy day: they are events that would not have happened had they not made sense to me. This is the other side of the truth noted by many philosophers that actions are actions only under a certain description. The description precedes the action and the action fulfils the description.

This last argument might be countered by examples of complex, sustained behaviour from the animal kingdom. Think, a determined determinist might argue, of the migration of swallows who return in successive years to the same nesting grounds at the end of a 3,000-mile journey from their winter habitat. It will require many thousands of movements and often include corrections when the birds have been blown off course. This example does not provide as powerful a counter-argument as it may seem because, although the target of a swallow's journey is singular, the driver for reaching it is programmed and general. For a start, swallows are not voluntary nomads. More importantly, the return to an address can be programmed into the bird's brain which utilizes magnetic fields, the sun as a compass, and other cues, for orientation. After all, an entirely insentient ballistic missile can be so programmed. The human subject's participation in Libet's experiment, by contrast, is bespoke all the way through: it is bespoke in its origin, bespoke in its realization, and bespoke in the goal to which it is directed. The sense necessary for it to happen is rooted in an individual life. No homing device would be sufficient to unite the participant with the experiment in the laboratory, even less take her through the steps involved in participation.[21]

The questions of a) the degree and b) the level at which actions are bespoke are connected. A man walking down a road is doing something that can be understood in biological terms and is analogous to a dog walking down a road or an insect climbing a blade of grass. Less so a man walking down the road in order to meet a friend in a pub. Even less so the same man walking down the road to discuss something particular with a friend in said pub. And less again a man walking down a road to discuss something with a friend in order to correct a misunderstanding as part of a project of being as kind and as helpful to others as possible. While this latter action can be biologized as an instance of a bonding instinct that has survival value for the species, the generalization is in the opposite direction to the increasing tailor-made character of the action. The evolutionary interpretation dissolves all that is particular, all that is thought through, all that is deliberate, all that is individual, about the action, into an unwarranted generalization that obscures the singular path that led to the action. It is not surprising that agency is lost; and that my very specific, and reflected upon, kindness is reduced to a biologically prescribed response to a fellow member of a species. Instinct does not weigh pros and cons, knows no dilemmas.

There is no shortage of philosophers who believe that we grossly overestimate the extent to which conscious decision-making is in our lives. Most prominent among them is the same Daniel Dennett who, as we discussed in Chapter 2, has argued for many decades against the centrality of both intentions and intentionality in our lives. In his most recent book – *From Bacteria to Bach and Back* – he has claimed that, overwhelmingly, our competencies do not require comprehension.[22] While there may be reasons for our doing what we do, he argues, we do not *have* those reasons. Of course, there are levels at what Dennett claims is true, but this does not include the level relevant to the exercise of genuine free will in everyday activity.

Consider again my going to a pub to meet with a friend. I will exercise many competencies without comprehending them. It is perfectly obvious that I do not have to know how to orchestrate the contraction of my muscle fibres to get to my meeting. Nor do I have to be able to explain to myself exactly why I want to meet with my friend at the level of (e.g.) "the human need for friendship", though I may have a general purpose in mind – for example to plan a walking holiday.

What is more, in order to make sure the meeting takes place, I have to consult my watch to check the time and work out how to get to the pub on the basis of the directions my friend has given me.[23] Those directions may not seem cutting-edge technology but they are worth a bit more of our attention. They are not stimuli – I may well write them down with a view to acting on them tomorrow or at some indefinite time in the future, "when they are needed". The knowledge the written directions make available to me when I decide they are needed, like all knowledge, is not implanted in the way that sense experiences are. Nor is it a cause in the direct manner of natural causes. (I will return to this presently.) Importantly, I will resist being blown off course by distractions en route offered by shop windows and chance meetings because I want to honour my appointment. I am committed, in short, only to responding to the stimuli to which it is appropriate for me to respond in the light of my chosen goals. What might be the occasion for a response at one time is not seen as such at another. If, opportunistically, I nip into the newsagent en route to buy a lottery ticket, this will happen only if I have enough time to do this and not be late.

The last point underlines something central to human volition: our capacity to *refrain* from re-action, to make space for action. We persist in whatever is necessary to realize our intentions against a countervailing current of pressures, experiences, and distractions to which under other circumstances we might be inclined to respond. "Man, the refraining animal" is a profound expression of our species' temporal depth, of the fact that we are not a succession of conscious moments, of depthless "nows". As agents, we are time travellers, inhabiting possible futures informed by experienced or reported pasts, so that the present has a chosen direction. Those pasts and futures may be personal or collective and they are present influences on our choice of actions.

To keep open a space for actions with long-term benefits, mere reactions must be resisted. We are patient creatures, willing to wait, planning ahead, attending to preparations, responding to remote possibilities, and distant prospects, which we envisage. Actions are often mediated, with many steps in the hinterland: I do this in order to do that, do that in order to do the other, and so on.[24] Notwithstanding potential distractions, we usually remain steadfastly on course, whether the course is a trip to the pub to meet someone or something that has a more long-term significance such as going to a pensions advisor about saving up for one's retirement. We still, of course, need to retain the capacity for reflex reactions, as when one trips and saves one's self from falling, or jumps on to the pavement to avoid an oncoming vehicle.

What makes this even more remarkable is that, irrespective of our ability to stick to a plan in a torrent of distractions, we are not confined to a single course. We have the ability, where appropriate, to interweave other actions that may have vastly different time scales; for example, saving up for my retirement and at the same time calculating that it is fine to go for a drink without threatening adequate provision for my old age by missing my appointment with the pension advisor. Alternatively, we can remain simultaneously on two or more courses as we multi-task, consciously alternating between one goal and another, between occupation and preoccupation, switching between narratives. We can also set ourselves going and persist with one element of a purposeful activity without continuing to will it, though we have to be ready to intervene if necessary. My two-hour journey down to London by train does not require a two-hour sustained urge, effort, or intention. I can, volitionally freewheel and my intentions can be left to look after themselves so long as they are being realized. I can therefore get absorbed in a book or a conversation, even fall asleep, though I may have to renew my intention if the train breaks down and it looks as if I will not make my appointment in time; and I will, anyway, be reminded of it as I near my destination. As we are engaged in actions that take a long time, we are of course surrounded by prompts, a scaffolding of implicit reminders, and we may rely upon or call on the support of others. And while we may be able intermittently to hand ourselves over to ongoing processes that do not require our agency, this does not alter the fact that our actions would not have taken place had we not intended them and been sustainedly conscious of our purposes: we still have to know what we are about in order to be about it. This remains true even where habits permit us to freewheel and to be taken over by acquired dispositions.

Even where our actions are relatively immediate responses to external events, we typically respond not to stimuli defined in terms of their physical properties but to *situations* characterized by their significance and by our goals. Crucially, a situation is not a constellation of mechanical, or more broadly physical, forces but a state of affairs unified by the sense we make of it. That sense is not defined by what (physically) it is now. My physical surroundings *qua* situation are invested with an aura of possibility and draw on a salient past and a salient future. It is part of the human world offset from the material universe that we *face* as our world and as the ultimate source of our agenda. In being situated, we to some degree create the environment that encircles us and transform what encircles the body – into threats, opportunities and duties, into intermediate means and ends; in short, the substrate for rational action. Material events as relevant causes and causes as "handles" emerge out of such a situation, rather than being strands in a putative net of a causally closed physical world.

As for the meeting with my friend in the pub, while there may be some off-the-shelf conventions that are honoured – the choreography of the buying of drinks and selecting a table and some of the content of the conversation – much of what happens will be singular to the occasion. What I say and when I say it will be directed by my sense of who you are and how we fit into each other's lives, all of which *pace Dennett* will draw on competencies that most certainly require consciousness and comprehension. Even the most stereotyped action of more than a certain duration will incorporate novel elements and require the actor to resist the blandishments of distractions, and they will have to be sustained through circumstances that are, seen as a whole, unique.

The example of using learned skills highlights another aspect of the balance between doing and happening, between comprehension and competence, in the exercise of volition. A competent pianist may be able to play a Beethoven sonata almost on automatic pilot. But all the time she is aware of what she is doing; and she can look critically at her performance and modulate it in response to the advice of a teacher whose judgement she trusts or her own assessment of how well she has played.

Manifest comprehension of what we are up to is even more clearly evident in joint enterprises. The building of a house is nothing like the construction of an ant-hill where each ant makes its contribution without having any sense of the whole that is aimed at. The humblest bricklayer still must exercise his understanding in order to follow instructions, to get to the workplace on time, and indeed successfully to complete an apprenticeship, even though it seems unlikely that he thinks about the placement of every brick, while he is talking to his work-mates about last night's football match. And while competencies are distributed between people and may be implicit in assistive technologies, the individual conscious agent comprehending what she is doing cannot be superseded.

The exercise of competencies in the hurly-burly of daily human life can never be freed of the need for comprehension – of what is being done and why – because we exercise our competencies in a singular world, in a context, that is specific to us, connected from a particular moment in our lives with unique personal pasts and personal futures. This remains true even when we are following explicit recipes, obey instructions, or being guided by measurements and calculations based on them. We can make an instructive comparison between on the one hand how my kidneys look after me (by helping to maintain homoeostasis necessary for life) and on the other how I look after my kidneys. The failure to recognize this normally obvious difference between mechanism and the exercise of conscious competencies is the result of an uncontrolled obsession with exorcising the Cartesian "ghost in the machine" from the human. The "willusionist" will not be satisfied until only machinery remains.

Actions are composed of events that would not have happened, even less occurred in an orchestrated sequence, if they had not been *requisitioned* with a future goal in (someone's) mind. While each walking step is a physical event, but it is also an element of a journey to the insurance broker with whom I plan to discuss my provision for my retirement. The step is not just a material effect of a prior material cause – though at a mechanical level it must be that as well. There is a "because" as well as a cause and "because" operates in a reverse temporal direction from what is seen in the natural world. The steps of my journey, instead of being driven by prior mechanical events – though they are assisted by the inertial ongoingness of my movements – are occasioned by desired consequences – for example my closer approximation to the insurance agent to discuss pension arrangements.[25]

The relationship between time and causation is turned around: instead of the past shaping the future, the future shapes what will become, for it, the past. Reasons (what we might call "becausation") reverse the asymmetry of influence – from prior cause to subsequent effect – seen in nature. The reason a stone flies through the air and the reason you threw it are entirely different. A falling stone is propelled by actual forces operating in an actual situation; a stone that is thrown is in part propelled by a future possibility – of hitting a target to fulfil some goal.

Beyond the causal net: freedom and the thatosphere

My aim has been to respond adequately to Jerry Coyne's seemingly knock-down argument against free will that it "would require us to step outside of our brain's structure and modify how it works". Free will most certainly does require this; and indeed, to act from outside not only of the brain but of nature understood as the causally closed material world subject to the physical laws that have that world in an unbreakable grip. To see how free will is possible, we must understand the nature of the "outside". It is to a great degree identical with the thatosphere we discussed in Chapter 4.

Let us remind ourselves of the central role of intentionality. It is courtesy of the space opened up by intentionality – most obviously in vision, where we make non-reciprocated contact with things "out there" – that we begin to be uncoupled from the material world and can import possibilities into a material realm of unrelieved actuality. While those possibilities are located in the future, they are nourished by the past.

Several features of the gaze are relevant to the freedom of voluntary action. Firstly, the direction of intentionality – reaching from sense impression registered by or within me to something "out there" – explicitly distinguishes the object of experience both from the experience itself and from the subject of experience. Secondly, the arrow of intentionality is *in the opposite direction to any putative causal arrow arising from the object and impinging on my sensorium.* Thirdly, the object is more than my present experience of it: there is a halo of possibility – the possibility of my own future experience of it from different perspectives, at different times, through different senses, and additionally of others' experiences of it.

Shared intentionality is the platform of collective action. As expressed by David Schweikard, it establishes "a basic sense of common ground on which other agents may be encountered in potential cooperation".[26] We not only take account of others' participation but count on it. This mutual awareness lifts agents beyond the herd behaviour seen in animals, that is rarely much more than the unwilled sum of individual intentions. The thatosphere, a cognitive product of shared intentionality, and the realm of further sharing of intentionality is an important source of the progressive uncoupling of the human subject from the surrounding world. When, as is customary, "That such and such is the case" is shared through testimony, what we know and expect is further separated from the direct causal impact of the material world on the conscious agent via our senses.[27] Courtesy of knowledge, action is far from reaction, a mere response to a stimulus. The quantity of knowledge that is mobilized in something as simple as my arranging to meet you at a particular time in the future is considerable, though it is largely unnoticed because commonplace.

Noting the centrality of knowledge to the exercise of free will is a cue for a further critical glance at the "causal theory of knowledge" and the false idea that the acquisition and deployment of knowledge and factual beliefs are causal processes within the natural order.[28] First, even more clearly than in the case of perceptions, the direction of the "aboutness" of knowledge, is not that of causation, least of all when it is deployed. Knowledge is neither the material effect of a material cause or a material cause of material effects.

Equally important is the nature of the *content* of factual knowledge. The latter is not a collection of material objects, events, charges, mass, or of anything else that we think of as being the substrate of causation in the natural order. Consider what happens when I use the instructions I have written down in order to find my way to a venue. "Take the 22 tram, alight at such-and-such a stop, take first left off the main road, walk for about 100 yards, and you will see the pub on your right". Not one of those instructions could plausibly be described as a *stimulus* definable by its physical properties or even as a representation of a piece of the material world, generated by that world, not the least because I have voluntarily mobilized them. We act in the light of knowledge: it is not something that shapes our actions by impacting on us. We take account of, rather merely react to, what we know.

Even the knowledge we deploy in strictly practical situations has more than merely local meaning or local content. Indeed, it owes its usefulness to the generality of its content, which obviously does not act as a cause. Consider this: my knowledge that you might be worrying about where I am that prompts me to phone you; my knowing that Africa is thousands of miles away explains why I book a plane to get there rather than walk; my being informed that the winter is predicted to be especially cold explains my going shopping in September for a warmer coat. None of these items can be thought of as either the product of natural, or more narrowly biological, forces or as exerting their influence through such forces. The material world does not have predicates. Knowledge operates within the thatosphere and, unlike sense experiences, are intrinsically public, being shared articulated perceptions, and not anchored in an individual human being, whose body might offer the diehard materialist a toehold for causal interaction. Items of knowledge, what is more, often have abstract elements. In addition, facts are typically held in store, available to be mobilized (or ignored) when they are relevant to my concerns. Even the homeliest exploitation of the simplest factual truths is remote from an effect of, or a response triggered by, the impingement of energy on my sense endings, such that they are part of the same causal net to which (for example) the neural activity occurring in my visual cortex belongs.

Let us return to my appointment and the use of directions. My asking you for instructions as to how to get to the location is not a mere effect of our agreeing to meet, though it makes sense in the light of the latter. Nor is my writing down those instructions. And even less is my consulting them when, a week later, I check my watch and decide that it is time to set out for our appointment. The fact that we may choose when to mobilize our knowledge

– determining when it is appropriate (and hence timely) to do so – also highlights how knowledge is not stitched into the flow of causes and effects passing through human persons via their sense organs. There is an interruption, a pause, and a resumption.

As has often been pointed out, knowledge is a matter not only of "knowing that" but also of "knowing how". The know-how, the skills, we acquire to extend the scope of our agency are typically not obtained at the point at which they are needed. In many cases, they are the product of extensive rehearsal at times when they are not needed. The skills are often self-taught but more often learned with the assistance of parents, teachers and colleagues, and they are enhanced by the wall-to-wall technology, purchased in advance, which amplifies our power and precision. There is typically an interval – which may be weeks, months, or even years – between the time of the acquisition of the know-how and the actions that exploit it.

Honing our skills is one of the many ways in which we "position ourselves", or tee ourselves up, in anticipation of the need for action or to pre-empt events that will interfere with the free expression of our wishes. "Positioning ourselves" begins in very humble or literal ways, that are also seen in non-human animals, such as building a permanent vantage point whence prey and predators are to be seen. It proceeds through the formation of cooperative groups and the accumulation of a store of weapons, to a long course of physical and cognitive training to prepare one for "the real thing". Skills, disciplines, tools and artefacts, are acquired at a time, and at a distance, remote from that in which they are used. These technologies and positioning habits, unlike those that may be utilized by non-human animals, are discretionary. This is the most clear-cut way in which we are self-fashioning agents, sometimes individually, sometimes in small groups, and sometimes as a tribe, a nation or even a species. Positioning may also take subtle forms – as when, for example, we encourage or train ourselves, or are encouraged or trained by others, to focus our attention in a certain direction or at a certain level – scaling up and down the acuity of observation.

Such self-fashioning is a reminder of the close relationship between selfhood and agency. *Ego ergo ago* ("I am therefore I act") also works in the opposite direction: *Ago ergo ego* ("I act, therefore I am"). Agency and selfhood ratchet each other up: they grow in parallel. And this is true of humanity as a whole: each generation delivers us to a higher level of agency. Our choices enhance our power to make future choices or to personalize our choices.

It is worth reflecting at this stage how far we are from the place where determinists find their arguments against free will. For determinists, the cause of our actions is the state of our body and the environment at a particular time t.

It will have been clear from what we have said in Chapters 3 and 4 that we are not identical in any meaningful way with the state of all, or even a privileged part, of our body at time t, when the action takes place or the decision to perform it is taken. I, as initiator of my actions, am not identical with the state of my body. What is more, the action reaches into an explicit future fashioned on the basis of an implicitly or explicitly present past. It follows, therefore, that even if the agent were identical with the present state of his body or his brain, that state as cause would be like no other. Causes do not look beyond themselves and give content to forward vision on the basis of the past. And causes are not self-extracting, putting a circle around something rather complex such as "the intention to deliver a better epilepsy service". The origin of actions is not to be located in the "it is" of the body in turn located in the "it is" of the material world but in the "I am" of the person, whose complex relationship to the body we have discussed.

Courtesy of our dwelling in the thatosphere, there is a radical transformation of the struggle to survive and prosper. Our days are remote from the push-pull, drag and lift, chase-and-flee life of beasts.[29]

Exploiting the laws of nature

> Having a special equipment of psychological abilities is a necessary factor in subjecting the energies of nature to use as instrumentalities for ends.   John Dewey[30]

We are now ready to address Jerry Coyne's challenge to explain our freedom: we *are* able to "step outside of our brain structure and modify how it works". Our freedom is rooted in the intentionality of experience, and in the sharing of intentionality that creates a uniquely human public realm, a multi-dimensional, immaterial "outside" from which we are able operate on the material world. Our actions draw on both a private and a collective past and reach into a future in which the private, the locally shared, and the public or collective, are interwoven. This is the outside which we inhabit.

It may still be argued that all of this remains subject to the laws of nature and intentionality, however widely joined, and offers us no escape from a causally closed world. This objection overlooks something fundamental. The laws of macroscopic nature operate in a fixed temporal direction – from t_1 to t_2 – and causes likewise. And they operate solely with actualities. Agency, by contrast, moves back and forth between many layers of the future informed by a private and shared many-layered past. As such, it operates with *possibilities*, whereas nature, the material world, is composed only of actualities. The past does not exist in the material world: its presence depends on its being preserved by humans in memories and in timeless facts. The future, present only as potent possibilities, necessarily of a general nature (unlike actualities which are particular) is likewise outside of nature. Actions are prompted by the sense that things might be different from the way they are. Thus the basis of a space which enables us to act on nature from outside: a space of possibilities outside of a nature of actualities. Yes, Professor Coyne, we act not merely from outside of the brain but from outside of nature. This outside is not to be identified with the inside of our body or our brain which belong to the "it is" of the material world.

And, yes, we can even act on our own brains: anyone who deliberately sets out to acquire a competence is changing the structure of her brain. In acting upon our brains, or the rest of our body, or indeed the natural world, we do not break the laws of nature; rather we exploit those laws insofar as they have come to light through our everyday understanding and, comparatively recently in the history of our species, through scientific understanding. Walking to a chosen destination involves exploiting the friction between our feet and the ground. Making walking safer and more efficient by manipulating the coefficient of friction by gritting a slippery surface is to work with, not against, the laws of nature. A grasp of "how things go" is the first step to making things go one way rather than another. We do not initiate action from a standing start but ride and shape the ongoingness of the world as it is refracted through our individual lives. We utilize the laws by taking events or states of affairs generated by natural processes and turning them into handles by which, or platforms from which, we bring about other events or states of affairs that we have identified as our immediate, intermediate, or ultimate ends. The ultimate origins of our voluntary actions, of course, go a long way back as will be evident from our discussion of "positioning".

The operation of free will does not therefore involve the impossibility of lifting ourselves by our hair. Actions are not supernatural self-caused causes, but rather the extra-natural use of causes to bring about a desired effect. Intentions are not local causes (*contra* Libet) but modes of consciousness that illuminate our world and make events, or possible events, into handles to realize possibilities.

To further our understanding of how we exploit the laws of nature, some remarks made by J. S. Mill in a posthumously published essay, *Nature* are helpful. Here Mill attempts to explain how we can act freely, even though we are material parts of a material world and consequently subject to the laws of nature; how we can maintain the distinction between the actions of agents on the one hand and, on the other, events arising in law-governed nature, without ascribing to our agency magic, independent material powers of its own.

Mill's argument is that, at any given juncture, there is more than one law of nature operating. By aligning ourselves with one law, we can use nature to achieve ends not envisaged in nature: "Though we cannot emancipate our-selves from the laws of nature as a whole, we can escape from any particular law of nature if we are able to withdraw ourselves from the circumstances in which it acts. Though we can do nothing except through laws of nature, we can use one law to counteract another".[31]

We do not break the laws of nature but utilize them by aligning ourselves with the one that leads to our goal. We can align ourselves in this way because we act from a virtual outside-of-nature just described: the human world woven out of temporal depth, possibilities, and knowledge – free-floating or embodied in artefacts and amenities. This is how, as Mill said, quoting Francis Bacon, we can "obey nature so as to command her".[32] An ever more powerful understanding of "how things go" will enhance our ability to make things go the way we want them to.

Our actions, therefore, are not uncaused, extra-legal miracles: they go with the grain of causation and their material expression is entirely law-abiding.[33] If it were not, no benefit would accrue to us from discovering nature's laws. But we are able to step back into the great extra-natural space that is the human world and from there use material causes as handles or levers on the material world. Mill again: "Every alteration of circumstances alters more or less the laws of nature under which we act; and by every choice we make either of ends or of means, *we place ourselves* to a greater or lesser extent under one set of laws instead of another"[34] (emphasis added). Our capacity to *position* ourselves in this way is complex and multi-layered as we have discussed. That this capacity operates at different time scales again highlights the fundamental misconception of thinking of agency (as neurodeterminists often envisage it) as being realized or mediated through discrete intentions which are special events, exotic assertions of quasi-physical power, inserted into a particular location in space-time to generate specific consequences.

To conclude our case for the compatibility of true agency and a law-governed natural world, two further points need to be made regarding the laws and causes with which we operate in exercising our agency.

Firstly, there is an important sense in which neither laws nor causes are part of nature. To say this is not to accept Kant's idea that "the synthetic activity of the mind is the lawgiver of nature";[35] only to make the less fundamental point that Nature does not utter the laws that describe its unfolding. The laws of mechanics, for example, are not part of the material world. If they were, then nature would have to update itself as science advanced and Aristotelian mechanics was replaced by Newtonian. The idea of laws that are *inherent* in nature seen from no viewpoint presupposes that there is a point where all laws converge and knowing and being are one. In reality, laws of actual science merely gather up *aspects* of the natural world – something that should be evident from their multiplicity. No material object obeys merely the third law of mechanics, or just the laws of mechanics, or just the laws of optics. To discover laws of nature is to highlight certain aspects of the natural world, in particular by removing the so-called secondary qualities (colour, taste, warmth, sound) that fill in the quantitative outlines of the experienced world.

Secondly, as the Nobel prize-winning physicist Eugene Wigner has pointed out, the laws of nature do not *mandate* anything: "classical mechanics, which is the best known prototype of a physical theory, gives the second derivatives of the positional coordinates of all bodies, on the basis of the knowledge of the positions etc. of these bodies. It gives no information on the existence, the present positions, or velocities of these bodies".[36] They do not, in short, specify any actuality. Rather they are the most general descriptions of aspects of how things unfold. Even less do they have legislative power to bring anything about. To imagine that the laws of nature have powers in themselves would be a kind of magic thinking.

Elsewhere in the extraordinary paper I have just quoted, Wigner designates as "initial conditions" those aspects of the physical world that lie *outside* the laws. They are the givens, the starting point, on which they operate and, additionally, include, the fact that there is something rather than nothing, that there are certain constants, that there is one set of laws and not another set, and so on.[37] All of this has to be put in place independently of the laws – hence the contested metaphysical status of the Big Bang. This is another way of highlighting the fact that the laws of nature do not make things happen. In virtue of their generality, they do not reach down to, and hence prescribe, actual happenings which, irrespective of their being general in character, are particular in their occurrence. And it is vain to look to "causes" – assumed to be sufficiently local – to fill this gap between timeless general laws and particular events taking place at a particular time and place. It is clearly absurd to think of causes exerting individual efficacy independently of the laws of nature, as it were to finish off the job left unfinished by the laws of making things happen. To see them this way would be to envisage them (mindless) local agents or (as Lichtenberg, following David Hume, pointed out) as "occult forces".[38] Seeing causes "at work" in this way is another way of projecting our own agency into the material world. (To reduce us to helpless lumps of flesh is to reverse the compliment by identifying our mindful agency with mindless forces delivered through electrochemical activity in the brain.)

Agents transform how things are at any moment, at a particular place, into those missing *initial conditions* Wigner referred to, upon which laws can operate and causes unfold.[39] It as it were puts them in by hand. Subjects wake up worlds within Being, creating a centre and a periphery and a beginning and an end, thereby turning actual events into handles to transform possibilities into actual events. In virtue of the "at" and "that" and the thatosphere from which agents face the material world, rather than merely being part of it, they can operate on it from the outside.

I have emphasized that the outside is not merely "outside the brain" but is the collective human outside, built up over hundreds of thousands of years, in which we support each other's agency and find our own. There is of course no such outside without the brain: chop my head off and pop goes my world, and with it my agency. But that outside is not to be found inside the standalone brain. Hence the failure to discover agency by peering into the darkness of the skull with devices whose technical sophistication has seduced even otherwise quite canny philosophers.

Distancing ourselves from nature

I have not entirely demystified the fact that there is, in a universe whose history is otherwise one of mere happenings, a subset of events that are *actions*. I have described the agent, the "I" who acts, as a point of origin, a *beginning*, an initiator, in a world of happening. The seemingly magical role of humanity in the order of things is captured by the poignant final sentence of Augustine's *City of God*, "God created man so that there might be a beginning in the world".[40] The status of that point of origin seems questionable and its own origin mysterious – especially if: a) we believe that everything has to be explained by the laws of nature, which do not accommodate beginnings, or initial conditions, as we have seen; and b) we do not overlook the fact that there *are* beginnings – the here and now from which actions take their rise, and provide the starting point for our journeys towards our goals.

For a start, we do not fabricate our flesh ourselves, nor drive our own growth, or indeed most of our development. Gaining head control, trunk control, walking, speech, are foreordained landmarks. What is more, if we believe what science tells us, first-person existence, and agency, far from being in at the beginning, were late entrants into the universe. Are we, after all, bubbles on a stream that has been flowing for billions of years before we emerged and so far as we know, will continue long after the last human agent has passed on? Such a thought makes it difficult to grasp that we, as it were, direct the flow of at least some events; that we live, rather than merely suffer, our lives. However, this way of framing the question takes too much, and too easily, for granted. Those "billions of years" are not unproblematic. The very idea that we are late entrants into the order of things is not something that fits into the notion of an unfolding, insentient material universe. "Billions of years ago" gathers up "years", "billions" and "ago" that do not inhere in the insentient, aconceptual universe outside of the human mind.

We shall return to this issue when we consider "the irruption of the subject" in Chapter 10. For the present, we note that something clearly has happened as a result of our arrival, making possible the seeming impossibility of bubbles on the stream directing themselves and, indeed, also part of the stream. We cannot deny ordinary agency in action, our capacity to redirect the planet when, motivated by explicit future possibilities, we requisition causes to produce certain effects. Fire has raged on the planet since there was material available for combustion; but only humans have turned this chemical rage into a handle to make the immediately future world cosier and nights brighter and food more digestible, and later, to fabricate more enduring and powerful artefacts. The distance between fire melting ice and fire smelting weapons is a measure of the distance between mere events (or processes) and causes-requisitioned-as-handles to magnify our power to shape the circumstances in which we live. This undeniable difference between actions and mere physical events should not be denied simply because it is difficult to accommodate in a world picture that limits itself to what can be revealed by natural sciences. Instead we should acknowledge that the reality of agency exposes the limits of the natural sciences. More specifically: that brain science seems to show that we don't have free will is a critique not of free will but of the metaphysical claims of brain science.

The arguments for free will have drawn on our undeniable "extra-natural nature". You don't have to suffer from the Darwinitis discussed in Chapter 2 to worry that an appeal to extra-natural human nature may seem to separate us from our evolutionary heritage and represent a regression to pre-Darwinian thought. While the fact of our unique freedom is incontrovertible, therefore, it would be reassuring if it were possible to show that it is compatible with what we know of our biological roots. We need, that is to say, a biological explanation of our escape from biology, though as we have already found, there is not going to be an evolutionary explanation of consciousness.

No biological story of the origin of the distance between ourselves as conscious agents and our nearest primate kin in whom the place of agency is largely taken up by programmed behaviour – unconditional and conditional reflexes and instincts – is going to be simple. As I mentioned in Chapter 2, I offered one in the trilogy on "human being" published a decade or so ago.[41]

The human hand was central to my explanation, combined with the upright position, and the emergence of vision, the most knowledge-like of the senses, as the dominant sense. Certain distinctive features transformed that organ into a proto-tool and this in turn informed the human organism with the sense of being the immediate agent of its agency.

It is entirely in the spirit of humanism to appreciate that there was nothing predestined about this journey or that it was humans rather than other primates that have taken, and being taken along, it. At its heart is cultural change driven at an accelerating speed by the pooling of experience, the shared intentionality we have discussed. We have consequently been able to build up and share agency through multiple modes of teamwork, the differentiation of labour, a protracted learning period mediated by teaching, and the vast legacy and treasury of knowledge (know-how and know-that) situated in an ever-richer landscape of artefacts, facilities, and amenities, in which our powers, collective memories, and accumulated skills are embodied. We act within a heritage of cooperation in which we draw on the sedimented insights, expertise, and powers of others. Togethering lies at the heart of much of what we can do and, in some cases, provides the rationale for doing it.

It is easy to overlook the multiple ways in which, through our co-presence as well as *in absentia*, we support each other's agency. Particularly striking is our willingness to accept others' expertise and authority (different others in different situations), to put ourselves in others' hands, and to cede some sovereignty for the sake of indirect empowerment. The manufacture of the means of subsistence – our own and that of others – or the provision of services to earn the universal means of exchange (money) is a ubiquitous (and for this reason deceptively ordinary) way of extending agency by spreading it, and dividing labour, among many, indeed countless, fellow agents.

Numerous examples of devolved agency are found quite close to the function of the hand, the primordial tool, Aristotle's tool of tools.[42] The strings that tie, or clips that hold, things together, or the nails and glue that stop them falling apart are outsourced power grips. Jars, bags, vats, and buckets and carts are outsize palms. Fingerposts point directions for a boundless community of strangers, anticipating their ignorance and consequent need for guidance. Such artefacts illustrate how agency can separate the standing possibility of assistance from occurrent actual delivery. The manufacture of the paper clip is a process quite separate from that of using the item to stand in for someone's grip. And the paper clip, numbered among one's possessions, is on stand-by for when it might be needed.

Our use of the laws of nature explicitly and consciously to bring about desired ends is not matched by any other organism. The species – humankind

– that shakes the palm tree to bring down the coconuts is also one that envisages the wind – that shakes the palm tree and brings down the nuts – as an agent, albeit an invisible and perhaps supernatural one: a divine being. Man is also the species that uniquely and typically exercises agency through the indirect causation permitted by complex tools or limitless intermediate events or "steps".

It may seem counter to common observation to claim that animals lack a fully developed causal sense. The issue, however, is addressed by Suddendorf in the light of empirical evidence. While primates may be able to solve puzzles by trial-and-error, they have no understanding of the causal relations involved. Small alterations in a learned task – as when the creatures have to push out, rather than rake in, food they have learned to release from a trap – result in dismal failure.[43] Even less are they aware of abstract or invisible causal forces such as gravity. They simply learn associations between observable events. They would have approved of David Hume's view of the nature of causation as mere superstition. In this, as in other respects, our primate kin seem to be Humean beings.

We are already sufficiently equipped to dispose of the view that the sense of agency is an illusion, but one that brings biological benefits. The conviction that you are bringing about, *doing* some of the things that befall you, that you are enacting at least part of your biography, must, so the story goes, be good for the morale and hence of survival value. And it is good for society if individuals believe they are responsible for their actions, even if it is untrue.[44]

There is an obvious response to the assertion that agency is an illusion: "by its fruits shall ye know it". The ability of the human race to control and create a novel, complex realm, outside of nature are those fruits. Human agency has *in actual fact* driven mankind ever further from the comparatively helpless and comparatively powerless state of other animals. It underpins the great institutions and monuments that embody the distinctive fruits of human endeavour. The mighty artefactscapes of cities speak for themselves: they are hardly the product of the mindless unfolding of nature.

NEITHER BIOLOGICAL MACHINES NOR GODS: THE LIMITS TO HUMAN AGENCY

While our agency is real and uniquely developed, we do not have to appeal to magic to explain it. It is due to our capacity to act upon the natural world – of which our own bodies are an important part – from a virtual outside. The claim that we are truly free, however, will be implausible if we also claim that our freedom is boundless. It is important, therefore, to emphasize that a defence of agency does *not* require us to believe any of the following:

1. That *everything* that happens to, or in, an agent is freely chosen. Self-evidently, it is not. I did not choose: to be born, to be born in 1946, to be born to white, middle-class parents in the UK, or many other determinants of, or at least influences on, my path through this world. In short, the new-born Raymond Tallis was put together by forces outside of his own control. But this does not undermine my claim to be a free agent. To the contrary: freedom must have something to work on. Maintaining that *any* aspects of the self that are "given" are incompatible with freedom would lead to the absurd conclusion that one could be free only if one had nothing to be free with, from, or for. In short, only if one was nothing.[45] If freedom is to be *someone's* freedom (as it has to be) it must be exercised within the context of a given, particular world, itself something that has been transformed from what-is into a given, and thence into a context for action. Unconditioned freedom would not be expressed in time: there would be no separation between present states and wished-for future states. There is no freedom without a platform from which to operate plus circumstances on which to operate. An important part of that platform is the community and the knowledge and expertise handed down to us. While we are not the sole architects of our path through life, we remain points of origin, initiators, who intervene in the flow of events and to do this we have to be someone we have not entirely chosen to be.

Many of my actions, for example, will make sense only in virtue of the situation in which I find myself as a result of previous actions, as well as unchosen circumstances and events. It is central to or having a coherent, not to speak of an honourable, life that we are bound by previous choices. We do not, and could not, and should not, act from a blank sheet.

The fact that not everything that happens to an agent is freely chosen actually highlights the reality of freedom. The difference between falling down the stairs as a result of having a seizure and walking down the stairs in order to set out for a journey to London to make the case for improved epilepsy services shows the freedom of the latter. And, the lack of freedom of a person in coma or of someone who has sustained a serious head injury illuminatingly contrasts with the freedom of the uninjured, alert human being. Likewise, the very fact that one can in certain anomalous conditions in psychological experiments be deceived into thinking one is *doing* something that is being brought about by other means, highlights that one is usually not deceived. The undeniable reality of our freedom is evident when we compare the helplessness of intra-uterine existence with actively led life of an adult human being.

So, while we may not be entirely responsible for how we are (and *a fortiori* for the fact *that* we are), this does not exclude a degree of freedom sufficient to make us morally responsible for our actions. That my "I" is tied to an "it" is the source of my (necessarily local) power as well as of my vulnerability.[46] Without my being – or identifying myself with – something unchosen, embracing something given to myself to be, there would be no basis for choosing one path rather than another, for doing this rather than that. Free will would have no platform or direction.

2. That *every part of a free action* is explicitly done and freely executed. On the contrary, if we had to will every detail of every action, we would not get anything significant done. I could not walk to the pub if I had consciously to contract all the muscle fibres involved in walking, and had deliberately to maintain my posture, and guide myself through the spaces that separate me from the pub. Likewise, when I deliberately reach out and pick up a glass, the aperture of my open hand, the control of the ballistic movement of my arm, and the regulation of the pressure with which I grip the glass, taking account of its expected weight and that of its contents and the slipperiness of its surface, are not parameters that I control deliberately. The autonomous functioning of our body and the automatic pilot of well-practised routines are necessary to free us in order to act freely. And this is true even of our thoughts. I have no idea of the processes that make thoughts possible but it does not follow from this that "I" do not have the thought and that "it" (e.g. my brain) has the thought while I am merely its involuntary host.[47]

3. That the agent must be free *to do anything*. There are varying degrees of volitional freedom depending on the circumstances. Internal and exter-nal constraints must arise because our freedom is dependent on, and acts through, our bodies and is framed by our, and to some extent its, history. Our conclusion from Chapter 3 – "I am because it is" – implies "I can act because it is" or "*I* can act only so long as *it* is". And indeed, so long as it is functioning.

4. Finally, that the only constraints on freedom are *metaphysical* ones result-ing from our being embodied subjects. On the contrary, our finite life, our species being, and our biology are only the most basic constraints. There are others. The many dimensions of our enculturation and the things we are schooled to take for granted also shape our agenda and our capacity to deliver on it. Beyond this, there are many modes of enslavement and self-enslavement. Slaves are no more enslaved by the laws of gravity than their masters but they carry the additional constraints of domestic, cultural, and political tyranny,

not to speak of the burdens of privation, of hunger, fear and degradation. And, short of enslavement, there is the pressure to conform or other sources of the curtailment of life chances.[48] Against this, there is the obvious point that the shared constraints on our freedom to do whatever we like are, if they are equitably applied, liberating. The famous "tragedy of the commons" – the unregulated access to grazing rights that leads to the destruction of the resource and starvation for all – is a straightforward example of how regulations may add to the sum total of human freedom.[49]

I have only gestured towards, not solved, the problems that remain outstanding once we have established that we have free will. Just how challenging are the remaining difficulties is captured in this passage from Roger Scruton:

> Any being who can say "I" and mean it is free; and any being who can say "I" is situated in a world of universally binding causal laws ... I am a free subject and a determined object: but I am not *two* things, a determined body with a free soul rattling inside. I am *one* thing which can be seen in two ways. This is something that I know to be true, but which lies beyond understanding. I can never know *how* it is possible but only *that* it is possible.[50]

Even so, it is evident that it is we who turn initial conditions into the site of initiation; or, rather, transform some states of the universe around us into initial conditions. The power of initiation is not, however, exercised at the level of an isolated event. We are not merely *points* of origin whose powers of volition are enacted through localized events such as intentions that occur at time t. Our interventions are the interventions of a temporally extended *self* – and in a world we have had a role in shaping in cooperation with countless others. The free act draws on our past that has been directed towards its possibility, most obviously through all the modes of preparation and positioning we undertake during our lives.

Much of our agency is joint agency and, unlike the situation where we, say, carry a basket by each holding one of the handles, our collaborators are largely unknown to us.[51] Catching a bus to a destination is the child of innumerable voluntary actions not only by ourselves but also by our fellows – innumerable inventors, engineers, vehicle manufacturers and maintainers, managers, administrators and accountants, making bus production and bus services possible, road makers and menders, creators of time tables and bus-stop marked routes – as well as the most conspicuous co-agent – the driver. Nature gave me legs and culture gave me wheels and engines to make them turn. In short, this most commonplace of actions (like most of the others that fill my days) is supported by a back office of many hundreds of interconnected agents servicing the service that I take for granted. Such group agency can seem to look after itself.

That agency is often plural, with others sometimes supplying not only the means, but also the motives and the opportunities, in no way diminishes the unique contribution of individual agents. Each member of the team, collective, or background chorus brings his or her own reasons and narratives and motivations to the action – indeed they are necessary conditions for participation. Past, present and future are present in my journey – a collective and a bespoke past, present, and future, fleshed out with intentions and attentions that belongs to individuals and the community of minds.

Over time, we humans increasingly rig the natural world in our favour and our capacity to do so has been massively amplified by science. Our evolving, collective agency makes the world more fit for us to live in – a trend opposite to that of Darwinian evolution in which organisms evolve to fit the world. We still, however, ride the ongoingness of the natural world, of which in one sense we are a part and in another sense are not, so that we can direct that ongoingness, exploiting its energy and properties – "obeying nature so that we may command her". The sense we make of the world in relation to our own needs – anticipated in general form before and after they are felt as clamant necessities – is amplified by the sense we seek in the world as we search out its laws and seek the connectedness of causes.

The irruption of the sense-making, suffering, rejoicing, striving, reflecting, inquiring subject into the universe – which it is both connected to and separated from by intentionality – is the ultimate discontinuity. It is a tear in what classical science sees as a gigantic law-govererned machine, an opening that ultimately creates the possibility of a human world in which regimentation by nature is mitigated. It is a consequence of the sense-making faculty of the human being that nature is unpicked into discrete, salient events, connected by causal relations instantiating laws of boundless generality, and available in some cases to become handles. Our freedom is not merely marginal for this reason: we not only increasingly create the conditions under which it operates but also its agenda. This is evident when we act on our desires which are not, as it were, internal causes (themselves effects of unchosen causes) of actions understood as effects. A desire is a way of interpreting, addressing, the relationship between one's self and the world. Unlike a physiological need, desire makes sense of itself, even narrates itself, and of the world to which it is directed.

To say all this is not to abolish the mystery of our freedom but to place it in a larger context: that of the mystery of the irruption of the subject into the natural world. While objective science sees the human subject as a recent product of the natural world, there is an alternative account according to which the human subject is responsible for making the universe into *the* or *its* world, given that, prior to his/her appearance on the scene, there was no "scene", no "here" or "there", or "before" or "after".[52] This irruption breaks the flux or continuum into discrete events that have distinctive significance in individual worlds. Causes then become handles on the unfolding world, expressive of laws that can be manipulated.

We may therefore envisage a primordial state of seamless ongoingness in the universe. It is the irruption of the subject that breaks it up into discrete events that may be connected with other events whose probability of occurrence they raise. We may be tempted to go further and argue that the very notion of a cause is a displaced sense of our own agency, that our intuition of causation in nature comes from our experience of being agents. The eighteenth-century philosopher Thomas Reid speculated that "our conception of an efficient cause may very probably be derived from the experience we have had … of our own power to produce certain effects".[53]

Such a view leaves conspicuously unanswered the question of the important role of the brain in the agent's capacity for freely chosen action. If, however, we accept that the brain is the necessary but not sufficient *condition* of there being a subject and a subject is the *condition* of there being agency, we can assign it an essential role without making it the proximate cause of our actions, even less the sole and sufficient one. We can accept what neuroscience tells us without becoming neuromaniacs.

Suffice it, anyway, to recognize that the notion of a (discrete) cause of (discrete) events is no more straightforward than that of a voluntary action. The idea of the mindless, natural cause of an event is no less mysterious than that of an action caused by an agent. Both require a pause in the seamless ongoingness of the material world. Causation and volition are, we might be tempted to say, equiprimordial. While this may be too much to swallow, it is reasonable to concede that we cannot simply "nod through" the idea of universal causation, en route to its making that of a voluntary action more mysterious and volition illusory.[54] Irrespective of whether or not our freedom is ultimately inexplicable, this cannot be denied: we *use* causes and *exploit* laws; we utilize the habits of nature observed initially through informal collective understanding and ultimately through the lens of the exact sciences.

When we think of an agent bringing about an action, both the "cause" (for example my wishing to argue the case for better epilepsy services) and the "effect" (my journeying to London) are wholes that do not correspond to, or even map on to, material events such as neural discharges bringing about muscular movements. There is a unity in both the subject (the "I") who does the action and in the action itself that is not appropriately analysable into elements such as activity in nerves and/or muscles. Agency is not a series of discrete events within the agent, any more than its expression is a succession of discrete, or at least self-defining, events in the natural world.

The very fact that my goal may *not* be achieved underlines the purpose that informs the elements of the action. Those elements are brought together by a desired possibility. Other than in relation to conscious agency, natural events per se can neither "succeed" or "fail": whatever happens just happens. By contrast, success and failure are built into the very idea of agency, which is fuelled by a sense of possibility, of something that does not yet, and may never, exist. Failure is impossible in the physical world – as is success. As for the aimed-at possibility, it could not, when realized be the mere effect of a cause in several respects. The nature of what is aimed at and how it is to be achieved – the level of its "whatness", and the fact that it might not be achieved, do not belong to the universe of matter, energy, forces, and charges.

CONCLUDING THOUGHTS

Dr Samuel Johnson noted with some irony that while all arguments are against free will all experience is for it, implying "so much the worse for the arguments".[55] His message, which I share, is this: we should resist an uncritical acceptance of the theoretical arguments that "disprove" the undeniable truth that some of the events in our lives are actions and many of those actions are events that occur only because they would take us closer to a freely chosen goal. One reason for valuing the lived reality of agency over the theory that denies its possibility is that to deny our freedom would undermine any claim we might have to dignity as humans. It might even encourage us to behave badly. Without a sense of responsibility – and an anticipation of justified guilt for the damage we may have done to others or the iniquities we have not prevented – we may be less inclined to resist the temptation to cheat on our fellows. Studies have suggested that this may be the case; that in a world without belief in free will, individuals may be less inclined to be good, altruistic, honest, or generous.[56]

It ill behoves a philosopher to suggest that, because determinism may encourage us to be wicked, it is an argument for free will. Truths with unpalatable consequences are no less true. "Yuk!" is not a valid argument. After all, the fact that we all die is an unpalatable truth, and no-one would claim that this is a proof of our immortality. But we do not need arguments to prove that we are truly agents because, notwithstanding that to some thinkers it looks impossible in theory, freedom is a ubiquitous practical reality of everyday life. Granted, the theory has not caught up with the reality; but this does not make the latter any less real. The (false) case against our freedom is easily stated while the true case in favour of it is more complex and elusive.

If the fact that we are, under one aspect, physical objects in a physical world really did make agency impossible, it would equally make it impossible that we should entertain the *illusion* of agency, or that the illusion would serve any purpose.

The emphasis on the cultural underpinnings of our agency may raise doubts about our individual freedom other than those we have focused on in this chapter. Is it not possible that our escape from physical or biological determinism has been bought at the cost of being *culturally* determined? Not at all. Our lives as embodied subjects mean that we have a unique trajectory through, and a unique take on, the human world. Culture distances us from biology; and our destination as unique beings distances us from the generalities of culture.

The mysteriousness of our freedom is not at all surprising. The intentionality out of which grows the "outside" from which we freely operate on nature is deeply mysterious. And this, too, is entirely to be expected, given that intentionality precedes any sense we may have of "a world" and any endeavour to grapple with its mystery – to make sense of it.

It remains true that we need to be physical objects of a certain very special kind – human organisms – to be agents acting within a material world. Discarnate spirits could exert no traction on nature. Our power is therefore inseparable from our bodily vulnerability.[57] We are consequently doomed sooner or later to lose our agency and to become as helpless as the physical material of which we are made; and we leave a world we did not make relatively little changed by our individual passage through it. In the next chapter, we shall discuss one secular response to this unwelcome truth: dreams of immortality entertained by the so-called transhumanists.

CHAPTER 7

Humanity against finitude: transhumanist dreams

CONFRONTING TRANSIENCE

In the preceding chapters, I have attempted to justify the belief that, while human beings are not supernatural entities, neither are they simply parts of nature. Unfortunately, that is only half the story. Our privileged mode of being is hedged about with terms and conditions: personhood is contingent on the continuing vitality of our bodies. Those bodies share the unwilled transience of all things in a restless universe. "I am" depends on "It is": sooner or later the relevant "it" disintegrates and the "I" is swallowed up in the wider "it" of the material world; the little "who" is lost in the boundless "what". Worse, since we are highly complex entities, and hence thermodynamic freaks, we are more transient than most of the material world that surrounds us. Pebbles, rivers, trees outlast us. Irrespective of whether or not mankind can bear too much reality, reality of a sort will sooner or later kick down the door, set fire to all our possessions, raze our property, and leave us naked to and beyond the bone, inert in the indifferent open. While we may in some sense be the makers of the world in which we live our lives, the natural realm outside of the thatosphere has us in its ultimate grip.

Thus, death the leveller, eloquently expressed by Bohuslav Brouk the Czech poet, biologist and philosopher: "The body is the last argument of those who have been unjustly neglected and ignored: it demonstrates beyond debate the groundlessness of all social distinctions in comparison to the might of nature".[1] And the Bible observes that notwithstanding man's special relationship with God: "For that which befalleth the sons of men, befalleth beasts; even one thing befalleth them; as the one dieth, so dieth the other; yes, they have all one

breath; so that a man hath no pre-eminence above a beast; for all is vanity".[2]
The "justice" of transience goes beyond human affairs. Our mortality reflects
the contingency of all particular things, the inadequacy of the reason for
their existence. Anaximander observed this in the famous opening sentence
of western philosophy, the only one preserved from his *oeuvre*: "But where
things have their origin, they must also pass away according to necessity; for
they must pay the penalty and be judged for their injustice, according to the
ordinance of time".[3] We do not deserve the lucky accident of our existence.
This, the scandal of our lingering, is hardly consolation when we meet "the
ruffian on the stair".[4]

Uniquely among transients, we are aware of our transience, though our own
non-being lies beyond the edge of our imagination. We know we are, as W.
B. Yeats expressed it, "fastened to a dying animal"[5] and in this sense "Man has
created death".[6] A pin-prick bubble is popped; nevertheless, the popping matters more than anything else in the universe since the pin-prick has a temporal
depth and can value her own past and future and fears an end she can foresee.
It is hardly surprising then that: "[T]he idea of death, the fear of it, haunts the
human animal like nothing else; it is a mainspring of human activity – activity
designed largely to avoid the fatality of death, to overcome it by denying in
some way that it is the final destiny for man".[7]

One of the chief functions of religions of salvation is to offer the hope of
escape from transience and from the contingency that makes our extinction
inevitable and loss total. The Given, so the story goes, was the Made – by a
Maker Who is reassuringly wise when not unnervingly angry – so that seeming accidents are part of His design. Tragedy may be the door to salvation
because there is something of His divinity within us. As God's favourites, we
will not be subject to Anaximander's implacable law. Better still, according to
Plato, the death of the body will free the transcendental subject from its subjection to the body and that which is truly one's self, which is most valuable in
us, will be saved for eternal life.

This is not the place to discuss the vexed idea of eternity – and its consolations are contestable, even if an eternity of Heaven rather than Hell were
guaranteed[8] – because the secular viewpoint that is the starting premise of
our present inquiry does not include the expectation of an afterlife granted by
a divine agent. Humanists need to look elsewhere than eternal life for consolation. Many have been proposed, with different degrees of sincerity.

There is much talk of "living on" in the memory of others. But such memories are patchy, scattered, and may be based on confusion. What is more
each of us is in competition not only with other dead for attention but also
with life and the living. The frequent calls to resurrect the memory of some

forgotten artist or writer or historical actor inevitably has the consequence of drowning someone else in collective oblivion, as we have limited capacity for recollection. Besides, the stay of ultimate extinction is only temporary. The memorial tended by those we leave behind lasts only as long as the lives of those whom we would have remember us. The last bubble, the last ripple, in our wake will soon be lost in the ocean. And it scarcely matters if this takes a handful of years or, in the case of a glorious few, several millennia. In "death's dateless night" there is no difference between an eye-blink and an aeon: both fall equally short of eternity.

Perhaps, we think, we may live on not in the capricious memory of humanity but in a substantive legacy we have left behind. The most obvious is our biological legacy. But genetic replication does not provide the difference between mortality and eternal life. This would make the accident of fertility carry too high an existential burden. Besides, genetic eternity is not especially privileged. As Mary Midgley put it jokingly, "If it is immortality you are after, an amoeba is just the thing to be!"[9] Besides, genetic drift ensures that, over time, the genomic afterlife carried by phenotypes similar to your own is limited. And, just as with being remembered, the fact that this might take a long time does not palliate the tragedy of ultimate extinction.

Our legacy is usually envisaged as cultural rather than biological, taking the form of benefactions to succeeding generations. There were many millions in the twentieth century for whom contributing to the Great Leap Forward, that would elevate humanity to a prescribed version of freedom, promised by totalitarian regimes, was the most commonly embraced (or more often imposed) promise of immortality. Individually, however, the legacy is not easily tracked: the signal is lost in the noise. Anything substantive in the way of scientific, technological, or social advance, may be reversed by other developments that have rendered an individual's contribution null and void. Alleviating the suffering of one's contemporaries, what is more, may have unintended consequences. We can never know that our net contribution has been positive, when offset against our cost to the world. Whether one joins "... the choir invisible / Of those immortal dead who live again / In minds made better by their presence ..."[10] remains uncertain. Besides, goodness is not a particularly important determinant of immortality. Wickedness may just as well secure an afterlife. Hitler and Stalin will have a more secure foothold on the future than the vast majority of good people. And even those monsters have limited tenure in the collective consciousness: their posthumous ripples will sooner or later cease widening from the ghastly event of their irruption into the world. That Stalin's name will be spoken in 40,000 years' time seems highly doubtful. The contrail of our passage through the world cannot be made over into concrete.

Posthumous fame is anyway wasted on the dead. It is like the sunshine on a statue's face. In 2016, the four hundredth anniversary of his death, Shakespeare was justly celebrated as one of the greatest writers of all time. It is unlikely, however, that the Bard relished 2016 any more than 2015 or any of the other years since 1616 when he took his last breath. Or indeed the years before he was born. It little profits us, therefore, to transfer the burden of our immortality to others, particularly as it seems unlikely that one will be understood any better in death than in life or remembered as if from within.

Secular humanists have to seek other consolations for sooner or later losing all that they are, have, know, and love. They might agree with St Paul that "The last enemy to be destroyed is death"[11] but they cannot envisage how this can be achieved, how its tragic sting might be removed. Enter, stage left, the notion of "the right time to die": "Many die too late, and some die too early. Still the doctrine sounds strange: 'Die at the right time'. Thus, Zarathustra teaches."[12] There may come a time when life is unbearable, as in the terminal stages of an incurable illness. That is certainly the right time to die but it does not abolish the tragedy of death; it simply merges it with the tragedy of dying, when the "it is" of the body remorselessly extinguishes the "I am" of the embodied subject.

A more cheerful version of "the right time to die" may be when one has achieved all that one wanted to achieve and has done all that one felt that one could do, so that one could say, wholeheartedly: "Mission accomplished". We think of this in relation to the artist or thinker who has said, composed, or painted, all that he or she has to say, compose, or paint, a state signalled in advance by "a late style" in which "ripeness is all". It is a romantic notion to which little corresponds. After all, any thinker or artist worth his or her salt feels that their works (as the great poet and thinker Paul Valéry said) are not completed, only abandoned.[13] And the same applies *a fortiori* to The Complete Works. The fact that Mozart's *Requiem* was finished by someone else – his pupil Franz Sussmayer – puts paid to the notion that the death of one of the greatest of all artists at the age of 35 was a moment of completion. And the same applies to those who have achieved greatness in other areas: many scientists, for example, feel they are leaving their chosen topic *in medias res* with much fascinating business unfinished.

There is the romantic idea that death may be redeemable if one dies not *of* a cause – a contingent, unchosen cause such as illness or accident – but *for* a cause. Unfortunately, the vast majority of causes for which people die also seem contingent, insufficient to justify the loss of the entire world. The tens of millions who died in, or as a result of, the First World War, had their lives squandered by the accidents of history, however much their pointless deaths were glamorized as sacrifice for the sake of the country. And there is worse. A suicide bomber may gather up all his days into one act which for him completes the meaning of his life, though at terrible cost to others.

The point is that there seems to be no appropriate end to one's life. Tennyson captured this with incomparable poignancy through the mouth of Ulysses in old age:

> ... Come my friends,
> 'Tis not too late to seek a newer world.
> Push off, and sitting well in order smite
> The sounding furrows; for my purpose holds
> To sail beyond the sunset, and the baths
> Of all the western stars, until I die.[14]

And this remains true, even of ordinary individuals such as the present writer. There is no foreseeable moment at which I want to say good bye to all those I know; to say "see you later" for the last time to my wife; to have the final glimpse of the grandchildren; to decide that I have seen enough of the world. In short, while I suspect many people may have had more than enough of Raymond Tallis, I cannot get enough of his world, his life and hence of him. My thirst for RT is unquenchable. And I suspect that this insatiable appetite for more self is true of pretty well everyone who reads this book.

TECHNOLOGY AGAINST DEATH

Assisting biology

The commonest secular response to our finitude is to look to technology to mitigate it. The passion with which this endeavour is pursued and the extravagance of the dreams that drive it is sometimes reminiscent of a religious cult.[15] This is particularly evident in the United States, notably in Silicon Valley, where Francis Bacon's dream expressed in New Atlantis of "the effecting of all things possible" has its firmest grip on the collective imagination. Mark O'Connell's engaging and thoughtful account of this "transhumanist" enterprise identifies several distinctive approaches to the battle against death.[16]

The least radical focuses on extending longevity by tinkering with the biology of the human body. The treatment and prevention of the diseases of old age, genetic modification of the organism, and a direct assault on the ageing process have seemed to some to promise great progress. Its suitably bearded senior prophet Aubrey de Grey has attracted huge funds and international celebrity on the basis of his claim that the "60-year-old who will live to be 1,000 is already among us". He argues that medical advances that extend life expectancy by, say, 30 years will buy time for further medical advances that will further extend life. By this means we shall achieve what he calls "biological escape velocity" and we shall be on course for a "post-ageing" world. Thus the promise of his Strategies for Engineered Negligible Senescence.

Writing for a moment as a gerontologist rather than as a philosopher, I must point out that the sequence of events he describes, while seeming to be logically unassailable, depends on assumptions that have no present foundation in biology. His views are regarded with suspicion, even derision, by most of the experts in the field of ageing. Even so, it is worth considering some of the issues raised by the possibility of achieving a four-figure lifespan.

Would it be worthwhile? Surely, we would tire of life, as did Emilia Marty in Karel Čapek's *Makropoulos Case* that Janáček made into such a wonderful opera. The philosopher Bernard Williams, reflecting on this story, wrote about "the tedium of immortality",[17] arguing that, like Emilia who had lived for several hundred years, we would soon run out of projects to pursue and things to enjoy. How many performances of *Don Giovanni* – however much we loved it – could we stand? A hundred, a thousand, ten thousand? Against this, there is always unfinished business and there are new projects, new lands to explore, new experiences to be had, new duties to take on. If 80 years seems a long life, this is only because this is the "going rate" for life expectancy in a developed country. If 150 were normal, we would think differently about dying at 80. Besides, we do not live accumulated time. At best we live only a year, a week, a day at a time; and, as hardly needs saying, short times and long times are only relative to subjective experience and to the nature, rather than the quantity, of its content.

There is a more troubling question posed by the possibility of vastly extended longevity. Inevitably, we would change as the centuries passed and so, too, would the world around us. At some point, the accumulated changes, however gradual, would be such that one no longer would be the same person in the same world. There is no definite point, of course, at which when, despite living on, one ceases to be one's self: the criteria for identity and sameness are not clear cut, as we discussed in Chapter 5. I will return to this later; I flag it up now only to indicate that life extension may not necessarily mean self-extension. And if only a subset of the population can enjoy the benefits of the interventional gerontology you may find that you are the only survivor of your group, a desolate outcome, given that our personhood is to an important extent interpersonal.

An alternative approach to biological life extension is *cryonics*, a process by which your brain – or, if you are very rich, your entire body – is frozen at death in such a way that it can be preserved until cures have been found for the conditions that killed you. Then you can be unfrozen, treated – in short "reanimated" – and you will resume your interrupted life, hoping that there are still people around who will recognize you and others who will guide you through a doubtless terrifying new world. It is overwhelmingly improbable that the brain or body of a dying person will pass through the process of freezing and unfreezing and emerge sufficiently undamaged to be able to support any kind of human life, even less to support the life of the very person who succumbed to the cryonic process. (For a demolition of the claims of the brain freezers, see Clive Coen[18]). And there are all the uncertainties around the responsibility for maintaining the frozen body or brain. What, for example, if the firm with curatorial responsibility goes bust? Or a war breaks out and the warehouse is bombed?

A more promising approach would seem to be the gradual replacement of body parts by machinery. This is already being employed in, for example, cardiac assist devices to take over the function of failing hearts, and "intelligent" prostheses that can be controlled from the brain to enact certain simple functions such as grasping objects. The Silicon Valley dreamers go further than that, imagining "cyborgs" – cybernetic organisms – that augment human function with machinery and replace an increasing amount of flesh with technological hardware not susceptible to those ills to which the flesh is heir. The ultimate destination of such developments would be a merger of people and machines permitting an almost complete emancipation from organic existence. It seems unlikely that such machinery would have any kinship with the fleshy organism it had replaced. Besides, while heart, lung, leg and kidney replacements seem feasible, developing a prosthesis to stand in for the most important organ, the brain, presents insuperable challenges – of which more presently.

Escaping biology

None of these strategies – biological life extension, cryonics, or the transformation of humans into cyborgs – would cancel death, even if they succeeded in postponing it. The residual biological, and even physical, elements remain vulnerable. Intrinsic ageing and disease may be arrested but there is still threat of extinction by accidents and natural disasters. Cyborgs can be destroyed by avalanches and by other cyborgs. Hybrids of body and machine would be susceptible to wear and tear, and their astronomical maintenance costs would depend on the good will of others, which is likely to be in short supply when a 900-year old valetudinarian presents yet again for even more advanced replacement therapy.

Something more radical is needed. And it is at this point that we move from science fantasy to pure fantasy. It is the theory of "technoimmortalization"[19] or "virtual immortality", according to which: "the fullness of our first-person mental selves (our "I") [can] be digitized and uploaded perfectly on to non-biological media so that [we] ... can live on beyond the death of our bodies and the destruction of our brains".[20]

These "substrate independent minds" can, if necessary be endlessly copied, so that persons can exist eternally as "code". And they can be copied on different media: if music can be stored on either CDs or an MP3, minds could likewise be preserved, with mortality being evaded by transfer to ever more robust substrates. Death is consequently abolished as the individual human essence is gathered up as software installed in hardware more enduring than the flesh on which we currently rely. We will "realize" ourselves on different and more dependable platforms. While we are grateful to Mother Nature for taking us so far, it is time to say thank you and good bye and to escape the tragic flaws of organic being, transcending "the confusion and desire and impotence and sickness of the body, cowering in the darkening shadow of its own decay".[21]

The future of humanity, in short, lies outside of the ontological slum of the human body. We unhitch our wagon from a fallen star, from perishable goods and become shiny, immortal machines. As Yeats expressed it in "Byzantium", we might become like the Golden Bird of Paradise who "... scorn aloud / In glory of changeless metal / Common bird or petal / And all complexities of mire or blood". Just how those machines will be maintained – and the collective enterprise of technology, logistics, low-grade tasks, nuts, and bolts – by substrate-independent minds is another matter.

We are entering the realm of fantasy but this is philosophically more familiar, and importantly, more interesting, territory. In assessing transhumanist dreams, we shall need to revisit issues that have exercised us in previous chapters. At the heart of these dreams are assumptions about embodiment, about our mode of being in time, and about the nature of the self – its identity and its agency.

The key idea is the replacement of the perishable embodied subject not with the immortal self-as-soul but with an immortal self-as-information. There are three additional assumptions:

1. To be a person is in some sense to be or to instantiate (an important distinction we shall return to) certain information;
2. The information constituting a person can be transferred to other substrates than the person's body (or brain) – such as computers attached to devices (a robotic or virtual body); and
3. The devices can emulate whatever functions (if any) are necessary for the replica to survive and flourish as a person.

The process by which it is envisaged that the "information" (a term that should usually be contained within inverted commas in this context for reasons that will become apparent) should be extracted from the human brain, depends heavily on the ruling ideas of computational neuroscience. According to this discipline – which sees the brain through the lens of computational theory – the mind, the self, the person, are identical with the computational activity taking place in the circuitry or "wetware" of the brain. The trick is to scan the brain and so extract the information contained within it and then copy it on to a new, longer-lasting substrate. When the new substrate starts to decay, the information can be copied on to another substrate. And so on *ad infinitum.*

There are many reasons for questioning the very idea of extracting ourselves or our minds from our brains and then "uploading" them on to a medium that is not only more enduring than the nervous system but also endlessly replicable, even if it were practically feasible. Leaving aside the many reasons for not identifying us with our brains (as discussed in Chapter 5), there are queries regarding the precise nature of what needs to be replicated. The very notion of copying is bedevilled by confusion and conflict – between, for example, snapshot copying of *activity* at a time, copying functions (general forms of activity) evident over time, and copying structures (standing dispositions to forms of activity).

A snapshot of the activity of a brain at any particular time would not reflect its irreducibly dynamic nature, that goes all the way down to the propagated wave that is a nerve impulse, the endlessly *changing* activation of different parts working together in response to changing inputs and ongoing needs. On the other hand, a sustained record – a time-lapse image – of brain activity would be a blur, with neurones at a given place that are in different states of activation at different times being represented simultaneously. Individual neurones or circuits would be both active and quiescent as successive states are superimposed.

This problem is compounded by the fact that temporal depth is central to personhood. A person at time t is not confined to time t: the experience and meaning of successive moments draws upon other moments. Every "now" is doubly impregnated – by the no-longer actual past and the not-yet possible future – to which it is attached not merely causally, or by means of objectively observable temporal connections, but by an intentional relation; indeed, a double intentional relation – the aboutness of an original experience and the aboutness of the memory of the experience. And the same applies to an intuition of the future, where there is a triple intentional relation: the aboutness of experience; the aboutness of the episodic or autonoetic memory of experiences; and the aboutness of the anticipation of possibilities drawing on those remembered experiences. By contrast the brain is confined to its successive states: a brain at time t is its material state at time t. This is what will be captured in the snapshot – or anything else – that is to be uploaded.

It is easy to miss this if, as is so often the case, the state of the brain and the nature of the mind are both described as "information". As we noted in Chapter 4, information, most evidently in the form of facts, is not anchored to any particular moment, in the way that experience is. While the Battle of Hastings took place in 1066, the fact *that* it took place did not take place in 1066 or at any other year. Information is timeless.

It might be argued that the "information" that is copied is not activity but relatively static circuitry. But precise replication of the structure at the level of a single neurone would be just as deficient as a portrait of a living mind as the gross structures seen in present-day brain scans. Leaving aside the difficulty that the micro-structure of the brain is dynamic, this model of brain emulation conflates: a) relatively fixed neural structures; b) the chemical behaviour of neurones; and c) their ongoing function. While it is difficult to see how these three could in practice be separated, they would have to be separated for transplantation to another medium to be possible. In fact, the structure of the brain's wetware is presumably inseparable from the micro-structure of neurones with all their biological properties – the very properties from which that technoimmortalization is supposed to liberate us. In short structure goes all the way down to the molecular level. This said, the brain, like any living tissue, is intrinsically messy: there is chaos inside the structure, as there is structure inside the chaos.[22] The juices inside the wetware and surrounding and sustaining it are not reducible to informational structures but the latter are not possible without the former. It is impossible to see how the means by which the neurones are kept alive and interact with each other could be reduced to a finite amount of "information", which sounds rather dry, frozen, general stuff. If on the other hand all the wet stuff was replicated, then we would essentially have another biological brain. More fundamentally, the appeal to the notion of information leaves it uncertain as to whether the information that it has to be replicated would count as information *about* the brain (its specification), information that is *in* the brain (what has been experienced by its owner, what is known, what its capabilities are), or information that *is* the brain, its supposedly digitizable matter.

The uncertainty as to what could be, and what should be extracted, copied or emulated (more uncertainty) is evident from the literature on mind-uploading. As Bamford and Danaher point out, in a brilliant critical article, the proposal:

> involves some attempt to copy information about a person (the functionality of the brain; their personality traits, etc.) and reproduce this information in a synthetic substance (robot, digital computer, etc.). They vary in terms of the information they try to capture and reproduce, and the methodology they use to transfer this information from the original, biological person to the synthetic analogue.[23]

Copying information about personality traits? Good luck with that one! What on earth would be the digital equivalent of a kindly disposition? The failure to be clear about what is replicated in whole mind-brain emulation is of course key to the plausibility of the very idea of copying the mind by copying the brain. There are other sleights of hand. Consider this passage from the celebrated futurologist Ray Kurzweil: "... my identity is rather like the pattern that water makes when rushing round a rock in a stream. The pattern remains relatively unchanged for hours, even years, while the actual material constituting the pattern of the water is replaced in milliseconds."[24] This would be a compelling analogy if it did not overlook the fact that the pattern in the water does not exist *for* the water, *for* the stream, or *for* the landscape of which it is a part. A standing wave, like a mistbow on a waterfall, exists only for an observer. Even less does it count as an observation or an element of an observer. The fixed patterns of activity in the brain need an observer to synthesize them across the brain and over time; they cannot themselves constitute that observer. And, as we discussed in Chapter 2, they lack intrinsic intentionality. The patterns do not extract themselves; even less do they transform themselves into information-bearing patterns, though the fact that they are more general than their components, and their successive moments, makes them seem abstract, quasi-informational. Needless to say, they do not abstract themselves.

At the heart of the fantasy of uploading the self is the identification of persons with their brains and brains with information or an information processor that can be reduced to information.

MYTH-INFORMATION

We have so far allowed the term "information" to pass through on the nod. The misuse of this term is one of the most important paths to misunderstanding, confusion, and error in contemporary philosophy and indeed the neurosciences.[25] It is a self-reinforcing error: the more often it is committed, the more it becomes consolidated as a habitual way of thinking about minds and brains. It is a case of the wrong tree being barked up where each bark increases the height of the tree.

Separating information from consciousness

The Original Sin is the mistake of believing that "information" can exist independently of conscious – and indeed self-conscious – individuals and that it can inhere in material objects such as brain or events such as nerve impulses or their patterns that are not being perceived by such creatures.[26]

Other than when it is employed explicitly as a metaphor, the proper use of "information" is to designate something that passes between a (conscious) informant and a (conscious) recipient. Informant and recipient may be the same person when I remind myself of something. That, however, is a secondary use. Information is primarily interpersonal, except when it is used to apply to the natural world. When, for example, I look up at the sky and see clouds, this will inform me of the possibility of rain; but the status of the cloudy sky as an "informant" warning me of rain, or as information, depends on my present consciousness (as a consumer of the implications of the clouds) and on my past consciousness when I learned either directly or from others the significance of clouds. Spots may mean measles but they don't mean to mean measles. A tree, likewise, may be informative – as when the number of rings in the trunk tell me how old it is – but not to another tree or indeed to itself. The rings on the tree tell knowledgeable humans, but not itself, how old it is. Trees do not know how old they are. The general point is this: there are no "data" – a term that etymologically means something that is "given" – without one to whom they are (ultimately) given. To describe the material world as being in itself "informative" without a conscious human being to receive or transmit information is to succumb to the pathetic fallacy on a grand scale. In the absence of a conscious recipient, there is no distinction between transmitter and receiver, between input and output, not the least because there is nothing to define a point of reception or a recipient. There is simply an unfolding of subjectless nature.

We forget this because during its passage from transmitter to receiver, information may be curated in the absence of consciousness. We are accustomed to libraries where information is "stored" on pages and in magnetic media. Strictly, however, when it is stored, it is only *potential* information. Consider the "information" that has been stored in the multi-billion-year history of the universe prior to the arrival of conscious human beings. Before the first sentient entities, the stratification of rocks was not information about the history of the earth. Overlooking this closes the gap between material processes taking place in nature or in artefacts and conscious experience. Information is suddenly everywhere, irrespective of whether there is anyone or anything to inform anyone about anything.

Astonishingly some may not see this as problematic. On the contrary, the suggestion that *everything* that happens is information is enthusiastically embraced. David Chalmers, who is regarded as a leading figure in the philosophy of mind, has made this extraordinary claim: "[W]herever there is causal interaction, there is information ... One can find information states in a rock – when it expands and contracts, for example – or even in the different aspects of an electron".[27]

The passage is worthy of quoting not only because it is bonkers – which of course it is – but because it illustrates what lies at the bottom of the slippery slope that begins with the idea that "information" can exist independently of conscious human beings. Information as envisaged by Chalmers is: a) confused with causal relations (a view that compounds the falsehood of the causal theory of perception); b) lacks any kind of subject – an informant or an informee; and c) because everything is information, it allows no space for "aboutness", or for separation between information and that which it is about. Lacking intentionality, it cannot uphold the distinction between self and world.

The careless use of the term "information", with the separation of information from conscious subjects, licenses the common assumption that, as computers have increasing processing power, so they are more likely to become conscious: put "super-" or "super-duper-" in front of computer and you seem to justify the expectation that it will wake up and even (as some futurologists fear) start to have ideas of its own. This is an expectation that is unshaken by the story so far that the most powerful computers in the world with terabytes of RAM and the capacity to handle the bits at trillions per nanosecond are no closer to being conscious, even less to having first-person experiences, or being a self, than a pocket calculator or the thermostat on the wall.

The consequences of misusing the idea of information are exacerbated by the lackadaisical use of another word: "intelligence" (artificial or otherwise) when applied to machinery. "Intelligence" becomes a bridging word linking increasing computing power to the emergence of consciousness: increasing artificial superintelligence or "cognitive computing" is, we are to believe, the path to artificial consciousness. For some, recent spectacular triumphs of AI – and they are truly awe-inspiring – justify this way of thinking.

Consider the recent victory of the computer programme AlphaGo over the human Grandmaster.[28] Given that the number of possible moves in the game "Go" is 10^{100} greater than chess, the victory represented an extraordinary feat of computer programming and data crunching. Even more extraordinary, the computer was "self-taught" – at least in the sense that its responses were sharpened and shaped by successive encounters with moves in self-generated games. However, that was all that the computer could do. It could not have made it alone to the place where the game took place, switched itself on at the right time, and most certainly did not understand the point of the game or feel satisfaction when victory was declared. Indeed, it had no sense of victory. AlphaGo "defeated" its opponent only in the sense that a falling stone kills a person in its flight path: the person is not a murder victim and the stone is not a homicide. The computer loaded with AlphaGo was not an agent, and most certainly not a conscious one. It was not even an *idiot savant* given that it would not match the skills of a one-year old in respect of perception and finding its way round the world. It did not know it was playing Go and had no sense of the world in which Go mattered.

The culpably lax use of the language of "myth-information" – or, more charitably, taking convenient metaphors for literal truth – prepares the way for the ever more widely received idea that human minds (selves, persons) can be "uploaded" on to alternative, non-biological platforms and, if necessary, replicated indefinitely. Computers handle and store information. As their processing and storing power increases, so (the story goes) they become more intelligent and, eventually, given that consciousness is lots and lots of information, they will become conscious intelligences like you and me. Alternatively – to return to our present concerns – supercomputers will be able to scan and store or effectively replicate all the "information" that is in our brains and dump it on some extra-biological platform, out of the reach of the Grim Reaper stalking persons who are unfortunate enough to be made of flesh.

Thus, the route by which the transhumanists arrive at their utopian (or dystopian) vision of a universe populated by disembodied or "disembrained" immortal subjects. Indeed, the real gap between conscious humans and non-biological minds is further seemingly narrowed by seeing the brain as mind as a super-computer defined by neural circuitry – though brains, we are told, are not as super as will be the computers of the future. The latter, will not be constrained by neuronal firing rates of a mere 200 times per second (in contrast with hundreds of thousands per second in the case of transistors), transmission speeds of 100 metres per second (compared with the speed of light in wires) and the need to be accommodated in the modest *atelier* of the human skull. This is a much more impressive version of the Aubrey de Grey "escape velocity" story: systems, self-replicating automata, far more intelligent than the humans that built them, would build other systems (without so much as a by-your-leave) that would be yet more intelligent. We would soon be left far behind by a technological evolution we had initiated.[29]

There is one further confusion. We have already noted that AlphaGo, despite its prowess in Go algorithms, was not exactly a rounded character. Its only capacity was the processing of what, for its minders, and the rest of the human world, was information. Not being conscious, however, AlphaGo was not itself informed by that information. Even if it *were* correct to claim that it was, would the information amount to consciousness? Is consciousness information? Can consciousness be built up out of the kind of information that streams out of computers? Of course not. The transmission and receipt of information is a higher-level manifestation of human consciousness. Attempting to build first-person consciousness out of bits of information is like trying to build the foundations of a house out of its upper storeys; or finding the foundations of the foundation in the roof. It is topsy-turvy to think of consciousness being constructed out of bits of information, unless like David Chalmers you think information is everywhere.

At the phenomenological level, information falls far short of consciousness. My being-in-the-world is not a matter of being in receipt of discrete streams of information. Even something as basic as sunbathing cannot be reduced to "information-bathing". We might extract information from the world around us, but that experienced world is not built up out of information. I may focus on a part of that world and articulate it but my ability to do this is limited. The strand that I pull out of my state of being-in-the-world and being-surrounded-by-the-world and, indeed, being the point of convergence of "I am" and "It is", makes sense only with respect to an existing multi-layered, multi-loculated, multi-dimensional reality, situated in a present, a future and a past, that has no clear boundary.

Even information in the legitimate sense of something that is shared when one person informs another of something, lacks the properties of the experienced world. Its most developed form is that of facts. Facts, as we noted in Chapter 4, are colourless, scentless, weightless, are neither tasty not toxic, hot or cold. That is why they can be represented in many forms: pictorially; in written words and numerals; and in spoken sounds. And when, for example, the facts are set down in writing, the size and font of the characters, what colour they are, and where they are located, do not matter. It does not matter whether I write the word "blue" in blue ink or red; or whether the word "large" is inscribed in small print or capitals. What matters is the relationship they have to one another and the place in the structure or system to which they belong.

Most importantly, information most obviously in the form of facts is *general* – that is why it can be shared. And why it can seem to be replicated as the technoimmortalizers require. The tokens – words or pictures on a screen, or 0s and 1s in the software – are instantiations of types. Unlike experiences, they are ownerless. Information, in virtue of the fact that it can potentially be communicated without limit, is disconnected from the personal (and the inter-personal) to the point of being impersonal: it is subsumed into the thatosphere. This is why mind-as-information is ripe to be united with other minds in a General Mind, as envisaged by one of Mark O'Connell's Silicon Valley interlocutors: "[W]hat he imagined himself being was an interconnected system of information-seeking nodes, travelling in ever-widening arcs throughout the universe, learning, expanding, collating".[30]

What the nodes would do with that information, what *information* would do with information – with another lot of information or itself somehow divided into transmitter and recipient – is not at all clear. Nor is it at all clear how they would qualify as *nodes* – as privileged points of convergence in a matrix. Be that as it may, this vision is an unsurprising end-point of the reduction of the mind and the self to information floating free from the body and indeed the individual embodied subject. Token minds are gathered up into mind-in-general. The fantasy of a vastly expanded thatosphere, which subsists without any "who" to taste and maintain it, is the ultimate consequence of the Original Sin of imagining that there could be information without individual informers and individual informees, or without even a differentiation into a) informers, b) those who receive information, and c) information itself.

Since individuation is set aside and the spatially extended body of the organism has been discarded, it is difficult to envisage how the separation of information into distinct items, corresponding to the entities that populate the thatosphere, would be possible. Such differentiation begins with, and must ultimately be rooted in, the succession of experiences of individuals, separated in space, time, and sensory modality (sight, sound, etc.) and anchored to a viewpoint. These all presuppose a localized substrate. Without such a connection with sensory experience – at the very least sufficient to secure the translation of transmissible facts into tokens corresponding to the acquisition of intelligence – information would seem to merge into a frozen totality; in short, a standing state of whatever is, in which incidentally there is no basis for the distinction between signal and noise.

We can see this particularly clearly if we return to the home territory from which the myth of universal information spilled out: the computer. What goes on in the circuitry of a computer does not itself amount to information without someone being informed by it, however indirectly. That is obvious. Less obvious is this: only a small part of what goes on in a computer counts as information. The user picks out the activity that is relevant. Molecular activity in the computer circuitry does not of itself ascend from meaningless noise or rise above its particularity to count as intelligible, and necessarily general, information. Uploading would require more than replication of the brain, the stuff of its circuits, or the messy actuality of its neural activity. There would have to be a process of abstraction of salient features. Something would have to guide this process and abstraction would have to be tailored to individuality, if the process was not simply to replicate a generic human being, or even generic brain, rather than a token me. Replication would be constrained by two criteria facing in opposite directions; towards generality to ensure that the information shall be salient; and towards particularity in order that I myself, not some general human being, or something even more general than a human being, should be preserved. And these requirements are in addition to the impossible challenge of making sure that what is replicated retains its connectedness with my singular past and future, essential to any moment of my replicated life making sense.

There is another problem. Information stored on an electronic platform would be worldless even at the fundamental level of being anchored to a particular place in space. It would have no existential tie to a world. At the basic level, I am where my body is, from which I am currently inseparable. Where would we locate the "uploaded" mind? The computer of which it is a part would presumably have to contact some kind of surroundings. This would presuppose that the device was wired into its surroundings by "sensors" and "actors". And what would those surroundings consist of? If it were the immediate physical surroundings of the device, it would be difficult to see how the inputs and outputs would harmonize with any world the uploaded self has brought along with it. The very fact that it could be envisaged as "an interconnected system of information-seeking nodes, travelling in ever-widening arcs throughout the universe, learning, expanding, collating" would suggest that it is not merely freed from the biological shackles but is not anchored anywhere.

All of these problems arise only when the more fundamental issues have been solved: determining what counts as information in the absence of an informant and an informee. Without that being settled, there is no clear boundary defining what has to be copied, separating the person-relevant information in the brain, the brain as information processor; that within the living tissues of the brain – juices, enzymes, membranes, etc., necessary for its functioning; and the random stuff and activity that, as it were, pads it out as a material object. There seems no prospect even if, in a sense difficult to define, the self was identical with the brain, of reducing what is essential to selfhood to a vast number of 0s and 1s and the meanings of processing them. This is relevant to the discussion that follows.

Personal identity and the uploaded self

The idea of "uploading" figures in many thought experiments that philosophers have appealed to in discussions of personal identity and (to use Derek Parfit's phrase) of "what matters" in survival. Squeezing the "who" out of information seems to enable the state of a material object such as the brain to be translated without remainder into information and for that information to be transmitted and, if necessary replicated, just as a page of print can be photocopied or a disc copied. As noted earlier, information, by definition, is impersonal, belonging to no individual – a necessary condition of its being transmissible, and intelligible, to be shared in a way that my experiences cannot. The person, it seems, is saved by being uprooted from a personal and interpersonal world, in short by becoming impersonal. Not much of a salvation.

Those who are deluded enough to believe that individuals – and their conscious experiences – are replicable information might argue that what is unique about an individual is not a particular piece of information but a unique *combination* of billions of items of information. This won't work because it does not close the gap between my first-person (actual) experience and memories and impersonal information. My experience of writing this sentence in a pub cannot be replicated, though *the facts that* I wrote it at a particular time and the factual details of my writing can be relayed, and hence replicated, any number of times. The multiplication of facts, of items of information, irrespective of whether they are broken down into any number of 0s and 1s, cannot close that gap between experience and information understood as something transmissable. The sum total remains impersonal.

Consider this passage from one of Parfit's many examinations of personal identity using thought experiments. He imagines a more ambitious uploading, not just of the brain or its states, but of his entire body. The principle in play is the same:

> Here on earth, I enter the Teletransporter. When I press some button,
> a machine destroys my body, while recording the exact state of all

my cells. The information is sent by radio to Mars, where another machine makes, out of organic materials, a perfect copy of my body. The person who wakes up on Mars seems to remember living my life up to the moment when I pressed the button and he is in every respect just like me.[31]

Parfit then asks whether the new arrival on Mars is or is not the same as the person who pressed the button. He does so not in order to arrive at a definitive answer but test our intuitions about personal identity and what matters in survival – intuitions that he himself feels are wrong as they incorrectly lead us to think personal identity is important. This is of less interest for our present concern than the seriously flawed assumptions built into the thought experiment.[32]

As always in assessing thought experiments, we need to scrutinize with particular care the scene-setting things that are nodded through before the argument begins. The machine, we are told, records "the *exact* state of all my cells". It can be assumed that Parfit refers to "cells" rather than to "my body" to give the fiction a quasi-scientific flavour and to indicate the degree of exactness of the record. We should not, however, allow this to distract us from the dubious nature of the idea of "an exact recording" that transforms an object into transmissible information. What would be an exact recording of the state of my body at time t? What form would it take? Clearly it would not be a verbal description, however extensive, because the words, necessarily general, cannot drill down to the singular reality of the transportee, least of all at a particular time. Nor would translation into 0s and 1s suffice – for the same reason. Any "exact description" would have to be something that left nothing out – that replicated every aspect of my cells. In short, nothing less than a physical replica – and this is not something that could be readily transmitted by radio: it would exceed the weight allowance. A complete recording of the state of a body, as opposed to the state of an aspect of it reduced to numbers (such as its temperature), could not be achieved except through the body itself. The nearest we could get to an exact presentation of the state of my cells at time t_1 would be the state of my cells a moment later.[33] An analogy would be a life-size map that left out nothing – not even, for example, the disposition of grains of sand.

Even an exact replica of a time-slice of the body would not suffice because this would leave out many states of the body outside of the time-slice. Hold on, you might say, what would be replicated in a time-slice would not only be the state of the body at time t but also the properties and dispositions of the body at time t that will guarantee that transitions to future states that will be true to the body and hence (according to the thought experiment) the person. However, as we have already discussed, an instantaneous snapshot, to whatever degree of exactitude, will not translate into dispositions and propensities that are implicitly extended over time.[34]

Perhaps what Parfit really envisages as being transmitted to Mars is nothing more than an exact *recipe* for recreating me, for reincarnation, at the other end of the journey. It would be rather like the kind of instructions that are sent to 3D printers for making boxes, paper clips, or tools. Recipes, however, are general and typically broad brush. They would not, could not, be a recipe for something utterly singular: *my* body. A recipe for an apple pie is a recipe for any apple pie not for this apple pie that is made at a particular time. We must not regard this problem as merely a temporary technical limitation to be overcome as more powerful teletransporters loaded with more precise recipes are developed. "My body" is not just "this body or something roughly like it", an instance of a range of bodies with a range of histories. My body, and in particular my brain, would have to be exactly like it if the recipe is to generate a sufficiently accurate copy for the resurrected me to "remember living my life up to the moment when I pressed the button". The question would then arise as to what the exact replica of a dynamic system such as my body would be. As we asked earlier, what would be replicated?

If one believes, as Parfit seems to do, that memories are states of the brain, they would have to be utterly particular states of that brain. What is more, autonoetic memories that are key to personal identity are inseparable from an awareness of the singular world and of the self to which the remembered experiences belonged. It is this that gives them their individuality, significance, and meaning: their very essence as memories.[35] To ensure that the teletransportee woke up with a sufficient quantity of his past, vast tracts of the actual, individual brain would have to be recorded with a fidelity that only complete material replication on the spot could secure. The person could not be resurrected from a general recipe, unless it were specified to the last molecule, by recording in full all the states of the cells. Such a full record would amount to the object itself. Only this would be enough and yet in a sense it would be too much: for aspects of the states of the cells would be irrelevant even to cellular function, never mind identity. And in an important sense, it would be too little. Because the specification must, of necessity, leave off the specific spatio-temporal history of the body prior to uploading. For when the body is reconstructed at the end of the journey the actual history of the materials from which it is made will be different from the history of the materials of the body prior to transportation. And we haven't even started to address the question of how, and by whom, things are to be sorted out on arrival; how the recipe is to be realized and the relevant materials are to be sourced. The intrepid tele-transportee would require a reception committee. Of this, more later.

How could such obvious objections to the very way in which the thought experiment is posed be overlooked? It will be clear by now that this is a symptom of the grip that pan-informationalism has on the contemporary mind: the assumptions that not only does consciousness boil down to information but that material objects (including brains) boil up to (necessarily general) information which, as in the thought experiment, can be transmitted from mechanism to mechanism. It is this that ultimately inspires the notion that the universe might be a computer simulation – of what, by what, and for whom, is not clear. And it also nods through the assumption that the incarnation of the teletransportee on arrival, using the transmitted recipe, would also amount to "waking up" – the restoration of the conscious person with all her memories, expectations, habits, attitudes, personality, etc., intact and her familiar world around her. The thought experiment removes the very aspects of personhood that reductionist materialists find most awkward. First-person, utterly singular, irreplaceable being, becomes, when reduced to information, impersonal and replicable because generalizable. If there were a general recipe for constructing Raymond Tallis, Tallis would be general. To assert this would give generality priority over individuals, *quidditas* over *haecceitas* – and in the very place where singularity – the irreplaceability of the individual – is of the essence.

Selves are irreducibly token and as such essentially irreplaceable and non-replicable.[36] I am, of course, when seen from a certain outside view, an instance of a type. Indeed, I instantiate many types: male human, husband, European, doctor, bearded, traveller, EU Remainer, boring old fart – the list is endless and I won't weary you by extending it any further. The point is that these types under which others categorize me do not reach all the way down to my personal identity. Personal identity is unique to a person who, unlike information in any quantity or combination which is intrinsically replicable, cannot be replicated. Raymond Tallis, with his body and his/its history, can alone fill the office of Raymond Tallis. My essence reaches all the way down to the level of the token.

Personal identity is not stipulated from outside, as if the "I" were an entity defined by a finite number of types, which could be realized in a multitude of tokens with general meaning, being a class with any number of members. And importantly, this is equally true of each of my experiences and my memories of my experiences. The information that I experienced the colour red can be shared with any number of people; my experience of red at time t is not shareable in this way. And so it cannot be reduplicated. The docking of the uploaded mind on to a new substrate would not restore to it the kind of "tokenhood" associated with being a person. Personhood is the primordial form of token-hood.

"Am" identity is not of course granted or achieved solely through meeting certain objective criteria. I do not have to qualify to be myself; and if I did, those qualifications would be insufficient to deliver my identity.[37] That is why someone else can ask: "Is that Raymond Tallis?" and it is not impossible that I might ask "Am I Raymond Tallis?" meaning "Am I the person that other people call Raymond Tallis?", but I could not ask "Am I this person?" or "Am I me?". My identity in this sense is as inescapable as my pains (and perhaps more loosely) my responsibilities.[38]

The apparent plausibility of mind-uploading or teletransportation by replication of bodies or brains depends on sliding between translating bodies or brains into (necessarily general) information – itself an impossible task – and appealing to the originating body or brain to underwrite unique, token identity. In short, on having the cake generally (so that it is replicable) and eating it singularly (so that it corresponds to a unique individual). At any rate, to transmit my conscious self into the teletransporter, it would be necessary to deliver more than a snapshot of the state of my body or brain, or a translation of those items into information. We are back with the problem of translating the material brain into transmissible information: the record of the exact states would have to be supplemented by the stuff that has that state. Neurones *and* their microanatomical modes of configuration *and* their patterns of activity (assumed to be self-defining for the machine), *and* the knowledge and skills they make possible, would all have to be boiled down to static, general, replicable, timeless, pieces of information. The distinctions between these things, however, are of the utmost importance and no account of personal identity can do without them.

The same blurring of reference is evident in the wider literature on "uploading" that talks of humans or their minds as "data". "Data" has to encompass, without clear distinction:

1. The original structure or "platform" (the biological brain or body) that has been left behind as the teletransporter is entered and will need to be replaced;
2. The software;
3. Knowledge and competencies; and
4. Conscious experience.

The only way to justify this would be to resort to the pan-informationalist ontology according to which everything – from tears of grief to an earthquake on an unvisited planet – is information. But this would have extraordinary, conflicting consequences. In one direction it would assimilate consciousness to a piece of the material world (states of the brain) and in the other it would swallow up the material world into something like consciousness.

The latter outcome is realized in the ultimate destination of pan-informationalism: the famous (or notorious) "IT from BIT" formulation of John Wheeler, according to which information is even more basic than quantum fields or energy.[39] The information in question is entirely digital, with the analogue bump-into-able reality of daily life boiling down to 0s and 1s. The self-transformation of the physical world into impersonal knowledge of said world means that the sense of stuff can be got from stuff itself, impersonal knowledge from the physical universe, without passing through "who". We cut out the middle man: man. What we are left with is a universe in which everything is realizing its potential as a source of potential information; but in the absence of a recipient, a user, there is no transformation of potential into actual information. The universe would be like a parliament with everyone talking and nobody listening, except the talking is done by no-one. What is more, there would be no distinction between matter and "matter" or the physics of speech and the meaning of what is spoken.[40]

The less radical, but no less vulnerable, idea that we are somehow "code" – a system of rules for converting one form of information into another form or representation – misses the "presentation" out of "representation". It also merges the communication channel with what is communicated and both of them with those who are communicating. Data, software, code, operating system, hardware, the casing, and the user are all merged, boiling down to free-floating on-off, 0 or 1, states. We cannot tell the dancer from the dance, or indeed from the dance hall. There would be no basis, in the computational theory of mind – succinctly summarized by Steven Pinker as the view that "mind is a naturally selected system of organs of computation"[41] – for the difference between the machinery of computation and what is computed or processed.

In conclusion, the tragedy of my transience cannot be pre-empted by "recording the exact state of my cells" and posting me out of harm's way.

Interpersonal identity and the shared world

Something absolutely fundamental missing in Parfit's discussion of the tele-transporter thought experiment is also missing from the transhumanist dreams of mind-uploading. It is nothing less than the human community and the human world and the interpersonal dimension of the self. "We" is conspicuously absent or marginalized; instead, the focus is on an "I" that, paradoxically, verges on being no-one.

This is lucidly expressed by Kim Atkins who argues that the attributes and processes of attribution which make up my identity exist, in a sense, "in between" myself and other people and not simply "in" me: "Because my identity is not a self-contained piece of information that can be abstracted from my body it cannot be transferred to another body to create an identical 'person'. It is just because my identity is discursive, a collaboration that is continually renewed and reformed in discourse, that it cannot be expressed in third-person terms alone."[42] Personhood has several persons – second-person "you" and first-person plural "we" as well as first-person singular "I" – something that is reflected in the profound human reality that the significance of our lives is not established purely within ourselves.[43]

In the light of this, let us have another look at the subject undergoing teletransportation. When she wakes up, what does she wake up to? Her journey is solitary: it is a journey of a snapshot of the *state* of a body undertaken without the body that fleshes out that state. There would be no room for the crowds of loved ones, friends, enemies, strangers, and the invisible hands that had made her world possible. Even if *per impossibile* the snapshot of her brain captured the dynamic, temporally deep world she demitted from when she entered the machine, the resumption of that world on arrival would be an hallucination; at best, a four-dimensional, multi-modal after-image of the community she has left. It would not really be "outside" in the way that the one she left behind when she entered the teletransporter was outside. It would be a construct sustained by contents of her consciousness; and their intentionality would be like antennae waving in emptiness, with no point of application. It would not be populated by other people and supplied with the material necessary to reconstruct her body and download her uploaded mind. Even this bleak prospect optimistically assumes that the intentionality suspended while the teletransportee is in the machine would be restored on arrival.

The arrivee would therefore have no valid current grounds for emotions, values, enjoyment, or even suffering. Given that there would be no new experiences in this *worldless* realm, with nothing real going on to trigger and justify new neural activity, she would be living off a diminishing capital of past experiences that would become progressively more irrelevant. In short, she would not have the wherewithal to continue anything like a human life. Or life of any kind. She would not even be able to make sense of herself. As Nikolas Kompridis points out: "[i]f personal identity is constituted in, and sustained through, our relations with others, such that were we to erase our relations with significant others we would also erase the conditions of our self-intelligibility".[44]

An intuition of an environment is necessary for a device to be truly "intelligent". AlphaGo impressed because it was "self-teaching" but it did this dumbly by means of number-crunching that generated probabilities and identified associations of which it was not, of course, conscious. It did not inhabit the world of Go-players. According to Judea Pearl, a truly intelligent device would have to have a sense of causal relationships and for this it would need to be equipped with a model of the environment.[45] In the case of intelligent humans the environment is not a brute given. It is crucially fashioned by the interests of the subject.[46]

We can see the absurd conclusion to which we are led when "I-hood" is reduced to the information contained in a brain, or a trickle of connected psychological contents, and it is forgotten that such contents presuppose the outside world they are *about*. The Parfitian or transhumanist person is already impoverished before it is rendered worldless. It is thereby readied for the final impoverishing reduction to general information that is paradoxically had by no-one, informs no-one, and is about nothing other than its empty self. The mind-uploaders and teletransporters inadvertently remind us that the continuity of the self is inseparable from the scaffold of the continuity of the world. The reduction of the self to a worldless quasi-person is an entirely predictable consequence of starting from the idea of the self as an internally connected stream of psychological material realized in a standalone brain. In real life, in human life, we "are born in someone's arms".[47] And, in a very fundamental sense, remain there. At any rate, there is no community of minds without the co-presence of bodies.[48]

As if being worldless were not enough, there is another problem for the teletransportee if it were merely the brain rather than the whole body that was recreated at the other end of the journey in the teletransporter. Even a cerebral idealist – according to whom the world is a construct of the brain – must accept that the standalone brain, detached from sense organs spread over a body, cannot sustain a viewpoint. What is more, viewpoints are scale-relative and to establish a scale something more than a "processor" is needed. Whether there is a beach or a sand grain "over there" depends on the acuity of attention, itself determined by interests of something (a person) that is concerned for itself, at least to the extent of being rooted in, and flowering out of, its own unique and uniquely owned history, and it will be influenced by its physical scale. If the mind is uploaded on to non-biological material – as opposed to being reincarnated in the body and the brain – that material would have no needs, other than say battery power. While an external observer may locate it, it would not be situated *for itself*, as the centre of surroundings with which it engages to meet its needs. It would, effectively, be nowhere; for the substrate would not provide the point of origin from which it relates to a material world.

These issues betray something chilling in the transhumanist vision. What is uploaded is at once monstrously egocentric to the point of being worldless and yet composed of information that by definition is transmissible and consequently ego-less. Unlike experiences, information (facts, knowledge) has no owner or even a home base. "The facts" are not tied to a time or place. That, as we saw in the last chapter, is why they are key to the enhancement of human agency. For Parfit, identifying personhood with transmissible information is central to his endeavour to make personal identity unimportant:

> The fact of personal identity through time consists only in taking account of certain particular facts which can be described without presupposing personal identity and without explicitly supposing that the experiences in the life of this person are possessed by them or without even explicitly supposing this person exists. One can describe these facts in an *impersonal* manner.[49]

Thus the entirely unsurprising discovery that, if one glosses experiences and other psychological contents as "facts" (which, of course, belong to no-one), then personal identity disappears and impersonality reigns. And information, likewise, has no intrinsic "who" in itself, no individual informant or informee embedded in it. That is why it can be transmitted – that is to say replicated. This is the necessary condition of its being intelligible to an indefinite number of persons, transmitters and recipients. And, as we have argued, facts as information existing independently of any conscious transmitter or recipient are not information at all. We are misled into thinking that information can exist in the absence of persons only because of the interval – which can be extended indefinitely – between transmission and reception, that we have referred to. That is why we mistakenly imagine that what is in unopened books, or the rings of a tree, or the strata in rocks is enjoying an existence as information in the absence of the consciousness of persons. Once we think of those rings as "standing information" – as if the tree were always telling itself how old it is – it is no great step to imagine that a person can be copied by the teletransporter and transmitted as information, especially if one's idea of a person is of something impersonal. Parfit's often repeated point that personal identity is not "a further fact" additional to "the existence of a brain and a body, and the occurrence of a series of interrelated physical and mental events" does not do away with personhood.[50] Nothing could be further from a fact – impersonal, and timeless – than being a person. No-one is, or could be, just the facts, dig-itized or otherwise, of their case.

Facts are not only homeless but also timeless, as discussed in Chapter 4. The information recoding "the exact state of my cells" that is sent up in the tele-transporter would be divorced from any particular time interval between its departure from the source and its arrival at the destination. While a memory is located in the past of a person, *the fact of there being such a memory* and the facts captured in the memory would not be located in the past of the transportee. And the future arising out of a past reduced to transmissible facts would likewise be divorced from any putative personal timeframe of the teletransportee. After all, if information had an intrinsic location in space or time, independent of any conscious transmitter or recipient, it could not be transmitted intact from one time or place to another. More fundamentally, it is difficult to see how, having been reduced to information, the teletransportee could arrive at any destination. If information is not located in time or place – that is why it can be replicated – it could not alight at a "there" or indeed a "now"; or, more precisely, transform a putative place of arrival into a "here" or "now" – even if it were somehow packaged in a spaceship that could travel and arrive. The dream that we could be entirely subsumed into the thatosphere for the purposes of replication has, as its down side, that we would be no-one nowhere at no time.

Curiously, this nightmare of being no-one is close to the transhuman-ist dream reported earlier of becoming "an interconnected system of information-seeking nodes, travelling in ever-widening arcs throughout the universe, learning, expanding, collating". The prospect of humanity as a nebula of rootless intergalactic consciousnesses hardly gives one a warm glow. It is difficult to imagine how this package of information would have any agenda, anything to live for, any mode of being that would be of concern to itself.

CONCLUSION

Transhumanist dreams, of indefinitely postponing the many ills that the flesh is heir to, collide with reality – or in the case of technoimmortalization a lack of it. Arresting the self-destructive processes built into the human body by preventing intrinsic ageing and treating the illnesses that give the "it" of the body the means of extinguishing the "I", may postpone, but will not cancel, the inescapable Appointment in Samarra. The marriage of the perishable body with enduring replaceable machinery does not seem likely to create a new class of privileged persons[51] enjoying countless centuries of extra life. The maintenance of the hardware and the care of the interfaces presents problems that will soon become insuperable for social as well as bioengineering reasons. While, for some, "machines sit at the pinnacle of human consciousness"[52] *l'homme machine* is fortunate to be embodied in flesh developed through millions of years of evolution and his birthday machinery seems unlikely to be bettered. The "delicate protein complexes with fairly pathetic use-by dates"[53] seem to have served us rather well.

And, finally, the Assumption of a human being into the thatosphere, into information – eternal through being endlessly replicable – would (if it were possible) mean the loss, not the salvation, of the self. The transhuman future would be inhuman if only because we cannot be reduced to generalizable, replicable information. Actual particulars cannot be translated from singular "thisness" to a confluence of general "whatness". Personal identity is *essentially* token; it is, well, personal. Uploading of mind-as-information does not preserve token identity and, consequently, it is difficult to see what remains of identity, indeed, of the person one was, in what is uploaded.[54] Uploading even the most precise recipe for my brain and body would involve reducing my flesh to necessarily general information. This would not provide the basis for a unique body, located in a particular point in space and time, not the least because that body could not take its world, or any world, with it. It could not, as it were, cadge situatedness from the biological medium on to which it had been uploaded. Its dissolution into information would remove the external or real objects of intentionality.

Engineered immortality therefore does not seem even a distant prospect. The tragedy of our finitude is unmitigated. We have to learn how to live in the presence of this gigantic truth of our life. This, along with understanding how to order our affairs individually and collectively such that all may flourish in their inevitably brief lives, are the most important challenges for secular humanity. It is thither that we shall direct our thoughts in the final chapters where we shall return to some of the territory traditionally occupied by religion.

PART III

Flourishing without God

CHAPTER 8

"The sky is empty"

PROLOGUE: ON THE PHILOSOPHICALLY EXAMINED LIFE

We have highlighted aspects of our nature often overlooked or even denied in secular thought. Given that we are neither apes nor angels, neither mere organisms nor pure spirits temporarily lodged in bodies, how shall we think of ourselves? How shall we live in the light of what we know, or might come to know, of our nature? More to the point, where shall we find meanings sufficiently enduring and profound to withstand knowledge of our own mortality and the certain loss of all that we love or value?

Rejecting religious responses to these questions does not mean that we can ignore the questions themselves. Or, come to that, ignore religion: a humanism that chooses not to think seriously about something that has played such an important role in human history must be impoverished. While we may live outside the interrogative grasp of these questions for much of our lives, we know that they are awaiting us. At times of grief, suffering, and fear we may be engulfed by them. We should therefore engage with them even, or especially, when they are not interrogating us.

Contemporary philosophy rarely aspires to teach us how to live. As a doctor who has cared for many seriously ill patients, I can report that philosophy of the kind that figures in the pages of this book rarely has much to offer people *in extremis* or in daily life. Even so, I would like to think that a rich sense of the mystery of our nature is an essential basis for secular living.

There is a danger hereabouts of endorsing the claim, ascribed by Plato to Socrates, that "the unexamined life is not worth living".[1] The Platonic idea that knowledge (of a philosophical nature) increases one's moral worth should be questioned, not the least because, measured against Socrates' criteria, most lives (including many that are truly admirable) pass without examination. Kant's confident assertion that "in all men, as soon as their reason has become ripe for speculation, there has always existed and will continue to exist some kind of metaphysics"[2] does not correspond to any kind of population-based observation. I seem to remember – though I cannot pin it down – a couple of Samuel Beckett's many tramps, domiciled in a ditch, arguing over Henry of Ghent's distinction between the "being of essence" and "somethingness", mocking the idea that the examined life, at least in its philosophical form, is the norm for humanity.

Even those who aspire to the examined life are too busy meeting life's multiple, legitimate demands to devote much of their days to the kind of reflection we associate with Plato. When life gets serious, metaphysics retreats to the margins and it may look like mere brain-teasing. Those of us who try to be philosophers find, even in the hours devoted to philosophy, and when we are not concerned with winning an argument rather than arriving at epiphanies, that more time may be spent on tying thoughts together, polishing sentences, and proof-reading than truly thinking, even less inhabiting, the thoughts one wants to share with others or realize in our own minds. The endeavour to assume an Archimedean position from which we can gather up our lives in the widest cognitive gaze may be displaced by worry over a feverish baby or irritation at someone nipping into a parking space. Awakenings seem doomed to be temporary – a reflection in miniature of the brevity of the interval of wakefulness between birth and death.

Nearly 2,500 years after Plato, Heidegger advanced the notion of "authentic being-towards-death".[3] The most important message that can be flushed out of the tangled shrubbery of his writing is a familiar exhortation to live each moment as if it were one's last, in full awareness that all lives come to an end and whoever is born is old enough to die; and that one should resist the temptation to take refuge in the world of a "they" who never die. Even this version of the examined life resists translation into a way of everyday being. In a responsive and responsible life "the long littleness" still demands attention to endless trivial details.

Heidegger's philosophy – and that of his phenomenological ancestors such as Husserl and his existential descendants such as Sartre – is essentially descriptive, rather than explanatory, of our ordinary modes of being-in-the-world. Their rich, sometimes revelatory accounts of everyday life leave the mystery of humanity intact. They awaken the wonder that is the traditional prompt to philosophical questioning. To see ourselves through their eyes, is to see the "Given" as a *gift*, not something that can be taken for granted. As Hannah Arendt expressed it, Heidegger "had regained for philosophy a thinking that expresses gratitude that the 'naked that' had been given at all".[4]

Notwithstanding their sometimes rather technical appearance, the arguments advanced in the previous chapters of this book are intended to be celebratory in the Heideggerian sense; thinking is thanking. Wonder and gratitude are legitimate starting points for meeting the humanist task of thinking clearly about ourselves. That we are finite, contingent beings who have only limited control over our lives in a universe that is overwhelmingly indifferent to us (as we are indifferent to the vast part of it), pixels in a picture that no-one can see because there is no eye to see it, is a staple of secular thought. What is less frequently observed is that we are also profoundly, indeed mysteriously, different from any other being in the order of things, not the least in the extent to which we are aware of our condition.

It is overlooked in the following admirably lucid definition of secular humanism: "a comprehensive life stance and world view which embraces human reason, metaphysical naturalism, altruistic morality, and distributive justice, and consciously rejects supernatural claims, theistic faith and religiosity, pseudoscience, and superstition".[5]

The missing element – and how we might restore it – is explored in this third part of *Seeing Ourselves*. How may we ensure that, as we accept the death of God, something within us does not also die?

DISENCHANTMENT

Dieu est mort! Le ciel est vide...   Gérard de Nerval[6]

Secularization is liberating but it comes at a price. What is most conspicuously absent is captured in the notion of "disenchantment", associated with the German sociologist Max Weber. For Weber, there were two phases of "the disenchantment of the world" (an enchanting phrase originally owed to the German poet and dramatist Friedrich Schiller). The first was a tidying up of the supernatural resulting in monotheistic religions. The second was the rejection of monotheism in favour of a god-free world picture.

The most frequently cited explanation for emptying the universe of divine agency is the rise of science. "Angry" clouds disintegrated into moodless droplets, the passage of air through wind-tossed foliage was no longer the whispering of spirits, and the hydrodynamics of water meant that brooks no longer babbled to themselves or anyone else outside of poetry.

The scientific revolution, however, did not arise out of a vacuum; nor did it exert its manifold influences in a world that was otherwise unchanging. After all, in Europe the sixteenth-century schism in the Christian church and the encouragement to engage directly with God via the sacred texts, cutting out layers of middle reverends (Most, Very, Right, or Plain), played an important part in promoting rational, critical Enlightenment thought. Brad Gregory has argued[7] that the headline doctrinal disputes in successive waves of reformation resulted in "the unintended self-marginalisation of theology through doctrinal controversy".

Some historians of thought have gone further and even questioned the independent role of science as a secularizing influence. Other forces have been invoked. They include industrialization, urbanization, universal education or at least literacy, modernization (marked by the establishment of a capitalist, and then an industrial-economic order), economic growth and the dissemination of affluence, the spread of egalitarianism and liberal democracy, and rights-based societies. These putative influences have in turn been challenged on the grounds that their rise is not temporally correlated with secularization or that it is unclear to what extent they are causes or effects, or sometimes causes and sometimes effect.[8]

Even if the Protestant affirmation of the right to think for one's self without the mediation of priests may have been an inadvertent trigger of secularism, the latter may have had a deeper theological origin. Marcel Gauchet has argued[9] that the God who is "distant" and "difficult", like the God of Geoffrey Hill's poem about Ovid,[10] carries within Him the seeds of his own destruction. Durkheim echoes this: "the apparent departure from religion that we see in the development of the modern West was always incipient in the Judaeo-Christian tradition with its emphasis on the transcendence of God, whose separation from mundane affairs leaves room for the development of a secular space".[11]

Gauchet characterized monotheistic Christianity, in which God's interventions are few and far between, as "the religion for departing from religion".[12] The result, as Paul Fitzgerald describes it is that: "Christianity ultimately frees people from all mediating structures of organized religion even as it encourages human curiosity to subdue and possess a disenchanted world".[13] The most conspicuous casualty of the scientific revolution has been the belief, as Feuerbach has described it, "that nature is ruled ... *by the same forces and motivations* as man ... that the only valid cause of natural effects or phenomena is a thinking being with intentions and desires".[14]

And it cannot be denied that the transition from worshipping the sun to measuring its output has represented and reinforced a transformation of our picture of nature from the scene of divine agency to that of actual or (increasingly) possible human agency, notwithstanding that we are alive only courtesy of forces of which we are largely unaware and which, ultimately, we cannot control.

The radical change in outlook is characterized by W. T. Stace in an essay, "Man Against Darkness", written shortly after the end of the Second World War and the 50-year season in Hell that was the first half of the European twentieth century:

> The founders of modern science – for instance, Galileo, Kepler, and Newton – were mostly pious men who did not doubt God's purposes. Nevertheless, they took the revolutionary step of consciously and deliberately expelling the idea of purpose as controlling nature from their new science of nature. They did this on the grounds that inquiry into purposes is useless for what science aims at: namely the prediction and control of events. To predict an eclipse, what you have to know is not its purpose but its causes. Hence science from the seventeenth century onwards became exclusively an inquiry into causes. The conception of purpose in the world was ignored and frowned on. This, though silent and almost unnoticed, was the greatest revolution in human history.[15]

Stace spells out the implications of this revolution – for ethics, politics, and the future of our species – and they are enormous.

Darwinism explicitly incorporated mankind into this godless, purposeless nature and paved the way for the Darwinitis we discussed in Chapter 2. One of Darwin's most influential early apostles, the philosopher and biologist Ernst Haeckel, saw Darwinism "as 'only a small fragment of a far more comprehensive doctrine' ... which recognized that the universe as a whole was no more than a vast impersonal machine, sublimely indifferent to the happiness, or indeed the existence, of the human race".[16]

The Galilean revolution not only marginalized the idea of intelligent purposes controlling nature. It also downgraded phenomenal experience and so-called "secondary qualities" on the grounds that they were mind-dependent. Qualitative aspects of experience, such as colours, or feelings of warmth and cold, were ontologically suspect. Compared with measurements, sense experiences were epistemologically inferior. Primary qualities – size, shape, number, etc. – alone were intrinsic to objective, that is to say real, reality. Even weight, effort, burden, are amenable to being transformed to weightless numbers. The reduction of organisms to "living matter" and hence to "matter" period was an important step towards dissolving what counts as reality into the purely quantitative fields of the subatomic realm. That the world is at bottom a system of magnitudes is an idea that has become increasingly dominant.[17]

It may be thought that enchantment abolished by macroscopic science has been restored at the fundamental, nanoscopic level, in the paradoxes of quantum mechanics. They are, however, revealed as impersonal and quantitative. Quantum reality remains a mindless realm of "it", notwithstanding the vexed question of the role of the observer in resolving uncertainty at the subatomic level. The gap between the hidden order of the universe and its human intelligibility remains unreduced.[18]

The progressive disenchantment brought about by scientific explanation is described by the Nobel Prize-winning physicist Steven Weinberg: "The explanatory arrow points downwards from societies to people, to organs, to cells, to biochemistry, to chemistry, and ultimately to physics. Societies are explained by people, people by organs, organs by cells, cells by biochemistry, biochemistry by chemistry, and chemistry by physics".[19] His seemingly shocking conclusion that "the more the universe seems comprehensible, the more it also seems pointless" is entirely unsurprising.[20] The more closely we identify the sum total of what there is with the physical universe as it is viewed from the impersonal viewpoint of natural science the less point it must seem to have. If we exclude subjective meaning from what qualifies as reality, we will find the universe empty of anything we recognize as our own. This is not an empirical discovery but the result of a methodology. The material dividends – increased life expectancy, health expectancy, comfort expectancy and enjoyment expectancy – seem, however, to validate a world picture in which mindless matter and energy have displaced the lesser minds of spirits and the greater minds of the gods.

Perhaps we have accepted the notion of a "meaningful" (or indeed meaningless) universe too easily. Surely meaning (and value) are *necessarily* local; the very idea of meaning (or value) visible from a standpoint that sees the universe as a whole is self-contradictory. What would correspond to them? Values felt or asserted by matter that (after all) by definition does not matter to itself? Values felt by the universe as a whole? Hardly. The complaint that the universe is "meaningless" is thus rather odd. Is it a complaint that the universe that does not care for a minute part of itself (humankind) – or not at least to the extent that that minute part cares for itself – does not share our ideas of what is meaningful? Leaving aside the fact that values are competitive and meanings (in the sense of what counts as meaningful, as significant) are viewpoint dependent, it is difficult to see what content a meaning of the universe-as-a-whole could have, what values would be expressed in its caring for me, for all human beings, or for itself. Such values would have to be agent-neutral or impersonal and, in addition, unshaped by any particular beings or types of beings in the sum total of things.

Be that as it may, Weinberg's unsurprising conclusion echoes Bertrand Russell's claim in "A Free Man's Worship" that "the world which Science presents for our belief" is "purposeless" and "void of meaning", that Man and all his manifestations "are but the outcome of accidental collocations of atoms" and that "the whole temple of Man's achievement must inevitably be buried beneath the debris of a universe in ruins".[21] We are a long way from the religious world picture where, according to Charles Taylor, "Human agents are embodied in society, society in the cosmos, and the cosmos incorporates the divine".[22] Thus, apparently, the metaphysical face of Weber's disenchantment of the world and the price of emancipation from religious belief.[23]

While secularism and disenchantment are tightly interconnected, they are not identical: "Disenchantment has two distinct aspects, each utterly implicated in the other. On the one hand there is secularization and the decline of magic; on the other hand, there is the increasing scale, scope, and power of the formal means-ends rationalities of science, bureaucracy, the law, and policy-making".[24] Divine purpose and divine justice are displaced by the seemingly endless mediations of the bureaucratic state and the rule of man-made but impersonal law. The progress of technology permits ever tighter bureaucratization of our lives. We are born and die in a blizzard of documents, of profane texts, defining our entitlements and responsibilities.

Scientific and bureaucratic sources of a disenchanted human world converge in our relationship to the landscape of artefacts, amenities, and institutions – made neither by God or nature – within which we pass most of our waking hours. Half a millennium of scientific thought and experimentation has created a material environment furnished wall-to-wall with science-based technology disinfected of spiritual forces and supernatural entities. Rationality, or the idea of it, is implicit in the machinery that surrounds us and mediates our interactions with the world. If the car breaks down, our first instinct is not to appeal to God but to call for a mechanic. And when our health breaks down, we may pray for a recovery but the real business is seeking medical advice and following it. It is from the surgery, or the Internet, not the hills, whence cometh our help and liberation from misfortune, notwithstanding that the hospital where we are treated may have been founded as a religious institution and be named after a saint.

Science fiction writer Arthur C. Clarke's famous Third Law was that "Any sufficiently advanced technology is indistinguishable from magic".[25] Perhaps; but any inclination to see the miraculous at work in the extraordinary devices we use is pre-empted by our engagements with them being mediated by monetary transactions and contracts. We are customers aware of our consumer rights. The wonderful devices are wrapped in many layers of instructions and guarantees. These are sufficient to extinguish any aura of magic, even around devices that enable us to converse with chosen individuals 10,000 miles away. We are more mindful of the number of free minutes that come with our contract than with the miracle of our ability to master invisible electromagnetic waves to cast our utterances to the other side of the earth via a space satellite that directs a billion voices to the particular ears to which they wish to speak. We are concerned not with what has made this possible – the laws of nature and the huge cooperative cognitive enterprise enabling us to uncover and to exploit them – but that they do what is said on the tin and give us value for money. Ironically, the artefactscape is all the more disenchanted precisely *because* its contents, unlike spirits, behave predictably rather than capriciously. The more efficient the technology, the less we are impressed by it. The nearest we get to seeing what is "under the bonnet" is when a device breaks down. Otherwise the painfully acquired knowledge and the million patented ingenuities on which it is built are concealed by its reliability.

Much of what is relevant to our lives comes to us as facts. Facts, as observed in previous chapters, belong to no-one: they are cognitive denizens of nowhere. This goes some way to explaining what would otherwise be paradoxical: that, as the human mind penetrates the universe, so the latter seems to be increasingly mindless, an epistemic desert populated in its macro- and micro-extremes largely by numbers which serve to make us ever more insignificant. As the known age of the universe grows to an unimaginable 13.8 billion years, so my lifespan shrinks to an eyeblink. It becomes all too clear that a world that has done without me for 99.9999 per cent of its duration will not miss me after I have gone. We are pin-pricks of "this" in a boundless "that". Truly did the prophet of Ecclesiastes cry that "he who increases knowledge increases sorrow"[26] even where that same knowledge may provide us the means to mitigate our sorrows – or to postpone them.

Some writers have questioned whether most humans live in a disenchanted world – or are equally immersed in that world. It has been claimed that three quarters of the population of the United States believe in the paranormal.[27] These beliefs, however, are isolated flowers in a stony ground, localized outbursts of metaphysical sentimentality in an otherwise hard-headed outlook that prompts individuals to reach for lawyers when things do not go as expected. The aficionados of seances expect as high a standard of consumer service as do those who would scoff at such scraps of the supernatural. It is salutary to recall what Brad Gregory said of Christianity in the United States: "[it] remains superficially strong by comparison with western Europe, but it is a mile wide and an inch deep".[28] The inch is provided by religious experience and the mile by social conformity and political expediency born up on an ocean of money.[29]

Religious fundamentalism is alive and well in the United States where about a third of the citizenry believe in the literal truth of the Bible, including its claim that the universe is a youngster of a few thousand years. And even an amoral character such as Donald Trump feels obliged to name-check God from time to time. He was a prominent participant in a recent (2018) National Day of Prayer. In the wake of large-scale disasters he affirms that his "thoughts and prayers" are with those who have suffered – though not those who have suffered at his hands. He regularly repeats this formula after each avoidable massacre sponsored by the Second Amendment (the right to bear arms even if you also bear lethal grudges), while conspicuously failing to criticize the National Rifle Association. (God, unlike the NRA, is not a direct donor to his campaign.) And his loyal lieutenant, Vice President Michael Pence, has been described as a Christian supremacist.[30]

Leaving aside fake and/or opportunist religion, it would seem to be difficult, therefore, to dispute Durkheim's famous characterization of what Matthew Arnold described in his poem "Dover Beach" as the "melancholy, long with-drawing roar" of the Sea of Faith in the western world:

> Yet if there is one truth that history has incontrovertibly settled, it is that religion extends over an ever-diminishing area of social life. Originally, it extended to everything; everything social was religious – the two words were synonymous. Then, gradually political, eco-nomic, and scientific functions broke free from the religious function, becoming separate entities and taking on more and more a markedly temporal character. God, if we may express it in such a way, from being at first present in every human relationship, has progressively withdrawn. He leaves the world to men and their quarrels.[31]

Nevertheless, as we discussed in Chapter 1, the story of secularization is not universal. Secularization narratives often conflate "religion" with Latin Christianity in Europe and North America and industrial democracies in Europe and North America with the world.[32] If we look elsewhere, we do not see such a clear parallelism in the development of secularization, moderni-zation, the rise of bureaucracy, and democracy. There are societies beyond western Europe where religion is resurgent or where, at least, traditional reli-gion seems to co-exist comfortably with science-based solutions to the soluble problems of everyday life. The fruits of advanced science can be enjoyed, and are widely employed, in theocracies. The use of the most sophisticated technology to broadcast religiously-inspired barbarisms such as crucifixions has a ghastly irony, exceeded only by the sickness of using Facebook to disseminate films of beheadings.[33] More innocently, the employment of loudspeakers to broadcast the mullah's message, or call the faithful to prayer, does not subvert the message as much as might be expected. The reliance on technology to spread the word of God does not seem to remind the faithful that not all help comes from Heaven.

Secular humanism, therefore, is not the guaranteed future of all humanity. For this reason, if for no other, it is essential for infidels to think how they might fill the spaces vacated by the withdrawal of religion in their own world. We cannot, or at least should not, neglect the profound, compelling questions to which religion has seemed, to a significant portion of humanity, to provide answers.

THE SEARCH FOR MEANING IN A GODLESS UNIVERSE

> In seeing ourselves from the outside we find it difficult to take our lives seriously. This loss of conviction, and the attempt to regain it, is the problem of the meaning of life.
>
> Thomas Nagel[34]

> Human life loses its value when seen from afar, either from distant space or from distant time.   Emil Cioran[35]

The absence of a search for meaning

> *Diversion.* Being unable to cure death, wretchedness and ignorance, men have decided, in order to be happy, not to think about such things.   Blaise Pascal[36]

Hunger for a different kind of meaning – deeper, wider, more intense, more coherent – in our daily life is sharpened by the knowledge that we shall die. Dissatisfaction with the meaning of life and with its brevity may seem contradictory – rather like diners complaining both that the food is terrible and that the portions are so small. Mortality, however, undermines, even mocks, the importance of the terribly important things that fill our days, making them seem futile, and yet sometimes more precious:

Life is real! Life is earnest!
And the grave is not its goal;
Dust thou art, to dust returnest,
Was not spoken of the soul.[37]

So long as "goal" is not interpreted as "terminus", secular humanists may respond to the first three lines of Longfellow's poem with an unhappy "Amen". They won't agree with the redemptive soul-talk in the fourth. Hence the search for a mode of flourishing that might mitigate the universal tragedy of our transience.

And yet the search for meanings resistant to awareness of mortality is not an obvious preoccupation, even less a continuous concern, in many lives. There is a disconnection between our everyday consciousness and the large ideas that should challenge, haunt, even undermine, it. What science has to tell us about our smallness and our ignorance does not invade our hours to the extent that it perhaps should. My home is located in the outer suburbs of one of billions of galaxies – and yet it is not. And I do not measure my brief time above ground against the 13.8 billion years of the universe, the 4 billion years of the life of the earth, the 500 million years of the history of multicellular life, or the 300,000 years of modern *H. sapiens.* While it may seem to the eyes of science that we are located in a vast, largely meaningless universe, we do not live in that universe; rather we inhabit a small parish within it, populated by those whom we love and hate, like and dislike, our friends and our adversaries, where we pursue our projects and are immersed in our preoccupations. The poet Paul Valéry acidly responded to Pascal's famous cry – "The eternal silence of these infinite spaces terrifies me"[38] with "However, the hubbub in the corner distracts me".[39] Being the most important character in the room, the life and soul of the party, can cancel one's objective insignificance.

In part this is because meaning, and meaninglessness, begins far nearer home than (for example) the rocks on distant galaxies. The most obvious reason for our unconcern with ultimate meanings is that we are often too closely examined – or at least tested – by life. The spaces which might house our search for cosmic meanings that we would choose, and embrace, are already occupied by unchosen meanings that embrace, indeed engulf, us.

For the overwhelming majority of mankind, life has been characterized by hunger, pain, fear, grief; in short, suffering. Most of our ancestors lived and many of our contemporaries live in terror of natural threats from within and without the body and of the power of their fellows to humiliate, oppress, enslave, torture, starve, and destroy them. The quest for meaning consequently seems like a luxury available only to those not under the yoke of meaning imposed by hunger, oppression, and the many sources of unbearable sorrow. As Hans Rosling points out "the main factor that affects how people live is not their religion, their culture, or the country they live in, but their income".[40] And that applies even more clearly to how, or whether, they think about the meaning of their lives.

The modes of imposed meaning are infinite in their variety. The horny-handed sons and daughters of traditional, analogue toil are crushed by the burden of labour – lifting, carrying, dragging – exacerbated by the bully with the lashing tongue or, indeed, the lashing lash. The rewards have been sub-sistence wages, aching limbs, a damaged body, and hungry, uneducated children who may die before reaching adulthood. In the twenty-first century, the gross exertions of manual labour have been succeeded by the semi-manual and cognitive sweatshops of the digital economy. Slavery is alive and well in developing countries and nations in the grip of reverse development such as the United Kingdom. The misery is, however, largely off-stage, scarcely exist-ing for those who are not subject to it.[41]

All work is characterized by repetition, waiting, and loss of the freedom to use our time and to act as we wish. This may be entirely benign and even fulfilling in the case of professional work; but for most of humanity even non-manual, reasonably well remunerated work demands that we enter a cog-nitive space far from the place where we pause to reflect on our lives and the meaning they may or may not have. It typically requires of us a close-minded attention to small-scale details which demand a focused and resolutely down-ward gaze. (We shall return to work in the next chapter.)

Such attention, too, is required of us when we discharge our unsalaried duties to others, notably in the universal responsibility of childcare. Looking after a one-year-old sometimes divides life into ten minute or even ten second epochs. Dry-mouthed anxiety over a sick child can squeeze the rest of the uni-verse to the margins. Those who selflessly take on the care of adult dependents are similarly engulfed. Here, as elsewhere, much of life boils down to localized attention and logistics, organization, and planning.

There are, of course, civic duties. At a time such as the present when, as in England, the barbarians are destroying the life chances of one's fellow citizens, picking apart the welfare state and leaving an ill-fare state in its place, these may be time-consuming. I speak as the veteran of many hours spent cam-paigning in the open air against the attacks on public service, chanting sim-plistic slogans in chorus, and writing endless dull letters, in a kind of existential sleep, far from any concern with the meaning of life. These are modes of seri-ousness that make questions about the significance of a godless universe seem less than serious, or at least a kind of luxury, an ultimate "first-world problem".

So much, so obvious. There are additional, less obvious, but no less effective, barriers to searching for an answer to "What it's all about?", to thinking about the All, and reflecting on one's own life against the background of the conditions that made it possible in the light of the hints we have as to its possible nature. What fills the remaining space, however, is shaped by the same habits of focused, that is to say narrowed, attention that have been developed in the hours on duty. When we are not externally propelled over the surface of sense, we are self-propelled, setting ourselves elective, semi-serious tasks.

There is no shortage of activities, recreations, hobbies, sports and other preoccupations to occupy hard-earned free time and fill the spaces where an ache for more meaning might arise. The Czech novelist Ivan Klíma who spent his childhood in Terezin concentration camp mordantly observed that, following the fall of the Soviet Union, the liberated eastern European authors had "traded totalitarianism for total entertainment".[42] The meaning we find in activities that engross us often seem unworthy of our lives – unworthy of what they cost, or might cost, those who live them and those others on which they depend. Even great art (of which more in Chapter 10) can become a mere diversion, bubbles on the pell-mell, in which each moment or hour erases the contents of its predecessors. It seems impossible to dismount from business or busyness to contemplation, except for the hour or so of yoga or mindfulness or church, though this may make further organizational demands. Hurrying to church to catch the eucharist, to honour a temporal appointment to meet with God, symbolizes the ironies of the intersection between time and eternity, for the most devout believer.

Beyond pastimes, there are other ways in which our attention may be consumed, and time passed. The joy of tidying up, sorting the book collection, or other small satisfying tasks, can be sufficiently diverting, if not all-consuming. And there is, for some, the business of incessant consumption of items, notwithstanding the usual finding that they do not translate into the joys that are promised in the idea of them, even or especially when what is promised is the glory of a brand that will bathe one's appearance in the eyes of others in its reflected light. It is easy to fill the spaces free of duty and toil with things that seem like "jobs to do" and which borrow some of the moral kudos of duty and toil: unforced house moves (just for a change), dealing with the consequences of a new kitchen, planning holidays in pursuit of experiences they may or may not deliver are a few examples.

Drugs and other addictions, sexual and other obsessions, may leave individuals drowning in a sea of unsolicited meaning, so alien as to be a form of anti-meaning. And this is even more true for those in the grip of pathological anxiety, when everything is a sign overloaded with meaning, or of an obsessive-compulsive disorder where the failure to take the endless steps that appear necessary to avoid imaginary harms to one's self or to others provokes unbearable distress.

The smallest concerns, that are the enemies of large ideas, can command our attention, even our passion. Small and large vexations, the things that warrant sighs of discontent rather than screams of pain or anger, also play their part. Mild disgust, irritation, jealousy, longing, resentment may leave little space for contemplation of our condition. Primo Levi spoke of how lesser pains and grief hide behind the greater "according to a definite law of perspective" such that "if the most immediate cause of distress comes to an end, you are grievously amazed to see that another one lies behind; and in reality a whole series of others".[43] Who can be exercised over the meaning of life, over the fact that one does not matter to the universe, when he has stubbed his toe or she has seen someone jump the queue in a supermarket? Horace Walpole's claim that this world is "a comedy to those who think, a tragedy to those who feel" is trumped by the meta-comical truth that the feelings that stop us thinking may have comically trivial causes.

There are especially telling examples of the triumph of vexation over the possibility of illumination in the lives of the great thinkers and artists. Arthur Schopenhauer was obsessed by the noise of coachmen gratuitously cracking their whips, which he described as "the only genuine assassin of thought".[44] Artists are notoriously a *genus irritibile*, touchy, for the sake of the buried treasure in their souls, about things that others would ignore. The life of that supreme artist Beethoven was beset by feuds with friends, petty offence-taking, by volcanic eruptions, sometimes followed by grovelling apologies. They culminated in a drawn-out battle with his sister-in-law and his nephew over nothing very clear, that darkened his last decade and led to his nephew's attempted suicide.[45]

Life, in short, has the habit of making sense through the imposition of unchosen meanings from toothache to terror. I have not even touched upon the profound, joyful, anxious, distressing and sometimes comic, dramas of loving and being loved, of acknowledgement and rejection, of being overlooked, of pride and shame, of the care for one's reputation and for the figure one cuts in the eyes of important others, of the desperate search for approval and that mythically concrete item "status", of the acid bath of shame, of consummation and frustration, of delight in companionship, and grief at loss, of loud and quiet satisfaction, of comedy and tragedy. These are too profound to be captured in asides. Fortunately, they hardly require elaboration for the reader.

So, there is no shortage of micro- and macro-purposes extended over seconds, hour, days, and weeks. Our dis-tracted (literally "pulled apart") state of purposiveness without over-arching purpose – and the butterflying of our intentions pursuing a mere tincture of *telos* – is compounded by the internal dynamic of trains of thought, memory, little bits of sense-making, unfolding without cessation from our earliest days to our last. James Joyce's *Ulysses* captured this lifelong soliloquy, exposing the truth of our inner life. Consider this randomly chosen excerpt from his 700-page masterpiece, much of which is devoted to Leopold Bloom's talking to himself:

> But for example the chap that wallops the big drum. His vocation: Mickey Rooney's band. Wonder how it first struck him. Sitting at home after pig's cheek and cabbage nursing in the armchair. Rehearsing his band part. Pom. Pompedy. Jolly for the wife. Asses' skins. Welt them through life, then wallop after death. Pom. Wallop. Seems to be what you call yashmak. I mean kismet. Fate.[46]

What is most striking about Bloom's thoughts is not their poverty but their overwhelming richness. We could spend many hours unpacking the allusions in his reflections. The flow of meaning, of self-distraction, of rehearsals, of prattle, is unremitting.

The monologue reminds us how often our self-presence is a procession of smithereens: pondering over an uninterpretable smile, considering the fact that global warming makes dogs more prone to a certain sort of worm, the outcome of a football match played in 1926. Our distractibility is not surprising: if, after all, attention is to be grabbed, it must be available to be endlessly interrupted. Thus, the fragmentary nature of the life of the mind. It took Joyce's genius to see what was not merely in front of our nose but actually behind it. We are self-deceived by seeing ourselves through lens of our structured speech, our accountable days, of the timetable and the diary and the CV. Our attention is too wedded to the habits of locality, and is often unnecessarily, as well as sometimes inescapably, imprisoned by particulars, to host a sustained quest for some over-arching meaning.

Dis-tracted (*sic*) into smaller pieces, we are satisfied with little bursts of significance, and sense bounded by a nearby horizon. This constricted meaning-space is pre-filled by items and emotions that, from the aspect of eternity, look unworthy of the attention we give them. The so-called distraction economy that thrives on tugging at our sleeves, click-baiting us into giving up our secrets, and stealing moments of our attention for advertisements, breaks the chains of "and then ... and then ... and then" into ever smaller elements. The permanent self-interruption of the digital world – in which we are emailed, Twittered, Facebooked, and Googled hundreds of times an hour – adds distractions and distractions from distractions, to obsessions, occupations and preoccupations, not to speak of getting and spending, to pre-empt the sense of disenchantment or terror at the eternal silences and the infinite spaces. They occupy the widening emptiness that would otherwise be created by the departure of God and his attendant prophets, priests and scholars. There is, it seems, more than a sufficiency of meaning in our lives to conceal any lack of overall significance. Or local inadequacies of meaning that make us long for local meanings.

We can discern here an answer to Jesus' question: "What went ye out into the wilderness to see? A reed shaken by the wind?"[47] The answer may be: in order to see nothing at all. To be relieved of all the local somethings and make space for a whole that is greater than the part. Or in modern parlance, for a cognitive detox, that may make it possible to dismount from the relentless dynamism of outer and inner distractions, of the lure of elsewhere (especially electronic or e-elsewhere) that makes it difficult to pause and meditate, to be serious about being serious in the sense of the examined life. Unfortunately, the journey into the desert may not deliver the tranquillity and stillness that is wanted: Heidegger's *Gerede*, gossip, gassing, will follow us into our solitude, as we continue the conversation with the cast of real and imaginary, particular and general, characters who inhabit our inner spaces.

We are close to something to which we shall return: the intrinsic dynamism of consciousness. It is most obviously reflected in the trains of thought that proceed at express speed, but it is implicit in a search for sense that is always forward-moving, pointing past any point of rest. It is also present in the manner in which thought is *un*thinking in virtue of thinking past itself. And is most inescapable in the present continuous of mean-ing – meaning as a process, a journey rather than arrival. We cannot, it seems, *inhabit* meaning, least of all when it takes the form of an answer to a large question, or the solution to a problem, or aspires to eternal truth, because it is intrinsically ongoing – going on – to the next thing. This is, however, disguised in the timeless words that seem to arrest it, particular when they are written down and puffs of speech, fading soon as spoken, are frozen on the page. Ultimately it seems that only meanings we can truly inhabit are those that inhabit us – such as pain, grief, hunger – but these seem as much anti-meanings as meanings.

The elusiveness of meaning and of ourselves is an immemorial preoccupation of religious thinkers. It is one of the many reasons why the future of humanism should involve the dialogue between infidels and believers discussed in Chapter 10.

The search for meaning

> Ever let the Fancy roam,
> Pleasure never is at home:
> At a touch sweet Pleasure melteth,
> Like to bubbles when rain pelteth ...[48]

We live, so it appears, for the most part free of any hunger for cosmic meaning. Even so, we may be assailed by a secular search for meaning, not prompted by a sense that we cut a negligible figure in the universe and that our lives are minute events in an unimaginable vastness. Rather, it may not be the question of the significance of our lives but of the unsatisfactoriness of meaning within our lives.

One source of dissatisfaction comes from the fact that our lives are marked by raw succession: this follows that, this experience that experience, this emotion that emotion, this preoccupation that preoccupation. We are always on to the next thing, held back only by things we might want to escape: sources of guilt, shame, embarrassment, fear and pain. It may be chastening to reflect on lives that are a whirligig of needs, of duties, of affections, of dreams, of pleasures and pains, gratifications and irritations, acted out in a multiplicity of situations chosen and unchosen, feeding into, and fed into by, a tangle of histories that lack the formal satisfaction of stories. A sense of raw sequence without addition – of "and then" where the "and" does not even have the dignity of the ampersand – threatens.

The shallow connectedness and repetitions of everyday life are the recipe for the *weltschmertz* expressed by the eponymous hero in Georg Büchner's extraordinary play *Danton's Death*:

> Time has lost us. It's very wearisome everyday first to drag on one's shirt and then one's breeches; and to crawl every night into a bed, and every morning out of it. And to set one foot always in front of another. And who can suggest another way?
> It's a sad thought. And that millions have done it already – that millions will do it all over again – ... that's a miserable thought![49]

This from a man who was a central figure in one of the turning points of world history: the French Revolution.

There is no shortage of sources of transient meanings. Anger, ambition, resentment, desire, lust, sexual obsessions and, yes joy can be all-consuming so long as they last, their succession filling our days with wall-to-wall meaning.

Tears, laughter, delight, and anguish follow each other in rapid succession. They are poignantly gathered together by Joe Moran: "Toddler rages, family dramas, adolescent strops, asymmetrical fallings in and out of love, toxic friendships and enmities, worrying over and delighting over children, thwarted or fudged ambitions, the slow-motion hurtle into ageing and dying – and, in between, snatched moments of laughter, enlightenment, of joy".[50]

Shakespeare's description of the course of lust:

> Enjoy'd no sooner but despised straight
> Past reason hunted, and no sooner had
> Past reason hated, as a swallow'd bait
> On purpose laid to make the taker mad.[51]

traces the abrupt transition from climax to anti-climax, from ecstasy to desolation, the descent from bibulous joy to the hangover when all vintages are vinegar. It is a paradigm of the self-cancellation of meaning. The trajectory was generalized beyond the obvious example of loveless sex by Schopenhauer: "Our days are devoted to ending, one by one, the achievements that give them meaning".[52]

That many goals are not achieved isn't the point. The trouble lies with those that are achieved: arrival means a new point of departure. They do not look or feel like the idea we had of them: those ideas cannot be translated into experiences, even less enduring states of ourselves. As points of arrival, goals seem uninhabitable; besides, they rarely if ever correspond to what they seemed in prospect. A fulfilled dream may turn out to be another form of quotidian wakefulness: the morning of the arrival is still Wednesday, after all, and a new point of departure for an unspecified destination. This should come as no surprise, given the distance we have highlighted (in Chapter 4 and elsewhere) of even ordinary facts from actual experience.

There are antidotes to the sense of endless "and". The most potent are *narratives* – of inner and outer growth, of slow-burning or hard-won success, betterment, aggrandisement, development, advance. Increasing salary, rising seniority, watching the business expand from start-up to healthy enterprise, a growing reputation, a swelling mountain of possessions. We are nourished by stories of increasing status, wealth, knowledge, and qualifications. Other dreams, small and large, realistic and unrealistic, of completing the stamp or Meissen collection, of improving one's personal best, of gaining and exercising power, of acquiring a skill, may pre-empt the sense of emptiness. Craftmanship may be an end in itself: an entire life may be satisfactorily filled by the achievement of seemingly pointless perfections, such as pin-head carvings. And there are other, more easily comprehensible or defensible, stories: of liberating one's self from those who are exercising power; or seeing one's children flourish, grow up, and have children of their own; or of achieving statistically improbable fame or fortune. Thus, the addition sums that make a virtue out of repetition, even if the addition delivers only further pages of that uninhabitable skeleton biography, the CV. The implicit or explicit narrative – like any looking forward to an eagerly awaited event or looking back in fond memory – elevates a raw sequence of steps to a journey, transforms the scalar succession of events and actions to a vector that has a clear direction.[53] It is consonant with Longfellow's path to salvation:

> Not enjoyment, and not sorrow,
> Is our destined end or way;
> But to act, that each to-morrow
> Find us farther than to-day.[54]

The most promising endeavour to redeem "and then ... and then ... and then" is most clearly seen in the *project*, the over-arching structure of actions that brings together so many moments, binding days and weeks, to a different kind of time, lifting the hours above what is felt and what happens in them, creating a footpath out of footsteps. This promise is captured by Schiller, "Time flies on restless pinions – constant never / Be constant – and thou chainest time for ever".[55]

But ... but ... but. Many goals are unachievable or not at least in the terms they are set. Or they have no natural point of completion. Consider even such modest aims as building up a stamp collection, improving one's Personal Best (formalized as PB), getting to know a country or a culture. Any limits placed are arbitrary. This applies as much to great projects – involvement in the affairs of state, campaigning for a better world, researching the fundamental nature of the universe, creating enduring monuments of art and architecture – as to the many smaller ones that engage the vast majority of mankind. And the vast majority of us have to be part of "the vast majority of mankind". We cannot all be leaders – in our field or in the world – because there would be no-one to lead. Nor can we all stand out of the crowd, or there would be no crowd to stand out of. We have to settle for less: obscurity, modest unchronicled achievements, being part of a following, in the audience rather than on stage. The great physicist Richard Feynman's advice, "No-one has figured out the meaning of life. Fall in love with some activity and do it",[56] seems more compelling when the activity in question is the pursuit of an understanding of the fundamental nature of things leading to Nobel prize-winning discoveries.

If it is a computer game you fall in love with, the advice may seem open to challenge.[57]

And this is a reminder that connectedness over time is shared with activities that are, or seem to an outside observer, intrinsically "trivial": completing a collection of cigarette cards, acquiring an astronomical score on a computer game, or building a shrine to a celebrity adorned with ephemera gathered over decades. The less defensible allure of such pastimes is an inadvertent critique of the binding power of projects that are of intrinsic value and it invites us to examine the latter more critically.

We are always therefore looking for something new, a fact whose motor can be boredom, distractibility, or a more laudable discontent with the smallness of achievement, the narrowness of ambition, and the unoriginality of one's aims. Our lives are littered with the debris of projects that seem to have lost their meaning and perhaps should not have meant so much in the first place. When we grow up, we put away childish things; next, we set aside adolescent things; and we "move on" from adult things; finally, we reach old age and find ourselves increasingly distant from so much that was of overwhelming importance in the preceding decades. We never stop putting away things that, for all that they are not childish, seem to belong to a person we are no longer, someone who valued things we no longer value. Our dreams, hopes, concerns, loves are replaced by other dreams, hopes, concerns, and loves. There are endless farewells of growing up – and away – and of our children's growing up – and away. There is the intimate self-betrayal of "getting over" this, that and the other, of learning to forget, of flourishing after loss, and other manifestations of outliving one's self.

Lurking in the background is an assumption – strikingly expressed in the Shakespeare sonnet cited earlier – that should not be allowed to pass unchallenged: that the later judgement must be superior to the earlier. A relationship that begins with passionate love and ends in indifference should not be regarded as being on that account meaningless. The earlier state should not be dismissed as "an illusion". Given that later word is not the last word, its judgement should not be treated as authoritative or even superior. The one who falls out of love may not be wiser than the one who fell in love. Meaning cannot be automatically wiped from the record, as something that has been exposed as illusory. Joy may have mistaken grounds but it cannot itself be mistaken. Sadder does not mean wiser, as nostalgia often proves. To remember what it was like to have been in love can restore respect for its meaning. Its transience, after all, may not discredit what was transient.

Perhaps the most fundamental challenge to redemption through projects and their accompanying narratives is that, during the greater part of the journey, the destination is not present; and memories of the staging posts and anticipation of the future trajectory may simply add to the torrent of "and then". Sustained projects are comprised of many thousands of often highly repetitive actions that hardly taste of the over-arching goal. Consequently, any given moment of even the most stellar life will be a tangled web of micro-scopic, medium-sized and macroscopic narratives, each diminished by the others to the status of "and then ... and then". The "long littleness" of life, of many hundreds of thoughts and actions, intentions fulfilled, frustrated, and discarded, may not be fully redeemed by the dim light of over-riding purposes.

Even a seemingly head-on pursuit of meaning such as composing a work of art or a philosophical treatise or advancing scientific knowledge breaks down into many sub-artistic or sub-philosophical or sub-scientific moments, separated by interruptions, parentheses, and asides. The fiddle of composi-tion, of getting thoughts or notes into some kind of order and, in the case of science and philosophy, the contingency of the place where one begins, the arbitrariness of the chosen end, and the tools one uses, betray how far one is from any kind of absolute. And there are the logistical heroics required to make the time and find the place, not to speak of the interruptions and the distractions – externally imposed and self-imposed – when time is made and place is found. For many, perhaps most, even those whose work is intrinsically interesting and satisfying, being "mad busy" is a distracted state that ends only when meaning is gathered up in sleep.[58]

While projects seem to offer something more than addition without sum-mation, increase without growth, they do not arrest the involuntary advance, as the years add up, towards total loss, the dwindling to the zero of our ulti-mate extinction. The growing CV is a disguised burial mound, an obituary-in-waiting. Even when we do not actively collude with the transience of their significance, the consequences of our cherished projects will be cancelled by events beyond the scope of our agency. We are aware that their importance is borrowed from the merely tautologous self-importance of our existence: my life is more meaningful because is it *my* life. And more meaningful does not mean absolutely meaningful; it may only mean "less unmeaningful".

For some thinkers, *infidelity* to one's projects, constant self-renewal, is a mark of authenticity. The determination "to kill the puppet"[59] in one's self, to deny the automaton, to refuse to continue along a pre-set trajectory, is not however consistent with being the kind of person who will contribute reliably to a bearable social order, to a civilization necessarily based upon kept prom-ises, agreements that are honoured, contracts that are fulfilled, and even con-ventional courtesies respected – in short, with being the kind of person one would wish, indeed expect, others to be. Unilateral shaking off the shackles of commitment and starting over may be the mark of the psychopath.

Meaning may after all be found elsewhere than personal satisfaction. This is a matter for the next chapter. For the present, let us reconnect with the endeavour to make sense of our lives in the light of a secular world picture.

The deepest barrier: solidarity

Our discussion has encompassed, and in places conflated, three different ways of construing the meaning of our lives: a) what our lives may mean to ourselves – their pleasures and pains, the satisfactions and dissatisfactions; b) our significance in the larger frameworks of human affairs – in our parish, in the nation, in history; and c) the objective importance of humanity in the order of things.[60] The domination of the first sense explains why we are rarely preoccupied by "the eternal silence of these infinite spaces"; why the vastness of those spaces is not a diluent. But something more profound, and in an important sense *honourable*, prevents us from approaching the "What's it all about?" question with the seriousness it seems to deserve. That "something more" is our fundamental nature as social beings.

The secular search for an over-arching or underpinning meaning may well be for something that lies outside the life we share with others – acquaintances, colleagues, friends, and those who we love – and the assumptions that are built into it. The struggle to wake out of quotidian wakefulness may therefore seem a rejection, even a betrayal – of the most profound kind – of the contract of sociality upon which our communal life depends. The quest for a reality beyond "the painted veil" of everyday understanding seems to imply that the shared life – with its small change of togetherness, in which we take so much for granted – is mistaken, even a dream. This is disturbing if we remember Heraclitus' aphorism that "only the waking share a common cosmos, while each sleeps alone".[61] The endeavour to wake up from our lives will be to wake *out* of them, and those who share those lives.

The deeper we dive, the further we descend from the community of our fellows, including or especially those who matter most to us in love and friendship. Exploring the depths means shaking off the necessarily quotidian places where we care for each other and where even the most profound love has to be lived. Although mortality is the common condition of humanity, when we truly engage with it in our thoughts we enter a solitude in which the death in question is our own, as it extinguishes the common world, and the voices of others die away. Even if the quest for deeper, more coherent, meaning is undertaken by more than one person, synchrony of descent or ascent is unlikely. Nietzsche's metaphor that we are like corks holding each other to the surface may say more about Nietzsche than human relationships but it helps us to see the connection between solitude and the will to understand our life and why the latter so often drives people to the wilderness, to retreats, and to other hermetic modes of life.

Philosophers must surely find, more often than they are prepared to admit, that it is difficult to inhabit the profoundly revisionary ideas to which their arguments take them. David Hume, with characteristic candour, famously set aside the radical scepticism we discussed in Chapter 5 – his claim that external objects and the internal self were "logical fictions" – when he joined his friends in a game of backgammon: "When, after three or four hours of amusement, I would return to these speculations, they appear so cold and strained, and ridiculous, that I cannot find in my heart to enter into them any further".[62]

An even more spectacular example of this disconnection is that of Leibniz and those who shared his viewpoint, beautifully described by Bertrand Russell:

> While their temper was social, their theoretical philosophy led to subjectivism. This was not a new tendency ... [and] it reached momentary culmination in Leibniz's windowless monads. Leibniz believed that everything in his experience would be unchanged if the rest of the world were annihilated; nevertheless, he devoted himself to the reunion of the Catholic and Protestant Churches.[63]

It is part of a wider problem, described by Ernest Gellner:

> The world in which men [and indeed women] think seriously, and to which serious thought refers, is no longer identical with the world in which one lives one's daily life. The instability, contestability and often incomprehensibility of the serious, and respect-worthy kind of cognition, and hence of its object, make it and them altogether unsuitable to be the foundation of a stable, reliable social order, or to constitute the milieu of life.[64]

Is this the most profound of the challenges that face humanist thought: how to engage with our metaphysical condition without losing contact with the places, and hence the persons, where we live our daily lives? We shall return to this when we consider what humanism can take from religion.

CHAPTER 9

Meaning and purpose

ON BEING USEFUL: THE DIGNITY OF LABOUR

Work keeps at bay the three great evils: boredom, vice, and need.

Voltaire[1]

Measured by the hour, work is the most important part of many, perhaps most, lives. Labour has occupied the greater part of the waking hours of the human race since time immemorial and one's job – or lack of it – is the most generally accepted marker of one's place in the social order.

Genesis 3:19 commanded that, as a result of that first disobedience, humans should live by the sweat of their brows. Work as a punishment captures some of the unappealing features by which it is defined. They are most evident in the kind of work where there is division of labour and of classes, numerically weighted towards the bottom. It is associated with: loss of freedom, and being bossed around, even bullied; the fear of failure, of making a mistake however trivial (missing a spoon in a table setting), of falling behind others, of looking a fool, of being mocked and pranked; unpleasant, gruelling and not infrequently damaging physical toil, mental strain, stress; inhospitable physical and social conditions; eternal repetition of the same actions, even in some cases of the same physical movements; uncontrolled interruption (politely called multi-tasking); being in attendance or on call; waiting (all work is riddled with waiting) and clock-watching; and sometimes acute danger with a risk to limb or even life. "Work" encompasses a wide range of human activities from the relatively elevated calling of the priest, doctor, or nurse to a frenzied repetition of simple actions, while one is harassed by progress chasers who in some cases do not even permit the toilet breaks necessary to prevent incontinence.

The fragmentation of labour in industrialized society into small elements may remove any claim to dignity. As a thoughtless schoolboy, I relished a comedy sketch in which an individual spoke enthusiastically of a job that consisted in putting the holes at the end of toothbrush handles, so that they could be hung up. I assumed the voice of the character affirming "how stimulating" he found this work – much to the apparent amusement of my school-friends, whose probable future lay in one of the professions. It seemed that I regarded the pathos of someone endeavouring to extract dignity from work reduced to endless repetition of a fragment of the process of producing a humble tool of everyday hygiene as appropriate for mockery. So much for "the dignity of labour" that occupies most of the waking hours of most adult people.

The negative aspects of work are, of course, offset by remuneration or some other direct or indirect reward, including future prospects and status. Most workers are employed directly or indirectly in growing, rearing, or extracting materials or making goods, or providing services, for others to consume or use. The actions involved in earning the wherewithal to live are remote from directly meeting our own needs, satisfying our appetites, or responding to our desires. Workers are like waiters who do not eat the food they serve.

Notwithstanding the unappetising nature of work, it can also seem to be a potent source of positive meaning. Some talk sincerely of their jobs as a source of "fulfilment": skilled labourers, craftsmen, professionals, and carers all value their work. There are micro-narratives of "doing a good job" and "getting the job done". There is the comfort of routines, of days filled, of some kind of structure to one's life. And there are larger-scale narratives: acquiring a skill, mastering the "mystery" of one's craft, becoming professionally competent, the pursuit of excellence – and the status that this may bring with it; competing with others, promotion to positions of increasing seniority, the ascent to "the top"; a rising salary and/or accumulation of resources supporting the purchase of a dreamed-of car, house, or a style of life.

The journey however lacks a clear point of arrival. Even being "at the top" does not mean leaving behind repetition often expressed in the daily, weekly, monthly, yearly cycle. The days and the seasons are flattened under the weight of mere recurrence until the final point of non-arrival – the departure that is retirement. Even the successful professional, looking back on a glittering career, may recall a working life lived in the meshes of the CV, where the microscopic details of what had to be done concealed any narrative sense. The story of ascent through the ranks, or of increasing remuneration, is a general shell, marginalized by the activity that fills the working day. Irina's lament that she cannot bear her job in the telegraph office because "there is not enough poetry in it" will find an answering echo in the heart of anyone who, like herself, takes on a job for idealistic reasons.[2] As Durkheim expressed it, "Duties are not fulfilled intermittently in a blaze of glory".[3]

There are, of course, adventures in work: setting up a business; building an empire; discovering new techniques and ways of understanding parts of the world; advancing knowledge. But these joys are available only to a small and decreasing minority of the employed. And there is collegiality – of shared vocational standards, of a joint mission, of the guild – or at least companionship or even the sense of being "all in it together", an "us" united against the "them" of the boss class. At the least we may meet friends – as well as enemies – through work and sometimes our lifelong partners.

But again, these are only a small part of the experience of work. With a continuation of trends towards an ever-narrowing contractual conception of employment, individuals hired as mere hands by the hour, the casualization and de-unionization of labour, and the destruction of any kind of human relationship between employers and employees, that small part is getting smaller. For many, perhaps most, the narrative of employment is drudgery and grind (the digital sweatshop replacing the analogue one), greater or lesser degradation (repetitive lowly tasks or having to sell one's self in some way – one's charm, or one's body, cleaning up literal shit or eating it metaphorically) or acting in the face of a variety of sources of disinclination – from aching muscles, a sense of pointlessness, boredom, or moral queasiness. Complaints are pre-empted by job insecurity and the threat of destitution. Overworked, underpaid, exhausted employees will keep silent for fear of being discarded. Hired hands log in to the "gig economy", zero-hours contracts, that offer no guaranteed living wage, no job security (though the workers may have to be available 24/7), no pensions, access to healthcare or insurance schemes, no career progression, and no community of workmates in a shared workplace. Increasingly, this is the condition of "the precariat":[4] ill-paid, ill-protected, ill-housed, ill-treated, of the disintegrating communities of domestic, manual, and clerical workers, in the richest economies in the world.

It is hardly surprising that only 13 per cent of workers worldwide felt engaged by or positive towards their work – something to which we shall return presently.[5] This is particularly concerning where, as is usually the case, one's employment is potentially an important source of self-worth. And some consequences of technological advance – en route to rendering workers redundant – have been to make work emptier. Many employees are "nothing but placeholders for machines that have already been invented" though it does not yet make economic sense "to permanently replace you and your work-mates who are very low-cost".[6]

The future of work

Disengagement is hardly the worst that can happen to someone seeking to make a living. Fit young men worked to their death in building the football stadia in Qatar in advance of the world cup in appalling conditions; the funding of a second yacht for a knighted fat cat at the cost of pensioners working in his business; the unpleasantness of labouring in the workhouses of the giant Internet retailers in the UK – these are just a few of countless examples of vicious exploitation in pursuit of wider profit margins that will add another billion to a personal fortune that is already far beyond what anyone could spend. The size of the gap in affluence between the workers and those for whom they work is a moral abhorrence. Given that the reality of work for many is unbearable toil – boring, stressful, humiliating, not infrequently dangerous – the end of work as we have traditionally understood it may be welcomed. Assuming that material needs are met by some means such as a universal basic income, unemployment may be seen as a liberation of human beings to be their most fulfilled selves. The idea of a workers' paradise without work was anticipated in a famous essay by John Maynard Keynes published in 1930.[7]

Keynes identified what he called *technological unemployment*, which he defined as "unemployment due to our discovery of means of economising the use of labour outrunning the pace at which we can find new uses for labour".[8] He saw this as "a temporary phase of maladjustment" en route to mankind's solving "its economic problem", the rescinding of Adam's immemorial curse, when humans could devote their energies to non-economic purposes. How temporary the "phase of maladjustment" may prove to be is a matter of intense debate today, nearly a century after Keynes' prescient essay, written before the emergence of electronic devices such as computers and robots capable of doing things thought to be possible only for humans. Unfortunately, for many, this latest industrial revolution has meant involuntary unemployment or under-employment and consequently relative or absolute impoverishment, not to speak of a lack of social status and even a sense of purpose. The understandable resentments and votes of these "left-behinds" has empowered populist politicians whose actions may set back any hopes of solving the economic problem.

Against this, it is notable that the rate at which machines render human workers redundant has been greatly slowed down. In the UK at present, the employment rate is the highest it has been for decades, though many jobs are deeply unattractive. According to a YouGov poll, 37 per cent of British workers thought that their jobs contributed nothing to the world.[9] It is a desolating thought that so many hours of the lives of so many individuals are squandered in being (to use David Graeber's categories) "flunkies, goons, duct tapers, box-tickers, and taskmasters". Graeber, noting the collapse of jobs in industry, agriculture, and domestic service, suggests that it is "as if someone were up there making pointless jobs just for the sake of keeping us all work-ing".[10] Pretending that what one does as a flunky or goon is something one wants to do, even what one *is* – as in the case of Sartre's famous waiter in *Being and Nothingness* pretending to be a waiter – is a classic example of what Sartre called "bad faith". It is easy to criticize this – just as my schoolboy self mocked the comedy character finding "stimulation" in his job overseeing the insertion of holes into the handles of toothbrushes – if one has alternative ways of making a living.

"The dignity of labour", and the idea of a job as a calling, romanticizes what is often a matter of scratching a living, or of serfdom. And yet, the automation of tasks that were once carried out by humans and the possibility of material needs, comfort, and leisure activities being secured with little or no hands-on labour, should have had positive effects on the nature of what work remains. So many tasks – passport control, ordering and even driving a taxi, shopping, banking, examining and so on – are or will be delegated to artificial intelli-gence. There should still be a demand for employees in entertainment, art, and the so-called "creative industries", and in jobs that require social intelli-gence. And there will be an increasing demand for truly empathetic hands-on carers to meet the needs of an increasing number of people who require and expect such care. The prospect of replacing hands-on carers by X-on-care, where X is a prosthetic hand attached to a robot with an artificial voice and a simulated kindness constructed out of programmed responses capable of aping empathy, is repugnant. The simulation of caring is the most profound deception. Professional hands-on caring for strangers can, of course, be unre-lieved drudgery marked by repetition. If, however, such caring was valued in proportion as it is valuable, and had the status it deserved, it would be easier to see it as it should be seen: a fundamental human interaction built on the purest gifts of attention and kindness.

The economics of caring, that grants low status to justify the minimal wages it attracts, and the fact that carers are not themselves cared for, may take the caring out of caring. It makes the idea of robot-supplied care less repugnant, so that the deception of cognitively impaired patients seems acceptable. The low status of caring is one of the many reasons why it is easy to overlook. But, as Raj Patel and Jason W. Moore have pointed out, "Writing a history of work without care work would be like writing an ecology of fish without mention-ing water".[11] The point is that the supply of jobs required to meet each other's wants and needs would not dry up, if the right priorities prevailed, and caring was valued as it should.

While manufacture, transport, and many other functions may be handed over to robots, it is perhaps a forlorn hope that, as the destructive rapacity of the wealth extractors is replaced by ever more agile algorithms, those who deliver hands-on care will be valued more than those who manipulate electronic money to turn it into monstrous piles of private wealth. Even so, there is no doubt that humans, rather than machines, helping humans will never be redundant. Robots as caregivers, companions, or sexual partners will fail at the most fundamental level. In her characteristically astute critique of the idea that robots, "mindless slaves", will take over our lives, Mary Midgley questions:

> Why ... should anyone expect these extra calculative powers to make the difference that is needed? The confusions that now afflict human life are not primarily due to lack of cleverness but to ordinary human causes such as greed, bias, folly, meanness, ignorance, ill-temper, lack of common sense, lack of interest, lack of public feeling, lack of team-work, lack of experience, lack of conscience, perhaps most of all to mere general lack of thought ... [w]e are distorting our own nature by attending to the working of these tools rather than directly using our own powers to solve the problems that threaten us.[12]

At any rate, the workless future is not a realistic prospect in the near future for a society that values caring for others. Even so, it is expected in the long run and it will bring deeper challenges than can be solved by a universal minimum wage, and are closer to the central preoccupations of this book. Those challenges, too, were anticipated by Keynes in his essay: "And there is no country and no people, I think, who can look forward to the age of leisure and abundance without a dread. For we have been trained too long to strive and not to enjoy."[13]

The possibility of the end of work is addressed thoughtfully by John Danaher.[14] He begins by separating issues of distributive justice from those of personal fulfilment and meaning, and proceeds on the assumption that the productive gains arising out of automation are equally and universally shared. He assumes, that is, that widening inequalities in those societies where automation is most advanced, with increasing numbers of digital slaves and a small minority of unimaginably rich wealth extractors representing opposite poles – the winner-take-all economy of Amazon – are not, after all, necessary consequences of technological unemployment.

Let us suppose, he says, that "the technologically unemployed future ... [is] ... one of *abundance* not deprivation", how will people fill their time and lead meaningful lives? If "working for a living confers a certain sense of well-being and individual flourishing that would be absent if one did not work for a living", is it not possible that "the absence of paid employment could lead to vicious forms of idleness, boredom, and depression?"[15] Danaher cites a study by Mihaly Csikszentmihalyi who identifies subjective well-being with "flow states" in which people are, as it were, carried away by activities they are engaged in. (It is hardly necessary to reiterate what we said earlier that much work is stressful, tedious, and sometimes degrading.)

Csikszentmihalyi studied this experimentally by interrupting people with questions about their overall levels of personal satisfaction and well-being. People seemed more likely to enter flow states at work than when they are at leisure. They more often report feeling anxious and bored when, outside of work, they are free to do as they like. Flow seems to reconcile the dynamic and the static, as we see in the case of a river that flows but does not move. Hence the so-called "paradox of work" that subjects claim, when asked, that they prefer play to work.

There may be a fairly straightforward explanation. At work we may be absorbed in what we are doing and not liable to an oppressive self-consciousness. In addition, there is no pressure to enjoy ourselves and we do not feel guilty of sloth. This may explain why our leisure activities often emulate the features – the logistical complexities, administrative demands, and the pressures – of paid employment and we often seek a sense of "achievement" after sustained effort. If some of the satisfaction of leisure activities lies in their replication of the seriousness of useful labour, it is hardly surprising that the ubiquitous pastime of sport is often associated with various aspects of "hard work". The pleasure that is to be found in (some) work is not a subjective sensation analogous to a sensory experience; rather the satisfaction of a job, most strikingly in the case of a vocation, that is not only done well but deemed to be worth doing, directly or indirectly of value to others, is something we shall address presently.

I want to round off this part of our discussion with a passage from an extraordinary essay by Adam Keiper and Ari Schulman which reflects the equilibrium state at which we have arrived in thinking about the implications for our human future if work proves to be a phase which humanity, through its own ingenuity, leaves behind:

> [T]here are basically just two visions of [a] future in which man coexists with super-intelligent machines. Each of these visions has an implicit anthropology – an understanding of what it means to be a human being. In each vision, we can see a kind of liberation of human nature, an account of what man would be in the absence of

privation. In each, some latent human urges and longings emerge to dominate over others, pointing to two opposing inclinations we see in ourselves.

The first vision is that of the techno-optimist or -utopian. Granted the proper rope, humanity clambers right up Maslow's pyramid of needs, takes a seat in the lotus position, and finally goes about the business of self-actualising and achieving inner peace. Thanks to the labour and intelligence of our robots, all our material wants are met and we are able to lead lives of religious fulfilment, practise our hobbies, pursue our intellectual and creative interests ... This is imagined in countless stories and films, in which our robots make possible a Golden Age that allows us to transcend crass material concerns and all become artists, dreamers, thinkers, lovers.

In the opposing vision, mankind decides that the bottom of Maslow's pyramid is a nice place for a nap ... [H]umanity becomes a race of Homer Simpsons, a leisure society of consumption and entertainment turned to endomorphic excess. The culminating achievement of human ingenuity, robotic beings that are smarter, stronger, and better than ourselves, transforms us into beings that are dumber, weaker, and worse than ourselves. TV-watching, video-game-playing blobs, we lose even the energy and the attention required for proper hedonism: human relations wither and ... natural procreation declines or ceases. Freed from the struggle for basic needs, we lose a genuine impulse to strive; bereft of any civic, political, intellectual, romantic, or spiritual ambition, when we do have the energy to get up, we are disengaged from our fellow man, inclined toward selfishness, impatience, and lack of sympathy. Those few who realize our plight suffer from crushing ennui. Life becomes nasty, brutish, and long.

These two visions are inherently anthropological, even teleological. They each suggest that if we had machines in charge of all the hard parts of life, we would get to know ourselves better – we would find out what being human truly is. In one vision, we become godlike; in the other more like beasts. The truth, of course, is that both of these visions are deformations of what is truly human: we are at one and the same time beings of base want and transcendent aspiration; dependent but free; finite but able to conceive of the infinite. Somewhere between beasts and gods, we are stuck stumbling and muddling along, alone and together – stuck, that is, with virtue.[16]

BEING USEFUL: THE GOOD LIFE

"Virtue" is a good place to continue our reflections on post-religious life. Work will not save us from the tragedy of transience, or even from the lesser curse of "and then ... and then ... and then", through being the foundation of the life-stories, in the form of careers, offered by some employment. The way we treat our loved ones, especially those dependent on us, our being domestic saints or domestic tyrants, may be of paramount importance. Nevertheless, work is the most sustained, organized, and in some cases and in some respects, the most significant mode of interaction with our fellows. Because the products of our labours directly or indirectly, intentionally or inadvertently, contribute to, or take away from, the common good – not to speak of how we treat our work-mates and colleagues, subordinates, peers, and bosses – it is an important element of our standing as moral beings. This may be less obviously true where work is not vocational and its contribution to the overall good of humanity is doubtful – as in the (entirely honourable) situation where one labours primarily for a wage given in exchange for enhancing the salary-earning capacity of some present, remote, or invisible boss.

There is a further sphere in which our activity may have sustained meaning, purpose, and significance. This is civil society, where we assume our role as citizens and contribute to making the world a better place through voluntary activities such as setting up food banks, political and non-political campaigning, offering a variety of services free – in short, acting in accordance with the belief that citizenship brings an obligation to support the health, well-being, life-chances, and freedom of one's fellow citizens through unpaid labour.

The divisions between these three areas – being a carer, paid employment, and active citizenship – are not sharp. How we care for our children will influence whether they become happy, productive citizens who care for their own children. And professionals who regard their jobs as vocations rather than trades, or even as callings, will perhaps look beyond their contractual responsibilities to the betterment of their fellows. I have known many idealistic doctors who try to advance the scientific basis of their practice, to improve how it is delivered, to reach out beyond the population they are contracted to serve, and even to contribute to advancing health in distant parts of the world. And there are many ways of going "above and beyond" in one's role as a public servant. The very idea of a calling is a secular residue of the notion of being called by God to serve the world.

My childhood, like that of many others, was inspired – and, yes, haunted or oppressed – by exemplary lives. Among them was that of Jonas Salk, the man who discovered how to vaccinate children against polio: "He grew up wanting to be a miracle worker, to perform heroic feats of compassion, to minister to suffering humanity in a way that would bring his own spirit comfort and might win him lustrous renown".[17] His legacy lives on in the near-abolition of this ghastly disease worldwide.

With such exemplars before me, I informed my father in my early teens, when he asked me what I intended to do with my life, that I wanted to be of benefit to society. He was shocked. He pointed out that this was irresponsible. My first duty was to ensure that I made enough money to support my wife and children. As I had neither and none was in prospect, our conversation was not a meeting of minds. It was not until many years later that I appreciated his suspicion of "do-gooders" – with their frequently empty or even self-serving rhetoric – and the dangers of the dream of being of net benefit to humanity and of giving more than one takes.

While Henry Adams' assertion that "it is always good men who do the most harm in the world" may deliver a frisson of pleasure, and it is open to empirical challenge, it is a warning. Bertrand Russell's classic "The Harm that Good Men Do" should be mandatory reading for the morally ambitious.[18] One element of that harm, highlighted by my father, may result from neglecting one's immediate responsibilities, concentrating instead on the greater, wider, more glamorous and morally more fluorescent cause. We might call this "Mrs Jellyby Syndrome". Mrs Jellyby, readers of Dickens' *Bleak House* will recall, spent much time fretting over her useless vanity projects to save the poor children in Africa. She neglected her own children who consequently lived in abject misery. Her "telescopic philanthropy" is a warning to those who want to do good in general rather than getting on with the good in particular that is a more immediate obligation.

Pessimists find other grounds to criticize even those who honourably seek to live a meaningful life through exercising their capacity to do good. They deny the reality of overall progress in the moral and even the material condition of humanity. The hope of progress is regarded as hubristic and consequently dangerous. Among the pessimists who despise those who are committed to improving the lot of their fellow men, one particular individual has exercised me over the years, if only because his views are so widely disseminated. The individual in question is the political philosopher John Gray.[19]

In *Straw Dogs* and other excessively popular books, Gray dismisses as vanity the humanist belief that man is fundamentally different from other animals. Any endeavour towards promoting material improvement is bound to fail, he argues, because our behaviour is determined by the forces that operate throughout the natural world. Man – whom he calls *Homo rapiens* – is not only an unredeemed beast but, on account of his superior cunning, a uniquely nasty one.[20] Dreams of progress, therefore, have always ended in tears and always will do so. Fortunately, there are enough people in the real world of practical action who ignore calls to quietism of the "resist not evil, it will only make things worse" kind.

Attacking the views of people like Gray is not just a question of shooting the messenger. The astonishing progress of humanity over the last century is undeniable. It is engagingly summarized in Hans Rosling's *Factfulness*. Whether you look at undernourishment, access to clean water, poverty, immunization, child mortality, child labour, education, literacy, suffrage, legal slavery, deaths from natural disasters, plane crash deaths, the story is the same: vast, and accelerating, improvements. As Rosling puts it, "Bad things are decreasing and good things are increasing". And he also offers various explanations as to why this good news is not known to, or believed by, so many people. Among them is "the feeling that as long as things are bad it's heartless to say they are getting better".[21] But those who believe in progress are not heartless Panglossians. On the contrary, it is the malign pessimists who are heartless, often looking from their position of comfort and security straight past the facts of the avoidability of some suffering and, also, past the humanity of those who are preoccupied by the continuing necessity of freeing their fellows from engulfing and degrading want. To be able to write an articulate sentence poo-pooing the possibility of progress one has to have been well-fed and well-schooled, in short a beneficiary of the very progress one denies.

The brevity of the timescale in which massive changes for the better have taken place is staggering. The race to end extreme poverty began only 200 years ago, an eye-blink in the 300,000 year history of *H. sapiens*. Worldwide, extreme poverty has fallen in the last 20 years from 29 per cent to 9 per cent. Infant mortality has declined from 15 per cent in 1950 to 3 per cent in 2016. The period in question (and the places where progress has been driven) is roughly that in which we have heard Matthew Arnold's "melancholy, long, withdrawing roar" of "The Sea of Faith" and the secularization of inquiry, knowledge, institutions, public space, governance, government, and the exercise of power, along with industrialization driven by new technology, a consideration highly relevant to our discussion, in Chapter 10 of the role religion may or may not play in our humanist future. Ever greater numbers of people – in absolute and proportionate terms – being lifted out of destitution, are freed to experience the transcendence implicit in our mode of consciousness, which would otherwise be repressed by sickness, oppression and hunger.

Whatever the rationale of pessimism, the consequences of negativity are themselves negative:

When people believe that nothing is improving, they may conclude that nothing we have tried so far is working and lose confidence in measures that actually work. Or, they may become radicals, supporting drastic measures that are counter-productive when, in fact, the methods we are already using to improve our world are working just fine.[22]

The apocalyptic nihilism of a philosopher such as Gray, therefore, is potentially dangerous. It is fortunate that he is ignored by, or more likely unknown to, those many millions of people – sometimes flawed, perhaps self-interested – who are working for incremental improvements in things of supreme importance to humans: their own life expectancy and that of those whom they love, their health, the mortality of children, nutrition, political order (promoting democracy and women's rights, abolishing the death penalty, outlawing slavery). They are doing so in places remote from the extraordinary luxury, the unprecedented comfort, of the academic world from which Gray and his fellow misanthropes look with contempt on their fellows toiling to improve the lot of humanity.

As Rosling made clear, there are no grounds for complacency. There are many threats to the planet and those who inhabit them. The possibility of weapons of mass destruction being deployed, a cataclysmic conflict permitted by the destruction of checks and balances, the upward spiralling of the population (though the curve is starting to flatten) and their per capita consumption, global warming and global poisoning, out-of-control biotechnology, robotics, and artificial intelligence, the huge concentrations of wealth in a minority,[23] and information, including personal data, in a few hands, giving power to non-state actors insulated from the will and wishes of any electorate or accountability to them – these are just some of the paths to a future in which mankind might manage to obliterate itself. The destabilization of the international order by leaders such as the Reality TV Star currently occupying the most powerful office in the world breaking everything within reach has exacerbated all of these threats. But this is no excuse for passivity, paring one's fingernails at the prospect of (other people's) Apocalypse. Rather, it is a call for more energetic and smarter action.[24]

The last few paragraphs have not been the digression they may appear to be. Contributing to the grand project of bettering the lives of our fellows, and reaching beyond the circle of care defined by those who belong to our small parish, may seem pointless or would do so, if there were no possibility of net, overall progress, or if endeavours to achieve this, however well-intentioned, would inevitably make things worse. A fundamental purpose in life – helping to leave the world a better place than we found it – would be unavailable. There is, however, clear evidence that progress is possible. It is therefore intrinsically worthwhile endeavouring to contribute to it.

This may, however, make other concerns more visible. The poignant example of one of the most admirable and profound thinkers, the nineteenth-century political philosopher, ethicist, metaphysician and logician John Stuart Mill should give us pause. Mill was committed from childhood to the great project of making the world a better place – more tolerant, more just, more peaceable, more prosperous – through developing, advocating, and applying the utilitarian philosophy of his father and his father's friend Jeremy Bentham, such that it would inform law and social policy. Shortly before his death, Bentham sent a letter to a friend's daughter:

> Create all the happiness you are able to create: remove all the misery you are able to remove. Every day will allow you to add something to the pleasure of others, or to diminish some of their pains. And for every grain of enjoyment you sow in the bosom of another, you shall find a harvest in your own bosom; while every sorrow you pick out from the thoughts and feelings of a fellow creature shall be replaced by beautiful peace and joy in the sanctuary of your soul.[25]

Alas, this peace and joy was by no means guaranteed, as Mill discovered. In his posthumously published *Autobiography* he described a catastrophic depression that overcame him at the age of 20. It removed his appetite for the great mission of making the world a better, more just, and more tolerant place:

> Suppose that all your objects in life were realized; that all the changes in institutions and opinions which you are looking forward to, could be completely effected at the very instant: would this be a great joy and happiness to you? And an irrepressible self-consciousness distinctly answered, "No!". At this my heart sank within me; the whole foundation on which my life was constructed fell down. All my happiness was to have been found in the continual pursuit of this end. The end had ceased to charm, and how could there ever again be any interest in the means? I seemed to have nothing left to live for.[26]

The reason for Mill's crisis is not clear. He reports that, with the aid of Romantic poetry, he came through it. It is, however, a striking example of the difficulty of discovering in secular life anything comparable to the fullness of meaning that religion, leaving aside crises of faith, seems to promise; of finding in good works and politics a replacement for religion as a means to a satisfactory definition of what one is or ought to be. His crisis may also have been triggered by the uneasy feeling that seeking meaning in our life by devoting ourself to making the lives of others better, safer, warmer, and more fulfilling, and promoting a more just, equitable, and prosperous world, is simply handing the problem on. The hope that those others will experience a plenitude of meaning may evade, rather than solve, the problem of living in such a way as to cancel the emptying effect of seeing our lives clearly and in full awareness of mortality. It is analogous to the claim that we fulfil ourselves through having children: it transfers any lack on to another. It is a distant echo of the notion, made explicit in evolutionary theory, that the aim of life is to make more life, more of itself.

There is, anyway, something close to a contradiction in seeking non-instrumental meaning through being the instrument of others' flourishing; or identifying something as an end in itself in virtue of being the means to another's end. The poet W. H. Auden's observation "We are all here on earth to help others; what on earth the others are here for, I don't know" is penetrating as well as wry.[27] The sentiment is echoed by Julian Baggini: "if the only point of living is to serve *somebody else's* purposes, then we cease to be valuable beings in our own right and we merely become tools for others, like paper knives or cloned workers".[28] Thomas Nagel spells out the problematic nature of the dependence of the meaning of life on things going wrong:

> Granted, one advantage of living in a world as bad as this one is that it offers an opportunity for many activities whose importance can't be questioned. But how could the main point of human life be the elimination of evil? Misery, deprivation and injustice prevent people from pursuing the positive goods which life is assumed to make possible. If all such goods were pointless and the only things that mattered was the elimination of misery, that really *would* be absurd. The same could be said of the idea that helping others is the only thing that really gives meaning to life. If no one's life has any meaning in itself, how can it acquire meaning through devotion to the meaningless life of others?[29]

Seeking the meaning of one's life in contributing to a collective pursuit of some distant good is, as history, particularly that of the last century, has shown us, an ideal prone to the foulest corruption, where the good will, altruism, and obedience of others can be appropriated for wicked ends. The subordination of the life of the individual to the will of a leadership guiding the state towards utopia has often resulted in unspeakable horror on an unimaginable scale.

Isaiah Berlin reminds us of the "dogmatic certainty that has been responsible for the deep, serene, unshakeable conviction in the minds of some of the most merciless tyrants and persecutors in history that what they did was fully justified by its purpose".[30]

This is not, of course, to contradict our earlier point that less high profile, genuinely altruistic, incremental interventions have ultimately produced those spectacular advances that Hans Rosling has summarized so brilliantly. That many tyrants have abused power under the cloak of beneficence is not an excuse for a passive attitude towards the iniquities and remediable sorrows of the world. It remains true, however, as Mill seemed to have felt, that dedication to a cause, even if pursued with unalloyed nobility, cannot elevate means-to-an-end to an ultimate end. The very notion of "making the right use of one's life" seems to subordinate to a particular purpose something upstream of "use" – the sum total of things, of what one is, or experience, or might become, in short, one's life. Nevertheless humanists, just like the poet "worthy of the name" according to John Keats, should be those "to whom the miseries of the world / Are misery, and will not let them rest".[31] It is perhaps too cynical to suggest that to give up on personal salvation may free us up to settle for the lesser but objectively more important satisfaction or destination of helping others. I would find it difficult to regret that the doctor who saved my life when I was six weeks old did so at the cost of some profound idea of personal development.

The difficult relationship between the (morally) good life and the meaningful one brings us to an issue that has featured prominently in the discussion of secular societies: whether or not there can be a godless ethics.

GOODNESS WITHOUT GOD

> Godlessness is the first step to the Gulag.
> Aleksandr Solzhenitsyn[32]

Secular humanists have to live inside the truth that, ultimately, there is nothing to underwrite the *mattering* that gives our lives their meaning. The universe matters only to the extent that it matters to us; it matters to us only because we matter to ourselves and to each other; and we cannot *objectively* matter individually or collectively with the intensity and continuity to which we matter to ourselves. For some, this opens the way to a psychopathic form of nihilism: rejection of moral principles as well as religious beliefs on the grounds that life is intrinsically, or ultimately, meaningless, not the least because it has been generated by, and is largely sustained by, biological and pre-biological processes that lack meaning. Ultimately, the conditions that made our lives possible were not informed by any intention or had any purpose.

This has been cited as a reason for fearing that ethics may eventually wither in a godless world. Another is this: the lack of a compulsion to remain on the straight and narrow that comes from the belief that our actions are observed by God and that, on the basis of divine judgement, we shall be assigned to an eternity of Hell or Heaven. For this, and other reasons, the absence of a divine legislator seems to remove the basis for moral obligation and the regulation of permission.

Is the humanist reassurance that we shall find a firm basis for ethical behaviour in a godless world well-founded? I will argue that it is; indeed, that finding a foundation for good behaviour is no more a challenge for secular societies than it is for religious ones.

The first obligation on anyone addressing this issue is not to add to the excessive attention that has been lavished on Ivan Karamazov's claim that "If God does not exist, then everything is permissible". There are several reasons for setting this aside. The first is that there is no apparent limit to the suffering humans are willing to inflict on one another in societies where God is a pervasive presence. Belief in God may amplify wickedness, even justify it, as much as it has restrained it; at any rate, many individuals, tribes and nations that have behaved monstrously, have not done so through lack of gods. The second is that the claim, which is an implicit warning, conflates the existence of God with belief in His existence and His moral authority. It is not clear whether Karamazov is saying that there had better be a God or that we had better believe in one – or both. We could not of course requisition God, and believe in that invented God, in order to control our own behaviour. Embracing a religious belief or persuading others to do so because it is prudent would hardly be in the spirit of religion – God cannot be instrumentalized in this way – and it would not work. Thirdly, it is not God, but other human beings – individuals and institutions – that permit, and define, the permissible. Behind the Karamazov muddle is the assumption that, absent a transcendental authority such as God to underpin ethics, there will be a universalization of the intermittent horrors that have disfigured our shared past in which religion has been the dominant cultural presence.

At the heart of morality is the sense of fairness and justice which is understood by children long before they are capable of developing a religious or secular world picture.[33] Implicit in their outrage at the transgressions of others, is the sense of a principled "ought" that they do not apply to the material world. It grows naturally into the sense that the bad behaviour of a few is parasitic on the good behaviour of the many. Extreme selfishness is not a generalizable position.[34] It can be acted out only by a powerful minority holding a majority in subjection. More narrowly, those who break promises in pursuit of their immediate wishes can do so only if others keep those promises. Psychopaths require conscientious individuals so that they can flourish in the manner of their choosing. The free-riders depend on others to create and maintain the means of transport. Without others honouring contracts, and acting out of duty rather than egocentric impulses, there are no contracts to be broken or duties to be dodged, people to be exploited. In a truly, consistently, universally nihilistic society none would survive much beyond adult life and the result would be extinction. Principled ethical nihilism, therefore, can be only a transitional, degenerate phase of a society that has previously been established on the basis of, or has organically developed out of, non-nihilistic principles.

A compelling, but misleading, image of such a society – in which every man's hand is raised against every other – is presented by Thomas Hobbes in his *Leviathan.* "During the time men live without a common power to keep them all in awe" the norm is the war of all against all and everyone is in constant fear of sudden, violent death:

> In such a condition there is no place for industry, because the fruit thereof is uncertain, and consequently no culture of the earth; no navigation nor use of the commodities that may be imported by sea; no commodious building; no instruments of moving and removing such things as require much force; no knowledge of the face of the earth; no account of time; no arts; no letters; no society; and, which is worst of all, continual fear and danger of violent death; and the life of man, solitary, poor, nasty, brutish, and short.[35]

Against this, so the secular argument proceeds, even though ethical principles are not underpinned by divine warrant, there are still the political necessity and social pressures to limit the pursuit of one's own appetites, desires, and interests without regard for the needs of others. Self-interest dictates that we shall further the interests of others who will in turn defend our interests. As society becomes more complex and our inter-relationships extend and proliferate, the constituency of those "others" becomes more wide-ranging and more various and the dovetailing of interests more intricate. We are remote from that state of nature which Hobbes described, if only because we are densely connected and interdependent. The functioning of an advanced society requires a million-stranded network of cooperation and trust that is presupposed rather than actively entered into, and sustained, as a matter of the independent, voluntary choice of individuals.

The consequences of the complexity of human society are described by Durkheim: "The division of labour, then, is the result of the struggle for existence, but it is a mellowed denouement. Thanks to it, opponents are not obliged to fight to a finish, but can exist one beside the other".[36] We are bound, like Gulliver, by a thousand bonds to cooperative and mutually advantageous behaviour without there being a need for a fellow-feeling, empathy, sympathy, mutual regard, going beyond instrumentality. Pacification is supported because the division of labour increases productivity and hence "furnishes the means of maintenance and survival to a greater number of individuals who, in more homogenous societies, would be condemned to mere existence".[37]

That Durkheim wrote this on the eve of what has been justly called "History's Age of Hatred"[38] – a half-century dominated by two world wars and genocides in Germany, Armenia and elsewhere – may suggest that he was somewhat starry-eyed about the consequences of the division of labour. What he did not take into account was the hatred between highly organized populations – between Great Powers or between ethnic groups – that apparently made the destructive price seemingly worth paying. Seen through the lens of patriotism and tribal loyalty, atrocities seemed ethical and dying for one's country the purest altruism even if in the lead up to one's death one killed any number of one's fellow human beings.[39] The division of labour – and the "organic solidarity" that comes with it – may have arrested anarchic, Hobbesian wars of all against all, but made wars between economies more effective because of the increased efficiency of the means of production.

The separation of socially-imposed codes of behaviour from the direct exercise of hand-to-hand violence has been discussed by Richard Wrangham.[40] He notes that our levels of crude "reactive aggression" have declined. Unfortunately, proactive aggression, usually mediated by the collective, mobilizing massively destructive weaponry, and occurring within the law, has become more common. We have a power to cause greater harm with less direct moral, or even emotional, engagement. This transformation, however, long preceded secularization and religion has done little to prevent, or even oppose, the bloodiest wars in history – for example the First World War where clerics on all sides and of all persuasions blessed the bombs that rained Hell on the combatants.

This notwithstanding, at least one fundamental moral principle seems likely to withstand secularization and the withdrawal of transcendental threats, promises, sanctions or Divine authority. It is one we touched on before our journey through the Hobbesian nightmare that even little children understand

and, in principle, subscribe to: to treat others as one would want to be treated one's self. This, the Golden Rule, is the most compelling and fundamental instantiation of the more sophisticated concept of universalizability set out by Kant in his *Groundwork of the Metaphysics of Morals*: the categorical imperative asks whether the maxim of your action could become one that everyone could act upon in similar circumstances. If the principle behind an action could be generalized, then it is morally acceptable. The Golden Rule is the maxim of maxims. Kant illustrates it with the example of seeking to borrow money without intending to pay it back. If everyone did this, the institution of lending money would fall into disrepute. Eventually no-one would lend money. The Golden Rule is also the founding ethic we would choose if we did not know our station in life – if it were hidden behind John Rawls' famous Veil of Ignorance, such that we would not know whether we would be near the top or near the bottom of the social heap, rich or poor, powerful or powerless.[41] This highlights the strength of the Golden Rule: that it is rooted in self-interest. Of course, free-riding scoundrels can disconnect their self-interest from the interests of others, undermining the principle of reciprocity that keeps the two aligned – just as in law-governed societies many individuals break the law.

Nevertheless, can we be sure that we would be overwhelmingly disposed to follow the Golden Rule without the threats and promises that come with a belief in God? What is to prevent society from reverting to the Hobbesian "state of nature" and the endless horror of "the war of all against all"? After all, we have seen examples of hideous regressions to barbarity, within the compass of the law and in a society towards which the overwhelming majority of citizens felt a duty of individual service. Those who committed the genocide of the Jews, perhaps the worst atrocity humankind has ever committed, were not breaking the laws of their country. And among those who perpetrated or facilitated the mass murder of the Gulags (20 million souls) or Mao's cultural revolution (up to 10 million) there were many individuals who were sincerely committed to what they believed to be the best future for their country. Many more, of course, were motivated by terror, the simple need to protect themselves or their loved ones, by ambition, or a joy in the exercise of power and cruelty, or murderous instincts.

To assume that the Hobbesian "war of all against all", however, is the default position of humanity in the absence of transcendental constraint, ignores the extra-natural state of humanity. More to the point, if it were the default position, by what means could we have left this "natural" state behind? The emergence of societies based upon the rule of law would be conspicuously unexplained. The Hobbesian story, according to which men escape from the state of nature by combining into communities that cede individual authority to that of the sovereign, does not sound like a natural way of putting an end to universal war. It presupposes a certain level of mutual trust and patience, and a capacity for communication and negotiation, that is not seen elsewhere in nature. The social covenant seems even less likely in the context of Hobbes' radical metaphysical naturalism, according to which human beings are machines lacking in free will, collections of atoms connected with the outside only by the impingement of material events on material senses, mechanical automata, and – most importantly – isolated units.

This is hardly the place (nor am I the scholar) to embark on a critique of Hobbes' political theory, even less to compare different accounts of the emergence of civil society out of a putative natural state of isolated humans ruthlessly pursuing their own interests with no regard to the well-being of others. Suffice it to note that the social contract or compact that Hobbes envisages as the means of lifting humanity out of the state of nature does not look like the kind of collective self-transformation that biological machines effect to elevate themselves above their intrinsic animal condition. Even less, do such machines seem likely to be disposed to draw up the innumerable sub-contracts that flow from or into the rule of law, and the agreement by which the state or its agents assumes the monopoly of (legalized) violence. If humans really did begin in a state of nature in which each is the enemy of all, it is not only inexplicable how advanced societies – with distinctive duties of individuals, groups, and states – emerged from this state but it is remarkable that we are unique in having done so. Evidence that the political organization of our nearest primate kin such as chimpanzees has changed in the last million years is entirely lacking. The relationship between (say) the alpha male and the troop is hardly comparable to that between sovereign and state. The human mode of socialization – explicitly rule- and role-governed – is even less like the programmed collective behaviour seen in, say, social insects.

The assumption that without the transcendental constraint such as that provided by religion, there would be a regression to the hideous bloody chaos of ruthless individualism, would make it impossible to see how we got from this supposed natural state in the first place. If, as secular humanists believe, God is a human invention, the appeal to God does not deliver an explanation of our escape from the war of all against all. If, as is assumed in secular thought, God is a projected self-image of humanity then it must mean that mankind, in the absence of God, is so committed to moral behaviour as to *invent* a transcendental warrant for the conscience that regulates our dealings with our fellows, connecting the small change of our hours with an Eternal, All-Powerful Being. A creature that goes to the trouble of inventing the idea of God to underwrite or enforce moral behaviour must have morality buried deep in its collective psyche.

Many have argued that, if sacred texts offer moral guidance, it is because they distil best practice from observing what has "worked" (for some at least) over a long time. In short, we get God's commandments from our morality rather than our morality from God's commandments. This has unhappy consequences, of course. Richard Holloway echoes this: "It is ... fairly clear to anyone with even a superficial understanding of divinely mandated moral systems that they always bear a striking resemblance to, and offer confirmation of, the social systems in which they emerged".[42] Biblical teaching may consequently commit us to a morality of more than 2,500 years ago. Even if we believe that humanity has made no moral progress in the interim, this must fit awkwardly into life lived under entirely different circumstances, shaped by different social and political expectations.

It is worth noting that the science which has contributed by its explanatory power to marginalizing the gods, or even, with its promise of total explanation without recourse to "the hypothesis" of God, to empty the universe of the possibility of a deity, is itself a remarkable tribute to the collective morality of humanity. Without honesty, patience, the capacity to work together collectively, science as we know it would not be possible. There would simply be a collection of competing alchemists, wizards, mages, and other charlatans, deceiving others and themselves, as they pursue impotent dreams of understanding and manipulating the occult forces that govern things, making their fortune by emptying the wallets of the credible. Science fraud would be 100 per cent of science, rather than (say) 5 per cent or 10 per cent.

It seems reasonable to conclude that a species willing to invent a god to underwrite its moral code must be committed to ethically-governed coexistence. And in this respect humankind must be fundamentally different from other species whose members are largely indifferent to the fate of their fellows. This difference is particularly evident when we embrace an impersonal (or "agent-neutral") ethic that requires us to act in the interest of all, friends and strangers alike, even if the moral pressure to do so is mediated by our immediate awareness of others and our need for approval.

The most pertinent difference between Hobbesian man and actual humanity is the extent to which personhood is interpersonal, and I is "we". We are inextricably invested in each other in a way that goes beyond mere cooperation in enterprises that are of benefit to ourselves or of mutual advantage. It is rooted in something much deeper than merely instrumental relationships: our unique and overwhelming desire for *recognition* – for love, and freely given admiration, along with a desire for union with and the good of the other. This, of course, takes us into territory covered in Chapters 6 and 7. It will also be familiar to anyone who has even a passing acquaintance with the writings of Georg Wilhelm Friedrich Hegel and his most celebrated work *The Phenomenology of Mind*. For Hegel, what is distinctive about humanity is self-consciousness. At the heart of self-consciousness is *desire* which wishes to possess its object without destroying it. Such possession is possible only when the object in question is a subject like ourselves, another self-consciousness which possesses itself. Desire, unlike appetite, is inseparable from the need for *acknowledgement* – crucially, mutual acknowledgement.[43]

Admittedly, the consequences of this are not entirely clear. One interpretation is that a self-consciousness can be satisfied only by the total possession of the other that occurs when he is killed or, short of that, utterly enslaved. This pessimistic interpretation[44] is undermined by the fact that the utterly enslaved other, not to speak of the slain one, ceases to be a source of satisfaction because he has lost his otherness, most arrestingly expressed in his freedom. A more optimistic interpretation is that the desire for another as he or she is in herself is the path to a relationship that goes beyond instrumentality: to what Aristotle would call "excellent friendship", or to romantic love, to companionate marriage, and to the kind of feelings we have for our children, and – by extension – to the possibility of more widespread feelings for our fellows. It is present in our love of the other's freedom and our joy in seeing them flourish. While such disinterested emotions are rare in their purest form, they are sufficiently present, even if only in the pale reflections of courtesy, respect, and institutionalized *mores*, to support a sense of what we owe to others that distances us from the Hobbesian *bellum omnium contra omnes*.

The entanglement of the sense of "I" in "we" and of the inseparability of "I" and "thou" locates us far from any putative state of nature which presupposes that humans are atomic individuals. Our sense of who we are is *inter*personal all the way down. To be an "I" – notwithstanding flights into solitude – is to be part of a "we" that acknowledges, and at an important level respects, others. Others are woven into the very fabric of our self-presence, our intelligibility to ourselves, irrespective of whether or not this truth is articulated. The profound interpersonality of our personhood entails the possibility of empathy.

One obvious consequence of this is that secular judgement of our fellows reaches as deep as any judgement by a barely conceivable God. Shame, guilt, a sense of lost honour, even embarrassment remain powerful inner agents for moral behaviour, even where love and empathy fail. How we judge and value ourselves is influenced by how we are judged and valued by significant others. If, as La Rochefoucauld said, "hypocrisy is the tribute vice pays to virtue" it does suggest a profound need to be seen as virtuous, independently of any divine judge. And the hunger for social approbation, can take us ethically beyond ourselves and our immediate circle of affection and beyond mere episodes of self-interested cooperation. Morality is inseparable from the tissues of the self, extended through time, that we discussed in Chapter 5. Our promises, kept, are the very fibre of our experience of our own being.

This should be enough to ensure that the Golden Rule maintains its power and influence in secular societies. We may think of this as the over-arching principle sufficient to keep us at a distance from a state of nature. There will be differences of opinion as to how the principle will or should translate into custom and practice. And it leaves plenty for theoreticians of philosophical ethics to argue over as they foreground utilitarian/consequentialist, deonto-logical, and virtue ethics. It will not, for example, bring to a conclusion seem-ingly interminable discussions of utilitarian thought experiments involving runaway trolleys. Most relevant to our present discussion is that there are no grounds for expecting that the Golden Rule will have greater authority over our behaviour through being ascribed to an invisible, incomprehensible, entity refracted through all sorts of conflicting and dubious discourses and their interpreters: God.

Indeed, the reverse is often the case. If history tells us anything, it is that we should not rely on religion to cool hatreds. The link between institutionalized religion and the massacre and/or persecution of the innocents is compelling enough to suggest that secularization may make the world a morally *safer* place, by removing the justification for transcendentally warranted wicked-ness. Not always, of course: we have alluded to the horrors of the explicitly anti-religious French Revolution and the totalitarian regimes of Mao's China and the Soviet Union and will return to them in the final section of this book. Suffice it to say that where religion has not actively fomented or condoned domestic and public violence, injustice, and oppression, it seems to have been remarkably unsuccessful in discouraging them, even where the prime movers are not rival religions but secular actors. And faith-based virtue may seem closer than is generally accepted to prudence and long-term enlightened self-interest.

Notwithstanding these arguments, many thinkers worry that secular soci-eties will revert to the state of nature once the "moral capital" inherited from a religious past has been used up. The employment of the term "capital" is particularly telling because it implies that there is a fixed quantity of moral resource which, if not being supplemented by new income, will gradually dwindle. Nietzsche, the patron saint of post-religious nihilism, famously attacked the English novelist George Eliot in *Twilight of the Idols* over this:

G. Eliot. – They are rid of the Christian God and now believe all the more firmly that they must cling to Christian morality ... In England one must rehabilitate oneself after every little emancipation from theology by showing in a veritably awe-inspiring manner what a moral fanatic one is. That is the penance they pay there.

We hold otherwise. When one gives up the Christian faith, one pulls the right to Christian morality out from under one's feet. This morality is by no means self-evident ... Christianity is a system, a *whole* view of things thought out together. By breaking one main concept out of it, the faith in God, one breaks the whole: nothing necessary remains in one's hands ... Christian morality is a command ...; it has truth only if God is the truth – it stands and falls with the faith in God.[45]

Nietzsche concludes that "For the English, morality is not yet a problem"; but trouble was lying ahead once they were no longer able to freewheel on the moral principles transcendentally underwritten by Christian faith. Dostoevskian Hell would then break out – for "everything would be permitted". This view is wittily characterized by Julian Baggini: "It's only a matter of time before, like Wile E. Coyote, we realize we have run off a moral cliff, impossibly suspended in mid-air only so long as we fail to realize there's nothing under our feet".[46]

The passage from Nietzsche reveals enough of its misunderstanding of the sources of morality to discredit its confident, indeed malicious, predictions. The irreducibly interpersonal nature of our personhood goes deeper than a higher order, remote transcendental pressure mediated through religious doctrine, notwithstanding the terrors religion may recruit to ensure our adherence to the mores (however cruel, however arbitrary) of our culture. And Nietzsche seems to overlook something that we have already noted; if our starting position is that religious beliefs are without foundation (as he himself believes) then the God who insists on our behaving well, or at least in accordance with customs and the law, must be the product (the alienated product, as Feuerbach would say) of our profound ethical sense, of our sense that "Thou art I", the asymptote of all generosity of spirit. We must have a deep moral instinct if we invent a God and his commandments, spoken or written, to underwrite our moral code.

For some, the question of the fate of ethics in a secular society is one to be settled empirically. We can test the assertion that, after religion, we shall be drawing on dwindling moral capital by looking at the historical record. The evidence for the benignity of secular societies is largely reassuring. Sociologist

Phil Zuckerman has pointed out that the most godless or god-free societies in history – Denmark and Sweden – are the happiest and have the lowest crime and disorder rate, social equality, and an often admirable record of concern for world affairs.[47]

Zuckerman's claims have, however, been challenged on various grounds. There is a failure fully to define what secularism involves: whether it relates to belief or doctrine, participation, or belonging. A detailed study in Copenhagen, has highlighted how being a believer is not a "yes or no" matter: there are many dimensions to religious belief, independent of whether one participates in organized religious events and visits religious spaces.[48] For example, a YouGov poll in the UK in 2017 found that only 16 per cent of *believers* accepted the creation myth. Conversely, it is argued, religion lives on even in secular societies, but in a private form.

Ina Rosen maintains, that, rather as is the case with high-level concepts such as culture, work, the family or gender, religion must be reconceptualized to be applicable to the study of society. She points out that "If we were to understand work as one did a century ago, not many of us would work".[49] While what Rosen calls "packaged religion" may be declining, "religion-as-heritage" – privatized believing, belonging, and sharing – may be surviving outside of religious spaces and places, without explicit membership of or affiliation to, a sect. Of course, many may seem to belong to a religion when they have ceased to be observant – they have just forgotten to cancel their subscription.

The multi-faceted nature of religion, the blurred boundary between believers and non-believers, and the many ways of being religious and being secular, are things to which I shall return. For the present, it may be enough to observe the contrast between godless, peaceable Copenhagen and Stockholm and devout blood-spattered Beirut, Baghdad, and Belfast, acknowledging as we have done that not all secular societies are benign. Steven Pinker's mighty 1000-page *The Better Angels of Our Nature* has noted a general trend towards a diminution of violence, of petty bad behaviour, and an increased regard for the welfare of an ever-widening circle of our fellow human beings in a time of increasing secularization, notwithstanding intermittent catastrophic regressions to barbarity.[50]

But even this is not decisive. There, after all, are many other historical, political, geographical differences between countries secularists would characterize as blessed with atheism and those cursed by religion. And some of the trends observed by Pinker have been contested.[51] So, we still cannot identify the distinctive contribution of religion to good behaviour or bad. Religious hatred, as we noted in Chapter 1, may simply be a manifestation of hatred that has other causes. However, to pre-empt the objection that it is yet too early to tell whether secularization will make us behave individually and collectively worse to each other, it is worth thinking of the example of ancient China which, as Stephen Law points out, "has survived and sometimes morally flourished, without grounding morality in religion".[52]

It may anyway be early to declare a victory for secularism. While only a very small percentage of philosophers are deists (14.6% according to a survey quoted by Stephen Law[53]), the world outside the seminar room looks very different. Law points out that:

> In many countries round the world, to reject the faith into which one was born is to risk social ostracism or worse. Apostate Muslims are executed in Saudi Arabia, Iran, Somalia, Qatar, Yemen, and Mauritania. In Malawi and Nigeria, Christian pastors condemn children for witchcraft who are then beaten, tortured, and sometimes killed in exorcisms. As a result of religious lobbying, Uganda is considering introducing life imprisonment as the minimum sentence for engaging in gay sex.[54]

Humanism, which requires only biologically human parentage for fully qualifying as a human being, and which defines our "species being" in the way that I have in previous chapters, is hardly likely to inspire the bloodbaths of the past. The advocates of brain-based and body-based accounts of personal identity may be wrong, but do not seem inclined to burn each other's villages or stone each other to death for blasphemy. The suggestion that historical events such as the fall of communism, and cultural trends such as the reaffirmation of traditional beliefs against a globalized world, signal a post-secular phase of humanity and a return to religion may strike chill in the humanist heart.

Even if religion has, or has had, an important civilizing role, lifting us above a putative savage state, it does not follow, supposing *per impossibile* it could be embraced by an act of collective will, that it would have a positive role in keeping us from regressing to savagery. The most obvious reason for saying this is that, the more passionately held are religious beliefs, the more aggressive, or at least adversarial, they are liable to be. One thing is clear: religion has been conspicuously unsuccessful in preventing us from harming each other.

A more provocative, and perhaps questionable, way of thinking about this would be to suggest that religion took us from Level 1 to Level 2 civilization and Enlightenment took us from Level 2 to Level 3. The contribution of religion was in the past and there are therefore no guarantees or grounds for thinking that it will continue to be a progressive force or, if restored to its former social dominance, even protect the gains that have been made hitherto. This seemingly arrogant suggestion is consistent with the secularization narrative of Dominic Erdozain, according to which "the origins of unbelief in the modern West lie in conceptions of moral responsibility and freedom generated from within Christianity itself ... [A] moral revolt, inspired by religious values, paradoxically leads to an undermining of Christian orthodoxy".[55]

Secularization is not the only threat to religion. Tolerance of other faiths may be more subtly undermining. The co-presence in public of religions that affirm different ideas of God, subscribe to different doctrines, and appeal to different sacred texts, cannot be entirely comfortable to all parties. Ecumenical sentiments contain an implicit admission of the relativity of belief, precisely in those areas where for many nothing less than absolute adherence to a doctrine is permitted. The church, the mosque, the temple, and the synagogue sharing the city space are existential challenges to each other, irrespective of any generous-spirited reaching across religious divides. Where there are fundamental disagreements, an agreement to disagree will seem to the most impassioned believers like a betrayal: doctrines of tolerance, the pursuit of inter-faith dialogue, and a commitment to multiculturalism, may seem to fail to take profound, life-and-death differences seriously enough. If you were hoping to broker peace in the Middle East, a debate between Shia and Sunni clerics about the heirs of Mohammed would be the least promising place to start.[56] And the suspicions of believers about the perils of mutual respect and understanding are not without foundation: historians have argued that after the Reformation had played such an important role in precipitating the hideous pan-European bloodbath of the Thirty Years (confessional) War, the doctrine of tolerance had a central role in secularization. It expressed what must have seemed to the most devout a fundamentally blasphemous idea – that there was something more important than worshipping the right version of God in the right way: peace on earth. So, notwithstanding the actions of persons of good will and often considerable courage, inter-faith reconciliation seems a distant prospect among those for whom their faith is, or they feel should be, the most important fact of their life. We shall talk about the possibility of dialogue between believers and secularists in the final chapter.

There seems sufficient evidence to argue that Karamazov's gloomy prediction about godless societies does not seem to be well-founded. There appears to be reassuring evidence that we may look beyond religion for the continuing underpinning of truly civil society. Our capacity for empathy, to respond to others' judgements, to reflect on what is right and wrong, and act on the outcome of our reflections, rooted in the interpersonal nature of persons, does not seem to be threatened by secularization. Such milk as there is of human kindness will not dry up in the absence of a divine warrant or mandate, threat or promise. What is more, it is delivered in the capillaries of society, remote from the great arteries which direct social behaviour in accordance with large, and often contested principles.

I will end by briefly picking up two additional strands of the argument about post-religious morality.

Firstly, for reasons that will be obvious from Chapter 2, I have not discussed the claim that commitment to the welfare of our fellow human is guaranteed by our evolutionary heritage. Human norms do not seem to follow from biological facts. Besides, observation of the behaviour of most other animal species does not encourage the belief that evolutionary forces, mediated through nature red in tooth and claw, promote a compassionate ethical stance towards conspecifics.[57] The process by which genetic replication is maximized does not typically draw on a general care for others. At any rate, the scope of that care does not extend to the crowds of non-kin with whom we interact in our work and play and with whom we shall need to cooperate in promoting the best future for our increasingly globalized lives. While reciprocal altruism may assist the survival of the species, it also lacks reach necessary for us to maintain a moral stance towards the strangers upon whom we may depend or who may depend on us for our welfare. The problem, as Diana Fleischman has pointed out, is one of scope.[58] It makes any putative "biologically evolved" morality unsuitable for the complexity of modern life, such that we might mourn a single person's death more than that of a million strangers.

The question of the reach of our moral sentiments is equally relevant to what we might call institutional morality, where there may be a vast distance between our actions and their consequences. It is illustrated most spectacularly in the finance system where the making of profit is remote from the costs borne by others. Monetarization crowds out finer feelings, accountability becomes "accountantability" (sic), and our interactions are reduced to morally empty transactions. It is also of particular concern not only because it is facilitated by instantaneous worldwide communication but also because individual greed has no limits when it is mediated by money (which we may not be able to spend) and used to purchase possessions beyond anything that can be truly possessed by being translated into experience. The appetite for wealth is boundless because numbers, like facts, have no nutritional value. Driven by an avarice that has no limits because it is disconnected from any desire other than for increase, the multi-billionaire, fretting that he is not a trillionaire, is willing to impoverish the world, enslaving his workers, in pursuit of self-enrichment. The cosy relationship between turbo-capitalism and the established and emergent religious faiths does not suggest that a religious revival would create a moral climate hindering wealth extractors in their pursuit of more, more, more, condemning their fellows to less, less, less.

SURPRISING A HUNGER IN OURSELVES

Religion: community and purpose

It was perhaps unnecessary to spend so much time defending secular humanism against the charge that, sooner or later, it will result in pandemic amorality that will return us to some version of the Hobbesian war of all against all. Besides, to judge the significance of religion in terms of its impact on morality may seem to instrumentalize it and bypass its primary claim of offering a metaphysical vision of the universe and our place in it. At any rate, the deed is done and the way is now clear to examine those things that religion really does seem uniquely to bring to our lives. It will set the agenda for a discussion of what humanism has yet to do to fill the voids opened up in those who have lost their faith.

In the case of those religions with which we in the West are most familiar, what is most obviously lost when we cease to believe is the hope of a salvation that will offset the total cancellation of death. It is not clear what this hope might mean. There is no account of the afterlife that is imaginable, never mind attractive, for all that it is often a source of consolation, even compensation, for non-attainment of worldly desires.[59] Another obstacle to clarity is that the idea of God, modified by ingenious theologians eager to immunize it against charges of contradictions, thins to the point where it is an "apophatic" being, of whom nothing can be said and nothing understood. God ceases to have personhood, a personal relation to humanity, a personal history or a history of interventions in human history. Most tantalisingly, existence as understood in the physical realm does not apply to God. He is not a thing; nor is He nothing, either. So, not only is God not knowable, He cannot be known to exist in a particular fashion, though he is somehow known to exist.[60]

And yet, and yet, the idea of God seems to answer to a fundamental human need for hope, for something that would be deep enough to counter our feeling of helplessness, our fear, our grief, our frustration, our sense of emptiness; for something that will answer the profound and ultimately tragic mystery of our lives. Certainly, we may reject religious answers – or those answers may reject us – but we must engage with their questions, if only because their depth honours the depth of our life and, correspondingly, the scale of what we shall ultimately lose. It is a fundamental, indeed existential, error to patronize religion merely as a metaphysical stop-gap invoked before science replaced mythology with truth, anthropocentric, inaccurate religious cosmology was superseded by accurate, evidence-based astrophysics, and universal human rights replaced the care and authority of a loving but capricious, partisan God, as the defender of the vulnerable from injustice.

The most obvious gifts that *Homo religiosus* has to offer his infidel conspecifics are monuments – literature, visual art, music, architecture – that may fill us with awe at human creativity and inventiveness, at the capacity to entertain visions of possible worlds utterly different from that of our daily life. We can visit cathedrals and exclaim "How mighty are the works of man!".

We may reject cosmological and other belief on the grounds that where they are not self-contradictory, they are literally unintelligible – or unintelligible to the literal-minded. This, however, is no occasion for superiority or smugness. We should remind ourselves how much of science, at the fundamental level, is unintelligible. It doesn't even have to pretend to make intuitively satisfying sense, because it "works", as measured by its extraordinarily accurate predictive and its huge practical power. But the familiarity of the iconic equations hides their incomprehensibility. Consider the most famous of all equations: $E = mc^2$. It proposes multiplying the mass of something (e.g. the chair you may be sitting on) by the velocity of light, separated from light itself, and then multiplied by itself. And consider how time is treated in physics. It is made to undergo all sorts of indignities such as being turned into a denominator (as in distance/time which is velocity) or multiplied by itself or by the impossibility of the square root of -1. These are not the kinds of things you could do to a real stretch of time such as a Bargain Break Weekend.

Fundamental science provides even easier targets. Foremost among them are the infinite number of parallel universes proposed by physicists trying to make sense of quantum mechanics or the dissolution of nature into a landscape of string theories as scientists try to reconcile quantum mechanics with relativity. One quote from physicist and gifted populariser of science Carlo Rovelli is a gem: "[Space is] made up of grains ... The theory describes these 'atoms of space' in mathematical form ... They are called 'loops' or rings because they are linked to one another, forming a network of relations that weaves the texture of space, like the rings of a finely woven, immense chain mail".[61]

There are serious, intrinsic, limitations to the intelligibility of physics. The Original (intellectual) Sin perhaps goes back to Pythagoras who extracted ideal triangles from the irregular shapes of things, their lengths from the sides of triangles, and then multiplied those lengths by their famished selves. As physics advances, so the very world in which physics is practised and physicists take their lunch breaks, becomes incomprehensible. If quantum mechanics really were the fundamental truth of things, the macroscopic actions of macroscopic physicists using macroscopic instruments to discover quantum mechanics would be impossible. We have already noted (in Chapter 4) that physicists find clocks and measuring rods – the fundamental apparatus of physics – an embarrassment. And there is the scandal of the impossibility of reconciling the non-locality of quantum mechanics with the locality of relativistic physics. The two most powerful, elegant and inspiring theories in science are fundamentally at odds with each other.

I highlight this to pre-empt the patronising sighs of secularists when theologians and other believers defend the unintelligibility of religious beliefs by arguing that they are not to be taken literally as factual assertions.[62] Even so, we cannot leave it at that, if we are to argue that secular societies can prosper only if something uniquely associated with religious belief is to re-enter the culture.[63] We cannot settle for a fudge that places the very idea of God beyond the reach of arguments about the evidence for His existence and questions about the intelligibility of His nature. After all, to name something that does not correspond to anything – but is everywhere rather than nowhere – seems self-undermining. It presupposes what, for the humanist, is yet to be established, seeming to justify the complaint that religion does not so much provide answers as promissory notes, asking us to accept on trust that an answer is on the way. At any rate, by the time theologians have insulated God from rationalist critique, He/She/It has been drained of those very characteristics that bring comfort or purpose to the lives of the devout.

If religion is to have a healthy afterlife in secular society, therefore, it cannot be entirely excused adherence to the standards of rational discourse, particularly when belief in God, as used in the Creed in an act of public worship, has to carry so much weight. After all, it "promises that life, and love, and all one's actions are henceforth set steadfastly on the mystery of God, and hence that we are thereby pledged to work towards that comprehensive healing of the world by which all things are brought into their peace and harmony in God".[64]

If religion is to be appropriated for secular humanism, there is still a mountain to climb, irrespective of whether or not it is intelligible or to be understood literally or metaphorically. The first, and steepest, slope is the transition from a proposition, or set of propositions, about our nature to a *creed*. A creed does not belong to an individual. It is not something held by me as a selection out of a range of views or opinions. It is a shared worldview, and sharing is the essential part. Religions exist only insofar they are collectively affirmed. That is why their worldviews can get by with little supporting evidence separate from the practices and rituals which endorse them. Most importantly, continuity between externally episodic experiences – the weekly service and private prayer – is provided by the community of believers to which one belongs and with whom one is joined in the act of worship. The hour or two of communal worship is situated in and supported by a calendar that extends throughout the year, connecting every week with a different aspect of belief; not just Christmas and Easter, but Advent and Epiphany, Whitsun, and Harvest Festivals. The sacred spaces are supported by sanctified times.

A creed, therefore, is not merely a cluster of propositions reached as the terminus of a series of arguments with one's self or with others. It is typically accepted before it is fully comprehended. Children learn to lisp the Lord's Prayer before they know what "trespasses" are. While the understanding implicit in affirming it is not entirely outsourced to the collective – otherwise prayer would be mere lip service – it is upheld by fellowship, rituals, sacred spaces, and the history. This is how it makes it possible at once to transcend everyday life and yet be brought closer to my fellows in a deeper belonging.

Secular humanists do not always appreciate this and are consequently puzzled that, when arguments for the existence of God are shown to be invalid, believers remain unshaken in their beliefs. As Roger Scruton has expressed it:

> Far from supposing the cult to be a secondary phenomenon derived from the theological beliefs that justify it, I take the opposite view … Theological beliefs are rationalizations of the cult, and the function of the cult is membership. It is through establishing a cult that people learn to pool their resources. Hence every act of settling and of turning the earth to the common needs of the community, involves the building of a temple and the setting aside of days and hours for festivity and sacrificial offering. When people have, in this way, prepared a home for them, the gods come quietly to inhabit it, maybe not noticed at first, and only subsequently clothed in the transcendental garments of theology.[65]

The key word in this profound passage is *membership*. Membership is emphasized by Tim Crane in his critique of a common secular image of religion as "cosmology plus morality". This image overlooks what is central: a sense of identity or belonging, expressed in certain modes of behaviour.[66] It is a profound misrepresentation to see religion as (flawed) cosmology or metaphysics: our relationship to God is in important respects personal, or indeed interpersonal. Most importantly, approached through the door of the cult, the transcendental is a source of closeness and belonging rather than a summons to solitude.

Religious belief, then, is one of the most fundamental markers of group identity. The belonging may be exclusive – from which comes much sorrow. As Neil MacGregor expressed it:

> Religious stories are part of a ... strategy ... for communal survival. Addressing conundrums of life and death, they offer not explanation but meaning. As much about the future as the past, they provide a society with a narrative that goes far beyond the self, embracing the living, the dead and those still to be born in one continuing story of belonging".[67]

Religion is *re-ligare*, "binding fast", binding us to each other in virtue of our being bound to the same god. This is echoed by Durkheim: "A religion is a unified system of beliefs and practices relative to sacred things, that is to say, things set apart and forbidden – beliefs and practices which *unite in one single community* called a Church, all those who adhere to them.[68] (emphasis added).

Bach's dedication of his music – embracing, at its most profound, ritual and art – "To the glory of God and the benefit of my neighbour" reflects this unity. The sacred music expresses emotions that conjoin the inward, the sideways, and the upwards, and offers an image of a coherent life in which one is part of a community of souls rather than a collection of selves and one serves one's ultimate interests by serving that of one's neighbour. The community of souls presupposes a mode of conviviality that addresses our solitude in everyday life and in the face of death, taking the interpersonal on to "the far side". Death becomes a point not of (absolute) departure but *arrival* in the bosom of Our Lord.

This remains true even where there is, as is so often the case, a tension between the "I-God" relationship and the "We-God" relationship, arising because the small details of cooperative life require a shallow connectedness that smooths our interactions with each other. Indwelling in Christ, all are bound together; and family life and other, more casual modes of collegiality, are gathered up into a shared life conducted in the presence of a God worshipped by all.

Collective worship, the hierarchy of priests, where the glory of God and the glory of prelates are inseparable, and the at least partly intelligible narrative of church services, enable believers to live out, or at least live with, that which surpasses all understanding. We can, as it were, outsource the duty of understanding to the community. The side-ways affirmation that comes from the presence of fellow worshippers in the same place lightens the burden of comprehension. St Anselm's famous (or for infidels infamous) profession of faith *Credo ut intelligam* – "I believe in order that I may understand" – has its echo in the heart of many believers: I feel that I understand because I am surrounded by the beliefs of others.

The unity of mission in Bach's dedication of his music "to the glory of God and the benefit of my neighbour" is a manifestation of the idea that God gives shape, direction, a point of convergence for our lives. Take the simple statement of faith that "the goal of all human existence is to praise, worship, and serve God".[69] Leaving aside the truth – or even intelligibility – of this claim, consider how attractive it might seem to the secular seeker for meanings, purposes, and truths that are equal to our condition: aligning one's self with an entity that is coterminous with the universe, One in whom Is and Ought, Being and Knowing, are one; and even engaging in communications with that entity that are not entirely one-way.

With such a god comes a guarantee of meanings "all the way down", reaching into the small details of daily life, and yet withstanding the assault of death and of privation. Diarmaid MacCulloch noted how "the sound of Christian passion is heard in the hymns of John and Charles Wesley, bringing pride, self-confidence, and divine purpose to the lives of poor and humble people struggling to make sense of a new industrial society in Georgian Britain".[70] The curse of "and then … and then … and then" is lifted. God completes our personhood, irrespective of what happens in our lives. We may move on, but also stand still. The Jacobean metaphysical poet George Herbert captures this sense of the service of God as perfect freedom:

> Teach me, my God and King,
> In all things Thee to see,
> And what I do in anything
> To do it as for Thee …
>
> A servant with this clause
> Makes drudgerie divine:
> Who sweeps a room as for Thy laws,
> Makes that, and th' action fine.[71]

The sentiment is wonderful, assuming of course that "drudgerie" is equally distributed and is not carried out for a pittance by a member of the precariat. The divinity of modern-spelling "drudgery" – order-filling carried out for the sake of a West Coast billionaire – is not easy to discern.

The central point is that religious vision at its purest, most majestic, and most innocent promises a convergence, between the minutiae of duty, and the Cosmos in a personal God who is both the creator of the universe and the place where the meaning of life is to be found. He is the place where all projects come together such that no action, if divinely approved, will lack significance, even as its often tedious details are worked out. And within our lives, there is a connection between the small spaces in which we live and the limitless All, in which we are cast. The transient facts of our minute existence are tinged with something of the significance that pervades the universe as a whole, a blush of boundless meaning throughout the whole of being. Our objectively negligible status is redeemed by our being in communion with One Who is the Author and Sustainer of everything.

We may therefore hold that the idea of God is unintelligible and that what counts as praising, worshipping, or serving him, is not clearly defined – indeed is often violently disputed – and still acknowledge the power of this religious image of a coherent life. Even the secular heart can wish for that "purity of heart" that Kierkegaard spoke of, which was "to will one thing".[72] That "one thing" cannot be the dreams of pleasure, honour, status, riches, or power which are always transient – indeed, instantiating a second-order transience within the transience of our lives – and are never achieved in the sense of being realized in a way that corresponds to what they promise in prospect. It corresponds to an ideal of meaning that applies to all one's life, that is additive, convergent, climactic, complete. This ideal would seem contradictory if meaning were sought *within* experience. After all, it is not possible to assign ultimate meaning to both the passion directed towards some object *and* subsequent indifference, unless one appeals to a narrative that transcends both states, that derives its ultimate meaning from outside of one's life.

A cautionary note

It is important not to be too starry-eyed about looking beyond one's life for meaning or forget that the ambition "to will one thing" may not have entirely admirable consequences. Such an absolute focus may not be compatible with the interruptions necessary for paying kindly attention to one's fellows. Convergence of meanings may result in a zero sum, as everything cancels everything else or a mixture of all colours adds up to white. And, by a supreme and terrible irony, it may lead to an ethical nihilism, expressed in a willingness to sacrifice one's life for a cause – something greater than "the long littleness" of life.

The proximity is evident in the many who have signed up to fight in wars because the possibility of sacrifice offered a resolution of the problems of an unsatisfactory life. There is no clearer expression of this than Yeats' "An Irish Airman Foresees His Death":

> I balanced all, brought all to mind,
> The years to come seemed waste of breath,
> A waste of breath the years behind
> In balance with this life, this death.[73]

In the foreground is the airman's own heroic death as a solution to his feeling of emptiness. The deaths he caused are off-stage, not included in the equation. The airman's sentiment, therefore, is nearer than is comfortable to recall to that of the suicide bomber who subordinates his entire life and all its possibilities to the realization of one idea. He saves his soul – and acts on behalf of his vision of the world – by spattering the brains of infants (whom it should not be necessary to call "innocent") on their prams.

Violent religious extremism is of course as repulsive to the vast majority of the most committed religious believers as to the rest of us. They would find it impossible to imagine a God worthy of worship who would approve of an individual placing his own salvation above the lives of others who do not worship Him in the same way. The often-deployed defence that "God moves in a mysterious way" – and hence is not to be judged – is, however, not reassuring.

While acknowledging the profound needs that religion endeavours to meet, therefore, it is important to acknowledge that there is no clear divide between a totality of commitment, as in admirably pure faith that makes a life coherent in the profoundest sense, and fanaticism. If the meaning of life is something you are prepared to die for, it may well be that, in ranking your own life below some cause, you may rank others' lives even lower. It is, anyway, uncomfortably close to the life-hating, misanthropic responses that seem to some to be appropriate responses to the profoundest truth about ourselves: that we are contingent, finite, indeed insignificant, beings who have limited control over our lives in a universe that is overwhelmingly indifferent to us, as we are equally indifferent to it (and indeed to the vast majority of creatures living on our home planet). That the secular life lacks a point of convergence in which everything of value adds up, therefore, may be part of its nobility. And the dangers of trying to find a non-religious collective substitute for that point of convergence in some political doctrine do not need spelling out.

Although the living truth of religion lies not in a set of propositions but in rituals and prayers shared with fellow believers extending across the world and over the centuries, in a way of life, might these not eventually lose their force if they were entirely detached from the union of a metaphysical world

picture with personal needs, and social ordinances? Or in the absence of peti-
tionary prayer which, by casting the believer on the mercy of a great power,
alleviates the sense of powerlessness in a life without hope? Church-, temple-,
and mosque-goers have to believe that "we are gathered together in the Lord's
name" not that "we are gathered together in our own name". Propositional
faith, in short, cannot give way entirely to attitudinal faith or the latter would
lack intentional direction.

And if the deal is that our lives, if they have been well spent, will open on to
an existence in which we are united with God in an eternal afterlife, this may
subvert, rather than sanctify, the meanings of our daily life. More to our present point, if eternity and afterlives – not to speak of the God Who is present
in them – are impossible to imagine, religious hope may (but not always) do
more to empty our lives of meaning than to underwrite any meanings they
have. Judged by some religious criteria, all lives in this world fall infinitely
short of the condition God or the gods intended for us. George Herbert's
cheerful hope of making "drudgerie divine" by doing it for God's sake will
seem even less compelling when the drudgerie in question is driven by terror
of a demanding, bullying boss, and is marked by endless, fatiguing repetition.
God has little presence in an Internet retailer's warehouse and His epiphanies
to the shelf-fillers are rare.

I mention this only to indicate the scale of the task and some of the contradictions that confront secular humanism when it attempts to take back from
religion what belongs to humanity. This, the task of "spiritual irredentism",
is the theme of the final chapter. It is motivated by an appreciation of "the
seriousness which a religious mentality brings to the mystery and misery of
human existence" and "the solemnity of the religious liturgy as a way of con-
fronting these problems".[74]

CHAPTER 10
Reclaiming ourselves

We may acknowledge the harm caused by institutionalized religion, with its power to amplify hostilities between human groups, and recognize that doctrines spread across 200 or more faiths are not imaginable by, never mind believable to, many, and still conclude that a human life without institutionally acknowledged transcendent meaning is impoverished. The personal meanings we find in our lives are parochial and transient. We often look back on them with wonder and even dismay, finding that we are indifferent to the things that we valued so much, and how we passed through, rather than arrived at, goals that were so important to us. And we acknowledge how the objective significance of our lives may have to humanity as a whole – "making the world a better place" and so on – seems unlikely to cancel deficiencies in our subjective experience. And, finally, when we envisage our place in a Godless universe, we hardly cut much of a figure. We seem to be the products of purposeless mechanisms that did not intend us. We are not here because we are needed or wanted. As the physicist Steven Hawking expressed it: "[T]he human race is just a chemical scum on a moderate sized planet, orbiting round a very average star in the outer suburbs of one among a billion galaxies".[1]

Thus, our self-image in the mirror of natural science; how we look when seen as pieces of nature. A primary purpose in writing *Seeing Ourselves* has been to highlight the extent to which we are *not* just pieces of nature, to describe the extra-natural nature of humanity and of the human world we have built. I have rejected the assumption that, if we are not supernatural beings, separately hand-crafted by God and uniquely related to him, we must be mere organisms; that persons are at bottom beasts. Yes, we are made of matter, but we are not just pieces of matter; yes, we are animals but we are not just animals. We are unique beings in the universe, as should be evident from the fact that, uniquely, we *speak* of "the universe"; or, more generally, have a world picture that transcends any kind of *umwelt* that other creatures may be immersed in.

REVISITING DISENCHANTMENT

Turning the tables: the enchanting mystery of the road to disenchantment

If you are looking for human transcendence of the world as seen in the disenchanted gaze of natural science, it is not necessary to look far. Perception – the very ground floor of science – which cannot be denied, is as inexplicable as the extra-sensory perception whose existence is certainly in doubt. While much fuss is made about "premonition" that some individuals are claimed (with insufficient evidence) to possess, "postmonition" – the ability to look back in time to particular events we are conscious of having experienced is no less extraordinary and has the additional virtue of being shared universally. And there is nothing matter of fact about those progenies of shared perception we tend to dismiss as "mere" facts, not the least the extraordinary facts that Hawking invoked in cutting us down to what he sees as our true size. It is not the way of chemical scum to see itself as chemical scum and to locate itself on a planet circling a star in turn lost in a billion galaxies. But less exotic facts take us far from our body and its experiences. Knowing "for a fact" that London is 200 miles away is remote from sense experiences. And we are even further from such experiences when we argue over whether London is 200 or 250 miles away.

In the foregoing pages we have examined our relationship to our own bodies, and to time, our selfhood, and our agency. They are the manifestations of the unique nature of human consciousness – of the full-blown intentionality that builds up into the "aboutness" of a complex mind facing a world, of a conscious subject, a person, who actively lives a life, participating in the community of minds that is the extra-natural realm that we inhabit. There are many reasons why we overlook this. The most important is the habit of scientism that extends the justified authority of natural science to places where it has nothing to offer, indeed to aspects of reality that are in fact excluded by natural science, the very exclusion to which applied science owes much of its predictive and practical efficacy. The undoubted power of science, and the astonishing scope of its truths, have led to the false conclusion that whatever science cannot see or accommodate is not real. If brain scans and other neuroscientific techniques cannot discover the self there is no such thing as the self. If agency doesn't fit into the mechanics of the material world, then it must be an illusion.

Many of those who acknowledge that human consciousness is currently mysterious still insist that its vexed relationship with the brain is a local difficulty that will one day vanish before advances in neuroscience. Ever closer inspection of the "it is" of the brain will, they maintain, explain the "I am" of the person. Natural science, so we are assured, will ultimately make sense of the very idea of nature and of we who face, and try to make sense of, nature. Meanwhile we are reduced by the scientific gaze to "chemical scum" on a remote planet, located in a not particularly distinguished part of the universe. It is time to dispute this assumption; indeed, to turn the tables.

Let us begin with a couple of table-turning arguments, one from a famous religious thinker and another from an equally famous opponent of religion. Let us begin with the most quoted of Pascal's *Pensées*:

> Man is only a reed, the weakest in nature, but he is a thinking reed. There is no need for the whole universe to take up arms to crush him: a vapour, a drop of water, is enough to kill him, but even if the universe were to crush him, man would still be nobler than his slayer, because he knows that he is dying and the advantage the universe has over him. The universe knows none of this.[2]

"The universe knows none of this". That our destroyer does so without malice and is unaware of doing so seems cold comfort. However, there is a seed of an interesting, if not entirely comforting, thought here. It is also present in the following passage from Russell's *A Free Man's Worship*:

> A strange mystery it is that Nature, omnipotent but blind, in the revolutions of her secular hurryings through the abysses of space, *has brought forth at last a child, subject still to her power, but gifted with sight, with the knowledge of good and evil, with the capacity of judging all the works of his unthinking Mother*[3] (emphasis added)

Russell here gives expression to a profound, and profoundly strange, truth. It is in us alone that the universe is gathered up as a whole, that, courtesy of us humans, matter not only matters but assumes inverted commas as "matter", and nature is "Nature". We are made larger by our possession of the very vision that sees us as vanishingly small. In our reflective consciousness, we enclose the world that encloses us. The idea of a universe that is meaningless, and hence shows us to be meaningless, transcends the supposedly meaningless universe.

The tough-minded naturalist Quine has beautifully encapsulated this mystery of the advance of scientific knowledge in a passage we have already quoted: it is the mystery of "how we, physical denizens of the physical world, can have projected our scientific theory of that whole world from our meagre contacts with it: from the mere impacts of rays and particles on our surfaces and a few odds and ends such as the strain of walking uphill".[4] This is how science looks if it looks at itself with an objective, scientific gaze: impossible. Quine concludes from this that Being and Knowing are inside each other. As expressed by his long-time colleague Burton Dreben: "In the classical tradition, the Order of Being ... took precedence over the Order of Knowing ... From Locke on ... the Order of Knowing has taken precedence over the Order of Being. For Quine, the two have equal standing; neither is prior to the other, they are reciprocally contained".[5]

Let us unpack this a little – while doing little justice to the complexity of Quine's thought. On the one hand, physical stuffs (belonging to the Order of Being) – objects, energy and the like – are "posits" constructed out of sense experience (belonging to the Order of Knowing). So Knowing has priority over Being. On the other hand, sense experiences (belonging to the Order of Knowing) are, according to Quine's naturalistic account of consciousness, the result of the stuff-on-stuff action: the impingement of the material world on the nervous systems of knowers (a physical interaction in the Order of Being). So, Being must have priority: Knowledge is an effect of causal interactions between Being and human beings, that is to say, human bodies. If this seems circular, it is because it *is* circular. Quine considered that the circularity must be inescapable because (as Dreben puts it) he believed that "there is no Archimedean point from which we can justify knowledge as a whole".[6] Philosophy cannot rise above science and, indeed, the whole cognitive realm to see, understand, and judge it from the outside.

We may disagree with this (as I have done throughout) but still accept that a tough-minded naturalism that characterizes us as minute, transient material objects in a gigantic billion-years-old material universe, seems to undermine itself. There is a crack through which enchantment may re-enter our disenchanted picture of the world. The inexplicable miracle of the thinking reed goes beyond mere knowledge of her lowly place in the universe: it also encloses the known universe in a relationship between Being and Knowing that is more equitable than science-based naturalism would allow. What the notion of reciprocal containment of Knowing and Being delivers is *a legitimate sense of possibility* that is not, after all, closed down by what natural science has to say about the world. There are no ultimate grounds for accepting that the last word on our nature, our place in the universe, and what we may expect, is of the kind spoken by Steven Weinberg. Specifically, we should not be bullied by the extraordinary predictive power of science and the astonishing success of science-based technology into deferring to science on matters that are strictly metaphysical.

We uncover the hidden enchantment in our world picture when we unpack the extraordinary steps that take us from the baseline envisaged by Quine – "the meagre contacts" with the world – to knowledge that enables the universe that encloses us to be enclosed in our thoughts.[7] We have taken our collective endeavour to make sense of the world, of which science is a spectacular expression, far too much for granted.[8] No-one was more aware of this than the greatest scientist of the twentieth century, Albert Einstein who asserted that "the eternal mystery of the world is its comprehensibility".[9] We are justified in turning the scientific disenchantment of the world on its head by reminding ourselves of the utterly mysterious achievements of *Homo scientificus*.[10] The cognitive endeavour which has contributed most to the disenchantment of our world picture – seeing nature as a meaningless self-contained system regulated by mindless immanent principles – is the most profound mystery and legitimate cause for wonder. We can feed this wonder by reminding ourselves: that we, with our pin-prick bonces, can entertain the idea of a universe trillions of miles across and billions of years old; and that we, who are a minute part of the universe can speak of "the universe". And we can identify laws that apply equally to our own bodies and to that of the entire material universe. We can wake up out of our subjectivity to the seemingly impossible wakefulness of scientific truth.

It is hardly surprising that we cannot make sense of our capacity to make sense of things. As we saw in Chapter 4, the endeavour that is natural science has no place in the natural world that it describes. The cognitive achievements that have made science possible are unexplained descendants of a putative initial primordial awareness that inexplicably emerged in an insentient universe.

It seems that the more disenchanted our picture of the world, the more enchanted must be we who can depict it. It is a pleasing irony that scientific naturalism – inadvertently – places our extra-natural nature in italics. Transcendence is always with respect to some baseline that is "exceeded" or "surpassed". By setting this baseline rather low, scientism makes the secular humanist case for the transcendence of human beings easier to make! When the science that places man on the edge of the universe, as a rather undistinguished element in it, is seen for what it is – a human achievement – man comes back to the centre of things. That humankind, a minute part of the universe, christened the universe "the universe" and measured its size and age and, despite being subject in many respects to the laws of nature, identified those laws and named them "laws" – these are markers of the extent to which we cannot be accommodated in the scientists' disenchanted picture of the world. It demonstrates that, if the scientific account of the world were the whole truth of things (including ourselves), these achievements would be as inexplicable as a soluble fish becoming an oceanographer.

It is time to consolidate this reverse Copernican revolution by meditating on the irruption of the subject into a subjectless universe.

The disenchanters' last stand

I want to first spend a little more time on the paradox that the disenchantment of the world is driven by science, itself the most extraordinary manifestation of an enchanted human world, that the reductive vision which sees us as "chemical scum" is a demonstration of how remote we are from the general run of scum. The explanation of the paradox is that the community of minds underpinning science is more or less hidden in what it says about the universe. This is not in the slightest bit surprising: while science begins with individual curiosity and interests, it can proceed only when we get ourselves out of the way; when we do not seek our own face, or the divine image of ourselves, in nature. When we look through or past ourselves.

It may still seem puzzling why we have to get ourselves out of the way to discover truths that will enhance our power to manipulate the world for our own benefit until we remember that the laws of nature we discover enhance our ability to manipulate the material world precisely *because* they apply not just to me, to us, to our culture, but to all living and non-living entities. That is why, as science advances, so the Nature we uncover returns less and less of our gaze. It is because it is a law that applies equally to human beings and rocks on as yet undiscovered planets that $E = mc^2$ mirrors none of our personal characteristics or our concerns. Science cuts a path through the thickets of subjectively experienced reality to this conclusion, setting fire to everything en route.

I rehearse this point because I want in due course to drill beneath science to something that is both the necessary condition of scientific inquiry and which, nevertheless, natural science makes more difficult to understand, indeed cannot accommodate: the emergence of the conscious human subject in a totality which is seen to be overwhelmingly subjectless. Science is a spectacular manifestation of knowledge in a universe which, according to the science's own picture of the order of things, has no means of making itself known, as it is made of insentient, purposeless, matter, energy, or charge – a description that incidentally encompasses the brain when it is construed, as the neuro-philosophers construe it, as a material object. It therefore presents us with the challenge of understanding the emergence of the Order of Knowing in the Order of Being, while avoiding (at least for as long as possible) the idealist position according to which beings are constructs of knowledge.

The inability of natural science to deal with human subjects is seen most clearly in something central to the inquiry of this book: the intentional relationship of our consciousness to what is "out there" and the joining of intentionality into the community of minds. The laws of nature cannot account for, or even accommodate, the non-material separation between ourselves and the natural world, a gap crossed and yet held open by intentionality. That is why – as we saw in Chapter 2 – the disciples of scientism were so keen to eliminate intentionality.

The scientific enterprise, and the knowledge and understanding it generates, is the most extraordinary product of the joined intentionality of human minds. Tracing the paths and pathways to scientific knowledge puts into italics a mystery that not only transcends science itself but also highlights the scale of our transcendence of the material world. To demystify the *aurora borealis* by seeing it as an electromagnetic storm created by solar flares rather than a manifestation of divine moods, pushes the mystery back to that of how energy is perceived, named, understood by creatures who care for themselves in a universe that lacks purpose or hope and does not care for them.

The disenchanters will not give up without a struggle. Eliminating intentionality is only one approach to naturalizing human consciousness and the extraordinary cognitive trajectory that has led to contemporary science. Another is to appeal to evolutionary theory. Evolutionary "explanations" of human consciousness – of the spontaneous emergence of mind out of a mindless universe by mindless mechanisms – have relied on two major assumptions. The first is that consciousness has survival value; and the second is that, having arisen spontaneously as the result of a mutation, it would then develop into the cognitive powers of *Homo scientificus*, by means of natural selection acting on spontaneous mutations. Both assumptions are highly contestable, as we discussed in Chapter 2.

The appeal to Darwin, therefore, does not advance our understanding of how a state of a material object such as an organism can reveal what there is beyond that organism; that matter can come to know some of matter as its surroundings, its world; and that it can ultimately come to value some states more than others and aim to manipulate the world accordingly. In short, that matter, obeying its own laws, can turn itself from what-is to what-is-there or what-there-is; what-is gets its "itness", and, in living beings, starts to mind its own "isness". That matter can give rise to "thatter".

For some, the problem can seem less challenging if a "gradualist" notion of the emergence of consciousness is adopted. This works on the dubious principle that if we break up a metaphysical transition into small steps, it can be plausibly mapped on to a series of physical transitions or sneaked into Being through tiny cracks. We start off with a teeny-weeny dot of consciousness which we get for free and then add to this, courtesy of nervous systems which are described as increasingly "complex" or "sophisticated", a widening, deepening and layering of consciousness and thus arrive at people like you and me. If this seems to ease the difficulty it is only because it blunts appreciation of the extraordinary fact (fact being a hopelessly inadequate word) that, so it appears, Being woke up in beings like ourselves and, ultimately, became a universe which we engage with, are conscious of, face, know, and endeavour to explain.

Gradualist accounts, allocating hundreds of millions of years to the journey from a smidgeon of sentience to a human person, are attractive because of their biological aura. They seem to be consistent with what we see in nature: that more recently emerged species have a more developed consciousness than the more ancient. They accord with the idea of an ascent up an evolutionary tree (or several such trees) from lowly insentient beings to lowly sentients to elevated, self-conscious, society-conscious, world-picturing, art-loving, God-worshipping, man.

At any rate, gradualists hope that consciousness can be smuggled through "on the nod" as if it were a little extra (un-designed) design feature, and as if the incomprehensible relationship between ever more complex consciousness and emerging nervous systems were just a little local difficulty, that science will one day solve. That it is nothing of the kind becomes evident when we see clearly the claim that is being made. For this we need to start in the right place with insentient matter and end in the right place with human subjects facing a universe that appears to be made up of overwhelmingly insentient matter.

A non-gradualist view, gathering up everything from the first tingle of sentience to the bearers of the highest-level theories, into the idea of an instantaneous irruption of the subject in an insentient, sensationless, mindless, thoughtless, pre-conscious stuff is even less attractive. The notion of a single universe-wide flash of Being awakening to itself does not take account of the fact that Being is appreciated by distinct beings – individual subjects – who have a different "take" on different parts of Being. Being does not become The Given, or "reality", all at once. Subjects have to form; and each subject tastes only a part of Being, including – and distinctly – that being which it is itself. Nor does this story account for the gradual acquisition of empirical knowledge of parts of Being by individual subjects and the community of minds. (In this respect, it shares some of the problems of one version of panpsychism according to which the entire universe is pervaded by a single mind.[11]) What is more, we know that human subjects emerge in succession into a world structured by prior and co-present subjects: I entered an already populated world in 1946. And we observe the development of humans from the ignorant foetus to the fully developed, knowledgeable adult subject in a seeming rehearsal of the genealogy of consciousness.

For these reasons, even though the notion of the gradual emergence of consciousness and its organization into subjects, selves, points of view, occurring as a result of natural selection operating on insentient or less conscious organisms, does not withstand examination, it may be more attractive than the idea of the sudden irruption of the subject or subjectivity into a subject-less universe, of "thatter" into matter. Gradualism can at least accommodate subjectivity being distributed through individual subjects whose emergence and continuing existence depends on the health of a living organism which organism also provides the most fundamental basis for the subject having a viewpoint, for being aware of this rather than that and having this interest rather than that interest.

Nevertheless, the distribution of subjectivity into individual subjects indexed to bodies seems to be accommodated within evolutionary theory only if we focus on the "what" of subjectivity, the particular conscious contents of subjects, and bypass the question of the "that" of its existence; if, that is to say, we glide past the transformation of Being into something that is, for certain beings, the Given, the Present, a World.

Evolutionary theory in sum offers nothing to help us make sense of the emergence of the "I Am" of human subjects from the "It Is" of the material universe. It offers even less to account for the escape of the conscious subject from the primordial state of a sentient organism, with a merely inchoate sense that it is, to a fully-fledged person with objective knowledge of a world that exceeds him or her many million-fold. Besides, the difference between an instantaneous irruption of subjectivity and a gradual emergence of consciousness over time does not appear so secure when we reflect that temporal ordering and duration may be something that is retrospectively imposed on the universe by fully fledged subjects – something to which we shall return.

THE MYSTERY OF THE SUBJECT: BE-ING TO AM-ING

> [T]here exists no viable, or even moderately convincing, explanation of how nonconscious physical matter gives rise to subjective experience.   Stan Klein[12]

> We feel that when all *possible* scientific questions have been answered, the problem of life remains completely untouched.
>   Ludwig Wittgenstein[13]

> The mind-body problem is not just a local problem, having to do with the relation between mind, brain, and behaviour in living animal organisms ... it invades our understanding of the entire cosmos and its history.   Thomas Nagel[14]

The universe before the subject

This may be the most difficult and controversial part of this book and certainly the most vulnerable. It may even lose me a few philosophical friends. Let us, nevertheless, run with the idea of the irrupted subject as a kind of flashlight that illuminates Being,[15] creating a layered "here" anchored on a viewpoint that reaches into the many "theres" that forms an environment plus an unlimited number of intuited "elsewheres" that encircle that environment.[16] At the same time, it develops into a "world", as shared intentionality, usually mediated by signs, delivers a public space which is ultimately an object of common knowledge; a common infrastructure for cognition.

Implicit in what we have concluded earlier, the laws of nature do not seem to have the wherewithal by which insentient matter would turn on itself and become an object of knowledge that includes knowledge of those laws of nature. If we try to imagine the universe in the absence of consciousness, we may arrive at a clearer idea of the explanatory gap between that universe and a human world in which it is revealed and to some extent understood. This gap is not narrowed even if we accept that (necessarily embodied) human subjects are subject to the laws of nature as the necessary condition for their continuing as (living) subjects. Indeed, the fact that there are objective, material conditions of the possibility of subjectivity, just as there are unconscious mechanisms necessary for the possibility of consciousness and of "mattering", of pieces of conscious, living matter being concerned for themselves, makes subjectivity yet more difficult to grasp. It is even more perplexing: while we cannot envisage the subject emerging out of material reality, it must some-how be indexed to it. If it were not, then its world would be a pure idea and everything, from the Big Bang to the arrival of *H. sapiens*, would exist only insofar as it was located in some mind. While such a view would bring us close to Kantian idealism and Kant's startling claim that "the synthetic activity of the mind is the lawgiver of nature",[17] it may be more helpful to examine our puzzle through the ideas of another philosopher. The philosopher is Merleau-Ponty who was an important, though mainly off-stage, presence in Chapter 3.

Towards the end of his major work, *The Phenomenology of Perception*, Merleau-Ponty argues that the original "nebula" – the initial state of the universe, proposed by the eighteenth-century physicist Laplace from which the conditions necessary for life were absent – "is not behind us, at our remote beginnings, but in front of us, in the cultural world":[18] "the sun exists only within a world, and a world emerges at the confluence of a perceiver and the perceived".[19] This sounds dangerously close to idealism, or to a philosophy in which the totality of the cosmos is internal to human awareness.[20] Common sense or ordinary understanding would hold that "I am" is surely a recent arrival in the order of things: the advanced organisms necessary to house first-person being emerged out of a long pre-existing "it is". Without the latter, the subject would have nothing to emerge from, or emerge into, and at the very least would not have any basis for a viewpoint. For Ted Toadvine, however, Merleau-Ponty's view "does not deny the [existence] of a time before the [human] world, a primordial prehistory that haunts the world from within, which is the truth of the naturalist's conviction about a time prior to humanity".[21]

It demands, however, that we look critically at the idea of "an elemental past *that has never been [for any subject] a present*"[22] (emphasis added); at the status, even privileged status, of a past located in a physical world prior to the human world – the very idea of something that was "there" but was not "there" for anyone. At the very least, we should be prompted to puzzle over the relationship between phenomenal, human time and a putative physical time which is supposed not only to precede humanity but also (given that, as seems likely, the human race will not last forever) to outlast it. The assumption that the sum total of human time – or the time in which there are subjects – is a mere episode in a vastly greater time span of nature should not be taken for granted.

There are two ways of approaching this issue. The first is to examine the nature of our (collective) backward glance to a pre-human universe. We shall find that the past, envisaged as the target of our glance, is not at all straightforward. Secondly, let us try to imagine the universe in the absence of human, or any other consciousness. It will dawn on us that the pre-conscious universe is not at all as we envisage it, even when our endeavour to imagine it draws on the latest and most reliable science.

Let us think first about the backward glance. Consider the assertion that "The earth was formed 4.5 billion years ago". When we subject the seemingly innocent word "ago" to the beady-eyed, critical attention it warrants, the statement is far from straightforward. "Ago" is a hybrid, combining quite different elements. The first element is a definite quantity – 4.5 billion years. The second is a *relationship* – of an event to a changing marker of the present. "The earth was formed 4.5 billion years ago" most obviously connects: a) a physical event; and b) an implicit "now" that gives the "ago" its reference point. There is a third relatum: a conscious being for whom a particular time is now and who brings the now and the event into a relationship. That third party tends to be overlooked because the "now" is a common now, belonging to no-one in particular. "Ago" is thereby gathered up into a seemingly impersonal world of fact, and hence a universe which appears to exist without any conscious support. When we remember the "now", however, and the "third party", we appreciate that "ago" does not travel outside the realm where human consciousness is at least possible.

"So, what?" you might ask. "You have reminded us that 'ago', like 'before' is a relational, not an intrinsic, property of an event." And this is pretty obvious: if the temporal relations of events were intrinsic to them, events would be a fever of contradictions, endeavouring to be both "before" some events and "after" others (not to speak of "at the same time as" yet other events). So they are external relations. They are not the properties of insentient events or the objects that are their substrate. They rely on observers to make the external relations between events.

But there is another twist. If we take the most authoritative account of the mechanics of the physical world, the general theory of relativity, which sums all possible viewpoints, and hence corresponds to no particular viewpoint, we find that nothing happens at a particular time, or in any order, or indeed at all. You may recall the passage from Herman Weyl quoted in Chapter 4: "The objective world simply *is*, it does not *happen*. Only to the gaze of my consciousness, crawling upward along the lifeline of my body, does a section of this world come to life as a fleeting image in space which continually changes in time".[23]

The timing and order of events is relative to an inertial frame of reference and the latter is not self-creating. There is, as discussed in Chapter 4, no "at" a time in the physical world. The physical world has to be haunted by a conscious observer to create, and certainly to privilege, a frame of reference. The time of occurrence of events is necessarily relational in that fundamental sense and relationships have to be picked out. More fundamentally, there is no definite happening without the subject to provide a frame of reference. This remains true, even if we imagine a single cosmic clock, connected with a preferred reference frame in which (for example) cosmic background radiation has the same temperature in all directions. This clock does not of itself tell the time and deliver past, present, and future, or "ago".

We need the present as a starting point for a history of the universe and the reconstruction of what counts as its past. The present in this case has a double face: the now of our present token thoughts about the formation of the earth (or indeed anything else); and the moment which is the most recent part of a series that extends backwards from now, giving "ago" its starting point. This second face disguises the true nature of "ago" if "now" is translated into a date (e.g. 24 January 2019) that, in virtue of not being indexed to a person, seems independent of human consciousness. The translation conceals the fundamental difference between an actual present and a (paradoxical) past present which was not, and indeed could not be, present to anyone. We are consequently misled into thinking of "now" and a pre-conscious past event (such as the birth of the sun) as the beginning and end of a line that connects them. Thus we arrive at a deceptively straightforward image of a relationship between "now" and a past (or a past event) that was never present, never "now". When this is appreciated, we can embrace Merleau-Ponty's rejection "of a time in-itself that would be entirely purified of any point of view, since we cannot think time apart from our own emergence within it and our subsequent reconstruction of it"[24] without committing ourselves to idealism.

The twists and turns do not end at this point. Yes, according to orthodox physics, there is no absolute order of events without viewpoint. Viewpoints, however, cannot *dictate* the order of events: the order of physical things is not the plaything of minds. The sequence "Big Bang", "Formation of the Earth", "Beginning of Life", "Emergence of Conscious Human Beings" is not negotiable; nor are the intervals between these steps. It does not lie within the jurisdiction of conscious individuals to determine that the Earth was formed after the Big Bang or that several billion years separated the two events. What is more, individual subjects do not choose their location in historical or astronomical time. The location of my own beginning in the very recent history of the universe is not up to me to decide. Yes, the subjectless universe does not know what time it is at; but, no, the subject does not have jurisdiction over the temporal duration, or temporal order of events.[25] Nevertheless, the notion of a time *at* which the conscious subject emerged is deeply problematic, given that consciousness is the bearer of a temporal "at" into any putative insentient physical world.

The idea of the subject irrupting in the universe either at a particular time or gradually emerging over a time therefore remains enigmatic. We cannot conceive of it as an event or a series of events at a particular time, given that subjectivity is that in virtue of which there are discrete events with definite temporal relations. The question of the status of the Big Bang in the absence of subjects remains. In what sense would it occur at a time? In virtue of what is it a beginning? What would make it a single event or multitude of events or a continuous process? The Big Bang is neither intrinsically bounded or boundless, located, or ubiquitous. The scale of attention determines whether it counts as one or many. And none of the contents of the universe other than human subjects makes the universe a *universe*.

The difficulty we are in is captured in this passage from Thomas Nagel: "Mind, as a development of life, must be included as the most recent stage of this long cosmological history [from the Big Bang], and its appearance ... *casts its shadow back over the entire process and the constituents and principles on which the process depends* (emphasis added).[26] The backward glance of consciousness over the remote pre-conscious past to that which led up to consciousness is a profound challenge to our understanding. There is something deeply mysterious, if we accept the standard ordering of events, in the comparatively recent emergence in the material universe of something – human consciousness – that gives an account, an image, of that universe. What we have on a grand scale is the paradox of something which is made the intentional object of part of itself: it loops back on itself.

So, while we may stop short at fully accepting Merleau-Ponty's claim that the sun exists only in a "world" and worlds await the emergence of human consciousness, we can understand the motivation behind this claim. There is something deeply problematic about the very notion of a state of affairs that has never been present to anyone (the universe prior to human consciousness) being present or now at a particular time. "Ago" is both backward facing – to the event which is located in a past that was never present – and connected sideways to a common Now. It can hardly exist in the absence of human consciousness. When "ago" is extended to events which occurred in the absence of any possible consciousness, it is like a bridge with only one pier: the present. Additionally, it connects two relata and yet keeps them apart. This is unique to all forms of intentional relationship, as when my awareness of an object "out there" connects me with something from which I am explicitly distinct.

The idea of there being a particular time at which, or a period of time over which, knowing subjects emerged in an insentient universe, is therefore difficult fully to grasp. How can we say that there was a "before" and an "after" of the emergence of the subject, given the nature already discussed of "before" and "after"? There is a further, perhaps deeper, problem associated with the idea of Being existing prior to subjects to which it appears. It prompts the question of whether Being has an intrinsic appearance. If it does not, then there seems to be nothing to justify what is revealed when the subject irrupts. We cannot appeal to the idea that appearances will be determined merely by what is of biological concern to the subject because the latter is an embodied being and the particular form of its concern with the nature of certain beings other than itself (food, prey) must have something to do with the intrinsic properties of those beings and, indeed, with those of its intrinsic properties that determine its needs. We need, in short, to find a source of the biological needs of the subject when we start from Being without intrinsic qualities. The idea of the true, intrinsic appearance of a material object is problematical.

The target of our backward glance – the nature of the universe in the absence of human, or any other consciousness – warrants further reflection.[27] Let us return to this startling passage from Merleau-Ponty: "the sun exists only within a world, and a world emerges at the confluence of a perceiver and the perceived".[28] What is the sun like in the absence of consciousness? It will have no appearance because there will be no sentient being to whom it appears. It will lack secondary qualities: it will not be yellow, warm, bright, etc. In a world without conscious subjects, electromagnetic radiation is not light as we experience it: a rose bathed in such radiation will be equally lacking in redness as a rose in daylight. The sun will not "have" a surface or depths for these are differentiated only from the viewpoint of a subject. The pre-conscious world will not even be dark and silent: as consciousness is removed, silence will lose its silence and the dark will go out with the light.[29] Nor will it have definite boundaries, insofar as its status as "one thing" or alternatively as a multitude of things with their individual boundaries will depend on the acuity of the attention paid to it. Intrinsically, it is not either a vast multiplicity of atoms, a single macroscopic object, or part of a galaxy. In short, without an observer, there is no basis for regarding the sun as a multitude of (uncollected) parts or as part of a greater whole such as a galaxy. This blocks the claim that, when the secondary qualities have been drained out of the universe, by the withdrawal of consciousness, it will still have primary qualities – size, shape, location, and number.

Few would see this as controversial. I want to go further, however, and suggest that the pre-conscious universe – notwithstanding that we accept that it unfolds according to laws – will not have dispositions or powers either. Let us, for simplicity, focus on a straightforward example of a disposition: the brittleness of ice. The brittleness is the *possibility* of the ice breaking when it is impacted upon. It is a connection between a present and a future state. Possibilities, future states, unlike actualities, exist only insofar as they are entertained. Material objects at any given time t_1 are what they are at time t_1. They are not what they might be at time t_2. They are confined to actuality and (as the other face of this), they do not have a future (or indeed their past) in their present. Dispositions such as brittleness towards a relatively limited range of future states are discerned by a generalizing consciousness that anticipates beyond actuality (the sum total of the material world) to future possibilities. It is easy to make the mistake of thinking of dispositions as being like states, and hence seem to be inherent and present in objects, because they are *standing* possibilities; nevertheless, they are future orientated. The brittleness of ice is expressed only in a future moment when it falls and is broken; neither its intact state at time t_1 or its fragmented state at time t_2 is in itself brittleness. A similar argument applies to powers: like dispositions, they subsist in the connection between successive states of a part of the universe and successive states are not co-present or self-connecting. A physical object at t_1 is what it is at t_1, end of story. Powers, being future-orientated, cannot be accommodated in a physical instant. Even absolutely basic dispositions such as inertia are dispositions – to continue in a particular state of being in motion or at rest; they correspond to law-like unfolding *over time* under the right conditions. In summary, dispositions and powers connect the universe at different times, when, in the absence of subjects, it can be only at one time at a time. If we are inclined to think that dispositions exist independently of consciousness, this is only because we imagine we can separate them from their *manifestations* for which consciousness is necessary.

The subjectless material world has total amnesia, lacking a present past and lacks a present future. The universe is what it is; only courtesy of conscious subjects does it become a realm of might-be (and couldn't be!). Only with the assistance of conscious subjects entertaining them is actuality a constellation of realized possibilities. There is no modality in the pre-conscious universe. Nothing is in itself (merely) possible, probable, certain, or (by necessary contrast with unreal) real.[30] And, as we have pointed out, universe in the absence of consciousness with its levels of attention is neither a collection of atoms, of macroscopic objects, or a unified cosmos. There is no privileged level of attention intrinsic to the material world.

We are now in a position to guess what the universe looks like prior to conscious subjects: nothing at all. It lacks (secondary) qualities, locations, scales, dispositions, powers, and so on. In short, it is featureless. The truism that there are no appearances in the absence of consciousness licenses the counter-intuitive conclusion that it is illegitimate to think of the irruption of the subject as the moment when the ready-to-be-given, finding a recipient, becomes The Given seeming to reveal how it was before the subject emerged.

To say this is not pure speculation. Featurelessness is evident in the most fundamental physical equations, which seem to encompass the totality of things. The universe insofar as it can be grasped by the general theory of relativity is a mathematical structure: tenseless, unchanging, it awaits a subject, the synthetic activity of the mind, to link its successive moments to a frame of reference and to one another and release its dynamism. This is how it is portrayed in the picture of the universe that relies on the very mathematics that has enabled us to arrive at the conclusion that the universe is nearly 14 billion years old.

We can now see the truth of the seemingly outrageous assertion that "the sun exists only within a world, and a world emerges at the confluence of a perceiver and the perceived". The sun that exists in the absence of conscious subjects or *even the possibility of such subjects* is not the hot, yellow, ball of fire, with a unity, a location, a trajectory, and dispositions and powers, that characterize the sun we know. The subjectless, "purely objective" appearance of objects is at best mathematical, though we should not perhaps overlook the strangeness, the almost paradoxical nature, of physics – which, until recently, has been ultimately rooted in experience, an empirical inquiry – reaching into places where there is not even the possibility of experience. (The less said about string theories and multiple universe hypotheses the better!).

Two questions now come into focus.

The first is this: How do we make the mistake of imagining that there was a present state of for example the sun at a time when, prior to the emergence of a conscious subject, it was not, and could not have been, present to anyone, since conscious subjects have not yet emerged? It is the consequence of our reaching into the world through the mediation of facts. Facts, as we discussed in Chapter 4, have two characteristics that distance them from (present tense) experience. First, they are impersonal and can seem to exist independently of any particular person's experience and hence (apparently) of anyone's or any experience. Secondly, they are timeless. This applies equally to facts about events that were experienced by conscious subjects as well as to those, such as the Big Bang, that were not witnessed. For example, the fact that the Battle of Hastings took place in 1066 is a) not translatable into a particular experience; and b) remains true for all time.[31] We may overlook this because timeless facts have a temporal face in the token thoughts and token sentences that express them. The disconnection between factual truths and experiences, which enable knowledge to take us to places beyond our own experiences, seem to lie beyond anything that anyone has experienced, and ultimately beyond

anything that *could* be experienced because they are prior to conscious subjects. Hence our capacity to talk authoritatively about the sun before there
were conscious subjects as if we were talking about something that has an
appearance, has evident properties, even in the absence of possible observers. So we think we can imagine the presence of the universe in the absence
of consciousness, notwithstanding that to do so is to think we can validly
imagine the visual appearance an object has before eyes have evolved. The
hybrid status of facts – impersonal generalities that are personalized tokens
emitted by persons – gives us the false impression we can reach beyond the
sum total of human experience and knowledge into the airless realm of the
subjectless universe, a universe into which a subject then irrupts courtesy of
natural selection or some such process.

The second question is this: What is given to subjectivity when it irrupts
from a subjectless universe? In short what is there to be *given* before the subject emerges as a *recipient*? It is evident from what we said earlier: precious
little. Experience consequently cannot simply be a revelation of what was
already there prior to experience as if consciousness were switched on like a
light illuminating a room, revealing the furniture that had been hidden in the
dark. What this tells us is that the pre-experienced universe does not have that
within itself to account for its being experienced or for what is experienced.
Being is not intrinsically the Given, even less is it responsible for the specific
contents of what is Given, for an experienced world that includes a sun in
space.[32]

The standard notion that the Given is the product of the physical interaction between that which is given (pre-conscious stuff) and that which receives
(the conscious subject or her body or brain) has already been ruled out. The
equally standard account of this interaction as causal, regulated by laws that
reign in the pre-conscious universe, exposes the impossibility of seeing how
such an interaction would make a minute part of the universe such as you, the
reader of this book, be aware of a larger part of the universe as *your* world.
Causal interactions between object A and object B (the body of a subject) are
not sufficient to make object B enjoy a consciousness that is a) about object
A, and b) true to the latter's putative intrinsic properties.

We have returned by a slightly different route to something that has
haunted this book: that intentionality cannot fit into the world picture defined
by what is revealed by the natural sciences. Consequently, there is nothing in
the material world to justify, account for, explain, the emergence of subjects,
experiencing a world – even less a world characterized by secondary qualities, locations, dispositions, powers, and so on. Evolving neural pathways have
nothing within them to make electromagnetic energy luminous, glowing and

bright, and capable of illuminating, revealing that which was not even concealed. The reality and the mystery of our transcendence of the natural world, of our own genesis within that world, and our individual and shared worlds within the universe, are beyond dispute. While science may be the most powerful approach to knowing, even understanding, and certainly controlling, the world in which we live, it has nothing to say to us about why, or how, Being became a given reality, with the irruption of the subject, of the "I am" within "It is". The idea of a time at which the subject emerges, marking the temporal boundary between the subjectless universe and one haunted by subjects, is deeply perplexing.

We are drawn back to the notion of the "reciprocal containment" that Quine spoke of and we referred to earlier in this chapter. The image of the super-ouroboros – a snake that swallows not only its own tail but its entire body, including its mouth – seems equally apt. The sinister overtones of the ouroboros are not entirely misplaced. The ascent up the cognitive ladder from sentience to world pictures, via awareness of material objects, a sense of a shared public space, and thence to theories that claim to encompass everything, delivers a view of the cosmos that cannot accommodate the experiencing subject – ourselves. The loss of the present tense, of the now that Einstein regretted his science could not accommodate, is only the most obvious aspect of the loss of presence, itself the ground floor from which all inquiry necessarily takes its rise.

Reciprocal containment is captured in the idea of our having a "double nature" lucidly expressed by Béatrice Han-Pile. We are world-constituting and an object in the world: "Man is both the epistemic condition of the possibility of knowledge ... and ... within the epistemic field thus opened. Without man nothing can be known, but as soon as there is knowledge Man appears to itself as empirically pre-existing his very opening of the epistemic field."[33]

This paradox haunts any endeavour to assume a metaphysical standpoint. E. J. Lowe observes that if we have no direct access to objects – there is filtration and projection – "we must ask: what place we ourselves have in such a world, seemingly so much of our own making. For we can hardly be supposed to make ourselves, in the object of which we speak".[34] There is an obvious echo here of the object-subject circularity discussed in Chapter 3. And it is replicated – though neuromaniacs are unaware of it – in the claim that the brain, an object in the world, is the very basis of there being objects experienced as being located in worlds. The wider point is this: the relationship "I" of the subject and the "it" of the objective world is complex, not to say knotted. The default notion of the human subject growing out of a pre-existing material world cannot be allowed to pass unchallenged.

Human transcendence

I hope I have said enough to justify: a) placing the human subject beyond the reach of the very science it has made possible; and b) acknowledging that we transcend nature.[35] We are transcendent creatures in virtue of which matter comes (at least in part) to be something that matters, its configurations being of importance to someone. Matter comes ultimately to be named as the most primordial and basic (and, let us be honest, the dimmest) stuff in the universe. There is nothing within it that enables it to become the Given. Givenness is a coproduction between what comes to be an object and the subject for whom it is an object.

A story based on natural science now seems even more problematic in view of the vexed relationship between natural and human time, a relationship that most certainly does not fall into a straightforward before-and-after sequence of natural time preceding human time.[36] The door is open to the development of what Paul Valéry's *M. Teste* called "mysticism without God".[37]

In the *Tractatus*, Wittgenstein asserted that "It is not *how* things are in the world that is mystical, but *that* it exists".[38] Against this, the entire argument of this book points towards a mystical understanding focused on the unfathomable mystery of the transformation of what-is into "that it is", into "that X is the case": the mystery of "I am" making a universe of matter into a world of thatter.

All of this is intended as a corrective (or part of one) to the assumption that secular humanism, informed by scientific knowledge of the world in which we live, must be committed to a disenchanted vision of ourselves in which we are a nano-nearly-nothing in a giga-something. Yes, there is an important sense in which the great spaces and times, when we locate ourselves in them, reduce us to something very insignificant indeed. But there is an equally important sense in which we are not thus reduced.

Accepting this is a necessary preliminary to any dialogue between believers and unbelievers, ensuring that it will not be a non-meeting of world-pictures: between unimaginably bleak scientific truths and rich, comforting, but sometimes poisonous myths; between secularists who bring nothing but desolate truths to the table and religious believers who offer only wishful thinking. The conversation should take place within one levelling observation; namely that the passage from sentience to world-pictures is a vast, mysterious jump, irrespective of whether we approach it from a scientific or a religious standpoint, from the standpoint of empirical inquiry or from that of religious doctrines. The competing accounts of the origin of subjectivity − stories and myths versus equations and tables − need a point of convergence, to be explored in dialogue.[39]

Before we consider the possibility of dialogue, we need to look more carefully at what a secular humanist might bring to the table, in the light of what our thoughts are about human nature.

SPIRITUAL IRREDENTISM

> Man is double. There are two beings in him; an individual being which has its foundation in the organism, and a social being which represents the highest reality in the intellectual and moral order. Paul Carly[40]

> The great things of the past which filled our fathers with enthusiasm do not excite the same ardour in us ... In a word, the old gods are growing old or are already dead. But this state of incertitude and confused agitation cannot last for ever. A day will come when our societies will know again those hours of creative effervescence, in the course of which new formulae are found which serve for a while a guide to humanity ... There are no gospels which are immortal, but neither is there any reason for believing that humanity is incapable of inventing new ones. Émile Durkheim[41]

The putative irruption of the subject is the point of origin of our human transcendence. Armed with this realization, we have prepared the ground for what I believe to be the supremely important philosophical, perhaps cultural, task for contemporary humanism. Let us call it "spiritual irredentism". We associate the term "irredentism" with political movements advocating the restoration to a country of any territory formerly belonging to it. Spiritual irredentism is the project of claiming back for humanity spiritual territory that we have donated to a divine being and which is curated, managed, mediated by churches, synagogues, temples, and mosques and their attendant hierarchy of priests, imams, and ministers.

In the previous chapters we have identified the multitude of ways in which we are offset from nature, and, in this sense, we are transcendent creatures. While our transcendence has its most impressive expression in the sciences, in art, and – of course – religion, it is implicit in every moment of our lives as conscious agents.

To say this may be to provoke the surprise of Moliere's M. Jourdain who is astonished to learn that he has been speaking prose all his life:

Monsieur Jourdain: Oh really? So, when I say: "Nichole bring me my slippers and fetch my nightcap" is that prose?
Philosophy Master: Most clearly
Monsieur Jourdain: Well, what do you know about that! These forty years now I've speaking prose without knowing it![42]

Some, like M. Jourdain, may have thought I have set the bar too low. Surely there is more to transcendence than the "mere" fact that we are persons as well as organisms, and that those persons are outside, as well as inside, of time, and that they are selves who are also, and centrally, agents who can act on the material world as if from without. By a nice irony, however, the miracle of the human person becomes especially clear when we see the universe through the eyes of the very science that is supposed to reduce us to organisms subject to the laws revealed by natural science. If reality were confined to the world as described by natural science, then we truly transcend that reality – if only (as pointed out in Chapter 10) because we have created the science that describes it. We should be grateful, therefore, to the profoundly mistaken idea that, if we are not supernatural beings, with eternal souls, created by God, it follows that we are mere pieces of nature, organisms ultimately to be accounted for by the laws of biology, chemistry, and ultimately physics. It does a brilliant job of highlighting by omission our transcendence of the physical world.

Some clarification is called for. To say of something that it is "transcendent" is to claim that it "exceeds usual limits" or "extends or lies beyond the limits of ordinary experience". There is, however, another aspect of the meaning of the term as it is used in theology: "transcending the universe or material existence". It typically designates those aspects of God's nature and power that are independent of the material universe and are beyond physical laws. While this latter may seem to place transcendence out of reach of secular humanity, my central thesis has been that we transcend the universe, understood as material stuff, at every moment of our daily lives. Transcendence originates with the intentional relationship between perceiving subjects and what they perceive; grows with the sharing of intentionality within and between subjects; and is expressed in the extra-natural human world of knowledge, norms and laws, institutions, and artefacts. In our capacity to understand the universe, we transcend that which we understand – most spectacularly in the case of science which, as we have observed, cannot be accommodated in the natural world it describes. To step back and see the laws of nature – as enablers, constraints, and a constant background to our lives – is to rise above them.[43]

It is this transcendence, encountered and acknowledged individually and collectively, as the human community emerges from the natural order, that humanity donates to divine beings when it invents, or is collectively possessed by, religion. There is a continuity between transcendence as the moment-to-moment reality of human consciousness, the quality of certain special experiences, and a realm of being that is posited as being beyond this world. Our sense of our extra-natural nature, our difference or distance from the world in which we find ourselves, is transformed into the intuition of a supernatural being to whom we, and the natural world, owe their existence. Spiritual irredentism is the endeavour to reclaim that territory which humanity, voluntarily or involuntarily, has ceded to a Being Who goes under the name of God; to recover for our collective self-awareness, self-understanding, and, yes, self-appreciation, what we have projected into the divine.

Some readers will detect a striking unoriginality in this project. Reversing the relationship between Man and God, so that God is seen as the creation of Man rather than Man as the creation of God, is most particularly associated with the nineteenth-century philosopher Ludwig Feuerbach and, of course, Durkheim whom we have already discussed. These two thinkers provide a useful starting point for anyone aiming to reclaim human transcendence for human beings, on the basis that the gods are projections of our collective transcendence.

Feuerbach's notion that The Holy Family is a projection of the human family is compelling.[44] As he points out, if gods were not formed in our own image, we would not know how to address them in order to seek their help and guidance. "God [must be] the super-human, the infinite being ... nevertheless, *the infinitely human, the super-human* human being – a being that is *more, infinitely more man* than man himself – a seeing, knowing, feeling, loving being as man is – a being that is *more, infinitely more man* than man".[45] God as an intentional object is the most spectacular product of our joined, collective, intentionality; and our distance from God is within our collective selves. It has been strikingly expressed by Scruton: "The gods spring from our unconscious needs and strivings – they are thrown off by that great explosion of moral energy, whereby the human community first emerges from the natural order and idealizes itself".[46]

Feuerbach's final work *Theogony* (even more than his better-known *Essence of Christianity*) spells out the extent to which our desires, in particular our desire for fulfilment or completion of our unfulfilled or incomplete nature, have been instrumental in the creation of God. Men have invented God in their own idealized image and then treated their creation as their supreme Lord who demands obedience and worship. Durkheim's view that God and the spiritual realm are symbolic expressions of the sense of the collective consciousness of society, that religious images encode social relations and the dominance of society over the individual, complements Feuerbach's vision of man-made God.

These insights, according to which "instead of the gods creating the cosmos, the cosmos in the individual form of human beings, giving rein to their imagination, created the gods", profound though they are, remain only a starting point for twenty-first-century humanism.[47] It is not sufficient to acknowledge that it is ourselves – explicitly our collective selves in Durkheim's interpretation and the perfections of our own species as well as the forces operating within nature in the later Feuerbach – that we have projected into the invisible, infinitely distant realm occupied by God. This is not enough to turn on its head the relationship between God and man by identifying worship of the divine as the most spectacular expression of humanity's capacity for transcendence. We need to look harder and more steadfastly at what it is that we have projected into the heavens and our (astonishing) capacity to do so: at our own nature and to that which is transcendent in human being. Much of this book has been devoted to this purpose.

We should hold fast to the thought that there must be something god-like in a creature that has the capacity to create gods. If God does not exist, this makes all the more remarkable our sense of a Beyond all beyonds, of an afterlife; the meaning we invest in sacred objects, places, and times; the rituals, creeds, the liturgies where rituals and creeds meet; the priestly hierarchies, and complex doctrines, myths, and allegories encompassing the totality of things; and the temples, cathedrals, the sacred music, art, and texts, that reflect our sense of the divine. Again, "How mighty are the works of man!" Anyone who doubts the capacity of man to transcend the "it is" of nature should reflect on the significance of the most commonplace stained-glass window, the huge organizational and discursive feat of the nearly 20-year Council of Trent, the thousands of years of commentaries on sacred texts. The transcendence that enables humanity to live a life backlit by the supernatural is not at a distance from the human world and our humanity but within that world and within our humanity.

So much for the case for spiritual irredentism. But what do we do with a sense of our own nature as undiminished by religion and unreduced by science? It may be reassuring that the metaphysical grounds for seeing ourselves as transcendent – intentionality, our relationship to time, "at", and "that", selfhood, the miracle of our agency – are a benign starting point for a new way of thinking about our lives. The fundamental thesis of this book – that we are neither fallen angels trying to please an irascible and capricious God nor unrisen apes acting out a biological prescription – should not of itself warrant conflict with, or persecution, or subjugation of our fellows. The markers of transcendence are universal. They would seem to offer nothing to justify hatred, contempt, conflict, persecution, or discrimination. They are, for example, distant from the idea of a Chosen People who have a not infrequent sense of historical destiny. They would scarcely justify: any claim by a subset of humanity that they are uniquely working out God's purposes for all mankind; a division into a superior "us" and an inferior "them"; or aggressive proselytizing, or an addition to the monopoly spiritualism of dominant religious institutions. Acknowledging the "thatosphere" – shared by all and equally – would not seem to offer much ground for despising one's fellows or to stoning them to death for blasphemy.

Its ungainsayable universalism would seem equally unlikely to lead to the spectacular horrors of the secular religions of Nazism and communism, where individuals, defined by class or race or both are seen as legitimate targets for state-sponsored injustice, and injuries ranging from privation of livelihood, to imprisonment, and execution that in the twentieth century exceeded in horror the worst outrages justified by religious belief.

Unfortunately, this makes the next step – mobilizing what we know of our fundamental nature to our individual and collective advantage – seem less clear. Its very benignity makes a philosophically founded humanism unlikely to arouse passions equal in strength to those directed against putative enemies of the faith and bind believers in a defensive fellowship against infidels.

It would be dishonest to suggest that I have a satisfactory answer to this most pressing question for a humanism that wants to define itself positively rather than merely in opposition to religious belief. Getting a clearer view of ourselves is only a starting point and we have to get beyond this, if humanism is to find a growing rather than a diminishing place in the world and human affairs, given that the trends towards secularization may well be in reverse.

The examples of secular religions – ranging from the high ambitions of Comte's Religion of Humanity with its Positivist Catechism to the School for Life with its Sunday services, god-free sermons, and sing-alongs of "It's a wonderful life" – are not encouraging. There is nothing to equal the visions that created the awe-inspiring places of worship, the spectacular ceremonials, and art of the religion whose spiritual spaces irredentist secularism would wish to reclaim. Comte's minutely prescriptive ritualism, J. S. Mill commented, could "never have been written by a man who had ever laughed".[48] And if we classify Marxist communism or fascism or neoliberalism as secular religions, the prospects seem even less encouraging.

In what follows I flag up some of the problems for the future of a positive humanism and suggest directions in which answers may be found. The reader who takes away the impression that I am stronger on problems than solutions is not mistaken.

What secularism cannot offer

Sacred places

When M. Jourdain discovers rather late that he has been speaking prose all his life, he may just as well have been disappointed as gratified. Perhaps prose is not all it is cracked up to be. Humanists likewise may feel that, in extending the sphere of transcendence to encompass most of our conscious existence is to cheapen the currency – even if it is allowed that, in the light of the dictionary definition, "transcendence" must be indexed to a baseline and hence is irreducibly relative rather than absolute. Nevertheless, my position may seem existentially or even ontologically too democratic.

The more traditional religious notions of the transcendent are associated with a *hierarchy* – of beings, of phenomena, of places, times and of course persons. The consensus among anthropologists and sociologists of religion is the essence of religious belief is bound up with the idea of the sacred encircled by the profane. Without the contrast between the ground of the ordinary and the figure of the extraordinary, to which latter praise and worship might be directed, there would appear to be no anchor for a sense of mystery and gratitude. A week that consists only of Sundays is not necessarily different from a week of Wednesdays. Or to make every day a private Sunday may downgrade every day to a Wednesday. The sacred *needs* the contrast of the profane for its special glow. If all places and all things are equal, they may seem equally profane rather than equally sacred. Even humanists may find it difficult, as Emmanuel Durand puts it, "to escape the injunctions of Leviticus. Holiness requires separating spaces, as well as rituals of consecration and purification".[49] When, as science advanced, miracles and epiphanies as well as ordinary events were gathered up into general laws, the result was disenchantment rather than universalization of enchantment. The wonder of sunrise was incorporated into a meaningless circulation of no-longer-heavenly bodies. A gaze in which the ordinary is extraordinary is not easily maintained. While, as Wittgenstein pointed out, flames are not more mysterious than furniture[50] – after all, the wood in a chair was fashioned out of the swallowed flames of the sun and the chair itself is the product of the marriage of the wood with the ingenuity of mankind – it is difficult to upgrade the mystery of furniture rather than downgrade the mystery of flames.

There seems to be a solution staring us in the face: infidels should appropriate the sacred spaces that have been involuntarily bequeathed by believers, acknowledging that they are part of the common heritage of humanity. Less obvious is how this may be accomplished. The afterlife of churches is neither encouraging nor inspiring: uncongenial community centres, exhibition halls, or emptiness, stained glass replaced by plywood, and ruin. Respecting sacred texts as part of a cultural heritage looks backward to what they have meant "to them" rather than forward to what they still mean or might mean in the future "to us". The Bible is a rich source of quotations and of titles for books and a gold-mine for anthropologists rather than a means of putting us in touch with the transcendence of our nature.

Philip Larkin's "Church Going" is a candid and penetrating meditation on the endeavour to engage with the monuments of beliefs that in increasingly secular England seem to belong irreversibly to history. Larkin's narrator who has "... no idea / What this accoutred frowsty barn is worth" is pleased, nevertheless, "... to stand in silence here" before he signs the visitor's book, donates an Irish sixpence, leaves and reflects "... the place was not worth stopping for". The poem, however, ends with something on the verge of a revelation as to what the church might mean – and we shall return to this.

Profound belonging

During the course of a public debate in a bookshop, my interlocuter, an eminent, extraordinarily gifted cleric, was challenged by a member of the audience to say why he believed in God. His reply was characteristically honest. In his youth, he said, he came to know people who were believers and was struck by the joy in their lives. Using a variation of the immortal words of a diner in *When Harry Met Sally*, he said "I wanted to have what they are having". There could be no more compelling support for the idea that, at the heart of religion, is the sense of *belonging* to a living community whose connectedness transcends the dozens of temporary, usually instrumental, associations to which we perforce belong in daily life. Participation, not the outcomes of arguments, is at the heart of religion. What Stuart Kelly said of Judaism, that "it began as an ethnicity and became a philosophy", is true of most religions. Belonging is first, believing second.[51]

Of course, humanists may identify their own community as "mankind" but, compared with the circles of family, other loved ones, friends, colleagues, chance acquaintances, "mankind" may be a colourless abstraction. Collegiate bodies, teams, campaigning groups, people united by other common interests may be the occasion for much camaraderie but they lack the vertical dimension of congregations who are gathered together in the name of God. There is nothing to equal the profound togetherness – or at least the idea of it – of those who are bound by a creed uttered in and rituals enacted in a sacred space, under the guidance of clerics who mediate between humanity and the divine. And what could compare with the promise posted outside my local church: "Jesus welcomes all with love and hope"?

We already noted how secular thinkers may find wider separation, rather than closer unity, in the depths of thought: the more profound our meditations, the more we retreat into solitude. Thoughts that endeavour to do justice to our transcendence do not fit easily in the overwhelmingly practical associations that serve us in daily lives. Whereas religious beliefs unite believers, secular metaphysical beliefs may be dis-affiliating. In my 40 years as a doctor, I recall only a handful of philosophical conversations with colleagues – all with the co-dedicatee of this book.

There are, of course, examples of belonging together for spiritual purposes without the apparatus of churches and priests and the lightest of light-touch creeds. An obvious instance is Quakerism, which is rooted in a belief in the ability of each human being to access "the light within" or the "God in everyone", and promulgates "a priesthood of all believers". Worship is not programmed: "the holy communion in the manner of friends", with an "expectant waiting upon God", takes place in meeting houses rather than churches. About 30 per cent of British Quakers are agnostic, atheist or humanist.[52]

The moral track record of Quakerism, whose closest approximation to a sacrament is a sacramental meal with others, is impressive by the standard of other religions. Quakers have been leaders in the fight to abolish slavery, in promoting prison reform, and in establishing programmes of social justice. An "extremist" Quaker might be one who is silent for two hours instead of one. The inter-tribal blood-baths of Christianity, Islam, Buddhism and other religions conducted in God's name are unknown to pacifist Quakers. They remain a small minority, albeit a beneficent one, in contemporary life and a good model for humanism – perhaps because they are (as has been suggested) humanists.

Convergence of meaning and purpose

Religious belief not only provides the basis for a profound connectedness with others – living and meeting in the sight of God – but also for a connectedness within one's self. In earlier chapters, we discussed the unsuccessful search for a fully coherent life, inwardly lit by a single sense of purpose, and overall source of meaning. This is one way of identifying a hunger that remains unappeased even when other hungers, ambitions, all appetites and desires, have been met. It is difficult to characterize this hunger, not the least because it is not easy to be sure when one is speaking for mankind, when one is speaking for one's own culture, and when one is speaking autobiographically.

Cue for a return to Larkin's "Church Going". The poet is drawn by "a hunger in himself to be more serious", that seems to be acknowledged in the sacred space of a church:

> A serious house on serious earth it is,
> In whose blent air all our compulsions meet,
> Are recognised, and robed as destinies.[53]

Thus the promise of a place of convergence, like the vanishing point in a perspectival painting, from which all our goals, ambitions, duties, occupations, preoccupations, can be seen in true perspective. If it cannot be found within ourselves, or our secular world, this is because our lives of necessity demand a division of attention. What is more, if the endeavour to sum the totality of meanings is not going to result in meaninglessness, that total cannot be located at the same level as the meanings that are summed. The fundamental challenge of secular humanism is to find something comparable to the believers' "goal of all human existence": "to praise, worship, and serve God".[54]

Thus, the challenge to secular thought of finding some comparable way of gathering up all the meaning, depth, variety, of one's life, its joy and sorrows, tying together all the narratives, transient and life-long, of one's days. Such a connectedness must also connect one with others in a fellowship that goes deeper than the many, largely instrumental, relations we have with one another – our personhood is, after all, interpersonal. Only this way could a heightened, more continuous, awareness of our own transcendence become a way of life, a way of being.

As we discussed in Chapter 9, the point where "all our compulsions meet" cannot be reliably supplied, as many secular thinkers have hoped, by working for a better future for mankind. Even where utopian visions do not end in catastrophe, we do not always know where that future lies or what will be the consequences of actions, however noble, of labouring to bring it about. What's more, we live only one life, and being a small part of a gigantic enterprise cannot redeem our transience, the inevitable obliteration of our world.

Consolation

If the science and the technology that has transformed our world largely for the better has been made possible by denying ourselves wishful thinking, we may need to learn how to reinsert our wishes into our thinking. The most profound of those wishes – what we might call the master-wish – is to evade extinction; and it is here that secular humanism has its most conspicuous failure. The tragi-comic endeavours of the Silicon Valley visionaries to cancel the death sentence that comes with life expose the futility of the endeavour to find permanent safety without relying on the protecting hands of God. It is a bitter irony that the fundamental limitation of an irredentist humanism is inseparable from the ultimate source, ground, or condition of transcendence: our nature as embodied subjects.

The "I" will share the transience of the "it". Comparing the "I" of the subject and the "it" of the body with recto and verso of a sheet of paper is reassuringly distant from dualism but in other respects rather less reassuring, given that recto is unlikely to outlive verso. Nothing in the secular reclamation of our transcendence can palliate anguish at our own mortality and grief at the mortality of those whom we love. Indeed, it is our very transcendence, our self-awareness and our capacity for objective knowledge, that elevates the fact of our transience into awareness of mortality. The objective standpoint reveals that whoever is born is old enough to die and our continuation through time is a journey into increasing improbability. Death may result from the most trivial of causes. A bang on the head can cancel all that was brought into being, nurtured, nourished, and educated. Alternatively, there may be a protracted process of losing faculties like a tree shedding its leaves, ending with a return to the original helplessness of material objects.

Secular humanism has not only to live with a tragic sense of life and acknowledge that there is no ultimate safety but must also accept that there is no justice or retribution – reward for goodness or punishment for wickedness. Nothing will distinguish the secular afterlife of Hitler from that neither enjoyed nor endured by those who devoted their lives to goodness, or the posthumous fate of tyrants from those whose innocent lives they made living Hell. As a commentator on Feuerbach expressed it: "What refuge would we find among the countless evils of life, if religions would not offer us some means of atonement and some calming of the terrors by which we are constantly plagued and driven?"[55]

Secular sources of salvation

Such are the obstacles in the way of any attempt to transform our transcendence into the life-blood of a *Weltanschauung* that can bring consolation and lighten the sense of the darkness encroaching on our joys and on celebration of the gift of life that has no Giver. In what follows, I want to explore some ways in which we might palliate secular despair: a grateful sense of our shared history; love; art; and philosophy.

Gratitude

The most solemn moment in the Christian ritual is the Eucharist. Holy communion reaffirms the community of souls as they share the body and blood of Christ, to become one in His name. Ex-communication – denial of the right to take communion and being expelled from the community – is the most profound punishment for a believer.

At the heart of the Eucharist is something that secular communities may share: gratitude. "Eucharist" is derived from the Greek word for "thank you" and taking Holy Communion is an act of Thanksgiving. The recipient of those thanks is God. Might it not be possible, therefore, if God is a human invention, to redirect those thanks to our fellow humans? The grounds for such thanks are self-evident: we are the inheritors of the riches – art, science, technology, government, civil society – that have been handed down to us by our forebears whose often agonising labours made them possible. We owe them gratitude for social and cognitive advances and for their practical applications that have liberated us, if only temporarily, from the mindless cruelty of nature. We are enabled by our fellows.[56]

Is this mere sentimentality? Some look back on history and see a blood-bath motivated by the base passions of individuals hungry for power and riches. Nietzsche spoke of history as "an experimental refutation of the so-called moral order of things".[57] Such freshman cynicism overlooks something fundamental: that in the absence of humanity, there is no such thing as history – the convergence of the experiences of hundreds of millions of conscious beings into a collective narrative; and that the profoundest aspect of human history is the insertion of "ought" into what merely "is" and (admittedly incomplete) transformation of "ought" into moral codes that regulate some of our lives all of the time and many of our lives most of the time. The very idea of a moral order is inconceivable without the complex societies that are a late consequence of the irruption of subjects that are distinct and yet communicating into the insentient universe.

It is against this fundamental understanding – and acknowledgement of the progressive trends we discussed in Chapter 9 – that we should remember and thank those to whom we owe so much for the pacification of nature and the self-pacification of humanity, as a consequence of which our lives are longer, healthier, safer, more comfortable, and (perhaps) richer than they would be in a state of nature. Such gratitude, encompassing those who fabricated the pebble chopper, tamed fire, and discovered electromagnetism, the legislators, campaigners, who have made civil society possible, acknowledging the greatness of the individuals and collectives, who contributed so much to human advance, would be an entirely appropriate form of ancestor worship.

This at least is one way of reclaiming from the gods what we humans have donated to them. Whether this should be bolstered by the establishment of shrines such as a Panthéon (itself the rededicated magnificent church of St Genevieve) to house the remains of secular saints is something that might be discussed, if only as a reminder that humanity's self-worship is sometimes connected with bloodshed. And there remains the question of the extent to which we should focus on individuals rather than the soil, water, and light, of the collective that made them possible.

Love

Love – of man for God and God for man – lies at the heart of many religions, most notably the Christian faith. In my discussion of meaning in our lives, I passed rather quickly over love. In his extraordinary reflection on the place of love in contemporary life, Simon May has argued that "consciously or unconsciously, we increasingly rely on human love to supply the consolations of the God in whom so many no longer believe – or, even if they do, no longer necessarily hold to be the source or catalyst of *all* genuine love";[58] "Human love – of almost any type, from romantic to parental – is widely expected to be unconditional, disinterested, enduring, and affirming of the loved one in just the all-encompassing manner (of remarkably recent origin) in which God is said to love".[59]

For May, love is:

> the joy inspired by whomever or whatever we experience as rooting, or as promising to root, our life ... This joy can be rapturous or quiet; unqualified or admixed with pain, hate, jealousy, and even disgust. It is born of self-interest: to be at home in a world that we supremely value, which I take to be among the greatest of all goods and of all human needs. It sets us on a trajectory of seeking to attain such rootedness in and through relationship with the loved one. And it can motivate the most devoted self-giving of which humans are capable. ... On this picture, therefore, love is grounded in a promise of

"ontological rootedness", a promise glimpsed in another "of a home" in the world – or ... in a very particular world that we supremely value – towards the attainment of which our lives become powerfully oriented, though the promise can never be perfectly fulfilled, for no final state of groundedness is available in a human life.[60]

There seems to be the possibility of the convergence of meaning and value on one focal place in our life: the "master-aim" of love can be the master-aim of our lives. We have the intuition of something non-accidental in an accidental life full of accidents: the missing other half, tailored to an aching hole in one's self. We experience the loved one as "calling us to our as yet unlived life or destiny".[61]

What can secular life find to replace the love of, or by, God? The most obvious place is romantic love, where the beloved is valued more than life itself. It has inspired some of the greatest art, the most poignant cries of joy and woe, in all cultures over the centuries. Sexual attraction, overwhelming admiration, a sense of the other's mystery (that echoes the previously unacknowledged mystery of one's own existence) converge in an emotion that seems to gather up all that one is. Nothing can seem more important than that one's feelings should be reciprocated. The accidents by which the other entered one's life are redeemed and so, too, is the contingency of one's own life. "She is the one; we were made for each other; this is my destiny". Devotion translates into a life directly or indirectly dedicated to the other.

Romantic love, if not unrequited, is always at risk of disillusionment. The *princess lointaine* loses the distance that lends enchantment. The handsome young hero becomes the boring middle-aged fart sharing the hum-drum reality of years in which each takes the other for granted and attention is redirected towards, or divided with, other preoccupations. Ecstatic co-presence subsides to a cohabitation, an interweaving of the banal routines of daily life. The longed-for togetherness becomes an inescapable condition. The tendrils of practical life choke the sense of mystery, of magic, as the partners to the romance work out their relationship in working and playing together and apart. Contingency returns with a vengeance: "He married a woman to stop her getting away / Now she's there all day".[62] This is not inevitable and, in many lives, the quiet joy of companionship, mutual affection, respect and concern, and shared dreams and projects, memories, interests, and hopes, a thousand modes of intimacy, is more than enough compensation for the loss of the long torments and the brief ecstasies of romance. But there remains the threat – always to be fulfilled – of loss, of bereavement, that is greater the happier the partnership.

May argues that, just as romantic love displaced love of God, the latter is "gradually giving way to parental love as the *archetypal* love: namely the love without which one's life cannot be deemed to be complete or truly flourishing; the love that traces, or points to, the domain of the sacred".[63] Parental love is rooted in the desire:

> to locate the sacred in the everyday world, instead of in transcendence of it, such as in God or in a romantic union that is taken to abolish the distinct individuality of the lovers; the war on risk and suffering that marks our age, a war to which the security of the child has become totemic; the unprecedented degree to which childhood has come to be seen as *the* key to a flourishing life; the value placed on individual autonomy, to which love for the child is (*pace* harassed parents!) far more attuned than is, say, romantic love; a turn away from the belief that love can have a final goal, such as union with the loved one, or be marked by an event that "consummates" it, in the sense that it could have in traditional conceptions of love for God or the romantic partner (a development that is one symptom of the long struggle to abandon teleological ways of thinking); and the will to empower women, by achieving equality or even superiority not merely in roles that men have hitherto played and defined, but through roles that, it is accepted, only she can play and define.[64]

Here is not the place to do justice to May's rich and thought-provoking thesis. A comment or two will have to suffice. Parental love has the advantage over the love of God, in that its object is at least undeniably present and the response of the loved one is visible, even if not always what is hoped. It can be utterly consuming: pride, joy, anxiety, practicalities of caring, grief, emotions large and small. And, unlike romantic love, it does not rely on a smokescreen of mystery that may not survive consummation or the "long littleness" of a shared life. Parental love is not rooted in fantasy based on desire: there are no scales to fall from the eyes. The power relationship has a different kind of asymmetry: it begins in total dependency of the beloved on the one who loves; between one who has overwhelming needs and another who meets them. Parental love has a kind of purity that comes from a profound longing (often anxious) for the happiness and well-being of another – the child. It is not conditional on the child having objectively admirable qualities. As Touchstone said, heartbreakingly, of his son "An ill-favoured thing, sir, but mine own".[65]

But, but, but … the initial power asymmetry, the control over the child that is the other side of overwhelming responsibility, must give way to a different kind of relationship. Parents have to learn to relinquish control. The intervals between episodes of care or between interventions lengthens, and the child's presence becomes more intermittent. The long-for stages of growing up are also signs of growing away. The child becomes more opaque as she develops her own life, countries of mind, heart, and soul, that she may or may not share with her parent. The parent, even when loved and respected, becomes a less constant point of reference. Eventually, the family home is merely a place to visit as the centre of gravity of her life moves away, when she finds new significant others, most importantly a partner with whom she has children of her own, and a home of her own.

Thus, the not entirely happy trajectory of parental love, even when it is not disrupted by the agony of conflict or greater agony of bereavement. As a substitute for the love of God, it falls short precisely because, when parenting is successful, it has a built-in trajectory beginning with the utter dependence of the loved one and proceeding to a more equal relationship between two adults. Divine love, by constrast, is not only absolute but also unchanging.

Art

With the decline of religion, at least among the articulate and affluent, in the West in the nineteenth century, a tradition emerged of looking to art for salvation. As Roger Scruton has expressed it:

> The romantic poets and painters turned their back on religion and sought salvation through art. They believed in the genius of the artist, endowed with a special capacity to transcend the human condition in creative ways, breaking all the rules in order to achieve a new order of experience. Art becomes an avenue to the transcendental, the gateway to a higher kind of knowledge.[66]

While "salvation through art" has become a familiar mantra, it has rarely been made clear what it might mean. In what respect does it provide salvation? And who is saved: the artists themselves; or those who read, listen to, or look at what they have created?

Perhaps the most ambitious and explicit endeavour to deliver redemption through art was in the work of Richard Wagner, described by Scruton as "one of the great humanists of modern times ... [but] a humanist of a peculiar kind who recognized humanity's religious need and tried to make man his own redeemer, so as to ennoble the human beyond the divine".[67] The church as theatre is turned on its head and we have the theatre as a church.[68]

Wagner saw his vision for the role of art as being realized in the *gesamt-kunstwerk* that united the arts in a spectacle in which music and drama were equal partners. The work would bring to life eternal myths that (in Scruton's words) "acquaint us with ourselves and our condition, using symbols and characters that give objective form to our inner compulsions".[69] And as Wagner himself expressed it: "It is reserved to art to salvage the kernel of religion, inasmuch as the mythical images which religion would wish to be believed as true are apprehended in art for their symbolic value, and through ideal representation art reveals the concealed deep truth within them".[70]

It is clear, however, as Scruton points out, that salvation through art does not promise life after death. Neither the artist nor the lover of art evades the fate of all living creatures. The spectacular posthumous existence of Wagner has not been lived, even less enjoyed, by the incomparable, if personally flawed, genius who died in 1883. Does art, however, offer salvation *within* life? If so of what kind? In particular does it release us from the tyranny of "And then … and then … and then", ever more powerful as the distraction economy penetrates more of our lives? Does it offer a point of convergence that the succession of transient meanings and purposes seem to deny us? Might it be a place where (to repeat Larkin) "all our compulsions meet / Are recognised, and robed as destinies"? Merely to ask these questions is to see the answers; but before we do so, we should remind ourselves of the extraordinary nature of art.

Nietzsche, initially a disciple and then an adversary of Wagner, famously declared that "without music, life would be a mistake".[71] And there are various ways in which the arts may seem to correct "the mistake" of life. A work of art, the product of a heightened and, perhaps more importantly, connected attention, invites us more fully to experience our experiences, and thereby to satisfy a profound human hunger to be more completely there. It is appropriate to explore this further; but first a few *caveats* are in order.

Any "theory of art" has to deal with, perhaps over-ride, certain awkward truths. The very notion of art is baggy, with much contested territory round the edges. That is why it's possible in certain circles to make a reputation as an artist simply by presenting as art something that isn't art and provoking, and mocking, the response that it isn't art. Here is not the place to dwell on the shocking yawn of most "conceptual" art.[72] And it is reasonable to be sceptical about a theory that tries to encompass statues, novels, and symphonies, or netsukes, poems, and string quartets. Any such theory much be cast in very general terms. And it won't of course help us to say what is good art and what is not. But this is not our task here.

Art has fulfilled many functions in the history of mankind and in the history of our own lives. It may sometimes be just another kind of fun, a pleasurable distraction, another way of passing the time. So what is the distinctive nature and significance of the satisfaction that art might afford us when it is at its best and we are at our most receptive?[73] I want to offer a thesis[74] about art in secular life: that it meets a need arising out of the very nature of our experience; more specifically, that it addresses what may be characterized as a hollowness in the present tense of human consciousness. At the heart of the thesis is the observation that we do not fully experience our experiences; as a consequence, we may be bothered by the sense that our lives are somehow eluding us. This would hardly matter when we are hungry, thirsty, afraid, or in pain, or suffering the many woes humans inflict on each other; or even when we go about our daily business of ensuring, however indirectly, our survival, or making a living, discharging our duties towards others. Art finds its ultimate place not in the Kingdom of Means but in the Kingdom of Ends – where we seek "life more abundant", to borrow the arresting phrase from St John's Gospel.

The need addressed by art has its roots in our curious and somehow unhappy condition as beings who have awoken, but only incompletely, out of the state of being an organism. Half-awakened, we are constantly engaged in making explicit sense of the world and of our fellow humans. This sense remains tantalizingly incomplete and stubbornly local. We may consequently be haunted by the feeling that we have not fully realized our own existence, have not fully realized that we exist, have not fully realized the scale and scope of what we are and of the world we live in. It is a kind of *existential numbness.*

Such numbness may present in different ways but it is most evident when we seek out experience for its own sake and note a mismatch between the experience we actually have and the idea we had of the same experience that led us to seek it out. At the very simplest level, experience does not measure up to expectation. At its root is the intrinsic dynamism of meaning; the "-ing" in meaning.

Our sense of not fully experiencing our experiences is compounded by the feeling that they are insufficiently connected. We may characterize this lack of connectedness in different ways: for example, that we are always small-sampling our lives and our worlds; that we have no overview on ourselves; and that we cannot close the gap between what we are and what we know, between our experiences and our ideas, our moment-to-moment realities and the life and world of which they are a part. This in part is what is behind the sense we have already discussed that we are condemned to live in "The Dominion of And". In "The Kingdom of And Then, And Then", in deserts of et cetera, or repetition or variety, of succession and parataxis, we pass on from one thing to the next, without ever arriving, without ever being entirely *at* any of them. We seem to advance through our days never *having been fully there* or *never having fully grasped our being there.*

How does art address this hollowness in the present tense? In part it does so through reconciling the particular experience of what is there with the general idea or ideal of what might be there, our abstract notions with concrete instances. A work of art is a concretely realized idea – an idea as large as those that haunt our consciousness through anticipation and memory. One approach to understanding how art unites these adversaries is through the general concept of artistic *form* – a complex and much-contested notion I could spend many pages discussing without reaching a satisfactory account. Let me however, throw out a few strikingly unoriginal, Aesthetics 101, hints.

"Form" designates "inner shape" or *arrangement of parts*. We may think of form in art as that by virtue of which things otherwise experienced or considered separately are brought together: that *unity in variety* which conveys the sense of sameness in difference: it is an explicit paradigm of what is implicit in the synchronic and diachronic unities of the self. Form gives a sense of *stillness underneath change*, and to the Aristotelian idea of form as the *moving unmoved*. The common function or effect of formal features that unify across variety is to integrate experiences that would otherwise be separate. Art sometimes brings incongruous and disparate things together: outrageous couplings, dissonant discourses, disjunct objects. More importantly, and most evidently in literary art, the nears and fars of the world, booty from the four corners of the empire of experience, may be gathered in a mind-portable space. This permits, indeed invites, expansion into something larger than the quotidian succession of experience; something, in short, answering to what we hope to experience when we seek out experience for its own sake. The formal structure integrates over time in music, over space in the visual arts (though we seem to unpack space from music and we experience paintings and sculptures in time), and over a multidimensional hyperspace in referential forms such as literature.

How does this palliate the hollowing of the present tense by experiences being eaten from within by the ideas of experience? The question is most readily answered in the case of the most formal of all the arts: music. It is only a weakly, or secondarily, referential medium whose materials belong to itself alone. The ordering of its elements is not significantly dictated by an external (extra-musical) reality. Form and subject matter are one – hence Walter Pater's famous assertion that "All art constantly aspires to the condition of music".[75]

Think of the relationship between a group of musical ideas, the form in which they are gathered up, and the acoustic sensations, in creating the experience of a melody. Each note is fully present as an actual physical event and yet it is manifestly and explicitly part of a larger whole because the music conforms to a form that shapes expectation and assists recall – through conformity to the rules of harmony, of contrast and symmetry, of progression and repetition. Our moments of listening are imbued with a sense of what is to come and what has passed. The form to which the music conforms – that ties what has gone and what is to come with each other and with what is present – shines through its individual moments. We seem to have the beginning of a reconciliation between the dynamic and static aspects of meaning.

Of course, the music has its journeys – it manifestly *is* a journey from a beginning to an end – and in great music we feel as if we have travelled great distances to and through an enchanted landscape of sound. But the journeying is never merely a stretch of en route: the unfolding of the form fills and fulfils the sensation of the present moment with the past and the future, rather than undermining it with the past and the future. The musical ideas, phrases, leitmotifs, recurring throughout the music like an involuntary memory, tie the beginning, the middle and the end, making song or symphony a unity, notwithstanding its variety. The retrospective light a motif casts on all that has gone before sometimes creates the feeling that we have been arriving all the time and that, indeed, we are arrived.

The perfected journeying that is music is continuous arrival. That is why, although it is so clearly temporalized, music liberates us from time: it has the forward movement of time, but in it the away and the towards of time are united. And that is why, also, there are moments when, listening to music, we have the sense of enjoying our own consciousness in italics: like a hurrying river dilating into a lagoon, our becoming has dilated into being. Invited to the possibility of a perfected, connected attention, we are liberated for a while from The Dominion of And. Meaning is replete.

The possibility of connectedness can be illustrated with a different art: fiction, where a complex tale brings together a beginning, a middle, and an end. At its height, literary art can give us the sense of recovering an entire world, as E. M. Forster describes so brilliantly in his essay on *War and Peace*:

> After one has read *War and Peace* for a while, great chords begin to sound and we cannot say exactly what struck them. They come from the immense area of Russia, over which episodes and characters have been scattered, from the sum total of bridges and frozen rivers, forests, roads, gardens, fields, which accumulate grandeur and sonority after we have passed them.[76]

Access to an entire world, an expansion of the guttering torchlight of our practical, linear consciousness, to a wide-horizoned sunlight, is made possible in a different way by the visual arts. Consider a Rembrandt self-portrait. You see the man's life in the painted surface. As Shakespeare put it: "Thus is his cheek, the map of days outworn".[77] The "and then … and then" of those out-worn days, is gathered up.

The examples also illustrate how the experience of art, where experience and emotion are cultivated for their own sake, not only lifts us out of the often self-emptying pell-mell of ordinary experience, but also enables us to realize to the full the potential freedom that our partial liberation from our biological destiny could afford us. Our temporal depth permits us spectatorial freedom that distances us from physical time. We are uniquely separated from nature as well as being part of it. This privileged state is taken to a further level when we look at the images of objects uprooted from places where we might be obliged to act in response to them or when we remember a past world we no longer have to respond to.

Consider what happens when the face is translated from a person who is present before us to a portrait on a wall or a landscape is lifted from the land to a gallery. This freedom is also exploited in virtual participation in the lives of fictional characters who engage our memory, knowledge, understanding, empathy and emotions. Sartre's characterization of art as "the world grasped by a freedom"[78] seems apt. And in music, our freedom is exercised in engaging with the *virtual causation* – to use the brilliant phrase of Roger Scruton[79] – that links one note, one chord, with another in the unfolding melody, a neces-sity that is elective rather than endured, an *aesthetic* necessity.

It hardly needs adding that scientistic accounts of the creation and appre-ciation of art and *faux* sciences such as "neuroaesthetics" and evolutionary accounts of art are entirely point-missing. They manage, by an extraordinary economy of effort to be wrong about neuroscience, about art, and about humanity.[80] Essentially, the significance of art is to be found not in any prac-tical even less biological value, but in its helping us to recover the wholeness of a world delivered in fragments, and in permitting us glimpse of what a full realization of our human freedom might be like. Art enables us to become from time to time what we, potentially, are. Or, if that is too ambitious, it gives us an image of what we might be.

That, at least, is one account of what art could mean in a secular society. No, it does not cancel our death sentence, it promises no eternal life, no reversal of our losses. But does it even work at the level I have suggested? Can the hunger for a coherent life be met through the experience of art? Yes, it can liberate (temporally) us from time. Yes, it can gather up the scattered pieces of our ordinary existence. And, yes, it can sometimes wake us out of our half-awoken state. But, no, it cannot round off the sense of the world: it is part of the "And" from which we seek liberation.

The lived reality, as opposed to the idealized experience, of art must always break down to successive experiences: the spectre of "mere and" re-emerges as music, painting, and literature, follow one another in a succession of episodes. As each episode ends, we return to quotidian life. This is captured by Thomas Mann in *Buddenbrooks*. Hanno Buddenbrooks, the life-denying artistically inclined son of the great mercantile family, comes out of an electrifying performance of *Tristan und Isolde* – Wagner's supreme attempt to realize redemption through art – to the banality of everyday life, represented by the wet overcoats in the cloakroom, where he waits with his ticket. The only solution to his search for transcendence seems to be his early death – which is precisely the consummation sought and found by Wagner's unhappy lovers. Nietzsche, notwithstanding his claim that without music life would be a mistake, reported how, after the music stopped, he had "a peculiarly exaggerated weary dread of everyday reality, because it no longer seemed real to me, but ominous".[81] Pater himself acknowledged that aesthetic experiences were only "momentary" and the exhortation "to burn always with this hard gemlike flame, to maintain this ecstasy"[82] seems only incompletely to exorcize the circling ghosts of "and then … and then".

It seems surprising that we overlook this obvious truth. It may be because we tend to conflate the place of art in the lives of artists, of full-time performers or commentators, with its place in the lives of the rest of us. While one might not agree with Nietzsche's assertion that "The artist is related to the lover of his art as a cannon to a flock of sparrows",[83] we must distinguish between how Proust might (or might not) be saved through writing *Remembrance of Things Past* and how we his readers might (or might not) be saved through reading his masterpiece. And it is important not to be too starry-eyed about the life of the artist; to think only of the moments of inspiration and forget the drudgery of composition and performance, of painstaking vision and revision, of correction and further correction. Idealizing the artist, we overlook the opportunistic and, indeed, accidental nature of the *oeuvre*. Borges tries to redeem this in a beautiful but alas misleading story: "A man sets out to draw the world … mountains, bays, ships, islands, fishes, rooms, instruments, stars, horses … A short time before he dies, he discovers the patient labyrinth of lines traces the lineaments of his own face".[84]

Of course, the transcendental experiences of observant religious believers are also episodic. Their daily lives, their practical activities, work and play, likes and dislikes, are largely godless. They are often too busy or merely distracted for intimations of divinity. For religious believers, however, there remains the possibility of as it were "outsourcing" continuity of vision to the community, to the institution, to which one belongs. There is a fundamental difference between an audience brought together by accidents of taste or curiosity and a congregation held together by fundamental convictions and commitment to a way of life. Yes, it may be difficult for believers to hold true to their deepest selves in a life which makes many different claims on them and in which they are inevitably scattered over many occupations and preoccupations. And yes, even if they are not distracted from without, the inbuilt dynamism of human thought that won't keep still dissipates them. But the church is a standing reality that underwrites or guarantees the continuity of something that is engaged with only intermittently. Above all, the continuing existence of the entity – God which is the ultimate intentional object of the religious consciousness – gives an objective underwriting to a coherence that cannot be directly experienced, even less lived out.

The fragmented personal experience of religion is held together by that community. There is, however, a danger to believers in outsourcing the continuity of the presence of God in their lives: He may become a marginal figure, or a mere presupposition, Who re-emerges only when He is needed. In short, the existence of churches permits spiritual coasting. This, notwithstanding, elective – even capricious – engagement with particular works of art is at odds with the ache for an over-arching meaning. Which works of art we encounter, embrace, visit and re-visit is largely accidental. Paintings, symphonies, novels, compete with each other for our attention. And our attitude to them is often far from reverential. We are consumers and we *judge* what we listen to, see, or read. We exercise our taste and argue over the merits of different works and the way they are performed. Our stance is often that of a discerning (or undiscerning) critic, even when we are applauding. While the Mass in church is, of course, a performance, it is not as judges of performances that we engage with it, as we do with Beethoven's *Missa solemnis*. We are aware that art is the human product of human beings, even where we subscribe to the notion of the divinely inspired artist and grant artists the status of demigods.

It is true that the picture is surrounded by a frame and located in a gallery; the wide margins round the poem enjoin attentive silence; and the darkened, silent auditorium commands undistracted attention. All of these seem to support the notion of art as sacrament. But that space is not situated in a larger ground, boundless because of its invisibility. The auditorium is next to the bar and the cloakroom. And we may listen to the Ring Cycle in the comfort of our own home, pressing the pause button when we hear the phone ring.

Philosophy?

> The old philosophy holds a two-fold truth – the truth for its own
> sake that did not have any consideration for man – philosophy
> – and the truth for man – religion. Contrary to this, the new
> philosophy, as the philosophy of man is, essentially, also the phi-
> losophy for man … It takes the place of religion, it incorporates
> the essence of religion within itself, it is, in truth religion, itself.
> Feuerbach[85]

What part might philosophy, more specifically a philosophical anthropology, play in advancing humanism in a world without God? How shall we address the concern, expressed in Chapter 8 that the deeper we take philosophical thoughts, the further we are distanced from the majority of our fellows. How might philosophical ideas build a community?

Philosophy, of course, has its institutions: associations, conferences, jour-nals, clubs, and academic departments. But they are often characterized less by agreement than by dissent; rivalry rather than true togetherness. The busi-ness of philosophy is often technical, with the community (or more precisely the aggregate) of philosophers being divided into labourers in different fields, and very little evidence of conclusions, never mind consensus, being reached. The vast majority of its practitioners are honourably content to contribute to a discipline that advances, if at all, piecemeal towards an undefined conclusion. The thoughts that click with editors of journals click shut rather than open. The full stop at the end of a philosophical paper is a marker of temporary satisfaction rather than true arrival.

The discipline seems unable, perhaps unwilling,[86] to provide definitive answers to any of its questions. Its conclusions, at best provisional or prelim-inary, are always contested. It often presents itself as a thicket of technicali-ties, of interminable quarrels in which footnotes are entangled with footnotes. Philosophy cuts a small figure in the life of most ordinary – and indeed extraor-dinary – people. Of little or no interest to their fellow man and women, philos-ophers' inquiries seem easy to dismiss as a "higher unseriousness".

Admittedly, these faults are mirrored in religious thought, which often takes the form of endless commentaries and commentaries on commentaries, and demonstrations of the extraordinary number of angels that can dance on a footnote. Obsession with the minutiae of scholarship, commentary, and dis-puted hermeneutics, seems remote from a vision of God and His relationship to mankind. What's more, philosophical disputes, unlike theological ones, do not lead to bloodshed. There is no record, so far as I know, of property dualists and substance dualists laying waste to each other's crops or burning each other's villages – though this may reflect how little is felt to be at stake. But there is another important difference.

The lived truth of religion is not conducted within the discipline of theology or textual elucidation or siphoned down footnotes. It is to be found in the community of believers led by clerics. One can live a full Christian life with little knowledge of what preoccupies scholars and fuels their arguments. Philosophy has no comparable realm where the inconclusiveness of the arguments and the exclusiveness of the community engaging in them are redeemed in daily life and the discipline makes way for a shared vision of a life more abundant. On the contrary, with a few exceptions, some of the most inventive, thoughtful, and brilliant contemporary philosophers would resist the very idea of such a place.

Cue for an anecdote. It concerns, as not many stories do, a taxi driver, a poet, and a philosopher.

> "You're T. S. Eliot" said a taxi driver to the famous poet as he stepped into his cab. Eliot asked him how he knew. "Ah, I've got an eye for a celebrity" he replied. "Only the other evening, I picked up that Bertrand Russell, and I said to him: 'Well, Lord Russell, what's it all about?' *And you know he couldn't tell me*".[87]

The shock of the man-in-the-street discovering that one of the last century's greatest and best-known philosophers could not deliver on what is often seen, at least by non-philosophers, as the central preoccupation of philosophy was palpable. What should be equally striking is the taxi driver's assumption that we can outsource the task of finding a meaning in life to specialists. It is a continuation of the religious tradition of wise persons (usually men) – prophets, saints, priests, textual scholars – who do our existential thinking for us, freeing us up to lead an *un*examined life.

Few contemporary philosophers regard the search for the meaning of life as central to their inquiries – least of all philosophers in the analytical tradition which Russell had such a key role in establishing – though, as we have seen, Russell himself wrote eloquently on this topic in essays such as "A Free Man's Worship". There are important contemporary exceptions.[88]

One is of particular relevance to our present preoccupations. David Cooper has argued for maintaining "a delicate balance" when addressing a tension between two claims.[89] The first is that the meaning of anything owes its place *within* a form of life. Unfortunately, as we discussed, meanings within life are transient, even where they do not cancel one another out, they usually derive from other things that in turn derive their meanings from yet other things *ad infinitum.* The second is that the meaning of life as a whole, or at least an entirely valid meaning, must be rooted in something beyond life: it requires a transcendent realm to underwrite that meaning. This can be discovered, it seems to me, only by starting a long way back; more specifically with something that we discussed in the previous section: *the emergence or irruption of the subject in an apparently subjectless universe.*

I will return to this but let me first make another observation. The disenchantment of the world can make the usual, more modest, goals of philosophy, seem insufficient. An unsatisfied hunger for meaning may make us impatient with a technical philosophy that is suspicious of visions, even less with one that is satisfied with addressing questions that interest only philosophers. There is a vacancy, which philosophers seem reluctant to fill.

The reason why philosophers might be reluctant to engage in anything that might smack of lay preaching was most influentially articulated by Wittgenstein. This passage in the *Tractatus Logico-Philosophicus* is particularly relevant: "The solution of the problem of life is seen in the vanishing of the problem. (Is this not the reason why those who have found after a long period of doubt that the sense of life became clear to them have then been unable to say what constituted that sense?)".[90] Our lives, it seems, neither lose their meaning nor acquire new meaning as the result of our arriving at the conclusion of an argument, even a philosophical one. Lived meaning is not propositional.

While philosophy may not even address the question "What's it all about?" – where "all" is the sum of things, the universe, our lives, and our place in the totality of things and "about" refers to something we might call "meaning" – it may at least offer a clearer understanding of the question, beginning with an acknowledgement of its strangeness. For behind the inquiry into "The Meaning of Life" is an important assumption that requires clarification: that human life – the sum of our lives, either individually or collectively or both – *has* a meaning; that that meaning can be uncovered by the traditional philosophical methods of argument backing up broader reflection, meditation, or even (on the basis that the meaning is existential rather than propositional) a way of living. Behind that assumption in turn is something else, more extraordinary and mysterious than any meaning we might ascribe to our own lives or to human life in general. It is the very fact that we humans are sense-making beings, endeavouring to comprehend the world and our place in it, nature and our own nature.

It is here that we may find the starting point from which philosophy may engage with the question of the meaning of life without ascending (or declining) into mere secular preaching. It will not make grandiose claims which cannot be believed, even less lived, but rather open up a dimension of possibility, and the possibility of waking out of wakefulness, through a critical examination of the assumptions built into everyday life, so that we become *un*used to ourselves. The justification for a transformative astonishment is the mystery of knowledge, indeed of ordinary human consciousness, reaching back to the relationship between mind and cosmos, the self and its world, the primordial mystery of the irruption of the subject, the "I am" that transforms what is or matter into thatter.

Thus might philosophy find its mission in a disenchanted world: unpeeling from the mystery of everyday consciousness the many-layered patina that results from our over-familiarity with ourselves and our world. This mission would be served equally well by the analytical philosophy of the concept and the phenomenological philosophy of consciousness. They are neither rivals nor opponents – something that in recent decades has become evident to practitioners on both sides. While the aims of analytic philosophy may seem at times to be over-modest, inquiring piecemeal into the geography of the concepts that underpin the way we think about and engage with the world, its examination of the basis for and limitations of our knowledge, seeing how everyday experience and scientific understanding are connected, and reminding us of what is in front of our nose, it is no such thing. As P. F. Strawson characterized it, the essential business of philosophy was "to get a clear view of our concepts and their place in our lives" and "to establish the connections between the major structural features of elements in our conceptual scheme".[91] Philosophy would not be about the meaning of life, as something life points to, or even the meaning *in* life, as something expressed in it, but about the way meanings are organized in our way of thinking, speaking, and otherwise engaging with what is there, including each other.

This might sound dull and technical. Technical it may sometimes be but not dull, especially if it is motivated by disenchantment. Against the concern that we are too easily satisfied with meaning – an "embarrassment of bling" – a philosophical gaze will argue that we are too easily *dis*satisfied because we overlook, look past or through the many layers of the cognitive infrastructure that underpins the most commonplace meaning. There is nothing matter of fact about the facts that we use to guide us through our supposedly ordinary but inexpressibly complex lives. There is nothing trivial about what makes the seeming trivia of our lives possible. Unpacking what is necessary for you to say to me "Let's meet next Wednesday in London" could be the contemplative work of a lifetime. Calendrical and tensed time, the shared intentionality of joint planned enterprise, the relationship between language and the world, abstractions such as "Wednesday" and concrete abstractions such as "London" – all things we take for granted – deserve an astonished, even reverential, attention they rarely receive outside of philosophy. Philosophy can serve us through formulating profound reminders of what kinds of beings we are by unpacking the depths hidden in the shallows. While it does not promise to reveal hidden meanings that lie beyond our lives, it can uncover and unshowily celebrate, the meanings that are made invisible with familiarity.

Our endeavours in philosophy to see – as Wilfrid Sellars put it – "how things in the widest sense hang together in the widest sense"[92] – will never reach a point of arrival. Nevertheless, the struggle to make connections is to widen and deepen our gaze. En route, however, as we attempt to make the world more visible and even intelligible, we are to some degree returned to ourselves. What is lost in daily life in the dynamism of meaning, the succession of our preoccupations, may be at least momentarily recalled. We may be un-dissipated; not completely of course – any more than the smoke can be ravelled up and returned to the embers of the firewood and the living trees reconstructed.

This sense of being "called back" overlaps – and I would submit not by accident – with the fundamental sense of the word "re-ligion" – "re-ligio" – which means to be bound back, to be returned. In the case of religion, this return is to God, to the foundation of being, and thence to the ground of one's self. A philosophy which allows one to be open to the fundamental mystery of human existence, explored through a steady gaze on the phenomena of consciousness, and on the conceptual framework that supports our being in, and relating to, it – has the capacity to gather us up, to allow us to be flooded with the world's own light and indeed our own light that is the light of the world. It permits re-enchantment.

At the heart of the philosophically examined life is a return to the primordial astonishment at our existence and at the boundless connectedness of things – the natural world, human institutions, or our individual consciousnesses. Yes, there is the work of argument – if only to fasten our attention to the large questions that belong to us all – but it needs to be preceded and succeeded, indeed enclosed in, the work of contemplation. A hard-won conclusion has to be won again – and again – as something that is realized in the imagination, in the widening pause between the dynamic elements of dialogue – with others and with ourselves.

The philosophical inquiry that has occupied most of this volume has endeavoured to connect specific, sometimes rather technical, arguments with a larger conception of our human nature. Irrespective of whether it persuades those to whom they were not already obvious, much work would remain to be done to ensure that its conclusions are imbued with the kind of shared, collective, seriousness that we associate with religious beliefs. While theological arguments are often seen as intellectually flawed, theological conclusions are expected to have existential weight. By contrast, the high technical standards of argument in philosophy often support a journey to conclusions that do not carry such weight; indeed, those conclusions are simply a pause in the arguments that seem unending.

What we do with the extraordinary facts of our extra-natural nature is, it seems to me, to be the central question of the philosophy of humanism and how we learn to live within those facts. To take the full measure of the depth and complexity of our daily existence is the key challenge of living as a humanist, responding to the call "Humanists, awake!" – in order to live inside the mystery of our human being and to be more continuously alive to it.

It is only relatively recently in the 2,500-year history of western philosophy that it has been entirely separated from theology. For a much longer period, philosophy has played a key role in the development of the Christian and Islamic religions. The union of Greek and Hebraic thought in the writings of Philo of Alexandria was crucial to the vision at the heart of Christianity, of the *logos* and of "the word become flesh.[93] In short, the modesty of contemporary philosophy (and, yes, it has much to be modest about) may be seen as a loss of, rather than an arrival at, its essential mission. James Tartaglia's observation is very much to the point:

> [T]he aim of engaging with the traditional problems of philosophy is to achieve an overall understanding of reality and our place within it – of a kind not available within the necessarily more fragmented perspectives offered by natural and social sciences. To this extent the aims of philosophy resemble those of religion and it remains rooted in the same kinds of human need.[94]

HUMANISM AND RELIGION

Philosophy at its most profound, and most relevant to the question of the meaning of life, is about demisting our awareness of the world, of untaking the taken for granted, seeing the ground on which we stand. So far, so good. Unfortunately, philosophical inquiry has a fundamentally solitary heart and its existential significance, in the gaps between philosophizing, cannot be sustained by others, outsourced to a community. Religious observance is, by contrast, a communal activity and the collective can as it were conserve the profundity of ideas even when they are merely parroted by fallible individuals. One can be devout without being a theologian but cannot be a philosopher without engaging in philosophical thought. And philosophy does not offer what certain religions offer: the consolation of a universe sustained by a benign, omnipotent being who created it, who ensured that ultimately justice would prevail, and that the death that cancels all meanings, and undermines them before it does so, is not fatal in any sense that matters. We must acknowledge those fundamental hungers to which religion responds and which humanism cannot satisfy: for a convergence of all meanings; and for something as deep as life to offset the tragic fact that we are all mortal. The chances of a religion of humanism based on philosophical thought therefore seem slim.

Humanism as a religion

Some have suggested that humanists already have their religion but – unlike a Comtean synthetic Religion of Man – it is so widely diffused that it is not visible. Sam Blumenfeld, a defender of religion, has argued along these lines, in relation to education in the United States. For Blumenfeld, the ubiquitous presence of humanist assumptions means the marginalization of the alternative. Religion (beyond lip- and wallet-service) has a relatively small part to play in huge swathes of culture – most importantly in education, though humanists would wish it were even less:

> Today, humanist beliefs are inculcated through such programs and concepts as values clarification, sensitivity training, situational ethics, evolution, multiculturalism, globalism, transcendental meditation, sex education, death education, humanistic and behavioural psychology etc. All of these programs are marbleized through the curriculum – in reading, language arts, math, social studies, health education, psychology, art, biology, and other subjects. It is impossible for a student in a government school to avoid or to escape the all-pervasive influence of humanist ideas and beliefs which confront and accost him daily every which way he turns.[95]

One may agree with Blumenfeld's empirical observations and still not accept his claim that humanism amounts to a religion and should be forbidden by the American constitution's First Amendment against the government establishment of religion to be propagated in publicly funded state colleges and schools. After all, humanism has no identified sacred places and spaces assigned to humanism; nor are there specific rituals or a clerisy.

Nevertheless, we should not abandon the hope of finding in sustained reflection on our own nature the source of a renewed solidarity between human beings, a solidarity observed within but not alas between religions. Our extra-natural status at any rate should provide us with rich material for meditation. We do not fit into the universe, not the least in virtue of our understanding of it. We are, as anthropologist Clifford Geertz pointed out: "incomplete or unfinished animals who complete or finish themselves through culture".[96]

The other side of this incompleteness is an openness to fundamental change, expressed in our history of endlessly surpassing ourselves – in cognitive and technological, if not moral, advance. The ultimate root of that openness is the intentionality, the sense of aboutness, which opens up the world, and worlds beyond worlds, possible worlds that may or may not exist but are there, possibly, to be realized, or at least imagined, and through being imagined (as in the case of the world of the supernatural) influential in our history.

This aspect of our unnatural nature is expressed by Feuerbach: "[God] is not another creature … only the completion of an incomplete creature, a completion of his limited ability to act, in contradiction to his desires".[97] Thus, the creative force of our sense of our own incompleteness. If we are capable of creating God, there is potentially no limit to the extent to which we may surpass ourselves. Durkheim highlighted the role of human society as an engine for changing the very nature of humanity: "Because society surpasses us, it obliges us to surpass ourselves, and to surpass itself, a being must, to some degree, depart from its nature".[98] We live out a dual nature, "one purely individual and rooted in our organisms, and the other social and nothing but an extension of society".[99]

There remains much work to be done to connect this with the project of spiritual irredentism, the reclaiming of our transcendence in the service of humanity, and to understand the role of fundamentally solitary, potentially asocial, philosophical thought in our collective development. At the very least we might identify this as a supremely important philosophical, perhaps cultural, task for contemporary humanism: learning to celebrate what is revealed to an unpeeled gaze and make of this a means of promoting human fellowship and quenching potentially lethal tribal and individual hostilities. It seems doubtful that this will be achieved by mobilizing, on a pick and mix basis, sacred spaces, rituals, creeds, and liturgies, gathered from faiths past and present. Resacralization of aspects of our life cannot be achieved by a *fiat*, that is voluntary or individualistic, not the least, because religion, is as Durkheim said, "an eminently collective thing"[100] – and one that seems to have a legitimacy, a warrant, that is not dependent on individual decisions.

There are examples of religions that facilitate collective acknowledgement of human transcendence without populating the universe with supernatural beings to be worshipped and appeased or the human world with prelates, wrapped in the grandeur of the God, who exercise a lethal combination of spiritual authority and temporal or political power. Quakerism, with its elusive non-doctrinal beliefs, is a useful reminder that the boundaries of religion are ill-defined and the division between religion and a free-floating spiritualism is not sharp or continuous. Lois Lee has emphasized the variety and degree of spirituality of those who identify themselves as non-religious.[101] Any *rapprochement* between "believers and non-believers" will therefore be complicated by the fact that both parties may be coming from a variety of places. And this would have particular relevance if it were felt that there was mileage in trying to gather up a free-floating sense that there must be "something more" into the vacated or abandoned structures of religion.

Tomas Halik, a Czech priest and academic who courageously chose to be ordained in 1978, a year after the brutal crackdown following the signing of Charter 77, has sympathetically discussed a church for unbelievers, "somethingists" for whom there is something unspecified "beyond" – an unknown God.[102] This, however, seems like making the best of a bad job; trying to compensate for what has been lost, and cannot be regained, or, if it exists, lies forever out of range. We need something beyond a "somethingism" taking residence on the periphery of religion and loitering in the ante-room of the church, if we are to achieve what Roy Wood Sellars described in his humanism manifesto of the 1930s as expressing religious emotions in "social passion".[103]

Easier said than done. Nothing about the journey from propositions that are reached by arguments to shared creeds, liturgies, and a community with a profound sense of common purpose motivated by a non-exclusive ethic of care is clear except that it will be, at best, long. Any endeavour to establish by *fiat* a humanist church addressing the "hunger ... to be more serious", a literal or metaphorical place where "all our compulsions meet / Are recognised, and robed as destinies" may result in cults, at best vacuous and at worst poisonous rather than the grandeur of the great religions. Humanism will not have anything to compare with the spectacular debut of a crucified Son of God, the *logos* made flesh, come to earth to save us from ourselves. Even then, Christianity evolved over a long period of time and survived at least in part as a result of historical accident: the path from minor cult to a world religion was slow and uncertain. Humanists, in any case, may feel ambivalent towards the idea of a religion of humanism, when the distinctive characteristics of most religions – belief on the basis of faith, powerful institutions unaccountable to civil authorities – are precisely those things from which they may most want to distance themselves.

What then remains to further the cause of humanism beyond the supremely important task of advancing the material well-being and freedom of human- ity? For a philosopher, it must come from digging deeper, by thinking harder, about our nature and our place in the universe. The "something more" that is intuited, sought for, desired, is a mode of imagining our humanity that goes beyond the way we understand ourselves when we are busy, necessarily in the grip of details. As such it would try to break the barrier, or close the gap, between our most elevated and our most closely focused moments, between the widest visions and the narrowest preoccupations.

We secularists cannot do this on our own. A dialogue is called for between humanists and believers who are, after all, fellow humans. The actuality of human transcendence and the needs it awakens, on which both parties are agreed, must lie at the heart of the construction of any kind of bridge across the "divide" between believers and those whom they characterize as "infidels". It might even prove a model for other dialogues such as those between differ- ent faith groups.

Dialogue between believers and infidels: beyond "the coalition of the reasonable"

In the opening chapter, I cited the Roman playwright Terence's prescriptive claim that "Nothing human is alien to me". This profound sympathy should be extended by humanists to those (the majority) of their fellow humans who are subscribers to religion faiths. As Durkheim observed, "the unani- mous sentiment of the believers of all times cannot be purely illusory".[104] To dismiss believers as cognitive children, espousing pre-scientific fairy stories about the nature of the world and of their place in it, and religion as merely false, merely wicked, or merely primitive, is hardly consistent with the spirit of humanism. Not to take seriously world pictures that have been central to the lives of most human beings throughout history is an odd way to embrace humanity, even if we were not, believers and infidels alike, inheritors of a rich treasure of religious artefacts, art, thoughts, and institutions. If we have yet to develop an adequate philosophy of humanism, it is perhaps because humanists have spent too much time congratulating themselves on escaping religious belief.

If only because they are going to have to live side by side for the foreseeable future it is time to take seriously the task of widening the dialogue between humanists and infidels. Besides, there is much that humanists could learn from religious institutions; notably how to connect our most profound thoughts, hopes, fears, and needs, with the prose of daily life. And, who knows, believers may learn something from infidels.

Such dialogues will be least successful where the parties enter the discussion primarily in the expectation or purpose – declared or undeclared – of persuading the other to concede defeat; where one party sees the other as damned and the other party sees the first as credulous or daft. Even a polite or peaceable echo of the doctrinal and tribal conflicts seen between organized religions will not take either party very far. Where they have avoided arguments over the existence or non-existence of God, or whether religion has or has not been a net force for evil, they have rarely gone much further than expressions of mutual respect (perhaps a veneer concealing mutual contempt) or even proposing what Julian Baggini has characterized with some irony as "a coalition of the reasonable".[105]

A polite exchange of views seems absurdly inadequate in view of what is, and has been, at stake. Many Christians may be mindful of St Paul's warning: "Beware lest any man spoil you through philosophy and vain deceit, after the tradition of men, after the rudiments of the world, and not after Christ".[106] Argument will anyway have little traction, given the religious tradition which subordinates argument to experience and revelation. Kierkegaard famously asserted that "it was one thing to stand on one leg to prove the existence of God and quite another to fling one's self to the ground to worship him".[107] Thomas Aquinas, who had spilled vast quantities of ink arguing for his vision of God, dismissed everything he had written as "seeming like straw to me compared to those things that I have seen and have been revealed to me".[108] At any rate, an argument about the existence or non-existence of God will not be a good starting point.

A necessary condition for a dialogue that transcends bickering will be that both parties have a clear idea of what each other actually believes. Many theologians have been exasperated by the cavalier way certain scorched earth atheists have dealt with religion, reducing complex religious doctrines to simplistic caricatures.[109] The temptation to reduce religious belief to a series of propositions, stripped to mere assertions, that are either unintelligible, self-contradictory, or simply lacking evidential support, should perhaps be resisted. It will not, anyway, make much progress against the defence – discussed in Chapter 9 – that religious creeds are not assertions of matters of fact but are metaphorical, symbolic, inseparable from a wider context of lived experience. While this may be true to the nature of religion – though not all theologians accept the dichotomy – it may, however, exasperate secular thinkers, seeming to close down the possibility of the kind of discussion unbelievers prefer to engage in. Surely, infidels say, there is a factual difference between "Jesus rose from the dead" and "Jesus did not rise from the dead" and even between "Jesus was the Son of God" and "Jesus was not the Son of God". One cannot, surely, live one's life in the light of beliefs that are neither true nor false. What is more, this take on religion does not seem consistent with the acts – good or evil – that have been done in their name. Much innocent Jewish blood has been spilt on the grounds that it was the Jews who murdered Christ.[110] Nevertheless, the secularist assumption that, say, to believe in an afterlife is to embrace a factual error, may seem to be tone deaf. The belief is a transforming intuition rooted in a sense of the extraordinary nature of humanity, one expression of which is our unique relationship to time, discussed in Chapter 4.

It is important that religious believers appreciate that humanism can be profound too; more particularly that a secular world picture need not, indeed should not, be committed to the notion that human beings are simply part of the natural world – beasts, or pieces of matter – entirely subject to, or defined by, the laws that operate throughout the universe. Secular humanists, too, bring something to the table, and they are not to be defined by what is absent from their lives, though this is always a risk if they self-define by their lack of belief in God, calling themselves "atheists". If humanists must know what they are talking about when they attack religious doctrines, religionists who oppose humanism have an equal duty to understand what they oppose.

In short, any dialogue worth having must begin with a recognition of shared ground. First and foremost is acknowledgement of fundamental hungers, common to believers and unbelievers alike, arising out of what is unresolved in the human condition. The sense of our transcendence, and of wonder at the kinds of beings we are, should also be in the forefront of both parties' minds. Both religious belief and humanism are manifestations of our exceptional nature and our individual and collective awareness of ourselves. This should pre-empt a patronising or superior attitude on either side of the debate. The interlocutors should be animated by a respectful astonishment that the person sitting across the table inhabits an entirely different imaginative universe.

Mutual respect should not be laid on so thick that it obscures the most important fact about the dialogue: that the interlocutors are starting from fundamentally different premises. Those for whom Man is made in the image of God and those for whom God is made in the image of Man will – indeed should – have to work hard to find things to say to one another. Even flat earthers and round earthers might agree on a middle position, acknowledging that the round earth is flat in parts and then deciding how much is round, and how much is flat. (To say this is not to allocate either secular humanists or believers to either category.) There seems to be no comparable meeting of minds between those who think of God as a transcendent Being Who created everything including humanity and those for whom the gods are projections of the community of human minds. What is more, they may have a different direction of travel. Believers may begin with answers which they try to understand and incorporate in their lives; while infidels may begin with questions prompting a piecemeal advance towards the unrealized possibility of complete answers.

For all these reasons, metaphors such as "crossing the divide", "reaching out" or "building bridges" underestimate the difficulties of arriving at a true meeting of minds. The putative "divide" that is to be crossed is ill-defined. If "reaching out" is from fundamentally different places, it is likely to result in two arms passing one another by. And two "bridges" – one building out from a set of metaphysical beliefs and a rich tradition of creeds, rituals, and arts and the other from everyday experience – are at risk of having two disconnected lanes and landing in different places, particularly as one bridge-builder tries to imagine religion from a secular starting point and the other endeavours to imagine a secular worldview from a religious viewpoint. The two ideas of God – as an ontological reality and as a socio-economic entity – have no meeting place.

The "bridge" metaphor highlights another problem. If there is to be a bridge between A and B, there have to be piers at A and at B to support the connection. The religious believer appears to have a rather larger pier than the infidel. One of the chief aims of *Seeing Ourselves* has been to find the material for a secular pier in the extra-natural nature of human beings. This should help to correct the imbalance between the believers for whom the general territory – sacred places, doctrines, rituals, liturgies – within which truth may be found is rich and complex and the humanist whose journey to truth seems to be more sparsely equipped. A *personal* God that can unite the "I am" of personhood with the giant "It is" of the universe is at odds even with a rich humanism that acknowledges the paradoxes that arise from a scientistic viewpoint that sees "I am" as a very late entry into the order of things.

The aim cannot be to remove difference. After all, the purpose of a bridge is not to abolish the river or road or canyon which it crosses. But we need to make the most of difference, so that both parties can be enriched. For this, we should reset the terms of any dialogue. After all, there is much in religion that may assist humanists in overcoming some of the challenges to the irredentist project of highlighting the undeniable reality of human transcendence, of reclaiming from the gods what belongs to mankind and of returning to civil society the solemnity, the mystery, and the grandeur of religion.

An obvious starting place is what religionists and secularists cannot disagree over: the urgent need to cope with the tragedy of transience and the struggle to live well; and the fact that we are mysterious creatures in a mysterious universe – made more, not less, mysterious by the science that claims to describe the general principles of all that is. As conscious creatures, we do not fit into the material world; and as self-conscious agents of the kind that builds cities, laws, history, etc., we do not fit into the animal kingdom. This should be enough to take both parties beyond the surface quarrels, point-scoring, mutual indifference, or surface cooperation.

I have skated over the question of the passions we should bring to the dialogue. Which brings us to a concern both parties have, or should have, in common. Secular humanism and organized religion need to understand how placing intimations of our transcendent nature at the heart of communal life may have evil consequences; to be aware of the path from non-trivial spirituality to the abuses, persecution, prejudices, exclusion, and bloodshed committed in the name of, or with the excuse of, defending or promoting life as it should be lived. The boundary between a belief-led community spirit and a coercive communitarianism is not clear, continuous, or stable, but the emphasis on a transcendental sense of ourself threatens to create an inward gazing sect that will look outwards only to cast baleful glances on the non-elect, on the unchosen. This should not be forgotten in the cosiness of a dialogue conducted between free individuals in a safe place, particularly as it is easy to forgive crimes from which one has not personally suffered.[111] How to prevent the spiritual communities, secular or religious, from becoming instruments of oppression should have a priority in any dialogue.

In that spirit, both parties should be honest about the iniquities committed in the name of their highest ideals and how the latter are easily weaponized. The evils promoted by religion have been well covered. But secularists have much to answer. From the French Revolution to the totalitarian regimes of the twentieth and twenty-first centuries, there is a shocking pattern, illustrated unforgettably by Albert Camus whom we quoted in the opening chapter, by the example of "slave camps [being established] under the flag of freedom, massacres justified by philanthropy".[112] This secular outrage matches the bitter irony by which the Franciscan heirs of the supreme Christian apostle of love contributed so much so quickly to the persecution and slaughter of the Jews in late-medieval Europe, and discharged their duties in the Inquisition with such enthusiasm. The quasi-religious worship of "the people" and of the Great Leaders who exert power over them for the sake of their good has justified atrocities that match and, in some cases, exceed those which have disfigured religions. Secular humanism and religion together face the challenge of placing our mysterious nature front and centre of our individual and communal lives – and perhaps making it that which binds us most closely together – without getting diverted so disastrously off course.

It seems a reasonable assumption that the vast majority of religious believers have an interest in distancing themselves from radical, militant, or fundamental religionists, who have attracted a large share – disproportionate or proportionate – of the secular world's image of all believers. Each party may have much to teach the other in the art of not taking lethal offence at others' different experiences and beliefs, even where the differences are as profound as that between seeing God as a socio-economic entity and seeing Him as an ontological reality. The question of how we get from wonderful sentiments ("all are beloved by God", "the inalienable rights of all mankind") to appalling behaviour, needs to be addressed by both.

Religionists can thus make a common cause with secular humanists in pursuing the goal of a peaceable, just world where all can flourish. We should be equally unsentimental about the capacity of secular and religious societies to inflict suffering. "I fear those big words that make us so unhappy" Stephen Dedalus thought to himself.[113] While we should not give up on "love", "justice", "freedom", "glory" and "happiness", we should not, at any rate, enter lightly, carelessly, thoughtlessly, into the establishment of institutions aimed to do honour to our intimations of transcendence without thinking very carefully how we might avoid the path that leads from idealistic, even beatific visions of humanity, and of our duties to each other to individual or collective thuggery or to more subtle abuses of power. Without, in short, recreating the aspects of religion that humanists repudiate. In order to overcome the episodic, and the solitary, nature of our profoundest thought, they need collective acknowledgement and institutional support and therein lies the danger of tribalism and bloodshed.

I am not sufficiently self-deceived to imagine that it is possible to eliminate the gap between humanism and the major religions, particularly the theistic ones that have a god, God, or a personal God at their heart. To turn the tables on God such that He (he) is interpreted as our (Our) instrument – a force for social cohesion and a source of ultimate meaning – rather than our being His instruments will be a Copernican revolution too far for religionists. Secularists and believers, however, may find a fruitful point of convergence if the invention of Gods is acknowledged as an extraordinary, mysterious aspect of our humanity, a measure of our human distance from nature. If, as Merleau-Ponty argued, life "is the power to invent the visible",[114] human life is the power to intuit, even invent, the invisible, and God-inventing humanity is the supreme expression of this.

Both parties, if they are honest, are agreed on something utterly fundamental: that the origin of the universe, of life, and of conscious life lack explanation. There must be something more at work to explain that there is anything at work and account for the fact that that "anything" is (albeit incompletely) known to part of itself. The something in question remains elusive for all parties. There is a convergence between the apophatic tendency according to which no predicates can be ascribed to God and atheism according to which God has the predicate of non-existence. At any rate, the gap between the "something more" of thoughtful religionists and that of secular thinkers who have not succumbed to scientism may not be as wide as either party assumes.

Nevertheless, Halik's "somethingism" – that "there must be something more but I don't know what it is"[115] – which we mentioned earlier – doesn't really offer much in the way of actual content. For that we need to look within our own being. And here we may find the territory of the most fruitful dialogue between secular and religious voices, one which may be conducted in a spirit of generosity and of mutual respect. It is the territory alluded to by Halik, in his talk of "the beliefs of disbelievers" and the "disbelief of believers" who envisages "a church for seekers".[116]

The dialogue should open the possibility of something entirely new rather than an infertile quarrel over the status of gods encrusted with the weight of history and compromised with the accidents and intentions of political, civil, and domestic powers. The sense of possibility, an awakening out of the deadening sense of the obvious, that humanists may bring to the conversation, may even assist in the evolving understanding of God that thoughtful theism is engaged in. There may be mutually illuminating reflections on the God of many believers Who is not a thing, an entity, a being, a force, an agent, even less a capricious, somewhat prejudiced, busybody intervening in human history. In return, religionists give to secularist thought the wonderful heritage of philosophy, literature, architecture, painting and music that has been inspired by the hunger to mediate between God and Man, to lift our lives above tragedy and to respond to the profound questions that ask us. And both parties can draw, in gratitude, on the inherited treasures of human spirituality, science and artistic creation.

We must never lose sight of what we can share: acknowledgement of our mysterious nature; a common concern with our vulnerability, our anxiety before death, our need to be loved, valued and significant, to cope with grief, guilt, lost opportunities for kindness or self-advancement, for coherence in our life, and for justice in the world; and awareness of being in a fog of uncertainty and ignorance. There may not be convergence in the belief that the profound hole in our understanding of our relationship to the material world – and to the universe of which we are seemingly such a minute, and dispensable part – is God-shaped or even spirit-shaped. It may, however, ensure that dialogue will do justice to the depth of our lives and our joyful, tragic condition.

Let the conversation begin.

Epilogue: an inconclusion

My finitude is not something I can escape. All I can do is to (try to) master the art of being finite.   Adrian Moore[1]

What I do take issue with is the assumption (typically implicit) that the scientific method has exhausted our ways of apprehending and knowing reality. Render to science what belongs to science, but we should not surrender all of reality too hastily lest we fail to encounter vast mysteries not accommodated by its unique set of assumptions and methodologies.   Stan Klein[2]

When it comes to personal reality, the language of philosophy is possibly the *only* way to speak well of who we are and what our humanity is like.   Rowan Williams[3]

Seeing Ourselves has been motivated by the hope that philosophy might do justice to our human nature and by the possibility that it might one day open up a way of thought that matches the profundity of religion. A particularly inspiring example in western philosophy is Baruch Spinoza, a philosopher who seems to have been poised on the cusp between religious and secular thought. He did not separate God from Nature, and denied that the deity was a transcendent, providential agent who intervened in history. Consequently, he has been accused of being both an atheist and a pantheist, as both godless and (to use the German Romantic poet Novalis' phrase) "God-intoxicated". He was expelled from his Jewish community for "abominable heresies".

There is a deeply moving passage at the beginning of his unfinished *Treatise on the Correction of the Understanding*:

> After experience had taught me that all things which frequently take place in ordinary life are vain and futile; when I saw that all the things I feared and which feared me had nothing good or bad in them save in so far as the mind was affected by them, I determined at last to inquire whether there might be anything which might be truly good and able to communicate its goodness, and by which the mind might be affected to the exclusion of all other things: *I determined, I say, to inquire whether I might discover and acquire the faculty of enjoying throughout eternity continuing supreme happiness.*[4] (emphasis added).

It is striking that Spinoza, who denied personal immortality, still hoped for "continual supreme happiness" – presumably personally enjoyed – "throughout all eternity". This sets the bar impossibly high. A clear-eyed view of the order of things and one's own place in it may not be entirely cheering. And a preoccupation with "continual supreme happiness" may seem distasteful in a world where ordinary happiness is denied to many; where indeed suffering may be lifelong. The hungry, destitute, oppressed, despised, bereaved would settle for alleviation of their many sources of sorrow. To suffer without pain the loss of what we love and treasure would be to mock or betray one's very self and those with whom one has shared one's life. The aspiration to an impersonal viewpoint seems to set ordinary, but precious, life at nought. And it has to ignore the accidents necessary to live long enough to arrive at this state, and of being spared the metaphysical bad luck of dying before one is capable of philosophical wisdom.[5] What is more, the search for meaning – an idea of a meaningful life – that can withstand the knowledge of finitude is frustrated at every turn, not the least by our dis-tractable selves, now e-ttenuated and e-roded, divided into ever smaller fragments by the electronic termites nibbling at the connectedness of our consciousness, illustrating the irony of a more densely connected world resulting in more disconnected individuals.

But we need to consider this somewhat more carefully before we give way to despair. Happiness does not have to be justified, to be underpinned by reason. Indeed, there is a pleasing asymmetry: while many things may make us unhappy for good reason – hunger, bereavement, shame – happiness may be free-floating. And if it is backed up by justified moral satisfaction at a life that has contributed to removing the sources of unhappiness from the lives of others, then it may float longer. And we need to look critically at the eternity that humanists believe they are denied.

The relationship between moments of consciousness, the experience of the things of our lives, and great finite or infinite stretches of time is not simply one of less and more. Conscious experiences are not located in the same time-frame as the material events of which we are conscious. And there is no sense in which objective eternity – eternity understood as endless time – adds up to itself: it is unexperiencable. If eternity is to be found, it is to be discovered (perhaps) in the fathomless moment seen aright: in moments of joy, in love, in being lost in something truly worthwhile. This was captured by William Blake, when he urged us:

> To see a World in a Grain of Sand
> And a Heaven in a Wild Flower
> Hold Infinity in the palm of your hand
> And Eternity in an hour[6]

The appeal to this kind of eternity – eternity as timelessness as opposed to infinite time – at least redresses the imbalance between the excessive respect shown for the measured time of the clock, the calendar and natural science, and the experienced time of our daily life. It invites us to see the magical contingency of the quotidian in the possibility of the intersection of the time that has us in its grasp with ourselves who grasp time.

We invoked the image of the Ouroboros to highlight the extraordinary fact that we, miniscule objects in the material world, are able to enclose and judge that universe with our thoughts. We seem to contain the vast container that contains us. Thoughts about our capacity for thought inspire consoling sentiments such as these in the concluding passage from Russell's "A Free Man's Worship": "[I]n thought, in aspiration, we are free, free from our fellow men, free from the petty planet on which our bodies impotently crawl, free even, while we live, from the tyranny of death".[7]

If this is persuasive, however, is it because Russell conflates thoughts as *types* (that give access to the unchanging features of the universe) and thoughts as tokens, had by individuals at a particular time? Thoughts, alas, have to be thought by thinking reeds. The series of token thoughts will be ended by death or, indeed something less than death – a mere bang on the head, or a distraction. The most abstract thoughts never achieve the Platonic ideal of pure intelligibility. They are always compromised by the sense experience of the living thinker. What will free us from the tyranny of death will be the thought types that will exist independently of our life and death. Perhaps we need to dig deeper.

What is behind the notion of a meaningful universe – an idea whose own meaning, as we have noted, is in doubt? Perhaps it is the vision of the "I am", pitched in the "It is" of our bodies, being replicated in, or permeating, the totality of things. It is reflected in that of the Old Testament God as "the great I am" incarnate in a Saviour.[8] But this only highlights a contradiction: for the entire universe to have meaning, it would have either to be arranged around the concerns of the sum total of sentient creatures who matter to themselves (assuming *per impossibile* they are not conflicting, competitive, or mutually cancelling) or be identical with God, whose (first-person) Being and Thoughts are One with each other and with the universe. This would, it seems, leave no space for the individual meanings, concerns, and preoccupations, of actual individuals – human or otherwise – such as you and I.

Even so, the familiar lament that we not only live in a disenchanted world but in a meaningless universe, cannot be dismissed as the stain left behind by the withdrawal of religion. It correlates with a need felt, when other more basic needs are not extinguishing or displacing any transcendental aches, by the kind of creatures we are, sufficiently awoken from our organic state to mourn our finitude. While we may mock the transhumanists with their ambitions for liberation from our biological heritage, we should acknowledge that their desire to be folded out of harm's way into a universe that is one great mind, or "an interconnected system of information-seeking nodes, travelling in ever-widening arcs throughout the universe" is not entirely alien to the philosophical hunger so poignantly articulated by Spinoza.[9]

Two thoughts – that the meaninglessness of the universe is itself a meaningless notion and that we humans, neither apes nor angels, are utterly unclassifiable – throw open the window of possibility. Combine these with the Ouroboros, the mystery of reciprocal containment, then the fact that we die – an existential outrage – does not cancel all meaning. We might be freed to see the human world for what it is, our opened eyes dazzled by the obvious that is rich beyond expression and comprehension; freed to be astonished at the self-evident; to hold common-sense metaphysics with a mystical intensity.

Such is the form of spirituality – without God or corruptible institutions – to which humanism may strive. It is animated by, among other sentiments, gratitude for a world built by our predecessors, for the cultural heritage of which we are beneficiaries, which will include those wonderful works of sacred art – music, literature, cathedrals and temples. They are all the more extraordinary for being inspired by the idea of a God to which there corresponds only the infinite depth of human yearning and the boundless fertility of our imagination. We are neither angels nor Gods: we invented both; but that we have invented them should not be taken for granted.

It will be evident that the quarrel that has motivated this book is at least with myself as with others – and that it is far from settled. My aim has been the modest one of opening up a landscape of possibility: a sense of what we might be, and what we may become, given that, as Pascal said *l'homme passe infiniment l'homme.* Our status as historically evolving, articulate, self-shaping beings is the other side of the fact that we are in important respects incomplete.[10] By underlining the mystery of the "I am" in a universe of "it is", that lies equally beyond the reach of religion and natural science, I have left a door ajar.

Others perhaps will open it wider and let in more light.

Notes

ACKNOWLEDGEMENTS

1. Sellars, "Philosophy and the Scientific Image of Man", 35.

PREFACE

1. Wittgenstein, *Philosophical Investigations*, para 66.
2. Hyland & Jiang, "Changing Patterns of Self-Citation", 1–24 is relevant.
3. Quine, "The Nature of Natural Knowledge", 67.
4. Tallis, *The Hand: A Philosophical Inquiry into Human Being.*
5. Gilles Deleuze, quoted in O'Sullivan, "The Finite-Infinite Relation", 215.
6. J. S. Mill, "Bentham", 39.

CHAPTER 1

1. Law, *Humanism: A Very Short Introduction.*
2. Humanists UK website; https://humanism.org.uk/.
3. A. C. Grayling quoted in Baggini, "Is Common Ground between Religion and Atheism Possible?".
4. A. C. Grayling quoted in Baggini, "Myth of *Mythos*", 46.
5. If, in its eagerness to oppose religion, humanism tends to homogenize its adversary, clumping together 200 or more denominations, this may be understandable but is nonetheless undesirable. After all, not all faiths offer an after-life or seem particularly concerned with it. Judaism, Christianity's closest neighbour, is focused on this life and the challenges it presents, rather than any putative next life. We tend to envisage

"religion" in terms of the faith with which we are most familiar. In my case, it is Christianity, which does have the advantage of being the world's largest religion, with a congregation of over 2 billion (over a quarter of the entire population of the planet).

6. Kant, "Answering the Question: What is Enlightenment?".

7. Taylor, *A Secular Age*.

8. Kung, *On Being a Christian*, 89.

9. Kodaj, "Religious Evil".

10. Strickland, "The Problem of Religious Evil: Does Belief in God cause Evil?" – an article to which I am indebted in the present discussion.

11. This was, however, rather late and the recent history of the Church has often appeared to be one of belated and reluctant catching up with the more enlightened judgements in society at large; of being morally behind the curve rather than demonstrating moral leadership; of resisting, rather than driving, progress.

12. Quoted in Strickland, "The Problem of Religious Evil".

13. Dostoyevsky, *The Brothers Karamazov*. The most recent translation (said to be most faithful to the spirit of the original) has Ivan asking whether "Without God and the future life? It means that everything is permitted now, one can do everything", 150.

14. British Humanist Association (Humanists UK), *The Case for Secularism*.

15. Clark, "Secularization and Modernization: The Failure of the 'Grand Narrative'", 176. Indeed, Clark suggests that one aspect of egalitarianism – individualism – "may even be pushed back to individual burials – in England to the Bronze Age, ca 2500 BCE"!

16. McGhee, "Our Proud and Angry Dust", 162. The suggestion that monotheistic religion, far from being an obstacle to scientific progress, inspired the search for the laws of nature, being a manifestation of God's design in the world, does not, however, look very impressive when we remember China whose technological advances (for many centuries ahead of those in Christian Europe) were independent of any religious influence.

17. "Hitler's religious beliefs and fanaticism", quotations from *Mein Kampf* compiled by Jim Walker; available at https://www.nobeliefs.com/hitler.htm.

18. Jean-Paul Sartre cited and translated by Robert Cumming in *Starting Point*, 225.

19. Camus, *The Rebel* [*L'homme Revolté*], 12.

20. *Ibid.*, 11.

21. McGrath & McGrath, *The Dawkins Delusion? Atheist Fundamentalism and the Denial of the Divine*.

22. *Ibid.*

23. Buckley, "China is detaining muslims in vast numbers".

24. It has been argued by many theologians and religious apologists that religious belief does not describe any kind of reality and believers do not make knowledge claims. Religion, in short, is not about believing in, for example, a God who is some kind of entity, judgement day, or the Incarnation. This entirely goes against the empirical truth of the beliefs of the vast majority of believers. There is a lucid demolition of the claim that religious beliefs cannot be contradicted, even less refuted, because they have no cognitive content by Stephen Law in "Wittgensteinian Accounts of Religious Belief".

25. Nijinsky (ed.), *The Diary of Vaslav Nijinsky*.

26. Béla Hamvas was a twentieth-century Hungarian polymath and philosopher who was forced by the communists to earn his living as a factory worker in appalling conditions. It is cited in his Wikipedia entry.

27. In 1808, the Bavarian minister for education invented the term *Humanismus* to designate the reformed classical curriculum he had devised for introduction into German secondary schools. In 1856, Georg Voigt used "humanism" with reference to the movement in the Italian Renaissance to revive classical learning. In the French Enlightenment, it had had a more extensive reference to refer to a general love of humanity.

28. Sen, "Greek, Roman, Hebrew or Arabic", 24.

29. Della Mirandola, *Oration on the Dignity of Man*. It is now generally accepted that Renaissance humanism was less of a philosophical movement than a body of knowledge about classical letters. It was not anti-religious or even conspicuously anti-clerical. However, it is reasonable to assume that, by giving credence to pre-Christian, indeed Pagan, thought, it opened the door to secular humanism. What is more, via the development of the principles of philology and careful scholarship, the Renaissance birth of the humanities paved the way for the future, corrosive "higher criticism" of the Bible, treating it as a (secular) text.

30. British Social Attitudes 36 (2018); available at: http://www.bsa.natcen.ac.uk/latest-report/british-social-attitudes-36/religion.aspx.

31. "Religion", YouGov poll (2012).

32. Johnson, *The Soul of China*.

33. *Wikipedia* "Christianity in Africa"; https://en.wikipedia.org/wiki/Christianity_in_Africa (accessed 2 August 2019).

34. Sherwood, "Religion: why faith is becoming more and more popular", 10–11.

35. Most presciently by Bell, "The Return of the Sacred? The Argument on the Future of the Religion".

36. Berger, "The Desecularisation of the World: A Global Overview".

37. Micklethwait & Wooldridge, *God is Back: How the Global Rise of Religion is Changing the World*.

38. Rée, "Atheism and History", 64–5.

39. Jeffries, "Is That All There Is?"

40. Harrison, "Narratives of Secularization", 3. I shall return to this in the last chapter.

41. Chesterton, *Orthodoxy*, chapter 2.

42. Marx, *Theses on Feuerbach*, number 6.

43. For a more detailed discussion, see "Worries about Universalism" in Tallis, *Enemies of Hope*. The Parisian anti-humanists are also discussed in this book.

44. Pascal, *Pensées*, 434.

45. Gordon-Reed, "Might vs Right", 12.

46. Barthes, "The Great Family of Man" in *Mythologies*.

47. *Ibid.*, 11. For a critique of Barthes' assault on The Great Family of Man, see Tallis, *Enemies of Hope*, 400. Norman, *On Humanism*, 79–82 also puts Barthes firmly in his place.

48. Discussed in Kronfeldner, *What's Left of Human Nature?* Kronfeldner wonders whether it would be better to do without the notion of human nature altogether. For

reasons that will become evident, I strongly disagree with this conclusion, although I am sympathetic to her concerns.

49. The Universal Declaration of Human Rights adopted by the UN General Assembly, 10 December 1948.

50. Brecht, "Posterity", 227. The full quote is "What times are these, when / To speak of trees is almost a crime / Because it passes in silence over such infamy!" I used to read it rather literally – that the traditional preoccupations of lyric poets were no longer appropriate in a world when there was so much wickedness to speak out against – but I am now persuaded that it is a sigh of complaint against the wearisome obligation to commit one's art to bringing about political change.

51. And we are not humans in the way that a particular chemical element is that element – otherwise we would lack free will. Our human essence is something that has to be (collectively and individually) asserted in order to be maintained and expressed. Our nature is profoundly influenced by the idea we have of our nature.

52. Tallis, *Not Saussure: A Critique of Post-Saussurean Literary Theory.*

53. Quine, *From Stimulus to Science*, 16.

54. Quine, "Mr. Strawson on Logical Theory", 446. The role of philosophy as the hand-maiden of science is clearly described by James Ladyman and Donald Ross: "If a metaphysical claim is to be taken seriously ... it should show how one or more *scientific hypotheses*, at least one of them *specific* and at least one of them both specific and drawn from fundamental physics ... jointly explain more than the sum of what is explained by the two hypotheses taken separately" (*Everything Must Go*, 37). However, in a later paper, "An Apology for a Naturalized Metaphysics", Ladyman admits that "science offers us ontologies at many different levels. The ontological commitments of the special sciences should be taken as metaphysically on a par with those of physics. For example, there are atoms, cells, organisms, agents, social structures and indeed tables."

55. Ernest Gellner cited in Merquior, *Foucault*, 150.

56. Wittgenstein, *Philosophical Investigations*, para. 127.

57. Yeats, "Death" in *The Collected Poems of W. B. Yeats*, 198.

CHAPTER 2

1. Less than 15 per cent of professional philosophers are theist; Law, *Humanism*, 143.

2. Stroud, "The Charm of Naturalism".

3. This is echoed in Cheng, "Quine's Naturalism and Behaviourism": "The distinguishing characteristic of this doctrine is that when someone regards herself as a naturalist, others cannot confidently attribute any specific thesis to her without making heavy assumptions – it may include views as to how we pursue knowledge, about the way we live, and about what there is", 548.

4. Armstrong, "Naturalism, Materialism and First Philosophy", 156.

5. Buchner, *Force and Matter*, lxxvii.

6. Quine, *From Stimulus to Science*, 16.

7. Quine, "Naturalism; Or Living Within One's Means", 251. The idea that philosophers

should not only take their cue from the findings of science but also judge the validity of any metaphysical theories by the extent to which they are consistent with cutting-edge natural science has been a constant theme in Anglophone philosophy since the early twentieth century.

8. Stroud, "The Charm of Naturalism", 54. Maddy has suggested an even more hospitable characterization of naturalism: "[N]aturalism, as I understand it, is not a doctrine, but an approach; not a set of answers but a way of answering questions. As such, it can hardly be described in a list of theses: it can be seen only in action", cited in Mendelovici & Bourget, "Consciousness and Intentionality", 37.

Even scientism can be defanged. James Ladyman's "Scientism with a Humane Face" argues that, though science studies the natural world, "we ourselves and our cultures and societies are part of the natural world". However, he also asserts in *Scientism: Prospects and Projects* that "there is something in the idea that every putatively non-physical thing, such as a mind, somehow depends on the physical stuff associated with it" and that "there are prima facie grounds for some kind of asymmetric supervenience of everything on the physical" (137).

Another manifestation of expansive naturalism is the liberal naturalism, discussed in the essays collected in De Caro & MacArthur (eds), *Naturalism and Normativity*. It emphasizes that the impersonal stance of a "dehumanized science" should not be privileged over other stances that acknowledge the reality of phenomenal experience and the norms (reasons and values) that regulate our lives, including scientific modes of inquiry.

9. G. Strawson, "Real Naturalism". Strawson argues that what is usually called naturalism is in fact "wildly anti-naturalist" because it treats "the basic data of experience ... as if it were its greatest problem and had tried to deal with it by questioning its existence or at least questioning its claim to be in a fundamental respect, exactly as it seems, and indeed it is" (142).

10. Tallis, *Aping Mankind: Neuromania, Darwinitis, and the Misrepresentation of Humanity*.

11. Ramachandran, *The Tell-Tale Brain: A Neuroscientist's Quest for What Makes Us Human*.

12. Tallis, *The Hand: A Philosophical Inquiry into Human Being*. This is the first part of a trilogy that sets out in a mere 1,000 pages the way in which we differ from other living creatures.

13. Suddendorf, *The Gap: The Science of What Separates Us from Other Animals*, 1.

14. De Waal, *Are We Smart Enough to See How Smart Animals Are?* It has also been pointed out that the dice may be loaded against animals by testing them "on tasks at which humans excel or are taken directly from human psychology, without consideration of the animal's own distinctive abilities or ecological niche" (Buckner, "Morgan's Canon meets Hume's Dictum", 859. Buckner also quotes research into "theory of mind" (or its absence) in non-human primates that "violates ideals of fairness by pitting captive chimpanzees against free-ranging humans, humans working with conspecifics against chimpanzees working with heterospecifics, humans with parents nearby against apes without parents nearby, or humans on familiar materials against apes on unfamiliar materials" (866). This argument would be more compelling if we

had evidence, arising from scientific studies performed by free-range, grant-awarded chimps on caged human subjects. The vast cognitive distance between ourselves and our nearest primate kin is evident in all the steps that have led to humans studying chimps and not vice versa.

15. Midgley, *Beast and Man: The Roots of Human Nature*, 210. In fact, those mental functions that I will identify as unique to humans still draw on capacities not seen in animal consciousness, even when they are performed very badly.

16. Charles Darwin quoted in Suddendorf, *The Gap*, 41.

17. See Clayton, "Ways of Thinking: From Crows to Children and Back Again".

18. Almost as far-fetched are the claims made by Peter Wohlleben, *The Inner Life of Animals*. They include bees that are self-conscious and can remember people who have harmed them and a brainless slime mold that can memorize a maze. The latter is derived from a study published in a top-rank scientific journal, Reid *et al.*, "Slime Mold Uses an Externalized Spatial 'Memory' to Navigate in Complex Environments". The mold preferentially avoids areas that contain extracellular slime from recent exploration, thus avoiding futile repetition of search for nutrition in areas that have been previously explored. This is clearly not a question of memory but of an avoiding response to a stimulus that marks its own previous track. We must not expect that it feels nostalgia for the past journeys and its youth when it set out with a pocket full of hope.

19. Jane Goodall quoted in Midgley, *Beast and Man*, 227.

20. Suddendorf, *The Gap*, 44.

21. Hippocrates, "On the Sacred Disease", 344–5.

22. Quoted in G. Strawson, "Real Naturalism", 139.

23. Many of the ways human dining differs from animal feeding are examined in Kass, *The Hungry Soul: Eating and the Perfecting of Our Nature*. There is a fascinating discussion of developments, such as the liberation of the mouth from a prehensile role, that are important precursors of the hedonistic, social and ritualistic aspects of human dining.

24. Wrangham, *Catching Fire: How Cooking Made us Human*.

25. The humblest "ingredient" draws on the most profound individual and shared cognitive activity. The separate cultivation, manufacture, synthesis, collection, storage and distribution of these materials, and the supply chains that link us with them, is not only a marker of the distance between human and animal nutrition but also an important reminder of something central to voluntary human activity: that we do, bring about, things only because we know what we are doing and why. We shall examine this in more detail in Chapter 6. For the present we may note that humans not only *make the means of their own subsistence*, as Marx pointed out, but they make the means to make the means of their own subsistence. This is particularly clearly instantiated in the case of ingredients manufactured separately and stored apart until they are required.

26. Donald, *The Origin of the Modern Mind: Three Stages in the Evolution of Culture and Cognition* has emphasized this. It explains why there is no "flexible, customised teaching of virtually indefinite content that is evident in humans" (Suddendorf, *The Gap*, 182). If we did not teach ourselves – by rehearsing and active memorizing – of course, we could not make sense of the action of teaching others. No wonder it takes

chimpanzees several years to learn to crack a nut (*ibid.*). Eva Jablonka among others has talked about the transmission of behavioural traditions in animals, but it is very limited. Examples include the passing on of food preferences. See, for example, Avital and Jablonka, *Animal Traditions: Behavioural Inheritance in Evolution*.

27. Suddendorf reports that "after decades of systematic observation, there are only two instances of proposed ape teaching in the literature" (*The Gap*, 183).

28. *Ibid.*, 182.

29. The centrality of learning to human life reflects the extent to which we are incomplete, as Arnold Gehlen argued, "Unlike animals, humans are endowed with stable innate instincts only to a very limited extent. They have only residual instincts and they are not adapted to any specific environment ... Human motor activity is for the most part acquired and learned, whereas in animals the range of learned motor skills is significantly limited. This fact is linked to the plasticity of human nature, which enables humans to adapt to a wide range of environments." Cited in Halák & Klouda, "The Institution of Life: Gehlen and Merleau-Ponty", 374.

30. Recently summarized in Tomasello, *A Natural History of Human Thinking*.

31. See Schweikard and Schmid, "Collective Intentionality".

32. Suddendorf, *The Gap*, 146.

33. Between the alternative interpretations of brute associative learning driven by trial and error, in response to sensory stimuli, and the sophisticated possession of general concepts, there is a third possibility: imaginative cognition. This is discussed by Christopher Gauker, "Visual Imagery in the Thought of Monkeys and Apes". The fundamental point, however, is untouched: the lack of generalization to solving similar problems, remains. By such fruits, or rather lack of them, shall you know them.

34. See Tallis, *Logos*. This is a riposte to the smart-Alec claim by the pathologically misanthropic John Gray that "Humankind is unique in its incapacity to learn from experience" ("Question and Answer", 7).

35. Goodall, *Through a Window: My Thirty Years with the Chimpanzees of Gombe*, 208.

36. See, for example, Tallis, *Michelangelo's Finger: An Exploration of Everyday Transcendence* for an extensive discussion.

37. The most detailed treatment is by Richard Dawkins in *The Extended Phenotype: The Long Reach of the Gene*.

38. Dawkins, *The Extended Phenotype*, 109.

39. See "The Sighted Watchmaker" in Tallis, *Aping Mankind*.

40. In this section, I have homogenized consciousness. Consciousness, of course, has many facets and dimensions. We may distinguish: sentience, object perception, propositional awareness "that", other propositional attitudes such as hope and fear, awareness of a world, unity of a self at and over a time, sense of one's own past and future, ascription of selfhood to others, entertaining individual and shared long-term goals, and a moral sense rooted in empathy, a sense of responsibility, and duty. Whether or not this is the whole story or the best way of distinguishing modes of consciousness, it is a useful reminder of its intrinsic complexity and irreducible variety.

41. Grant Bartley has argued (I believe correctly) in "Why Physicalism is Wrong" that it is self-contradictory to identify experience with physical events because a physical event involves physical things that are incompletely revealed in experience and this

could hardly be true of experiences. The argument holds up even if it is argued (as I will do in the next chapter) that our sense of the opaque "in-itself" of physical objects is derived from the experience of our body which is *lived* as a whole, though it is *experienced* patchily.

42. Described in harrowing detail in Thomas de Quincey, "The Last Days of Kant".

43. Salomons *et al.*, "'The Pain Matrix' in Pain-Free Individuals".

44. Feinstein *et al.*, "Preserved Emotional Awareness of Pain in Patients with Extensive Bilateral Damage to the Insula, Anterior Cingulate, and Amygdala".

45. Summarized by Wilder Penfield in "Memory Mechanisms". The stimuli used by Penfield were gross and so gave little insight into the relevant neural pathways. More recent work in waking subjects stimulating the particular area of the brain associated with perception of faces resulted in visual distortions of actual faces but not of other objects; see Parvizi *et al.*, "Electrical Stimulation of Human Fusiform Face-Selective Regions Distorts Face Perception". More precise stimulation studies have been carried out in waking Macaques, showing that the activity of a single neuron in a particular visual area predicts the animal's visual discrimination of motion; see Ruff and Cohen, "Relating the Activity of Sensory Neurons to Perception".

46. There are particularly tricky questions around the possibility of the neural activity that is supposed to underpin the experiences of those neuroscientists to whom it is supposedly revealed that experience is underpinned by neural activity.

47. Crane, "Intentionality as the Mark of the Mental".

48. Jacob, "Intentionality", 1.

49. Franz Brentano quoted in Jacob, "Intentionality", 3. Brentano rather regretted adopting the medieval term.

50. The contained object is described as being "intentionally inexistent".

51. In the second edition of Brentano's seminal *Psychology from an Empirical Standpoint* (180–1): "Intentionality" as been misunderstood in that some people thought that it had something to do with intention and the pursuit of goals. In view of this, I might have done better to avoid it altogether. There is an important overlap between the two terms in the Latin root of "tendere" to reach out.

52. Dennett, *Consciousness Explained*, 33. This is supplemented by Dennett's "ground rule" – "to explain every puzzling feature of human consciousness within the framework of contemporary physical science" (40).

53. Searle, *The Mystery of Consciousness*, 6. Searle believed that consciousness is caused by brain activity but the mode of causation is non-event causation. What does he mean by this? He holds that brain activity stands to consciousness as water molecules (which are not slippery or shiny) stand to drops of water (which are slippery and shiny). There are many faults in this position. The most important is that it draws on the fact that stuffs *seen* at different levels may appear to have different properties. This way he thinks to avoid a form of dualism in which material neural causes have conscious effects. But the seeing – necessary for seeing at different levels – is precisely what we are trying to explain. Vision at a macroscopic level is necessary to turn water molecules into slippery, shiny stuff. If the analogy were valid, we would need to experience neural activity at a macroscopic level (and hence to be conscious of it in a different way) to make it conscious. In short, Searle requires different modes of

consciousness to explain how neural activity, without being a distinct cause, can be the basis of consciousness. His "non-event causation" is anyway dubious: it amounts to the notion that a stuff seen at one level (molecules of H_2O) can *cause* the properties of the stuff seen at another level (slippery, shiny, macroscopic water). We are asked to imagine one level of a stuff causing *itself* as seen at another level.

54. Astonishingly, a recent survey found that 50 per cent of American adults believed in extramission as the basis of vision; see Winer *et al.*, "Fundamentally Misunderstanding Visual Perception: Adults' Beliefs in Visual Emission".

55. I owe this point to William Rosar, *The Localization of the Mind: Why We Think the Mind is in the Head*.

56. Grice, "The Causal Theory of Perception", 121. The critique that follows applies *a fortiori* to the so-called "causal theory of [linguistic] reference" whereby the referent of a word is fixed by an original act of naming (a baptism) to which later references are causally linked.

57. Grice, "The Causal Theory of Perception", 108.

58. Items such as pains and floaters "seem to have location and extension in space and time, and we effortlessly talk about them using singular terms and we predicated properties of them as we do of objects and events" (Crane, "Intentionality as the Mark of the Mental", 6).

59. Andrew Pinsent has questioned this claim (personal communication). The causal sequence leading from an acorn to a full-grown tree, he argues, has a natural end-point. There are two reasons why this is not the case. Firstly, there is no point at which the tree is full-grown. And, secondly, the causal sequences continue, without interruption or discontinuities, past any stage in the tree's development to an eventual state in which the tree has become a rotting log dissolving in the soil. It is we, the observers, who confer unity upon the tree (which is the site of innumerable causal processes) by gazing at it at a macroscopic level, and we who stipulate a particular state of the tree as an end-stage.

60. A complementary point is made by Galen Strawson when he asks why perceptions reach all the way to objects, rather than being experiences of the photons impacting on the retina or any other of the causal way-stations en route to neural activity in the visual cortex. See G. Strawson, "Real Intentionality 3: Why Intentionality Entails Consciousness".

61. Quinton, "The Problem of Perception", 61.

62. It is evident that the actual existence and the location of the relevant object in the vicinity of a functioning eye is a necessary condition of a truthful perception. This does not make it a sufficient condition. One version of the causal theory of perception, therefore, might seem to hold up: the counterfactual theory. We can say that if light arising from the glass did not enter the visual system of the subject, there would be no seeing of it. To say this, however, is only to highlight the inadequacy of the counterfactual theory of causation, which I discuss at some length in *Of Time and Lamentation*; see Section 11.2.2.3 "Causes as Counterfactuals".

63. Dennett, "Facing up to the Hard Question of Consciousness", 2.

64. Fodor, "Semantics, Wisconsin Style", 232.

65. Rosenberg, "Eliminativism without Tears: A Nihilistic Stance on the Theory of Mind", 13.

66. Daniel Dennett quoted in Crane, "Intentionality as the Mark of the Mental", 14.

67. Dennett's most detailed exposition of this idea (which he has been promoting since his earliest publications in the 1960s) is in *The Intentional Stance*, especially the chapter "True Believers".

68. Dennett, *The Intentional Stance*, 29. This formulation of Dennett's position seems to deny objective or any other kind of reality to beliefs and desires. And he consistently claims that they do not correspond to brain states. At other times, he seems to concede that they are real and objective. This is discussed with great subtlety in Eronen, "Interventionism for the Intentional Stance: True Believers and their Brains".

69. Dennett, *The Intentional Stance*, 42.

70. Dennett, "Intentional Systems Theory", 87–8.

71. Dennett, "Philosophy as Naïve Anthropology: Comment on Bennett and Hacker", 89.

72. Quassim Cassam defines them as "particular items which are capable of being perceived and of *existing unperceived*" (*Self and World*, 28, emphasis added).

73. The most informative senses are those that, as it were, get themselves, their phenomenal content, out of the way, and there is less "what it is like" to have them. A pain *is* almost entirely what it is like to have (and is private and so cannot be pointed to – although we may point to the place where it is at or describe its general characteristics), whereas a view of a landscape is what "the landscape" is like. The phenomenal, as it were, gets in the way of the intentional. That is why, for some philosophers, the contrast is between intransitive and transitive contents of consciousness.

74. The explicit separation between the conscious subject and its object of consciousness was central to the phenomenological ontology of Sartre in *Being and Nothingness*: that which separated consciousness from it, or any object, was Nothingness. To be a conscious subject was to be other than any object, including the self-as-object. The process by which consciousness opens up a nothingness-filled space between it and the object of which it is conscious is called "nihilation".

75. Discussed in Suddendorf, *The Gap*; see also Tomasello and Carpenter, "Shared Intentionality". The experiments reported by Daniel Povinelli in *Folk Physics for Apes* suggest that object permanence and the sense of causal properties intrinsic to objects are poorly developed. A more recent ingenious study, which involved providing chimps with faulty tools, confirms that they are not blessed with "a mechanism for causal diagnostic reasoning"; see Povinelli and Frei, "Constraints on the Exploitation of the Functional Properties of Objects in Expert Tool-Using Chimpanzees (Pan Troglodytes)".

76. Anthony Quinton: "The terminology of objects is used to refer to what is invariant between the private worlds of experience" ("The Problem of Perception", 61).

77. The uniqueness of collective intentionality in humans – how it is unlike pack, herd, flock, or swarm behaviour – is discussed in Kaufman, "Collective Intentionality: A Human Not a Monkey Business". To look at this another way: where we do act as a member of a group, the other members are often invisible, unlike packs, herds, etc. There is a non-cognitive aspect to this uniqueness. Rosas and Bermuzez in "Viewing Others as Equal: The Non-Cognitive Role of Shared Intentionality" have discussed the extent to which the intuition and acknowledgement of another as equal to one's self is part of the infrastructure of shared intentionality.

78. For further discussion, see Tallis, *Michelangelo's Finger*.
79. See, in particular, Tomasello and Carpenter, "Shared Intentionality".
80. For a more detailed discussion of the unique characteristics of human tool use, see Tallis, "*Homo Faber*".
81. Suddendorf, *The Gap*, 38.
82. Steven Weinberg quoted in Stuart, "Breaking the Galilean Spell", 1. For Weinberg, the crock at the end of the rainbow of scientific inquiry is meaninglessness. As he said "the more the universe seems comprehensible, the more it also seems pointless" (*The First Three Minutes*, 144). Given that Weinberg summarizes the most advanced theory in his home discipline of physics as explaining the universe as "various modes of vibration in tiny one-dimensional rips in space-time known as strings" (quoted in Strawson, *Selves*, 295), the pointlessness seems built into what counts as comprehensibility.
83. Strawson, *Real Naturalism*, 125.
84. See, for example, Tallis, *Logos*, Chapter 4, Addendum 2. One way of addressing the so-called combinatorial problem – the problem of explaining how sequins of consciousness spread through the world add up to a subject – is to deflate the subject. The subject is reduced to successive experiences, or time-slices of a flow of experience: there are no persisting subjects; each distinct experience has its own experiencer. This merely transfers the problem to that of explaining how experiences add up to a subject who has a sense of herself at a time and over time and is acknowledged to be a person by other subjects also acknowledged to be persons. It is not at all clear by what means, by who or what, the thin subjects are stitched together and how we would survive sleep or episodes of unconsciousness.

    There is an excellent discussion in Nesic, "Against Deflation of the Subject" in which the unity, the subject-summing, and the boundaries of consciousness are discussed. We shall return to this in Chapter 5.
85. Galen Strawson's reference to the "well-known difficulty in the whole area of the adaptive function of experience", is pertinent: "it seems that all behavioural responses that have adaptive value could possibly have existed in the absence of experience" (Strawson, "Real Naturalism", 150). The example of "blindsight", in which patients who have lost the experience of vision and who seem nonetheless able to sense where objects are located, raises further questions about the function of conscious experience.

    Lawrence Weiskrantz, who studied such patients over many years, did, however note that they lacked the capacity to think about or to image the objects that they can respond to in other sensory modalities, and this was seriously disabling; see Weiskrantz, "Introduction: Dissociated Issues". We also note that while blind-sight is rare, seeing-sight is overwhelmingly typical. What is more, there is an alternative explanation of apparent blindsight: the tendency to be very cautious in reporting stimuli under near-threshold conditions; see Campion, Latto and Smith, "Is Blind-Sight an Effect of Scattered Light, Spared Cortex, and Near-Threshold Vision?" (This argument addresses only the point that, if a species is typically conscious, then to be deprived of aspects of consciousness, is to be disadvantaged). Anyone unpersuaded by what can be achieved without consciousness should read about microbial intelligence; a good starting place is Ford, "Revealing the Ingenuity of the Living Cell".

86. Flanagan, *Consciousness Reconsidered*.

87. Hassin, "Yes it Can: On the Functional Abilities of the Human Unconscious", 195.

88. Gutfreund, "The Neuroethological Paradox of Animal Consciousness", 199.

89. Oxenberg, "Why Does Pain Hurt? An Inquiry into the Limits of Evolutionary Explanation".

90. Schmidt and Dejean, "A Dolichoderine Ant that Constructs Traps to Ambush Prey Collectively: Convergent Evolution with a Myrmicine Genus".

91. Nagel, *The View from Nowhere*, 78–9.

92. Strawson, "Real Naturalism", 142.

93. Goff, "Panpsychism is Crazy but it is also Most Probably True", 1.

94. Fodor, "Semantics, Wisconsin Style", 232.

95. Dennett, *From Bacteria to Bach and Back: The Evolution of Minds*. If our comprehension were so thin on the ground, it is difficult to see how we could have built up the huge database that supports Dennett's argument that our competencies are overwhelmingly void of comprehension. The emphasis on competence without comprehension is simply another aspect of this thinker's desire to abolish that awkward customer intentionality – through denying qualia, dismissing propositional attitudes such as beliefs and desires, reducing intentionality to something that is merely ascribed for methodological reasons, and libelling the self as a user illusion (see Chapter 5). Consciousness is a problem for a fundamentalist Darwinian such as Dennett. He emphasizes (correctly) that evolution is a mindless process but cannot accommodate the fact that mind pops up and is very prominent in the lives of his conspecifics. He tries to incorporate sighted watchmakers such as you and me in the blind processes, the unconscious algorithms, of the material universe. Enough already.

96. Baird Callicot, "The Wilderness Idea Revisited: The Sustainable Development Alternative", 350.

97. Ground, "The Stupendous Intelligence of Honey Badgers", 9. This review of Frans de Waal's *Are We Smart Enough to See How Smart Animals Are?* is a wonderful essay.

98. Elwood, "Evidence for Pain in Decapod Crustaceans".

99. Chittka, "Bee Cognition".

100. "Cooperative Pulling Paradigm", *Wikipedia* (accessed October 2018) – an article to which the discussion that follows is heavily indebted.

101. Krupenye *et al.*, "Great Apes Anticipate that Other Individuals will act According to False Beliefs".

102. Quoted in Kaufman, "Collective Intentionality", 121.

CHAPTER 3

1. "If we would have true knowledge of anything, we must quit the body", Plato (*Phaedo*) quoted in Russell, *A History of Western Philosophy*. Knowledge – or thought – which has only a toe-hold at best on experience, is the mode of self-presence most distant from the body. The fantasy of thought perfected by escape from our corporeal being is therefore unsurprising. The idea of thoughts being thought without being instantiated in tokens thought by an individual thinker necessarily located in space and time is, however, self-contradictory.

Andrew Pinsent (personal communication) has commented on the tendency to go straight from the classical Greeks to post-Cartesian early-modern philosophy is to miss out important figures, notably Aquinas, for whom the soul is the form or the intelligible constitution of the body (*Summa Theologia* 1.76.a.1). The medieval account, he says, is not dualist but that of an embodied soul. Pinsent has also drawn my attention to Tertullian: "The truth is that the flesh is the very condition on which salvation hinges" (*De Resurrectione Carnis* 8–9).

2. Scruton, *I Drink Therefore I Am*, 53–4.
3. Patocka, "Being-in-the-Body and Phenomenology", 70.
4. *Ibid.*
5. The frame of reference that arises from the point of view tethered to the body is not a mathematical one. The latter is a virtual position, liberated from experienced intervals.
6. "According to Merleau-Ponty living beings' bodily-perceptive relationship with environment can be understood neither as a mere centripetal registration of empirical contents, nor as a centrifugal 'grasping' of meanings intelligible by themselves thanks to some pre-established *a priori* logic (e.g. instincts)", Halák & Klouda, "The Institution of Life", 883. English translation kindly provided to the author by Jan Halák.
7. Philip Larkin, "Ignorance" (1955) in *Collected Poems*.
8. While I am not sure that Jan Halák would entirely agree with all of what follows, his luminous and suggestive paper "Merleau-Ponty on Embodied Subjectivity from the Perspective of Subject-Object Circularity" has proved very helpful to me.
9. Henry Head quoted in Halák, "Merleau-Ponty on Embodied Subjectivity", 33.
10. Merleau-Ponty's interpretation of the body schema as summarised by Halák & Klouda "Institution of Life in Gehlen and Merleau-Ponty", 385.
11. Merleau-Ponty quoted in Halák & Klouda, "Institution as a General Model of Meaning".
12. Merleau-Ponty's lifelong endeavour was "to understand how man is simultaneously object and subject".
13. Locke, *Two Treatises of Government*, Second Treatise, para 27.
14. Shakespeare, *Sonnets* 94.
15. For a more detailed investigation of the body-as-agent, see Tallis, *The Hand*.
16. See Chung, "Gesticulation as the Integration of Body and Mind: Semantics of Nodding".
17. Anthony Burgess, *Earthly Powers*, 201 (US edition).
18. Sartre, *Nausea*, 143–4. Readers familiar with Sartre's writing, especially *Being and Nothingness*, will be aware of his ghost co-haunting these pages with his one-time friend and ultimate adversary Merleau-Ponty.
19. See Nagel, "What is it Like to be a Bat?", 436.
20. Hacker, "Is there Anything it is Like to be a Bat?". It is arguable that certain experiences such as itches and pains are neither intransitive nor fully transitive.
21. *Ibid.*, 157.
22. *Ibid.*, 167.
23. The postulated boundary between hard problems of consciousness – such as understanding phenomenal experiences – and the easy problems such as various cognitive

functions is highly dubious; see Tallis, "David Chalmers' Unsuccessful Search for the Conscious Mind" in *Reflections of a Metaphysical Flaneur*.

24. When the brain is given over to overwhelming spontaneous activity, as in a generalized seizure, the subject is blotted out: consciousness and agency are temporarily lost.

25. Wittgenstein, *Philosophical Investigations*, II, xi, 223e.

26. Koch *et al.*, "Neural Correlates of Consciousness". Koch *et al.*'s conclusion from a review of the vast literature on NCC is admirably honest. Progress in the search for NCC "will require, in addition to empirical work, testable theories that address in principle what consciousness is and what is required of a physical substrate" (317). I would suggest that once we have a clear idea of what consciousness is, we will cease to try to identify a physical substrate, even less one to be found in a subset of neurones.

27. The distinction between the object of experience and the phenomenal content of experience, has profound implications. We have already noted that it is possible, indeed common, to have an experience and not know what it is an experience of. This ignorance can seem to characterize even experiences which have restricted intentionality, for example an itch. The intervention of language widens this gap. I cannot be mistaken in having a certain sensation, but I can be mistaken in naming, that is to say, classifying it as (say) "an itch" and, of course, in ascribing it to a certain cause. Experiences are not self-identifying, self-naming, or self-classifying. My younger son's claiming as a five-year old that he had a headache in his knee illustrates this. The gap between sentience and knowledge, between sense experience and factual knowledge is an important element of the distance that enables us to engage with the natural world from without, which I will discuss in Chapter 6.

28. The "heteroscope" of collective knowledge presents just as many challenges to the idea that being RT is being "What it is like to be RT's brain". If I were my brain – so that my brain would not be outside of me as an object of knowledge, never mind as an object of general knowledge – how would I get to know that I was certain activity in a certain brain? How would my brain get to know that it was me, or even that it was *my* brain?

29. Schilder and Wechsler, quoted in Rosar, *The Localisation of the Mind*, have highlighted this:

> [A]s far as direct experience goes, we know nothing of the organs inside our bodies; all that we are aware of is a heavy mass ... Bodily sensations, except that of weight, are concentrated on the surface and what we know of our organs is acquired intellectual knowledge ... Our direct experience of our own body is based on visual and tactile impressions, on perceptions of the weight of the body and its various parts, and on happenings on the sensitive surface. (5)

And Rosar quotes a survey which showed that the average person "typically did not know the accurate position of viscera such as heart, stomach, kidneys, and liver, and were often grossly in error as to their actual size" (6).

30. Patocka, *Body, Community, Language, World*, 155.

31. Hume, *A Treatise of Human Nature*, 3.1.1.27.

32. Evolutionary ethicists think they have cracked this by focusing on living matter and the replicative imperative: you can get an ought – for example, that we should treat each other well – in order to secure an is – that this will maximize the replicative potential of the genes we share with our conspecifics. This does not deliver what is needed for the reason we gave in the last chapter. If consciousness cannot be explained as a product of evolutionary pressures, evaluative consciousness, and the normative sense, most certainly cannot.

33. P. F. Strawson, *The Bounds of Sense: An Essay on Kant's Critique of Pure Reason*, 88.

34. As Strawson expressed it, "objective experiences" include "judgements about what is the case irrespective of particular subjective experiences of them" (*Bounds of Sense*, 24) and "experiences of objects that are distinct from experiences of them" (65).

35. This passage from the theologian Emmanuel Durand is highly pertinent: "Perceiving implies a synthesis of adequate and inadequate perception. Perfect and integral perception is only some ideal since we always perceive phenomena in temporal and partial ways, by multiplying visual angles and by superposing memories. That which appears to us always leaves some space which does not appear at all or does not yet appear. 'No perception of the visible without a co-perception of the invisible' contends [Jean-Yves] Lacoste" (Durand, "God's Holiness: A Reappraisal of Transcendence", 421).

36. The argument that follows overlaps the famous discussion by Edmund Husserl of touching my own body, helpfully summarized and critiqued in Romano, "After the Lived-Body":

> The lived-body (*Leib*) is my body inasmuch as it reveals it-self to me in a sin-gular experience: for example, my hand coming into contact with any other part of my body. In that experience, the part of my body to which I apply my touch (for example, my other hand) appears not only as "touched", but in turn, as the seat of tactile sensations, in such a way that we have here a double-sensation in each body part, a phenomenon in which each of these parts of my body appears alternatively as touching and touched; these two characteristics keep exchanging themselves, repeating to each other in a reciprocal, mirror-like way. (452)

However, as Romano points out, Husserl's conception of the fundamental "life-world" does not provide a basis for objective, physical bodies. As earlier noted, I do not *discover* my body as mine. Romano makes the point, against Husserl, that "My body reveals itself from the start as a primordial location that I occupy first of all by virtue of the radical difference between the sensibility by which I relate to this body and my general sensibility to the world around me" (457).

He calls the former "egocentric sensibility" and the latter "allocentric sensibility". For this reason, the experience of double-sensation is "radically insufficient" for our sense of embodiment. Romano also draws attention to Husserl's excessive emphasis on one sense: touch. Additionally, it is worth pointing out that the relation between the two hands is not always symmetrical – the dominant hand is the toucher and the other the touched. This asymmetry is even more clearly evident when the hand touches another part of the body. This is discussed in Tallis, *The Hand*.

37. Quassim Cassam discusses this in "The Embodied Self". We need to specify the nature of that "inside" carefully. It is not identified with the subcutaneous interior. After all, the burning of my skin after sunbathing is just as inside as a fullness in my stomach. Indeed, "from the inside" is not a literal viewpoint, or the locus of a viewpoint. Nevertheless, it remains the case that, as argued in the main text, our awareness of the body "from within" presents itself as the archetype of an object that has a "metaphysical inside", or an in-itself.

    It is worth comparing this claim with the less radical (and perhaps less reckless) one made by Cassam in "Representing Bodies". According to Cassam, "awareness of one's one body is the necessary condition for the acquisition and possession of primary qualities such as force and shape", 315.

38. And both thought the same of minds. As Hume expressed it: "The identity we ascribe to the mind of man is only a fictitious one, and of a like kind with that which we ascribe to animal and vegetable bodies" (*A Treatise of Human Nature*, Book 1, Part 4, Section 6, 234).

39. Quine, "Two Dogmas of Empiricism". This sits uneasily with Quine's hard-headed naturalism. After all, an object that owes its existence to the synthetic activity of the mind – to something other than the object itself – does not look like the kind of thing that can physically impact on the nervous system.

40. Treated with great lucidity and depth by Cassam in *Self and World*. I also address the issue in "The Necessity of Embodiment" in *I Am: A Philosophical Inquiry into First-Person Being*.

41. An adjacent viewpoint is expressed by Ingmar Persson: "My claim is that this felt three-dimensional 'model' of our bodies, centre-piece of our perceptual or phenomenal world, taking as presenting a real, physical thing, constitutes the subject to which we ordinarily attribute our perceptions and other mental states. If correct, this account of the subject of experience has the merit *of undercutting scepticism about the physical world*" ("Self-Doubt: Why We Are Not Things of Any Kind", 307, emphasis added).

42. My argument that the "itness" of objects is existentially grounded is not as original as I thought it was when it first occurred to me. Other philosophers have explored this link between the body that "I" am and the "it-body" that is. And in my broader view, I find a perhaps surprising ally in Quine: "Bodies are our first reification: the first objects to be taken as objects. It is on analogy to them that all further positing of objects takes place" (Quine, *From Stimulus to Science*, 24).

43. Patočka, *Body, Community, Language, World*. We are also *cognitively* born in someone's arms. See, for example, Bredlaw, "Husserl's 'Pairing' Relationship and the Role of Others in Infant Perception".

44. Suddendorf, *The Gap*, 49.

45. Kant, *Critique of Pure Reason* A293/B350.

46. I am aware that this is a radical claim. It is at odds with the naturalistic world picture that has prevailed since the Galilean revolution according to which primary qualities (size, shape, location, and quantity) – properties of "it" – are deemed to be more real than secondary qualities (colour, smell, taste, etc.) – mind-dependent properties experienced by "I". Romano expresses this very clearly:

[Thinking of] the body from the phenomenological viewpoint, far from being a simple and immediate undertaking, actually requires us to rethink the history of philosophy as a whole, to question that history in a most radical way possible and to challenge some of its most central claims. That is why the problem of the body is not just one problem, one task among others for phenomenology. It is one that compels phenomenology to re-think itself through and through (Romano, "After the Lived-Body", 468).

That challenge needs to go further back and question the dogma that secondary qualities are "secondary" in the sense of being ontologically inferior to, or dubious compared with, primary qualities. A world purely of size, shape and number is not much of a world (as we shall discuss in Chapter 10). It is also difficult to understand how, say, the yellow of a daffodil is daffodil-shaped, and daffodil-located, if it does not really belong to a real world to which daffodils are supposed to belong, a world purely of quantities.

47. Quoted in Halák, "Merleau-Ponty on Embodied Subjectivity", 37. As Halák puts it, according to Merleau-Ponty, "the subjective and objective dimensions of the body are not only juxtaposed or systematically correlated … Their relationship is rather that of mutual implication and circular dependence or conditioning, for we would be unable to understand the orders as separate if we did not understand the embodied subject as one totality" (31).

48. I am aware of having simplified what may be meant by "object", by focusing on seemingly self-bounding items such as glasses, cups and chairs. I have left unaddressed the many cases in which the object, rather than being intrinsically "one" through having continuous physical boundaries, requires a concept to cut it out as a unitary whole. The "oneness" of artefacts such as cups is reinforced by the fact that they are defined by the use for which they were made. Even so, there are artefacts such as rooms that do not seem to have clear, continuous boundaries, and this applies *a fortiori* to suburbs, woods, and items that are defined within the realm of discourse such as "The Nineteenth Century". Repeated reference to them, according to agreed rules, gives such objects (and even non-existent ones such as unicorns) the appearance of having stable edges. Nouns are the ultimate arbiters of what count as objects that belong to public spaces, giving them boundaries that go beyond any directly visible limit, audible direction, or the tactile surface. The self-bounded material objects I have focused on, however, seem to present the toughest challenge to my thesis. The "I" or more precisely the "we", is clearly deeply implicated in the unity of "a room", "a landscape" or "The Nineteenth Century", not at all clearly in the case of rocks, and trees, and tables.

CHAPTER 4

1. Some of the territory covered in this chapter has been discussed in more detail in Tallis, *Of Time and Lamentation.*

2. According priority to human time should not, however, trigger alarm at the possibility of a regression to Kantian idealism which locates time inside the mind. I hope this will become apparent.

3. I will leave open the question of whether mental events such as perceptions can be said to be occurrences that take place at particular times. If I look at an accurate clock and see that it is 12 noon, then we might conclude that my seeing must be at 12 noon. However, it does not seem quite right to locate the seeing in the same time frame as that which is seen in order to support the judgement that the one is simultaneous with the other. Simultaneity belongs to events in phenomenal space not to that in virtue of which there is phenomenal space.

4. The points made in this part of the chapter are dealt with at greater length in "Mathematics and the Book of Nature" especially Section 3.5.3 "The Erasure of the Observer", 149–83, *Of Time and Lamentation.*

5. Einstein, "On the electrodynamics of moving bodies", 2.

6. Or until recently. The "many worlds" interpretation of quantum mechanics amounts to what leading astrophysicist Paul Steinhardt (*Edge*, 13 January 2016) has cuttingly described as "A Theory of Anything" and such a theory is "*useless* because it does not rule out any possibility and *worthless* because it submits to no do-or-die tests". Such theories, he argues, should be retired. Unger and Smolin (in *The Singular Universe and the Reality of Time*, 120) talk about "the massive underdetermination of reality by theory in some of the variants of particle physics now commanding the greatest respect". George Ellis and Joe Silk have argued in leading science journal *Nature* that they undermine the credibility of physics ("Scientific Method: Defend the Integrity of Physics").

7. André Metz quoted in Canales, *The Physicist and the Philosopher: Einstein, Bergson, and the Debate that Changed our Understanding of Time*, 315.

8. Bertrand Russell (*ABC of Relativity*) quoted in Canales, *The Physicist and the Philosopher*, 315.

9. Einstein, "Autobiographical Notes", 59.

10. Maudlin, *Philosophy of Physics: Space and Time*, 106.

11. Laplace's imaginary demon – who could predict the future state of the universe if provided with a set of initial conditions and the laws of nature – could not be accommodated in Laplace's system.

12. Carnap, "Intellectual Autobiography", 37.

13. Savitt, "Time in the Special Theory of Relativity", 551.

14. Heidegger, *Being and Time*, 382.

15. I shall refrain from any joke about there being no time like the peasant.

16. This is in addition to its more obvious role in underpinning the quantitative "before" and "after" that forms such a central element of the "system of magnitudes" that is the world according to the physical sciences.

17. From "at" there grows the possibility of "today", "this week", "this year", "nowadays".

18. Savitt, "Time in the Special Theory of Relativity", 551.

19. There is another challenge to the relativistic interpretation of time. The very assumption that there is no temporal ordering of events independent of a frame of reference is at odds with the generally accepted idea that the cosmos has a unitary history, with a definite order of events (Big Bang first, planets later, life later still, and eventually humans) over a definite period of time so far (nearly 14 billion years ago). This is particularly perplexing because the assumption that the Big Bang happened at a

particular time is derived from general relativity. Ouch! The attempt to deal with this by arguing that the clock of cosmic time is the universe itself is a desperate endeavour to incorporate the observer into the observed universe, by conflating the clock (or clock-face) with the viewpoint that uses it, the time-teller with the time that is told.

20. Weyl, *The Philosophy of Mathematics and Natural Science*, 122. This unintentionally highlights the truth of Merleau-Ponty's observation that "we need absolutes within the relative". That absolute is the human body "as a system of possible actions" (*The Phenomenology of Perception*, 127. An action is an event that happens at a particular time, and a particular point in space. If not, there could not be cooperation in a coherent world, spectacularly instantiated in the great cognitive adventure of science. Einstein's ego-less space-time manifold cannot accommodate actions or the convergent actions that made physics possible.

21. An even more shocking conclusion is that, if the universe is essentially processual, a sum total of events, an eventless universe would also be thing-less.

22. Reported by Karl Popper in "Why I Reject Metaphysical Determinism: A Conversation with Parmenides", 90.

23. This history is not merely the prior causes implicit in the present state or properties of a part of the material world. It is a past that is actively present in itself, present *now* so that it is referred to, argued over, something to guide the present, or to be contested.

24. Hannah Arendt cited in Strhan, "Matters of Life and Death", 150.

25. A view echoed by L. A. Paul: "Making sense of the features of temporal experience is fundamental to our ability to make sense of the world and of ourselves as agents in the world and bears important connections to one's having a point of view and to one's sense of being a self." ("Temporal Experience", 334).

26. The force of "mental" in "mental time travel" is that nothing material is transplanted to the future in anticipation of it. The "journey" is undertaken by a self but not a body.

27. Clayton, "Ways of Thinking: From Crows to Children and Back Again".

28. Suddendorf, *The Gap*, 104–5.

29. Clayton, Russell and Dickinson, "Are Animals Stuck in Time or are they Chronesthetic Creatures?". There is a powerful defence of the uniqueness of human mental time travel into the past and future in Tulving, "Episodic Memory and Autonoesis: Uniquely Human?". Tulving focuses on autonoetic memory, on remembering personally experienced events, rooted in a sense of one's self – memories of experiences that are owned *now*, though they are of what was *then* – and are connected with explicit travel in inner, private time, alighting at a destination that belongs (if the memories are true) to a shared world. (Future-orientated time travel depends on memory to populate the future with possibilities and to connect them with the traveller). We shall return to this when we discuss selfhood in Chapter 5.

30. Reviewed in Clayton, "Ways of Thinking".

31. Daniel Gilbert quoted in Buonomato, *Your Brain is a Time Machine: The Neuroscience and Physics of Time*, 199.

32. Wittgenstein, *Philosophical Investigations*, para 650, 166e.

33. Suddendorf, *The Gap*, 108.

34. Nietzsche famously described man as "the promising animal" in the second treatise of *The Genealogy of Morals*.

35. Yuri Lotman introduced the term "semiosphere" to capture the sphere in which signification operates. The analogy is with the "atmosphere" and, more closely, the "biosphere".

36. The original is "Out of the crooked timber of humanity, no straight thing was ever made" (Kant, *Idea for a General History with a Cosmopolitan Purpose*, proposition 6).

37. This difference was asserted in a rather muddled – or muddling – way by Quine in the distinction he made between "occasion" sentences that are true on some occasions and false on others and "eternal sentences" that are true for all time (see *The Pursuit of Truth*, 3). Let us suppose that it rained in Manchester between 12 noon and 1 p.m., 16 August 2018 but at no other time in that day. The sentence "It is raining in Manchester" would be true at 12:30, 16 August 2018 and false at 1:30 p.m. the same day. The assertion that "It was raining in Manchester at 12 noon on 16 August 2018", by contrast, is true for all time. No change in circumstances after that date can change its truth value. Quine glimpsed something big – incompatible with his naturalism – and then blinked. Both kinds of sentences – occasion and eternal sentences – are outside of time in the sense relevant for our discussion.

    It is worth examining, however, why there may be a temptation to exaggerate the significance of the difference between the two kinds of sentences. The eternal sentence clearly does not belong to the same timeframe as the happening it is referring to. "*That* it rained in Manchester at 12 noon, 16 August 2018" does not itself happen on 16 August whereas "It is raining" has to be uttered in the same timeframe as the rain in order to be true. There is, however, an important sense in the facts corresponding to both sentences do not happen at *any* time, though the utterances that assert the happenings do of course happen at particular times.

38. Fodor, "Semantics, Wisconsin Style", 232. This is entirely consistent with the way meaning has frustrated the attempts of neuroscientists to identify any locality in the brain responsible for processing of word meaning. It's happening "everywhere" (or nowhere in particular) in the brain should raise alarm bells in the minds (or brains) of neo-phrenologists; see Uttal, *The New Phrenology*, 200.

39. Quine, *From Stimulus to Science*.

40. Quine, "Epistemology Naturalised".

41. W. V. O. Quine quoted in Stroud, "The Charm of Naturalism", 46.

42. The contrast between "brute" and "institutional facts" – originally put into circulation by G. E. M. Anscombe and then elaborated by John Searle (in *The Construction of Social Reality*) – is seriously point-missing. Searle's example of a brute fact – "That there is snow on Mount Everest" – is a piece of "thatter" that has no part in nature, even though it is what is true of nature that makes it a (true) fact. That Mount Everest is snow-bound would not have become a truth-maker without the assistance of an assertion vulnerable to empirical testing. This is not, of course, to suggest postmodernly that "all facts are (mere) interpretations"; rather that in crossing over from nature to facts about nature we have moved into the thatosphere. In sum, that there are facts is not a matter of brute or natural fact. All facts are in this sense institutional.

43. See Tallis, *Michelangelo's Finger* for further development of some of these points.

44. There is of course interrogative pointing, in which a child points to something it does not understand and seeks some explanation, or even the name of the item it is pointing to. This may be regarded as, perhaps, a hybrid: a cognitive "gimme!".

45. One can say this without being committed to the naïve idea that the natural and the semantic realms are linked by one-to-one correlations, as if language were a heap of separate words reflecting a heap of material objects or types of such objects. I reference pointing merely to identify a half-way house between the direct intentionality of object perception and the derivative intentionality of vocalized or unvocalized propositional attitudes such as beliefs articulated in language.

46. Quine, *Theories and Things*, 20.

47. The suggestion that what impinges on our nervous system is not something arising from objects but simply energy, seems to give ontological primacy to energy over objects but that is hardly consistent with physics whose most famous equation – $E = mc^2$ – seems to give matter and energy equal standing.

48. The intuition of an object as the permanent underpinning of a succession of experiences is reinforced when it is referred to, on separate occasions, by a singular referring term. It is frozen only as a referent: "the question of the identity of a body from one time to another is generally meaningless apart from the choice of a governing predicate" (Quine, *From Stimulus to Science*, 39).

49. We must also reject the causal theory of verbal meaning, even when it is applied to seemingly simple terms such as proper names. If there were a simple causal relationship between a name and its referent, it would be difficult to see how the name could be "about" the referent. And when it comes to sentences – in particular written sentences – we are outside the network of causation that unfolds in time. They have a frozen significance, available to be liberated when they are used.

50. Events do not become truths or truth-makers simply in virtue of happening. For them to become truth-makers they require propositions that assert that they are the case; and the propositions will assert things only if they are they themselves asserted.

51. Quine, "Two Dogmas of Empiricism", 344.

52. In the light of this, the desperate endeavours of the very influential teleosemantic brand of naturalism to incorporate reason into the biosphere are revealing. Jacob Rump in "On the Use and Abuse of Teleology for Life: Intentionality, Naturalism and Meaning Rationalism in Husserl and Millikan" (54) quotes Ruth Millikan as follows: "all of basic norms applied to cognition are biological norms"; "rationality is biological norm effected in an integrated head-world system under biologically ideal conditions" and adds that she speaks of biological norms in terms of "mechanisms" and rationality in terms of "heads in good mechanical order". A brave, but futile, attempt to get purpose without intentionality.

53. The passive trains of thought of the wool-gathering mind may seem to be an example of meaningful, cognitive events that are causally linked in the way that successive physical events are. There are two reasons for not accepting this. First, and most obviously, while the elements are token-events, their meaning is general and the connections are between meanings, firmly situated in the thatosphere. They still have their splinter of eternity. Secondly, we are able to interrupt the train of thought at any stage, can reflect on it (even to the extent of wondering what set it going), and can report it to another: hardly features of a causally linked sequence of events, that do not interrupt, reflect upon, or report themselves. For further discussion, see Tallis, "Just a Little Tune I Found in my Mouth" in *In Defence of Wonder*.

54. The ownerlessness of facts is connected with the necessary ejection of the individual from the limitations of subjective perspective in order to arrive at factual truth. The need to get one's self out of the way in order to access truths that may be of benefit to said self is less obvious than it should be.

55. It is significant that mental time travel separates space and time. When I remember what happened yesterday, there is a definite time interval between what happened and my memory of it. There is not, however, a definite space interval between the location of the event and the location of the memory of the event. My memory of a walk in Samos is a memory of something that is several months before itself. But there is no definite distance between the here of the memory and the there of what is remembered. Indeed, both took place in some sense in myself.

56. The timelessness of facts is echoed at a higher level in the distances between use and mention of assertions.

57. They seem to hate it even more than they hate purpose and value which they believe they can biologize. Organs and behaviour seem to have purposes in the sense of biological functions. Value seems to be translatable into that which promotes or threatens biological survival. This seems to extend purpose and value beyond its proper location: explicit, entertained purpose and value as judgement. These require the individual to stand out of their current state at time t_1 and imagine future states – something that is unique to humanity.

CHAPTER 5

1. Hume "Of Personal Identity", *A Treatise of Human Nature*, Bk 1, Pt 4, Section 6, 228.
2. *Ibid.*, 229.
3. *Ibid.*, 251.
4. *Ibid.*, 235.
5. This is a point to which we shall return. As Terence Penelhum expresses it "I can only wonder if I am the same person I was yesterday, if I am, not if I am not" (Penelhum, *Themes in Hume: The Self, the Will, and Religion*).
6. Some Buddhists make much of the idea that the self is an illusion. Did Buddha have a self? If not, then who or what are we talking about when we talk about Buddha and tell the story of "his" life? In fairness, it should be pointed out that a) Buddha discouraged idle speculation about the self; and b) his doctrine of *anatta* is that there is no eternal, unchanging, autonomous self; that there is nothing corresponding to the *atman* of the Vedic teaching prevalent when Buddha was teaching.
7. A similar point is made by William James: "Take a sentence of a dozen words, take twelve men, and to each assign one word. Then stand the men in a row or jam them in a bunch and let each think of his word as intently as he will; nowhere will there be a consciousness of the whole sentence" (James, *Principles of Psychology* Volume 1, 160).
8. There is no awareness of belonging-together in as a whole cloud or in the drops that compose it – as the very possibility of correctly seeing the cloud both at the level of a single object and at the level of vast numbers of droplets indicates. They are separable because the coherence of the drops in the cloud, unlike that of the many experiences of a person, is contingent.

9. For example, Harry Frankfurt (*The Importance of What We Care About*, 267): "It is like a source of light which, in addition to illuminating whatever other things fall within its scope, renders itself visible as well". A candle is not, of course, self-lit.

10. Hume, *A Treatise of Human Nature*, 162.

11. As Hume, *A Treatise of Human Nature*, 230 observes: "In order to justify to ourselves this absurdity, we often feign some new and unintelligible principle, that connects the objects together, and prevents their interruption or variation. Thus we feign the continuing existence of the perceptions of our senses, to remove the interruption; and run into the notion of a *soul*, a *self*, and substance, to disguise the variation."

12. Dennett, "The Self as a Center of Narrative Gravity". Dennett's autocidal tendencies are also evident in his claim that the self, and its apparent unity of consciousness, is a transient "virtual captain" – a momentary me – emerging as a result of a small group of information parcels coming to dominate over other groups to control cognitive activities such as self-monitoring and self-reporting. These virtual captains add to their legitimacy by their connections with autobiographical memory. What we are to make of his use of expressions such as "self-monitoring", "self-reporting", and "*auto*-biographical memory" is dazzlingly unclear. Dennett's notion of the self as analogous to a construct like "centre of gravity" has a distant echo in Russell's argument in *The Analysis of Mind* (141) that: "the subject appears to be a logical fiction, like mathematical points and instants ... introduced, not because observation reveals it, but because it is linguistically convenient and apparently demanded by grammar".

13. This is at least an improvement on being designated (as *per* Russell – see previous note) as a merely grammatical or linguistic entity, such that the subject exists only insofar as he/she is the subject of a sentence.

14. Ulrich Meixner quoted in Klein, "Sameness and the Self: Philosophical and Psychological Considerations", 3.

15. There is a third objection to Dennett's comparing the self with a centre of gravity. Items such as a rock, to which the centre of gravity is ascribed have a solid, independent existence. This does not seem to be on offer in the case of the self – unless we identity it with the human body – of which more (much more) presently.

16. See Schechtman, "'The Size of the Self': Minimalist Selves and Narrative Self-Constitution" for a critique of this idea.

17. Louis Althusser argued that the human subject was "hailed" into being. Indeed, the subject, in virtue of being captured for bourgeois capitalism, was an "abject". For a critical view of this idea see Tallis, *In Defence of Realism*. It would be interesting to speculate how the subject could be "hailed" into existence without there being (other) subjects to do the hailing.

18. Helpfully set out and criticized in McClelland, "Against Virtual Selves".

19. *Ibid.*, 30.

20. *Ibid.*, 22.

21. *Ibid.*, 21.

22. Thomas Metzinger is another brain-based autocide. He argues that there is no such thing like the self. Nobody ever had or was a self (Metzinger, *Being No One*) because the self "is an ongoing process" and what exists are "phenomenal selves". Neuroscience, he claims. demonstrates that there is no objective basis for the self in neural activity. Of course, the objective tools of brain science are hardly equipped for detecting the

self – or, indeed, first-person being, or subjectivity. Metzinger's additional claim that the illusion that we are selves – that the systems that we are simulate or emulate the self – is of biological value because it allows us to plan for the future, falls victim to the arguments about the biological uselessness of consciousness put forward in Chapter 2. The arguments apply with added force to self-consciousness.

23. As psychologist Stan Klein has pointed out in "The Unplanned Obsolescence of Psychological Science and an Argument for its Revival", 361: "it is never made clear by proponents of physical determinism how the qualitative experience of an illusion fits into a non-qualitative universe".

24. Chater, *The Mind is Flat: The Illusion of Mental Depth and the Improvised Mind*.

25. *Ibid.*, 82.

26. This may be true of bees. Recent work has pointed to the role of sequential visual information in the bee brain, such that if they are tethered and unable to move their eyes, they behave as if they are blind (quoted in Chittka, "Bee Cognition"). But we ain't bees.

27. Chater, *The Mind is Flat*, 15.

28. *Ibid.*, 37.

29. *Ibid.*, 54.

30. *Ibid.*, 153.

31. Some of the points that follow are made in an excellent article by Jonathan Cohen, "The Grand Illusion Illusion".

32. Cohen, "The Grand Illusion Illusion", 145.

33. There can be no *re*presentation without prior presentation. The latter *requires*, rather than being the basis, or stuff, of a conscious mind. Besides, the theory assumes that neural activity can represent the world outside of the brain in virtue of having some-thing in common with it, most obviously its structure. This fails at the most basic level. There is no respect in which for example pain is structurally similar to its cause – for example, burnt skin. The failure of the theory is even more profound when applied to phenomenal consciousness, as does Fred Dretske in "Experience as Representation". A neural echo of the object in the brain would no more make the object be present than the reflection of a cloud in a puddle would make the cloud present to the puddle.

34. Unless statements like "Yesterday I completed Chapter 1" or "I will deliver the manu-script in 3 months' time", which have a temporally extended self as their subject, refer to illusions cooked up by the brain.

35. Wittgenstein, *Philosophical Investigations*, part I, paragraph 464, 130e.

36. Chater, *The Mind is Flat*, 183.

37. *Ibid.*, 202.

38. *Ibid.*, 203, emphasis added.

39. Nešić, "Against Deflation of the Subject", 1104.

40. Chalmers, "Panpsychism and Panprotopsychism", 271.

41. The PhilPapers survey on philosophers' views on the nature of personal identity found that 33 per cent of respondents believed that personal identity inhered in psychologi-cal continuity; 17 per cent in biological continuity; 12 per cent thought personal iden-tity was a further fact; and 37 per cent had other views; see Bourget and Chalmers, "What Do Philosophers Believe?".

42. Derek Parfit's first fully developed statement of his views was in *Reasons and Persons* (1984). His later views were set out in, for example, "The Unimportance of Identity" (1995) and "We Are Not Human Beings" (2012).

43. Olson, *The Human Animal: Personal Identity without Psychology*, 76.

44. Olson, "Parfit's View That We Are Not Human Beings", 1.

45. Parfit, "The Unimportance of Identity", 424. Parfit has not always held to this view. As noted, in his early writings (such as *Reasons and Persons*), identity over time involved only psychological connectedness and/or psychological continuity. This change of view is discussed in "Parfit's Retreat: 'We Are Not Human Beings'".

46. Olson, *The Human Animal*, 76.

47. Olson is not alone in suggesting this. For example, Quine: "We can say of John's body not only that it broke a leg, but that it thinks it sees how to prove Fermat's Last Theorem" (*From Stimulus to Science*, 85).

48. Hume, *A Treatise of Human Nature*, 234 (emphasis added). This view was echoed by Ernst Mach who took his phenomenalism to a logical conclusion: "Thing and Ego are provisional fictions of the same kind", cited in Schrenk, "Ernst Mach on the Self".

49. The classic expression of this philosophical conundrum is the Ship of Theseus story. Theseus has a ship which requires repairs at frequent intervals. Damaged parts are replaced with new wood. Eventually, there will be no part of the ship composed of the materials from which it was originally built. Is the ship still the same ship? Supposing all the wood was preserved and a second ship was constructed out of the material that had been replaced. Would there now be two ships laying claim to the same identity? I leave the reader to decide between intuitions based on continuity or sameness of form and intuitions based on continuity or sameness of stuff.

50. Hume, *A Treatise of Human Nature*, 233.

51. Atkins, "Personal Identity and the Importance of One's Body: A Response to Derek Parfit", 343. The importance of others in every aspect of our mental life extends of course to intelligence – and to so-called artificial intelligence. As Mark Lee puts it: "artificial intelligence has to face the fact that intelligence is not just a single entity, bounded by the skull, but is also diffuse and requires social interaction" ("A Frame of Mind", 47). We shall return to this in Chapter 7.

52. See Suddendorf, *The Gap*, 49.

53. Atkins, "Personal Identity and the Importance of One's Body", 332.

54. Her source is Cassam, "Kant and Reductionism".

55. This should not be taken to imply that my personal identity is something that can be entirely settled from within. The intra-personal core requires interpersonal scaffolding as we shall discuss.

56. Hume "Of Personal Identity", *A Treatise of Human Nature*, Bk 1, Pt 4, Section 6, 235.

57. A currently popular neural theory of consciousness, Guilio Tononi's "Integrated Information Theory", is fundamentally deficient because it offers no satisfactory account of the neural basis for the unity of the conscious moment. In addition, it plays on an ambiguity at the heart of the notion of "information" – something I will discuss in Chapter 7. The ambiguity enables the brain-consciousness barrier to be crossed without any empirical or conceptual work being done.

58. This is one of the many reasons why the increasingly popular notion of the brain

as a "predictive device", as a Bayesian engine, is invalid. Prediction involves a sense of possibilities located in a future, based on actualities that occurred in the past. A material object does not entertain possibilities or reach into an explicit future with a grasp guided by an explicit past.

59. Locke, *An Essay Concerning Human Understanding*, 335.

60. Parfit, "We Are Not Human Beings", 7.

61. In a late paper – "The Unimportance of Identity" – Parfit makes an assertion that appears to be contradictory: "Though persons are distinct from their bodies, and from any series of mental events, they are not independent or separately existing entities" (423). Distinct from but not independent of? The following "clarifications" only makes things worse: "Personal identity over time just consists in physical and/or psychological continuity" (423); "A person is reducible to but not identical to bodily and psychological events" (424); "Though a person is distinct from that person's body, and from any series of thoughts and experiences, the person's existence just *consists* in them" (431).

62. Parfit, "The Unimportance of Identity", 429.

63. Most clearly set out in Parfit, *Reasons and Persons*, 206ff.

64. It would be interesting to know who or what is keeping count. Any book-keeping would seem to require in advance precisely what is to be established: a unified, continuous subject, owning the perceptions – in short a book-keeper. The same applies to the resemblances between successive moments of the psyche that, according to Hume, deceive us into thinking that we are a definite self that transcends the flux of individual impressions. Who, or what, is judging that successive states are sufficiently similar to seem to belong to the same entity? Who or what is deceived? It must be *someone* capable of comparing the successive moments of a moving total of impressions. Without such a subject, there would be no viewpoint from which the totality of impressions can be judged as changing only gradually.

65. There is controversy in how we should understand the associative mechanisms that seem to "drive" the succession of thoughts. Darcy, "Rethinking Associative Mechanisms in Psychology" suggests that "association" should be treated as a filler term that would be compatible with many ways of understanding the direction of trains of thought.

66. Parfit, *Reasons and Persons*, 429.

67. Cassam has pointed out that the common feature of various forms of the reductive account of the self is "the impersonalisation of subjectivity" ("Kant and Reductionism").

68. Klein, "What Memory Is", 2. The role played by memory in the constitution of the self is of course very complex. This is illustrated by Mark Rowland's discussion of "Rilkean" memories. These are memories without specific content that contribute to making us who we are. They are inscribed patterns of behaviour and bodily habitus, general attitudes and outlooks, moods and feelings, that originated in repeated, often childhood, past experience. Such cladding is in part evident to others as well as to one's self (Rowlands, *Memory and the Self: Phenomenology, Science and Autobiography*).

69. Klein, "What Memory Is", 1.

70. *Ibid.*, 2. Klein usefully develops this point: "To qualify as an act of memory, the content in awareness must present itself as reexperience of an experience previously had. This

feeling of reexperiencing is directly given to consciousness, rather than as the product of an act of inference or interpretation" (6). The widening, indeed debasement, of the term "memory" to encompass alterations in behaviour of brainless slime molds is discussed in Chapter 2.

71. That I have such a past makes sense of what psychologists call auto-cueing, of "racking my brains", even if what I rack out of my sluggish brain are timeless, ownerless matters of fact – such as the date of the Battle of Hastings – rather than personal memories.

72. At a very basic level, it misses something that we discussed in Chapter 2: two intentional relationships. There is first of all the intentional relationship between *P* and *E which points in the opposite direction* to the causal relation. And there is the intentional relationship between *M* and *P, which also points in the opposite direction to any putative causal relation* and which (see Chapter 4), unlike causes and effects, transcend the present. In the material world, effects do not reach back to their causes.

73. Interestingly, Hume almost accepts this when he alights upon memory as "chiefly, … the source of personal identity" because "memory alone acquaints us with the continuance and extent of the succession of perceptions" (*A Treatise of Human Nature*, 237). Memory "does not so much *produce* as *discover* personal identity, by showing us the relations of cause and effect among our different perceptions" (*Ibid.*).

74. Tulving, "Episodic Memory of Autonoesis: Uniquely Human?".

75. Fugazza, Pigany and Miklosi, "Recall of Others' Actions after Incidental Encoding Reveals Episodic-Like Memory in Dogs". .

76. Tulving, "Episodic Memory of Autonoesis", 14–15.

77. Marcel Proust, *A La Recherche de Temps Perdu*, 904.

78. J. Butler (*The Analogy of Religion*) quoted in Parfit, *Reasons and Persons*, 219.

79. Parfit, *Reasons and Persons*, 220.

80. The circularity of Parfit's "quasi-memory" approach has also been exposed by Schechtman in "Personhood and Person Identity".

81. However, the role of the memory in sustaining the sense of self is complex as is evident from the literature on acquired amnesia due to brain damage – reviewed by Klein and Nichols in "Memory and the Sense of Personal Identity".

82. Hume (*A Treatise of Human Nature*, 229) argues that "we must distinguish betwixt personal identity, as it regards our thoughts and imagination, and as it regards our passions or the concerns we take in ourselves". Even so, he focuses on the former in arriving at the conclusion that personal identity is a fiction.

83. The referent of a memory is an object, event or state of affairs liberated from its place in space and time; or rather an aspect, a presentation, a time-slice-from-an-angle, of an object, event, or state of affairs, liberated from its original location. The referent not available to be revisited. The past is beyond vision, cannot be heard, and is not there to be touched, even less to be altered.

84. And yet we have to agree with Kant that we have a mode of consciousness in virtue of which we are conscious that we are the single or unifying subject of all our conscious mental states. For a discussion of this, see Gomes, "Kant, the Philosophy of Mind, and Twentieth-Century Analytic Philosophy".

85. Or, at the very least, there would be no grounds for differentiating between hallucinations and perceptions and awarding the truth value "true" to the latter.

86. That we are not "things" is also comprehensively argued by Persson, "Self-Doubt: Why We Are Not Identical to Things of Any Kind".

87. The elusiveness of the self in philosophical discourse cannot be entirely explained by the fact that that which is trying to reach it is that which is to be reached. The reaching takes place via the community of minds.

88. Marsh, *Admissions: A Life in Brain Surgery*, 12.

89. Parfit, "We Are Not Human Beings", 6.

90. Parfit, "The Unimportance of Identity", 441.

91. Hume, *A Treatise of Human Nature*, 29.

92. Heidegger, *Being and Time*, *passim* but especially Section 41, "The Being of Da-sein as Care".

93. Lucretius, "The Folly of the Fear of Death", *On the Nature of Things*.

94. Scruton, "Living With a Mind".

95. Wittgenstein, *Philosophical Investigations*, para 304, 102e.

CHAPTER 6

1. It is widely quoted and re-quoted but I have never been able to trace its location in Gibbon's works.

2. Qur'an 2.30. Andrew Pinsent (personal communication) has pointed out that "Islam has an ambiguous relation with [the idea of] free will. The general tendency [of the universe] is located in a single cause like a black rock in an empty desert".

3. Kane, *The Significance of Free Will*, 4.

4. Libet *et al.*, "Unconscious Cerebral Initiative and the Role of Conscious Will in Involuntary Action".

5. Soon *et al.*, "Unconscious Determinants of Free Decisions in the Human Brain".

6. Haggard, "Human Volition: Towards a Neuroscience of Will". The most consistent and articulate of the "willusionists" was Daniel M. Wegner who argued that "conscious will … is an indication that we *think* we have caused an action, not a revelation of the causal sequence by which conscious action was produced" (precis of "The Illusion of Conscious Will", 649). Wegner reaches this position by examining instances – both naturally occurring in neurological disease or in laboratory conditions – in which individuals are deluded into thinking that they are causing events for which in fact they are not responsible. The fundamental error of Wegner's claim is that shared by any Argument from Illusion: just because we are sometimes deceived it does not follow that we are always deceived. The extraordinary examples he cites underlines how they are abnormal and therefore not the norm. The norm is that I have a feeling of consciously willing actions that I have in fact done.

7. Blackmore, "Mind over Matter?". *The Guardian*, 28 August 2007; available at: https://www.theguardian.com/commentisfree/2007/aug/28/mindovermatter.

8. Coyne, "Why You Don't Really Have Free Will", *USA Today*, 1 January 2012.

9. Nahmias, "Why We Have Free Will".

10. See Tallis, *Of Time and Lamentation*, Section 12.3.3, "The Impossibility of Free Action" for a further discussion of the methodological problems of the neurodeterminist literature.

11. What follows is closely based on a presentation of the arguments in *Of Time and Lamentation* and "How on Earth Can We be Free?" in *The Mystery of Being Human: God, Free Will, and the NHS*.

12. I have given Libet something of a free pass neurologically. There is now considerable doubt whether the Readiness Potential (RP) really does represent the brain readying itself for the movement the subject is going to make. It might signal the subject's decision to divide her attention between looking at the clock to time the intention and planning the movement to come; see Miller, Shepherdson and Trevena, "Effects of Clock Monitoring on Electroencephalographic Activity". Alternatively, the RP may be a spontaneous build-up of neural activity of which the subject takes advantage – "catching the wave" as it were – resulting in a conscious intention to move; see Shields, "Neuroscience and Conscious Causation".

   There are also serious methodological questions around the scanning studies of John-Dylan Hayes *et al.* The most striking criticism has been directed at the claim that scientists can predict which hand the subjects are going to use several seconds before the hand is chosen. It is possible that this is due to pattern recognition (because subjects find it difficult to stick to random choices) which statistically would have a predictive power at least as powerful as that obtained through observing neural activity.

   These doubts are, however, less relevant philosophically than the misrepresentation of the nature of voluntary action.

13. It is interesting how timing of the urge – a sophisticated metacognitive task – is not itself highlighted by the experimenters. (This was first pointed out by Gerald Wasserman – "Neural-Mental Chronometry and Chronotheology"). It may be because it is an unquestionably voluntary action which could not be the material effect of an unconscious material cause. And it seems irreducibly conscious. Also overlooked is the *intention to time the intention*. What is more, in the light of our discussion of "at time t" in Chapter 4, this meta-action of reflection on an action in order to time it clearly does not fit into the timeframe of physical events. "*At* time t_1" is not part of the series to which t_1, t_2 and t_3 belong. What is more, recent research – summarized in Shields, "Neuroscience and Conscious Causation" – has shown that timing one's decision or urge to move relies on inference not perception. At any rate, noting the simultaneity between the position on a clock face and the urge to move is itself a rather complex action which it makes more sense to ascribe to a person rather than a bit of a brain.

14. The design of Libet's experiments typifies the tendency within scientific psychology of "losing the human context" – brilliantly described in Velden's *Psychology: The Study of a Masquerade*, 10.

15. And it is worth reminding ourselves that there are no forking paths in material reality. The physical world lacks possibilities which later exist only so far as they are entertained. The co-presence of opposite possibilities does not correspond to the co-presence of opposing actualities.

16. Libet's seeing intentions as causes is driven by the mistaken idea that free will presupposes mental causation operating in a quasi-physical way. Only if they were identical with physical events in the brain could mental phenomena cause physical events without breaking fundamental physical laws, notably the first law of thermodynamics,

according to which energy may be exchanged but not lost or created. If they were physical events, they would lose their status of initiators. In reality, our intentions are not packets of extra-material oomph that deliver volition but belong to our mode of being outside of the physical world freeing us to manipulate it according to the laws of nature, as we shall discuss presently.

17. Sam Harris quoted in Nahmias, "Defining Free Will Away", 112.

18. Coyne, "You Don't Have Free Will", *Chronicle of Higher Education*, 18 March 2012.

19. This is a specific illustration of a general truth enunciated by the early twentieth-century German philosopher Arnold Gehlen, summarized by Halák and Klouda in "Institution as a General Model of Meaning":

> Unlike animals, humans are endowed with stable innate instincts only to a very limited extent. They have only residual instincts and they are not adapted to any particular environment. Human behaviour is therefore not rooted in instinctive motoric patterns. Human motor activity is for the most part acquired and learned, whereas in animals the range of learned motor skills is significantly limited. This fact is linked to the plasticity of human nature, which enables humans to adapt to a wide variety of living environments (374).

It is worth noting that those living environments are largely man-made. As Halák and Klouda put it (*ibid*., 4), according to Gehlen, "[H]umans can purposefully act only because supra-personal, external institutions 'free' them from their unstable internal motivations and needs. An authentic human action, characterized by its purposeful nature, freedom and ethical relevance, is therefore possible thanks only to institutions, that is complexes of actions habitual to a degree where they become autonomous and purpose-free". This is another aspect of the exoskeleton that supports the self discussed in Chapter 5.

20. The improbable nature of our actions, in which we requisition causes to bring about effects, is italicized in the humble activity of tidying up and repairing things. Cleaning up a spillage or glueing together a shattered vase is counter to the general tendency of the universe as expressed in the second law of thermodynamics which dictates that the world gets messier with time. Extraction, distillation, and purification are even more strikingly counter to the natural tendency of the universe. When, over a period of four years, Marie and Pierre Curie retrieved a tenth of a gram of radium from a ton of pitchblende, their incredible exercise of agency produced a result that went against the fundamental direction of the natural world, although they did this by utilizing natural forces.

21. The same argument applies to nest-building which involves many separate actions. The goal does not need to be envisaged by the bird because, although the construction is bespoke, being dependent upon local circumstances, its purpose is general rather than singular. One marker of the difference between nest-building and house-building is that the former has not evolved to anything like the degree that house-building has. The style of a fifth-century ordinary wren's nest is not profoundly different from that of a twentieth-century wren's nest. There is nothing corresponding to fashions that draw on, or rebel from, previous fashions. (There is some evidence of what geneticist

Eva Jablonka has called "animal traditions" and cultural inheritance but it has neither the scope of human cultural development or the conscious radicalism or conservatism of human fashions.)

22. There is a vast literature claiming that we do not know what we are doing, or why, when we are doing it. I have already discussed the experiments by Libet and others. Anyone who has been seduced by the arguments – particularly those that focus on unconscious social priming – should read Newell and Shanks, "Unconscious influences on decision making: a critical review". At any rate, if we are aware of our unawareness (as psychologists claim), then we must be aware. At the least, the psychologists who argue that we are unaware must, by some myserious dispensation – perhaps as the result of obtaining a university degree – be aware of what they are doing.

23. While goals are general in the sense that they are intelligible and communicable, and can be realized in different ways, they still have to be given a singular *point d'appui* through the body of the agent. My intention to go to the pub to meet a friend to apologise for an unkindness has to be enacted in a particular stretch of space–time. It is this requirement that (incorrectly) makes reasons seem like causes. This example, however, where the goal is expressed in abstract terms, is a reminder of how rarely our expressed goals have a meaningful translation into a set of physical events.

24. One of the most widespread expressions of such patience is the interval between tool-making and tool-using. The most striking expression is theoretical research, and blue skies thinking, where there is typically a long delay before practical benefits accrue. We have already noted the nearly 600 years that intervened between the Copernican understanding of the universe that kicked off the scientific revolution and the GPS systems that help us to find our way in the wilderness.

25. Reference to inertia is a reminder of the impact of the sixteenth-century scientific revolution, one consequence of which was to render the natural world increasingly mindless. For Aristotle, movement continued only because it was maintained by a final cause; whereas for post-Galilean mechanics objects set in motion continued moving unless acted upon by an arresting force. The Aristotelean universe is haunted by the ghost of agency.

26. Schweikard and Schmid, "Collective Intentionality".

27. Our existential uncoupling from the material world is particularly evident when our role is entirely spectatorial, where what we see does not require any action of us. Reading, looking at pictures, listening to music, watching television or films are obvious examples.

28. The appeal to *evidence* (gathered at another time, often by another person) in order to defend a claim about a matter of fact is another aspect of man, the Knowing Animal that does not fit with the causal theory of knowledge. Material events are not in or of themselves "evidence": they do not turn themselves into evidence before reverting to mere causes of beliefs that are in turn the causes of actions.

29. It is striking how often philosophers overlook the hours, weeks or years of preparation that go into positioning ourselves to act. The idea of "genius" – and of being possessed by it as well as possessing it – imports an impossible helplessness into those places where, in fact, human freedom has its most complete development. A work of genius is hard work, requiring the most deliberate racking of brains and sustained attention

to the world, to the work, to the technical factors, and to keeping the vision alive: "an infinite capacity for taking pains".

30. Dewey, *Experience and Nature*, 13.

31. J. S. Mill, "Nature", 152.

32. *Ibid.*

33. As Kant pointed out in *Critique of Pure Reason*, an unconditional causality of freedom would "abrogate the rules through which alone completely coherent experience is possible"; "Side by side with such a lawless faculty of freedom, nature [as an ordered system] is hardly thinkable; the influence of the former would so unceasingly alter the laws of the latter that the appearance which is their natural course as regular and uniform would be reduced to disorder and incoherence" (414). This is part of the reason why Kant looked for the origin of freedom outside of the phenomenal world, where the laws of nature operated, and located it in the transcendental realm. At any rate, we can't shake off the laws of nature when we want to act freely and then expect them to deliver predictable consequences of our actions. It would be rather like the anarchist hippies, returning to their burgled flat, exclaiming "We've been robbed. Get the pigs!".

34. Mill, "Nature", 152–3.

35. Kant, *Critique of Pure Reason*, 148, A126.

36. Wigner, "The Unreasonable Effectiveness of Mathematics in the Natural Sciences", 6.

37. The most profound constant – 1/137 – that determines how stars burn, the fundamental nature of chemistry, and whether atoms exist, was described by Richard Feynman as "one of the greatest damn mysteries of physics: a magic number that comes to us with no understanding".

38. I think this is Georg Christoph Lichtenberg's phrase.

39. This is perhaps distantly reflected in the idea that the God who was at the beginning of the world was also the First *Cause*. When Laplace, challenged by Napoleon over the absence of God in his world picture, asserted that he had "no need of that hypothesis". That's as maybe but he certainly had need of something outside of his scheme: initial conditions.

40. "*Initium ergo ut esset, creatus est homo, ante quem nullus fuit*", Augustine, *City of God* Bk XII, Ch 27, final sentence.

41. The first volume – *The Hand* – is the most directly relevant.

42. Aristotle, *De Partibus Animalium* IV, X, 681a.

43. Suddendorf, *The Gap*, esp. 149. The following passage is also of considerable interest:

> There is no sign yet of the construction of explicit theories that describe the relationship of forces. Some animals make tools but none so far seem to design and refine tools by assembling various components and with various functions. Without embedded scenario building, without the benefits of human mental time travel, theory of mind, and language, it would not be surprising that their capacities for reasoning are limited even in the simplest tasks. (153)

44. Leading AI developer Judea Pearl has suggested that it would be useful to provide robots with the sensation of free will because it would make them more effective; see

the interview with Kevin Hartnett, "To Build Truly Intelligent Machines, Teach Them Cause and Effect". No comment required.

45. It would be unnecessary to make this point had there not been some philosophers (including myself at age 15) who advanced this argument. A contemporary example is Galen Strawson who argues as follows: "(1) Nothing can be *causa sui* – nothing can be the cause of itself. (2) In order to be truly morally responsible for one's actions one would have to be *causa sui*. (3) Therefore, nothing can be truly morally responsible." ("The Impossibility of Moral Responsibility", 5). In short, since we did not make ourselves, we cannot be responsible for our properties and dispositions, and hence our actions. Strawson requires that we have to be self-created as well as self-caused in order to be agents.

The argument fails because we do not have to cause ourselves at time t_1 in order to act freely at t_1 and be held morally responsible for that action. Actions, as we have discussed, are not mere effects of causes; and agents are not mere causes of effects in the sense we use the term when we apply it to the material world. By the time we come to be agents, we are remote from the pure givenness of the intra-uterine organism from which we developed. Our life's work is in making ourselves. Nevertheless, something has to be given, something that is not self-caused, in order for actions to have a locus, a *point d'appui*, a meaning, a purpose. The necessity of such a given does not remove moral responsibility but gives it content and, yes, limits. Just because we cannot be entirely responsible for what we are – because we cannot bring ourselves into being – it does not follow that we are not responsible for what we do. Actions do not follow from something as a mere cause defined by its standing properties: agency is not itself an effect of material causes, though it has material conditions, as we have discussed. It is a gift that emerges as we develop from infancy and increasingly, we have a role in developing it.

Some aspects of the conception of freedom that Sartre developed in *Being and Nothingness* seemed to have been prompted by intuitions similar to Strawson's, though he drew precisely the opposite conclusion. Freedom, Sartre argues, has to be free of any circumstances that make it possible. Hence it is allied with the Nothingness that breaks the plenum of Being and enables the self to be non-identical with itself: it is what it is not and is not what it is. Sceptics (among whom I number myself) may note that Nothingness is somewhat busy intervening in this way. Its power seems to come from the "-ness" that distances it from mere nothing. It is at any rate difficult to see how it could provide the necessarily *local* interventions to free the self from being identical with itself. Not being identical with itself and not being weighed down with the given would seem to make freedom of the self at once boundless and empty.

46. There is an element of luck in the scope of one's free will. We are free by permission of circumstances, which we do not always choose, under which we grow up or courtesy of the many accidents that may befall us on the way. Luck is not only upstream but also downstream of agency. It influences the opportunities that make action possible and the consequences they may have. Even successful actions will have unintended effects. My driving into town will leave tyre-prints on the road, add to air pollution, contribute to the noise of the traffic, bringing it above a threshold at which a baby wakes much to the distress of the parent, stimulate the economy by my act of

consuming petrol, cause fatal damage to an insect, and so on. We tend to reserve the title "consequences" for *significant* effects. This is something that is recognized in courts of law.

At a deeper level, however, human agents *transform* circumstances and consequences into (good or bad) luck. Pebbles and most animals have neither good luck nor bad. What's more, we have a role in making – or ruining – our luck. Even so, to listen to the haunting, endless, distinctive cry of a child born to drug addicts, suffering the horror of withdrawal and arrested development in its first day of life, is a shocking reminder of how the lottery of life is many-layered.

47. Another point I would not have seen as necessary to make were it not seen by some as relevant to the argument against free will. Sam Harris, for example, argues as follows: "Consider what it would take to actually have free will. You would need to be aware of all the factors that determine your thoughts and actions, and you would need to have control over all those factors" (*Free Will*, 24).

48. It is a reminder of how, as in the case of the rules of grammar, there are *enabling* constraints; and, more broadly, of the fallacy of the notion that the structures within which we operate necessarily compromise our freedom.

49. We must not exaggerate the limits imposed on our freedom that come from social pressures. Square-bashing soldiers may seem to lack agency but they may have made choices upstream of the parade ground and resume making them downstream after dismissal. Each soldier arrives at the drill square by a different route with different economic, political, and social constraints, which he experiences, interprets, and acts upon differently.

50. Scruton, *I Drink Therefore I Am*, 106.

51. This illustrates the point made by Arnold Gehlen – as summarized by Halák and Klouda: "Human action attains its solid form and a character intelligible both to the agent and to others only thanks to external support that is non-biological, culturally acquired support that stabilizes it and guides it on the basis of habitual behavior" ("Institution as a General Model of Meaning", 3).

52. I discuss this in Tallis, "Time, Reciprocal Containment, and the Ourobouros". Another "Ourobouros" example is the claim that our consciousness, including our consciousness of our brain as a small part of the world of which we are conscious, is identical with activity in our brain.

53. Reid, *Essays on the Active Powers of the Human Mind*, 367.

54. At the most basic level, according to the most powerful scientific theories, discrete events do not occur at particular times (general theory of relativity) nor are they discrete (quantum theory). I discuss this at some length in *Of Time and Lamentation*, especially Chapter 3.

55. Boswell, *Life of Johnson*, 273.

56. See Shariff & Vohs, "The World Without Free Will". The studies examining the impact of believing that free will is an illusion are well summarized in Steven Cave "There's No Such Thing as Free Will. But We're Better Off Believing in it Anyway". Cave cites research which reveals that people are less creative, more likely to conform, less willing to learn from mistakes, less grateful to one another, have a lower threshold for cheating. "In every regard, it seems, when we embrace determinism, we indulge our

dark side". For some, this constitutes a case for concealing the truth about free will from the people at large. Lucky, then, that the truth about free will is that it is real.

57. Kant's claim that the source of our freedom lies outside of the phenomenal realm in which the laws of nature operate does not help us to understand the scope and limits of our individual freedom. In the so-called noumenal realm of things-in-themselves, freedom would have no object – no location, no succession, no agenda – and there would be no basis for discrete actions, for a determination of what is to be done, how it is to be done, and what the doing amounts to. Nor would there be any basis for the distinction between the expression of, and frustration of, our freedom or between voluntary actions and the unwilled events that constitute the overwhelming majority of occurrences in the universe. As Jan Patocka has put it: "We need to think through anew our Kantian heritage from the standpoint of activity and practice, which Kant and his successors left suspended; we need to think through all of philosophy anew" (*Body, Community, Language, World*, 72–3); "Agency is inseparable from bodily movement: We realize possibilities only by moving, by being physical. Every realization takes place ultimately through movement" (*Ibid.*, 79).

CHAPTER 7

1. Bohuslav Brouk quoted in Sayer, *Prague: The Capital of the Twentieth Century*, 268.
2. Ecclesiastes 3:19.
3. Quoted in Heidegger, "The Anaximander Fragment", 32–3.
4. W. E. Henley, "Madame Life's a Piece in Bloom".
5. W. B. Yeats, "Sailing to Byzantium".
6. W. B. Yeats. "Death".
7. Becker, *The Denial of Death*, xvii.
8. The idea of eternity is discussed in "Temporal Thoughts on Eternity" in Tallis, *Of Time and Lamentation*.
9. Midgley, *Beast and Man*, 153.
10. George Eliot, "The Choir Invisible".
11. 1 Corinthians 15:26.
12. Nietzsche, "On Free Death", *Thus Spake Zarathustra*, 183.
13. "A poem is never finished, only abandoned" seems to have been sincerely meant. Valéry spent nearly five years revising one particular poem of just over 500 lines – *La Jeune Parque*. And even then André Gide had to drag it from him.
14. Alfred, Lord Tennyson, "Ulysses".
15. James Hughes ("Buddhism and Our Post Human Future") has claimed that "Buddhism and human enhancement have some affinities and some useful complementarities". It has been sympathetic to science and the technological advancement of mankind. Since, however, in "Buddhism human beings routinely evolve into gods and superbeings" a less expensive approach to immortalization might be to meditate and wait patiently for the universe to have its benign way with you.
16. O'Connell, *To be a Machine: Adventures Among Cyborgs, Utopians, Hackers, and the Futurists Solving the Modest Problem of Death*.

17. Williams, "The Makropoulos Case: Reflections on the Tedium of Immortality".
18. Coen, "To Store, Perchance to Thaw?".
19. As M. Rothblatt expressed it: "the software-based mind is a technoimmortalized continuation of the predecessor's identity"; quoted in Bamford and Danaher, "Transfer of Personality to a Synthetic Human Mind ('Mind Uploading') and the Social Construction of Identity", 9. Interestingly, the belief that consciousness can be instantiated on non-biological platforms is dependent on a functionalist interpretation of consciousness: all that matters are systems with the right causal structures and right causal roles. I owe this point to Danaher, "Philosophical Disquisitions: Chalmers v Pigliucci on the Philosophy of Mind-Uploading". Functionalism bypasses the question as to whether what it is like to be Raymond Tallis is the same irrespective of whether he is realized in a body or in a non-biological substrate.
20. Kuhn, "Virtual Immortality: Why the Mind-Body Problem is Still a Problem".
21. O'Connell, *To be a Machine*, 164. And, as Kuhn ("Virtual Immorality") says, "If 'I' can be duplicated once, then I can be duplicated twice; and if twice an unlimited number of times" (33). The vision of a vast crowd of "I's" all competing to be the I of I and to downgrade the others to "you", "him" or even "it" is not cheering.
22. See Tallis, "The Soup and the Scaffolding".
23. Bamford and Danaher, "Transfer of Personality to a Synthetic Human Mind", 9–10.
24. Quoted in Bamford and Danaher, "Transfer of Personality to a Synthetic Human Mind", 10. "Patternism" is essentially the idea that identity is a question of functional patterns and that identity can be preserved if patterns of organization and behaviour are realized in or on different substrates.
25. I have summarized the key points in the entry on "Information" in *Why the Mind is Not a Computer: A Lexicon of Neuromythology*.
26. Claude Shannon, "the father of the information age" anticipated this error when he emphasized that the engineering sense of "information" should not be confused with the everyday sense; see Shannon, "A Mathematical Theory of Communication". The idea of information as the resolution of uncertainty, needs uncertainty to be entertained. A range of possibilities has to be established. There are, of course, no possibilities in the material world – or not at least at the macroscopic level – without there being envisaged by a conscious being.
27. Chalmers, *The Conscious Mind: In Search of a Fundamental Theory*, 297.
28. Silver *et al.*, "Mastering the Game of Go Without Human Knowledge".
29. This is the story of the "singularity" that would signal the development of super-intelligent artefacts that would continue to upgrade themselves and leave the beastly organism *H. sapiens* far behind. It invites us to imagine a future in which machines might organize a conference to decide on the criteria for ascribing consciousness to human beings.
30. O'Connell, *To be a Machine*, 156. This is the point at which it seems justified to describe the valley as "Silly-Con" Valley.
31. Parfit, "The Unimportance of Identity", 1.
32. According to a survey conducted by PhilPapers, the proportion of philosophers who believe that the individual survives teletransportation (36%) is not much different from those who do not (42%); see Bourget and Chalmers, "What Do Philosophers

Believe?". The proportion who accept the validity of the experiment is not reported but clearly there are enough people out there who share Parfit's general assumptions to make his view resistant to being dismissed as the eccentric fantasy of a solitary thinker.

33. The temptation to compare this with Jorge Luis Borges' "Pierre Menard: Author of the *Quixote*" (collected in his *Fictions*) who recreated the novel by replicating its actual text is overwhelming. And, as you can see, I have not resisted it.

34. The idea of an "exact" recording is not at all clear for other reasons. If we think about brain cells, we have a choice. Either they are replicated: in some sensory image – for example, their image on a scan – in which case much will be left out, not the least the properties that are available to other senses; in some abstract form, such as 0s and 1s; or in (interminable) verbal descriptions – in which case even more is left out. There would have to be some way of translating these "recordings" into something that could be a living brain.

35. For a more detailed defence of this view, see, for example, Persson "The Involvement of Our Identity in Experiential Memory" and Klein, "What Memory Is" (discussed in Chapter 5).

36. Only God perhaps is both singular and general: an irreplaceable token that cannot be replicated who is also the type of all types.

37. This is reflected in "the distinction between the *feeling* of sameness of self and the *evidence* marshalled in support of that feeling" explored by Klein in "Sameness and the Self: Philosophical and Psychological Considerations", 1.

38. Parfit's determination to remove the personal from personal identity is connected with his overall project to construct a reformed utilitarianism that can head off the criticism that its "felicific" calculus that treats all pain and pleasure equally goes against our human nature. It is quintessentially human to care more for one's self and for those connected with one's self than for the generality of mankind.

39. Wheeler, "Sakharov Revisited: 'It from Bit'".

40. The idea that matter is information effectively amounts to the idea that matter is at the same level as the description of it or parts of it. This would result in conflicts between descriptions, especially at different scales – for example, a beach as a stretch of sand and a beach as a collection of trillions of sand grains. Fortunately, matter is *not* description and so is not conflicted by trying to be itself at different scales of description.

41. Pinker, "So How Does the Mind Work?", 22. Just as brainifying the person is greatly helped by personifying the brain, so the notion that the mind is a set of computational organs is made more plausible by mentalizing computers, taking literally notions such as computer memory. It is made easier still by regarding what goes on in the universe as a whole, not just the brain, as data transmission and processing.

42. Atkins, "Personal Identity and the Importance of One's Own Body", 343. Although this was not his intention, Parfit exposes the impossibility of the idea of the windowless Leibnizian self-conscious monad that is complete in itself without others and which upholds an entire world single-handedly – or at least single-mindedly. Similar arguments against Parfit have been expressed more recently by Bamford and Danaher, "Transfer of Personality to a Synthetic Human Mind". They remind

us that "our personal identities are constructed by social factors both causally and constitutively" (7). Personal identity is to an important degree established and maintained through our relations with others. My sense of who I am cannot be maintained monadically.

43. Hannah Arendt has expressed this: "Our being born means being woven into a whole 'web of human relationships, which is, as it were, woven by the deeds and words of innumerable persons, by the living as well as the dead'"; quoted by Anna Strhan in "Matters of Life and Death", 150.

44. Kompridis, "Technology's Challenge to Democracy: What of the Human?", 27.

45. See Hartnett, "To Build Truly Intelligent Machines, Teach Them Cause and Effect".

46. This may be why, as Velden has put it, "The project of simulating mental function by computers has now for decades been one of announcements rather than result" (*Psychology*, 48).

47. Patocka, *Body, Community, Language, World*, xxiv.

48. There is another important, dubious assumption, in Parfit's thought experiment. It is that reincarnation – as the "information" is translated into a body – will guarantee wakefulness. This is particularly clear in another description by Parfit of his thought experiment: "Travelling at the speed of light, the message will take three minutes to reach the Replicator on Mars. This will then create, out of new matter, a brain and body exactly like mine. *It will be in this body that I shall wake up.*" (Italics added) (Parfit, *Reasons and Persons*, 199). Even if if did wake, what would it wake up to, given that it has been transported, worldless and alone?

49. Parfit, *Reasons and Persons*, 210.

50. *Ibid.*, 211.

51. A "Cyborgoisie" perhaps. The term was suggested to me by Howard Makin, though a computer search reveals that others may have hit on it independently.

52. Scharf, "Where Do Minds Belong?".

53. *Ibid.*

54. A similar point is made by Walker, "Personal Identity and Uploading", especially Section 9, "The type-token solution to personal identity": "[i]t is argued that what is important in personal identity involves both token and type identity. While uploading does not preserve token identity, it does save type identity" (37).

CHAPTER 8

1. Plato, *Apology* 37e–38a.

2. Kant, *Critique of Pure Reason* Introduction B21, 56.

3. Heidegger, *Being and Time*, 235–67.

4. Hannah Arendt quoted in Safranski, *Martin Heidegger: Between Good and Evil*, 427.

5. "Humanism", *Wikipedia*; https://en.wikipedia.org/wiki/Humanism.

6. Gérard de Nerval, "Le Christ aux oliviers", taken from the German novelist Jean Paul.

7. In the arrestingly titled *The Unintended Reformation: How a Religious Revolution Secularized Society*, 28.

8. J. C. D. Clark has gone further and questioned whether there was a unitary

secularization process. His fascinating paper, "Secularization and Modernization: The Failure of the 'Grand Narrative'" is sharply critical of the conflation of sociological analysis with historical inquiry. He disputes pretty well every aspect of the standard sociological account of secularization – Marx, Durkheim, Simmel, Weber, Tonnies and others – and questions not only the cause of the process but the process itself. Among his targets is Weber's famous idea that a unitary Protestant Reformation in the sixteenth century generated a unitary Protestant ethic driving the rise of capitalism. "The once-celebrated strong correlation between Protestant dissent and entrepreneurship in finance and manufacture has been shown to be largely inaccurate" (171). Not the least of the problems of the historians of secularization is the question of what secularization is. We shall return to this question in Chapter 10.

9. Cited in Harrison, "Narratives of Secularisation", 5.
10. Geoffrey Hill, "Ovid in the Third Reich".
11. Durkheim, *Emile Durkheim Selected Writings*, 245.
12. Gauchet, *The Disenchantment of the World: A Political History of Religion*, 101.
13. Paul J. Fitzgerald's review of Gauchet's *The Disenchantment of the World: A Political History of Religion*.
14. Quoted in Walther, "Is Man's Wish the Father of the Gods? Comments on the Theogony by Ludwig Feuerbach".
15. Stace, "Man Against Darkness", 9.
16. Ernst Haeckel quoted in Rée, "Atheism in History", 66. There is an echo of this in Daniel Dennett. In his defence of Darwinitis in *Darwin's Dangerous Idea*, he argues that, the idea that evolution is mindless, and design can occur without a designer, is "a universal acid" that eats through every traditional concept. Mmm. The idea of the universe as a vast impersonal machine has a long tradition in western thought.
17. For a further discussion, see Tallis, *Of Time and Lamentation*, Chapter 3 "Mathematics and the Book of Nature".
18. It is highlighted by the striking contingency of the fundamental constants, such as the speed of light or the mass of a proton, that underpin that order. The hugely improbable "fine-tuning" of the universe necessary for the emergence of the elements, and hence life, and hence ourselves is deeply mysterious. It has prompted some pretty wild suggestions by physicists, foremost among them the proposal that there are billions of non-communicating, parallel universes. At present, no story of the universe – secular or sacred – makes it any less improbable. Physicist Sean Carroll recently pointed out in a tweet (@seanmcarroll 21 June) that fine-tuning is an argument *against* theism because God could make life whatever the laws of physics were. "Fine-tuning is only necessary if life is purely physical and God doesn't exist".
19. Weinberg, *The First Three Minutes*, 149. This is, of course, untrue, as we have seen from previous chapters. Good luck to anyone trying to create an atomic account of consciousness or the community of minds.
20. Quoted by Kauffman in "Breaking the Galilean Spell". The idea that there should be an over-arching meaning evident in every moment of every life, or human life, and that it should have an existence beyond moments and lives into the massive acreage of the universe is not as straightforward as it sounds. At best, it may suggest a convergent or additive meaning, something that we shall consider presently. Certainly, when it

comes to liveable meaning, it seems unlikely that the totality of things could provide it. See, however, the next chapter.

21. Russell, "A Free Man's Worship" in *Mysticism and Logic and Other Essays*, 51.

22. Taylor, *A Secular Age*, 152.

23. See especially "Science as a Vocation" in Weber, *Essays in Sociology*, 155.

24. Jenkins, "Disenchantment, Enchantment, and Re-Enchantment", 12. Bureaucracies, he argues, are not entirely disinfected of pre-rational spirits, as they may be associated with "a broad panoply of collective enchantments, in the form of rituals, symbols, legends, traditions and so on" (14). What is more, the Church – particularly the intensely hierarchical Catholic Church – is highly bureaucratic.

25. Arthur C. Clarke, "Hazards of Prophecy: The Failure of the Imagination". Our stubborn resistance to appreciating the magic of technology is beautifully summarized by Jacques Ellul: "Technique worships nothing, respects nothing. It has a single role: to strip off externals, to bring everything to light, and by rational use to transform everything into means" (*The Technological Society*).

26. Ecclesiastes 1:18.

27. Josephson-Storm, *The Myth of Disenchantment: Magic, Modernity, and the Birth of Natural Sciences*.

28. Gregory, *The Unintended Reformation*, 175. The close relationship between religion and the market in the US is highlighted by John Micklethwait and Adrian Wooldridge in *God is Back*. The absence of a state-authorized religion central to the Constitution opened the path to a lucrative and flourishing competitive market in the sacred.

29. Lloyd Blankfein, CEO of Goldman Sachs, the firm that was a poster child for bad behaviour on Wall Street, and whose contribution to human happiness is not clear, described his role as a banker as "doing God's work" (*Sunday Times*, 8 November 2009). God, it seems, moves in a mysterious way, through surprising agents. Thus, the self-branding of wealth-extractors as wealth-creators, dropping trickle-down mammon from Wall Street as the ante-chamber of Heaven, seeing themselves as acting as the deputies of God. The presence of the moneylenders in the temple is one aspect of the religious tradition that seems still to be going strong. The Church of England was surprised to discover that it drew income from its shares in the infamous pay-day loan company Wonga.

30. D'Antonio and See, *The Shadow President: The Truth about Mike Pence*.

31. Durkheim, *The Division of Labour in Society*, 119–20.

32. See Clark, "Secularization and Modernization" and James Spiegel's review of Keith Ward's *The Christian Idea of God*.

33. P. W. Singer and Emerson Brooking note the savage irony of "a terrorist group with a seventh-century view of the world that, nonetheless, could only be understood as a creature of the new Internet". They instance Omar Mateen who killed 49 people in an Orlando nightclub: "As he waited to kill himself, he periodically checked his phone to see if his attack had gone viral"; see "Jihadi Digital Natives", 87.

34. Nagel, *The View from Nowhere*, 217.

35. I have been unable to track down the source of this quote.

36. Pascal, *Pensées*, 37.

37. Henry Wadsworth Longfellow, "A Psalm of Life".

38. Pascal, *Pensées*, 206.

39. Paul Valéry, *Collected Works of Paul Valéry*, vol 4, 125. We do not require astronomers to tell us how small we are. A view from a mountain top or membership of a crowd are sufficient.

40. Rosling, *Factfulness: Ten Reasons We're Wrong about the World – and Why Things are Better than you Think*, 155.

41. Vividly described in David Wong, "Shit Jobs: 9 Types of Job that Will Destroy Your Soul".

42. Klíma, *My Crazy Century: A Memoir*.

43. Levi, *If This Is a Man / The Truce*.

44. Schopenhauer, "On Noise" in *Studies in Pessimism*.

45. Documented in the admiring biography by fellow composer Jan Swafford, *Beethoven: Anguish and Triumph*.

46. Joyce, *Ulysses*, 38.

47. Gospel According to Luke 7:24.

48. Keats, "Fancy".

49. Buchner, *Danton's Death*, 148.

50. Moran, *First You Write a Sentence: The Elements of Reading, Writing ... and Life*, 206.

51. Shakespeare, *Sonnets* 129.

52. Schopenhauer quoted in Setiya, *Midlife: A Philosophical Guide*.

53. Moran (in *First You Write a Sentence*, 26) cites the anthropologist Tim Ingold who argues that "humans live, and give their lives meaning, by making lines. In a world of continual growth and movement – a world of life – lines are how we make it all cohere, how we hold things together in what would otherwise be a formless flux".

54. Longfellow, "A Psalm of Life".

55. Friedrich von Schiller, *The Immutable*.

56. I am not sure where he said this but, given that it has his tone of voice, I am confident that he said it.

57. Not everyone would agree with this dismissal. Tom Chatfield in *Fun Inc.* mounts a robust defence of videogames. Some might be persuaded.

58. Just as we are more likely, in the course of a serious illness, to think more about the symptoms than our transience.

59. "When he spoke he never lifted an arm or a finger; he has *killed his puppet*", Paul Valéry, *An Evening with M. Teste*, 10.

60. I am grateful to James Tartaglia's *Philosophy in a Meaningless Life: A System of Nihilism, Consciousness and Reality* for this clarification and for much else in this chapter.

61. The aphorism is cited by Plutarch, *On Superstition* and gathered (in a slightly less racy translation than the one I have used) in Jonathan Barnes' wonderful *Early Greek Philosophy*, 62.

62. Hume, *A Treatise of Human Nature* section vii, Conclusion.

63. Russell, *A History of Western Philosophy*, 577.

64. Gellner, *Conditions of Liberty: Civil Society and its Rivals*, 95.

CHAPTER 9

1. Voltaire, *Candide.*
2. Anton Chekhov, *The Three Sisters* Act 2.
3. Durkheim, *Moral Education: A Study in the Theory and Application of the Sociology of Education*, 34.
4. Standing, *The Precariat: The New and Dangerous Class.*
5. Steve Crabtree, "Worldwide 13% of Employees are Engaged at Work", Gallup, 8 October 2013.
6. Heike Geissler quoted in "Employees are exploited and humiliated in the new precarious world of work. How to make a change?", *The Guardian*, 29 December 2018.
7. Keynes, "Economic Possibilities for Our Grandchildren".
8. *Ibid.*, 360.
9. Cited in David Graeber, "On the Phenomenon of Bullshit Jobs: A Work Rant".
10. *Ibid.*
11. Patel and Moore, (*A History of the World in Seven Cheap Things*) quoted by Mark O'Connor in his review in *The Guardian*, 14 June 2018.
12. Midgley, *What is Philosophy For?*, 186-7.
13. Keynes, "Economic Possibilities for Our Grandchildren", 265.
14. Danaher, "Will Life be Worth Living in a World Without Work? Technological Unemployment and the Meaning of Life".
15. *Ibid.*, 47.
16. Keiper and Schulman, "The Problem with 'Friendly' Artificial Intelligence", 89.
17. Valiunan, "Jonas Salk, the People's Scientist", 100.
18. Russell, "The Harm that Good Men Do", 51-2.
19. See Tallis, "Fifty Shades of Black".
20. See Gray, *Straw Dogs: Thoughts on Humans and Other Animals.*
21. Rosling, *Factfulness*, 65.
22. *Ibid.*, 69.
23. A recent report by Oxfam (2019) "Threat to the Future" notes that 26 people own as much as 50 per cent of the planet's population. Quoted in Aditya Chakraborty, "Paris is on the agenda at Davos, but it's too little, too late", *The Guardian*, 23 January 2019.
24. See Bostrom, "The Vulnerable World Hypothesis".
25. Jeremy Bentham quoted in Layard, *Happiness: Lessons from a New Science*, 235-6.
26. J. S. Mill, *Autobiography*, 112.
27. According to Edward Mendelson, Auden's most assiduous editor, the observation, which Auden did not claim for himself, is probably picked up from a radio music-hall comedian who called himself "The Vicar of Mirth".
28. Baggini, *Atheism: A Very Short Introduction*, 59.
29. Nagel, *The View from Nowhere*, 27.
30. Berlin, *The Proper Study of Mankind*, 239.
31. John Keats, *The Fall of Hyperion. A Dream.* Canto 1, line 147.
32. Solzhenitsyn, Templeton Address, 1983.
33. Given that childhood morality is internalized from the precepts and examples of parents, it might be argued that it will depend on parental morality and this may wane as religion retreats.

34. It is a matter of concern that Ayn Rand, whose loathing of altruism and praise of self-centeredness articulated the implicit morality of a two-year old, has had such an influence on powerful politicians in the US (notable the godfather of the 2007–08 crash Alan Greenspan) and, more recently, in the UK, where her worshippers include the (as of 2019) Chancellor of the Exchequer Sajid Javid. The key text is Rand's *The Virtue of Selfishness.*

35. Hobbes, *Leviathan* Chapter 13, "Of the Natural Condition of Mankind as Concerning their Felicity and Misery", 64.

36. Durkheim, *The Division of Labour in Society*, 270.

37. *Ibid.*

38. Ferguson, *The War of the World: History's Age of Hatred.*

39. Norman Angell's *The Great Illusion* (1909) argued, a few years before the outbreak of the bloodiest war in history to date, that, because the integration of the economies of European countries was so close, war between them would be futile – there would be no spoils for the victors. Militarism should therefore be obsolete. As Angell pointed out, this might not prevent war, only make them more destructive. At any rate, it would serve the interests of none of the combatants.

40. Wrangham, *The Goodness Paradox: How Evolution Made Us More and Less Violent.*

41. Rawls, *A Theory of Justice.* Rawls argued that under such circumstances, we would choose that society should be run on egalitarian principles and be committed to distributive justice.

42. Holloway, *Godless Morality: Keeping Religion out of Ethics*, 18.

43. For an excellent brief exposition of this central aspect of Hegel's thought, see Singer, *Hegel. A Very Short Introduction*, 77–81.

44. Spelled out at length in Sartre's *Being and Nothingness* Part 3, Chapter 3 "Concrete Relations with Others", 361–413.

45. Nietzsche, "Skirmishes of an Untimely Man" in *Twilight of the Idols*, paragraph 5.

46. Baggini, "How to Compare Fruit: The Limited Ambitions of Ethical Thinking", 7.

47. Zuckerman, *Society without God: What the Least Religious Nations Can Teach Us About Contentment.* Andrew Pinsent (personal communication) points out that even "godless" Denmark is actually a weakly religious country with a constitutional monarchy. He also notes that nations in which religion is forbidden – communist Albania, North Korea, and a few others we have mentioned – have the most appalling human rights record.

48. Rosen, *I'm a Believer – But I'll be Damned if I'm Religious.*

49. *Ibid.*, 8.

50. Pinker, *The Better Angels of Our Nature: Why Violence Has Declined.* I covered much of the same territory in *Enemies of Hope: A Critique of Contemporary Pessimism.*

51. Pinker's thesis has been challenged by theologians (not surprisingly) and by some historians. An entire issue of the academic journal *Historical Reflections* (vol. 44:1, 2018) has been devoted to Pinker's book and concludes that it is "seriously, if not fatally, flawed".

52. Law, *Humanism: A Very Short Introduction*, 26.

53. *Ibid.*, 26.

54. *Ibid.*, 27. There are, of course, secular societies such as the Soviet Union where homosexuality was severely punished. The recent revival of the brutal treatment of gay

people in Russia, however, is closely connected with the resurgence of the explicitly homophobic Orthodox Church.

55. Dominic Erdozain cited in Harrison, "Narratives of Secularisation".

56. It has often been argued that inter-faith dialogue has been integral to Islam from the beginning. See, for example, Hussain, "Muslims, Pluralism, and Interfaith Dialogue". Unfortunately, the attitude of the *Qur'an* is unclear: some verses support bridge-building and some mutual exclusion. The Ahmadiyya sect of Islam, which is committed to peace and tolerance between Islamic sects, is regarded by many Muslims as heretical and the Ahmadi are often subject to persecution and violence.

57. I question whether there are "Biological Reasons for Being Cheerful" in *In Defence of Wonder*. Richard Wrangham ("The Goodness Paradox") reflects on the fact that, while we are more domesticated and less aggressive than our nearest primate kin, particularly chimpanzees, we still have an extraordinary capacity for violence. We may be less directly or reactively violent, but organized, proactive aggression may be on a much greater scale than seen in other species. Technological advance – notably in weaponry and communication – has facilitated bloodshed on a vast scale, often, ironically, in defence of law and order, peace, and an idea of civilization.

58. Fleischman, "The Origins of Human Morality".

59. See Chapter 9 "Beyond Time: Temporal Thoughts on Eternity" in Tallis, *Of Time and Lamentation*.

60. Denys Turner mocks atheists ("poor bewildered things") for failing to keep up with the evolving idea of the God of the theologians; see "How to be an Atheist", inaugural lecture delivered at the University of Cambridge, 12 October 2001. Even by the standards of negative theology, Turner's footwork is particularly fancy. For example: "Negative theology does not mean that we are short of things to say about God; it means just that everything we say of God falls short of him". How can we know that what is said "falls short", if we do not know what it is supposed to fall short of? And how do we know that it merely falls "short". Could it not be entirely wrong?

61. Carlo Rovelli quoted in Matlack, "Quantum Poetics", 60.

62. There is an interesting analogy between the embarrassment faced by science at the highest level in explaining how anything actually happens in the spatio-temporal continuum and the embarrassment of theologians in trying to explain how God can intervene in history – the so-called puzzle of Special Divine Action. In general theory of relativity, which gathers up all possible viewpoints, we have no events happening at any particular time, which, as we saw in Chapter 4, invited a Parmenidean vision of the universe as an unchanging unity. The observer alone can provide the frame of reference that will assign a time to events and permit them to happen. In quantum theory there is no definite state of the universe without an observer. Analogously, if as Rowan Williams puts it (*Being Human: Bodies, Minds, Persons*, 25), God's "will or purpose or character it is to share what His life is", it is hard to see how this intersection between His life and ours, could be possible. Behind this looms the greater puzzle of divine causation: how something as big as God can interact – at a particular time and place – with something as (comparatively) small as history, a nation, or an individual.

63. What follows has been greatly influenced, and assisted, by Stephen Law's excellent "Wittgensteinian Accounts of Religious Belief: Noncognitivist, Juicer, and Atheist-Minus".

64. Nicholas Lash quoted in Law, "Wittgensteinian Accounts of Religious Belief", 5.
65. Scruton, *I Drink Therefore I Am*, 136–7.
66. See Crane, *The Meaning of Belief: Religion from an Atheist's Point of View*, summarized by Crane in "Join the Club".
67. Neil MacGregor, "Belief is Back", *The Guardian*, 6 October 2018.
68. Durkheim, *Elementary Forms of Religious Life*, 47.
69. Carroll, "Beyond Theism and Atheism", 100.
70. MacCulloch, *A History of Christianity*, 10.
71. George Herbert, "The Elixir".
72. The title of Soren Kierkegaard's treatise is *Purity of Heart is to Will One Thing: Spiritual Preparation for the Office of Confession*.
73. W. B. Yeats, "An Irish Airman Foresees His Death" (1918).
74. MacCulloch in the introduction to his magisterial *A History of Christianity*, 11.

CHAPTER 10

1. Steven Hawking speaking on a 1995 television series, "Reality on the Rocks".
2. Pascal, *Pensées*, 66.
3. Russell, "A Free Man's Worship", 51–2.
4. Quine, *From Stimulus to Science*, 16.
5. Dreben, "Putnam, Quine – and the Facts", 294.
6. *Ibid.*, 309.
7. We see this recapitulated in miniature in the journey each of us must take from the dim intuitions of the foetus to the knowing adult human being. The post-natal part of the journey, however, is not taken alone: in our ascent from the buzz of sensation to a world-picture we are borne up by our fellow humans.
8. This is explored in Tallis, *Logos*.
9. Einstein, "Physics and Reality", 351.
10. In *Logos*, I spell out some of the steps that would be necessary to reach our present state of knowledge and understanding, if we began from the starting point so vividly described by Quine.
11. See, for example, Appendix 1 to Chapter 3 in *Logos*.
12. Klein, "The Unplanned Obsolescence of Psychological Science and an Argument for its Revival", 19.
13. Wittgenstein, *Tractatus Logico-Philosophicus*, paragraph 6.52.
14. Nagel, *Mind and Cosmos: Why the Materialist Neo-Darwinian Conception of Nature is Almost Certainly False*, 3.
15. The use of vision as a proxy for fully developed human consciousness is irresistible, given that vision is the most epistemic of the senses.
16. This is particularly tricky for natural science, which, at a fundamental level, homogenizes the universe. The very universality of the quantitative equations obliterates the qualitative variousness of things. The more the universe is explained in terms acceptable to fundamental science, the more subjectivity vanishes from it.
17. Kant, *Critique of Pure Reason*, 82.

18. Merleau-Ponty, *The Phenomenology of Perception*, 432.

19. *Ibid.*, 264.

20. Merleau-Ponty as an idealist may seem surprising to those who associate him with the central doctrine of the subject as being essentially embodied. A paper by Sebastian Gardner examines Merleau-Ponty's idealism with great subtlety: "Merleau-Ponty's Transcendental Theory of Perception". It is however subjected to a strong critique by Jan Halák.

21. Toadvine, "The Elemental Past". I am grateful to Jan Halák for drawing this article to my attention.

22. *Ibid.*, 264.

23. Weyl, *The Philosophy of Mathematics and Natural Science*, 122. This highlights a problem; the universe begins no-where as well as no-when. There is no zero point in space–time and yet every series seems to require such a starting point.

24. Toadvine, "The Elemental Past", 271.

25. Facts – about atoms, people, continents, planets, the universe – are about subjects that are unified. Prior to consciousness, the universe is neither one nor many. The Milky Way, planet Earth, items such as pebbles, are intrinsically neither single entities nor collections of entities. It is the subject that divides the world into discrete, stable objects hosting events, determining whether they are one or many. In summary, there are no levels or scales in a subjectless universe and hence the basis for differentiation is undetermined.

26. Nagel, *Mind and Cosmos*, 8.

27. We enter a territory associated in English philosophy with Owen Barfield and his classic work *Saving the Appearances: A Study in Idolatry*. Barfield argues that "the world ... (apart from the special inquiry of physics) experts of all kinds methodically investigate – is a system of collective representations" (18).

28. Toadvine, "The Elemental Past", 264.

29. The question about the sound a tree falling unheard makes seems difficult only because other falling trees have been heard on other occasions. We can know what it *would* sound like if it were within earshot of those who have ears to hear. We then extend our experience of heard sounds to unheard sounds that have similar causes. The emptiness of the question can be exposed by rephrasing it as "What does the unfulfilled possibility of a sound sound like?"

30. It might be objected that probability amplitudes are inherent in the material world, not least at the quantum level. They are not. The probability amplitude is a relationship between the wave function of a system and the results of *observation* of that system. Ultimately, the probabilities are entertained, that is to say hosted, by physicists.

31. Factual claims are exposed, howsoever indirectly, to what Quine called "the tribunal of experience" that will check whether it really is a fact. They do not face the tribunal individually but "corporately".

32. Romano, "After the Lived-Body" points out that taking the natural sciences as having the last word on the matter "consists in taking the truths of physics for the expression of an 'in-self' of things, and consequently in treating the phenomenal world, the pre-scientific world in which our life unfolds, as a mere appearance" (449). Given that

science has grown out of this world and faces the tribunal of everyday experience, this would undermine the credentials of science. And ultimately measurements require appearances.

33. Béatrice Han-Pile glossing Michel Foucault in "The Analytic of Finitude", 130.

34. Lowe, *A Survey of Metaphysics*, 113–4.

35. I have left open the nature of the subject. He/she is not a Cartesian substance emerging out of an already formed machine-world. Such a ghost would not only be incapable of acting on the material world – the standard anxiety about the impossibility of mental causation – but it could not learn anything from the material world, even less something relevant to its mode of being. Nor is the subject a Wittgensteinian "limit" to the world, as set out in the *Tractatus Logico-Philosophicus*: "The subject does not belong to the world: rather, it is a limit of the world" (5.632). On the contrary, the subject is that in virtue of which what-is is a world or what-is is a "what". The (embodied) subject is in its world, as well as offset from it.

36. One way of closing the gap between the physical world and subjective experience is to mobilize the notion of "sense-data". The term seems to bridge the gap between experience and that which justifies the experience. The characterization of what is experienced as "data" merges the experience, the experiencing subject, and that which is experienced.

37. Valéry, *An Evening with M. Teste*.

38. Wittgenstein, *Tractatus Logico-Philosophicus*, 6.4.

39. It is important not to dwell too much on the improbability of the emergence of the subject as viewed through the lens of physics. Yes, the universe needs to have certain highly improbable properties – it needs to be "fine-tuned" – for there to be carbon, and hence life, and consequently conscious life, etc. The truth is the odds are against *any* actuality. All *a posteriori* actualities have a low *a priori* probability unless there is something in advance to restrict the range of possibilities.

40. A paraphrase by Paul Carly of the famous passages in Durkheim's in which he describes the "double" nature of man.

41. Durkheim, *Elementary Forms of Religious Life*, 475–6.

42. Moliere, *The Bourgeois Gentleman* (1670). This is quoted in an essay by Rebecca Neuberger Goldstein "Speaking Prose All Our Lives", highlighting the ubiquity of religion-independent rational moral reasoning in our lives.

43. They are the broadest expressions of possibility. As discussed in the previous section, possibilities do not exist in nature. Strictly laws of nature are not laws in the sense in which they are usually understood because they are unbreakable.

44. In some respects, the gods in polytheistic religions are an even clearer view of humanity (and its attendant inhumanity) than the God of monotheism, who is distant and defined by abstract properties to which emotions – anger, love – are attached with difficulty. The Christian Holy Family provides theologians and Church fathers with endless puzzles, not the least regarding the status of the Son, the Virgin Mary, and the Holy Ghost. MacCulloch's *A History of Christianity* records some of the impressive volumes of blood that have been spilt over this matter.

45. Ludwig Feuerbach quoted in Walther, "Is Man's Wish the Father of the Gods? Comments on the Theogony by Ludwig Feuerbach".

46. Scruton, *Death-Devoted Heart: Sex and the Sacred in Wagner's Tristan and Isolde*, 13.

47. Lamont, *The Philosophy of Humanism*, 145.

48. Quoted in *Auguste Comte's Religion of Humanity*.

49. Durand, "God's Holiness: A Reappraisal of Transcendence", 420.

50. Wittgenstein, *Zettel*, para. 125.

51. Kelly, *The Minister and the Murderer: A Book of Aftermaths*, 142.

52. Dandelion, *A Sociological Analysis of the Theology of Quakers: The Silent Revolution*. Andrew Pinsent (personal communication) has pointed out that "the problem with 'the light within' is that it does not allow for irruption of the new light from without to be implanted in the everyday world (which, as a by-product, gives sacred spaces and times)". And there is a question as to the extent to which profound thought, even arrived at in a common silence, can be shared.

53. Philip Larkin, "Church Going" (1955) in *Collected Poems*.

54. Carroll, "Beyond Theism and Atheism", 100.

55. Ludwig Feuerbach quoted in Walther, "Is Man's Wish the Father of the Gods?".

56. I cannot leave the notion of a secular Eucharist without quoting this passage from Joe Moran:

> For those of us without faith, the sentence feels in some small way devotional. It pays homage, not by thanking God for the world's existence but by thanking the world itself for existing. The thanking happens not by worshipping but by noticing. We are the only animals who are truly paying attention. No other living thing seems to be curious about things they cannot mate with, play with, scrounge off, or eat. We humans are the noticers. (Moran, *First You Write a Sentence*, 206).

57. Nietzsche, *Ecce Homo*, "Why I am a Destiny".

58. May, *Love: A New Understanding of an Ancient Emotion*, 9.

59. *Ibid.*, 10.

60. *Ibid.*, 11.

61. *Ibid.*, 15.

62. Philip Larkin, "Self's the Man" (1958) in *Collected Poems*.

63. May, *Love*, 19.

64. *Ibid.*, 21.

65. Shakespeare, *As You Like It*, Act 5, Scene 4.

66. Scruton, "Faking It" in *Confessions of a Heretic*, 3.

67. Scruton, *Death-Devoted Heart*, 3.

68. It is no coincidence that the opera seems to have grown out of the church mass.

69. Scruton, *Death-Devoted Heart*, 5.

70. Richard Wagner quoted in Scruton, *Death-Devoted Heart*, 9.

71. Friedrich Nietzsche quoted in Safranski, *Nietzsche: A Philosophical Biography*, 19.

72. The reader might be interested in a tetchy outburst, Tallis, "The Shocking Yawn: Art up its *Ars*" in *Epimethean Imaginings: Philosophical and Other Reflections on Everyday Light*.

73. And this is closely connected with another point: anyone who talks about art is entering a conversation that has been going on for rather a long time. These include the

views that art primarily serves religious, ethical, therapeutic, political, and economic functions. More often perhaps than is admitted it may sometimes be just another source of pleasure, a distraction, another way of passing the time, up there with computer games, football fanaticism, and other pastimes.

74. The argument is presented in more detail in Tallis and Spalding, *Summers of Discontent: The Purpose of the Arts Today.*

75. Pater, "The School of Giorgione" in *The Renaissance: Studies in Art and Poetry*, 95.

76. Forster, *Aspects of the Novel*, 170.

77. Shakespeare, *Sonnets* 68.

78. It is a thesis explored *in extenso* in Sartre's *What is Literature?*

79. Scruton, *Understanding Music: Philosophy and Interpretation*, 5.

80. Tallis, "Was Schubert a Musical Brain?" in *Reflections of a Metaphysical Flâneur* develops the case against (neuro-)scientific "explanations" of music.

81. Quoted in Safranski, *Nietzsche: A Philosophical Biography*, 19.

82. Pater, "Conclusion" in *The Renaissance: Studies in Art and Poetry*, 158.

83. Nietzsche, *Untimely Meditations*, "Schopenhauer as Educator", Section 7.

84. Jorge Luis Borges, *The Aleph and Other Stories.*

85. Quoted in Walther, "Is Man's Wish the Father of the Gods?".

86. The brilliant philosopher of language J. L. Austin famously had as his motto "Neither a be-all nor an end-all be".

87. The story is quoted by Julian Baggini in *What's It All About? Philosophy and Meaning of Life.*

88. A contemporary exception is James Tartaglia whose engrossing *Philosophy in a Meaningless Life* I have found particularly helpful in distinguishing sources of meaning/meaninglessness: a) what our lives may mean to ourselves – their pleasures and pains, the satisfactions and dissatisfactions; b) our significance in the larger frameworks of human affairs – our parish, the nation, history; and c) the objective importance of humanity in the order of things. Nagel's *The View from Nowhere* – cited on several occasions in this book – manages to be both closely argued and horizon lifting on this matter.

89. Cooper, "Life and Meaning", 133.

90. Wittgenstein, *Tractatus Logico-Philosophicus*, paragraph 6.521.

91. P. F. Strawson quoted in Hacker, "Critical Notice of Timothy Williamson *The Philosophy of Philosophy*", 337.

92. Sellars, "Philosophy and the Scientific Image of Man", 35.

93. For a discussion of this, see Tallis, *Logos*, Chapter 2, "A Brief Backward Glance".

94. Tartaglia, *Philosophy in a Meaningless Life*, 79. Tartaglia's observation that contemporary philosophy occupies "a precarious cultural position between science and religion" hits the spot (81).

95. Blumenfeld, "Is Humanism a Religion?".

96. Geertz, *The Interpretation of Cultures*, 49.

97. Ludwig Feuerbach quoted in Walther, "Is Man's Wish the Father of the Gods?".

98. Durkheim, *The Elementary Forms of Religious Life*, 163.

99. *Ibid.*, 163.

100. *Ibid.*, 47.

101. Lee, "Polar Opposites? Diversity and Dialogue Among the Religious and Non-Religious". More recent research – Buillivant *et al.*, *Understanding Unbelief: Atheists and Agnostics Round the World*, an interim report – has confirmed the heterogeneity of the beliefs and unbelievers.

102. Tomas Halik quoted in Koci and Roubic, "Searching the Altar of an Unknown God: Tomas Halik on Faith in a Secular Age", 117.

103. The Humanist Manifesto drafted in 1933 by Raymond Bragg and the philosopher Roy Wood Sellars, asserted that the "the purpose of a man's life is the complete realisation of human personality ... the quest for the good life is ... the central task for man". Importantly, any religious emotions should be expressed in "social passion", in "a heightened sense of personal life and in a cooperative effort to promote social well-being".

104. Durkheim, *The Elementary Forms of Religious Life*, 417.

105. Baggini, "The Myth of *Mythos*", 38.

106. St Paul Letter to the Colossians 2:8. There is no record of any reply.

107. Kierkegaard, *Purity of Heart Is to Will One Thing: Spiritual Preparation for the Office of Confession*.

108. However, MacCulloch has pointed out that "Christianity has never ceased to debate the relationship between truth revealed from God in sacred texts and the restless exploration of truth by human reason, which on a Christian account is itself a gift from God" (*A History of Christianity*, 141).

109. See McGrath and McGrath, *The Dawkins Delusion? Atheist Fundamentalism and the Denial of the Divine*. It is important not to exaggerate the failure of atheists to engage with real rather than cartoon religion. Edmund Standing ("Are the 'New Atheists' avoiding the 'real' arguments?") has pointed out that the Nicene Creed central to Christian doctrine contains many of the claims that the New Atheists challenge: that God created Heaven and Earth; that Jesus was an historical figure born of the Virgin Mary and the Holy Spirit; that he was crucified and ascended into Heaven; and so on.

110. It is not actually true: it was the Romans who did it. As Stuart Kelly points out, "The long and inglorious history of Christian anti-Semitism began with a non-murder" (*The Minister and the Murderer: A Book of Aftermaths*, 71).

111. Polly Toynbee, "The culture of respect for religion has gone too far", *The Guardian*, 28 August 2018, makes this point with characteristic passion, humanity, and brilliance.

112. Camus, *The Rebel*, 12.

113. James Joyce, *Ulysses*, 38.

114. In *Nature: Course Notes from the College de France*, quoted in Toadvine, "The Elemental Past", 265.

115. Halik, "Church for the Seekers".

116. *Ibid.*

EPILOGUE

1. Moore, "Finitude", 62.

2. Klein, "The Self and its Brain", 508.

3. Williams, *Being Human: Bodies, Minds, Persons*, 8.
4. Spinoza, *On the Correction of the Understanding*, 227.
5. The life of the philosopher is riddled with accident: the contingency of the philosophical arguments you encounter, the small subset of philosophers you get to know of, and the opportunity and capacity to engage with philosophical thought, is chastening. Religious belief seems equally susceptible to accident. Axtel, *Problems of Religious Luck: Assessing the Limits of Religious Disagreement* has examined the awkward fact that worshipping the right gods must be a matter of chance. It is an accident to be born a Hindu or Muslim and yet some regard this as a crucial determinant of their likelihood of salvation and eternal life.
6. William Blake, *Auguries of Innocence*.
7. Russell, "A Free Man's Worship", 55.
8. Exodus 3:13-14. "I am Who I am".
9. The full passage is remarkable:

> "For me", he said, "the endgame is when the entire population of humanity, minus a few douchebags, basically flies into space. My goal, personally, is to peacefully and passionately explore the universe for all eternity. And I'm sure as s*** I'm not going to be doing that in this body"
>
> "But what would you be?" I asked. "And would it be you?"
>
> Tim said that what he imagined himself being was an interconnected system of information-seeking nodes, travelling in ever-widening arcs throughout the universe, sharing intelligence across the vastness, learning, experiencing, collating. And his guess, he said, was that this unimaginably expansive system would be as much him as the six-foot-high assemblage of bone and tissue that happened to be his current form. (O'Connell, *To be a Machine*, 156.)

10. An idea particularly associated with Arnold Gehlen – discussed in Halák & Klouda, "Institution as a General Model of Meaning". I am grateful to Jan Halák for sight of this manuscript – and for many other sources of intellectual stimulation.

References

Angell, N. *The Great Illusion.* New York: Putnam, 1911.

Arendt, H. *The Life of the Mind.* New York: Harcourt, 1981.

Aristotle. *De Partibus Animalium* [On the Parts of Animals]. Translated by William Ogle. Available at: http://classics.mit.edu/Aristotle/parts_animals.html.

Armstrong, D. M. "Naturalism, Materialism and First Philosophy". In *The Nature of Mind and Other Essays.* St Lucia: University of Queensland Press, 1980.

Atkins, K. "Personal Identity and the Importance of One's Body: A Response to Derek Parfit". *International Journal of Philosophical Studies* 8:3 (2000), 329–48.

Augustine. *City of God.* Translated by M. Dods. New York: The Modern Library, 1950.

Avital, E. & E. Jablonka. *Animal Traditions: Behavioural Inheritance in Evolution.* Cambridge: Cambridge University Press, 2000.

Axtel, G. *Problems of Religious Luck: Assessing the Limits of Religious Disagreement.* Lanham, MD: Lexington Books, 2018.

Baggini, J. *Atheism: A Very Short Introduction.* Oxford: Oxford University Press, 2003.

Baggini, J. *What's It All About? Philosophy and Meaning of Life.* Oxford: Oxford University Press, 2007.

Baggini, J. "Is Common Ground between Religion and Atheism Possible?". *The Guardian,* 25 November 2011.

Baggini, J. "Myth of *Mythos*". In A. Carroll & R. Norman (eds), *Religion and Atheism: Beyond the Divide.* Abingdon: Routledge, 2016.

Baggini, J. "How to Compare Fruit: The Limited Ambitions of Ethical Thinking". *Times Literary Supplement,* 25 May 2018.

Baird Callicot, J. "The Wilderness Idea Revisited: The Sustainable Development Alternative". In J. Baird Callicot & M. Nelson (eds), *The Great New Wilderness Debate.* Athens, GA: University of Georgia Press, 1998.

Bamford, S. & J. Danaher. "Transfer of Personality to a Synthetic Human Mind ('Mind Uploading') and the Social Construction of Identity". *Journal of Consciousness Studies* 24:11/12 (2017), 6–30.

Barfield, O. *Saving the Appearances: A Study in Idolatry*. London: Faber, 1957.

Barnes, J. (ed.) *Early Greek Philosophy*. London: Penguin, revised edition, 2001.

Barthes, R. "The Great Family of Man". In *Mythologies*. Translated by Annette Lavers. London: Paladin, 1973.

Bartley, G. "Why Physicalism is Wrong". *Philosophy Now* (June/July 2018), 28–31.

Becker, E. *The Denial of Death*. New York: The Free Press, 1973.

Bell, D. "The Return of the Sacred? The Argument on the Future of Religion". *British Journal of Sociology* 28 (1977), 419–49.

Berger, P. L. "The Desecularisation of the World: A Global Overview". In P. L. Berger (ed.), *The Desecularization of the World: Resurgent Religion and Politics*. Washington, DC: Eerdmans, 1999.

Berlin, I. *The Proper Study of Mankind*. London: Chatto & Windus, 1997.

Blake, W. "Auguries of Innocence". *The Complete Poems*. London: Penguin, 1977.

Blumenfeld, S. "Is Humanism a Religion?" *The New American Magazine*, 23 February 2010.

Borges, J. L. "Pierre Menard: The Author of Quixote" In *Fictions*. London: Penguin, 2000.

Borges, J. L. *The Aleph and Other Stories*. London: Penguin, 2004.

Bostrom, N. "The Vulnerable World Hypothesis". Working Paper 3.22, Future of Humanity Institute, University of Oxford.

Boswell, J. *Life of Samuel Johnson*. London: Everyman, 1992.

Bourget, D. & D. Chalmers. "What Do Philosophers Believe?" PhilPapers, 27 April 2013. Available at: https://philpapers.org/archive/BOUWDP.

Bragg, R & Sellars, R. W. "The Humanist Manifesto" 1933.

Brecht, B. "To Posterity". In M. Hamburger & C. Middleton (eds), *Modern German Poetry*. London: McGibbon & Kee, 1960.

Bredlaw, S. "Husserl's 'Pairing' Relationship and the Role of Others in Infant Perception". *Journal of Consciousness Studies* 23:3/4 (2016), 8–30.

Brentano, F. *Psychology from an Empirical Standpoint*. London: Routledge & Kegan Paul, 1973.

British Humanist Association. *The Case for Secularism*. London: 2007.

Buchner, G. *Danton's Death*. In *The Plays of Georg Buchner*. Translated with an Introduction by Geoffrey Dunlop. London: Vision Press, 1952.

Buchner, L. *Force and Matter* [1855]. Cambridge: Cambridge University Press, 2011.

Buckley, C. "China is detaining muslims in vast numbers. The goal: transformation". *New York Times*, 8 September 2018.

Buckner, C. "Morgan's Canon meets Hume's Dictum: Avoiding Anthropofabulation in Cross-Species Comparisons". *Biological Philosophy* 28 (2013), 953–71.

Buillivant, S. *et al. Understanding Unbelief: Atheists and Agnostics Round the World*. An Interim Report, University of Kent and other institutions, June 2019

Buonomato, D. *Your Brain is a Time Machine: The Neuroscience and Physics of Time*. New York: Norton, 2017.

Burgess, A. *Earthly Powers*. New York: Simon & Schuster, 1983.

Butler, J. *The Analogy of Religion*. London: J. & P. Knapton, 1736.

Campion, J., R. Latto & Y. Smith. "Is Blind-Sight an Effect of Scattered Light, Spared Cortex, and Near-Threshold Vision". *Behavioural and Brain Sciences* 6:3 (1983), 423–48.

Camus, A. *The Rebel*. Translated by Anthony Bower. Harmondsworth: Penguin, 1971.

Canales, J. *The Physicist and the Philosopher: Einstein, Bergson, and the Debate that Changed our Understanding of Time*. Princeton, NJ: Princeton University Press, 2015.

Carnap, R. "Intellectual Autobiography". In P. A. Schilpp (ed.), *The Philosophy of Rudolf Carnap.* LaSalle, IL: Open Court, 1963.

Carroll, A. "Beyond Theism and Atheism". In A. Carroll & R. Norman (eds), *Religion and Atheism: Beyond the Divide.* Abingdon: Routledge, 2017.

Cassam, Q. "Kant and Reductionism". *Review of Metaphysics* 42 (1989), 72–104.

Cassam, Q. *Self and World.* Oxford: Clarendon Press, 1997.

Cassam, Q. "Representing Bodies". *Ratio* 15:4 (2002), 314–34.

Cassam, Q. "The Embodied Self". In S. Gallagher (ed.), *Oxford Handbook of the Self.* Oxford: Oxford University Press, 2011.

Cave, S. "There's No Such Thing as Free Will. But We're Better Off Believing in it Anyway". *The Atlantic*, June 2016.

Chakraborty, A. "Paris is on the agenda at Davos, but it's too little, too late". *The Guardian*, 23 January 2019.

Chalmers, D. *The Conscious Mind: In Search of a Fundamental Theory.* Oxford: Oxford University Press, 1996.

Chalmers, D. "Panpsychism and Panprotopsychism". In A. Nagasaway (ed.), *Consciousness in the Physical World: Perspectives on Russellian Monism* 246–77. Oxford: Oxford University Press, 2015.

Chater, N. *The Mind is Flat: The Illusion of Mental Depth and the Improvised Mind.* London: Allen Lane, 2018.

Chatfield, T. *Fun Inc.* London: Virgin, 2010.

Cheng, T. "Quine's Naturalism and Behaviourism". *Metaphilosophy* 49:4 (2018).

Chesterton, G. K. *Orthodoxy.* Guttenberg e-book, 1994.

Chittka, L. "Bee Cognition". *Current Biology* 27 (Oct 2017), R1049–53.

Chung, D. "Gesticulation as the Integration of Body and Mind: A Semantics of Nodding". PhilArchive; available at: https://philarchive.org/rec/CHUGAT-2

Chung S. *et al.* "Unconscious determinants of free decisions in the human brain". *Nature Neuroscience* 11:5 (2008), 543–5.

Clark, J. C. D. "Secularization and Modernization: The Failure of a 'Grand Narrative'". *Historical Journal* 55 (2012), 161–94.

Clarke, A. C. "Hazards of Prophecy: The Failure of the Imagination". In *Profiles of the Future.* London: Orion, 1962.

Clayton, N. "Ways of Thinking: From Crows to Children and Back Again". *Quarterly Journal of Experimental Psychology* 68:2 (2015), 209–41.

Clayton, N., J. Russell & A. Dickinson. "Are Animals Stuck in Time or are they Chronesthetic Creatures?". *Topics in Cognitive Neuroscience* 1:1 (2009), 59–71.

Coen, C. "To Store, Perchance to Thaw?" *New Humanist*, 18 November 2016.

Cohen, J. "The Grand Illusion Illusion". *Journal of Consciousness Studies* 9:5/6 (2002), 141–57.

Cooper, D. "Life and Meaning". *Ratio* (New Series) XVIII (2002), 125–37.

Cornwall, G. "Parfit's Retreat: 'We Are Not Human Beings'". The Phantom Self; http://phantom self.org/parfits-retreat-we-are-not-human-beings/.

Coyne, J. "Why You Don't Really Have Free Will". *USA Today*, 1 January 2012.

Coyne, J. "You Don't Have Free Will". *Chronicle of Higher Education*, 18 March 2012.

Crabtree, S. "Worldwide 13% of Employees are Engaged at Work". Gallup, 8 October 2013.

Crane, T. "Intentionality as the Mark of the Mental". In A. O'Hear (ed.), *Contemporary Issues in the Philosophy of Mind.* Cambridge: Cambridge University Press, 1998.

Crane, T. "Join the Club". *Times Literary Supplement*, 1 November 2017.

Crane, T. *The Meaning of Belief: Religion from an Atheist's Point of View.* Cambridge, MA: Harvard University Press, 2018.

Cumming, R. *Starting Point.* Chicago, IL: University of Chicago Press, 1979.

Danaher, J. "Will Life be Worth Living in a World Without Work? Technological Unemployment and the Meaning of Life". *Science Engineering and Ethics* 23 (2017), 41–54.

Danaher, J. "Chalmers v Pigliucci on the Philosophy of Mind-Uploading". Philosophical Disquisitions; https://philosophicaldisquisitions.blogspot.com/2014/09/chalmers-vs-pigliucci-on-philosophy-of.html.

Dandelion, P. *A Sociological Analysis of the Theology of Quakers: The Silent Revolution.* Lewiston, NY: Edwin Mellen Press, 1996.

D'Antonio, M. & P. Eisner See. *The Shadow President: The Truth about Mike Pence.* New York: Thomas Dunne Books, 2018.

Darcy, M. "Rethinking Associative Mechanisms in Psychology". *Synthese* 193:12 (2016), 3783–6.

Darwin, C. *The Descent of Man* [1871]. London: Penguin, 2004.

Dawkins, R. *The Extended Phenotype: The Long Reach of the Gene.* Revised edition. Oxford: Oxford University Press, 1990.

De Caro, M. & D. MacArthur (eds). *Naturalism and Normativity.* New York: Columbia University Press, 2011.

Della Mirandola, G. P. *Oration on the Dignity of Man (De hominis dignitate)* [1496]. Available at: https://ebooks.adelaide.edu.au/p/pico_della_mirandola/giovanni/dignity/.

De Quincey, T. "The Last Days of Immanuel Kant" [1827]. *Blackwood's Magazine.* Available at: https://ebooks.adelaide.edu.au/d/de_quincey/thomas/last-days-of-immanuel-kant/

Dennett, D. *The Intentional Stance.* Cambridge, MA: MIT Press, 1987.

Dennett, D. *Consciousness Explained.* London: Penguin, 1991.

Dennett, D. "The Self as a Center of Narrative Gravity". In F. Kessel, P. Cole & D. Johnson (eds), *Self and Consciousness: Multiple Perspectives.* Hillsdale, NJ: Erlbaum, 1992.

Dennett, D. "Philosophy as Naïve Anthropology: Comment on Bennett and Hacker". In *Neuroscience and Philosophy.* New York: Columbia University Press, 2007.

Dennett, D. "Intentional Systems Theory". In A. Beckermann, B. McLaughlin & S. Walter (eds), *Oxford Handbook of Philosophy of Mind*, 339–50. Oxford: Oxford University Press, 2009.

Dennett, D. *From Bacteria to Bach and Back: The Evolution of Minds.* New York: Norton, 2017.

Dennett, D. "Facing up to the Hard Question of Consciousness". *Philosophical Transactions of the Royal Society B: Biological Sciences* 373:1755 (2018).

De Waal, F. *Are We Smart Enough to See How Smart Animals Are?* New York: Norton, 2016.

Dewey, J. *Experience and Nature.* New York: Dover Publications, 1958.

Donald, M. *The Origin of the Modern Mind: Three Stages in the Evolution of Culture and Cognition.* Cambridge, MA: Harvard University Press, 1991.

Dostoyevsky, F. *The Brothers Karamazov.* Translated by Richard Pevear and Larissa Volkhonsky. San Francisco, CA: North Point Press, 1990.

Dreben, B. "Putnam, Quine – and the Facts". *Philosophical Topics* 20:1 (1992), 293–315.

Dretske, F. "Experience as Representation". *Philosophical Issues* 13:1 (2003), 67–82.

Durand, E. "God's Holiness: A Reappraisal of Transcendence". *Modern Theology* 34:3 (2018), 419–33.

Durkheim, E. *The Elementary Forms of Religious Life*. Translated by J. Swain. New York: Free Press, 1954.

Durkheim, E. *Moral Education: A Study in the Theory and Application of the Sociology of Education*. Translated by E. Wilson & H. Schnurer. Glencoe: Free Press, 1961.

Durkheim, E. *Emile Durkheim Selected Writings*. Edited with an introduction by Anthony Giddens. Cambridge: Cambridge University Press, 1972.

Durkheim, E. *The Division of Labour in Society*. Translated by W. Halls. New York: Free Press, 1997.

Einstein, A. "On the Electrodynamics of Moving Bodies". In *The Principles of Relativity*. London: Methuen, 1923.

Einstein, A. "Physics and Reality". Translated by Jean Piccard. *Journal of the Franklin Institute* 221 (March 1936), 349–82.

Einstein, A. "Autobiographical Notes". In P. A. Schilpp (ed.) *Einstein: Philosopher Scientist* Volume 1. Lasalle, IL: Open Court, 1949.

Eliot, G. "The Choir Invisible". In E. C. Stedman (ed.), *A Victorian Anthology 1837–1895*. New York: Houghton Mifflin, 1895.

Ellis, G. & J. Silk. "Scientific Method: Defend the Integrity of Physics". *Nature* 516 (Dec 2014), 321–3.

Ellul, J. *The Technological Society*. Translated by J. Wilkinson. New York: Knopf, 1964.

Elwood, R. "Evidence for Pain in Decapod Crustaceans". *Animal Welfare* 21:S2 (2012), 23–7.

Eronen, M. L. "Interventionism for the Intentional Stance: True Believers and their Brains". *Topoi*, 2 December 2017.

Feinstein, J. S. *et al.* "Preserved Emotional Awareness of Pain in Patients with Extensive Bilateral Damage to the Insula, Anterior Cingulate, and Amygdala". *Brain Structure and Function* 221:3 (2016), 499–511.

Ferguson, N. *The War of the World: History's Age of Hatred*. London: Penguin, 2006.

Fitzgerald, P. "Review of *The Disenchantment of the World: A Political History of Religion*". *Theological Studies* 59.3 (1998), 548–52.

Flanagan, O. *Consciousness Reconsidered*. Cambridge, MA: MIT Press, 1992.

Fleischman, D. "The Evolution of Human Morality". Darwin Day Lecture 2018.

Fodor, J. "Semantics, Wisconsin Style". *Synthese* 59 (1984), 231–50.

Ford, B. "Revealing the Ingenuity of the Living Cell". *Biologist* 53:4 (2006), 221–4.

Forster, E. M. *Aspects of the Novel*. London: Pelican, 1962.

Frankfurt, H. *The Importance of What We Care About: Philosophical Essays*. Cambridge: Cambridge University Press, 1988.

Fugazza, C., A. Pigany & A. Miklosi. "Recall of Others' Actions after Incidental Encoding Reveals Episodic-Like Memory in Dogs". *Current Biology* 26 (Nov 2016), 1-5.

Gardner, S. "Merleau-Ponty's Transcendental Theory of Perception". In S. Gardner & M. Grist (eds) *The Transcendental Turn*. Oxford: Oxford University Press, 2015.

Gauchet, M. *The Disenchantment of the World: A Political History of Religion*. Princeton, NJ: Princeton University Press, 1997.

Gauker, C. "Visual Imagery in the Thought of Monkeys and Apes". In K. Andrews & J. Beck (eds), *Routledge Handbook of Philosophy of Animal Minds*, 25–33. New York: Routledge, 2017.

Geertz, C. *The Interpretation of Cultures.* New York: Basic Books, 1973.

Gellner, E. *Conditions of Liberty: Civil Society and its Rivals.* London: Hamish Hamilton, 1995.

Goff, P. "Panpsychism is Crazy but it is Also Most Probably True". *Aeon*, undated.

Goldstein, R. N. "Speaking Prose All Our Lives". *The Humanist* (Jan/Feb 2013).

Gomes, A. "Kant, the Philosophy of Mind, and Twentieth-Century Analytic Philosophy". In A. Gomes & A. Stephenson (eds), *Kant and the Philosophy of Mind: Perception, Reason and the Self*, 5–24. Oxford: Oxford University Press, 2017.

Goodall, J. *In the Shadow of Man.* London: Collins, 1971.

Goodall, J. *Through a Window: My Thirty Years with the Chimpanzees of Gombe.* Boston, MA: Houghton Mifflin, 1990.

Gordon-Reed, A. "Might vs Right: The Development of the Eurocentric 'Law of Nations'". *Times Literary Supplement*, 28 September 2018, 12.

Graeber, D. "On the Phenomenon of Bullshit Jobs: A Work Rant". *Strike Magazine* 2015.

Gray, J. *Straw Dogs: Thoughts on Humans and Other Animals.* London: Granta, 2002.

Gray, J. "Question and Answer". *New Humanist.* Autumn 2018, 6–8.

Gregory, B. *The Unintended Reformation: How a Religious Revolution Secularized Society.* Cambridge, MA: Harvard University Press, 2012.

Grice, H. P. "The Causal Theory of Perception". *Proceedings of the Aristotelian Society*, Supp. Vol. 35 (1961), 121–68.

Ground, I. "The Stupendous Intelligence of Honey Badgers". *Times Literary Supplement*, 26 May 2017, 9.

Gutfreund, Y. "The Neuroethological Paradox of Animal Consciousness". *Trends in Neurosciences* 40:4 (2017), 196–9.

Hacker, P. M. S. "Is There Anything it is Like to be a Bat?" *Philosophy* 77 (2002), 157–74.

Hacker, P. M. S. "Critical Notice of Timothy Williamson *The Philosophy of Philosophy*". *Philosophical Quarterly* 59 (April 2009), 337–46.

Haeckel, E. *The History of Creation*, volume 1 [1884]. Translated by E. Ray Lankester. London: Henry S. King.

Haggard, P. "Human Volition: Towards a Neuroscience of Will". *National Review of Neurosciences* 9 (2008), 934–46.

Halák, J. "Merleau-Ponty on Embodied Subjectivity from the Perspective of Subject-Object Circularity". *Acta Universitatis Carolinae Kinanthropologica* 52:2 (2016), 26–40.

Halák, J. & J. Klouda. "The Institution of Life in Gehlen and Merleau-Ponty: Searching for the Common Ground for the Anthropological Difference". *Human Studies* 41:3 (2018), 371–94.

Halák, J. & J. Klouda. "Institution as a General Model of Meaning: Gehlen and Merleau-Ponty on the Anthropological Difference". *Filosoficky Casopis* 66:6 (2018), 869–88.

Halik, T. & P. Hosek (eds), *A Czech Perspective on Faith in a Secular Age.* Washington, DC: Council for Research in Values and Philosophy, 2015.

Halik, T. "Church for the Seekers". In T. Halik & P. Hosek (eds), *A Czech Perspective on Faith in a Secular Age.* Washington, DC: Council for Research in Values and Philosophy, 2015

Han-Pile, B. "The Analytic of Finitude". In A. Morgan (ed.) *The Kantian Catastrophe? Conversations on Finitude and the Limits of Philosophy.* Newcastle: Bigg Books, 2017

Harris, S. *Free Will.* New York: The Free Press, 2012.

Harrison, P. "Narratives of Secularization". *Intellectual History Review* 21:1 (2017), 1–6.

Hartnett, K. "To Build Truly Intelligent Machines, Teach Them Cause and Effect", Interview with Judea Pearl. *Quanta Magazine* 15 May 2018.

Hassin, R. "Yes it Can: On the Functional Abilities of the Human Unconscious". *Perspectives on Psychological Science* 8 (2013), 195–207.

Heidegger, M. *Being and Time.* Translated by Joan Stambaugh. New York: SUNY Press, 1996.

Heidegger, M. "The Anaximander Fragment". In *Early Greek Thinking: The Dawn of Western Philosophy.* Translated by D. Farrell Krell & F. Capuzzi. New York: Harper & Row, 1975.

Hill, G. "Ovid in the Third Reich". In *New and Collected Poems, 1952–1992.* New York: Houghton Mifflin, 1994.

Hippocrates. "On the Sacred Disease". In *The Genuine Works of Hippocrates*, volume 2. Translated by Francis Adams. London: Sydenham Society, 1886.

Hobbes, T. *Leviathan.* London: Routledge & Sons, 1886.

Holloway, R. *Godless Morality: Keeping Religion out of Ethics.* Edinburgh: Canongate, 2004.

Hughes, J. "Buddhism and Our Post Human Future". *Sophia* (2018), 1–10.

Hume, D. *A Treatise of Human Nature.* New York: Dolphin Books, 1961.

Hussain, A. "Muslims, Pluralism, and Interfaith Dialogue". In O. Safi (ed.), *Progressive Muslims: On Justice, Gender and Pluralism.* Oxford: Oneworld, 2003.

Hyland, K. & K. Jiang. "Changing Patterns of Self-Citation: Cumulative Inquiry or Self-promotion?". *Text and Talk*, March 2018.

Jacob, P. "Intentionality". *Stanford Encyclopedia of Philosophy* (Spring 2019 Edition), Edward N. Zalta (ed.), avaliable at: https://plato.stanford.edu/archives/spr2019/entries/intentionality/.

James, W. *Principles of Psychology* Volume 1. London: Macmillan, 1890.

Jefferies, R. *The Story of My Heart: An Autobiography* [1883].

Jeffries, S. "Is that all there is?" *The Guardian*, 8 December 2007.

Jenkins, R. "Disenchantment, Enchantment, and Re-Enchantment". *Max Weber Studies* 1 (2000), 11–32.

Johnson, I. *The Soul of China: The Return of Religion after Mao.* London: Allen Lane, 2017.

Josephson-Storm, J. *The Myth of Disenchantment: Magic, Modernity, and the Birth of Natural Sciences.* Chicago, IL: University of Chicago Press, 2017.

Joyce, J. *Ulysses.* London: Bodley Head, 1960.

Kane, R. *The Significance of Free Will.* Oxford: Oxford University Press, 1998.

Kant, I. "Answering the Question: What is Enlightenment?" [1784]. In M. Gregor (ed.), *Practical Philosophy: The Cambridge Edition of the Works of Immanuel Kant.* Cambridge: Cambridge University Press, 1996.

Kant, I. "Idea for a Universal History with a Cosmopolitan Purpose" [1784].

Kant, I. *Critique of Pure Reason.* Translated by Norman Kemp Smith. London: Macmillan, 1963.

Kass, L. *The Hungry Soul: Eating and the Perfecting of Our Nature.* Chicago, IL: University of Chicago Press, 1999.

Kauffman, S. *Reinventing the Sacred. A New View of Science, Reason, and Religion.* New York: Basic Books, 2008.

Kaufman, A. "Collective Intentionality: A Human Not a Monkey Business". Available at: http://www.fupress.net/index.php/pam/article/view/19629.

Keats, J. "Fancy". *Selected Poems.* London: Penguin, 2007.

Keats, J. "The Fall of Hyperion: A Dream". *Selected Poems*. London: Penguin, 2007.

Keiper, A. & A. Schulman. "The Problem with 'Friendly' Artificial Intelligence". *The New Atlantis* 32 (2011), 80–89.

Kelly, S. *The Minister and the Murderer: A Book of Aftermaths*. London: Granta, 2018.

Keynes, J. M. "Economic Possibilities for Our Grandchildren". In *Essays in Persuasion*, 358–73. New York: Norton, 1963.

Kierkegaard, S. *Purity of Heart Is to Will One Thing. Spiritual Preparation for the Office of Confession*. Translated by Douglas Steere. New York: Harper & Row, 1956.

Klein, S. "The Self and its Brain". *Social Cognition* 30:4 (2012), 474–518.

Klein, S. "Sameness and the Self: Philosophical and Psychological Considerations". *Frontiers in Psychology* 5:29 (Jan 2014); available at: https://www.frontiersin.org/articles/10.3389/fpsyg.2014.00029/full

Klein, S. "What Memory Is". WIREs *Cognitive Science* 6:1 (2015), 1–38.

Klein, S. "The Unplanned Obsolescence of Psychological Science and an Argument for its Revival". *Psychology of Consciousness: Research, Theory and Practice* (2015).

Klein, S. & S. Nichols. "Memory and the Sense of Personal Identity". *Mind* 121:483 (2012), 677–702.

Klíma, I. *My Crazy Century: A Memoir*. New York: Grove Press, 2013.

Koch, C. *et al.* "Neural Correlates of Consciousness". *Nature Reviews Neuroscience* 17 (2017), 07-321.

Koci, M. & P. Roubic. "Searching the Altar of an Unknown God: Tomas Halik on Faith in a Secular Age". In T. Halik & P. Hosek (eds), *A Czech Perspective on Faith in a Secular Age*, 98–126. Washington, DC: Council for Research in Values and Philosophy, 2015.

Kodaj, D. "Religious Evil". *Philosophy Compass* 11:5 (2016), 277–86.

Kompridis, N. "Technology's Challenge to Democracy: What of the Human?" *Parrhesia* 8 (2009), 20–33.

Kriegel, U. (ed.) *The Oxford Handbook of the Philosophy of Consciousness*. Oxford: Oxford University Press, forthcoming.

Kronfeldner, M. *What's Left of Human Nature? A Post-Essentialist Pluralist, and Interactive Account of a Contested Concept*. Cambridge, MA: MIT Press, 2018.

Krupenye, C. *et al.* "Great Apes Anticipate that Other Individuals Will Act According to False Beliefs". *Science* 354:6308 (2016), 110–14.

Kuhn, R. L. "Virtual Immortality: Why the Mind-Body Problem is Still a Problem". *Skeptic Magazine* 21:2 (2016), 26–34.

Kung, H. *On Being a Christian*. New York: Doubleday, 1976.

Ladyman, J. & D. Ross. *Everything Must Go: Metaphysics Naturalized*. Oxford: Oxford University Press, 2007.

Ladyman, J. "An Apology for a Naturalized Metaphysics". In M. Slater & Z. Yudell (eds), *Metaphysics and the Philosophy of Science: New Essays*. Oxford: Oxford University Press, 2017.

Ladyman, J. "Scientism with a Humane Face". In J. Ridder, R. Peel & R. Van Woudenberg (eds) *Scientism: Prospects and Projects*. Oxford: Oxford University Press, 2018.

Lamont, C. *The Philosophy of Humanism*. New York: Frederick Ungar, 1982.

Larkin, P. "Church Going". In *The Less Deceived*. Hull: Marvell Press, 1955.

Larkin, P. "Self's the Man". In *The Whitsun Weddings*. London: Faber, 1964.

Larkin, P. "Ignorance". *Collected Poems*. London: Faber, 1988.

Law, S. "Wittgensteinian Accounts of Religious Belief: Non-Cognitivist, Juicer, and Atheist-Minus". *European Journal of Philosophy* 25:4 (2017), 1186–207.

Law, S. *Humanism: A Very Short Introduction*. Oxford: Oxford University Press, 2011.

Layard, R. *Happiness: Lessons from a New Science*. Harmondsworth: Penguin, 2005.

Lee, L. "Polar Opposites? Diversity and Dialogue Among the Religious and Non-Religious". In A. Carroll & R. Norman (eds), *Religion and Atheism. Beyond the Divide*, 166–76. Abingdon: Routledge, 2016.

Lee, M. "A Frame of Mind". *RSA Journal*, Issue 2 (2018), 46–7.

Levi, P. *If This Be a Man / The Truce*. London: Penguin, 1979.

Libet, B. *et al.* "Unconscious Cerebral Initiative and the Role of Conscious Will in Involuntary Action". *Brain* 106 (1983), 623–42.

Locke, J. *An Essay Concerning Human Understanding*. Edited by P. Nidditch. Oxford: Clarendon Press, 1975.

Locke, J. *Two Treatises of Government*. Cambridge: Cambridge University Press, 1988.

Lowe, E. J. *A Survey of Metaphysics*. Oxford: Oxford University Press, 2002.

Lucretius. *On the Nature of Things*. Translated by Cyril Bailey. Oxford: Clarendon Press, 1910.

MacCulloch, D. *A History of Christianity*. London: Penguin, 2009.

Mann, T. *Buddenbrooks*. Translated by J. Woods. London: Everyman, 1994.

Marsh, H. *Admissions: A Life in Brain Surgery*. London: Weidenfeld & Nicolson, 2017.

Marx, K. *Theses on Feuerbach* [1888]. Available at: https://www.marxists.org/archive/marx/works/1845/theses/theses.htm.

Matlack, S. "Quantum Poetics". *The New Atlantis* (Summer/Fall 2017), 47–67.

Maudlin, T. *Philosophy of Physics: Space and Time*. Princeton, NJ: Princeton University Press, 2012.

May, S. *Love: A New Understanding of an Ancient Emotion*. Oxford: Oxford University Press, 2018.

McClelland, T. "Against Virtual Selves". *Erkenntnis* 84:1 (2019), 21–40.

McGee, M. "Our Proud and Angry Dust". In A. Carroll & E. Norman (eds), *Religion and Atheism: Beyond the Divide*. Abingdon: Routledge, 2016

McGrath, A. & J. C. McGrath. *The Dawkins Delusion? Atheist Fundamentalism and the Denial of the Divine*. London: SPCK, 2007.

McGregor, N. "Belief is Back". *The Guardian*. 6 October 2018.

Meixner, U. "The Reduction of Reductive and Non-Reductive Materialism: A New Start". In A. Antonietti, A. Corradio & E. J. Lowe (eds), *Psycho-Physical Dualism: An Interdisciplinary Approach*, 143–66. Boulder, CO: Rowman & Littlefield, 2008.

Merleau-Ponty, M. *The Phenomenology of Perception*. Translated by Colin Smith. London: Routledge, Kegan Paul, 1962.

Merleau-Ponty, M. *The Phenomenology of Perception*. Translated by Donald A. Landers. London: Routledge, 2012.

Merleau-Ponty, M. *Nature: Course Notes from the College de France*. Translated by Robert Vallier. Evanston, IL: Northwestern University Press, 2003.

Merquior, J. G. *Foucault*. London: Fontana, 1985.

Metzinger, T. *Being No One: The Self-Model Theory of Subjectivity*. Cambridge, MA: MIT Press, 2018.

Micklethwait, J. & A. Wooldridge. *God is Back: How the Global Rise of Religion is Changing the World*. London: Penguin, 2011.

Midgley, M. *Beast & Man: The Roots of Human Nature.* London: Routledge, 1978.

Midgley, M. *What is Philosophy For?* London: Bloomsbury, 2018.

Mill, J. S. "Bentham" [1838]. In *On Coleridge and Bentham.* London: Chatto & Windus, 1971.

Mill, J. S. "Nature" [1874]. In H. D. Aiken (ed.), *The Age of Ideology: The Nineteenth-Century Philosophers*, 149–60. New York: Mentor, 1956.

Mill, J. S. *Autobiography.* Edited by J. M. Robson. Harmondsworth: Penguin, 1989.

Miller, J., P. Shepherdson & J. Trevena. "Effects of Clock Monitoring on Electroencephalographic Activity: Is Unconscious Movement Initiation an Artefact of the Clock?" *Psychological Science* 22 (2011), 103–9.

Moore, A. "Finitude". In A. Morgan (ed.) *The Kantian Catastrophe?* Newcastle upon Tyne: Bigg Books, 2017.

Moran, J. *First You Write a Sentence: The Elements of Reading, Writing ... and Life.* London: Penguin, 2018.

Morgan, A (ed.) *The Kantian Catastrophe? Conversations on Finitude and the Limits of Philosophy.* Newcastle upon Tyne: Bigg Books, 2017.

Nagel, T. "What Is It Like To Be a Bat?" *Philosophical Review* 83 (1974), 435–50.

Nagel, T. *The View from Nowhere.* Oxford: Oxford University Press, 1986.

Nagel, T. *Mind and Cosmos: Why the Materialist Neo-Darwinian Conception of Nature is Almost Certainly False.* Oxford: Oxford University Press, 2012.

Nahmias, E. "Defining Free Will Away". *Philosopher's Magazine*, third quarter 2012.

Nahmias, E. "Why We Have Free Will". *Scientific American* 26 (2017), 24–7.

Nešić, J. "Against Deflation of the Subject". *Filozofija I Društvo* 28:4 (2017), 1102–21.

Newell, B. & D. Shanks. "Unconscious Influences on Decision Making: A Critical Review". *Behavioural and Brain Sciences* 37 (2014), 1–61.

Nietzsche, F. *The Genealogy of Morals.* Oxford: Oxford University Press, 2008.

Nietzsche, F. *Untimely Meditations.* Cambridge: Cambridge University Press, 1997.

Nietzsche, F. *Ecce Homo.* London: Penguin, 1992.

Nietzsche, F. "Skirmishes of an Untimely Man". In *Twilight of the Idols* in *The Portable Nietzsche.* Edited and translated by Walter Kaufmann. New York: Viking, 1954.

Nietzsche, F. "On Free Death". In *Thus Spake Zarathustra* in *The Portable Nietzsche.* Translated by Walter Kaufmann. New York: Vintage, 1954.

Nijinksy, V. *The Diary of Vaslav Nijinsky.* Edited with a preface by Romola Nijinsky. London: Panthe, 1966.

Norman, R. *On Humanism.* London: Routledge, 2004.

O'Connell, M. *To be a Machine: Adventures Among Cyborgs Utopians, Hackers, and the Futurists Solving the Modest Problem of Death.* London: Granta, 2017.

Olson, E. *The Human Animal: Personal Identity without Psychology.* Oxford: Oxford University Press, 1997.

Olson, E. "Parfit's View That We Are Not Human Beings". *ResearchGate*, May 2015.

O'Sullivan, S. "The Finite-Infinite Relation". In A. Morgan (ed.), *The Kantian Catastrophe?* 209–22. Newcastle upon Tyne: Bigg Books.

Oxenberg, R. "Why Does Pain Hurt? An Inquiry Into the Limits of Evolutionary Explanation". Available at: https://philpapers.org/reg/OXEWDP.

Parfit, D. *Reasons and Persons.* Oxford: Oxford University Press, 1984.

Parfit, D. "The Unimportance of Identity". In H. Harris (ed.) *Identity*, 13–45. Oxford: Oxford University Press, 1995.

Parfit, D. "We Are Not Human Beings". *Philosophy* 87 (2012), 5–28.

Parvizi, J. *et al.* "Electrical Stimulation of Human Fusiform Face-Selective Regions Distorts Face Perception". *Journal of Neuroscience* 32:43, (2012), 14915–20.

Pascal, B. *Pensées*. Translated by A. Krailsheimer. London: Penguin, revised edition, 1995.

Patel, R. & J. Moore. *A History of the World in Seven Cheap Things*. London: Verso, 2018.

Pater, W. "The School of Giorgione". In *The Renaissance: Studies in Art and Poetry*. New York: Mentor Books, 1959.

Patočka, J. *Body, Community, Language, World*. Translated by Erazim Kohák, edited by James Dodd. Chicago, IL: Open Court, 1998.

Paul, L. A. "Temporal Experience". *Journal of Philosophy* 107:7 (2010), 333–59.

Penelhum, T. *Themes in Hume: The Self, the Will, and Religion*. Oxford: Clarendon Press, 2000.

Penfield, W. "Memory Mechanisms". AMA *Archives of Neurology and Psychiatry* 1952, 178–98.

Persson, I. "The Involvement of Our Identity in Experiential Memory". *Canadian Journal of Philosophy* 27:4 (1997), 447–65.

Persson, I. "Self-Doubt: Why We Are Not Identical to Things of Any Kind". *Ratio* (new series) XVII (2004), 390–408.

Pinker, S. "So How Does the Mind Work?" *Mind and Language* 20 (2005), 1–24.

Pinker, S. *The Better Angels of Our Nature: Why Violence Has Declined*. New York: Viking 2011.

Plato. *Complete Works*. Edited by J. M. Cooper. Indianapolis, IN: Hackett, 1997.

Popper, K. "Why I Reject Metaphysical Determinism: A Conversation with Parmenides". In *The Open Universe: An Argument for Indeterminism*. London: Routledge, 1982.

Povinelli, D. *Folk Physics for Apes*. Second edition. Oxford: Oxford University Press, 2011.

Povinelli, D. & S. Frei. "Constraints on the Exploitation of the Functional Properties of Objects in Expert Tool-Using Chimpanzees (Pan Troglodytes)". *Cortex* 82 (2016) 11–23.

Proust, M. *A La Recherche de Temps Perdu*. Translated by Terence Kilmartin. London: Penguin, 1983.

Quine, W. V. "Two Dogmas of Empiricism". *Philosophical Review* 60 (1951), 20–43.

Quine, W. V. "Mr. Strawson on Logical Theory". *Mind* LXII (Oct 1953), 248–53.

Quine, W. V. "The Nature of Natural Knowledge". In S. Guttenplan (ed.), *Mind and Language*, Wolfson College Lectures 1974. Oxford: Clarendon Press, 1975.

Quine, W. V. *Theories and Things*. Cambridge, MA: Harvard University Press, 1981.

Quine, W. V. "Epistemology Naturalised". Reprinted in Hilary Kornblith (ed.), *Naturalizing Epistemology*. Cambridge MA: MIT Press, 1985.

Quine, W. V. "Naturalism; Or Living Within One's Means". *Dialectica* 49:2–4 (1995), 251–61.

Quine, W. V. *The Pursuit of Truth*. Revised edition. Cambridge, MA: Harvard University Press, 1992.

Quine, W. V. *From Stimulus to Science*. Cambridge, MA: Harvard University Press, 1998.

Quinton, A. M. "The Problem of Perception". *Mind* 64 (1955), 28–51.

Ramachandran, V. S. *The Tell-Tale Brain: A Neuroscientist's Quest for What Makes Us Human*. New York: Norton, 2011.

Rand, A. *The Virtue of Selfishness*. New York: New American Library, 1964.

Rawls, J. *A Theory of Justice*. Cambridge, MA: Harvard University Press, revised edition, 1999.

Rée, J. "Atheism in History". In A. Carroll & R. Norman (eds), *Religion and Atheism: Beyond the Divide*. Abingdon: Routledge, 2016.

Reid, C. *et al.* "Slime Mold Uses an Externalized Spatial 'Memory' to Navigate in Complex Environments". *Proceedings of the National Academy of Sciences* 109:43 (Oct 2012).

Reid, T. *Essays on the Active Powers of the Human Mind*. Cambridge, MA: MIT Press, 1969.

Romano, C. "After the Lived-Body". *Continental Philosophy Review* 49 (2016), 445–68.

Rosar, W. *The Localization of the Mind: Why We Think the Mind is in the Head*. 1982, revised 2014. Available at: https://www.academia.edu/4042688/The_Localization_of_the_Mind.

Rosas, A. & J. Bermudez. "Viewing Others as Equal: The Non-Cognitive Role of Shared Intentionality". *Review of Philosophy and Psychology* 9 (2018), 485–502.

Rosen, I. "I'm a Believer – but I'll be damned if I'm religious". Belief and Religion in the Greater Copenhagen Area: A focus group study, University Lund Studies in Sociology of Religion Volume 8 (2009).

Rosenberg, A. "Eliminativism without Tears: A Nihilistic Stance on the Theory of Mind". Unpublished manuscript. Available at: https://www.semanticscholar.org/paper/Eliminativism-without-Tears/0466d508aedb8c8e53fd4666aa71382aec7e24a7.

Rosling, H., with O. Rosling & A. Rosling Ronnlund. *Factfulness: Ten Reasons We're Wrong about the World – and Why Things are Better than you Think*. London: Hodder & Stoughton, 2018.

Rowlands, M. *Memory and the Self: Phenomenology, Science and Autobiography*. Oxford: Oxford University Press, 2016.

Ruff, D. A. & M. Cohen. "Relating the Activity of Sensory Neurons to Perception". In M. S. Gazzaniga & G. R. Mangun (eds), *The Cognitive Neurosciences*, 349–62. Fifth edition. Cambridge MA: MIT Press, 2014.

Rump, J. "On the Use and Abuse of Teleology for Life: Intentionality, Naturalism and Meaning Rationalism in Husserl and Millikan". *Humana.Mente: Journal of Philosophical Studies* 34 (2018), 41–75.

Russell, B. *The Analysis of Mind*. London: Allen & Unwin, 1927.

Russell, B. "The Harm that Good Men Do". *Sceptical Essays*. London: Allen & Unwin, 1928.

Russell, B. *A History of Western Philosophy*. London: Allen & Unwin, 1946.

Russell, B. "A Free Man's Worship". In *Mysticism and Logic and Other Essays*. London: Penguin, 1953.

Safranski, R. *Martin Heidegger: Between Good and Evil*. Translated by Ewald Osers. Cambridge MA: Harvard University Press, 1998.

Safranski, R. *Nietzsche: A Philosophical Biography*. Translated by Shelley Frisch. London: Granta, 2002.

Salomons, T. V. *et al.* "The 'Pain Matrix' in Pain-Free Individuals". *Journal of the American Medical Association Neurology* 73:6 (2016), 755–6.

Sartre, J.-P. *What is Literature?* Translated by Bernard Frechtman. London: Methuen, 1950.

Sartre, J.-P. *Being and Nothingness. An Essay on Phenomenological Ontology*. Translated by Hazel Barnes. London: Methuen, 1957.

Sartre, J.-P. *Nausea*. London: Penguin, 1965.

Savitt, S. "Time in the Special Theory of Relativity". In C. Callendar (ed.), *Oxford Handbook of the Philosophy of Time*. Oxford: Oxford University Press, 2011.

Sayer, D. *Prague: The Capital of the Twentieth Century. A Surrealist History*. Princeton, NJ: Princeton University Press, 2013.

Scharf, C. "Where Do Minds Belong?" *Aeon*, 22 March 2016.

Schechtman, M. "Personhood and Person Identity". *Journal of Philosophy* 87 (1990), 71–92.

Schechtman, M. "'The Size of the Self': Minimalist Selves and Narrative Self-Constitution". In A. Speight (ed.) *Narrative, Philosophy and Life* (BSPR Vol. 2), 33–47. Dordrecht: Springer, 2015.

Schmidt, M. & A. Dejean "A Dolichoderine Ant that Constructs Traps to Ambush Prey Collectively: Convergent Evolution with a Myrmicine Genus". *Biological Journal of the Linnaean Society* 124:1 (Apr 2018), 41–6.

Schopenhauer, A. "On Noise". In *Studies in Pessimism.* Translated by T. B. Saunders. Cosimo Classics, 2007.

Schrenk, M. "Ernst Mach on the Self: The Deconstruction of the Ego as an Attempt to Avoid Solipsism". Available at: http://www.philosophie.hhu.de/professuren/prof-dr-markus-schrenk/mitarbeiterinnen/markus-schrenk/publikationen/aufsaetze/ernst-mach-on-the-self.html.

Schweikard, D. & H. Schmid, "Collective Intentionality", *Stanford Encyclopedia of Philosophy* (Summer 2013 Edition), Edward N. Zalta (ed.), https://plato.stanford.edu/archives/sum2013/entries/collective-intentionality/.

Scruton, R. *Death-Devoted Heart: Sex and Sacred in Wagner's Tristan and Isolde.* Oxford: Oxford University Press, 2003.

Scruton, R. *Understanding Music: Philosophy and Interpretation.* London: Continuum, 2010.

Scruton, R. *I Drink Therefore I Am.* London: Continuum, 2010.

Scruton, R. "Living With a Mind". *First Things*, December 2015; https://www.firstthings.com/article/2015/12/living-with-a-mind

Scruton, R. "Faking It". In *Confessions of a Heretic.* London: Notting Hill Editions, 2016.

Searle, J. *The Construction of Social Reality.* New York: The Free Press, 1995.

Searle, J. *The Mystery of Consciousness.* London: Granta, 1997.

Sellars, W. "Philosophy and the Scientific Image of Man". In R. Colodny (ed.), *Frontiers of Science and Philosophy*, 35–78. Pittsburgh, PA: Pittsburgh University Press, 1962.

Sen, A. "Greek, Roman, Hebrew or Arabic". In *Reason before Identity*, 1998 Romanes Lecture. Oxford: Oxford University Press, 1999.

Setiya, K. *Midlife: A Philosophical Guide.* Princeton, NJ: Princeton University Press, 2017.

Shannon, C. "A Mathematical Theory of Communication". *The Bell System Technical Journal* 27 (1948), 379–423.

Shariff, A. & K. Vohs. "The World Without Free Will". *Scientific American* 310:6 (June 2014), 76–9.

Sherwood, H. "Religion: Why Faith is Becoming More and More Popular". *The Guardian*, 27 August 2018.

Shields, G. "Neuroscience and Conscious Causation: Has Neuroscience Shown that We Cannot Control Our Own Actions?" *Reviews in Philosophy and Psychology* 5 (2014), 565–82.

Silver, D. *et al.* "Mastering the Game of Go without Human Knowledge". *Nature* 550 (Oct 2017), 354–58.

Singer, P. *Hegel.* Oxford: Oxford University Press, 1983.

Singer, P. & E. Brooking. "Jihadi Digital Natives". *The New Atlantis*, Winter 2019, 83–9.

Solzhenitsyn, A. Templeton Address, 1983.

Spiegel, J. "Review of Keith Ward: *The Christian Idea of God*". *European Journal for Philosophy of Religion* 10:2 (2018), 213–18.

Spinoza, B. *On the Correction of the Understanding*. In *Spinoza's Ethics and De Intellectus Emendatione*. Translated by A. Boyle. London: Everyman's Library, 1913.

Stace, W. T. "Man Against Darkness" *Atlantic Monthly*, September 1948, 53–9.

Standing, E. "Are the 'New Atheists' Avoiding the 'Real' Arguments?" *Butterflies and Wheels*, 31 October 2007.

Standing, G. *The Precariat: The New and Dangerous Class*. London: Bloomsbury, 2011.

Strawson, G. "The Impossibility of Moral Responsibility". *Philosophical Studies* 75:1/2 (1994), 5–24.

Strawson, G. "Real Intentionality 3: Why Intentionality Entails Consciousness". In *Real Materialism and Other Essays*, 281–305. Oxford: Oxford University Press, 2008.

Strawson, G. *Selves: An Essay in Revisionary Metaphysics*. Oxford: Oxford University Press, 2009.

Strawson, G. "Real Naturalism". *Proceedings and Addresses of the American Philosophical Association* 86:2 (Nov 2012), 125–54.

Strawson, P. F. *Individuals*. London: Methuen, 1959.

Strawson, P. F. *The Bounds of Sense: An Essay on Kant's Critique of Pure Reason*. London: Methuen, 1966.

Strhan, A. "Matters of Life and Death". In A. Carroll & R Norman (eds), *Religion and Atheism: Beyond the Divide*. Abingdon: Routledge, 2017.

Strickland, L. "The Problem of Religious Evil: Does Belief in God Cause Evil?" *International Journal of the Philosophy of Religion* 84:2 (2018), 237–250.

Stroud, B. "The Charm of Naturalism". *Proceedings and Addresses of the American Philosophical Association* 70:2 (1996), 43–55.

Suddendorf, T. *The Gap: The Science of What Separates Us from Other Animals*. New York: Basic Books, 2013.

Swafford, J. *Beethoven: Anguish and Triumph*. London: Faber, 2014.

Tallis, R. *Not Saussure: A Critique of Post-Saussurean Literary Theory*. London: Macmillan, 1988, 1995.

Tallis, R. *In Defence of Realism*. London: Edward Arnold, 1990.

Tallis, R. *Enemies of Hope: A Critique of Contemporary Pessimism. Irrationalism, Anti-Humanism, and the Counter-Enlightenment*. London: Palgrave Macmillan, 1997.

Tallis, R. *The Hand: A Philosophical Inquiry into Human Being*. Edinburgh: Edinburgh University Press, 2003.

Tallis, R. *I Am: A Philosophical Inquiry into First-Person Being*. Edinburgh: Edinburgh University Press, 2004.

Tallis, R. *Why the Mind is Not a Computer: A Lexicon of Neuromythology*. Exeter: Imprint Academic, 2004.

Tallis, R. *Michelangelo's Finger: An Exploration of Everyday Transcendence*. London: Atlantic, 2010.

Tallis, R. "The Soup and the Scaffolding". *Philosophy Now* 83 (2011), 54–5.

Tallis, R. *Aping Mankind: Neuromania, Darwinitis, and the Misrepresentation of Humanity*. Durham: Acumen, 2011.

Tallis, R. *In Defence of Wonder and Other Philosophical Reflections*. Durham: Acumen, 2012.

Tallis, R. *Reflections of a Metaphysical Flâneur and Other Essays*. Durham: Acumen, 2013.

Tallis, R. *Epimethean Imaginings: Philosophical and Other Reflections on Everyday Light*. Durham: Acumen, 2014.

Tallis, R. & J. Spalding. *Summers of Discontent: The Purpose of the Arts Today*. London: Wilmington Square Books, 2014.

Tallis, R. *The Mystery of Being Human: God, Free Will, and the NHS*. London: Notting Hill Editions, 2016.

Tallis, R. *Of Time and Lamentation: Reflections on Transience*. Newcastle upon Tyne: Agenda, 2017.

Tallis, R. "Time, Reciprocal Containment, & the Ourobouros". *Philosophy Now* Oct–Nov 2017, 54–5.

Tallis, R. *Logos: The Mystery of How We Make Sense of the World*. Newcastle upon Tyne: Agenda, 2018.

Tallis, R. "Fifty Shades of Black". *Philosophy Now* 227 (Aug/Sep 2018), 54–5.

Tallis, R. "*Homo Faber*". *Philosophy Now* (Feb/Mar 2019), 54–5.

Tartaglia, J. *Philosophy in a Meaningless Life: A System of Nihilism, Consciousness and Reality*. London: Bloomsbury, 2016.

Taylor, C. *A Secular Age*. Cambridge, MA: Harvard University Press, 2007.

Tennyson, A. "Ulysses". In *A Choice of Tennyson's Verse*. Selected and with an Introduction by David Cecil. London: Faber, 1971.

Tertullian: *De Resurrectione Carnis*. Available at: http://www.tertullian.org/articles/evans_res/evans_res_04english.htm.

Toadvine, T. "The Elemental Past". *Research in Phenomenology* 44 (2014), 262–79.

Tomasello, M. *A Natural History of Human Thinking*. Cambridge, MA: Harvard University Press, 2014.

Tomasello, M. & M. Carpenter. "Shared Intentionality". *Developmental Science* 10:1 (2007), 121–5.

Toynbee, P. "The Culture of Respect for Religion has Gone Too Far". *The Guardian*, 28 August 2018.

Tulving, E. "Episodic Memory and Autonoesis: Uniquely Human?". In H. Terrace & J. Metcalf (eds), *The Missing Link in Cognition*, 4–51. New York: Oxford University Press, 2005.

Turner, D. "How to be an Atheist". In *Faith Seeking*. London: SCM, 2002.

Unger, R. & L. Smolin. *The Singular Universe and the Reality of Time*. Cambridge: Cambridge University Press, 2015.

Uttal, W. *The New Phrenology*. Cambridge, MA: MIT Press, 2001.

Valéry, P. *An Evening with M. Teste*. Translated with an Introduction by Jackson Matthews. In J. Matthews (ed.) *The Collected Works of Paul Valéry*. Princeton, NJ: Princeton University Press, 1973.

Valiunan, A. "Jonas Salk, the People's Scientist". *The New Atlantis* (Summer/Fall 2018), 99–128.

Velden, M. *Psychology: A Study of a Masquerade*. Gottingen: V&R Unipress, 2017.

Walker, M. "Personal Identity and Uploading". *Journal of Evolution and Technology* 22:1 (Nov 2012), 37–51.

Walther, H. "Is Man's Wish the Father of the Gods? Comments on *The Theogony* by Ludwig Feuerbach". Lecture given at Gesellschaft fur Kritische Philosophie Nurnberg, 18 June 2003.

Warnock, G. (ed.) *The Philosophy of Perception.* Oxford: Oxford University Press, 1967.

Wasserman, G. "Neural-Mental Chronometry and Chronotheology". *Behavioural and Brain Sciences* 8 (1985), 556–7.

Weber, M. "Science as a Vocation". In M. Weber, *Essays in Sociology.* Translated and edited by H. H. Gerth & C. Wright Mills. New York: Oxford University Press, 1946.

Wegner, D. "Precis of *The Illusion of Conscious Will*". *Brain and Behavioural Sciences* 27 (2004), 649–92.

Weinberg, S. *The First Three Minutes: A Modern View of the Origin of the Universe.* New York: Basic Books, 1977.

Weiskrantz, L. "Introduction: Dissociated Issues". In A. Milner & M. Rugg (eds), *The Neuropsychology of Consciousness.* London: Academic Press, 1992.

Weyl, H. *The Philosophy of Mathematics and Natural Science.* Princeton, NJ: Princeton University Press, 1949.

Wheeler, J. "Sakharov Revisited: 'It from Bit'". In M. Man'ko (ed.) *Proceedings of the First International A. D. Sakharov Memorial Conference on Physics, Moscow, USSR 1991, May 21-31.* Commack, NY: Nova Science Publishers, 1991.

Wigner, E. "The Unreasonable Effectiveness of Mathematics in the Natural Sciences". *Communications in Pure and Applied Mathematics* 13:1 (1960), 1–14.

Williams, B. "The Makropoulos Case: Reflections on the Tedium of Immortality". In *The Problems of the Self.* Cambridge: Cambridge University Press, 1973.

Williams, R. *Being Human: Bodies, Minds, Persons.* London: SPCK, 2018.

Winer, G. A. *et al.* "Fundamentally Misunderstanding Visual Perception: Adults' Beliefs in Visual Emission". *American Psychologist* 57 (2002), 417–24.

Wittgenstein, L. *Philosophical Investigations.* Translated by G. E. M. Anscombe. Oxford: Blackwell, 1963.

Wittgenstein, L. *Zettel.* Translated by G. E. M. Anscombe. Oxford: Blackwell, 1967.

Wittgenstein, L. *Tractatus Logico-Philosophicus.* London: Routledge, 2001.

Wohlleben, P. *The Inner Life of Animals.* London: Bodley Head, 2017.

Wong, D. "Shit Jobs: 9 Types of Job that Will Destroy Your Soul". *Cracked.com* 2011.

Wrangham, R. *Catching Fire: How Cooking Made Us Human.* New York: Profile, 2010.

Wrangham, R. *The Goodness Paradox: How Evolution Made Us More and Less Violent.* London: Profile, 2019.

Yeats, W. B. "An Irish Airman Foresees His Death" (1918). In *The Wild Swans at Coole.* London: Macmillan, 1919.

Yeats, W. B. *The Collected Poems of W. B. Yeats.* London: Wordsworth, 1994.

Zuckerman, P. *Society Without God: What the Least Religious Nations Can Teach Us About Contentment.* New York: New York University Press, 2008.

Index